Altruism

Also by Matthieu Ricard

Happiness

The Monk and the Philosopher (with Jean-François Revel)

The Quantum and the Lotus (with Trinh Xuan Thuan)

Buddhist Himalayas (with Olivier and Danielle Föllmi)

Journey to Enlightenment

Monk Dancers of Tibet

Tibet: A Compassionate Eye

Altruism

The Power of Compassion to Change Yourself and the World

Matthieu Ricard

Translated by
Charlotte Mandell and Sam Gordon

Little, Brown and Company
New York Boston London

Little, Brown and Company
Hachette Book Group
1290 Avenue of the Americas, New York, NY 10104
littlebrown.com

First North American Edition: June 2015
Originally published in France as *Plaidoyer pour l'altruisme* by NiL éditions, September 2013

Little, Brown and Company is a division of Hachette Book Group, Inc.
The Little, Brown name and logo are trademarks of Hachette Book Group, Inc.

ISBN 978-0-316-20824-6 (hc) / 978-0-316-29725-7 (int'l ed)

LCCN 2015935986

10 9 8 7 6 5 4 3 2 1

RRD-C

Printed in the United States of America

To my spiritual masters, His Holiness the Dalai Lama, Kyapje Kangyur Rinpoche, and Kyapje Dilgo Khyentse Rinpoche, and all those who have opened my eyes to compassion.

To my mother, Yahne Le Toumelin, and to my sister Ève, who taught me altruism by example. To Christophe and Pauline André, accomplices in altruism.

To my scientific mentors and friends thanks to whom this book has some credibility: Daniel Batson, Richard Davidson, Paul Ekman, Paul Gilbert, Jane Goodall, Richard Layard, Antoine Lutz, Tania Singer, Dennis Snower, Frans de Waal, and all those who enlightened me on numerous points.

To my friends, fellow workers, and benefactors in the Karuna-Shechen Association, who put compassion into action through their contribution to over a hundred humanitarian projects.

To Raphaële Demandre, who never misses an opportunity to help those who are in need.

To those who have contributed so much to improving this book: Christian Bruyat, Marie Haeling, Carisse Busquet, and Françoise Delivet.

Finally, to all beings, who are altruism's reason for existence.

Contents

II
The Emergence of Altruism

III
Cultivating Altruism

IV
Contrary Forces

V
Building a More Altruistic Society

Nothing is more powerful than an idea whose time has come.

— Victor Hugo

Every man must decide whether he will walk in the light of creative altruism or in the darkness of destructive selfishness.

— Martin Luther King Jr.

Altruism

Introduction

I have little inclination to talk about myself and would rather expound the views of the great thinkers who have inspired my existence. Telling you about a few stages of my personal journey, though, will help you understand how I came to write this book and to substantiate the ideas presented in it.

After growing up in France, I went to India for the first time in 1967, at the age of twenty, in order to meet the great masters of Tibetan Buddhism including Kangyur Rinpoche, who would become my main spiritual master. That same year, I began a dissertation on cellular genetics under the direction of François Jacob, at the Institut Pasteur. It was those years of scientific training that taught me to appreciate the importance of intellectual rigor and honesty.

In 1972, having finished my dissertation, I decided to move to Darjeeling to be near my teacher. During the many years that followed that encounter, whether in India, Bhutan, Nepal, or Tibet, I led a simple life. I received barely one letter per month; I had neither radio nor newspapers, and scarcely knew what was going on in the world. I studied with my spiritual master, Kangyur Rinpoche, and after his death in 1975, Dilgo Khyentse Rinpoche. I spent a number of years in contemplative retreat. I also devoted myself to the activities of the monasteries to which I had become linked: Orgyen Kunzang Chöling in Darjeeling and Shechen Tennyi Dargyeling in Nepal, while working also toward the preservation of Tibet's cultural and spiritual heritage.

Thanks to the teachings I received from these masters, I became aware of the incalculable benefits of altruism.

In 1997, I received a message from a French publisher, proposing I engage in a dialogue with my father, the late philosopher Jean-François Revel. The publication of the book that resulted from these conversations, *The Monk and the Philosopher,* marked the end of a quiet, anonymous life, but it also offered me new opportunities.

After a quarter of a century of immersion in the study and practice of Buddhism, far from the scene of the West, I found myself again confronted with contemporary ideas. I renewed my ties with the scientific world by conversing with the astrophysicist Trinh Xuan Thuan (*The Quantum and the Lotus: A Journey to the Frontiers Where Science and Buddhism Meet,* published in 2000 in France as *L'Infini dans la paume de la main*). I also took part in meetings at the Mind & Life Institute, an organization inspired by the Dalai Lama and founded by the neuroscientist Francisco Varela and the entrepreneur Adam Engle, with the aim of encouraging exchanges between science and Buddhism. In 2000, at Richard Davidson's lab in Madison, Wisconsin, I began to take part actively in research projects in psychology and neuroscience whose object is to analyze the effects, both short- and long-term, of training the mind through meditation. Over the years, Richie and I developed a close friendship and collaboration. The same happened with several other scientists including Paul Ekman, Tania and Wolf Singer, Daniel Batson, and Antoine Lutz.

So my experience has taken place at the confluence of two major influences: Eastern Buddhist wisdom and Western sciences.

When I returned from the East, I had become used to living within a culture and among people whose priority was to become better human beings by transforming their way of being and thinking. Ordinary preoccupations with loss and gain, pleasure and displeasure, praise and criticism, fame and anonymity, were regarded there as puerile and as causes of suffering. Above all, altruistic love and compassion comprised the cardinal virtues of all human life and were the heart of the spiritual path. I was, and still am, particularly inspired by the Buddhist vision in which every human being possesses an indestructible potential for goodness and enlightenment.

The Western world in which I found myself, a world where individualism is often appreciated as a strength and a virtue—sometimes to the point of selfishness and narcissism—was a bit puzzling, since it did not seem to foster an optimal way to live in society.

When I considered the cultural and philosophical sources for the difference between "other-oriented" and "self-oriented" societies, I remembered Plautus, for whom "man is a wolf to man,"[1] an assertion taken up and developed by Thomas Hobbes, who speaks of the "war of every man against every man";[2] Nietzsche, who states that altruism is the mark of the weak; and finally Freud, who asserts he has "found little that is 'good' among human beings on the whole."[3] I thought it merely a question of a few pessimistic thinkers; I hadn't realized the extent of the impact of their ideas.

Anxious to understand this phenomenon better, I noticed how taking for granted that all our deeds, words and thoughts are motivated by selfishness has long influenced Western psychology and theories of evolution and economies, to the point of acquiring the force of a dogma whose validity has until recently scarcely been challenged. The most surprising thing is the persistence of intellectuals to try to spot, at all costs, a selfish motivation at the origin of every human action.

Observing Western society, I was forced to conclude that the "wise" were no longer the main objects of admiration, but that famous, rich, or powerful people had taken their place. The excessive importance accorded to consumption and a taste for the superfluous, as well as the reign of money, made me think that many of our contemporaries had forgotten the ends of existence—to achieve a sense of fulfillment—and gotten lost in the means.

In the reality of every day, despite the share of violence that afflicts the world, our existence is usually woven from deeds of cooperation, friendship, affection, and care. Nature is not merely "red in tooth and claw," as the poet Alfred, Lord Tennyson deplored.[4] What's more, contrary to conventional wisdom and to the impression the media give us, all in-depth studies, gathered together by Harvard professor Steven Pinker in *The Better Angels of our Nature,* show that violence, in all its forms, has continued to diminish over the course of the last few centuries.[5]

From spending time with my scientist friends, I was reassured to note that, during the last thirty years, the deformed vision of human nature had been challenged by an increasing number of researchers demonstrating that the hypothesis of universal selfishness was disproven by scientific investigation.[6] Daniel Batson, in particular, was the first psychologist to investigate, through rigorous scientific protocols, whether real altruism existed and was not limited to a disguised form of selfishness.

THE FORCE OF EXAMPLE

When I was young, I often heard it said that kindness was the most admirable quality in a human being. My mother demonstrated this constantly by her actions, and many people I respected urged me to be kind-hearted. Their words and actions were a source of inspiration and opened up to me a field of possibilities that were not limited to self-centered preoccupations and that fed my hopes for living a good and meaningful life. I was raised in a secular environment and so I was not inculcated with dogmas on altruism or charity. Only the force of example taught me.

Since 1989, I've had the honor of serving as a French interpreter for the Dalai Lama, who often states, "My religion is kindness," and the essence of whose teaching is: "Every sentient being, even my enemy, fears suffering as I do and wants to be happy. This thought leads us to feel profoundly concerned for the happiness of others, be they friends or enemies. That is the basis for true compassion. Seeking happiness while remaining indifferent to others is a tragic mistake." This teaching is embodied by the Dalai Lama on a daily basis. With everyone, visitors or strangers met in the airport, he is always totally and immediately present, with a gaze overflowing with kindness that touches your heart.

A few years ago, when I was getting ready to go on retreat in the mountains of Nepal, I sought some advice from the Dalai Lama. "In the beginning, meditate on compassion; in the middle, meditate on compassion; in the end, meditate on compassion," he told me.

Every practitioner must first transform himself before he is able to serve others effectively. Still, the Dalai Lama insists on the necessity of building a bridge between contemplative life and active life. If compassion without wisdom is blind, compassion without action is hypocritical. It is under his guidance and that of my other spiritual masters that I have devoted my resources and a large part of my time since 1999 to the activities of Karuna-Shechen.[7] This is a humanitarian organization made up of a group of devoted volunteers and generous benefactors, which builds and finances schools, clinics, and hospices in Tibet, Nepal and India.

THE CHALLENGES OF TODAY

In this current era we are confronted with many challenges. One of our main problems consists of reconciling the demands of the economy, the search for happiness, and respect for the environment. These imperatives correspond to three time scales—short, middle, and long term—on which three types of interests are superimposed: ours, the interests of those close to us, and those of all sentient beings.

The economy and finance are evolving at an ever-faster pace. Stock markets soar and crash from one day to the next. New methods of ultra-high-speed transactions, developed by the teams of certain banks and used by speculators, allow 400 million transactions to take place per second. The lifecycle of products is becoming extremely short. No investor is willing to place his money in treasury bonds redeemable in fifty years! Those who live in ease are often reluctant to alter their lifestyle for the good of those less fortunate and for the benefit of generations to come, while those who live in need aspire understandably to more wealth, but also to enter a consumer society that encourages acquiring not only what is needed to live a decent life, but to keep on chasing after superfluous things.

Satisfaction with life is measured in terms of a life plan, a career, a family, and a generation. It is also measured according to the quality of each passing instant, the joys and sufferings that color our existence, and our relationships to others; it is given or denied by the nature of external conditions and by the way in which our mind translates these conditions into happiness or misery.

As for the environment, until recently its evolution has been measured in terms of geological, biological, and climatic eras over dozens of millennia or millions of years, except for the occurrence of a few global catastrophes such as the collision of a giant asteroid that caused the fifth massive extinction of species on earth. In our day, the rhythm of change keeps accelerating because of ecological upheavals provoked by human activities. In particular, the swift changes that have occurred since 1950 have defined a new era for our planet, the *Anthropocene* (literally the "era of humans"). This is the first era in the history of the world when human activities are profoundly modifying (and at present degrading) the entire system that maintains life on earth. This is a completely new challenge that has taken us by surprise.

Wealthy countries, which profit the most from exploiting natural resources, do not want to alter their standard of living. But they are the nations chiefly responsible for climate change and other scourges (such as the increase of illnesses related to climate change—malaria, for example, is spreading in new regions and at higher altitudes as minimum temperature increases) affecting the poorest populations—precisely the ones that have contributed the least to these upheavals. An Afghan produces two thousand five hundred times less CO_2 than a Qatari and a thousand times less than an American. About the rising level of the oceans, the American magnate Stephen Forbes declared on Fox News: "To change what we do because something is going to happen in one hundred years is, I would say, profoundly weird." Isn't it actually a declaration like that that is absurd? The head of the largest meat company in the United States is even more openly cynical: "What matters," he says, "is we sell our meat. What will happen in fifty years is none of our business."

But it all concerns us, as well as our children, those close to us, and our descendants, along with all beings, human and animal, now and in the future. Concentrating our efforts solely on ourselves and our relatives, in the short term, is one of the regrettable manifestations of egocentrism.

If we continue to be obsessed with achieving growth, with consumption of natural resources increasing at its current exponential rate, we would need three planets by 2050. We don't have them. In order to remain within the environmental safety zone in which humanity can continue to prosper, we need to curb our endless desire for "more." "Voluntary simplicity" does not involve living in poverty, but in moderation. It also facilitates social justice and does not encourage the disproportionate concentration of resources in the hands of a few.

For many of us, the notion of "simplicity" evokes a privation, a narrowing of our possibilities and an impoverishment of existence. Experience shows, however, that a voluntary simplicity in no way entails a diminution of happiness, but on the contrary brings with it a better quality of life. Is it more enjoyable to spend a day with your children or friends, at home, in a park or outside in nature, or to spend it trotting from store to store? Is it more pleasant to enjoy the contentment of a satisfied mind or constantly to want more—a more expensive car, brand-name clothes, or a more luxurious house?

The American psychologist Tim Kasser and his colleagues at the University of Rochester have highlighted the high cost of materialist values.[8] Thanks to studies spread over twenty years, they have demonstrated that within a representative sample of the population, individuals who concentrated their existence on wealth, image, social status, and other materialistic, extrinsic values promoted by consumer society are less satisfied with their existence. Focused on themselves, they prefer competition to cooperation, contribute less to the general interest and are unconcerned with ecological matters. Their social ties are weakened and they have fewer real friends. They show less empathy and compassion for those who suffer and have a tendency to use others for their own ends. They are in less good health than the rest of the population. Excessive consumerism is closely linked to extreme self-centeredness and lack of empathy.[9]

Individualism, in its good aspects, can foster a spirit of initiative, creativity, and going beyond norms and old-fashioned and restrictive dogmas, but it can also very quickly degenerate into irresponsible selfishness and rampant narcissism, to the detriment of the well-being of all. Selfishness is at the heart of most of the problems we face today: the growing gap between rich and poor, the attitude of "everybody for himself," which is only increasing, and indifference about the generations to come.

THE NECESSITY FOR ALTRUISM

We need a unifying concept, an Ariadne thread that will allow us to find our way in this labyrinth of serious, complex preoccupations. Altruism is this thread that will allow us naturally to connect the three scales of time—short-, middle-, and long-term—by reconciling their demands.

Altruism is often presented as a supreme moral value in both religious and secular societies. It scarcely has a place, though, in a world entirely governed by competition and individualism. Some people, notably the philosopher Ayn Rand, even rise up against the ethics of altruism, which they perceive as a demand for sacrifice, and they advocate the virtues of selfishness.

In the contemporary world, though, altruism is more than ever a necessity, even an urgent one. It is also a natural manifestation of human kindness, for which we all have potential, despite multiple, often selfish, motivations that run through and sometimes dominate our minds.

What, in fact, are the benefits of altruism with respect to the major problems we have described? Let's take a few examples. If each of us cultivated altruism more, that is, if we had more consideration for the well-being of others, financiers, for example, would not engage in wild speculation with the savings of small investors who have entrusted themselves to them, just to gather larger bonuses at year's end. Financiers would not speculate on commodities—food, grain, water, and other resources vital to the survival of the poorest populations.

If they had more consideration for the quality of life of those around them, the ones who make decisions and other social agents would be concerned with the improvement of working conditions, family and social life, and many other aspects of existence. They would be led to acknowledge the divide that is growing ever wider between the poorest and those who represent 1% of the population but who control 25% of the wealth.[10] Finally, they could open their eyes to the fate of the society itself from which they profit and on which they have built their fortunes.

If we evince more concern for others, we will all act with the view of remedying injustice, discrimination, and poverty. We would be led to reconsider the way we treat animals, reducing them to nothing but instruments of our blind domination which transforms them into products of consumption.

Finally, if we care about the fate of future generations, we will not blindly sacrifice their well-being to our ephemeral interests, leaving only a polluted, impoverished planet to those who come after us.

We would on the contrary try to promote a caring economy that would enhance reciprocal trust, and would respect the interests of others. We would envisage the possibility of a different economy, one that is now advocated by many modern economists,[11] an economy that rests on the three pillars of true prosperity: nature, whose integrity we must preserve; human activities, which should flourish; and financial means, which ensure our survival and our reasonable material needs.[12]

Most classical economists have for too long based their theories on the hypothesis that people exclusively pursue selfish interests. This hypothesis is wrong, but it still comprises the foundation of contemporary economic systems based on the principle of free exchange theorized by Adam Smith in *The Wealth of Nations.* These same economists have argued against the necessity for each individual to attend to the well-being of others so that society can function harmoniously—a necessity clearly formulated, nevertheless, by the same Adam Smith in his *Theory of Moral Sentiments.*

Also forgetting the emphasis placed by Darwin on the importance of cooperation in nature, certain contemporary theories of evolution think that altruism makes sense only if it is proportional to the degree of biological kinship linking us to those who carry some part of our genes. We will see how new advances in the theory of evolution allow us to envisage the possibility of an extended altruism that transcends the ties of family and tribal proximity and emphasizes the fact that human beings are essentially "super-cooperators."[13]

Contrary to what the avalanche of shocking news often presented in media headlines would have us think, many studies show that when a natural catastrophe or some other kind of tragedy occurs, mutual aid is more the rule than every-man-for-himself, sharing more common than pillaging, calm prevails more than panic, dedication more than indifference, courage more than cowardice.[14]

Furthermore, the experience of thousands of years of contemplative practices attests that individual transformation is possible. This age-old experience has now been corroborated by research in the neurosciences that has shown that any form of training—learning how to read or learning a musical instrument, for example—induces a restructuring in the brain at both the functional and structural levels. This is also what happens when one trains in developing altruistic love and compassion.

Recent studies by theoreticians of evolution[15] stress the importance of the evolution of cultures: slower than individual changes but much faster than genetic changes. This evolution is cumulative and is transmitted over the course of generations by education and imitation.

That is not all. In fact, cultures and individuals continue to influence each other mutually. Individuals who grow up in a new culture are different, because their new habits transform their brain through neuroplasticity, and the expression of their genes through epigenetics. These individuals will, in turn, contribute to causing their culture and their institutions to evolve so that this process is repeated in every generation.

To recapitulate, altruism seems to be a determining factor of the quality of our existence, now and to come, and should not be relegated to the realm of noble utopian thinking maintained by a few big-hearted, naïve people. We must have the perspicacity to acknowledge this and the audacity to say it. But what is altruism? Does real altruism exist? How does it appear? Can one become more altruistic, and, if so, how? What are the obstacles to surmount? How can we build a more altruistic society and a better world? These are the main questions we will try to examine in this work.

I

What Is Altruism?

To live is to be useful to others.

— Seneca

1

The Nature of Altruism

Some Definitions

Is altruism a *motivation,* a momentary state of mind that aims at accomplishing the good of others, or a *disposition* to care for others in a benevolent way, pointing to a more lasting character trait? Definitions abound and, sometimes, contradict each other. If we want to show that real altruism exists and help it spread throughout society, it is necessary to clarify the meaning of this term.

The word "altruism," derived from the Latin *alter,* "other," was used for the first time in the nineteenth century by Auguste Comte, one of the fathers of sociology and the founder of positivism. Altruism, according to Comte, implies "the elimination of selfish desire and of egocentrism, as well as leading a life devoted to the well-being of others."[1]

The American philosopher Thomas Nagel explains that altruism is "a willingness to act in consideration of the interests of the other person, without the need of ulterior motive."[2] It is a rational determination to act stemming from "the direct influence of one person's interest on the actions of another, simply because in itself the interest of the former provides the latter with a reason to act."[3]

Other thinkers, confident in the potential for benevolence present in humans, go further and, like the American philosopher Stephen Post, define altruistic love as "unselfish delight in the well-being of others, and engagement in acts of care and service on their behalf. Unlimited love extends this love to all others without exception, in an enduring and constant way."[4] The *agapē* of Christianity is an unconditional love for other human beings, while altruistic love and compassion in Buddhism, *maitri* and *karuna,* extend to all sentient beings, humans and non-humans.

Some authors emphasize putting intentions into practice, while others think it is motivation that defines altruism. The psychologist Daniel Batson, who has devoted his career to the study of altruism, points out that "altruism is a motivational state with the ultimate goal of increasing another's welfare."[5] He clearly distinguishes altruism as ultimate goal (my explicit aim is to accomplish others' welfare) from altruism as means (I accomplish others' welfare with a view to fulfilling my own well-being). In his eyes, for a motivation to be altruistic, the well-being of others must constitute a *goal in itself.*[6]

Among the other modes of altruism, *goodness* corresponds to a way of being that translates into actions as soon as circumstances allow; *benevolence,* from the Latin *benevole,* "to want the well-being [of the other]," is a favorable disposition toward others, accompanied by a desire to act upon that desire. *Solicitude* consists of caring in a lasting way and with vigilance about another's fate: concerned about his situation, one is anxious to provide for his needs, promote his well-being, and remedy his suffering. *Dedication* consists of selflessly placing oneself in the service of persons or a cause beneficial to society. *Kindness* is a form of caring, warm-hearted consideration that is manifested in the way we behave toward others. *Fraternity* stems from the feeling of belonging to the great human family whose every representative is perceived as a brother or sister whose fate matters to us; fraternity also evokes the ideas of harmony, cohesion, and union. The feeling of *solidarity* with a more or less extensive group of people is born when all must confront together common challenges and obstacles. By extension, this feeling can be experienced for the most destitute, or for those who are affected by a catastrophe; it is the community of fate that unites us.

ACTION ALONE DOES NOT DEFINE ALTRUISM

In her book entitled *The Heart of Altruism,* Kristen Monroe, professor of political science and philosophy at the University of Irvine at California, suggests we reserve the term "altruism" for *actions* carried out for the well-being of others at the price of some risk for ourselves, without expecting anything in return. According to her, good intentions are indispensable for altruism, but they are not enough. One must act, and action must have a precise goal, that of contributing to the well-being of another.[7]

Monroe does acknowledge, however, that motivations for an action count more than their results.[8] So it seems preferable to us not to restrict the use of the term *altruism* to external behavior, since actions do not in themselves allow us to know with certainty the motivation that inspired them. Just as the appearance of *undesirable and unforeseen consequences* does not call into question the altruistic nature of an action meant for the good of the other, so a *hindrance to taking action,* which is beyond the control of the one who wants to act, does not at all diminish the altruistic nature of his motivation.

Moreover, for Monroe, an action cannot be considered altruistic if it does not bear a risk and has no "cost," however potential, for the one who performs it. In our opinion, an altruistic individual will indeed be ready to take risks to accomplish good for others, but the simple fact of taking risks for someone else is neither necessary nor sufficient to qualify as altruistic behavior. One can imagine an individual putting himself in danger to help someone with the idea of gaining his trust and drawing personal advantages from it sufficiently desirable to justify the perils encountered. What's more, some people agree to court danger for purely selfish reasons—to seek glory, for instance, by carrying out a dangerous exploit. On the other hand, a behavior can be sincerely devoted to the good of the other, without bearing any notable risk whatever. The one who, moved by benevolence, gives away part of his wealth or devotes years to a charity organization helping people in need does not necessarily take a risk; but his behavior deserves to be qualified as altruistic, in our sense of it.

It Is Motivation That Colors Our Actions

Our motivations, whether they are benevolent, malevolent or neutral, color our actions. One cannot distinguish altruistic behavior from selfish behavior, a lie meant to do good from another uttered to harm, by the sole appearance of actions. If a mother suddenly pushes her child to the side of the street to prevent it from being run over by a car, her action is violent only in appearance. If someone approaches you with a big smile and showers you with compliments with the sole aim of swindling you, his conduct may seem benevolent, but his intentions are obviously selfish.

Keeping in mind our limited ability to control outer events or anticipate the turn they will take in the long run, we cannot qualify an act as either altruistic or selfish on the basis of the simple observation of its immediate consequences. Giving drugs or a glass of alcohol to someone who is undergoing a detox cure, with the excuse that he is suffering from abstention symptoms, will no doubt provide him with much-appreciated temporary relief, but such an action will do him no good in the long run.

On the other hand, in every circumstance, it is possible for us to examine our motivations attentively and honestly, and to do our best to determine if they are selfish or altruistic. More often than not, we neglect to do so. It is also easy to misperceive our true motive. This is why Buddhist teachings emphasize the need to look again and again into the mirror of one's mind to check our motivations.

In his book *Altruism in Humans,* Daniel Batson offers a set of criteria by which we can qualify our motivations as altruistic.[9]

Altruism requires a motivation: an instinctive reflex or automatic behavior cannot be qualified as either altruistic or selfish, whatever the beneficial or harmful consequences may be.

The difference between altruism and selfishness is qualitative: it is the *quality* of our motivation and not its *intensity* that determines its altruistic nature.

Various motivations, altruistic and selfish, can coexist in our minds, and create a motivational conflict when we simultaneously consider our interests and the other's.

Moreover, we sometimes act in ways that benefit others for reasons that are neither altruistic nor selfish, especially out of a sense of duty or to respect the law.

Carrying thought into action may depend on various factors that are beyond our control. This alone does not fundamentally change the altruistic or selfish nature of our motivations.

Altruism does not require a personal sacrifice: it can even lead to personal benefits, provided that those benefits do not constitute the ultimate goal of our behavior, but are only secondary consequences of it.

In essence, altruism does indeed reside in the motivation that animates one's behavior. Altruism can be regarded as authentic so long as the desire for the other's welfare constitutes our ultimate goal, even if our motivation has not yet been transformed into actions.

By contrast, a selfish person considers others as instruments in the service of his own interests. He does not hesitate to neglect, or even to sacrifice, the good of the other when that turns out to be useful to reach his ends.

The Importance of Valuing the Other's Welfare

Valuing the other and being concerned about his situation are two essential components to altruism. When this attitude prevails in us, it manifests itself in the form of benevolence toward others, and it is translated into an open-mindedness and a willingness to take care of them.

When we observe that the other has a particular need or desire whose satisfaction will enable him to avoid suffering or to experience well-being, empathy first makes us become aware of this need. Then, concern for the other gives rise to a desire to help satisfy that need. On the other hand, if we grant little value to the other, we will be indifferent to him: we will ignore his needs; perhaps we will not even notice them.[10]

ALTRUISM DOES NOT REQUIRE "SACRIFICE"

The fact of experiencing joy in working for the good of others, or of coming away with unexpected benefits for oneself, does not, in itself, make an action selfish. Authentic altruism does not require that you suffer from helping others and does not lose its authenticity if it is accompanied by a feeling of profound satisfaction. What's more, the very notion of sacrifice is relative: what seems a sacrifice to some is felt as a gain by others, as illustrated by the following story.

Sanjit "Bunker" Roy, with whom our humanitarian organization Karuna-Shechen collaborates, relates that at the age of twenty, as the son of a good family educated in one of the most prestigious schools in India, he was destined for a fine career. His mother already pictured him as a doctor, an engineer, or an official in the World Bank. That year, in 1965, a terrible famine broke out in the province of Bihar, one of the poorest states in India. Bunker, inspired by Jai Prakash Narayan, friend of Gandhi and a great Indian moral figure, decided to go with friends his age to see what was happening in the villages most affected. He returned a few weeks later, transformed, and told his mother he wanted to go live in a village. After a period of worried silence, his mother asked him: "And what are you going to do in a village?" Bunker replied: "To work as an unskilled laborer, digging wells."

"My mother almost went into a coma," Bunker says. The other members of the family tried to reassure her, saying: "Don't worry, like all teenagers, he's having his crisis of idealism. After toiling there for a few weeks, he'll soon become disillusioned and will come home."

But Bunker did not come home, and remained for four decades in villages. For six years, he dug three hundred wells with a pneumatic drill in the countryside of Rajasthan. His mother stopped talking to him for years. When he settled in the village of Tilonia, the local authorities didn't understand either: "Are you running away from the police?"

"No."

"Did you fail your exams?"

"No."

"Were you unable to get a government job?"

"No."

Someone of his social standing and with such a high level of education was out of place in a poor village.

Bunker realized he could do more than dig wells. He observed that the men who had completed their studies left for the cities and contributed nothing whatsoever to helping their villages. "Men are untrainable," he proclaimed mischievously. It was better, he thought, to educate the women, especially the young grandmothers (aged 35–50) who had more free time than mothers with families. Even if they were illiterate, it was possible to train them so they could become "solar engineers," able to make solar panels. And there was no risk of their leaving the village.

Bunker was ignored for a long time, then criticized by the local authorities and international organizations, including the World Bank. But he persevered and trained hundreds of illiterate grandmothers who supplied solar energy to almost a thousand villages in India and in many other countries. His activity is now supported by the Indian government and other organizations; it is cited as an example almost everywhere in the world. He has also come up with programs that use the ancestral know-how of farmers, especially ways to collect rainwater to fill tanks big enough to provide for the yearly needs of the villagers. Before, women had to walk several hours every day to bring back heavy jars of often polluted water. In Rajasthan, he founded the Barefoot College, in which even the teachers have no college degree but share their experience based on years of practice. Everyone lives very simply at the college, like Gandhi's communities, and no one is paid more than 100 euros a month.

He has since reconciled with his family, who are now proud of him. So, for many years, what seemed to those close to Bunker to be an insane sacrifice has constituted for him a success that has filled him with enthusiasm and satisfaction. Far from discouraging him, the difficulties he encountered on his way have only stimulated his intelligence, his compassion, and his creative faculties. To this day, and for forty years, Bunker has led to fruition a multitude of remarkable projects in nearly sixty-seven countries. What's more, his entire being radiates the calm contentment of a meaningful life.

To teach villagers in a lively way, Bunker and his collaborators organize representations featuring large papier-mâché marionettes. As a sly wink to those who used to look down on him, these marionettes are made from recycled reports of the World Bank. Bunker quotes Gandhi: "First they ignore you. Then they laugh at you. Then they fight you. Finally, you win."

TEMPORARY MENTAL STATES AND LASTING DISPOSITIONS

For Daniel Batson, altruism is not so much a way of being as a motivating force directed toward a goal, a force that disappears when that goal is attained. Batson thus envisions altruism as a temporary mental state linked to the perception of a particular need in another person, rather than as a lasting disposition. He prefers to speak of *altruism* instead of *altruists,* since, at any time, a person can harbor in himself a mixture of motivations, some altruistic and some selfish. Personal interest can also enter into competition with the interest of others and create an internal conflict.

It seems legitimate, then, to speak also of altruistic or selfish *dispositions* according to the mental states that usually predominate in a person—all the stages between unconditional altruism and narrow-minded selfishness are conceivable. The Scottish philosopher Francis Hutcheson said about altruism that it was not "some few accidental motions of compassion, natural affection, or gratitude; but such a fixed humanity, the desire for the public good of all those to whom our influence can extend, a desire that regularly urges us to all acts of benevolence, and leads us to learn correctly the best way to serve the interests of humanity."[11] For his part, the American historian Philip Hallie states that "Goodness is not a doctrine or principle. It is a way of living."[12]

This lasting internal disposition is accompanied by a particular view of the world. According to Kristen Monroe, "altruists simply have a different way of seeing things. Where the rest of us see a stranger, altruists see a fellow human being. While many disparate factors may contribute to the existence and development of what I identify as an altruistic perspective, it is the perspective itself that constitutes the heart of altruism."[13]

The French psychologists Jean-François Deschamps and Rémi Finkelstein have also demonstrated the existence of a link between altruism regarded as a *personal value* and prosocial behavior, especially voluntary work.[14]

Further, our spontaneous reactions faced with unforeseeable circumstances reflect our deep-set dispositions and our degree of internal preparedness. Most of us will extend a hand to someone who has just fallen into the water. A psychopath or a person dominated by hatred might watch the unfortunate person drown without lifting a finger, even with a sadistic satisfaction.

Fundamentally, to the extent that altruism permeates our minds, it is expressed instantaneously when we are confronted with the needs of the other. As the Canadian philosopher Charles Taylor wrote: "Much modern moral philosophy has focused on what it is right to do rather than the nature of the good life."[15] This view of things allows altruism to join a vaster perspective and lets us envisage the possibility of *cultivating* it as a *way of being.*

2

Extending Altruism

Altruism is like rings in the water when you toss a pebble. At first the circles are very small, then they get larger, and finally they embrace the entire surface of the ocean.

— Alexandre Jollien[1]

For most of us, it is natural to feel benevolently inclined toward someone dear to us, or to anyone who is well-intentioned toward us. It seems a priori more difficult to extend that benevolence to many individuals, especially to those who treat us badly. But we have the ability, through reasoning and through mental training, to include them in the sphere of altruism by realizing that kindness and compassion are not simply "rewards" given for good behavior, but that their essential aim is to promote the happiness of beings and to remedy their suffering. I will discuss the methods suggested by Buddhism to this end. In doing this, my aim is not to urge the reader to adopt this spiritual way, but to emphasize the universal value of certain points emerging from the philosophy and practice of Buddhism. These qualities are part of what the Dalai Lama calls the *promotion of human values or secular ethics,* an ethics that is not opposed, in principle, to religions, yet depends on none of them.[2]

Altruism and compassion have the aim of spreading themselves as widely as possible. We must simply understand that our own well-being and the world's cannot rest on indifference to the happiness of the other or on a refusal to care about the sufferings around us.

Altruistic Love, Compassion, and Empathy

Buddhism defines *altruistic love* as "the wish that all beings find happiness and the causes of happiness." By "happiness," Buddhism means not just a temporary state of well-being or a pleasant sensation, but rather a way of being based on an array of qualities that include altruism, inner freedom, and inner strength, as well as an accurate view of reality.[3] By "causes of happiness," Buddhism is referring not merely to the immediate triggers of happiness, but to its profound roots, namely the pursuit of wisdom and a more accurate understanding of reality.

This altruistic wish is accompanied by a steady readiness and availability to others allied with the determination to do everything in our power to help each individual being to attain authentic happiness. On this point, Buddhism joins Aristotle, who wrote: "We may describe friendly feeling toward any one as wishing for him what you believe to be good things, not for your own sake but for his, and being inclined, so far as you can, to bring these things about."[4]

It is not a question here of a simple dogmatic assertion that "suffering is evil"; it is taking into consideration the desire of every sentient being to escape suffering. A purely normative attitude, the aim of which would be to bring an end to suffering as an abstract entity, might involve a risk that one might be less attentive to the beings themselves and to their specific sufferings. That is why the Dalai Lama gives this advice: "We must use a real individual as the focus of our meditation, and then enhance our compassion and loving-kindness toward that person so that we can really experience compassion and loving-kindness toward others. We work on one person at a time. Otherwise, we might end up meditating on compassion for all in a very general sense, with no specific focus or power to our meditation."[5] What's more, history has shown us that when one defines good and evil in a dogmatic way, all kinds of distortions become possible, from the Inquisition to totalitarian dictatorships. As my father, Jean-François Revel, often said: "Totalitarian regimes proclaim: 'We know how to make you happy. You just have to follow our rules. However, if you disobey, we will regretfully have to eliminate you.'"[6]

Altruistic love is characterized by unconditional kindness toward *all beings* and is apt to be expressed at any time in favor of *every being in particular.* It permeates the mind and is expressed appropriately, according to the circumstances, to answer the needs of all.

Compassion is the form that altruistic love takes when it is confronted with others' sufferings. Buddhism defines it as "the wish that all beings be freed from suffering and the causes of suffering" or, as the Buddhist teacher Bhante Henepola Gunaratana poetically writes: "Compassion is a melting of the heart at the thought of another's suffering."[7] This aspiration should be followed by putting every method possible into action to remedy his torments.

Here again, the "causes of suffering" include not only the immediate and visible causes of suffering, but also the deep-seated causes of suffering, chief of which is *ignorance.* Ignorance here is understood as a mistaken understanding of reality leading us to have disturbing mental states like hatred and compulsive desire and to act under their influence. This kind of ignorance leads us to perpetuate the cycle of suffering and to turn our backs to lasting well-being.

Loving-kindness and compassion are the two faces of altruism. It is their object that distinguishes them: loving-kindness wants all beings to experience happiness, while compassion focuses on eradicating their suffering. Both should last as long as there are beings and as long as they are suffering.

We define *empathy* here as the ability to enter into *affective resonance* with the other's feelings and to *become cognitively aware of his situation.* Empathy alerts us in particular to the nature and intensity of the sufferings experienced by the other. One could say that it *catalyzes the transformation of altruistic love into compassion.*

The Importance of Lucidity

Altruism *should be enlightened by lucidity and wisdom.* It is not a question of inconsiderately gaining access to all the desires and whims of others. True love consists in combining unlimited benevolence with flawless discernment. Love thus defined should involve taking into account the full picture of each situation and asking oneself: "What will be the short- and long-term benefits and drawbacks of what I am about to do? Will my action affect a smaller or larger number of individuals?" Transcending all partiality, altruistic love should lucidly consider the best way to carry out the good of others. Impartiality demands that you not favor someone simply because you feel more sympathy for him than for some other person who is also in need, if not more so. How can we reconcile this unconditional and impartial love with the fact that we naturally have preferential relationships with certain people and that we are programmed genetically to show particular care for our kin and our friends? We may take the image of the sun. It shines over all people equally, with the same brightness and the same warmth in every direction. Yet, there are people who, for various reasons, are closer to it and receive more heat, but that privileged situation does not entail exclusion. It seems therefore possible to develop the kind of goodness that embraces all living beings while caring the best we can for those who fall within the sphere of our responsibilities.

Rejoicing in the Happiness of Others and Cultivating Impartiality

To altruistic love and compassion, Buddhism adds *joy when perceiving the happiness and good qualities of others* as well as *impartiality.*

Rejoicing consists in feeling from the bottom of your heart a sincere joy at the accomplishments and qualities of others, toward those who work for the good of others, whose beneficial projects are crowned with success, those who have realized their aspirations at the cost of persistent efforts, and also those who possess multiple talents. This joy, appreciation, and celebration are accompanied by the wish that their happiness and qualities never diminish, but persist and increase. This ability to be pleased about the qualities of others also serves as an antidote to competitiveness, envy, and jealousy, all of which reflect an inability to rejoice in the happiness of others. Rejoicing also constitutes a remedy to a somber, despairing view of the world and humanity.

Impartiality is an essential component of altruism—the desire that beings find happiness and be free from suffering should not depend either on our personal attachments or on the way others treat us or behave toward us. Impartiality adopts the attitude of a kind, dedicated physician who rejoices when others are in good health and concerns himself with curing all sick people, whoever they are.

Altruism can be influenced by sentimentality and lead to attitudes of partiality. If, during a trip to a poor country, I meet a group of children and one of them seems nicer to me than the others, granting him any special treatment stems from a benevolent intention, but also testifies to a lack of fairness and perspicacity. It is possible that the other children present are more in need of my aid.

Similarly, if one is concerned about the fate of certain animals simply because they are "cute," and if one remains indifferent to the suffering of those that are considered "ugly," this is just a pretense of altruism, induced by prejudices and emotional preferences. Hence the importance of the notion of impartiality. According to Buddhism, altruism should be extended to all sentient beings, whatever their appearance, behavior, and degree of closeness to us.

Like the sun that shines equally over both the "good" and the "bad," over a magnificent landscape as well as over a pile of trash, impartiality extends to all beings without distinction. When compassion thus conceived is directed at a person who is causing great harm to others, it does not consist of tolerating, or encouraging by inaction, his hatred and his harmful actions, but in regarding that person as gravely ill or stricken with madness, and wishing that he be freed from the ignorance and hostility that are in him. This does not mean that one will consider anyone who does not share one's moral principles or deeply disagrees with them, as being ill. It refers to people whose views lead them to seriously harm others. In other words, it is not a matter of contemplating harmful actions with equanimity, even indifference, but of understanding that it is possible to eradicate their causes the way one can eliminate the causes of an illness.

The universal, impartial nature of extended altruism certainly does not create a diluted, abstract feeling, disconnected from beings and from reality. It does not prevent us from lucidly evaluating context and circumstances. Instead of being diluted by the multitude and diversity of beings, extended altruism is reinforced by their number and by the variety of their particular needs. It is applied pragmatically to every being who presents himself or herself in the field of our attention.

What's more, it does not require that we achieve immediate success. No one can expect all beings to stop suffering overnight, as if by a miracle. The immensity of the task should be matched by the magnitude of one's courage. Shantideva, a seventh-century Indian Buddhist master, says:

As long as space endures,
And as long as sentient beings exist,
May I, too, remain
To dispel the misery of the world.

One of the important aspects of altruistic love is courage. A true altruist is ready to move unhesitatingly and fearlessly toward others. Feelings of insecurity and fear are major obstacles to altruism. If we are affected by the slightest vexation, rebuff, criticism, or insult, we find ourselves weakened by it and think above all of protecting ourselves. The feeling of insecurity leads us to close in on ourselves and to keep our distance from others. To become more altruistic, we have to develop an inner strength that makes us confident in our inner resources that let us face the constantly changing circumstances of existence. Fortified with this confidence, we are ready to open ourselves up to others and to display altruism. That is why Buddhism talks about "courageous compassion." Gandhi too said: "Love fears nothing and no one. It cuts through fear at its very root."

Expanding One's Understanding of Others' Needs

The more concerned one is by the fate of someone experiencing difficulties, the more the motivation to relieve his suffering is reinforced. But it is important to identify clearly and correctly the needs of the other and to understand what is truly necessary in order to be able to provide for his various degrees of well-being.[8] According to Buddhism, the *ultimate need* of every living being is to be free of suffering in all its forms, including those that are not immediately visible and that stem from ignorance.

Recognizing the fact that this need is shared by all beings lets us extend altruism to both friends and enemies, to those close to us as well as to strangers, to human beings as well as to all other sentient beings. In the case of an enemy, for example, the need one takes into account is certainly not the accomplishment of his malevolent aims, but the necessity of uprooting the causes that engendered these aims.

From Biological Altruism to Extended Altruism

The Dalai Lama distinguishes two types of altruistic love: the first manifests spontaneously because of the biological dispositions that we have inherited from evolution. It reflects our instinct to take care of our children, those close to us, and more generally whoever treats us with kindness.

This *natural altruism* is innate and requires no training. Its most powerful form is parental love. Still, it remains limited and partial, for it usually depends on our links of parentage or the way we perceive others, favorably or unfavorably, as well as the way they treat us.

Solicitude toward a child, an elderly person, or a sick person is often born from our perception of their vulnerability and their need for protection. We indeed have the ability to be moved by the fate of children other than our own and people other than those close to us, but natural altruism is not easily extended to strangers, and even less so to our enemies. It is also fickle since it can disappear when a friend or a parent who until then had been well-disposed toward us changes their attitude and suddenly treats us with indifference, or even hostility.

Extended altruism, however, is impartial. In most people, it is not spontaneous and must be cultivated. "The social instinct, together with sympathy, is, like any other instinct, greatly strengthened by habit,"[9] wrote Darwin. Whatever our point of departure, we all have the possibility of cultivating altruism and transcending the limits that restrict it to the circle of those close to us.

Instinctive altruism, acquired in the course of our evolution, especially the mother's for her child, can serve as a basis for more extended altruism, even if that was not its initial function. This idea has been defended by a number of psychologists, like William McDougall, Daniel Batson, and Paul Ekman, and supported by some philosophers, including Elliott Sober and the evolutionary specialist David Sloan Wilson.[10]

This extension has two main stages: on one hand, one *perceives the needs* of a larger number of beings, especially those we had regarded till then as strangers or enemies. On the other hand, one *learns to value* a vaster totality of sentient beings, beyond the circle of those close to us, our social, ethnic, religious, or national groups, and even extends beyond the human species.[11]

It is interesting to note that Darwin not only envisaged this expansion, but also deemed it necessary, writing of "sympathy, which was originally acquired as part of the social instincts, but subsequently rendered, in the manner previously indicated, more tender and more widely diffused. Nor could we check our sympathy, even at the urging of hard reason, without deterioration in the noblest part of our nature."[12]

This approach begins with the following realization: If I look deep inside myself, I want not to suffer. I do not wake up in the morning thinking: "May I suffer all day and, if possible, all my life." When I have recognized this aspiration not to suffer within myself, what happens if I mentally project myself into the awareness of another being? Like me, he is perhaps under the sway of all kinds of torments and great mental confusion, but, like me, wouldn't he too prefer, if possible, not to suffer? He shares my desire to escape suffering, and this wish is worthy of respect.

Unfortunately there are people who, lacking the conditions that would have allowed them to do well, turn to harming themselves willfully, self-mutilation, or acts of despair, going as far as suicide.[13] Lack of love, of meaning, of confidence in oneself, and the absence of a clear direction in their lives weigh so heavily that it sometimes leads them to self-destruction. These extreme actions are a cry of despair, a call for help, a way of self-expression for those who do not know how to find happiness, or who have been prevented from doing so by the brutality of external conditions.

EMOTIONAL AND COGNITIVE ASPECTS OF ALTRUISM AND COMPASSION

Being moved by others' suffering, feeling suffering oneself because they are suffering, being happy when they are happy and sad when they are afflicted—all these stem from emotional resonance.

On the other hand, discerning the immediate or long-lasting, superficial or profound, causes of others' suffering and giving rise to the determination to alleviate them stem from wisdom and "cognitive" compassion. The latter is linked to the comprehension of the causes of suffering at various levels. For that reason, its dimension is vaster and its effects more extensive. These two aspects of altruism, affective and cognitive, are complementary and do not comprise two separate, airtight mental attitudes. In some people, at first altruism takes the form of an emotional experience that can subsequently transform into cognitive altruism when the person begins to analyze the causes of suffering. Altruism, however, remains limited if it is confined solely to its emotional component.

In fact, according to Buddhism, *the fundamental cause of suffering is ignorance,* the mental confusion that deforms reality and gives rise to an array of mental obscurations such as hatred, compulsive desire, jealousy, and pride. If we are solely interested in the secondary causes of suffering, that is in its visible manifestations, we will never be able to alleviate them completely. If a ship gets damaged, it is not enough to summon all hands to pump water out of the hold. It is absolutely necessary to plug the gap through which the water is rushing.

Love and Compassion Based on Discernment

In order to extend altruism, it is therefore necessary to become aware of the various degrees of suffering. When the Buddha spoke of "identifying suffering," he was not referring to the obvious sufferings of which we are so often witnesses or victims: illnesses, wars, famines, injustice, or the loss of someone dear to us. These sufferings, the ones that touch us directly (our relatives, ourselves) and indirectly (via the media or experiences we have lived through) and the sufferings stemming from socioeconomic injustice, discrimination, and war, are obvious to everyone. It is the latent causes of suffering that the Buddha wanted to bring to light, causes that might not manifest immediately in the form of difficult experiences, but that still constitute a constant source of suffering.

In fact, many of our sufferings are rooted in hatred, greed, selfishness, pride, jealousy, and other mental states that Buddhism groups under the term "mental poisons" because they literally poison our and others' existences. According to the Buddha, the origin of these mental obscurations is ignorance. This ignorance does not stem from a simple lack of information, such as not knowing the names of all the trees in a forest, but from a distorted vision of reality and from a misunderstanding of the first causes of suffering. As the contemporary Tibetan master Chögyam Trungpa explains: "When we talk of ignorance, it has nothing to do with stupidity. In a way, ignorance is very intelligent, but it is an intelligence that works exclusively in one direction. That is, we react exclusively to our own projections instead of simply seeing what is there."[14]

This fundamental ignorance is linked to a lack of comprehension of reality, that is, the true nature of things, free of the mental fabrications we superimpose upon it. These fabrications hollow out a gap between the way things appear to us and the way they are: we take as permanent what is ephemeral and as happiness what is usually a source of suffering—thirst for wealth, power, fame, and fleeting pleasures.

We perceive the external world as a totality of autonomous entities to which we attribute characteristics that seem to us to belong to them by their nature. Things appear to us as intrinsically "pleasant" or "unpleasant" and we rigidly divide people into "good" or "bad," "friends" or "enemies," as if these were characteristics inherent to people. The "self," or the ego that perceives them, seems to us equally as real and concrete. This mistake gives rise to powerful reflexes of attachment and aversion and, as long as our mind remains obscured by this lack of discernment, it will fall under the sway of hatred, attachment, greed, jealousy, or pride, and suffering will always be ready to appear.

If we refer to Daniel Batson's definition of altruism as a mental state linked to the perception of a particular need in the other, the ultimate need defined by Buddhism consists of dissipating the mistaken view of reality. It is in no way a question of imposing a particular dogmatic view of what is, but of providing the knowledge and the tools necessary to be able, through rigorous investigation, to bridge the gap that separates our perception of things from their true nature. This attitude consists, for example, of not taking as permanent what is by nature changeable, of not perceiving independent entities in what are only interdependent relationships, and in not imagining a unitary, autonomous, and constant "self" in what is nothing but an endlessly changing stream of experiences dependent on countless causes and conditions.

This attitude does not satisfy solely an intellectual curiosity; its aim is essentially therapeutic. Understanding interdependence notably allows us to destroy the illusory wall that our minds have raised between self and other. This makes obvious the mistaken foundations of pride, jealousy, and malevolence. Since all beings are interdependent, their happiness and their suffering concern us intimately. To want to build our happiness on others' suffering is not only immoral, but unrealistic. Universal love and compassion are the direct consequences of a correct understanding of this interdependence.

So it is not necessary to feel *emotionally* the state of mind of others in order to nurture an altruistic attitude. On the other hand, it is indispensable to be aware of their desire to escape suffering, to learn to value it, and to be deeply concerned to carry out their profound aspirations. The more altruistic love and compassion are cognitive, the more amplitude they give to altruism, and the less they are affected by emotional obscurations like the empathic distress aroused by seeing others' suffering. Instead of giving rise to benevolence, this perception of pain might lead one to retreat into oneself, or else might favor the development of a sentimentality that risks making altruism deviate into favoritism.

ADOPTING THE ATTITUDE OF THE PHYSICIAN

Extended altruism does not depend on the behavior of the people it is directed toward, since it operates at a more fundamental level. It manifests itself when we become fully aware of the fact that beings behave in a harmful way because they are under the sway of ignorance and the mental poisons that ignorance engenders. We are then able to move beyond our instinctive reactions faced with the behavior of malevolent people, since we understand that it does not differ in any way from the behavior of a mentally ill person attacking those around him: we then act like a physician. If a patient suffering from mental disturbances strikes the doctor examining him, the latter won't hit back but, on the contrary, seek the best ways to cure him from his madness.

At first sight, it may seem incongruous to treat an enemy with kindness: "He wants to harm me, why should I wish him well?" But Buddhism's reply is simple: "Because he doesn't want to suffer either, because he too is under the sway of ignorance. Because this ignorance makes him harm others." True altruism consists of wishing that the harm-doer become aware of his deviance and thus stop harming his fellow beings. This reaction, which is the opposite of the wish to avenge and punish by inflicting more suffering, is not a sign of weakness, but of wisdom.

Compassion does not exclude doing anything possible to prevent the other from continuing to harm. It does not prevent us from using all means available to put an end to the crimes of a bloodthirsty dictator, for example, but it is necessarily accompanied by the wish that hatred and cruelty vanish from his mind. In the absence of any other solution, it will not forbid recourse to force, provided this is not inspired by hatred, but by the necessity to prevent greater suffering.

Altruism does not consist in minimizing or tolerating the misdeeds of others, but in alleviating suffering in all its forms. The aim is to break the cycle of hatred. "If we practice an eye for an eye," said Gandhi, "and a tooth for a tooth, soon the whole world will be blind and toothless." More subtly, Shantideva wrote: "How many malicious people can I kill? They are everywhere and one can never come to an end of them. But if I kill hatred, I will overcome all my enemies."[15]

"No matter how mean or hideous a man's life is, the first thing is to understand him,"[16] writes the American philosopher Alfie Kohn. Asbjorn Rachlew, the police officer who supervised the questioning of Anders Breivik, the fanatic mass murderer recently sentenced in Norway, declared: "We don't bang our fists on the table, like in movies; instead we must let the person speak as much as possible, and do 'active listening', and at the end, we ask 'what is your explanation for what you did?' "[17] If we want to prevent the recurrence of evil, it is essential to grasp first why and how it can arise.

Altruism Is Neither a Reward Nor a Moral Judgment

The practice of altruistic love and compassion does not have the aim of rewarding good conduct, and its absence is not a penalty for punishing bad behavior. Altruism and compassion are not based on moral judgments, even if they certainly do not exclude those judgments. As French philosopher André Comte-Sponville writes, "We only need morality if we lack love." Compassion in particular has the aim of eliminating all individual sufferings, whatever they may be, wherever they are, and whatever the causes might be. Considered in this way, altruism and compassion can be impartial and limitless.

The Possibility of Bringing an End to the Suffering of Beings Reinforces Altruism

"One grows out of pity when it's useless,"[18] wrote Albert Camus. Powerless and distant pity becomes *compassion*, that is, an intense desire to free others from suffering, when one becomes aware of the *possibility* of eliminating this suffering and when one recognizes the ways to accomplish this aim. These various stages correspond to the *Four Noble Truths* stated by the Buddha during his first teaching, at the Deer Park in Sarnath, near Varanasi. The first Noble Truth is the *truth of suffering* which must be recognized for what it is, in all its forms, visible and subtle. The second is the truth of the *causes of suffering,* ignorance, which leads to anger, greed and many other mental obscurations. Since these mental poisons have causes that can be eliminated, the *cessation of suffering*—the third Noble Truth—is thus possible. The fourth Noble Truth is that of the *path* that transforms this possibility into a reality. This path is the process that puts into play all the methods allowing us to eliminate the fundamental causes of suffering.

Since ignorance is finally nothing more than an error, a distortion of reality, it is always possible to dissipate it. Mistaking a piece of rope for a snake in the twilight can give rise to fear, but as soon as you shed light on the rope and recognize its true nature, this fear has no reason to exist. Ignorance, then, is an adventitious phenomenon that does not affect the ultimate nature of things: it simply hides it from our comprehension. That is why knowledge is liberating. As we can read in the *Ornament of Sutras*: "Liberation is the exhaustion of delusion."

If suffering were a fate linked to the human condition, worrying endlessly about it would only add uselessly to our torment. As the Dalai Lama said playfully: "If there is no remedy for suffering, think about it as little as possible, go to the beach and have a nice beer." On the other hand, if the causes of our sufferings can be eliminated, it would be regrettable to ignore that possibility. As the Seventh Dalai Lama wrote in the eighteenth century:

If there is a way to free ourselves from suffering
We must use every moment to find it.
Only a fool wants to go on suffering.
Isn't it sad to knowingly imbibe poison?[19]

Realization of the possibility of freeing oneself from suffering gives compassion an entirely different dimension that differentiates it from impotent pity. In a teaching given in Paris in 2003, the Dalai Lama gave the following example:

Imagine that from the cockpit of a small private plane flying at low altitude, you see a survivor from a shipwreck swimming in the middle of the Pacific Ocean: it is impossible for you to help him and there is no one nearby whom you could alert. If you think: "How sad!", your pity is characterized by a feeling of powerlessness.

If, then, you see a small island that the survivor cannot see because of fog, but that he could reach if he swam in the right direction, your pity would transform into compassion: aware of the possibility of the unfortunate person surviving, you wish from the bottom of your heart that he will see this nearby island, and you will try by any means possible to point it out to him.

Authentic altruism rests, then, on understanding the various causes of suffering and on the conviction that everyone has the necessary potential to free oneself from it. Since it relies more on discernment than on the emotions, it does not necessarily show itself in a wise person by the intense emotions that usually accompany the expression of affective empathy. Further, it has the characteristic of being free from egocentric attachments based on concepts of subject and object regarded as autonomous entities. Finally, such altruism applies impartially to all beings.

Because of this, on the path of Buddhism, altruistic love and compassion lead to the unwavering determination to attain Enlightenment (the understanding of ultimate reality associated with freedom from ignorance and the mental afflictions) for the good of others. This courageous resolution, called *bodhicitta,* has two aims: Enlightenment and the good of others. One frees oneself of delusion in order to become capable of freeing others from the causes of suffering.

This view of things also leads to envisaging the possibility of *cultivating* altruism. We do have the ability to grow acquainted with new ways of thinking and with qualities already present in us in an embryonic state; we can only develop them through training. Contemplating the benefits of altruism encourages us to take this path. What's more, understanding better the mechanisms of such a training allows us to realize more completely the potential for change that we have within ourselves.

3

What Is Empathy?

Empathy is a term more and more commonly used, both by scientists and in everyday language. It in fact covers several distinct mental states that we will try to pinpoint. The word "empathy" is a translation from the German word *Einfühlung,* which refers to the ability to "feel the other from within"; it was used for the first time by the German psychologist Robert Vischer in 1873 to designate the mental projection of oneself onto an external object—a house, a gnarled old tree, or a windswept hill—with which one subjectively associates.[1] Later, the philosopher Theodor Lipps extended this notion to describe the feeling of an artist who projects himself by his imagination not only into an inanimate object but also into the experience lived by another person. He offered the following example to illustrate the meaning of the word: We participate intensely in a tightrope walker walking on his wire. We cannot prevent ourselves from *entering* into his body and mentally we take each step with him.[2] What's more, we add feelings of anxiety and vertigo from which the tightrope walker is very fortunately exempt.

Empathy can be set off by an *affective perception* of feeling for the other, or by *cognitive imagination* of his experience. In both cases, the person clearly makes the distinction between his own feeling and the other's, unlike *emotional contagion* in which this differentiation is blurred.

Affective empathy occurs when we enter into resonance with the situation and feelings of another person, with the emotions that are shown by the person's facial expressions, gaze, tone of voice, body language, and behavior.

The cognitive dimension of empathy is born by mentally evoking an experience lived by another person, either by imagining what the *other* person is feeling or the way the experience affects the person, or by imagining what *we* would feel in the same situation.

Empathy can lead to an altruistic motivation, but it can also, when we find ourselves confronted with another person's suffering, give rise to a feeling of distress and avoidance that leads us to close in on ourselves or turn away from the sufferings we're witnessing.

The meanings attributed by various thinkers and scientists to the word "empathy," as well as to other similar concepts like sympathy and compassion, are manifold and can hence easily lead to confusion. Still, scientific research conducted since the 1970s and 1980s, notably by the psychologists Daniel Batson, Jack Dovidio, and Nancy Eisenberg, as well as, more recently, by the neuroscientists Jean Decety and Tania Singer, allow us to discern the nuances of this concept more clearly and to examine its relation to altruism.

Entering into Resonance with the Other

Affective empathy consists, then, of entering into resonance with others' feelings, joy as well as suffering. Inevitably our own emotions and mental projections mingle with our representation of others' feelings, sometimes without our being able to distinguish between the two.

According to the psychologist Paul Ekman, eminent specialist in emotions, this empathic awareness occurs in two stages: we begin by recognizing how someone else feels, then we enter into resonance with the other person's feelings.[3] As Darwin showed in his *The Expression of Emotions in Man and Animals,* evolution has equipped us with the ability to read others' emotions from their facial expressions, their tone of voice, and their body language.[4] This process is distorted, however, by our own emotions and biases, which act as filters. It took some time before Darwin spoke passionately in favor of abolishing slavery. To do this he had to be deeply troubled by the way the slaves he had met during his voyages on the *Beagle* were treated. According to theories current in his time, whites and blacks had different origins; blacks were supposed to occupy an intermediate level between man and animal, and they were treated accordingly. It was only after being confronted with the fate of slaves and having felt their sufferings deep within himself that Darwin became an ardent advocate for abolishing slavery.

Convergent and Divergent Resonances

Ekman distinguishes two types of affective resonance. The first is identical, or *convergent* resonance: I suffer when you suffer; I feel anger when I see you angry. If, for instance, your spouse comes home in a state because the boss was mean, you are indignant and you exclaim angrily, "How could he have treated you that way!"

In reactive or *divergent* resonance, instead of feeling the same emotion as your spouse and becoming angry, you distance yourself and, while still showing your concern, you say, "I'm so sorry you have to deal with such a jerk. What can I do for you? Would you like a cup of tea, or would you rather we go for a walk?" Your reaction goes along with your spouse's emotions, but in a different emotional tone. Your calm, soothing concern allows you to help by defusing the feelings of anger and bitterness your spouse is feeling. In both cases, people appreciate the fact that you are concerned with their feelings.

On the other hand, if you don't enter into resonance with your spouse's feelings, you'll say something like, "You had a tough time? Well, what about me! You'll just have to get used to it," which is not much comfort.

Empathy and Sympathy

In everyday language, the word "sympathy" has preserved its etymological sense, stemming from the Greek *sumpatheia,* "natural affinity." To feel sympathy for someone means you feel a certain affinity with that person, you feel in harmony with that person's feelings, and you feel kindly toward that person.[5] Sympathy opens us up to the other and breaks down the barriers that separate us from him or her. When we say to others, "You have all my sympathy," that indicates that we understand the difficulties they are having and that we agree that their aspirations to free themselves are justified, or else that we show them our benevolent support.

But Darwin, and psychologists like Nancy Eisenberg,[6] a pioneer in the study of altruism, define sympathy more precisely as altruistic concern or compassion for another person, a feeling that leads us to wish that others be happy or that their condition improve.

According to Nancy Eisenberg, we begin by feeling an emotional resonance generally associated with cognitive resonance, which makes us take into consideration the situation and viewpoint of the other. The memory of our own past experiences is added to these feelings to set off an interior mobilization. This entire process leads to a vicarious reaction to another's fate. This reaction will depend notably on the intensity of our emotions and the way we control them. A reaction of aversion or avoidance can also occur.

Depending on the individual, these reactions will lead to sympathy and to altruistic prosocial behavior, or else to egocentric distress, which will be evinced either by a behavior of avoidance, or by a selfish prosocial reaction that leads us to come to others' assistance mainly in order to calm our own anxiety.

The primatologist Frans de Waal regards sympathy as an active form of empathy: "Empathy is the process by which we gather information about someone else. Sympathy, in contrast, reflects concern about the other and a desire to improve the other's situation."[7] Let's try to pinpoint the relationships between empathy and altruism to see our way more clearly through all these definitions.

Is It Necessary to Feel What Others Feel in Order to Show Altruism for Them?

Entering into affective resonance with another can indeed help induce an altruistic attitude, but it is not at all necessary for me to feel what the other feels. Imagine I'm sitting on a plane next to a person terrified of air travel and obviously frozen in speechless unease. The weather is beautiful, the pilot is experienced, and even though I personally feel at ease, that does not prevent me from feeling and showing sincere concern for that person and trying to reassure him or her as best I can by a calm, warm presence. For my part, since I feel no anxiety, I am not disturbed *by* what the other feels, but I feel concern *for* the person and for what he or she is feeling. It is precisely this calm that allows me to soothe that person's anxiety as much as possible and reassure him.

Similarly, if I know the person opposite me has a serious illness, even though the other person doesn't yet know it or isn't yet physically suffering from it, I can experience a powerful feeling of love and compassion. In this case, there is no question of feeling what the other feels, since the other is not yet suffering.

That said, imagining what the other is feeling by entering into affective resonance with him or her can certainly awaken in me a more intense compassion and a more active empathic concern, because I will have clearly become aware of the other's needs through my personal experience. It is this ability to feel what the other is feeling that is lacking in those who feel indifferent about the fate of others, psychopaths in particular.

Putting Oneself in the Other's Place

Picturing oneself in the other's place, imagining what their hopes and fears are, and regarding the situation from their point of view are, when one takes the trouble to act this way, powerful ways to feel empathy. To be concerned by the fate of others it is essential to consider their situation attentively, to adopt their point of view, and to realize what you would feel if you were in the same situation. As Jean-Jacques Rousseau noted: "The rich man has little compassion for the poor man, since he can't imagine himself poor."

It is in fact important to give a face to the suffering of the other: the other person is not an abstract entity, an object, a remote individual fundamentally separate from me. We sometimes hear about tragic situations that remain disembodied for us. Then we see images, bodies, facial expressions, we hear people's voices, and everything changes. More than verbal appeals from humanitarian organizations, the emaciated faces and skeletal bodies of children in Biafra, broadcast by organizations and media all over the world, did more to mobilize nations and urge them to remedy the tragic famine that raged between 1968 and 1970.[8] When we see people obviously suffering, no question arises: we value them and feel concerned by their fate.

An American teacher tells how, during the first years of the AIDS epidemic, when the illness bore the mark of shame, most students in his class showed a negative attitude toward people stricken with this illness. Some went so far as to say that they "deserved to die." Others preferred to turn away from them, saying, "I want nothing to do with them." But after the teacher showed a documentary about AIDS that gave a face to the sufferings of dying people, most of his students were shaken, and some had tears in their eyes.[9]

Many soldiers have related how, when they found in their dead enemy's pockets or kit his identity papers and family photos, they suddenly visualized this man's life and understood he was like them. In his novel *All Quiet on the Western Front*, inspired by what he himself lived through, Erich Maria Remarque describes the feelings of a young German soldier who has just killed an enemy with his own hands and now talks to his body:

> *You were only an idea to me before, an abstraction that lived in my mind and called forth its appropriate response. It was that abstraction I stabbed. But now, for the first time, I see you are a man like me. I thought of your hand-grenades, of your bayonet, of your rifle; now I see your wife and your face and our fellowship. Forgive me, comrade. We always see it too late. Why do they never tell us that you are poor devils like us, that your mothers are just as anxious as ours, and that we have the same fear of death, and the same dying and the same agony—Forgive me, comrade; how could you be my enemy?*[10]

The American philosopher Charlie Dunbar Broad very correctly notes: "A large proportion of the cruelty which decent people applaud or tolerate is applauded or tolerated by them only because they are either too stupid to put themselves imaginatively into the position of the victims or because they deliberately refrain from doing so."[11]

Is it necessary to reflect for a long time to picture the suffering of an adulterous woman mercilessly stoned, or the feelings of a man condemned to death, guilty or innocent, about to be executed, or the despair of a mother who sees her child dying? Do we have to wait for the other's suffering to be imposed on us with such an intensity that we can no longer ignore it? Isn't it this same blindness that leads to murder and war? Kafka wrote, "War is a monstrous lack of imagination."

In my childhood, I lived for several years with one of my grandmothers who tended to spoil me, little boy that I was. When we were on vacation in Brittany, this sweet grandmother often spent her afternoons fishing on the quays of the harbor of Le Croisic, next to a group of old Breton ladies who wore the white lace headdress of the Bigoudens. It would never have occurred to me that all these charming ladies could take part in anything but an honorable activity. How could my grandmother have wished to harm anyone? The little wriggling fish she took out of the water looked like toys sparkling in the light. True, there was a difficult time when they suffocated in the wicker basket and their eyes became glassy, but I would quickly look away and preferred to watch the little cork that floated on the surface of the water, hoping it would go under again, sign of another catch. Obviously, I didn't for an instant put myself in the fish's place!

A few years later, when I was thirteen, a friend asked me point-blank: "What? You go fishing?" Her tone was both surprised and reproachful.

"You go fishing?" Suddenly, the scene appeared to me in all its reality: the fish pulled out of its vital element by a metal hook that pierced its mouth, "drowning" in air as we drown in water. To attract the fish to the hook, I had also pierced a living worm to make it into bait, thus sacrificing one life to sacrifice another more easily.

This sweet grandmother didn't have a soft touch for everyone, then. Neither she nor I had till then taken the trouble to put ourselves in the other's place. How could I have turned my thoughts for so long away from these sufferings? With a lump in my throat, I immediately gave up fishing, which was no more than a sinister pastime for me, and a few years later I became a vegetarian for the rest of my life.

I know that such concern for little fish may well seem excessive or laughable compared to the tragedies that devastate the lives of so many human beings all over the world, but it seems to me that it is important to understand that real compassion should not know any boundaries. If we lack compassion for certain sufferings and certain beings, we risk lacking compassion for all sufferings and all beings. We are more inclined to feel sympathy for people with whom we perceive the links they have in common with us, links that could be familial, ethnic, national, religious, or that simply reflect our affinities. Nevertheless, empathic concern should be extended to the point of becoming a resonance that is born from our shared humanity and from the fact that we share with all sentient beings the same aversion to suffering, even though they may experience suffering in ways that are different than ours.[12]

In everyday life, putting ourselves in the place of others and looking at things from their point of view is a necessity if we want to live in harmony with our fellows. Otherwise, we risk closing ourselves up in our mental fabrications which deform reality and give rise to useless torments. If I think the conductor on a subway train "is slamming the door in my face," I am upset and demand, "why did he close it just for *me?* He could at least have let me through!" In that case, I've forgotten to adopt the conductor's point of view, who sees nothing but a constant flow of anonymous passengers, and will inevitably have to close the doors in front of *someone* before starting the train moving.

THE VARIOUS FORMS OF EMPATHY: THE POINT OF VIEW OF THE HUMAN SCIENCES

The psychologist Daniel Batson has shown that the various meanings of the word "empathy" ultimately stem from two questions: "How can one know what another person is thinking and feeling?" and "What leads one person to respond with sensitivity and care to the suffering of another?"

Batson has enumerated eight different modalities of the term "empathy," which are all linked yet do not constitute simply different aspects of the same phenomenon.[13] After analyzing them, he came to the conclusion that only one of these forms, which he calls "empathic concern," is both necessary and sufficient to engender an altruistic motivation.[14]

The first form, *knowing another person's internal state,* can provide us with reasons for feeling concern for him or her, but is neither sufficient nor necessary to give rise to an altruistic motivation. One can in fact be aware of what someone is thinking or feeling, while still remaining indifferent to his or her fate.

The second form is *motor and neural mimicry.* Based on earlier works by Brothers, Damasio, and others, Preston and De Waal suggested a theoretical model for the neural mechanisms that underlie empathy and emotional contagion. According to these researchers, the fact of seeing someone in a given situation induces our neural system to adopt a similar state to the other's, which leads to bodily and facial imitation accompanied by sensations similar to the other's.[15] This process of imitation by observation of physical behavior is also the basis for learning processes transmitted from one individual to another. According to the neuroscientist Tania Singer, Director at the Max Planck Institute for Human Cognitive and Brain Sciences in Leipzig, however, this model does not clearly distinguish empathy, in which one unambiguously establishes the difference between self and other, from mere emotional contagion, in which we confuse our own emotions with the emotions of the other. According to Batson, this process can contribute to engendering feelings of empathy, but is not enough to explain them. In fact, we do not systematically imitate others' actions: we react intensely when we watch a soccer player score a goal, but we do not necessarily feel inclined to imitate or emotionally resonate with someone who is organizing his papers or eating a dish we do not like.

The third form, *emotional resonance,* allows us to feel what the other is feeling, whether that feeling is joy, sadness, or any other emotion.[16] It is impossible for us to live through exactly the same experience as someone else, but we can feel similar emotions. Nothing can get us into a good mood better than watching a group of friends overjoyed at seeing each other; on the other hand, the spectacle of people prey to intense distress moves us, even makes tears well up in our eyes. Feeling approximately the other's experiences can give rise to an altruistic motivation, but here again, this kind of emotion is neither indispensable nor sufficient.[17] In certain cases, the fact of feeling the other's emotion risks inhibiting our altruistic response. If, faced with a terrified person, we too begin to feel fear, we could grow more concerned with our own anxiety than with the other's fate.[18] What's more, to engender such a motivation, it is enough to become aware of the other's suffering, without it being necessary to suffer oneself.

The fourth form consists of *intuiting or projecting oneself into another's situation.* This is the experience to which Theodor Lipps was referring when he used the word *Einfühlung*. However, in order to be concerned with the other's fate, it is not necessary to picture all the details of his experience: it is enough to know he is suffering. Moreover, one risks being mistaken when imagining what the other is feeling.

The fifth form is *imagining how another is thinking and feeling* as clearly as possible according to what he tells you, what you observe, and your knowledge of that person, his values, and his aspirations. Still, the simple fact of imagining the other's interior state does not guarantee the emergence of an altruistic motivation.[19] A calculating and ill-intentioned person can use knowledge of your interior state to manipulate you and harm you.

The sixth form consists in *imagining how one would think and feel in the other's place* with one's own nature, aspirations, and view of the world. If one of your friends is a great opera lover or rock fan and you can't bear that kind of music, you can indeed imagine him feeling pleasure and you can be happy about that, but if you yourself were in the first row, you'd feel nothing but irritation. That's why George Bernard Shaw wrote, "Do not do unto others as you would have them done unto you. They may have different tastes."

The seventh form is the *empathic distress* one feels when one witnesses another's suffering or when it is spoken of. This form of empathy runs more of a risk of resulting in avoidance behavior than in an altruistic attitude. In fact, it does not involve feeling distress *for* the other or putting oneself *in place of* the other, but a feeling of anxiety provoked *by* the other.[20]

Such a feeling of distress will not necessarily lead to a reaction of concern for the other or a response appropriate to the other's suffering, especially if we can diminish our anxiety by turning our attention away from the suffering we see being experienced.

Some people can't bear seeing upsetting images. They prefer to look away from these representations that make them feel bad, rather than confronting their reality. Choosing a physical or psychological way out is hardly useful to victims, and it would be better to become fully aware of the facts and to act with a view to remedying them.

Thus, when the French philosopher Myriam Revault d'Allonnes writes, "It's in order not to suffer myself that I want the other not to suffer, and I am interested in the other out of love for myself...

compassion is not an altruistic feeling,"[21] she is describing *empathic distress* and not compassion in the sense we mean in this book, namely a state of mind that stems directly from altruistic love and is manifest when that love confronts suffering. True compassion is centered on the other and not on oneself.

When we are mainly concerned with ourselves, we become vulnerable to everything that can affect us. Trapped in this state of mind, egocentric contemplation of the suffering of others undermines our courage; it is felt as a burden that only increases our distress. In the case of compassion, on the other hand, altruistic contemplation of others' suffering greatly increases our courage, our readiness, and our determination to remedy these torments.

If resonance with others' suffering leads to personal distress, we should redirect our attention to the other and revive our capacity for kindness and altruistic love. To illustrate this, I would like to relate the following story, which a psychologist friend told me.

> *In Nepal one day a young woman, Sita, came to consult me because her sister had just killed herself by hanging. She was haunted by guilt at not having been able to prevent such an action, obsessed with images of her sister, whom she sought everywhere in crowds and for whom she waited at night. Unable to concentrate, she cried all day long and, when she ran out of tears, she was plunged into a prostration from which it was difficult to emerge. During one of our sessions, she looked me straight in the eyes; she was the embodiment of suffering. She said to me point-blank: "Do you know what it's like to lose a sister like that? I'll never get over it; ever since I was born, we shared the same bedroom, we did everything together. I wasn't able to hold her back."*
>
> *I took her hand and, faced with the unbearable intensity of her suffering, I felt caught off-guard. I remembered the suicide of my sixteen-year-old first cousin and I had to make a huge effort to get control of myself so as not to break out crying too. I was overwhelmed by a conscious emotional resonance. And I knew that if I cried with Sita, I couldn't help her. I waited for a bit, holding her hands in mine, I asked her to cry her fill and to*

> *breathe slowly. I did the same to calm my own emotions. I was aware of being filled with the onslaught of her despair. I managed to calm down, to look at her, Sita, to stop thinking about my own pounding heart, my eyes that were misting over with tears, and to erase the memories of my cousin.*
>
> *Finally, when the emotional crisis had diminished and I felt that Sita was slowly emerging from the sway of traumatic images, I simply said to her, "I understand your sorrow; I really understand it. But, you know, you're not alone." I waited a while to see if she was listening to me, before continuing: "I too lost a cousin almost at the same age as you. I know how painful it is. But I understood and accepted the fact that I couldn't do anything at that time. That it wasn't my fault. And that one can get over this pain." She suddenly raised her head to look me again straight in the eyes, to see if I was telling the truth, and also to check if it was really possible to get over such a shock. To my great surprise, she stood up and hugged me, murmuring, "I'll try. Thank you."*

In the first part of the consultation, the therapist was clearly under the sway of empathic distress. For a few minutes, even though she felt compassion, she was powerless to help her patient, so much did she share and project her emotions. It was only when she got hold of herself by re-centering on the other and her pain that she was able to find words that could help her get over her suffering.

The eighth form, *empathic concern,* consists of *becoming aware of the other's needs* and then feeling a *sincere desire to come to his or her aid.* According to Daniel Batson,[22] only this empathic concern is a response directed *toward the other*—and not *toward oneself*—an answer that is both necessary and sufficient to result in an altruistic motivation. In fact, faced with people's distress, the essential thing is to adopt the attitude that will bring them the greatest comfort, and to decide on the most appropriate action to remedy their sufferings.

Daniel Batson concludes that the first six forms of empathy can each contribute to engendering an altruistic motivation, but that none of them guarantees the emergence of such a motivation, no more than they constitute indispensable conditions. The seventh, empathic distress, goes clearly against altruism. Only the last, empathic concern, is both necessary and sufficient to make an altruistic motivation arise in our mind and urge us to action.

Pity and Compassion

Pity is an egocentric, often condescending, feeling of commiseration, which in no way testifies to an altruistic motivation. One might give alms, for instance, full of a feeling of superiority. As an African proverb says, "The hand that gives is always higher than the hand that receives." The Swiss philosopher Alexandre Jollien is more precise: "In pity, there is a humiliation for the one receiving. Altruism and compassion stem from equality, without humiliating the other." Paraphrasing Spinoza, Alexandre adds, "In pity, sadness comes first. I am sad that the other is suffering, but I don't really love him. In compassion, love comes first."[23]

The novelist Stefan Zweig had also grasped the difference between the two when he wrote, "There are two kinds of pity. One, the weak and sentimental kind, which is really no more than the heart's impatience to be rid as quickly as possible of the painful emotion aroused by the sight of another's unhappiness…; and the other, the only kind that counts, the unsentimental but creative kind, which knows what it is about and is determined to hold out, in patience and forbearance, to the very limit of its strength and even beyond."[24] That sentimental pity is like the empathic distress described above.

The Point of View of the Neurosciences: Emotional Contagion, Empathy, and Compassion

Slightly different nomenclature and analysis were proposed by the neuroscientist Tania Singer and the philosopher Frédérique de Vignemont. Basing their findings on studies of the brain, they distinguished three states: emotional contagion, empathy, and compassion.[25] For them, these three affective states differ from a *cognitive* representation that consists of imagining the other's thoughts and intentions and adopting the other's subjective perspective, without, however, entering into *affective* resonance with the other.[26]

Singer and Vignemont define empathy as (1) an affective state (2) similar (*isomorphic* in scientific language) to the other's affective state (3) produced by the observation or imagination of the other's affective state which involves (4) an awareness that it is indeed the other who is the source of our own affective state.[27] Such an approach to empathy is not basically different from the one proposed by Daniel Batson, but it helps us explore further the modes of this complex mental state.

An essential characteristic of empathy is entry into affective resonance with the other, while making a clear distinction between self and other: I know my feeling comes from the other, but I am not confusing my feeling with that of the other. It turns out that people who have difficulty clearly distinguishing their emotions from another's can easily be submerged by emotional contagion and, because of this, do not reach empathy, which is the next stage.

The intensity, the clarity, and the quality—positive or negative—of the emotion expressed by the other, as well as the existence of affective ties with the person suffering, can have a great influence on the intensity of the empathic response of the observer.[28] Resemblances and the degree of closeness between the protagonists, precise evaluation of the other's needs,[29] and the attitude of the person suffering toward the one who perceives the suffering (the fact, for example, that the person suffering is angry with the interlocutor) constitute just so many factors that will modulate the intensity of empathy.

The characteristics of the person who feels empathy will also have an influence. If, for example, I am not subject to vertigo, I will have trouble entering into empathic resonance with a person who is prey to that distress, but that will not prevent me from being aware of the fact that the other needs help or comfort.

Context will also be a factor. If I think, for instance, that someone's joy is inappropriate, or even completely out of place (in the case of someone who is gloating over an act of revenge, for example), I will not enter into affective resonance with that person.[30]

In the case of *emotional contagion,* I automatically feel the other's emotion without knowing that he or she is the one who provoked it, and without being really aware of what is happening to me. Depending on the case, the diameter of my pupils changes, my heart slows down or speeds up, or I look right and left anxiously, without being aware of these physical manifestations. As soon as I think, "I am anxious because he is anxious," this is no longer emotional contagion but *empathy*, or *conscious affective resonance.*

Emotional contagion, distress, for example, exists in animals and young children. Thus, a baby starts crying when it hears another baby crying; but that does not necessarily mean they feel empathy, or that they are concerned with each other. We would have to know if they can make the distinction between themselves and others, which is not easy to determine, since we can't ask them. Among young children, the first signs of distinction between self and other, as well as the first signs of empathy, appear between eighteen and twenty-four months.

Compassion is here defined by Tania Singer and her colleagues as the altruistic *motivation* to *intervene* in favor of someone who is suffering or is in need. It is thus a profound awareness of the other's suffering, coupled with the desire to relieve it and do something for the other's benefit. Compassion, then, implies a warm, sincere feeling of concern, but does not require that one feel the other's suffering, as is the case for empathy.[31]

Olga Klimecki, who was then a researcher in Tania Singer's laboratory, summarizes the researchers' point of view this way: In the affective dimension, I feel something for you; in the cognitive dimension, I understand you; and in the motivational dimension, I want to help you.[32]

To illustrate these different mental states, let's take the example of a woman whose husband is terrified by airplane travel and let's consider the various reactions this woman can have toward him.

1. She is seated next to her husband. As he begins breathing more quickly, without her becoming really aware of it, her breathing accelerates and she becomes more agitated. This is *emotional contagion.* In fact, if someone asks her how she's feeling, she could reply, "Fine," or, at most: "I don't know why, but I don't feel very relaxed." If you measure her heart rate, the dilation of her pupils, or other physiological parameters, you will observe the presence of signs of anxiety. Under the sway of emotional contagion, this woman is not aware of the other's feelings and has only a confused perception of her own.

2. She realizes she is concerned and is moved by the fact that her husband is very anxious. She is now feeling *empathy* for him. She

herself feels a certain unease; she feels her breathing and pulse accelerate. She is aware of feeling distress because her husband is prey to this emotion. There is no confusion between her and him. She is entering into affective resonance with him, but will not necessarily try to help him. These are the characteristics of empathy. This has not yet given rise to an altruistic motivation.

3. She is not anxious; she feels rather a warm sensation of care and a motivation to do something to relieve his torment. She thinks, "I'm fine, but my husband is upset. What can I do so he won't be so affected? I'll take his hand and try to calm and comfort him." This, according to Tania Singer, is *compassion*.

4. When the perspective is *purely cognitive*, the affective component is absent. The woman is functioning only in a conceptual way. She says to herself, "I know my husband is afraid on planes. I have to take care of him and be attentive to him." She feels neither anxiety nor warmth. She just has a mental schema that reminds her that people who have phobias on plane trips don't feel well and deduces that that is her husband's case, and she takes his hand, thinking it will help him.

The researches of Tania Singer and her team have shown that empathy, compassion, and cognitive awareness all rest on different neural bases and thus correspond to clearly distinct mental states.[33]

THE BENEFITS OF EMPATHY

Neuroscientists think that empathy has two important advantages. First of all, compared to the cognitive approach, affective empathy probably offers a more direct and more precise path to predict another's behavior. It has actually been observed that the fact of sharing similar emotions with someone else activates in us reactions that are better adapted to what the other feels and to the other's needs.

Secondly, empathy allows us to acquire useful knowledge about our environment. If, for example, I see someone suffering from being burnt by touching a machine, the fact of entering into affective resonance with the victim gives me a feeling of aversion to that machine, without myself having to undergo the painful experience of being burned. Empathy is thus an effective tool to assess the world around me, through another's experience. Finally, empathy is also a precious tool of communication with the other.[34]

What Mental State Leads to Altruism?

We have seen that among the eight types of empathy listed by Daniel Batson, only *empathic concern* was necessary and sufficient to engender an altruistic motivation. What about the categories outlined by Tania Singer and her neuroscientist colleagues?

Emotional contagion can serve as a *precursor* to empathy but, in itself, it does not help to engender an altruistic motivation since it is accompanied by a confusion between self and other. It can even constitute an obstacle to altruism—if one is overwhelmed by this emotional contagion and disoriented, one is concerned only about oneself.

Empathy, or affective resonance, is also neutral a priori. According to the circumstance and the individual, it can transform into concern and give rise to the desire to provide for another's needs. But empathy can also provoke a distress that focuses our attention on ourselves and diverts us from the other's needs. For this last reason, empathy is not enough in itself to engender altruism.

The *cognitive approach,* on the other hand, can constitute a step toward altruism but, like empathy, it is neither necessary nor sufficient for the genesis of an altruistic motivation. It may even engender completely selfish behavior, as in the case of psychopaths who feel neither empathy nor compassion, but are expert in guessing others' thoughts and use this ability in order to manipulate them.

There remains *compassion* whose essence is an altruistic motivation, necessary and sufficient so that we will desire the good of the other and will give rise to the wish to accomplish it by taking action. Compassion is awareness of the other's situation, and is accompanied by the wish to relieve suffering and to procure the other's happiness. Finally, it is not distorted by confusion between the emotions felt by the other and our own.

Thus the importance of compassion for all suffering beings is emphasized by psychologists, who speak of empathic concern, by neuroscientists, and by Buddhism, where it occupies a central place.

4

From Empathy to Compassion in a Neuroscience Laboratory

In 2007, along with Tania Singer, I was in Rainer Goebel's neuroscience laboratory in Maastricht, as a collaborator and guinea pig in a research program on empathy. Tania would ask me to give rise to a powerful feeling of empathy by imagining people affected by great suffering. Tania was using a new fMRI (functional magnetic resonance imaging) technique used by Goebel. It has the advantage of following the changes of activity of the brain in real time (fMRI-rt), whereas data usually cannot be analyzed until later on. According to the protocol of this kind of experiment, the meditator, myself in this case, must alternate twenty or so times between periods when he or she engenders a particular mental state, here empathy, with moments when he relaxes his mind in a neutral state, without thinking of anything in particular or applying any method of meditation.

During a pause, after a first series of periods of meditation, Tania asked me: "What are you doing? It doesn't look at all like what we usually observe when people feel empathy for someone else's suffering." I explained that I had meditated on unconditional compassion, trying to feel a powerful feeling of love and kindness for people who were suffering, but also for all sentient beings.

In fact, complete analysis of the data, carried out subsequently, confirmed that the cerebral networks activated by meditation on compassion were very different from those linked to empathy, which Tania had been studying for years. In the previous studies, people who were not trained in meditation observed a person who was seated near the scanner and received painful electric shocks in the hand. These researchers noted that a part of the brain associated with pain is activated in subjects who observe someone suffering. They suffer when they see another's suffering. More precisely, two areas of the brain, the anterior insula and the cingulate cortex, are strongly activated during that empathic reaction, and their activity correlates to a negative affective experience of pain.[1]

When I engaged in meditation on altruistic love and compassion, Tania noted that the cerebral networks activated were very different. In particular, the network linked to negative emotions and distress was not activated during meditation on compassion, while certain cerebral areas traditionally associated with positive emotions, with the feeling of affiliation and maternal love, for instance, were.[2]

Only Empathy Gets Fatigued, Not Compassion

From this initial experiment was conceived the project to explore these differences in order to distinguish more clearly between empathic resonance with another's pain and compassion experienced for that suffering. We also knew that empathic resonance with pain can lead, when it is repeated many times, to emotional exhaustion and distress. It affects people who emotionally collapse when the worry, stress, or pressure they have to face in their professional lives affect them so much that they become unable to continue their activities. Burnout affects people confronted daily with others' sufferings, especially health care and social workers. In the United States, a study has shown that 60% of the medical profession suffers or has suffered from burnout, and that a third has been affected to the point of having to suspend their activities temporarily.[3]

Over the course of discussions with Tania and her collaborators, we noted that compassion and altruistic love were associated with positive emotions. So we arrived at the idea that burnout was in fact a kind of "empathy fatigue" and not "compassion fatigue." The latter, in fact, far from leading to distress and discouragement, reinforces our strength of mind, our inner balance, and our courageous, loving determination to help those who suffer. In essence, from our point of view, love and compassion do not get exhausted and do not make us weary or worn out, but on the contrary help us surmount fatigue and rectify it when it occurs.[4]

When a Buddhist meditator trains in compassion, she or he begins by reflecting on the sufferings that afflict living beings and on the causes of these sufferings. To do this, the meditator imagines these different forms of distress as realistically as possible, until they become unbearable. This empathic approach has the aim of engendering a profound aspiration to remedy these sufferings. But since this simple desire is not enough, one must cultivate the determination to put everything to work to relieve them. The meditator is led to reflect on the profound causes of suffering, such as ignorance, which distorts one's perception of reality, or the mental poisons, which are hatred, attachment-desire, and jealousy, which constantly engender more suffering. The process then leads to an increased readiness and desire to act for the good of others.

This training in compassion goes hand in hand with training in altruistic love. To cultivate this love, the meditator begins by imagining someone close to him or her, toward whom he or she feels limitless kindness. The meditator then tries little by little to extend this same kindness to all beings, like a shining sun that illuminates without distinction everything in its path.

These three dimensions—love of the other, empathy (which is resonance with another's suffering), and compassion—are naturally linked. When altruistic love encounters suffering it manifests as compassion. This transformation is triggered by empathy, which alerts us to the fact that the other is suffering. One may say that when altruistic love passes through the prism of empathy, it becomes compassion.

The Meditator's Point of View

Let's return to the experiment: the first session the next morning was devoted to empathy. This involved engendering as intensely as possible a feeling of empathy for the suffering of another person, a close relative for instance. The idea was to concentrate exclusively on empathy, without making altruistic love or compassion come into play, and to keep them from manifesting spontaneously. By isolating empathy in this way, we hoped to distinguish it more clearly from compassion and identify more precisely the specific areas of the brain it activates.

During the meditation, I concentrated the best I could in order to engender the chosen mental state—empathy—to make it as clear, stable, and intense as possible. I would revive it if it weakened, and give rise to it again if a distraction had temporarily dissipated it. During the session, which lasted about an hour and a half, the periods of meditation, which lasted around a minute, alternated with thirty-second periods of rest.

On that day, the subject of meditation on empathy had been provided for me by a disturbing BBC documentary I had seen the night before. It was about the living conditions of physically and mentally handicapped children in a Romanian hospital; although the children were fed and washed daily, they were practically abandoned to their fate. Most of them were horribly thin. One was so frail he had broken his leg just by walking. The nurse's aides were content to attach a makeshift splint to his leg and left him on his pallet. When the children were washed, most of them groaned in pain. Another child, also skeletal, was sitting on the ground in the corner of a bare room, vaguely nodding his head, his eyes empty. They all seemed so lost in their powerless resignation that they didn't even raise their eyes to the aides when they came toward them. Every month, several children died.

I also imagined a person close to me who had been terribly injured in a car accident, lying in his blood by the side of a road at night, far from help; disgust at this bloody spectacle became mingled with my distress.

So, for almost an hour, alternating with brief neutral periods, I pictured as intensely as possible these nameless sufferings. Entering into resonance with this pain soon became intolerable. In my mind, I did not know how to engage with these children and felt rather powerless. Merely an hour of intense feeling of empathy dissociated from love and compassion had led me to burnout.

I then heard Tania say to me in the earphones that if I was ready to do one more session in the scanner, we could move right away onto meditation on compassion, which had been scheduled for the afternoon.

I agreed enthusiastically, so intensely did I feel how much love and compassion were lacking from empathy experienced on its own. Scarcely had I shifted the orientation of my meditation to love and compassion before my mental landscape transformed completely. The images of the children's suffering were still just as present and strong, but instead of creating in me a feeling of distress and powerlessness that was hard to bear, I now felt a profound, heart-warming courage linked to limitless love for these children.

Meditating now on compassion, I felt like I had opened a gate loosing floods of love that permeated the suffering of these children. Each atom of suffering was replaced by an atom of love. The distance that separated me from them was erased. Instead of not knowing how to approach the fragile child groaning at the slightest contact, or that blood-soaked person, I now mentally took them in my arms, bathing them with tenderness and affection. And I was convinced that, in a real life situation, I could have surrounded these children with a tenderness that couldn't fail to bring them comfort.

Some people will object that there is nothing altruistic in all that and that the meditator is only benefiting himself by relieving his distress. My first reply to that would be that there is no harm in the meditator freeing himself from symptoms of distress, which can have a paralyzing effect and risk re-centering his concerns on himself, to the detriment of the attentive presence he could offer to the one suffering. Then, and this is the most important point, emotions and mental states undeniably have a contagious effect. If someone who is in the presence of a suffering person feels an overwhelming distress, that can only aggravate the mental discomfort of the person suffering. On the other hand, if the person who comes to help is radiating kindness and gives off a peaceful calm, and can be attentive to the other, there is no doubt that the patient will be comforted by this attitude. Finally, the person who feels compassion and kindness can develop the strength of mind and desire to come to the aid of the other. Compassion and altruistic love have a warm, loving, and positive aspect that "stand alone" empathy for the suffering of the other does not have.

To return to my personal experiment, while I observed that meditation on empathy came up against a limit, that of burnout, on the contrary it seemed to me that one could not tire of love or compassion. In fact, these states of mind both fed my courage instead of undermining it, and reinforced my determination to help others without increasing my distress. I continued to be confronted with suffering, but love and compassion conferred a *constructive* quality to my way of approaching others' sufferings, and amplified my inclination and determination to come to their aid. So it was clear, from my perspective, that if there was an "empathy fatigue" leading to the syndrome of emotional exhaustion, there was no fatigue of love and compassion.

Once the data were fully analyzed, Tania explained that the reversals in my experience were accompanied by significant modifications of activity in specific zones of my brain. These modifications had principally affected the anterior insula and the anterior cingulate cortex associated with empathy. The team saw in particular that, when I moved on to compassion, certain regions of the brain usually stimulated by positive emotions were more activated than when I remained in empathy. These studies are continuing today and scientific publications are coming out.[5]

By combining a precise introspective investigation with an analysis of data provided by the scanner, the "first person" experience—the experience of the meditator—is joined instructively with the "third person" experience, that of the researcher. Here we can appreciate the benefits of such collaboration between seasoned meditators and scientists for research.

Tania Singer and her colleagues have since undertaken a longitudinal study,[6] a project dubbed "ReSource," which aims at training a group of novice volunteers over the course of a year in different cognitive and socio-affective faculties crucial for the development of prosocial motivation and compassion.[7]

Before engaging in such a far-reaching project, the researchers carried out a week-long training program with novice subjects who practiced meditations on altruistic love and on empathy. This preliminary study has already shown that, among most people, empathy felt when faced with another's suffering is correlated with entirely negative feelings—pain, distress, anxiety, discouragement. The neural signature of empathy is similar to that of negative emotions. Generally, we know that the neural networks involved in empathy for another's pain (the anterior insula and the cingulate cortex) are also activated when we ourselves feel pain.

Tania Singer and her colleagues divided subjects into two groups. One meditated on love and compassion, while the other worked only on empathy. The first results showed that after a week of meditations oriented toward altruistic love and compassion, novice subjects perceived in a much more positive and benevolent way video clips showing suffering people. "Positive" does not in any way mean here that the observers regarded the suffering as acceptable, but that they reacted to it with constructive mental states, like courage, motherly love, determination to find a way to help, and not "negative" mental states, which instead engender distress, aversion, discouragement, and avoidance.[8]

Furthermore, empathy stops being systematically correlated with a negative and disturbing perception of others' suffering. This change is attributed to the fact that these subjects were trained in feeling benevolence toward others in all situations. They were thus able to approach a difficult situation with love and compassion, and to show resilience when faced with others' pain. Resilience is defined as the ability of a patient to live through and overcome a traumatic or challenging situation by summoning his or her inner resources. It is also the observer's ability to overcome his or her initial feeling of distress and to substitute for it active benevolence and compassion. Data measuring the cerebral activity of these novice subjects also showed that the neural network of feelings of affiliation and compassion is activated, which is not the case in the group that meditated only on empathy.

On the other hand, when subjects devoted a week to cultivating empathy alone, and entering into affective resonance with others' sufferings, they continued to associate their empathic response with negative values, and showed an increased perception of their own suffering, sometimes to the point of not being able to control their emotions. For these subjects, negative effects increased when they watched videos showing scenes of suffering. This group of participants also experienced more negative feelings toward ordinary, everyday scenes, which shows that training in empathic resonance increases sensitivity to negative affect in ordinary situations. One of the participants disclosed that as she looked at the people around her when she took the train in the morning, she was beginning to see suffering everywhere.[9]

Aware of these destabilizing effects, Tania Singer and Olga Klimecki added a training in altruistic love (one hour a day) after the week devoted to empathy. They then observed that this addition counterbalanced the negative effects of training in empathy alone: negative affects fell back to their initial level and positive affects increased. Here too, these results were associated with corresponding changes in the cerebral networks associated respectively with compassion, positive affects, and maternal love.[10] Moreover, the researchers were able to demonstrate that a week of training in compassion increased prosocial behavior in a virtual game specially developed to measure the tendency to help others.[11]

In Richard Davidson's neuroscience laboratory in Madison, Wisconsin, the French researcher Antoine Lutz and his colleagues have also studied this phenomenon. They have shown that among sixteen advanced meditators who engendered a state of compassion, the cerebral areas involved in maternal love and feelings of affiliation—like the medial insula (and not the anterior insula as in pain)—as well as areas linked to "theory of mind" (imagining others' thoughts) are activated by listening to recordings of voices expressing distress, which is not the case among novice meditators.[12] These observations confirm the fact that experienced meditators are both more sensitive to and more concerned by others' sufferings and that they react not by experiencing increased distress, but by feeling compassion, and that one can "train" in acquiring these states of mind.

Imbuing Empathy with Compassion

I was talking recently with a nurse; like most of her colleagues, she is constantly confronted with the sufferings and problems of the patients she cares for. She told me that in the new training that health care personnel undergo, accent is placed on the "necessity of keeping an emotional distance from the patients," who are now often called "clients," to avoid the infamous burnout which affects so many health care workers. This woman, who was very warm and whose mere presence is reassuring, then confided to me: "It's strange, I feel as if I'm gaining something when I take care of people who are suffering, but when I speak of this 'gain' to my colleagues, I feel a little guilty about feeling something positive." I briefly described to her the differences that seem to exist between compassion and empathic distress. This difference agreed with her experience and proved that she had no reason to feel guilty. Contrary to empathic distress, love and compassion are positive states of mind, which reinforce one's inner ability to confront others' suffering and to care better for them. If a child is hospitalized, the presence of a loving mother at his side who holds his hand and comforts him with tender words will no doubt do him more good than the anxiety of a mother overwhelmed with empathic distress who, unable to bear the sight of her sick child, paces back and forth in the hallway. Reassured by my explanations, my nurse friend told me that despite qualms she occasionally had, this point of view agreed with her experience as a caregiver. Empathy is indeed needed to trigger the arising of compassion, but the space of that compassion should be vast enough so that empathy does not turn into uncontainable distress.

In light of this preliminary research, it would seem logical for those whose profession consists of attending to suffering people on a daily basis to be trained in altruistic love and compassion. Such a training would also help close relatives (parents, children, spouses) who take care of sick or handicapped people. Altruistic love creates in us a positive space that serves as an antidote to empathic distress, and prevents affective resonance from proliferating until it becomes paralyzing and engenders the emotional exhaustion characteristic of burnout. Without the support of love and compassion, empathy left to itself is like an electric pump through which no water circulates: it will quickly overheat and burn. So empathy should take place within the much vaster space of altruistic love. It is also important to consider the cognitive aspect of compassion, in other words understanding the different levels of suffering and its manifest or latent causes. We will be able thus to place ourselves in the service of others by helping them effectively while still preserving our inner strength, our kindness, and our inner peace. As the French psychologist Christophe André writes, "We need the gentleness and the strength of compassion. The more lucid we are about the world, the more we accept seeing it as it really is, the easier it is to accept that we cannot face all the suffering that is encountered in the course of our lives unless we have this strength and this gentleness."[13]

5

Love, Supreme Emotion

Up to now we have presented altruism as a *motivation,* as the intention to act for the other's welfare. In this chapter, we will present the research of Barbara Fredrickson and a few other psychologists on an approach to love, regarded here as a *positive resonance* between two or several people, an emotion that may be fleeting but that is infinitely renewable. This *emotion* tallies with the notion of altruism on some points yet differs from it on others.

Barbara Fredrickson, at the University of North Carolina, is, along with Martin Seligman, one of the founders of positive psychology. She was among the first psychologists to draw attention to the fact that positive emotions like joy, contentment, gratitude, wonder, enthusiasm, inspiration, and love are much more than a simple absence of negative emotions. Joy is not the simple absence of sadness; kindness is not a simple absence of malevolence. Positive emotions have an additional dimension that is not reducible to neutrality of mind: they are a source of profound satisfaction. This implies that in order to flourish in life, it is not enough to neutralize negative and disturbing emotions; one must also foster the blossoming of positive emotions.

Fredrickson's research has shown that these positive emotions open our minds in that they allow us to view situations with a vaster perspective, to be more receptive to others, and to adopt flexible and creative attitudes and behavior.[1] Unlike depression, which often provokes a downward spiral, positive emotions cause an upward spiral. They also make us more resilient, and allow us to manage adversity better.

From the point of view of contemporary psychology, an emotion is an often intense mental state that lasts only a few instants but that is apt to reoccur many times. Specialists in emotions, Paul Ekman and Richard Lazarus in particular, have identified a certain number of basic emotions, including joy, sadness, anger, fear, surprise, disgust, and contempt—recognizable by facial expression and characteristic physiological reactions—to which are added love, compassion, curiosity, interest, affection, and feelings of elevation, shame, and guilt.[2] As the days go by, the accumulation of these temporary *emotions* influences our *moods,* and the reiteration of moods little by little changes our mental dispositions—our personality traits. In light of recent studies, Barbara Fredrickson avers that, of all the positive emotions, love is the *supreme emotion*.

Dictionaries define love as "the inclination of one person for another" (Larousse), or as a "strong affection for another arising out of kinship or personal ties" (Merriam-Webster). Beyond this, the variety of definitions of love are not surprising, since, as the Canadian poet and novelist Margaret Atwood wrote, "The Eskimos had fifty-two names for snow because it was important to them, there ought to be as many for love."[3]

As for Barbara Fredrickson, she defines love as a *positive resonance* that manifests when three events occur simultaneously: the *sharing* of one or several positive emotions, a *synchrony* between the behavior and physiological reactions of two people, and the *intention* to contribute to the other's well-being, an intention that engenders mutual care.[4] This resonance of positive emotions can last for a certain amount of time, or be amplified like the reverberation of an echo, until, inevitably, as is the fate of all emotions, it vanishes.

According to this definition, love is both vaster and more open, and its duration shorter than we generally think: "Love is not lasting. It's actually far more fleeting than most of us would care to acknowledge. On the upside, though, love is forever renewable." The research of Fredrickson and her colleagues has in fact shown that although love is very sensitive to circumstances and requires certain preliminary conditions, once these conditions have been identified, one can reproduce this feeling of love an incalculable number of times each day.[5]

In order to grasp what this research can teach us, we must step back a little from what we usually call "love." It is not a question here of filial love or romantic love, or of a wedding betrothal or any ritual of fidelity. "The bedrock for my approach to love is the science of emotions," writes Fredrickson in *Love 2.0,* her recent book published in the United States for a mass audience, which is a synthesis of all her studies.[6]

Psychologists do not deny that one can regard love as a profound connection that can last years or even an entire lifetime; they have stressed the considerable benefits of these connections for physical and mental health.[7] However, they think that the enduring state called "love" by most people is the *result* of the accumulation of many moments, much shorter, during which this positive emotional resonance is felt.

Similarly, it is the accumulation of *affective dissonances,* repeated moments of sharing negative emotions, that erodes and ends up destroying profound, long-lasting connections. In the case of possessive attachment, for example, this resonance disappears; in the case of jealousy, it becomes poisoned and is transformed into negative resonance.

Love allows us to see the other with caring, kindness, and compassion. Thus it is linked to altruism insofar as one becomes sincerely concerned for the fate of the other and for the other's own welfare.[8] That is far from being the case in other types of relationships related to attachment. Earlier on in her career, Fredrickson was interested in what she regards as being the polar opposite of love, namely the fact of regarding the woman (or the man) as a "sexual object," which can have as many harmful effects as love has positive effects. Here there is an investment not in others' well-being but in their physical appearance and their sexuality, not for *the other,* who is then regarded only as an instrument, but for *oneself,* for one's own pleasure.[9] To a lesser degree, possessive attachment stifles positive resonance. Feeding such attachments signifies that one is concerned above all with loving oneself through the love one claims to have for the other.

Love is altruistic when it manifests as the joy of sharing life with those around us—friends, companions, spouses—and contributing to their happiness, moment by moment. Instead of being obsessed by the other, one is concerned with the other's happiness. Instead of wanting to possess others, one feels responsible for their well-being; instead of anxiously expecting gratification from them, one can give and receive with joy and kindness.

This positive resonance can be felt at any moment by two or more people. Such a love is not reserved only for a spouse or romantic partner; it is not reduced to feelings of tenderness that one feels for one's children, parents, or relatives. It can occur at any time, with a person sitting next to us on a train, when our benevolent attention has given rise to a similar attitude, in mutual respect and appreciation.

This notion of love conceived as a mutual resonance still differs from extended altruism as we have previously defined it, which consists of an unconditional benevolence, not necessarily mutual, and which does not depend on the way the other treats us or behaves.

The Biology of Love

Love as positive resonance is profoundly inscribed in our biological makeup and results, on the physiological level, in the interaction of activity of certain areas of the brain (linked to empathy, maternal love, and feelings of reward and contentment) with oxytocin (a polypeptide created in the brain which influences social interactions), and the vagus nerve (which can have the effects of calming and facilitating connections with others).

The scientific data collected over the course of the last two decades have shown how love, or its absence, fundamentally changes our physiology and the regulation of a group of biochemical substances, substances that can even influence the way our genes are expressed in our cells. This ensemble of complex interactions profoundly affects our physical health, our vitality, and our well-being.

When Two Brains Become Attuned to Each Other

It often happens that two people who converse and spend time together feel perfectly in tune with each other. In other cases, communication does not get through, and one does not enjoy the time shared together at all.

This is precisely what Uri Hasson's team studied at Princeton University. These neuroscientists were able to show how the brains of two people linked by a conversation adopt very similar neural configurations and enter into resonance. They noted that the simple fact of listening attentively to someone else's words and talking to him activates similar brain areas in both brains in a remarkably synchronous way.[10] Hasson speaks of "a single act, performed by two brains." Colloquially, one could speak of a "meeting of minds." Uri Hasson thinks that this "brain coupling" is essential to communication.[11] He has also shown that it is very pronounced in the insula, a part of the brain that, as we have seen,[12] is at the core of empathy and indicates emotional resonance.[13] Synchronization is particularly elevated during the most emotional moments of the conversation.[14]

These results led Fredrickson to deduce that micro-moments of love, of positive resonance, are also a single act performed by two brains. Good mutual comprehension is, according to her, a source of mutual caring, starting from which benevolent intentions and deeds will organically manifest.[15] Our subjective experience thus expands from an attention usually focused on "me," on the self, to a more generous and open focus on "us."[16]

But that's not all. Uri Hasson's team also showed that our brain went so far as to *anticipate* by a few seconds the expression of the other's brain activity. In such a conversation a positive empathic resonance leads to an emotional anticipation of what the other person is about to say. It's a fact that being very attentive to the other usually leads us to anticipate the unfurling of what the other is telling us and the feeling that will be expressed.

People often refer to "mirror neurons." They are present in minute areas of the brain and are activated when one sees, for example, someone else making a gesture that interests us.[17] These neurons were discovered by accident in the laboratory of Giacomo Rizzolatti, in Parma, Italy. The researchers were studying the activation of a particular type of neuron in a monkey picking up a banana. As they were eating their lunch in the laboratory, however, in the presence of the monkeys, they noticed that the recording device crackled every time a researcher carried food to his mouth: the monkeys' neurons were being activated as well. This discovery revealed that the same cerebral zones are activated in a person who carries out a gesture and in the one observing him. Mirror neurons can thus provide an elementary basis for imitation and intersubjective resonance. Still, the phenomenon of empathy, which includes emotional and cognitive aspects, is much more complex, and involves many areas of the brain.

Oxytocin and Social Interactions

Research in the field of brain chemistry has also led to interesting discoveries in the realm of social interactions, after Sue Carter and her colleagues highlighted the effects of a peptide, oxytocin, which is created in the brain by the hypothalamus and also circulates throughout the body. These researchers studied prairie voles, which are monogamous, unlike their counterparts in the mountains. They noted that the level of oxytocin was higher in the brain of the prairie vole than in the mountain vole. They then demonstrated that if one artificially increases the level of oxytocin in the brain of prairie voles, their tendency to stay together and to huddle next to each other is even stronger than usual. On the other hand, if one inhibits the production of oxytocin in male prairie voles, they become as fickle as their mountain cousins.[18]

Oxytocin is also linked to maternal love. If one inhibits the production of oxytocin in ewes, they neglect their newborn lambs. On the other hand, when a mother rat licks her babies and pays a lot of attention to them, the number of oxytocin receptors within the amygdala (a small region of the brain essential for the expression of emotions) and in subcortical brain regions increases.[19] The baby rats that were treated with affection turned out to be calmer, more curious, and less anxious than the others. Studies by Michael Meaney have also shown that in baby rats who are surrounded by their mothers' care during the first ten days of life, the expression of genes that induce stress is blocked.[20]

In humans, the level of oxytocin increases markedly during sexual relations, but also during labor and just before lactation. Even though it is difficult to study the subtler fluctuations in humans with non-invasive techniques, research was greatly facilitated when it was perceived that oxytocin inhaled by a nasal spray reached the brain. This technique allowed researchers to demonstrate that people who breathe in a single blast of oxytocin perceive interpersonal signals better, look more often into others' eyes, and pay more attention to their smiles and to subtle emotional nuances expressed by facial expressions. They thus show an increased ability to apprehend correctly others' feelings.[21]

In the laboratory of Ernst Fehr in Zurich, Michael Kosfeld and Markus Heinrichs asked volunteers to take part in a "trust game" after having inhaled either oxytocin or a placebo.[22] During the game, they had to decide what amount of money they would agree to lend to a partner, who might then either reimburse them or keep the loan. Despite the risk of disloyalty, the people who had inhaled the oxytocin trusted their partner twice as much as those who had inhaled a placebo.[23] Other researchers have proven that, when sharing a piece of information that had to remain confidential, trust in the other increased by 44% after inhaling oxytocin.[24] Other studies have now established that inhaling sprays of oxytocin made people more confident, more generous, more cooperative, more sensitive to others' emotions, more constructive in communications, and more charitable in their judgments.

Neuroscientists have even demonstrated that a single inhalation of oxytocin was enough to inhibit the part of the amygdala that is activated when one feels anger or fear or when one feels threatened, and to stimulate the part of the amygdala that is usually activated during positive social interactions.[25]

More generally, researchers have demonstrated that oxytocin plays an important role in reactions that consist of "calming and connecting," in contrast to the "fight or flight" reflex.[26] In effect, it calms social phobia and stimulates our ability to connect to others.[27] Since beings need enriching connections, not only to reproduce, but also to survive and prosper, oxytocin was described by neurobiologists as "the great facilitator of life."[28]

Oxytocin is experiencing its hour of fame and is often referred to in the popular media as the "love hormone" or the "bonding hormone." The situation is in fact more complex. Oxytocin has an unarguable effect on the nature of social interactions, but not solely in a positive way. It turns out that, although it encourages trust and generosity in certain situations and for certain people, in other circumstances and for individuals endowed with different character traits, it can also increase envy, a propensity to rejoice at others' unhappiness, and favoritism for members of one's own clan.[29] One study has shown that after inhaling oxytocin, some volunteers were more cooperative with people they thought of as being "one of them," but less cooperative with people who belonged to other groups.[30]

So it seems that, depending on the situation and the individual, oxytocin can in certain cases reinforce our prosocial behavior, and in others, our tendency to discriminate between those close to us and those who do not belong to our group. Observation of these seemingly contradictory effects led Sue Carter to advance the hypothesis that this cerebral peptide might participate in a system for regulating social behavior, and that its action could be superimposed on the backdrop of our personal history and our emotional traits. Oxytocin could also act by intensifying our attention to social signals, helping us to notice them. Under the effect of this neuropeptide, a sociable nature will fully manifest itself, whereas in an anxious or jealous temperament, oxytocin will only exacerbate those feelings of anxiety or jealousy. To date, no specific study has been done on the potential effects of oxytocin on our altruistic motivations, and so much remains to be explored concerning its role in human relations.

CALMING DOWN AND OPENING UP TO OTHERS: THE ROLE OF THE VAGUS NERVE

The vagus nerve links the brain to the heart and to various other organs. In situations involving fear, when our heart is pounding wildly and we're ready to take flight or face an adversary, it's the vagus nerve that restores calm to our organism and facilitates communication with the other.

Further, the vagus nerve stimulates the facial muscles, allowing us to adopt expressions in harmony with our interlocutor's and to make frequent eye contact with him. It also adjusts the tiny muscles in the middle ear that allow us to concentrate on someone's voice in the midst of ambient noise. Its activity thus favors social exchange and increases the possibilities of positive resonance.[31]

One's *vagal tone* reflects the activity of the vagus nerve and can be evaluated by measuring the influence of one's breathing rate on one's heart rate. A high *vagal tone* is good for physical and mental health. It accelerates heartbeats when we breathe in (which allows freshly oxygenated blood to be quickly distributed) and slows them down when we breathe out (which occurs at a time when it is useless to make blood circulate quickly). Normally, our vagal tone is extremely stable from year to year, influencing our health as time goes by. It differs markedly, however, from one person to another.

It has been noted that people who have a high vagal tone adapt better physically and mentally to changing circumstances, are more apt to regulate their internal physiological processes (glucose levels, response to inflammation) as well as their emotions, their attention, and their behavior. They are less subject to heart attacks, and recuperate more quickly if they do have one.[32] The vagal tone is also an indicator of the robustness of the immune system. Moreover, a high vagal tone is associated with a diminution of the chronic inflammation that increases the risks of a cerebral vascular accident, diabetes, and certain types of cancer.[33]

These somewhat technical data took on particular importance when Barbara Fredrickson and her team demonstrated that it was possible to improve the vagal tone considerably by meditating altruistic love.

Cultivating Love on a Daily Basis

Having noted the qualities of positive emotions in general and love in particular, Barbara Fredrickson wondered how to disclose the links of cause and effect (not merely simple correlations) between an increase of altruistic love and the increase of qualities we have described in this chapter: joy, serenity, and gratitude, for example. She decided to compare under rigorous conditions a group that was supposed to feel more love and other beneficial emotions every day with a control group that was not meditating, the division of the two groups having been decided by lot. It remained to be seen how to lead the subjects in one of the groups to feel more positive emotions.

That was when Fredrickson became interested in an ancient technique practiced for 2,500 years by Buddhist meditators: training in loving kindness, or altruistic love, often taught in the West under the name *metta* (the Pali term, the original language of Buddhism). Fredrickson realized that this practice, whose aim is precisely to produce a methodical and voluntary change over the course of time, corresponded precisely to what she was looking for.[34]

For the experiment, she enrolled 140 adults in good health (70 in each group), without any particular spiritual inclination or experience in meditation. The experiment lasted seven weeks. During this time, the subjects of the first group, divided into teams of twenty, received a teaching on meditating on altruistic love given by a qualified instructor, and then practiced, generally alone and for about twenty minutes a day, what they had learned. During the first week, emphasis was placed on loving kindness for oneself; during the second, on relatives, and during the last five weeks, the meditation took as its object not only people close to the participants, but also everyone they knew, then strangers, and, finally, all beings.

The results were very clear: this group, which was made up only of novices in meditation, had learned how to calm their minds and, even more, to develop remarkably their capacity for love and kindness. Compared to people in the control group (who were given a chance to take part in the same training once the experiment was over), the subjects who had practiced meditation felt more love, involvement in their daily activities, serenity, joy, and other beneficial emotions.[35] In the course of the training, Fredrickson also noticed that the positive effects of meditation on altruistic love persisted throughout the day, outside of the meditation session, and that, day after day, a cumulative effect was observed.

Measurements of the participants' physical condition also showed that their state of health had clearly improved. Even their vagal tone, which normally does not change much over time, had increased.[36] This reminded me of something the psychologist Paul Ekman had suggested during one of our conversations, that we create "gyms for altruism and compassion"; he was thinking of those physical culture venues one finds pretty much everywhere in cities, because of the benefits on health—also amply demonstrated—of regular physical exercise.

Love and Altruism: Temporary Emotion and Enduring Disposition

At the close of this chapter, a few thoughts arise. The research studies we have just discussed are certainly fascinating, and the various practices that Barbara Fredrickson describes are likely to improve considerably the quality of life for each one of us. For Barbara, with whom I had the opportunity to discuss these matters, "first and foremost, *love is an emotion*, a momentary state that arises to infuse your mind and body alike."[37] It also requires, according to her, the presence of the other:

> *This means that when you're alone, thinking about those you love, reflecting on past loving connections, yearning for more, or even when you're practicing loving-kindness meditation or writing an impassioned love letter, you are not in that moment experiencing true love. It's true that the strong feelings you experience when by yourself are important and absolutely vital to your health and well-being. But they are not (yet) shared, and so they lack the critical and undeniably physical ingredient of resonance. Physical presence is key to love, to positivity resonance.*[38]

Without in any way denying the importance and special quality of physical interactions with another human being, we should still not lose sight of two additional and essential dimensions of altruism.

Although emotions do not last, their repetition does end up engendering more lasting *dispositions*. When a person who has an altruistic disposition enters into resonance with another person, this resonance will most of the time be imbued with kindness. When this disposition is weak, temporary positive resonances can be, in the ensuing instants, associated with selfish motivations that will limit their positive effects. Hence the importance, as in the Buddhist meditation studied by Barbara Fredrickson, of cultivating with perseverance not only positive moments of resonance, but also a *lasting* altruistic motivation.

That leads us to the second dimension: the cognitive aspect, even vaster than the emotional aspect and less vulnerable to mood changes. This cognitive dimension allows us to extend a limitless altruism to a great number of beings, including ones whom we have never even met. By integrating these different dimensions linked to temporary and renewable emotions with cognitive processes and with lasting dispositions, altruistic love can fully flourish.

6

The Accomplishment of a Twofold Benefit, Our Own and Others'

According to the Buddhist way, as in many other spiritual traditions, working for the benefit of others is not only the most desirable of activities, but also the best way to serve indirectly our own benefit. The pursuit of a selfish happiness is doomed to failure, whereas accomplishing the good of others constitutes one of the main factors for fulfillment and, ultimately, progress toward Enlightenment.

The ideal of Buddhism is *bodhicitta:* "the aspiration to attain Enlightenment for the benefit of all beings." Moreover, this aspiration is the only way to attain happiness for oneself, as Shantideva, a seventh-century Indian Buddhist master, writes in his work, *The Path Towards Awakening:*

All the joy the world contains
Has come through wishing happiness for others.
All the misery the world contains
Has come through wanting pleasure for oneself.

Is there need for lengthy explanation?
Childish beings look out for themselves;
Buddhas labor for the good of others:
See the difference that divides them![1]

This point of view is not foreign to Western thought. The philosopher Bishop Joseph Butler, one of the first to refute the theories of Thomas Hobbes on the universality of selfishness, wrote:

> *Thus, it appears, that private interest is so far from being likely to be promoted in proportion to the degree in which self-love engrosses us, and prevails over all other principles, that the contracted affection may be so prevalent, as to disappoint itself, and even contradict its own end, private good.*[2]

In *Émile: Or on Education,* Jean-Jacques Rousseau distinguishes self-love—the fact of feeling contentment when our aspirations are satisfied—which is entirely compatible with benevolence for others, from selfish conceit, which causes us systematically to place our own interests above others', and demands that the entire world take our desires into consideration.

Still, the accomplishment of the benefit of others does not involve sacrificing our own happiness—quite the contrary. To remedy others' sufferings, we can choose to pay with our own person, give up some of our possessions or comfort. In fact, if we are moved by a sincere, determined altruistic motivation, we will experience this action as a success and not a failure, a gain and not a loss, joy and not mortification. Abnegation called "sacrificial" and, under that description, decried by partisans of egocentrism,[3] is a sacrifice only for the egoist. For the altruist, it becomes a source of fulfillment. The quality of our life does not seem to be diminished, but rather increased. "Love is the only thing that doubles every time it's given," said Albert Schweitzer. So we can no longer talk of sacrifice since, subjectively, the accomplished action, far from having been felt as a suffering or a loss, has on the contrary brought us the satisfaction of having acted in a correct, desirable, and necessary way.

When we speak of the "cost" of an altruistic action, or of sacrifices made for others, it is often a matter of external sacrifices—our own physical comfort, our financial resources, our time, etc. But this external cost does not correspond to an internal cost. Even if we have devoted time and resources to the accomplishment of the good of others, if this act is experienced as an inner gain, the very notion of cost evaporates.

What's more, if we recognize the value of the common wish of all sentient beings to avoid suffering, it will seem reasonable and desirable to us to accept certain difficulties in order to ensure great benefits for them. From this point of view, if an altruistic action indirectly does us good, so much the better; if it does us neither good nor bad, it doesn't matter; and if it requires certain sacrifices that are meaningful, it is worth the trouble, since our sense of fulfillment becomes deeper.

Everything is a question of proportion and common sense: if the diminution of suffering is the main criterion, it would be foolish to sacrifice our lasting well-being so that the other can enjoy a minor advantage. It would be absurd to risk our lives to fish out a ring that someone else dropped in the water, or to spend a large amount of money to give a crate of vodka to a sick drunkard. On the other hand, it would be highly desirable to save the life of a person if she had fallen in the water with her ring on her finger, and to use our money to help the drunkard escape the alcoholism that is killing him.

Is an Action Selfish if One Benefits from It?

A disinterested action is no less so when one is satisfied with carrying it out. One can draw satisfaction from an altruistic gesture without this satisfaction having motivated our action. Moreover, the individual who carries out an altruistic action for purely selfish reasons risks being disappointed when he does not obtain the expected effect. The reason is simple: only a benevolent action stemming from an equally benevolent motivation can give rise to true satisfaction. Altruism thus appears to involve a synergy between the accomplishment of both the good of others and one's own. In order for this synergy to bear fruit, the altruistic act must be done primarily for the sake of another. Yet the mere knowledge that such an act is likely to yield one's own fulfillment as well does not tarnish its altruistic nature, provided one does not crave that outcome.

When a farmer cultivates his field and plants wheat, it is with an aim to harvest enough wheat to feed his family. At the same time, the stalks of wheat provide him with straw. But no one would argue that the farmer devoted a year of labor to the sole aim of amassing straw.

John Dunne, professor in the religion department at Emory

University in the United States, speaks jestingly of "Buddhist economics" to designate the way Buddhists perceive real profits and losses. Thus, if I emerge a winner from a financial conflict, I am richer externally, but I pay the inner price of the hostility that disturbs my mind, leaving a residue of resentment. So I have gotten poorer internally. On the other hand, if I carry out a disinterested act of generosity, I am poorer externally, but richer internally in terms of well-being. The material "cost" that can be recorded as an external "loss" turns out to be an internal "gain." In fact, from the point of the view of "psychological economics," everyone wins: the one who gives with generosity and the one who receives with gratitude.

According to the great Tibetan master Dilgo Khyentse Rinpoche, the true altruist is one who "never hopes for a reward. He responds to the needs of others out of his natural compassion. Cause and effect are unfailing, so his actions to benefit others are sure to bear fruit—but he never counts on it. He certainly never thinks that people are not showing enough gratitude, or that they ought to treat him better. But if someone who has done him harm later changes his behavior, that is something that will make him rejoice wholeheartedly and be totally satisfied."[4]

This concept of an internal economics is related to the often misunderstood notion of "merit." In Buddhism, merit is not an accumulation of "good points" for good behavior, but positive energy that allows us to do others the greatest good while being content oneself. In this sense, merit is like a farm of which one has taken great care and which provides an abundant harvest, capable of satisfying everyone.

EVERYONE LOSES OR EVERYONE GAINS

Seeking selfish happiness seems doomed to failure for several reasons. First of all, from the point of view of personal experience, selfishness, born from an exaggerated sense of self-importance, turns out to be a constant source of torment. Egocentrism and excessive self-cherishing multiply our hopes and fears and makes us brood on what might affect us. Obsession with "me," with the ego, leads us to magnify the impact on our well-being of the slightest event, and to look at the world in a distorted mirror. We project onto our surroundings judgments and values fabricated by our mental confusion. These constant projections make us not only miserable, but also vulnerable to external perturbations and to our own habitual thoughts, which lead to feelings of permanent malaise.

In the bubble of the ego, the slightest annoyance becomes overblown. The narrowness of our inner world means that by constantly bumping up against the walls of this bubble, our states of mind and emotions are magnified in a disproportionate and overwhelming way. The slightest cheerfulness becomes euphoria, success feeds vanity, affection freezes into attachment, failure plunges us into depression, displeasure irritates us and makes us aggressive. We lack the inner resources necessary to manage the highs and lows of existence in a healthy way. This world of the ego is like a little glass of water: a few pinches of salt are enough to make it undrinkable. On the other hand, one who has burst the bubble of the ego is like a great lake: a handful of salt does not change its flavor in the least. Essentially, selfishness makes everyone lose: it makes us unhappy and we, in turn, pass that unhappiness on to those around us.

The second reason stems from the fact that selfishness is at odds with reality. It rests on an erroneous postulate according to which individuals are isolated entities, independent of each other. The selfish person hopes to construct his personal happiness in the bubble of his ego. He says to himself basically, "It's up to each of us to construct our own happiness. I'll take care of mine, you take care of yours. I have nothing against your happiness, but it's not my business." The problem is that reality is quite otherwise: we are not autonomous entities and our happiness can only be constructed with the help of others. Even if we feel as if we are the center of the world, that world remains the world of other people.

So selfishness cannot be regarded as an effective way to love oneself, since it is the prime cause of our frustrations and unhappiness. It constitutes a particularly clumsy attempt to secure one's own happiness. The psychologist Erich Fromm, in line with Buddhist thinking, sheds light on selfish behavior in this way: "The love of my own self is inseparably connected with the love of any other self. Selfishness and self-love, far from being identical, are actually opposites. The selfish person does not love himself too much but too little; in fact he hates himself."[5] The selfish person is someone who does nothing sensible to be happy. He hates himself because, without realizing it, he does everything possible to make himself unhappy, and this permanent failure provokes an internal frustration and rage that he turns against himself and against the outer world.

If egocentrism is a constant source of torment, it is quite otherwise for altruism and compassion. On the level of lived experience, altruistic love is accompanied by a profound feeling of fullness and, as we will see, it is also the state of mind that activates the most brain areas linked to positive emotions. One could say that altruistic love is the most positive of all the positive emotions.

What's more, altruism is in harmony with the reality of what we are and what surrounds us, the fact that everything is basically interdependent. Common perception of our daily life can lead us to believe that things have an objective and independent reality, but, in fact, they exist only in dependence on other things.

Understanding this universal interdependence is the very source of the deepest altruism. By understanding how much our physical existence, our survival, our comfort, our health, and so on, all depend on others and on what the external world provides us—remedies, food, and the like—it grows easier to put ourselves in the place of others, to wish for their happiness, to respect their aspirations, and to feel closely concerned with the accomplishment of these aspirations.

The superiority of altruism over selfishness does not rest only on moral values, then, but also on common sense and on a clear perception of reality.

Is Altruism Intrinsically Linked to Our Well-Being?

Just as warmth inevitably occurs when one lights a fire, true altruism goes naturally hand-in-hand with profound personal satisfaction. When we accomplish a benevolent action—by allowing, for example, someone to regain health or freedom, or else to escape death—don't we feel as if we are in harmony with our deepest nature? Wouldn't we wish to experience such a disposition of mind more often, a disposition which makes the illusory barriers invented by egocentrism between the "self" and the world disappear, even for an instant, and which makes us feel at one with nature, a feeling that reflects the essential interdependence of all beings?

On the other hand, when we get hold of ourselves after having been temporarily overwhelmed by a feeling of violent anger, don't we often say to ourselves: "I was beside myself," or: "I wasn't really myself"? Harmful mental states always tend to distance us a little more from that feeling of harmony with oneself that the French philosopher Michel Terestchenko calls "fidelity to self." He suggests we substitute a concept of altruism envisaged as "giving up, abolition, dispossession of self, a sacrificial disinterestedness that abandons itself to a radical alterity (god, moral law, or the other)," with the notion of a "benevolent relationship with the other that results from presence to self, fidelity to self, from the obligation, experienced deep within oneself, to make one's actions agree with one's convictions (philosophical, ethical, or religious) and at the same time with one's feelings (empathy or compassion), and sometimes even, more simply, to act in agreement with one's self-image, independently of any regard or judgment of the other, indifferent to any social desire for recognition."[6]

The nature of the relationship between kindness and happiness becomes clear. Each engenders and reinforces the other; they stem from a feeling of harmony with ourselves. Plato said, "The happiest man is he who has no trace of malice in his soul."[7]

Altruism, kindness, and happiness also make sense from the point of view of the evolution of the social animals we are. Love, affection, and concern for others are, in the long run, essential to our survival. The newborn baby would not survive more than a few hours without the tenderness of its mother; an invalid old man would quickly die without the care of those around him. We need to receive love in order to be able to know how to give it.

7

Self-Interested Altruism and Generalized Reciprocity

Many seemingly altruistic behaviors do not truly stem from altruistic motivations. One can benefit others with the expectation of reward, with the desire to be praised or to avoid blame, or else to relieve the feeling of discomfort felt when witnessing others' suffering. "Self-interested altruism" is a mixture of altruism and selfishness. It is not a hypocritical façade, since it aims sincerely to contribute to the good of others, but it remains conditional and is practiced only when it contributes to our own self-interest.

Human beings are ready to help each other and, while watching out for their own self-interest, use these favors as a bargaining chip. Fair trade, rituals of exchange in traditional societies, gift and counter-gift, are examples of this. This practice is compatible with feeling respect for others, insofar as one acts in a fair way and takes care not to harm anyone. Self-interested altruism is not necessarily deceitful, then. Nevertheless if an action that is profitable for an individual performing it is carried out with the intention of benefiting from it, one cannot qualify it as true altruism. What's more, when it is not animated by a benevolent attitude, the mere practice of exchange often ends up in mistrust, dissimulation, manipulation, even hostility.

Self-interested altruism can also stem from selfishness, pure and simple. As La Rochefoucauld observed, "We often persuade ourselves to love people who are more powerful than we are, yet interest alone produces our friendship; we do not give our hearts away for the good we wish to do, but for that we expect to receive."[1] Mightn't the altruist be only a "reasonable egoist," in the words of Remy de Gourmont? Are we incapable of doing any better?

SELF-INTERESTED ALTRUISM AND THE REALIZATION OF THE COMMON GOOD

Some think that a quest for self-interested, rational, equitable altruism is a more realistic objective than the emergence in our societies of a selfless altruism. The French writer and political analyst Jacques Attali evokes the interdependence of human behavior as the foundational principle of this self-interested altruism:

> *Self-interested altruism is the transition between liberty and fraternity. I think our civilization will survive only if it can make it possible for each person to find happiness in the happiness of others.[2]... Our self-interest lies in the happiness of others; peace at home depends on the reduction of poverty elsewhere.[3]*

For the French economist and former Harvard and Stanford professor Serge-Christophe Kolm, the way to achieve this transition between liberty and fraternity is "general reciprocity":

> *The voluntary, unconstrained altruism of reciprocity... founds on individual liberties those positive actions toward others that are the fabric of communal feeling: it is the reconciliation of liberty with fraternity.[4]*

A harmonious society would be one that discovers a fair balance between the interests of each individual and those of the community, and one that favors an atmosphere of reciprocal benevolence. This benevolence is born from understanding that only when one respects such an equitable balance can the good of each person have a real chance of being accomplished. Philosopher André Comte-Sponville expresses it this way: "I think that the whole art of politics is to make selfish individuals more intelligent, which I call 'solidarity' and which Jacques Attali calls 'self-interested altruism.' It is a question of making people understand that it is in their own self-interest to take into account the interests of others."[5]

Long-Term Reciprocity

A reciprocity that turns out to be equitable over the long term is an essential component of every human society and of a large number of animal societies. Cooperation is in fact essential to the survival of social animals. According to Darwin, "social instincts lead an animal to take pleasure in the society of its fellows, to feel a certain amount of sympathy with them, and to perform various services for them.... Social animals aid one another in many important ways...and warn one another of danger."[6]

An often cited example of reciprocity among animals involves a particular species of bat, the vampire bat of Latin America. These vampires live in groups of about twenty, mainly females and their offspring. At night, they hunt farm animals, whose blood they drink. But many of them come back empty in the early morning, on an average of one night out of three. If, by misfortune, a vampire bat can't find anything to feed on for two nights in a row, which is frequent among the young, she will probably not survive until the third night because of her high metabolic requirements. The starved bat will then approach one of her fellows to ask for food. The other bat almost always agrees to regurgitate some of the blood collected during the night.

The ethologist Gerald Wilkinson, who has studied bats for a long time, has shown that these regurgitations are not only offered among related females (mother-daughter or close relative), but also non-related females who have established alliances that can last as long as a dozen years. These females often remain together and engage in more mutual grooming than the others. If a female refuses several times to regurgitate blood for others, she will be shunned by the group, or even be expelled from the community roost. Because of this, she will risk dying of starvation when she in turns needs blood.[7]

In human societies, reciprocity constitutes the texture of a balanced community within which everyone is ready to help everyone else and shows gratitude when helped in turn. In a community where people know each other well, everyone takes it for granted that others will behave in a beneficial way toward them when the need arises. If a member of the community doesn't play the game, such as by benefiting from a service performed by another without repaying it, he will quickly be ostracized by his peers.

In the high valleys of Zanskar, in the extreme northwest of India, community life is regulated by such a lasting reciprocity. In the villages, every year, a neighborhood of a dozen homes is chosen to take charge of the preparations for the New Year festivities. Each family must take turns offering a banquet to the neighborhood, during which a rich and abundant meal is prepared. Here it is out of tacit understanding that everyone feels obliged to respect. Associations are also formed in Zanskar of people not linked by blood, but by an oath taken during a religious ritual. At every important family event, like births, marriages, or deaths, the members of this fraternity help each other. At a death, for instance, they take charge of the expenses and organize the funeral. Over the course of recent years, a number of young people have emigrated to cities in the Indian plains, so these conventions of reciprocity have become harder to carry out for those who have remained in the village. [8]

This system of reciprocity is very different from an agreement or a commercial transaction. No one is bound by a contract and no one can force anyone to repay his debt. No external authority is involved. It would be inconceivable, even laughable, to go find the chief of the village to complain that Family X hasn't sponsored the festivities in a long time. Talk and reputation is enough. Either one remains within the circle of reciprocity, or one leaves it, with the consequence that withdrawal would have: isolation.

Tribes in the Andes who lived before and during the Inca Empire, were structured in social units that resembled large families. Members of the community helped each other in working the fields, building houses, and the like. A very precise account was kept of the tasks carried out, and reciprocity implied equivalent hours of service: they were well aware of having helped to plow five furrows or having given a piece of cloth that had required a certain number of hours to weave, and a return was expected in service that was in proportion to its value or to the number of hours of work. Here too, reciprocity had a great value in enriching and preserving the social cohesion.[9]

Quantified reciprocity can lead to extreme situations, as it has for the Ik people in Africa, where a person might, against the owner's will, plow his field or repair his roof while his back is turned, in the aim of imposing a debt of gratitude on him that will unfailingly be demanded when needed. "At one time I have seen so many men thatching a roof that the whole roof was in serious danger of collapsing, and the protests of the owner were of no avail,"[10] reports Colin Turnbull, an anthropologist who studied the rituals of gift exchange among the Ik. One individual in particular "always made himself unpopular by accepting such help and by paying for it on the spot with food (which the cunning old fox knew they could not resist), which immediately negated the debt." As an old Scandinavian adage says, "The greedy are always afraid of gifts."[11]

But, in general, as Paul Ekman notes, "In small communities and villages, the more people cooperated, the more they became prosperous and their children had a better chance to survive. Among the people in New Guinea, where I worked fifty years ago, from cooking to childbirth to dealing with predators, they needed to work together. As for people who are only squabbling with others, no one wants to work with them. In a village, you can't get away with exploiting others for long and you can't run away from bad reputation either. So over time, the gene pool should be biased towards cooperation."[12]

Reciprocity may also include a solidarity that goes beyond reciprocal giving. Among Tibetan nomads, for example, the birth rate, but also unfortunately the mortality rate among both mothers and infants, remains high. When a mother dies in labor, the orphans are almost automatically taken charge of by a related family living in a neighboring tent, and the two households merge into one, until the children are big enough or the widowed father remarries.

Everyone who practices this kind of community cooperation, from the Ik men who keep the trails clear in the African bush to the Papuans of New Guinea, testify to the joy they feel in uniting their efforts to achieve a common aim; they assert that these moments of shared labor and cooperation are among the most valued in daily life.

Still, in a much vaster community, like a metropolis, it is impossible to know all the other members of the community. That facilitates the emergence of those champions of "everyone for himself," and profiteers who can thus evade the tacit commitment of reciprocity.

TOWARD A GENERALIZED RECIPROCITY?

Cooperatives represent a form of voluntary, quasi-anonymous reciprocity (according to the size and function of these organizations). At the state level, institutions like Social Security and aid for the elderly, the impoverished, orphans, and the unemployed represent a form of generalized reciprocity.

The economist Serge-Christophe Kolm contends that the two economic systems that divided the world in the twentieth century—the capitalist, individualistic, market economy and the totalitarian, entirely state controlled economy—"are both based on selfishness, the pure and simple instrumentalization of the individual."[13] This economist defends the alternative model of a general reciprocity, "based on the best qualities in humans, on the best social relationships, which reinforce them." He clarifies this notion of reciprocity: each person gives to society and receives from the totality of the others. As a general rule, the origin of the gift is not known. There is no specific donor. It's "all for one, one for all."[14]

We see, then, in light of this chapter, that self-interested altruism and reciprocal altruism are different from narrow-minded selfishness in that they allow constructive relationships to be woven between members of society. They can also be a springboard for selfless altruism. In fact, as people become aware of the virtues of benevolence, they may become more inclined to abandon the need to receive something in return, deciding instead that altruism deserves to be practiced with the sole aim of doing others good, without any egocentric consideration interfering with it.

8

Selfless Altruism

We can all think of examples of actions that have seemed perfectly selfless to us. A single anecdote by itself qualifies as a testimonial, but an accumulation of anecdotes that reinforce each other, like the ones that follow, ends up having something of the value of a proof.

A bassoonist in a New York opera company, Cyrus Segal was waiting for the bus on a Manhattan sidewalk when his precious instrument, which he had set down next to him, was stealthily snatched away. Cyrus had been playing that instrument for twenty-five years; even though it was insured, he was devastated. Each bassoon has its own personality, and he knew he would never again find exactly the same companion. A little later on, a homeless man walked into a music store and offered the bassoon for the modest fee of ten dollars (whereas it was estimated to be worth more like $12,000). The salesman, who came from a family of musicians, could easily picture what the owner must have been feeling, and decided right away to buy the instrument, not without first bargaining the man down to three dollars! Then he asked all the musicians who visited his shop if they had heard about a colleague who was the victim of a bassoon theft. In the days that followed, the news reached the ears of Cyrus, who quickly went to the shop and recognized his beloved instrument. The salesman, Marvis, didn't ask for any reward, and even refused the three dollars that Cyrus tried to repay him.[1] That may not be as brave as jumping into freezing water to save someone from drowning, but it obviously constitutes a fine example of a generous, selfless act.

In 2010, Violet Large and her husband, Allen, who lived in Nova

Scotia, won over eleven million dollars in the lottery. Instead of buying a new house and living more luxuriously, the couple decided "it was better to give than to receive" and distributed 98% of the sum to local and national charities. "We didn't buy a single thing," said Violet, "we didn't need anything."[2] To which Allen added: "You can't buy happiness. That money that we won was nothing. We have each other."

British-born Stan Brock, a former cowboy in British Guyana, was an adventurous naturalist and conservationist who spent years in the Amazon forest among the Wapishana Indians, a twenty-six hour walk from the nearest doctor. He saw so many people die from lack of medical care that he vowed he would bring medical aid to the region. After becoming famous on the Emmy Award–winning TV wildlife series *Wild Kingdom,* which showed him on horseback catching wild animals with a lasso and fighting in a swamp with an anaconda, he said to himself that all this had no meaning and it was time to do something worthwhile. Stan gave away everything he owned to start RAM (Remote Area Medical Foundation), a charity that delivers free medical treatment to Guyana's jungles and other very remote lands.

He later settled in the United States, where he was galled to see so many US citizens deprived of health care, especially dental and ocular care. He decided to organize traveling medical clinics that would provide treatment to thousands of poor patients. Thanks to its hundreds of volunteers, RAM has now treated over half a million patients in the United States. Using old airplanes, he also goes back to Guyana to bring medical supplies to remote regions. Now seventy-seven, Stan has made a vow of poverty and owns neither a house nor a car; he has no bank account, nor any kind of property. He sleeps on a rug that he unfurls on the floor of his office. To a BBC journalist who remarked during an interview, "That must be quite miserable!" Stan replied: "Not at all, I enjoy every moment of it."

These are only a few examples. We shouldn't rush to conclude that they're rare simply because they're remarkable. There are hundreds of similar stories, and they all say more than long arguments.

Unselfishness Evaluated in the Laboratory

The selfless quality of a person's behavior can be demonstrated by experiments.[3] The psychologist Leonard Berkowitz asked a group of volunteers to make paper boxes under the direction of a supervisor. Half of the volunteers were then told that their performance, although anonymous, would influence the way the supervisor was graded.

It turned out that the participants of that group worked better and for a longer time than the members of the other group, who had been told nothing about the supervisor. The former acted anonymously for the good of a supervisor they would never see again. So one cannot attribute their behavior to the hope for any kind of reward.

Moreover, sociologists have shown that the frequency of altruistic actions diminished when they were linked to some material reward. A study carried out on a large number of blood donors revealed that less than 2% of donors hoped for payment for their donation. Almost all the donors simply expressed a desire to help those who needed it.[4] What's more, a famous study carried out in England revealed that rewarding donors made their numbers fall. Offering remuneration degraded the quality of their altruistic action, so the usual donors were less inspired to volunteer.[5] In fact, the quantity of blood donated in relation to the number of inhabitants was, until then, clearly higher in England than in the United States, where donations are paid for.

The Simplest Explanation

When we sincerely offer a real gift to someone, the beauty of the gesture stems from the wish to bring happiness to the other, and not from a hope for something in return. The other person receives your present with all the more joy since he knows your gesture is not prompted by any calculation. That is the difference between a gift offered wholeheartedly to a person one loves and, for instance, a commercial gift, which everyone knows has strings attached.

Two American researchers, Nancy Eisenberg and Cynthia Neal,[6] worked with three- to four-year-old children, with the assumption that it wasn't very likely that their answers would be influenced by hypocrisy or by an intention to manipulate their interlocutor. When the nursery-school children observed by these researchers shared, unprompted, what they had with others or when they comforted a sad or upset child, the researchers sought to learn the reasons for their actions by asking questions like, "Why did you give that to John?" In their answers, the large majority of children explicitly referred to the fact that the other child needed help: "He was hungry," for example, was the answer from one of them who had shared his snack. The children never mentioned a fear of being punished by the teacher or reprimanded by their parents if they didn't help their comrades. Only a few replied that they hoped for something in return, like being well-thought of, for instance.

Lucille Babcock, who received the Carnegie Commission medal for "acts of heroism,"[7] didn't feel she had deserved it: "I was not ashamed that I got it, but I'm self-conscious about it, because I don't think about myself that way." The same goes for men and women called the "Righteous Among the Nations," who saved Jews during Nazi persecutions: the honors they were later accorded were regarded as incidental, unexpected, embarrassing, even "undesirable" by quite a few of them. The prospect of such honors had never entered into the motivation for their actions. "It was very simple," reports one rescuer, "I didn't do anything major. I never thought of the risks or imagined that my behavior could lead to rebuke or recognition. I just thought I was doing what I had to do."[8]

So there are situations in which selfless altruism is the simplest and most likely explanation for behavior that occurs constantly in our daily lives. The usual arguments of those who strive to find selfish motivations behind every altruistic action hardly hold up to scrutiny.

The philosopher and moralist C. D. Broad emphasizes this: "As so often happens in philosophy, clever people accept a false general principle on a priori grounds and then devote endless labor and ingenuity to explaining away plain facts which obviously conflict with it."[9]

Father Ceyrac, who over sixty years has taken care of thirty thousand poor children in southern India, told me one day: "Despite everything, I am struck by the immense kindness of people, even those who seem to have closed hearts and eyes. It is other people, all the others, who create the fabric of our lives and form the matter of our existences. Each person is a note in the 'great concert of the universe,' as the poet Tagore says. No one can resist the call of love. You always give in after a while. I actually think that humans are intrinsically good. You always have to see the good, the beautiful, in a person, never deny, always look for the greatness of people, without any distinction of religion, caste, or way of thinking."

Ridding Ourselves of Cynicism

A critical mind is indeed a prime quality in scientific investigation, but if it turns into cynicism and systematic denigration of everything that seems to stem from human kindness, it is no longer a proof of objectivity, but a sign of narrowness of mind and chronic pessimism. I had proof of this when I mixed for several weeks with a television team that was preparing a report on the Dalai Lama. I interacted with the members of this team in Nepal, the United States, and France, where I helped them as best I could to film various private events in which the Dalai Lama was participating, as well as to obtain an interview with him. But then I finally realized that their main objective was to look for the faults they suspected were concealed in the actions and person of the Dalai Lama.[10] Near the end of the filming, I said to the director: "When you deal with some of the great moral figures of our time, people like Nelson Mandela, Desmond Tutu, Vaclav Havel, or the Dalai Lama, don't you think it's better to try to reach their level, instead of attempting to lower them to your own?" His sole response was a slightly embarrassed chuckle.

We are all a mixture of qualities and defects, shadow and light. Under the sway of defeatist laziness, it is no doubt easier to give up becoming better than to recognize the existence of human kindness and make efforts to cultivate it. That is why, when one witnesses this goodness, it is better to be inspired by it than to denigrate it, and to do one's best to give it a larger place in our existence.

9

The Banality of Good

A beggar is given two fifty-rupee notes—a relatively large sum in Nepal—and gives half to his companion in misfortune. A nurse exhausted after a difficult night watch still stays a few hours more to help a dying man who is alone. My sister, Ève, who all her life has taken care of children with behavioral problems, has never hesitated to get up in the middle of the night to welcome a child running away from home. At the end of a too-busy day, an engineer coming home from his office walks an extra quarter-mile to show a stranger lost in the capital the way back to his hotel.

There have been discussions about the banality of evil.[1] But one could also talk of the "banality of good," picturing the thousand and one expressions of solidarity, consideration, and involvement in favor of others' good, which punctuate our daily lives and exercise a considerable influence on the quality of social life. And those who carry out these countless acts of mutual aid and solicitude generally say that it is quite "normal" to help one's neighbor. If it is justifiable to evoke this notion of ordinariness, it is also because everyday good does not make much commotion and people rarely pay attention to it; it doesn't make the headlines in the media like an arson, a horrible crime, or the sexual habits of a politician. If there is "banality of good," it's also a sign that we are all potentially capable of doing good around us.

The Omnipresence of Voluntary Work

"Assistance is a deed that is in accordance with nature. Never get tired of receiving it or giving it,"[2] said Marcus Aurelius. Between a fifth and a third of Europeans, depending on the country, or over 100 million individuals, take part in volunteer activities.[3] In the United States, this number is close to 50% of the population and includes a majority of women and retired people who, when they have free time, think it their duty to help other members of society.[4] American volunteerism is

---

Contentment at Every Instant

In 2010, I met Chompunut, a Thai woman in her forties radiating physical and mental health. She told me her story: "When I was little, I was always attracted by the idea of helping people that society abandons. I had heard that the conditions of prisoners were horrible in my country. I became a nurse and I volunteered to work a few years in a prison in Bangkok. Then I heard that conditions for prisoners were even worse in Surat Thani, a coastal town on the Gulf of Thailand. I've been working there for ten years now. Due to a lack of funds, there's no doctor in the prison, and I'm all alone in taking care of the health of 1,300 prisoners. Some of them are supposed to be dangerous and I'm authorized to see them only through bars. But I always find a way to care for them or simply hold their hands and tell them a few comforting words. I've never had any problems. They respect me, since they know better than anyone that I'm only there for them and I'm doing everything I can to help them. The crimes they committed don't concern me."

Being the only woman in a prison, in charge of the health of 1,300 men, could be a psychological ordeal difficult to surmount. Propelled by her determination, Chompunut carries out her mission without difficulty: "There's so much to do and they're so sick. Each one of my actions relieves suffering, which for me is a contentment at every instant."

THE INCREDIBLE STORY OF JOYNAL ABEDIN

At the age of sixty-one, in Bangladesh, Joynal Abedin pedals a rickshaw all day long, a common method of transportation in Asia. A rickshaw is a big tricycle with a bench on the back that is supposed to be for two people but on which it is not rare for three or four people to sit. Abedin earns the equivalent of 1 to 2 dollars per day.

"My father died because we couldn't take him to the hospital, which was a two-day walk from here. I was so angry! People from here think that, because we're poor, we're powerless. I wanted to prove them wrong."

Joynal Abedin left for the city to become a rickshaw driver with a single goal in mind: to build a clinic in his village, Tanhashadia. He vowed not to return until he had enough money to begin construction.

He pedaled for thirty years, placing a portion of his earnings aside every day. At the age of sixty, he had saved the equivalent of 4,000 dollars, enough to carry out his project. He returned to the village and built a small clinic! In the beginning, he couldn't find any doctors. "They didn't trust me," he confides. So he began with paramedics. But soon people appreciated the incredible work he was doing, and he received help. Now, the village clinic, although modest, treats about 300 patients a day. To maintain it, Abedin has patients pay a small contribution. Anonymous donations, which began to flow in after newspapers related his story, are often made, too. After one particularly large donation, he also built, on his small piece of land, an education center that can welcome 500 children.

At the age of sixty-two, Abedin still drives his rickshaw, indefatigably transporting his passengers, dedicating every stroke of the pedals to the well-being of the patients in his clinic.

particularly high in the realm of the arts, and contributes to the functioning of many cultural institutions. About 1,500 people, for instance, work without pay for the Museum of Fine Arts in Boston. What's more, three-fourths of the inhabitants of the United States donate every year to charity organizations.

In France, the number of volunteers is about 12 million, or one Frenchman out of five (a third of them over sixty).[5] Those who devote at least two hours a week to their volunteer activity number a little over 3 million.[6] In 2004, the work accomplished by volunteers represented the equivalent of 820,000 full-time jobs.[7]

The Emergence of NGOs

About 40,000 international nongovernmental organizations (NGOs) have been counted throughout the world, and an even larger number of national NGOs. Russia has almost 280,000 national NGOs; in 2009, India had over 3 million. The number of charity organizations has doubled in the United States since 2000 (numbering almost 1 million now). Certainly not all of them are effective, and the management of some of them has been criticized at times. Nevertheless, this movement, by its very amplitude, is one of the great innovations of the last fifty years, and represents a major factor in the transformation of society. Some NGOs have a political aim or are focused on sports or the arts. Most have a social calling: reduction of poverty, environmental cleanup, education, health, emergency aid during wars or natural catastrophes. Others work toward promoting peace or improving the condition of women or children.

BRAC (Bangladesh Rural Advancement Committee), the largest NGO in the world, has helped over 70 million women in Bangladesh and in seven other countries to emerge from poverty. Other NGOs, both globally like Greenpeace and EIA (Environmental Investigation Agency) and locally like tens of thousands of smaller NGOs, devote themselves to the protection of the environment or of animals.

Some organizations like Kiva, GlobalGiving, and MicroWorld[8] directly and effectively connect people in need to donors who want to improve others' lives via the Internet. Founded in 2005, Kiva has facilitated over half a million donors to offer 300 million dollars in microcredit-type loans in sixty countries; 98% of these loans have been repaid. Similarly, since 2002, GlobalGiving has financed the completion of over 5,000 charity projects. MicroWorld connects potential lenders with people in need of financing to start up an activity that will help them get their families out of poverty. These are just a few examples among so many others.

Myths About Panic, Selfish Reactions, and Powerless Resignation

In a chapter from his inspiring book *La Bonté humaine* (Human Kindness), the psychologist Jacques Lecomte has compiled a number of studies showing how during catastrophes solidarity wins out over selfishness, discipline over looting, and calm over panic.[9] We are too often led to believe that it's the opposite that occurs. Lecomte describes the emblematic case of Hurricane Katrina, which, in August 2005, ravaged New Orleans and the Louisiana coast, rupturing the Mississippi River dams. This was one of the most devastating natural catastrophes in the history of the United States:

> *To this tragedy another was quickly added. For, as soon as the media started covering the event, it reported frightening human behavior. On August 31, a CNN reporter declared there was gunfire and pillaging, and that "New Orleans looks more like a war zone than a modern American metropolis."*

The situation seemed so alarming that Ray Nagin, mayor of New Orleans, ordered 1,500 police officers to interrupt their rescue operation to devote their efforts to stopping the looting.[10] The media reported rapes and murders, with the policemen themselves being the targets of the shooters. The governor of Louisiana, Kathleen Blanco, declared: "We will restore law and order. What angers me the most is that disasters like this often bring out the worst in people. I will not tolerate this kind of behavior."[11] She sent National Guard troops to New Orleans, with the authorization to shoot at looters, stating: "These troops are fresh back from Iraq, well-trained, experienced, battle-tested, and under my orders to restore order in the streets. These troops know how to shoot and kill and they are more than willing to do so if necessary and I expect they will."[12] This apocalyptic vision of New Orleans was broadcast throughout the world. The military force deployed to reestablish order amounted to more than 72,000 men and women. All this seemed to confirm the belief that, as Lecomte says, "left without government control, humans would return to their vilest, most hurtful natural leanings, without any sensitivity to others' suffering. Except for one thing: these frightening descriptions were totally false. The consequences of this falsification of facts were tragic."[13]

In fact, this hysteria of alarmist news managed to persuade emergency services that they were facing a wild pack of criminals—which kept them from arriving in time and acting effectively. What actually happened? The journalists reported the situation based on secondhand rumors. Once the media frenzy was over, they critiqued their own work. A month after the hurricane, the *Los Angeles Times* acknowledged: "Rumors supplanted accurate information and the media magnified the problem. Rapes, violence, and estimates of the dead were wrong."[14] *The New York Times* quoted Edward Compass, the New Orleans chief of police, who had declared that vandals had taken over the city and that rapes (of children especially) and assaults had taken place. He admitted that his previous declarations were wrong: "We have no official reports to document any murder. Not one official report of rape or sexual assault. The most alarming stories that coursed through the city appear to be little more than figments of frightened imaginations.... It seems that the overall response of the inhabitants of New Orleans did not correspond in any way to the general image of chaos and violence described by the media."[15]

In reality, hundreds of mutual aid groups were formed. One of them, which was nicknamed "Robin Hood Looters," was made up of eleven friends, soon joined by the inhabitants of their working-class neighborhood. After leading their families to a safe place, they returned to the site despite the danger to help save the inhabitants.

For two weeks, they requisitioned boats and looked for food, water, and clothing in abandoned houses. They followed some self-imposed rules, such as not carrying any weapons. This group collaborated with the local police and the National Guard, which entrusted them with getting survivors out of the danger zone.[16]

Finally, "while some antisocial behavior did occur, the overwhelming majority of the emergent activity was prosocial in nature."[17] According to one New Orleans law enforcement officer: "Most people by and large really, really, really just helped one another and they didn't ask for anything back."[18]

According to the investigations of the Disaster Research Center, the decision to militarize the zone also had the consequence of increasing the number of victims. Some people refused to leave their houses because of information that the city was infested with looters, and emergency services were afraid of approaching the damaged zones.[19] Thus, by focusing on the fight against imaginary violence, "the officials in charge failed to take full advantage of the goodwill and altruistic spirit of the inhabitants and resources of the community.... By transferring people from rescue operations to maintaining order, the authorities placed law and order above the lives of hurricane victims."[20]

What happened in New Orleans is not an isolated case. A widespread myth claims that, during catastrophes, people react with panic and that an "everyone for himself" mentality prevails. The media and movies have acclimated us to scenes of panic, sequences of entire crowds fleeing and screaming with terror in complete disorder. This exposure can lead to reactions of fear, which are entirely legitimate, and which lead us to get away as quickly as possible from danger, to be confused with reactions of "panic" in the course of which people lose control of themselves and behave irrationally.[21] According to sociologists, a person is overcome with panic when he feels cornered; when flight, which seems his sole chance for survival, seems impossible (as when trapped in a burning night-club with all emergency doors closed); and when he thinks no one can come to his aid.[22] In such cases, fear becomes uncontrolled panic.

The Disaster Research Center at the University of Delaware has developed the largest database in the world on human reactions to catastrophes. It emerges from analysis of all these data that three widespread beliefs are actually myths: general panic; a massive rise in selfish, even criminal, behavior; and the feeling of powerlessness while waiting for help.

The sociologist Lee Clarke wrote that during the attack on the World Trade Center on September 11, 2001, witnesses all agreed that panic was almost absent, while cooperation and mutual aid were prevalent. Despite the high number of victims, almost everyone below the floors where the planes struck survived, essentially thanks to the absence of panic.[23]

The English sociologist John Drury and his collaborators support Clarke's observation. During the London bombings in 2005 (three in the underground and one on a bus), which took the lives of 56 people and wounded 700, "Rather than personal selfishness and competition prevailing, mutual helping and concern were predominant amongst survivors, despite the fact that most people were amongst strangers rather than affiliates. There is also evidence that this helping behavior took place in spite of perceived danger rather than because people felt that they were now out of danger."[24] None of the people interviewed made any statements stemming from selfishness. On the contrary, they showed "at least as much concern for the strangers around them" as for their friends, and "they also used a variety of their own terms to describe the experience—'unity,' 'together,' 'similarity,' 'affinity,' 'part of a group.' "

Enrico Quarantelli, co-founder of the Center for Disaster Research, concludes: "I no longer believe that the term 'panic' should be treated as a social science concept. It is a label taken from popular discourse... During the whole history of our research involving nearly 700 different field studies, I would be hard pressed to cite...but a few marginal instances of anything that could be called panic behavior."[25]

During most catastrophes, acts defined as looting are quite rare. According to Enrico Quarantelli, one must in fact make a distinction between "looting" and "justified appropriation." The latter consists of taking urgently needed available objects and commodities—unused or abandoned—with the intention of returning them if possible, except when products for immediate consumption (food, water, medicine) are considered indispensable for survival. Researchers also noted that, when there is looting, it is rarely done by organized groups, but by individuals who do so furtively, and whose behavior is condemned by the other survivors.[26]

In the case of the tsunami that devastated the Japanese coastline in 2011, the absence of the slightest instance of looting, theft, or undisciplined behavior was so marked that the media, which were present at the heart of the tragedy, could only wonder at the fact, faced with the admirable prosocial qualities of the Japanese people. No doubt such qualities are explained by the feeling of belonging to a community in which everyone feels close to and responsible for everyone else, and by the civility and sense of duty that, in Japanese culture, outweigh individualism.

Natural catastrophes, attacks, accidents...these are all, of course, exceptional circumstances that have nothing commonplace *(banal)* about them. But by mentioning them in this chapter on the "banality of good," I intend to emphasize the fact that, even in such circumstances, the most common behavior is mutual aid, help, and solidarity, while indifference, selfishness, violence, and greed are rare.

10

Altruistic Heroism

How far can selfless altruism go? A number of studies show that, when the cost of aid is too high, altruistic behavior becomes less frequent. But it is far from being nonexistent. Though examples of courage and determination in coming to the aid of others despite considerable risks are certainly heroic, they are not necessarily called that because of their rarity—we hear about heroic actions almost daily—but because we measure the degree of boldness and dedication that such actions require, while no doubt wondering what our own reaction would have been in the same situation.

On January 2, 2007, Wesley Autrey and his two daughters were waiting for the subway at the 137th St.-Broadway station in New York. All of a sudden, their attention was drawn to a young man having an epileptic fit. Wesley quickly intervened, using a pen to keep the man's jaw open. Once the fit was over, the young man got up but, still half-dazed, he stumbled and fell off the platform.[1]

While the sick man was lying on the tracks, Wesley saw the lights of an approaching train. He entrusted his daughters to a nearby woman to keep them away from the edge of the platform; then he jumped onto the tracks. He planned to carry the young man back to the platform but realized he wouldn't have time. So he threw himself over the man's body and pinned him on the ground in the drainage ditch between the two rails. Despite the conductor braking as hard as he could, the train passed almost completely over both of them. The underside of the train left grease on Wesley's cap. Later on, Wesley told journalists: "I don't feel like I did something spectacular; I just saw someone who needed help. I did what I felt was right. I just said to myself, 'Somebody's got to help this guy or he's toast.'"

He explained that, because of his previous experiences, he was able to make his decision in a fraction of a second: "Since I do construction, we work in confined spaces a lot. So I looked, and my judgment was pretty right. The train did have enough room for me."

According to Samuel and Pearl Oliner, emeritus professors at Humboldt University in California, who have devoted their careers to the sociology of altruism and more particularly to the study of the Just, the "Righteous Among the Nations," who saved many Jews during Nazi persecutions, altruism can be thought of as heroic when:

- it has the aim of helping someone else;
- it involves a major risk or sacrifice;
- it is not linked to a reward;
- it is voluntary.[2]

Like the previous account, the following situation, reported by Kristen Monroe, amply fulfills all four criteria:

> *This hero was a man in his forties who liked to hike in the southern California hill country. On one of his hikes, he heard a mother screaming that a mountain lion had carried off her small child. The man ran to where the mother told him the lion had disappeared with the child; [he] tracked the animal until he found it. The child, still alive, was held tightly in the lion's jaws. The man picked up a stick and attacked the animal, distracting the lion so that it dropped the little girl and attacked him instead. He managed to beat off the attack and returned the child, badly mauled but still alive, to the mother. As soon as he got the mother and child safely en route to the hospital, he disappeared.*[3]

The event was reported by the grateful mother, which earned the man a notoriety he scarcely wanted, including the Hero medal awarded to him by the Carnegie Commission, which every year recognizes particularly heroic deeds in the United States. The rescuer did everything he could to escape the public's attention, refusing all interviews, including the one that Kristen Monroe had solicited when she was writing her book, *The Heart of Altruism.* In his polite but firm refusal letter, he explained that "the local honors were unwanted, the national press and television attention unpleasant, and the public acclaim abhorrent."[4]

Most of us have no way of knowing how we would act if confronted with the same situation. In general, a mother always reacts by saving her child and, when she risks her life for her child, she doesn't need to think twice about it. But some people also act in a similar way for complete strangers. Despite the powerful preconception that we are all basically selfish, examples of heroic rescues call that preconception into question.

HEROISM AND ALTRUISM

For Philip Zimbardo and his psychologist colleagues at Stanford University, heroism implies voluntary acceptance of a level of danger or sacrifice that goes well beyond what is usually expected of people.[5] The performer of a heroic act has no moral obligation to accept this risk. In instances involving potential physical danger, he must also transcend personal fear so as to act quickly and decisively.[6]

Zimbardo identifies three major forms of heroism: martial, civil, and social. *Martial (military) heroism* involves deeds of courage and abnegation that go beyond what is required by military discipline and sense of duty; giving one's own life to save one's companions is an example. *Civil heroism*, the heroism of someone diving into freezing water to save a drowning person, implies a peril for which the performer is generally not prepared; he or she is not guided by a code of obedience or honor. *Social heroism*—the heroism of activists against racism during apartheid in South Africa, or of whistle-blowers exposing a scandal in their company or government—is less spectacular and usually transpires over a longer period of time than actions linked to the first two forms of heroism. If social heroism doesn't generally include immediate physical danger, the price to pay can be very high, leading, for instance, to the loss of a job or to ostracism by one's colleagues or society.[7]

In 1984, Cate Jenkins, a chemist at the Environmental Protection Agency in Washington, DC, received a file from Greenpeace showing that scientific studies carried out by the Monsanto company that were supposed to prove the harmlessness of PCB (polychlorinated biphenyl) had been falsified, and that Monsanto knew that these chemical products were highly toxic. Jenkins alerted her superiors and submitted a damning report to them. But the vice president of Monsanto intervened with her superiors at the EPA, and the report was buried until, outraged, Jenkins decided to deliver it to the press herself. Misfortune dogged her: she was transferred, than harassed for years until her life became hellish. But it was thanks to her that the collusion between the government and Monsanto was brought out in the open and that many victims of PCBs and "Agent Orange" (used in Vietnam as a spray) could be paid damages.[8]

Zimbardo proposes a *situational* vision of heroism. He argues that most people are capable of heroism when conditions require a swift, courageous intervention. Although situations serve as catalysts indispensable to heroism, the decision of the people who intervene is made in the privacy of their own consciences. For many heroes, like those who saved Jews hunted by Nazis, heroic engagement is linked to an examination of conscience guided by moral norms that are deeply anchored within the person.[9]

Altruism can be the main motivation behind a heroic act, but that is not always the case. In some heroic acts, concern for fellow human beings is certainly present, but other motivations such as the sense of duty for one's nation (as in the case of martial heroism), or indignation in the face of injustice and abuse (in the case of whistle-blowers, for instance) can play a prominent role.

In the story that follows, there is clearly a mixture of altruistic concern for someone in great distress, and of fiery indignation against perpetrators of injustice, discrimination, and abuse.

THE STORY OF LUCILLE

Lucille had an eventful life. From the time she was very young, she performed courageous acts, coming to the aid of others. When she was little, when the America of the 1950s was still living in an age of intense racial discrimination, she resolutely took the side of a black girl whom the bus driver refused to allow on the bus with the chicken she was carrying. Lucille had the little girl get in and sit next to her grandma in the part reserved for white people, which was regarded as scandalous at the time, and took the chicken in her lap. This behavior brought the wrath of the local population down on Lucille and her mother. Later on, when she had enlisted as an officer in the US army, Lucille was sent to Africa. Despite her frailty, one day she rescued a Sudanese man whom a US soldier had thrown in the river and ordered the soldier back to the camp. On another occasion, a colonel who hated women soldiers let a frozen beef half fall on her back when they were unloading food supplies. Lucille had four ruptured vertebrae and remained handicapped for the rest of her life. That did not prevent her from continuing to help others, as her account shows, recorded by Kristen Monroe.[10]

> *On July 29—I'll have to double-check that, but I think it's the twenty-ninth—I was working at my desk... when I heard some terrible screaming.... I looked out and saw this man grabbing this young girl. It was my neighbor, washing her car. He threw her onto the pavement of the driveway.*
>
> *At this time, I knew that something had to be done and done now, and no time could be wasted. There was nobody in our neighborhood. They all work. I'm very crippled. I wear a back brace and a leg brace....*

But Lucille went outside. Despite the fact that she needs a cane to walk, she rushed down the steps of her house as best she could and began running toward the rapist and the young woman. When she arrived, she found herself in the presence of a 6'2" giant who had already torn off the young woman's shirt and was about to rape her. She shouted at the man to let her go, but he paid no attention to the old woman.

> *He didn't pay any attention to me. Well, he kind of turned his head and looked at me, and then he went back to her. I hauled off and hit him across the neck and the head with my cane. This caused him to get up. He started toward me. I said, "Come on, I'm gonna kill you. Just come on. I'm not foolin' with you."*

> *And I yelled at the girl, "You get in the house and lock the door, and don't even let me in. I don't care who comes; just don't let 'em in."*
>
> *People said, "Were you afraid?" Yes, I was. I kind of felt this was it for me, because he was so vicious-looking. I thought this was a death-to-death fight: I'm gonna kill him or he will kill me. Because he was hurting another human being, an innocent human being. I just can't take that. I wasn't trained that way....*
>
> *When she did get in the house, I realized that if I didn't catch him, he'd be another case where they'd say, "Well, you don't have any evidence."*
>
> *So Lucille went after the man, "whaling out with her cane.*
>
> *"He told me he was gonna kill me. 'You bitch,' he said. 'I'll kill you right here.' 'Alright, come on,' I told him. 'Let's do it.' And finally he turned and ran to his car."*

Finally, another man turned up, sent Lucille back to safety, and the police arrived. The attacker was overpowered and arrested. Lucille got out of it with bruises. According to her: "It's that you care enough about someone, about the human person, that you feel that you have to help no matter what."

Kristen Monroe asked Lucille why it was she, and not someone else, who had stopped the rape, when so many people might not have had the courage or even thought of helping. "I've thought about that," replied Lucille. "My mother and grandmother taught me to fight injustice in any form. If I'm there, I'm responsible. They taught me to love all of humanity."

Let's remember as well the boldness of the "unknown rebel" who, on June 5, 1989, on an avenue in Beijing, stood in front of a tank, immobilizing for thirty minutes a column of seventeen other tanks that had just broken up the freedom demonstration by the Chinese movement for democracy in Tiananmen Square. He managed to climb up onto the front of the tank and supposedly said to the driver: "Why are you here? My city is in chaos because of you. Turn around and stop killing my people." Here again we see a blend of resolute indignation against tyranny and concern for others. No one knows what happened to him, but the image of his confrontations with the blind power of totalitarianism was broadcast all over the world, and he became a universal hero.

Purely out of compassion, Maximilien Kolbe, a Franciscan priest imprisoned in Auschwitz, volunteered to be executed to take the place of another prisoner, a man with a wife and children. This man, along with nine others, had been condemned to die of hunger and thirst as revenge for the escape of another prisoner. Such examples seem to surpass our ordinary abilities, even though many parents, mothers especially, feel ready to sacrifice their lives to save their children. In the end, stories of heroic deeds emphasize the depth of kindness inherent in human nature and remind us that human beings are capable of the best as well as of the worst. About the "banality of heroism," Philip Zimbardo writes, "Most people who become perpetrators of evil deeds are directly comparable to those who become perpetrators of heroic deeds, alike in being just ordinary, average people."[11] In given situations at particular moments, the interaction between circumstances and each person's temperament tips the scale toward altruism or selfishness, toward pure compassion or the worst cruelty.

11

Unconditional Altruism

Altruism takes on an additional dimension when it manifests not only in urgent situations but also over the long-term, by repeated and difficult actions that are particularly dangerous for the person or group that hurries to the aid of those whose lives are threatened.

Otto Springer, a German, was living in Prague during the Second World War. He acquired a company whose previous owner was Jewish. He took advantage of his position to save a number of Jews from deportation to concentration camps by providing them with false papers, and by bribing Gestapo officers. He worked with Austrian Resistance networks. He married a Jewish woman in order to protect her and was finally himself arrested and deported. Even as a prisoner, he managed to save hundreds of Jews from death and to escape himself. Afterward, he retired to California where Kristen Monroe met him.[1] She describes him as a man overflowing with humanity and enthusiasm, confident while at the same time full of humility. He acknowledged having saved many Jews, but said, "I don't know whether I'd consider what I did altruistic," adding that he had a friend who was "an absolutely clear case" of altruism, a man named Kari, who knew that by marrying a Jewish woman, he could protect her. So he asked his friends, "Where is a Jew that I can marry?" There was a woman who had lost her husband and was living alone with her two daughters. Kari married her and everything was fine for a while. But one day the Gestapo came to arrest his wife and one of her daughters. Both were sent to Auschwitz. Kari hid the remaining little girl. A little later, everyone who had married a Jew was forced to divorce, under penalty of being imprisoned. All Kari's friends pleaded with him to sign divorce papers, since his wife was unfortunately already in Auschwitz. But Kari replied that since the Germans were very detail-oriented, if he divorced, they would examine his file and wouldn't fail to discover that they had only arrested one of the two daughters and would come looking for the other. Kari thought it his duty to remain married to prevent the Gestapo from finding any trace of the little girl. "He went to the concentration camp even though his wife had already been arrested, just in order to avoid the slight possibility that the child would be discovered. *That* is a clear case of altruism," said Otto Springer.

Why had Otto risked his own life to save other people? He wasn't religious, and didn't think of himself as especially virtuous (he said jokingly that his morality was just slightly above that of an average American congressman's). His explanation: "I just got mad. I felt I had to do it. I came across many things that demanded my compassion.... No big deal. Nobody could stand by and do nothing when the Nazis came." Kristen Monroe comments, "Yet at a deeper level, both Otto and I knew that most people did precisely that: nothing. If everyone had been normal in the way Otto defined the term, then the Holocaust would not have occurred." At the end of their interviews, Monroe writes:

> *I knew Otto put me in the presence of something extraordinary, something I had never before witnessed in such intensity and purity. I thought it was altruism. I knew it was real. I did not know if I could understand it myself, let alone explain it satisfactorily to others.*

The rescuers all knew that if they were discovered, they risked not only their lives, but also the lives of their families. Their decision was often sparked by an impromptu event, like meeting someone in flight who risked being sent to a death camp. But living up to their commitment required a complex, perilous strategy. Their actions have often remained unacknowledged, and they have never sought to boast about them. In almost every case, far from drawing the slightest advantage from their altruistic behavior, they suffered for a long time from its consequences on their health or their financial and social situation. But none of them regret what they did.

The Story of Irene

Irene Gut Opdyke is the very embodiment of courage and the purest altruism, in that all her actions were dictated by her invincible determination to save other lives, and at the constant risk of losing her own.[2]

She was born in a little village in Poland to a Catholic family where love of one's neighbor was a given. She had a happy childhood, surrounded by her four sisters and loving and attentive parents.

On September 1st, 1939, Poland was partitioned between Germany and the USSR. She was studying to be a nurse in Radom when German bombs razed much of the city. She was suddenly cut off from her family—she wouldn't see them again for two years. She was seventeen at the time. She fled with a group of combatants and nurses to Lithuania where she was raped by Soviet soldiers, beaten, and left for dead. She woke up in a Russian hospital, her eyes so swollen she couldn't see anything. She had been saved by a Russian doctor who found her lying unconscious in the snow and took pity on her. Restored to health, she worked for some months in this hospital as a nurse before she was repatriated back to Poland.

In 1941, Irene returned to Radom where her parents had taken refuge; they had lost everything and were trying to survive. That was when Irene witnessed the first roundups and pogroms against the Jews. Forced to work in an assembly line in a munitions factory, she met Major Rügemer, who was head of the factory. Impressed by her mastery of German (Irene speaks four languages fluently: Polish, Russian, German, and Yiddish), he offered her a job in his service, in the German officers' mess in town.

It was there, at the age of twenty, that she began to save dozens of Jews. She began with a seemingly insignificant gesture that could have cost her life: every day she slipped some provisions under the barbed-wire fence that separated the officers' mess from the Tarnopol ghetto. Then she got bolder. Responsible for the mess's laundry, she took advantage of her position to get Jews who were employed in the neighboring work camp out and integrated into the laundry team, where the work was less difficult and where they were better fed.

No one suspected this frail but efficient employee: "In this way, I made my weakness an advantage," she says.[3] She was able to spy on conversations between Major Rügemer and Rokita, the cruel SS commander in charge of exterminating all the Jews in the city of Tarnopol and the western Ukraine. Each time she obtained information about a roundup or reprisals, she passed it on to her Jewish friends. She herself lead people into the forests of Janowka who were trying to flee from the work camps and the ghettos; she hid them behind a *dorozka,* a horse-drawn cart. "I didn't ask myself, 'Should I do it?' but 'How will I do it?' " she said. "Every step I took in my childhood had led me to this crossroads. I had to follow this path, otherwise I wouldn't have been myself anymore," she said later on. Not only did she lead fugitives into the forest, but she regularly brought them provisions and medicine.

In 1943, Germany began to retreat before the onslaught of Stalin's armies. Major Rügemer decided to move to a villa in Tarnopol. In July 1943, the fearsome Rokita swore to exterminate all the Jews in the region by the end of the month.[4] Faced with the urgency of the situation, Irene took unheard-of risks: she hid her friends in an air duct located in the Major's own bathroom. Then, when everyone was sleeping, she brought them to the new villa requisitioned by Rügemer and put them in the cellar, which she had made ready for them. For over a year, Irene hid eleven people in the villa in which Major Rügemer was living!

One day, the Major came home unexpectedly and discovered Clara and Fanka, two of Irene's protégées, in the kitchen. Irene unwillingly agreed to become his mistress in order to save her friends' lives. "The price I had to pay was nothing compared with what was at stake. I had the blessing of God. I was completely sure of the rightness of my actions." Against all expectations, the Major kept her secret; he even went so far as to spend his evenings in the company of Irene's two young friends, unaware that his villa's cellar was still concealing nine other Jews.

In 1944, the Red Army advanced on Tarnopol and Major Rügemer ordered Irene to evacuate the house and make her two friends disappear. As the region was being shelled by Soviet artillery and German patrols were crisscrossing the countryside, Irene led her eleven friends by night into the forest of Janowka, where they joined other escapees who had found refuge there.

In 1945, exhausted by her struggles, malnutrition, and illness, Irene was living in the refugee camp of Hessisch-Lichtenau, in Germany, until a delegation from the United Nations, led by her future husband, William Opdyke, recorded her story and obtained American citizenship for her. In 1949, she emigrated to the United States. In 1956 she got married, and a new life began for her in California. Discussing her past, she concludes:

> *Yes, it was me, a girl, with nothing but my free will, clutched in my hand like an amber bead.... The war was a series of choices made by many people. Some of those choices were as wicked and shameful to humanity as anything in history. But some of us made other choices. I made mine.*

Who Are the Rescuers?

Six million Jews, 60% of the Jews living in Europe, were exterminated by the Nazis. According to Samuel and Pearl Oliner, the number of rescuers who not only helped but also risked their lives, without any compensation, totals about 50,000.[5] Many of these rescuers will never be known, and many others died for having helped the Jews, an action that was punishable by death in Germany, Poland, and France. The Yad Vashem organization has collected the names of 6,000 rescuers whose heroic deeds were reported to it by those who owed their lives to them. According to the Oliners, these 'Righteous Among the Nations' were more likely to have received an education based on concern for others and on values transcending individualism than people who lived at the same time in the same regions, but who did not intervene in favor of the oppressed. The parents of the rescuers spoke more often to their children about respect for others, sincerity, honesty, justice, equality, and tolerance than about material values. What's more, they put little stress on obedience or observance of strict rules. We know that a tendency to submit to authority led a number of citizens to carry out orders that their conscience ought to have dissuaded them from obeying.

Most rescuers didn't hesitate to transgress the conventional rules of morality—not to lie, not to steal, not to forge false documents—in view of a greater good, that of saving the people they were protecting. When asked about the motives for their actions, rescuers very often mentioned *concern for others* and *fairness,* as well as feelings of *indignation* about the horrors perpetrated by the Nazis.

Rescuers often have a *universalist* approach to humanity. Over half of them emphasized the importance of the profound conviction that "the Jews, like themselves and others, belonged to the universal class of humans, all of whom had the right to live and to be free from persecution."[6] Motivations linked to empathy are cited by a majority of the rescuers, who mention *compassion, pity, concern, affection.* This compassion is generally accompanied by the determination to do anything necessary to save others: "I decided that even if I had to die, I would help . . . I could not stand idly by and observe the daily misery that was occurring. It was unacceptable to watch idly while compatriots perished. It was necessary. Somebody had to do it."[7]

One of them, Stanislas, who protected a large number of people, said, "Can you see it? Two young girls come, one sixteen or seventeen, and they tell you a story that their parents were killed and they were pulled in and raped. What are you supposed to tell them—Sorry, we are full already?"[8]

UNITED IN ALTRUISM

In some cases, entire communities united to save Jews from deportation. This mobilization occurred notably in Denmark and Italy, where some of the population joined together to protect and systematically hide Jewish families. The same was true in France, in isolated regions of the Haute-Loire where Protestant populations were very active in helping a number of Jews to pass into Switzerland. The case of the village of Chambon-sur-Lignon is exemplary. The refugees to reach Chambon were Spanish Republicans who had escaped Franco's troops. Then came Germans who were fleeing the Nazi regime, followed by young Frenchmen escaping obligatory service under the Vichy government. But by far the most important group was the Jews. It was they who were most in danger and exposed those who hid them to the most risks.

In one way or another, the entire community of this village, itself only numbering 3,300 inhabitants, organized to secretly shelter more than 5,000 Jews over a few years. Under the urging of their minister, André Trocmé, parishioners put all kinds of strategies into play to hide and feed a large number of people, but also to procure false papers for them and lead them to a safe place. In his book *Lest Innocent Blood Be Shed,* devoted to the rescuers in Chambon, American historian Philip Hallie describes how the events unfolded.[9] One winter night in 1940–1941, when she was putting logs into the kitchen oven, Magda Trocmé, the minister's wife, heard a knock on the door and jumped. When she opened it, she found herself face to face with a trembling woman, obviously terrified and frozen by the snow. That was the first Jew fleeing Nazi persecutions to present herself at the vicarage. In the years to come, hundreds of others would also find refuge there. The woman asked her in a weak, worried voice if she could come in. "Of course, come in, come in," Magda Trocmé replied.

"For the rest of the Occupation," writes Hallie, "Magda and the other people of Chambon would learn that, from the refugee's point of view, closing your door to someone is not just a refusal to help: it's a way of harming the person. Whatever your reason for not welcoming a refugee, your closed door puts him in danger."[10]

All these activities were of course extremely dangerous, and they became even more so as the tide of war turned against the Nazis and they grew more and more pitiless. Philip Hallie reports these statements by Magda Trocmé: "If we had depended on an organization, it wouldn't have worked. How could a large organization have made decisions about the people crowding around our doors? When the refugees were there, on your doorstep, decisions had to be made right away. Bureaucracy would have prevented many of them from being saved. This way, everyone was free to decide quickly all alone."[11]

In his book *Un si fragile vernis d'humanité* (Such a Fragile Veneer of Humanity), Michel Terestchenko concludes:

> *The duty to help others was like "second nature" in them, a "lasting disposition."...Altruistic deeds in favor of the Jews arose spontaneously from the deepest part of their beings like an obligation they could not ignore, one that no doubt bore considerable dangers, but that had nothing sacrificial about it. By acting in this way, they did not renounce their profound being or "self-interests": quite the contrary, they responded to them in complete conformity and fidelity to themselves.*[12]

A Vision of the World: "We All Belong to the Same Family"

After the war, some governments offered financial compensation to rescuers who found themselves in great material difficulty after having protected Jewish families. But almost all of them refused this compensation.[13] It should be stressed that many of them were also ostracized by their fellow citizens, both during and after the war. They were sometimes called "Jew-lovers" and their heroism was often the object of sarcasm.

Some of them got married in another country and didn't even mention to those close to them what they had done.[14] "For all the altruists I interviewed," writes Monroe, "whatever honors they later received—and it is important to remember that, at least for the rescuers, these honors were usually awarded more than thirty years after the altruistic act—were peripheral. For most, they were unexpected; for a surprising number, unwanted. While the majority were pleased by them, they had nothing to do with the intent of, the motive for, the original act of altruism. For no rescuer was the honor ever central." They all evinced profound satisfaction in having saved lives.

According to Monroe, the sole point in common that emerges from so many testimonies of rescuers is a *vision of the world and of others* based on an awareness of the interdependence of all beings and their shared humanity.[15] This leads to a feeling that everyone deserves to be treated with kindness. "I always thought of Jews as brothers," confided a German rescuer to the writer Marek Halter.[16]

For many, people are not fundamentally "good" or "bad," but rather just individuals who have led different lives. This understanding seems to give altruists great tolerance and a remarkable ability to forgive. As a rescuer explained to Samuel and Pearl Oliner:

> *The reason is that every man is equal. We all have the right to live. It was plain murder, and I couldn't stand that. I would help a Mohammedan just as well as a Jew.... It's like saving somebody who is drowning. You don't ask them what God they pray to. You just go and save them.... These people just had the right to live like other people.*[17]

As proof of this, the Oliners provide the example of a woman who was part of a group hiding Jewish families. One day, as she and her husband were passing by a German barracks during an air raid, a German soldier came running out with a deep gash in his head—he was losing a lot of blood. Immediately, the husband put him on his bicycle, transported him to the German command post, rang the bell, and left when the door was opened. Later, some of their friends from the Resistance called him a traitor for having "helped the enemy." The husband replied, "No, the man was seriously wounded, he was no longer an enemy but simply a human being in distress." This man did not accept being seen as a "hero" for saving Jewish families or as a "traitor" for helping a gravely wounded German soldier.[18] When heroic altruists are faced with suffering, labels having to do with nationality, religion, or politics fall away.

Mordecai Paldiel, who was Chairman of the Righteous Among the Nations in Israel, concludes that it is the basic goodness present in each of us that allows us to understand this behavior of unconditional altruism. He writes in the *Jerusalem Post:*

> *The more I delve into the deeds of the Righteous among the Nations, the greater my doubts about the validity of the current tendency to magnify those deeds to unreasonable proportions. We are somehow determined to view these benefactors as heroes: hence the search for underlying motives. The Righteous persons, however, consider themselves as anything but heroes,*

and regard their behavior during the Holocaust as quite normal. How to resolve this enigma?

For centuries we have undergone a brain-washing process by philosophers who emphasized man's despicable character, highlighting his egotistic and evil disposition at the expense of his other attributes. Wittingly or not, together with Hobbes and Freud, we accept the proposition that man is essentially an aggressive being, bent on destruction, involved principally with himself, and only marginally interested in the needs of others. . . .

Goodness leaves us gasping, for we refuse to recognize it as a natural human attribute. So off we go on a long search for some hidden motivation, some extraordinary explanation, for such peculiar behavior. . . .

Instead of attempting to distance ourselves politely from them while at the same time lauding their deeds, would it not be better to rediscover the altruistic potential within us? That occasionally helping one another, even at great discomfort, is part and parcel of our human nature, of our behavioral patterns. . . .

Let us not search for mysterious explanations of goodness in others, but rather rediscover the mystery of goodness in ourselves.[19]

12

Beyond Imitations, True Altruism:

An Experimental Investigation

If someone steals, cheats, or commits a violent action, people might say nonchalantly: "That's human nature coming to the surface," or: "He showed his true face." On the other hand, when someone shows great kindness and devotes himself tirelessly to the service of the suffering, people might say: "He's a real saint," implying that his or her behavior is heroic, out of the reach of ordinary mortals.

Those who argue that humans are driven by nothing but egoism will offer many examples of behavior in which an altruistic façade hides a selfish motivation. The American philosopher and naturalist of Spanish origin, George Santayana, proclaims:

> *In human nature generous impulses are occasional and reversible.... They form amiable interludes like tearful sentiments in a ruffian, or they are pleasant self-deceptive hypocrisies acted out, like civility to strangers because such is in society the path of least resistance. Strain the situation however, dig a little beneath the surface and you will find a ferocious, persistent, profoundly selfish man.*[1]

An Example

Imagine that I'm hiking in the Himalayas with some close friends and a few strangers who joined us when we set out this morning. A farmhouse and a meal await us in the late afternoon after we climb a pass, but we don't have enough provisions for lunch at noon. During a break, I notice as I look through my bag that I still have a large piece of cheese and a hunk of bread that I had forgotten. First possibility: I walk a little way apart and eat all of it on the sly. Second possibility: I share it with my close friends. Third possibility: I head joyfully toward the whole group, saying, "Look what I found!" At first glance, these three different behaviors correspond, respectively, to strict selfishness, altruism limited by my personal preferences, and impartial altruism.

But the situation is not so simple, for even if I share with everyone, everything depends on my motivation. I can act in keeping with my benevolent nature. But it is also possible for me to share the bread and cheese for much less altruistic reasons: fear of being surprised as I eat my snack all alone in a corner; the fact that I like to be complimented, and that sacrificing a piece of cheese would give me the opportunity to improve my image with those around me and earn their sympathy; the calculation that once we reach the stopover point, conditioned by my affability, the others will pay for my dinner; or else a sense of duty, since my parents had taught me that "you should always share."

This simple example illustrates the various pretenses that should be distinguished from true altruism.

It is clear that certain actions that are beneficial to others actually stem from a self-interested, hypocritical calculation, for example when one offers a gift to someone in the hope of profiting from it. Other seemingly altruistic actions are not necessarily inspired by a desire to deceive, but remain principally motivated by the pursuit of our own interests or by noble sentiments, like a sense of duty, that are not, however, pure altruism.

The evolutionary biologist Michael Ghiselin expressed this point of view in a more brutal way:

> *Given a full chance to act in his own interest, nothing but expediency will restrain him from brutalizing, from maiming, from murdering his brother, his mate, his parent, or his child. Scratch an "altruist," and watch the "hypocrite" bleed.*[2]

In La Rochefoucauld's opinion, even friendship is no exception to universal selfishness:

> *What men term friendship is merely a partnership with a collection of reciprocal interests, and an exchange of favours—in fact it is but a trade in which self love always expects to gain something.*[3]

ALTRUISM PUT TO THE TEST OF EXPERIMENTAL INVESTIGATION

In the previous chapters, with the help of real-life experiences, we illustrated some of the many manifestations of human kindness, even in the most challenging and dangerous situations.

To persist in attributing *all* of human behavior to selfishness stems from a bias, and we would be hard pressed to find even a single empirical study in the scientific literature that could confirm this prejudice. Indeed, motivations for an action can be of various kinds, some altruistic, others selfish. Nothing, however, allows us to deny the existence of real altruism.

From the 1930s to the 1970s, the term "altruism" appeared rarely in psychology books. In 1975, in his speech as president of the American Association of Psychology, Donald Campbell summarized the general thinking of the time: "Psychology and psychiatry... not only describe man as selfishly motivated, but implicitly or explicitly teach that he ought to be so."[4]

This led the psychologist Daniel Batson to reflect that if we wanted to cut all these objections short, we must have recourse to a systematic experimental approach. He justifies his observation in this way:

> *It may seem tasteless to scrutinize the motives of a person who risked his or her life to shelter those trying to escape from the Holocaust, of firemen who died while directing others to safety after the attack on the World Trade Center, or of a person who pulls an injured child from shark-infested waters. But if we really want to know whether humans can be altruistically motivated, such scrutiny is necessary.*[5]
>
> *Cases like these are at once heart-warming and inspiring. They remind us that people—and other animals—can do wonderful things for one another. We are not simply "red in tooth and claw"; there is more to us than that. This is an important reminder.*
>
> *But cases like these do not provide persuasive evidence that altruism exists.... Altruism does not refer to helping, even heroic helping. Altruism refers to a particular form of motivation, motivation with the ultimate goal of increasing another's welfare....*
>
> *We must face the possibility that even a saint or martyr may have acted with an eye to self-benefit. The list of possible self-benefits to be gained by helping is long. One may help to gain gratitude, admiration, or a good feeling about oneself. One may help to avoid censure, guilt, or shame. One may help to put oneself in line for help if needed in the future. One may help to secure a place in history or in heaven. One may help to reduce one's own distress caused by another's suffering. To find persuasive evidence for the existence of altruism, we shall have to move beyond dramatic cases. They simply are not up to the task.*[6]

When he undertook his research, Daniel Batson knew better than anyone that most scientists attributed seemingly altruistic behavior to selfish motivations. It led him to believe that only experimental tests could produce clear conclusions about the nature of the motivations involved and invalidate the hypothesis of universal selfishness in a manner sufficiently rigorous to convince the most skeptical minds.[7]

Studying Altruism on a Daily Basis

Batson's proposal was not to study heroic altruism in all its exceptional aspects, but to highlight altruism in daily life.

> *The altruistic motivation for which I wish to make a case is not the exclusive province of the hero or saint. It is neither exceptional nor unnatural. Rather, I shall argue that altruism is a motivational state that virtually all of us frequently visit.... As long as we assume that altruism, if it exists at all, is rare and unnatural, we are likely to seek it on the edges of our experience in acts of extreme self-sacrifice.... I wish to argue that it is in everyday experience that we can find the clearest evidence of the role altruism plays in human life.*[8]

How to go about highlighting this everyday altruism? In the middle of the last century, behaviorists, led by John B. Watson and B. F. Skinner, decided to devote themselves exclusively to the study of observable behavior without concerning themselves with what happens in the "black box" (the inner world of subjectivity), refusing to speak of motivations, emotions, mental imagery, and even consciousness. By forbidding investigation into the domain of motivations, behaviorism could not increase our knowledge of altruism.

The observation of our external behavior alone does not allow us to discern the profound motivations that animate us. Experimental tests had to be conceived that would allow us to determine, without ambiguity, the motivations of the subjects being studied. Batson explains it this way:

> *For those seeking to understand human nature and the resources that might enable us to build a more humane society, the motivation counts at least as much as the behavior. We need to know not only* that *people (and other animals) do such wonderful things; we also need to know* why.[9]

Daniel Batson and his wife Judy devoted the majority of their careers to investigating this question.

Why do people help each other? They can be moved by an authentic altruism, but they can also be obeying motivations of a selfish nature, which can be subdivided into three main groups, depending on whether the goal aimed at is to *reduce a feeling of distress*, to *avoid punishment*, or to *obtain a reward*.

In the first case, the fact of feeling empathy for someone who is suffering can provoke in us a disagreeable sensation. What we want then is to reduce the feeling of anxiety. Helping the other person is then one of the ways to reach our goal. Any alternative allowing us to reduce our distress—especially by avoiding being confronted with others' suffering—would also be adequate. This is one of the most often cited reasons for helping behavior in the psychological literature of the last fifty years and in the philosophical literature of the last few centuries.

The punishment that the second type of selfish motivation wishes to avoid can be a loss of material goods and of various advantages, the deterioration of our relationship with the other person (reproach, rejection, tarnished reputation), or again the discomfort of a bad conscience (guilt, shame, or a feeling of failure).

Finally, as we have seen, the expected reward can also be of a material or relational order, stemming from others (material advantages, praise, reputation, improvement of our status, etc.) or coming from oneself (self-satisfaction, having done one's duty, etc.).

Let's examine a few of these selfish motivations and the way Batson and the members of his team showed that they cannot explain all human behavior.

Helping Others in Order to Relieve Our Own Distress

We have seen earlier that witnessing another's suffering has the potential to induce a feeling of discomfort and upset in us that can evolve into distress. This self-oriented vicarious distress is the emotional state that Daniel Batson defined as 'personal distress.' We withdraw into ourselves and are chiefly concerned with the effect of suffering and the emotions it arouses in us. In this case, whatever the mode of intervention chosen—helping the other or turning away from their suffering—the action does not stem from an altruistic motivation.

If it is impossible for us to hide from the spectacle of the other's suffering, the assistance we offer will be, above all, motivated by the desire to relieve our own distress. If a convenient evasion presents itself and allows us to avoid confronting the other's torments, we will generally favor this escape route.

For altruists, such a feeling of discomfort will function, initially, as an alarm that alerts them to the other's suffering, and will make them aware of the level of distress in the situation. Thus warned, altruists will use all means available to remedy this confusion and its causes. As the American philosopher Thomas Nagel puts it, "Sympathy is the pained awareness of their [the other's] distress as *something to be relieved*."[10]

EXPERIMENTATION IN THE LABORATORY

If the stimulus presented by another person's suffering is the main cause for my distress, two solutions occur to me: either I help the other get rid of his suffering (and, at the same time, put an end to my unease), or I find another way to escape this stimulus by distancing myself physically or psychologically. Psychological flight is the most effective, for if I simply turn my eyes away while remaining concerned about the other's suffering, I still won't have gotten rid of my own feeling of discomfort—"far from sight" remains "close to the heart." How can one verify by experimentation if a particular individual is driven by this first selfish motivation, or if he is behaving in a truly altruistic way?

The participants in one of the experiments conceived by Daniel Batson are placed in individual cubicles and watch on the monitor a student named Elaine. The observers are told that Elaine is a student volunteering for an experiment on her performance while working in unpleasant situations. She will receive electric shocks of an intensity that does not endanger her, but is unpleasant nonetheless. She will receive these shocks at irregular intervals over a certain number of sessions, between two and ten, each lasting two minutes. The participants are also told that they will not meet Elaine in person.

There are over forty participants, who are divided by lot into two groups.[11] The first group is told that Elaine will do between two and ten sessions of tests, but that they are required only to observe the first two. This is the situation of "easy escape." The second group is also told that Elaine will receive between two and ten series of electric shocks, but that they will have to observe her the entire time. This is the situation of the "difficult escape."

At the start of each session, one of the participants, seated alone in a cubicle, sees on a closed-circuit television screen Elaine entering the cubicle next to hers. Actually it's a video recording, as it is important that the experimental protocol be identical for all participants. Elaine is actually an actress who is not really receiving any electric shocks, but the participants don't know this.

On the video, we also see Martha, who is in charge of the experiments, explain to Elaine the protocol for the experiment. An electrode is attached to Elaine's arm. It is clear from Elaine's facial expressions that the shocks are extremely painful to her, so much so that at the end of the second session, Martha interrupts the experiment and leaves the room to get her a glass of water.

During this time, another person in charge questions the observer about her emotional reactions, especially about her degree of distress, and also her degree of empathy at seeing Elaine's painful reactions.

Then Martha asks Elaine how she feels. Elaine confesses that, when she was little, she landed on an electric fence when she fell off a horse and that after this traumatic experience, she reacts very strongly to electrical shocks, even slight ones. Martha suggests to Elaine that they stop the experiment, but Elaine replies, "I started; I want to finish. I'll go on.... I know your experiment is important, and I want to do it."

Martha then suggests a solution: "The person who is observing you is another psychology student; maybe she would be willing to help you out by taking your place." With a mixture of hesitation and relief, Elaine ends up agreeing.

The person in charge of the observer explains to her, "I guess you saw, Elaine's finding the aversive conditions pretty uncomfortable. I was wondering if maybe you'd like to help Elaine out by taking her place.... First of all, let me say that you're under no obligation to take Elaine's place.... If you decide to help Elaine, you'll take her place for the last eight sessions, and she'll observe you."

The experimenter adds an additional choice depending on the groups: to each of the participants in the "easy escape" group, she says, "If you don't want to take Elaine's place and you decide to continue as an observer, you've finished observing the two trials, so all you need to do is answer a few questions about what you're feeling now (anxiety, empathy, etc.) and then you'll be free to go."

To the participants in the "difficult escape" group, the experimenter announces, "If you decide to continue as an observer, I'll need you to watch Elaine's remaining eight trials."

Among the participants whose empathic distress has been induced to be predominant over their empathic concern (half of the participants), only 18% of them choose to take Elaine's place in the case of the "easy escape" group. But in the case of the "difficult escape" group, 64% of the participants decide to take her place, since they can't relieve their distress by escaping.

On the other hand, on average 91% of the observers who feel strong empathy but little personal distress (the other half of the participants) take Elaine's place when escape is easy, and 82% when escape is difficult. A compilation of data from four studies with slightly different experimental protocols shows (see graph) that on average 85% of observers with a "predominant empathic concern," are willing to take Elaine's place.[12] The conclusion, then, is that the empathic solicitude shown by these latter participants stems from real altruism, since they are intervening for the sake of Elaine's own welfare, and not merely out of a desire to relieve their own distress.

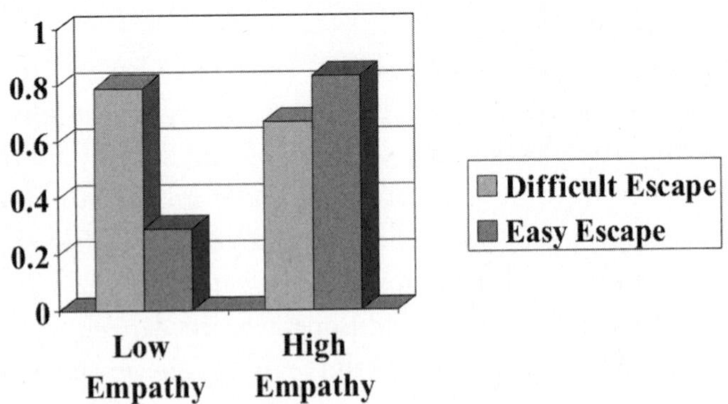

We can see that the people for whom empathic solicitude predominates choose to take Elaine's place when they could easily refrain from doing so. This is not the case for people with strong empathic distress, who take Elaine's place only when escape is difficult.

Helping Others in Order to Avoid Punishment: Guilt Feelings

Some people prefer to help others, even if they are not inclined to do so, because this effort is psychologically less costly for them than being prey to a feeling of guilt.

Thomas Hobbes, who constantly proclaimed that humans are motivated solely by self-preservation—which leads them systematically to privilege their own personal interests—was seen one day as he was giving a coin to a beggar. Seeing this, a friend who was familiar with the philosopher's opinions remarked that it looked very much like a selfless deed. To which Hobbes retorted: "Not at all, I did it to relieve my bad conscience."

We'll consider another famous anecdote. As he was traveling in a stagecoach, President Abraham Lincoln confided to one of the passengers his conviction that anyone who does good is in the end motivated by selfishness. Scarcely had he spoken than their vehicle passed over a bridge and they heard, below, the distraught squeals of a sow whose piglets had fallen into the water. Lincoln asked the coachman to stop, leaped to the ground and pulled the piglets onto the shore. When they had started up again, his companion remarked, "Well, Abe, where's the selfishness in this little episode?," to which Lincoln replied, "Why, that was the very essence of selfishness. My mind wouldn't have been at peace all day if I had gone by leaving that old sow worrying about her little ones. Don't you realize that I did this only [to] appease my own conscience?"

We should note, though, that the mere fact of feeling distress or guilt at the idea of neglecting another person's welfare is not in itself a sign of selfishness. If we were exclusively selfish, we would have no reason to be troubled by others' suffering. A person in whom selfishness is preponderant will stifle the timid protestations of any guilt feelings by fabricating moral justifications for inaction, likely to be expressed in the form of sentiments like, "Well, he was asking for it"; "Those people are just getting what they deserve"; or, "Poor people just have to work harder."

At the extreme limit, in order to rid themselves of all feeling of distress at the idea of behaving selfishly, some go so far as to invent a philosophical system based on a reversal of values. This was the case for the American thinker and novelist Ayn Rand. "Ethical selfishness," which she called "objectivism," asserts that altruism is immoral because it requires us to make intolerable sacrifices, and represents an unacceptable constraint imposed on our desire to live happily.[14]

How then can it be shown that people don't help out simply to avoid feeling guilty? In the laboratory this time, the participants, all of them students, divided into two groups, are told that by passing a test that is given to them they can prevent another student, Julie, from receiving electric shocks. But the test is so difficult that none of the participants pass it. One of the groups is then told that the test was relatively easy (which makes them feel guilty) and the other is told that it's not their fault, since the test was too difficult.[15]

The results of the experiment show that subjects induced to feel strong empathy by asking them to imagine vividly Julie's situation remain concerned with her fate no matter the explanation given for their failure, whereas the subjects conditioned to feel little empathy are *reassured as soon they are told it's not their fault* that Julie received a shock. The conclusion here is that those induced to feel empathic concern do not come to the aid of a person in need simply in order to have a good conscience.

One of the arguments that was made to Batson is that a physical escape (leaving the laboratory) does not necessarily imply a psychological escape (forgetting the person one has declined to help). The participants with strong empathy, the ones who volunteered to help, could have said to themselves: "Yes, but if I don't help her now, I'll feel bad later on,"[16] which is a selfish motivation. So it was important to find out if, at the time of the experiment, they anticipated the distress that thinking about the person's fate would cause later.[17]

Eric Stocks and his colleagues designed two experiments to provide easy psychological escape.[18] In the first one, participants were told that the study was part of a trial for two highly effective memory training techniques (both actually fictitious), one designed to enhance a specific memory and one designed to eliminate it. They were told that the human memory system works very much like the hard drive of a computer and that one technique could be used to permanently "save" a particular memory, whereas a different technique would permanently "delete" it. They were also informed that previous research had shown that the success rate was 93% for "saving" memories and 97% for "deleting" memories. Questionnaires showed that most participants did firmly believe what was told to them.

To provide a target for their memory training, participants listened to the audiotape of a radio broadcast which described the plight of Katie Banks, a university student struggling to take care of her younger brother and sister after her parents were killed in an auto accident.

Half of the participants were asked to remain objective while listening to the broadcast (thus inducing a low empathic concern), while the other half were asked to imagine how Katie felt and how her plight was badly affecting her life (thus inducing high empathic concern). Within each empathic condition, high or low, half of the participants were randomly assigned to the "Deleting Memories" training, which provided an easy psychological escape, and the other half were assigned to the "Saving Memories" training, which made psychological escape less likely to succeed.

After listening to the broadcast, participants were provided an unexpected opportunity to volunteer time to help Katie in any of a variety of ways—babysitting her younger brother and sister while she attended class, helping out around the house, providing transportation, and assisting with a fund-raising event.

The results showed that individuals in whom strong empathy was induced volunteered much more to help, whether or not they believed that they would most likely forget about Katie's plight. It thus seems that people who are sincerely concerned about someone's fate will offer help, whether or not they expect to be bothered by a lingering feeling of guilt if they had chosen not to help.

It now had to be demonstrated that people don't act solely in order to avoid having to justify their non-intervention to themselves either. In this case, the participants are asked to donate some of their time to help a woman in difficulty. The first group learns that the majority of the other participants volunteered to help. The second group is told that only a minority has offered to help. They understand that, if a participant doesn't want to help, she can say to herself that, after all, she isn't the only one in this situation, since most of the others have acted likewise. The results show that the participants who feel strong empathy for the young woman do offer their help in both instances, whereas people with weak empathy decline to help in the second instance, since it allows them to justify their inaction.

Helping Others in Order to Avoid Disapproval

If we act in an altruistic way because we're afraid of being criticized, then the action we accomplish is subordinate to the consideration that we are counting on other people's opinion. The personal "cost," in terms of time and effort, of carrying out such an action for the other person seems to us not as high as the opprobrium of our fellows. That is a frequent motive for the hypocritical altruist.

How can one be sure that people aren't helping with the sole aim of avoiding others' censure? To test this hypothesis, a new group of participants was formed who were given an opportunity to spend some time with Janet, who is introduced to them as a woman going through a difficult time in her life, suffering from loneliness and looking for friendship. Two subgroups are formed. The first is told that the experimenter and Janet will be informed of their decision to spend time with her or not. The second is guaranteed confidentiality with regards to their decision.

Half the participants are asked to imagine Janet's fate for a few moments, so as to arouse empathy for her; whereas the other half is simply asked to read Janet's request in which she expresses her desire to meet people. The results show that three-quarters of the participants with a high degree of empathy agree to meet Janet, whether or not their choice is confidential. On the other hand, most subjects with weak empathy decline the offer to meet Janet when they enjoy the shield of anonymity. This supports the idea that those induced to feel empathic concern were *not motivated by social acknowledgement.*[19]

The Calculated Expectation of Compensation

I am doing you a favor, but I expect a favor in return, now or in the long run. This expectation can be explicit, implicit, or hidden. This kind of altruism is often observed among animals—I scratch your back and you scratch mine. Impalas have a custom of licking each other's necks, but if one stops doing it, the other stops as well.

If the hope of benefiting from an advantage is our ultimate goal, our self-interested calculations can take on the appearance of altruism with the sole objective of inducing in the other person behavior favorable toward us, without regard for his welfare.

We know that such calculations sometimes have long-term aims. For instance, one might lavish attention on an elderly person for years in the hope of benefiting from an inheritance; one might heap favors on important officials with the prospect of ultimately drawing personal profit from it.

Another form of false altruism consists of doing someone a favor with the aim of receiving compliments or being appreciated by that person, or else making charitable donations in order to win a good reputation.

Still, nurturing the desire to establish friendly relations with others and, to do so, breaking the ice by performing a kind deed is not in itself selfish, insofar as we aren't proposing to use the other for our own personal interests.

Praise is not pernicious in itself. If one is sincere in the beneficial actions one undertakes, the fact that these actions are being praised can constitute a welcome encouragement (provided that vanity isn't mixed up in it); further, offering compliments is a celebration and a proof of gratitude for the good that others do. In this respect, still, a Buddhist saying enjoins prudence: "Think that the praise people give you is not addressed to you, but to the virtue embodied by your actions, and that criticism, on the other hand, is indeed addressed to you and your imperfections."

The fact is, though, that if we carry out an action, even one useful to others, in the sole aim of being complimented and well thought of socially, this is only a simulacrum of altruism. To accomplish the good of others while still bringing ourselves a feeling of fulfillment, altruism and compassion should not be self-centered.

Helping in the Hope of a Reward: The Experimental Test

If we help someone in the hope of obtaining a reward, we would be less satisfied if, in the course of the action, someone else comes to his aid in our place, since then we could no longer receive the expected reward, material or social. But if we are altruistically motivated, what counts above all is that the person is helped: it doesn't matter who does the helping. Our satisfaction would still be the same. This suggests a way to determine whether, when we feel empathic concern, we help in order to feel good about ourselves for helping.

Do people help because they get a subjective reward out of it, for instance, because it makes them feel good? Let's return to the experiment with Katie: if the participants with strong empathy help because they feel good after having helped—an explanation often advanced—they should help less readily when they have no way of knowing whether their help is effective. The experiment showed that the participants with strong empathy, placed in this new situation, help just as much when they are told that they won't hear any further news about the orphaned student as when they are told that they will be kept informed about her progress.

What's more, altruists are concerned with Katie's fate, and most of them want to receive news of her when offered the option of hearing an update on her situation a month later, even when the prognosis isn't very good. If they helped solely to please themselves, they would not choose to expose themselves to the risk of receiving bad news.

And what if people helped in order to feel proud of being "the one who made a difference"? How can we know if a supposedly altruistic person is simply helping to experience a feeling of pride in having accomplished a kind action? It is enough to determine if the person will be just as satisfied if someone else acts in his or her place. For a true altruist, it's the result that counts, not the satisfaction of being the hero in the situation.

This is precisely what another experiment demonstrated. The participants hear through headphones the voice of another individual of the same sex, Janet or Brian, who tells them about having to undergo an attention test in which being wrong results in an electric shock. "Wow! (nervous laugh)...Those shocks kinda hurt! I mean, they weren't terrible and I guess I'll go through with it, but I'm not looking forward to making mistakes on my task," the individual adds, in order to arouse a feeling of empathy.

The participant will carry out the same task as Janet (the experiment is the same with Brian) at first, without any risk of receiving a shock, and, every time the participant succeeds, it cancels the shock Janet is supposed to receive when she is wrong. The degree of empathy the participants have for Janet is also evaluated in a questionnaire.

Then, later, this same group of participants is told that in the end, Janet will not receive any shocks, and the experimenter will be content to point out to her the mistakes she commits. The results reveal that the real altruists (the ones who showed more empathy for Janet) are just as satisfied when told that Janet won't receive any shocks—and so will not need their help—as when told they will be able to remove her shocks. So their satisfaction is linked to the fact of knowing that Janet *herself* hasn't suffered and not to the idea that it is *they* who spared her the pain of the shocks.[20]

As Daniel Batson was publishing his research, other researchers set out to find selfish explanations for the results he had observed.[21] In response, Batson and the members of his team imagined new protocols meant to counter the objections advanced and put to the test all conceivable selfish explanations.[22] After eighteen years and thirty-one experiments, conducted by himself and other psychologists and designed to test the nature of the motivation to help created by empathy, Batson came to the fundamental conclusion that, "The results of these experiments support the empathy–altruism hypothesis. None of the egoistic explanations proposed have received more than scattered support."[23]

These studies have given rise to a number of discussions,[24] but to this day they have not been refuted. In fact, the altruistic hypothesis offers a better explanation for behavior of mutual aid, generosity, and kindness. It is up to the proponents of universal selfishness, then, to justify their hypothesis despite the overwhelming evidence to the contrary. As Daniel Batson concludes, "Altruism is a more pervasive and powerful force in human affairs than has been recognized. Failure to appreciate its importance has handicapped attempts to understand what motivates our action and what brings us satisfaction. It has also handicapped efforts to build better interpersonal relations and a more caring, human society. Recognizing the scope and power of altruism is not all that is needed to overcome these handicaps. But it is a crucial first step."[25]

This conclusion is key: If real altruism does indeed exist, if it is not the privilege of exceptional beings who are heroes or saints, and if its presence can be pointed out in countless actions of ordinary life, as shown by studies conducted by Daniel Batson, Nancy Eisenberg, Michael Tomasello, and others, we can draw important lessons. Like any other quality, altruism can be cultivated on a personal level and encouraged on a societal level. At school, it is not pointless to place more stress on cooperation, prosocial behavior, solidarity, compassion, non-discrimination, and all the attitudes that stem from altruism. It is not a sign of naïve idealism to envisage the development of an economy that would integrate the voice of care, along with the voice of reason, into its system.

Everyone knows that selfishness exists—it seems that, on this point, we don't need to convince anyone—but when we have acknowledged that altruism, too, is inherent in human nature, we will have made a great step toward the birth of a culture that is open to the other instead of one that withdraws into purely individualist interests.

13

The Philosophical Arguments Against Universal Selfishness

Viewing humans as seeking to promote their own personal interests in every circumstance is a concept that took shape under the influence of the English philosopher Thomas Hobbes, who presents the individual as a basically selfish being. The notion was adopted by a number of contemporary thinkers.[1] Specialists in human sciences have termed this "universal selfishness," or "psychological selfishness," the theory that postulates not only that selfishness exists, which no one doubts, but that it motivates *all* of our actions. Even if we want others to be happy, it would only be viewed as a roundabout way to "maximize" our own interests. Although no one denies the fact that personal interest can be one of the reasons we help others, the theory of universal selfishness goes far beyond that by asserting that personal interest is the only reason.

David Hume, one of Hobbes' main opponents, was not kindly disposed toward the proponents of universal selfishness, and thought this point of view stemmed from "the most careless and precipitate examination."[2] He was more inclined to observe human behavior empirically than to construct moral theories. Speaking about the thinkers of his time, he remarked, "It is full time they should attempt a like reformation in all moral disquisitions; and reject every system of ethics, however subtle or ingenious, which is not founded on fact and observation." For him, denying the existence of altruism went against common sense:

> *The most obvious objection to the selfish hypothesis is, that, as it is contrary to common feeling and our most unprejudiced notions, there is required the highest stretch of philosophy to establish so extraordinary a paradox. To the most careless observer there appear to be such dispositions as benevolence and generosity; such affections as love, friendship, compassion, gratitude.*[3]

Nonetheless, when confronted with the numerous examples of altruism which, like us, they witness in their daily lives, the supporters of universal selfishness set to work proposing explanations that often defy common sense. In other cases, they simply take for granted that genuine altruism can't exist. Concerning a man who rushed out of his car and plunged unhesitatingly into freezing water to save someone from drowning, the American sociobiologist Robert Trivers asserts boldly, without offering any evidence whatsoever, that without a selfish motive "it is clear that the rescuer should not bother to save the drowning man."[4]

This theory is problematic because it reflects a narrow and reductive vision of human motivations. The philosopher Joel Feinberg notes:

> *If the arguments for psychological egoism consisted for the most part of carefully acquired empirical evidence (well-documented reports of controlled experiments, surveys, interviews, laboratory data, and so on), then the critical philosopher would have no business carping at them. After all, since psychological egoism purports to be a scientific theory of human motive it is the concern of the experimental psychologist, not the philosopher, to accept or reject it. But as a matter of fact, empirical evidence of the required sort is seldom presented in support of psychological egoism.... It is usually the "armchair scientist" who holds the theory of universal selfishness, and his usual arguments are either based simply on his "impressions" or are largely of the non-empirical sort.*[5]

The Theory of Universal Selfishness Evades Every Fact-Based Refutation

On the philosophical level, the main arguments advanced by proponents of universal selfishness are the following: we help others because in the end we draw satisfaction from doing so; whatever we do, we can desire only one thing—our own well-being—which is in itself a selfish motivation; since everything we do freely is the expression of our will and our desires, our actions are consequently selfish; or, conversely, a heroic deed is not really altruistic because its agent is acting impulsively and doesn't really make a choice.

The theory of universal selfishness shows its weakness when it sets out to explain by itself alone *all* of human behavior. It is selfish to refuse to give a plum to a child (you want to keep it for yourself), and it is selfish to give it to the child (you are doing so in order to have a good conscience or in order to put an end to the child's insistent demands, which are exasperating you). Without experimentally verifying the real motivation of the person, one could advance, just as arbitrarily, the opposite hypothesis: it is just as altruistic to give a plum to a child (you know the child likes plums) as it is to refuse it (you know that plums make the child sick to his or her stomach).

Applying the word "selfish" to all behavior without exception leads to absurd interpretations of situations: the soldier who throws himself onto a grenade in order to keep his companions from being killed would be just as selfish as the one who pushes his comrade onto the grenade to save his skin. Being selfish would thus become synonymous with existing and breathing. As Abraham Maslow cautions, "It is tempting, if the only tool you have is a hammer, to treat everything as if it were a nail."[6]

A scientific hypothesis must not only be able to be put to the test by experimental verification, but it must also present the possibility of being refuted by facts. If a theory is formulated in such a way that it is always verified, whatever the facts observed, it does not advance the state of knowledge. A theory that is in principle unfalsifiable is not scientific; it is an ideology.

DO WE DO GOOD TO OTHERS BECAUSE IT DOES US GOOD?

People often say, "I've helped others a lot, but I've drawn immense satisfaction from doing so. They are the ones I have to thank." They speak of the 'warm glow' which accompanies the satisfaction born from accomplishing acts of kindness.

But such a hypothesis could not be applied to all altruistic behavior. When a fireman rushes into a house on fire to get someone out, it is quite absurd to imagine him thinking, "OK, I'm going into the blaze. I'll feel so good afterwards!"

As the psychologist Alfie Kohn emphasizes, "The egoist must do more than point to the smile on the face of the rescuer if she means to show that the rescuer had that pleasant afterglow in mind."[7]

What's more, the fact of feeling satisfaction when accomplishing an altruistic action does not make the action selfish, since the desire for that satisfaction does not constitute its main motivation. If you go for a hike in the mountains to bring provisions to a friend who is stuck in a small cabin, the walk is indeed good for your health and you appreciate its benefits, but wouldn't it be specious to argue that it's because the walk does you good, bodily, that you went to help your friend?

Satisfaction is born from true altruism, not from calculating selfishness. Herbert Spencer, a nineteenth-century English philosopher and sociologist, remarked, "This increase of personal benefit achieved by benefiting others, is but partially achieved where a selfish motive prompts the seemingly unselfish act: it is fully achieved only where the act is really unselfish."[8] In short, those who call any altruistic action that brings an advantage to the one who accomplishes it selfish are confusing primary with secondary effects.

One can also argue that altruistic actions are not always accompanied by pleasant emotions. Rescues carried out in emergencies and those that consist of protecting victims of persecution are often preceded or accompanied by more or less intense moments of fear on the part of the rescuer. During World War II, Irene Gut Opdyke risked her life many times to save Jews threatened with death in Poland. She clearly explains the difference between the emotions felt in the heat of the moment and the feeling of fulfillment experienced when she recalls the deeds. Was she aware of the nobility of her actions? "I did not realize then," she says, "but the older I get, the more I feel I am very rich. I would not change anything. It's a wonderful feeling to know that today many people are alive and some of them married and have their children, and that their children will have children because I did have the courage and the strength."[9] The fact of retrospectively appreciating the rightness of an action only adds to its admirable character; it takes nothing away from its altruism.

There is a variant to the theory of universal selfishness: the theory called *psychological hedonism,* the constant search for pleasure, which is described in the writings of the English philosopher John Stuart Mill.[10] It asserts that, "We are selfish because the only thing we really want is to have pleasant experiences, to prolong them, and to avoid or curtail unpleasant experiences." According to the theory of psychological hedonism, we are altruistic only to the extent that it brings us pleasure, and we would avoid being so if it allowed us to avoid any kind of unpleasantness. But this argument doesn't make much sense.[11] A runner who reaches the finish line, a builder who completes a house, a painter who finishes a painting, a person who has just finished washing the laundry, all take pleasure from having brought their work to completion. But we do laundry in order to have clean clothes, not to feel the satisfaction of having "done the laundry." Similarly, the simple fact that the achieving of another person's benefit gives us satisfaction does not imply that our motivation is selfish, since it is for the good of the other and not for our own satisfaction that we have acted.

Further, as Feinberg emphasizes, the fact that we felt satisfaction upon completing an altruistic action presupposes that we are naturally inclined to favor the other's happiness. If we were completely indifferent to others' fates, why would we feel pleasure in taking care of them?[12]

IS WISHING FOR ONE'S OWN WELL-BEING INCOMPATIBLE WITH ALTRUISM?

We should not confuse "self-love" or, to be more precise, "wanting one's own well-being" with selfishness. As the philosopher Ronald Milo explains, self-love leads to wishing for one's own welfare, while selfish love leads to wanting *only* that. Joseph Butler, the eighteenth-century

English philosopher and theologian, stressed the plurality of our concerns as well as the compatibility of wanting one's own welfare with also wanting that of others. He defends an "enlightened love of self" by which one of the secondary effects of altruism can be a contribution to the realization of our own happiness—without that making our initial motivation selfish. What's more, there are actions that contribute to our own well-being—breathing, walking, sleeping—that are neither selfish nor altruistic.

If the egoist had a better understanding of the mechanisms of happiness and suffering, he would accomplish his own well-being by showing kindness to others. Jean-Jacques Rousseau noted, "I know and I feel that doing good is the truest happiness that the human heart can taste."

Does Acting According to Our Own Will and Desire Make All Our Actions Selfish?

According to this argument, we are selfish because we act out of our own desires: when we act freely, in the end we do only what we want; consequently we are selfish. In other words, in order to be altruistic, an action should not have been desired by the agent who performs it, which is absurd. Norman Brown, a philosopher at Cambridge University, refutes this argument, explaining that it "amounts simply to saying that man is motivated by his own desires, a statement which is irredeemably trivial; for it is not praiseworthy but logically impossible to be motivated by someone else's desire, seeing that a desire just is the agent's tendency towards action."

What's more, if we acted for the other solely in order to satisfy our immediate desire to help, it would be enough to distract ourselves and to make this desire that bothers us go away. But that is not the case: as soon as our attention returns to those who need help, the desire to come to their aid re-arises and is maintained so long as we haven't *done something useful* for that person.

The difference between altruism and selfishness does not stem from the fact that I want something, but from the *nature of my desire,* which can be benevolent, malevolent, or neutral. It is our motivation, the ultimate goal we pursue, that colors our actions by determining their altruistic or selfish nature. I can wish for another's welfare, just as I can desire my own. Selfishness does not consist simply of desiring something, but of satisfying desires centered exclusively on personal interests, without taking into account others' interests. We are far from being able to control the development of external events, but, whatever the circumstances may be, we can always examine our intentions and adopt an altruistic attitude.

Further, it is possible, in most cases, to infuse altruism into activities that are seemingly ethically neutral. One can, for example, want to live a long time with good health in order to better devote oneself to the twofold accomplishment of one's own happiness and that of others. If this vision remains constantly present in the heart of our thoughts, whatever we do, our mind will always remain imprinted with kindness. There is a Buddhist practice that aims at turning ordinary activities into ways of training the altruistic mind. When opening a door, for instance, one thinks, "May the door of happiness be opened to all beings," and when closing a door, "May the door of suffering be closed for all beings." When lighting a fire, one thinks, "May the fire of wisdom be lit in my and everyone's mind and burn away the toxins of hatred, greed and arrogance," and so forth.

You Had No Choice?

In the case of intrepid rescuers, proponents of universal selfishness have another argument up their sleeves. Consider the explanation offered by many ordinary heroes after helping others, often at the risk of their own lives: "I didn't have a choice." Margot, a woman who had taken considerable risks to protect Jews persecuted by the Nazis, explained it this way to Kristen Monroe: "Suppose somebody drowns. If you stop to think, 'Shall I? Shall I not? Eeny, meeny, miney, mo.' You can't do that. You either help or you don't. You don't walk away. You don't walk away from somebody who needs real help."[13]

Partisans of universal selfishness conclude from this that one cannot describe automatic behavior as altruistic, since it is not preceded by an intention. But the fact of having acted unhesitatingly does not mean one had no choice, or that no intention presided over the action. It simply means that the choice was so clear that it led to immediate action.

Daniel Batson observes, "You may afterward report—as do many who rush into burning buildings or dive into dangerous waters—that you didn't think before you acted. In spite of this report, it seems likely that you—and they—did think. Otherwise, impulsive helping responses would not be as adaptive as they are.... It seems more accurate to say that you—and they—may not have thought carefully, but you did think. Your response was still goal directed."[14]

When we are faced with the need to make a decision in an unexpected situation that's evolving very quickly and doesn't allow for any hesitations, our behavior is the expression of our inner state. What seems like instinctive behavior is actually the natural manifestation of a way of being acquired over time.

If Altruism Did Not Exist, What Feelings Would We Have for Other People?

Joseph Butler suggested a reductio ad absurdum: if it were true that humans are purely selfish, then it follows that they are not at all concerned about other people. If that were the case, they would never wish for anything for other people, *either good or bad,* since these two desires, although opposite, both imply that one is interested in the other's fate, positively or negatively. A complete egoist could harm another or do good for the sake of his own self-interests, but he should not sacrifice his interests for any motivation whatsoever. If some people risk their lives to harm others out of hatred, why would they not be able to so do out of altruism?

Universal Selfishness Is Incompatible with the Existence of Morality

All morality is based on taking into consideration what is fair and desirable for others. A radical egoist regards others only as a means to arrive at his own ends. So he can't have any sincere consideration for their lot. In an "everyone for himself" world, there could be no moral sense, only at most contractual agreements established between egoists to limit the damages they risk inflicting on each other.

If selfishness were really the sole component of all our motivations, why would we experience the slightest feeling of surprise and indignation when we think of others' misdeeds? Why would we rise up against people who cheat others or against the captain who leaves his sinking ship before evacuating the passengers? We would regard such actions as perfectly normal.

Actually, even the most selfish people sometimes praise the kind or generous actions carried out by others. By doing so, they implicitly recognize the possibility of altruism in others. But in order to recognize it in others, one has to spot the possibility in oneself. We cannot assign feelings to others that are completely unknown to us.

Even the most inveterate egoist will think it normal to be treated fairly and will be indignant if made the victim of injustice. But the egoist cannot demand fair treatment without implicitly recognizing the value of fairness in itself. If that is the case, the egoist must also accept his responsibility to be fair to others, which means caring for others.

A growing number of researchers, including the psychologist Jonathan Haidt, have verified experimentally that moral sense is innate in humans. According to Haidt, it turns out that, in many situations, we sense first in an instinctive, or intuitive, way whether or not a certain kind of behavior is acceptable, and then a posteriori we justify our choices by reasoning.[15]

In brief, according to Norman Brown, "Psychological egoism is, I suppose, regarded by most philosophers as one of the more simple-minded fallacies in the history of philosophy, and dangerous and seductive too, contriving as it does to combine cynicism about human ideals and a vague sense of scientific method, both of which make the ordinary reader feel sophisticated, with conceptual confusion, which he cannot resist."

Nothing in the realm of lived experience, of sociological studies, or of scientific experimentation allows us to pass from questioning the existence of selfishness to dogmatically asserting that *all our actions* without exception are motivated by selfishness. The idea of universal selfishness seems to rest more on an intellectual a priori than on knowledge acquired by investigation into human behavior.

Escaping Defeatism and Choosing Altruism

Acknowledging that altruism and kindness are part of human nature encourages the full expression of this potential in our thoughts and actions. By presupposing a natural egoism, we seek to justify some of our antisocial behavior, and undermine any desire to remedy our defects. How many times do we hear it said about selfishness: "In any case, it's human nature"? Jerome Kagan, a Harvard professor, describes North Americans' tendency to accept the idea that personal self-interest takes precedence over all other considerations in this way:

> *Rather than acknowledge that the structure and philosophy of our society invite each of us to accept self-interest as the first rule, many Americans find it more attractive to believe that this mood, along with jealousy, hatred, violence, and incest, is the inevitable remnant of our animal heritage and so we must learn to accept it.*[16]

Our opinion about the existence of real altruism is not just a theoretical question, since it can considerably influence our way of thinking and acting. As Martin Luther King Jr. said, "Every man must decide whether he will walk in the light of creative altruism or in the darkness of destructive selfishness."

IS KINDNESS MORE NATURAL THAN HATRED?

The Dalai Lama often says that love is more natural than hatred, altruism more natural than egoism, since from birth to death we all need, in order to survive, to give and receive love to accomplish both our own welfare and others'. In general, he adds, we feel "good" when we show kindness to others, and "bad" when we harm others. We prefer the company of kind people; even animals move away from someone who is angry, brutal, or unpredictable. According to him, the relationship between kindness and well-being can be explained by the fact that the human being is a "social animal" who depends closely on the mutual aid and kindness from which we will benefit and which we in turn will show to others.

How, in that case, can we explain why humanity is subject to so many conflicts and so much violence? We can understand kindness as the expression of a human being's state of mental equilibrium, and violence as disequilibrium. Hatred is a deviance that causes suffering for both the one who is hated and the one who hates. When one follows a mountain path, it doesn't take much to make a wrong move and fall down the slope. When we lose our reference points and deviate from our state of equilibrium, anything becomes possible.

It is clear, then, that we must learn to master our malevolent thoughts as soon as they arise in our minds, just as we must put out a fire at its first flames, before the entire forest catches fire. Without this vigilance and this control, it is all too easy for us to stray far from our potential for kindness.

Nurturing the Potential for Goodness Present in Every Human Being

Many exceptional people have stressed the fact that, even in unfavorable circumstances, it is almost always possible to call on the good side of human nature, so that it manifests in behavior. Nelson Mandela, in particular, showed how such an attitude could be put to the service of a social or political cause:

> *I always knew that deep down in every human heart, there is mercy and generosity. No one is born hating another person because of the color of his skin, or his background, or his religion. People must learn to hate, and if they can learn to hate, they can be taught to love, for love comes more naturally to the human heart than its opposite. Even in the grimmest times in prison when my comrades and I were pushed to our limits, I would see a glimmer of humanity in one of the guards, perhaps just for a second, but it was enough to reassure me and keep me going.... [Human] goodness is a flame that can be hidden but never extinguished.*[17]

The Dalai Lama often reminds us that humans, unlike animals, are the only species capable of doing immense good or bad to their fellows. How can we act in such a way that it's the good side of human nature that gains the upper hand? We can find an inspiration in these words attributed to an old Cherokee giving advice to his grandson: "A fight is going on inside me," he said to the boy. "It is a terrible fight between two wolves. One is evil—he is hatred, anger, greed, envy, arrogance, grudge, resentment, miserliness, and cowardliness. The other is good—he is happiness, joy, serenity, love, kindness, compassion, hope, humility, generosity, truthfulness, and confidence. They are also fighting inside you and inside every other person, too." The child thought about it for a minute and then asked his grandfather, "Which wolf will win?" The old Cherokee simply replied, "The one you feed."

II

The Emergence of Altruism

14

Altruism in Theories of Evolution

Revolutionary Insights into the Evolution of Life: Charles Darwin

In 1859, Charles Darwin published *On the Origin of Species,* a text followed by several other foundational works on the theory of evolution. In it, he describes the mechanism and successive stages that allow the most elementary life forms to evolve into other, more complex forms, especially into acquiring the mental states and emotions that characterize humans and numerous animal species.

Darwin recognizes in humans "instincts of sympathy and goodwill to his fellows, which is still present and ever in some degree active in his mind."[1] He conceives of sympathy as "a basic element of social instincts" and concludes that "the man who did not possess similar feelings would be a monster." Contrary to a widespread misconception that Darwinism leaves no place for altruism, evolutionist theory insists on cooperation between individuals and on the development of empathy.

At a time when almost nothing was known about genetics, Darwin's detailed observations and perspicacity revolutionized our understanding of the relationships between animal species and their history. Darwin understood that the diversity of species was the result of a long and continuous process of adaptation to surrounding conditions. Showing remarkable discernment in the study of the nature of relationships and particularities that had escaped his predecessors, Darwin collected his discoveries into a theory of evolution of species, based on the combination of three essential elements:

- genetic mutations, which occur at random and cause hereditary variations that lead to differentiation in members of a species;
- variations that allow individuals to survive better and thus reproduce are favored by natural selection, so that the individual bearers of these mutations become increasingly numerous over the course of generations;
- adaptation: If external conditions change, individual bearers of other features might be better adapted to the new conditions; under the selective pressure exercised by the surrounding environment, they in turn prosper over the course of generations.

The notion of genes emerged from discoveries made by Gregor Mendel (1822–1884), a contemporary of Darwin (1809–1882), but not until after Darwin's death, and the structure of DNA wasn't elucidated by Watson and Crick until the 1950s, which made Darwin's discernment all the more remarkable. Today, we speak of genes rather than "hereditary traits," but the foundations of the theory of evolution remain unchanged.

From the Appearance of Life to the Emergence of Cooperation and Altruism

The birth of life corresponds to the appearance of entities capable of maintaining their integrity in a given environment, of reproducing and transmitting to the next generation the information necessary to the formation of new individuals. This information is coded in an ensemble of molecules that comprise the genes. Entities that have similar genomes and characteristics, and that, in the case of sexual reproduction, reproduce among themselves, form a species. They enjoy a certain degree of autonomy while still constantly being in dynamic interaction with their environment.

How does the transition from the most elementary forms of interactions to the most complex forms of psychological mechanisms occur? The various biological processes and behavior, first of all, have specific functions. For instance, the function of photosynthesis is to allow plants to use the energy of light; the function of incubation, that of keeping eggs warm until they hatch; that of hunting, as practiced by wild animals, of procuring food.

To this notion of *function* is added that of *need*. In order to grow, a tree needs water, oxygen, light, and nutritive elements drawn from the soil. These growth processes have become increasingly complex over the course of evolution. The needs of a bacterium, an oyster, a mouse, or a human being are all different, but within the biosphere all these species are *interdependent* on one another.

In the animal kingdom, these needs give birth to *tendencies*, which can go from the simple tropism of a bacterium which moves along a gradient of concentrated nutritive factors, onward to the propensity of an earthworm to move away from a dry, hot surface that endangers its survival, all the way to the complex tendencies and impulses among more evolved organisms.

The dimension of *desire* or *aspiration* is added to needs and tendencies when an organism acquires the ability to become aware of itself in a subjective way. Aspirations direct and facilitate the accomplishment of the organism's functions, needs, and tendencies. The most elementary conscious aspiration of a sentient being is one that consists of avoiding suffering and searching for well-being. Aspirations become more and more complex as the appreciation for suffering and well-being moves from the physical realm to the mental realm.

When a predator kills its prey, the vital function of the prey is interrupted, and it acquires the function of food for the predator. The needs and aspirations of the prey are thwarted, but those of the predator are satisfied. The desirable or undesirable nature of a situation is thus a relative notion, depending on individual points of view.

The ability of an organism to become aware of its identity and its aspirations goes hand in hand with a corresponding ability to become aware that the other also has its own identity and aspirations. From this, *empathy* is born.

The aspirations of self and other agree or disagree; it's at this stage that *ethics* enters the scene. Ethics is based on an appreciation of the desirable or undesirable nature of behavior (beneficial or harmful), or of a situation (fair or unfair), an appreciation that takes into account the other's aspirations without neglecting our own. This evaluation is associated with a value judgment depending on the altruistic or selfish nature of our motivations.

An individual who takes no account whatsoever of others' needs or aspirations uses others as tools in order to satisfy his or her own needs, without questioning the validity of his or her motivation and actions.

Altruism based on *reciprocity* leads to the "social contract," that is, to a collection of rules regulating relationships between individuals, rules that people agree to follow because they themselves draw advantage from them.

Through empathy and reasoning, which culminate in the human, individuals are now able to put themselves in the other's place, to consider the other's point of view, to become aware of the other's aspirations, and to understand that they are just as legitimate as their own. They then *respect* the other and stop considering the other as an instrument in the service of their own personal interests, and ethics takes on an additional dimension.

When this realization of the *value of the other* gives rise to a *motivation* and behavior whose *final goal is to accomplish the other's well-being*, we speak of *altruism* and of *compassion* when the goal is to *relieve the other's suffering.* An altruistic action may happen to benefit us personally without that being the ultimate goal of our action. It can also cost us, when we willingly decide to renounce some of our advantages for the sake of the other.

The quality and validity of an ethic increases with its degree of universality. Criminals, for example, can spend their time robbing people while still respecting a "criminal code of honor" that leads them to share their loot fairly. A malefactor or a tyrant can observe familial ethics, and be concerned for the well-being of his children, while he mercilessly oppresses the rest of the population.

We should note that most of our ethical systems take into consideration only human beings. That does not call into question the usefulness of these systems, but it considerably limits their extent. An ethic can be universal only if it takes into account the aspirations of all living beings, in all their modalities, and with all their degrees of complexity.

According to such an ethic, the desire not to suffer that all sentient beings feel should be respected, even if it is not felt by a being endowed with a superior intelligence, and even if it is not expressed in a language that we humans are able to decipher. Those who enjoy a superior intelligence should, by that very fact, use this ability to recognize and respect among other beings the same desire to avoid suffering.

Ethics is *fundamentally linked* to *altruism.* It begins with altruism limited to those close to us and to those who wish us well, and then extends to strangers who belong to the same human family as we do, and it culminates in an interest in the fate of all sentient beings.

Are we able to practice such an ethic? We are biologically programmed for *limited altruism,* toward our kind and toward those who treat us well, but this ability can serve as a foundation for cultivating *extended altruism.*

COOPERATION VS. COMPETITION

Darwin envisaged three types of behavior: purely automatic and instinctive behavior (that of the simplest organisms); behavior of pursuing individual interests (often to the detriment of other individuals); and behavior stemming from social instincts that are notably expressed by parental care and sympathy for other members of a group. Darwin clearly envisaged the possibility among humans of extending this sympathy beyond the family circle, the clan, and even the human species:

> *As man advances in civilization, and small tribes are united into larger communities, the simplest reason would tell each individual that he ought to extend his social instincts and sympathies to all members of the same nation, though personally unknown to him. This point being once reached, there is only an artificial barrier to prevent his sympathies extending to the men of all nations and races. [If they appear different from him]... experience unfortunately shews us how long it is before we look at them as our fellow creatures. Sympathy beyond the confines of man, that is humanity to the lower animals, seems to be one of the latest moral acquisitions.... This virtue, one of the noblest with which man is endowed, seems to arise*

> *incidentally from our sympathies becoming more tender and more widely diffused, until they extend to all sentient beings. As soon as this virtue is honoured and practised by some few men, it spreads through instruction and example to the young, and eventually becomes incorporated in public opinion.*[2]

In 1880, the Russian biologist Karl Fedorovich Kessler, then at St. Petersburg University, stressed the fact that, compared to the law of reciprocal struggle, the law of reciprocal aid is much more important for success in the struggle for life and for the progressive evolution of species. This idea inspired Peter Kropotkin to devote himself to the study of mutual aid among animals, the outstanding points of which he outlined in his *Mutual Aid: A Factor of Evolution*.

As for the phrase "struggle for life," Darwin himself used it in a metaphorical sense. In fact, two dogs can fight over a piece of meat and two plants can "fight" against drought to survive in a desert. The two dogs are fighting *against one another,* whereas the two plants are both struggling *against drought*.[3] In the latter case, the "struggle for life" does not imply any hostility between species. Some species emerge victorious from the evolutionary process without having to engage in the slightest battle; they have, for instance, a better immune system, or are equipped with eyes or ears, which allow them better to detect predators.[4] Moreover, although organisms are sometimes in direct competition with members of other species or their own species in appropriating rare and precious resources, or else in establishing their rank in a social hierarchy, if we consider *the totality of interactions* over time, we note that in the majority of cases, this competition is neither violent nor direct.[5, 6]

Competition is generally more visible and more spectacular than cooperation. A brawl in a public place immediately draws a crowd of people, and attracts much more attention than a group of people who have been cooperating in various ways for hours. However, it is fair to state that human life is more reliant on cooperation than on competition. In fact, as Martin Nowak, Director of the Program for Evolutionary Dynamics at Harvard, explains, evolution *needs* cooperation in order to be able to construct new levels of organization: genes collaborate in chromosomes, chromosomes collaborate in cells, cells collaborate in organisms and more complex structures, these structures collaborate in bodies, and these bodies collaborate in societies.[7] One thus finds cooperation among units sharing the same genes as well as among units carrying different genes. Throughout the history of life, units that were at first independent got together in a cooperative way and, over time, ended up constituting entire individuals, a human being for instance, or "superorganisms," as in the case of a colony of ants. Thought of in this context, the word "cooperation" does not imply any conscious motivation, since it can be applied just as well to genes as to bacteria or to superior animals.[8]

In general, animals co-exist in various, more or less complex ways. Some remain solitary aside from brief periods of procreation. Gregarious animals, on the other hand, are drawn by the company of their fellows, and tend to share in common grounds, without necessarily interacting. On the scale of complexity, we then move on to the *subsocial* stage, characterized by the occurrence of *parental care*. At this stage, animals become considerably involved in raising their young until they are grown. In certain species, the next stage is the *colonial* stage, occurring in large colonies of birds, for example, in which although the parents take direct care only of their own offspring, they also oversee a common terrain that ensures the group's security. At the *communal* stage, the females cooperate in taking care of the young, feeding them and protecting them. Finally, at the stage called *eusocial*, the most complex stage, one can observe the construction and defense of a communal habitat—an ants' nest, for instance—in which the adults cooperate over the long term in raising the young, as well as in a division of labor and a specialization in tasks.[9]

Explaining altruistic cooperation has been one of the great challenges posed to the theory of evolution. This type of cooperation implies a cost for the individual, and so it is hard to explain from the point of view of "survival of the fittest," a term coined by Thomas Huxley, the forefather of what became known later as "Social Darwinism," since the individual seemingly draws no advantage for his own survival from it. However, examples of this kind of behavior abound among humans, whom we constantly see engaging in strong, diverse, and repeated forms of collaboration, often costly or risky, which extend well beyond the limited circle of relatives to individuals without any kinship to them.[10]

Is Altruism Compatible with the "Struggle for Life"?

Darwin noted the existence of altruistic behavior in situations where it turned out to be useful to the group, but useless to the individual, as in the case of sterile workers in a society of insects. He found himself, he said, faced with "by far the most serious special difficulty, which my theory has encountered."[11] Natural selection should "never produce in a being anything injurious to itself, for natural selection acts solely by and for the good of each."[12] In order to exist, then, altruism must have a fundamental usefulness for the species:

> *In however complex a manner this feeling may have originated, as it is one of high importance to all those animals which aid and defend each other, it will have been increased, through natural selection; for those communities, which included the greatest number of the most sympathetic members, would flourish best, and rear the greatest number of offspring.*[13]

Theoreticians who developed and completed Darwin's ideas have always come up against the question of altruism. The question posed a thorny problem for them, since a priori it seemed that an individual who behaved in a completely selfish way had an advantage in the "struggle for life." The egoist would unhesitatingly appropriate food and other limited resources for himself, would brutally oust his potential rivals at the time of reproduction, and would not hesitate to kill altruists if that favored his survival. Because of this, it was hard to see how genes that manifested in an altruistic temperament could have become implanted in any sort of population.

From this perspective, willingly giving the other an advantage seems to be a major counter-indication to the optimization of the individual's chances of survival. Altruists should logically be the eternal losers in the struggle for life. However, that is far from the reality.

What Kind of Altruism Is Being Discussed?

We have thus far defined altruism as a mental state, a motivation, an intention to fulfill others' needs, a desire to do good for them or spare them suffering. Elliott Sober calls this motivation "psychological altruism" as opposed to "evolutionary altruism." We should keep in mind, though, in this chapter, that when evolutionists speak of "altruism," they are not interested in motivation, but solely in *prosocial behavior*—that is, in behavior that is *beneficial* to other individuals, and that entails a greater or lesser cost to their agents.[14]

For an evolutionist, the term "altruist" can be applied to sterile worker ants whose behavior benefits the ant colony, or else to a bird that emits an alarm call at a predator's approach, allowing its fellows to flee to a safe place, but drawing the raptor's attention to itself—a behavior that is often deadly for it. According to the view of survival of the fittest, such sacrificial behavior doesn't make sense, since, by prematurely losing their lives, these "altruists" leave behind fewer descendants than the survivors. Such behavior should be naturally eliminated over the course of generations. Even bacteria, according to Dugatkin, can be regarded as "altruistic," if their behavior leads to a diminution of their potential for reproduction while still being beneficial to that of other bacteria.[15]

This misappropriation by evolutionists of the terminology usually used to designate motivations is regrettable, since it continues to create pointless confusion. It would have been preferable for evolutionists to use other terms, such as "beneficial," "useful," "advantageous," or "favorable" to others, for instance, in order to prevent their discussions on the nature of evolutionary altruism from influencing our vision of real altruism in human nature, as so often happens.

Favoring Those Who Share Our Genes

The problem of "evolutionary altruism" would eventually be clarified to some extent by a young English student fascinated by the question of altruism. In the 1960s, at Cambridge University, William Donald Hamilton decided, against everyone's wishes, to concentrate in the genetic evolution of altruistic behavior. Solitary and shy, Hamilton didn't even ask for a desk or an office. He worked at home, in libraries, and even on train station benches when the libraries were closed. He faced repeated criticisms from his professors and even considered terminating the course of his scientific career. But he persevered and published two articles, one in 1963, the other in 1964, which were received with complete indifference.[16] His thesis advisers, who were of the opinion that he didn't deserve his doctorate in science, refused to award it to him until 1968. However, these two articles would profoundly influence the science of evolution. In them, Hamilton describes, with the help of a relatively simple equation, what would be regarded as one of the great discoveries of the twentieth century in the field of evolution.[17]

Darwin spoke of the transmission of hereditary "traits" that were more or less favorable to the survival of the individual, hence to his ability to engender descendants who would bear that individual's traits. Hamilton demonstrated that engendering the greatest possible number of descendants was not the only way to ensure the transmission of one's genes to future generations. The same objective can be reached if close relatives, who also carry some of the genes, reproduce.

In his two articles, Hamilton proposes an equation, which has since become famous, that accounts for what we now call "kin selection," by which behavior that helps a genetically related individual is favored by natural selection. Until then, the "reproductive success" of an individual was measured by the number of that individual's descendants. But Hamilton showed that this selective value is not only commensurate with the success of the individual himself, but also with the success of *all those who are genetically related to him,* his brothers and sisters, nieces and nephews. In fact, they too carry a part of the genes of the individual in question (the sister of a given individual has an average of 50% of genes in common with him, a first cousin, 25%, a niece, 12.5%, and so on).

The *overall reproductive success* (or else the selective overall value called *inclusive fitness* by Hamilton) is then the sum of his *direct* reproductive success (his descendants) and his *indirect* reproductive success (that of his parents, who carry part of his genes). In the final analysis, what matters is the overall quantity of copies of our genes transmitted to the next generation, directly or indirectly.

Altruistic behavior in certain animals seemed suddenly to take on meaning from the evolutionary perspective. Hamilton's equation formalized the intuition of the great geneticist J.B.S. Haldane, according to which it is worth giving one's life to save the lives of at least two brothers or sisters, or four cousins, or eight nephews or nieces. If a wolf sacrifices itself by breaking away from the pack when it's being pursued by hunters in order to attract attention to itself, saving the lives of a sufficient number of its brothers and sisters, nieces and nephews, who carry its genes and who can reproduce, then its sacrifice represents a clear benefit for the propagation of its own genes.

Since then, Hamilton's equation has been verified many times in nature, in more complex situations. It has been demonstrated that among a species of ground squirrel, the Belding spermophile, for instance, individuals that most often give the alarm at the approach of a predator—very risky behavior, since when the predator catches its prey, in half the cases, it's the unfortunate individual that gave the alarm—are those who have the greatest number of relatives in the immediate surroundings.[18]

In 1965, the great specialist in social insects Edward O. Wilson discovered Hamilton's work and contributed greatly to its diffusion in the scientific community. Hamilton's equation was verified in a spectacular way in eusocial insects like ants (which alone comprise half the biomass of all insects), certain bees, and other Hymenoptera.[19]

It follows from all this that a mutation predisposing behavior of the "evolutionary altruism" kind is favored by natural selection (and not penalized as previously thought) provided that the cost of the act borne by the "altruistic" individual is less than the corresponding gain for the propagation of his genes by his relatives.

The Odyssey of George Price

Before he was recognized as a brilliant innovator, William D. Hamilton was joined in his intellectual quest, which till then had been solitary, by a man named George Price.[20] Born in a poor family, son of an electrician and an opera singer, George Price studied chemistry, then at the age of twenty was recruited by the Manhattan Project, which was developing the atomic bomb. He worked for a time for IBM as an inventor, then emigrated to London. In a library, he came upon some articles by Hamilton. They intrigued him, and he wrote to Hamilton. Thus began a correspondence that led George Price, who initially was a novice in the field of evolution, to construct mathematical models to explain not only cooperation and altruistic behavior, but also intimidation, aggressiveness, and behavior that was generally harmful.

Finally, after some other exchanges with Hamilton, George Price formulated an equation, called the "covariance" equation, which accounted for various types of behavior, benevolent and malevolent, and for observations made in the animal world according to which altruistic behavior decreases when one goes from the immediate family to the group, and then changes into aggressiveness between individuals of different groups. Price showed too that, given adequate conditions, altruistic behavior could develop within a *group* of individuals.

As was the case for Hamilton, Price's ideas were at first ignored. The article he sent to the journal *Nature* was rejected and, even though they ended up accepting it, it was solely because Hamilton refused to publish his next article[21] until Price's was published, explaining that he was basing the developments of his new article on Price's equation. The article, called "Selection and Covariance,"[22] was therefore published, but no one paid any attention to it. Hamilton seemed to be the only person who understood its importance at the time. Years later, Price's contribution was recognized as one of the major breakthroughs of the twentieth century in evolution.

The Reciprocity of Beneficial Behavior

For over 98% of human history, our ancestors lived as hunter-gatherers,[23] in small cooperative tribes. The children were raised with the help of members of the extended family and, usually, of the tribe as a whole. Both sexes took part in the search for food, with men hunting and women gathering edible plants.[24] These societies were based on reciprocity and cooperation.

In 1971, Robert Trivers suggested that the creation of long-term relationships of exchange and mutual aid can facilitate reproduction and survival for each individual. Those who respect the law of reciprocity will derive long-term advantages from it that those who go it alone will not. According to his theory of "reciprocal altruism," it is therefore in the interest of individuals to help each other over the long term, even if they are not related. Although Trivers was not concerned with motivations and did not address the question of "psychological altruism," the theory of reciprocal altruism enlarges the circle of beneficial behavior, if one compares it to Hamilton's theory, which concerns only individuals genetically related. According to Trivers, reciprocal altruism is likely to have evolved among species with relatively long lifespans who are interdependent, know each other well enough to be able to distinguish a trustworthy individual and one apt to return the favor from some other individual who is only an unprincipled profiteer. Such species also have an egalitarian organization, and are collectively involved in the care of their young.[25]

The research carried out by Kim Hill on the Ache tribes in the mountains of Paraguay have shown that 10% of the time spent gathering food by men and women in fact helps members of the tribe not related to them, but who themselves helped others. It also appears that, more than the degree of relation, it's concern for fairness and taking into consideration the actual needs of each individual that govern the sharing of food. Such a reciprocity has even more meaning among the Ache since the provisioning of food is irregular and chancy. Reciprocal altruism thus comprises a form of insurance for periods when food is scarce. Here again, researchers focus on altruistic behavior, not on the motivation underlying such behavior.

Kim Hill and her colleagues also examined the social structures of groups of hunter-gatherers who still survive to this day throughout the world. Hill saw that because of the propensity of children of both sexes to leave the family home, most members of these communities are more often friends than relatives. The emergence of kindness to strangers thus seems to have appeared among humans not via the intermediary of genes (as one would expect if Hamilton's model were applied to humans, which, obviously, is not the case), but as the result of the gradual evolution of cultures.[26]

Selfish Genes?

In 1976, Richard Dawkins published a book that met with great success, *The Selfish Gene,* in which he explains that the most fundamental aspect of the process of evolution is not the survival of individuals, but that of genes.[27] Dawkins' main contribution was to show that

Darwinian selection and competition are not exercised at the level of species or even of individuals, but at the level of the fundamental replicators of heredity, which are the DNA molecules that make up genes. Dawkins expresses this idea unambiguously when he writes, "We are survival machines—robot vehicles blindly programmed to preserve the selfish molecules known as genes."[28]

Whereas Darwin saw the possibility for sympathies "to extend to the men of all nations and races," even "beyond the confines of man," that is, to animals, Dawkins leaves us with no illusions:

> *The argument of this book is that we, and all other animals, are machines created by our genes.... I shall argue that a predominant quality to be expected in a successful gene is ruthless selfishness. This gene selfishness will usually give rise to selfishness in individual behavior. However, as we shall see, there are special circumstances in which a gene can achieve its own selfish goals best by fostering a limited form of altruism at the level of individual animals.... Much as we might wish to believe otherwise, universal love and the welfare of the species as a whole are concepts that simply do not make evolutionary sense.*[29]

Dawkins is of course not opposed to the idea of creating a better world, but he thinks that we are not naturally predisposed to do so and that, to attain that objective, we have nothing working in our favor:

> *If there is a human moral to be drawn, it is that we must* teach *our children altruism, for we cannot expect it to be part of their biological nature.*[30]

As we will see in the chapter devoted to animals and childhood, that is not at all what emerges from research, for example the research of Felix Warneken and Michael Tomasello, in which they conclude: "Our claim is thus that the altruistic tendencies seen in early human ontogeny reflect a natural predisposition." The fact that not only humans, but also chimpanzees, help each other altruistically also indicates that "The phylogenetic roots of human altruism—at least in the form of instrumental helping—may reach as far back as to the last common ancestor of humans and chimpanzees some six million years ago."[31]

Although the stress Dawkins placed on the central role of genes in the evolutionary process does not lend itself to controversy, the use of psychological terms in his book to designate processes of an entirely different order is unfortunate. The very title of Dawkins' book—*The Selfish Gene*—no doubt contributed to its success: what would have become of the book if it had been called *On the Self-Perpetuation of Genes*? Still, according to the great ethologist Jane Goodall, this book became a bestseller "in part, I think, because for many people it provided an excuse for human selfishness and cruelty. It was just our genes. We couldn't help it...It was comforting perhaps to disclaim responsibility for our bad behavior."[32]

As Frans de Waal notes, "Genes can't be any more 'selfish' than a river can be 'angry,' or sun rays 'loving.' Genes are little chunks of DNA."[33] Even if Dawkins claims that he "is not interested in the psychology of motivations," by using a term like "selfishness," which inevitably evokes a motivation, he only aggravates the confusion that already reigned over the question of the nature of altruism.

This ambiguity did not fail to strike the imagination and to provide a justification for some of the most self-serving and selfish behavior of our time. Frans de Waal cites the case of the Enron company, which went bankrupt thanks to embezzlement: "The company's CEO, Jeff Skilling—now in prison—was a great fan of Richard Dawkins' *The Selfish Gene,* and deliberately tried to mimic nature by instigating cutthroat competition within his company."[34]

In fact, Skilling set up a system of internal evaluation among colleagues, who were ordered to evaluate each other. Then he fired anyone who got a weak score. Up to 20% of employees were turned away every year, after they had been humiliated on an Internet site where unflattering portraits of them were posted. To be able to survive in the world of Enron, you had to relentlessly attack/hound your colleagues!

A Return to Sources

Despite its remarkable consonance with many eusocial insects, Hamilton's theory fails spectacularly to explain human behavior, and, generally, any behavior characterized by a high level of cooperation independent of blood relationship. Humans are, in fact, capable of enlarging the circle of their altruism not only to include other non-related humans, but also to other non-human species, which is even less conceivable from the perspective of kin selection.

A science journalist for the British newspaper *The Guardian* wrote about the 180 Japanese workers in the Fukushima nuclear plant who continued working for months up to fifty hours in a row in order to cool down the damaged reactors, thus voluntarily exposing themselves to radiation levels that were seriously harmful to their health:

> *Although kin selection works well in the animal kingdom it seems an unlikely mechanism to account for human altruism and co-operation. A Japanese nuclear plant worker who wanted to benefit his genes would serve them better by buying train tickets to take himself and all his relatives far from Fukushima.*[35]

As for animals that take care of other species, like the tigress in the Calcutta zoo that suckled a litter of orphaned piglets instead of devouring them, Richard Dawkins declared in a televised documentary that this was a case of "a misfiring of selfish genes."

Not only are genes supposed to be "selfish," but in order to be faithful to them, we are supposed to behave solely in a selfish way. However, while still remaining in agreement with the Darwinian principles of evolution, extended altruism is fully explicable by taking into account the basic role of cooperation in evolution. That, in any case, is what emerges from recent discoveries in the field of evolution, which combine a considerable mass of observations about animal behavior with new mathematical models on the dynamic of populations.

E. O. Wilson was, as we have seen, one of the great promoters of the theory of kin selection. "I must say that I've had to concede that Hamilton—even though I think I knew more about social insects—beat me to it to produce the main idea, the most original, important idea, on social insects of this century,"[36] Wilson wrote in 1971. For forty years, this theory based on the importance of kinship has dominated evolutionist thinking. Today, having reached the summit of a long and distinguished career as a researcher, E. O. Wilson thinks he was mistaken: he is now convinced that it is generalized cooperation, compatible with classical Darwinian selection, that explains the emergence and success of social species, as the title of his most recent book attests: *The Social Conquest of Earth.*[37]

Other voices, those of eminent geneticists like Luca Cavalli-Sforza and Marcus Feldman, had, starting in the 1970s, drawn attention to the limitations of Hamilton's theory in explaining altruism.[38] His successors have tended to regard kin selection as being the universal principle of evolution, and have tried to make everything factor into this theory as well as they could, including altruistic cooperation. Over the years, Wilson also developed growing doubts about the validity of this theory. These doubts crystallized when he began collaborating with Martin Nowak, biologist, mathematician, and Director of the Program for Evolutionary Dynamics at Harvard. Wilson thought that Hamilton's theory was brilliant mathematically, but increasingly doubted its applications to the real world as practical observations, ever more numerous, came to contradict it. Nowak, on the contrary, was of the mind that Hamilton's theory was indeed verified in nature, but, from the mathematical point of view, he deemed it obscure and limited. Their meeting contributed to "a mutual liberation."[39]

Nowak and Corina Tarnita, a brilliant mathematician on the Harvard team, conceived of a more rigorous mathematical model, based on the classic Darwinian concept of natural selection, which encompasses kinship relationships, when they are involved, as well as the cooperative behavior involved in evolution. This model, based on the dynamics and genetics of populations, takes into account the variety of interactions that occur within a population, on both the individual and collective level.[40]

The necessity for this new formulation was twofold: to provide a theory that transcends the limitations of Hamilton's theory concerning "extended altruism," and to take into account the increasing number of exceptions to the theory of kin selection. Two wasp specialists, notably—James Hunt, at North Carolina State University, and Raghavendra Gadagkar, at the Indian Institute of Science in Bangalore—discovered that kin selection did not apply to the species they were studying.[41] Philip Johns and his collaborators also showed that after an antagonistic encounter between two non-related colonies of termites, the survivors of each colony cooperated successfully, forming a single colony.[42]

In particular, according to Wilson, the main factor that leads to the appearance of large animal societies (eusociality) is not fundamentally the link of kinship, but the building of "nests"—understood here in the wider sense of collective places for habitation and reproduction, an underground anthill, for instance—which can be defended and in which several generations of young are raised. When a female, the queen of an anthill, for instance, and her adult descendants remain in the nest to look after the next generations, a eusocial community can thus be established. The kinship links existing in such a community would thus not be the necessary cause (as Hamilton thought), but one of the consequences of the formation of this community. In brief, kinship links are useful, but not necessary, and we are now aware of many examples of eusocial colonies comprised of non-related individuals.[43]

The mathematical explanatory model by Nowak, Tarnita, and Wilson roused a storm of controversy in the field of evolutionists who, for several decades, have centered their vision of evolution on kin selection. An intense exchange of publications and arguments ensued in the scientific journal *Nature,* and the debate is still continuing today.[44] Still, this model brings new arguments to the idea of natural selection operating on multiple levels: that of individuals, that of groups of individuals, and that of cultures which influence the behavior of these groups.

The Notion of a "Group" from the Point of View of Evolution

Ever since Darwin, the idea that natural selection could favor or place at a disadvantage not only individuals, and more specifically their genes, but also the group of individuals which could be regarded as itself an entity, has met with varied reactions and continues to give rise to endless debate. Envisaged by Darwin, it was dismissed at the end of the 1960s,[45] brought back by Hamilton and Price in 1975 without much success, and finally reformulated with new arguments by David Sloan Wilson, Elliott Sober,[46] E. O. Wilson, and Martin Nowak.

Generally, a *group* is defined here as a collection of individuals constituted over a certain period of time during which they mutually influence their future (and their reproductive success).[47] Bees in a hive, for instance, have more influence over the fate of the other inhabitants of their own hive than on those of a neighboring hive. This group can have a varying duration of existence, from a few days to a whole lifetime. A dozen explorers preparing to leave in search of treasure in a jungle in Central America comprise such a group: they can all draw benefits from it and they will also all expose themselves to danger. The actions of each member will have repercussions on the fate of all the others.[48]

CAN ALTRUISM BE PROPAGATED?

Selective pressure occurs at all levels of the organization of life, from the cells of a multicellular organism to ecosystems, from individuals to groups. Group selection does not in any way oppose individual selection, but it goes beyond its limitations. Essentially, when *individuals* are all in competition with each other, those who cooperate the least and profit the most from the kindness of others succeed best, but when it is *groups* that enter into competition, the aptitude of groups to cooperate is a determining asset: strongly cooperative groups survive better than other groups.[49]

According to the mathematical models presented by David Wilson and Sober, groups that contain a majority of altruistic individuals prosper because of the advantages that cooperation and mutual aid bring to the group as a whole, despite the presence of a certain number of selfish individuals, or freeriders, that profit from the altruism of others. The members of this group will thus have more descendants, the majority of whom will exhibit altruistic behavior.

Groups containing a majority of selfish individuals do much less well, because the dominant attitude of "everyone for himself" harms the overall success of the community. In such a group, the minority altruists are less favored, and find themselves too isolated for their spirit of cooperation to influence the others. One on one, selfish individuals may have an advantage here over altruistic individuals, but their group stagnates as a whole, and will thus produce fewer descendants.

If this pattern is repeated from generation to generation, the proportion of individuals bearing the altruistic trait will increase. The lesson of this model, tested mathematically over a large number of generations, is encouraging: once the percentage of altruists in a population surpasses a certain threshold (which could be around 20% of the population), the altruistic characteristic is amplified over the course of generations.[50]

In collaboration with Sober and Wilson, Martin Nowak and Corina Tarnita have pinpointed the conditions that allow altruistic cooperation to prosper. It turns out, in fact, that human societies can be described in terms of collections of people who share certain interests, values, and activities. The more points you have in common with someone, the more you will interact with him, and the more your shared interests will encourage you to cooperate.

The eternal problem, in a community of cooperating individuals, is the presence of profiteers, whom economists call "freeriders," who profit from the kindness of cooperators in order to use them and get the best of the deal. When the majority of people trust each other and cooperate, freeriders can easily exploit others. And when their number increases too much, the community declines. Thus the rate of trust and cooperation will fluctuate over time.

Little by little, cooperators will tend to find each other and to work together, while groups where freeriders are predominant will decline with time. Fluctuations will still be repeated, however, since new freeriders will regularly introduce themselves into a group of prospering cooperators.[51]

By testing various mathematical models over hundreds of virtual generations, Nowak and his collaborators have shown that, aside from mobility, the success of cooperation depended in the end on the frequency with which cooperators associated with each other. If this frequency is higher than the frequency with which freeriders collude with other freeriders, altruistic cooperators will become the majority. In short, in order to progress toward a more altruistic society, it is essential that altruists associate with each other and join forces. In our time, this synergy between cooperators and altruists no longer requires them to be gathered together in the same geographical location, since contemporary means of communication, social networks in particular, allow the emergence of movements of cooperation joining together large numbers of people who are geographically scattered.

15

Maternal Love, Foundation for Extended Altruism?

Although the evolutionary origins of altruism have not yet been entirely elucidated, Daniel Batson believes that "they lie at least in part in the nurturant impulse of human parents to care for their young. This impulse has been strongly selected for within our evolutionary history; without it, our species would have vanished long ago. Perhaps because altruism based on nurturance is so thoroughly woven into the fabric of our lives, is so commonplace and so natural, its importance has failed to be recognized."[1] For Batson, among humans, it is more logical and empirically more easily verifiable to look for the genetic bases for altruism in a *cognitive generalization of feelings of tenderness, empathic concern, and nurturance which have emerged from the parental instinct,* which is deeply inscribed in our genes, than to attempt to prove that stems from Hamilton's kin selection, Trivers' reciprocal altruism, or a genetic tendency to socialization and formation of coalitions.[2]

The idea traces back to Darwin, for whom love of the other was based on parental and filial affection and linked to the emotion of sympathy.[3] Species of mammals that did not concern themselves with the well-being of their offspring would quickly disappear.[4] William McDougall, a social psychologist who was very influential in the early twentieth century, outlined a psychological approach based on Darwin's natural selection in which he stressed parental instinct, the "emotions of tenderness" associated with it, and, by extension, the concern we feel for all vulnerable beings who need protection. McDougall developed the idea that parental care, which he regarded as the most powerful of all instincts, is the basis for altruism extended to non-related individuals.[5]

Several contemporary researchers, including Elliott Sober, Frans de Waal, Paul Ekman, and, as we have cited above, Daniel Batson, have taken up this hypothesis and argued that, frequently, a quality selected over the course of evolution will be called on later to fulfill a different function. Thus, the tendency to be kind to our children and those close to us would not only have played a major role in the preservation of our species, but would also be at the origin of extended altruism.[6] As Paul Ekman notes:

> *Research has shown that when mothers hear their infants cry, there is a biological response, but not in females who have not yet been mothers. Mothers show a larger response to their own infants, but show response to others as well. Not only that, but when our parents grow old and become helpless, our concern, love, and care for them increase strongly, and they become like our children.*[7]

Among animals, we also find surprising cases of altruistic adoption among different species, like the female dog in Buenos Aires that became famous for having saved an abandoned human baby by placing him among her pups. Similarly, in a striking documentary, we see a leopard chase and kill a mother baboon. Before dying, the baboon gives birth.[8] At the sight of the newborn, the stunned leopard hesitates for a second, then changes its attitude: he treats the little baboon gently and, when other predators approach, takes him delicately in his jaws and places him safely on a tree branch. The baby baboon, frightened at first, tries to climb higher, is caught by the leopard, and then, exhausted, lies motionless between the paws of the leopard, which begins to lick and groom him. The two fall asleep leaning against each other. It's finally the cold of night that takes the life of the baby baboon.

"Mothers" in Large Numbers

Human procreation is distinguished from that of the great apes in several ways. Until a period considered very recent from the viewpoint of evolution, women had children at frequent intervals, and these children, more vulnerable at birth, depended for a longer time on their mothers for survival. It is thought that among hunter-gatherers, women had an average of one child every four years. A female chimpanzee has a baby only every six years, an orangutan every eight years. A young chimpanzee is almost entirely autonomous by the age of six; it takes years for a human child to develop its independence. The combination of these two factors—more frequent procreation and a longer period of dependence in offspring—implies that human mothers have more need of help to raise their children. The appearance among hominids of parental care in which many individuals take part could go back to as far as 1.8 million years ago.[9]

Sarah Blaffer Hrdy devoted her career to studying this question, and the sum of her own studies and those of a number of other anthropologists and ethologists led her to formulate this theory:

> *I hypothesize that novel rearing conditions among a line of early hominids meant that youngsters grew up depending on a wider range of caretakers than just their mothers, and this dependence produced selection pressure that favored individuals who were better at decoding the mental states of others, and figuring out who would help and who would hurt.*[10]

In other words, the fact that newborns interact quickly with a large number of people may have contributed considerably to raising the degree of cooperation and empathy among humans. Aside from affective empathy, adds Michael Tomasello, psychologist at the Max Planck Institute in Leipzig, one of the main capacities acquired by humans more than animals is to feel more concerned about what others think, and to factor that constantly into their own behavior.

Among the Hadza in Africa, a newborn is handled by eighteen people in the first twenty-four hours of its birth.[11] It has been demonstrated that "alloparents" (secondary parents) play a crucial role in the child's cognitive development, including empathy and autonomy. During its first year, the mother remains the main person taking care of the child, but the child is very often looked after by grandmothers, great-aunts, brothers and sisters, fathers, and even visitors. Breastfeeding by other women besides the mother was practiced in 87% of hunter-gatherers, and still to this day in a number of rural societies, as I have observed in Tibet and Nepal.[12]

During the first months after birth, a mother chimpanzee lets hardly anyone touch her child, except, according to Jane Goodall, for elder siblings whom she sometimes allows to groom her small infant. By four months, small chimps play gently with siblings and others.[13]

This situation has consequences for social communications and for the development of empathy: a young chimpanzee has a relationship almost entirely with its mother, and, what's more, it doesn't have to worry about her eventual absence or to check if she is nearby, since it is constantly carried by her. In contrast, a human newborn is in visual, auditory, and emotional contact (via facial expressions it recognizes and can copy from birth) not only with its mother, but also with its father and a large number of other people who all speak to it, gesture at it, exchange looks with it, take it in their arms, etc.

A study carried out between 1950 and 1980 by the United Kingdom Medical Research Council followed the growth rate of children in Mandinka horticulturist tribes in Gambia. Out of over 2,000 children, almost 40% of those raised solely by their two parents died before the age of five. But for a child whose siblings—sisters, especially—and maternal grandmother lived in the immediate neighborhood, the probability of dying before the age of five fell from 40% to 20%.[14] In particular, the proximity of a grandmother from birth influences strongly the child's state of health and cognitive abilities three years later.[15] For Hrdy, without the help of "alloparents," there would never have been a human species. The notion of "family" as limited to a couple and their children developed only in the twentieth century in Europe, and as late as the 1950s in the United States.[16] Before that, most families included members of three generations, often comprising uncles and aunts, cousins, etc.

In the 1930s, especially in the United States, mothers followed the theories of Dr. John Watson—as famous as they were harmful—who recommended they take their newborns in their arms as little as possible and let them cry as long as they liked, in order to make them strong and independent. Mothers, he said, should be ashamed of the "mawkish, sentimental" way they have been handling their offspring.[17] Studies of Romanian and Chinese orphans, however, have testified to the catastrophic effects of privation of physical contact and emotional interactions on the physiological and intellectual development of young children.

What About Fathers in All This?

Among the great apes, the young sometimes play with adult males, but a male gorilla, for example, never carries or takes care of an infant. There are, however, a few exceptions to this rule in other primates; among titi monkeys, for instance, the father is constantly on duty, taking care of the baby. The mother takes her child only to feed it and sleep with it. Baby titis spend most of their time on the backs of their fathers, and show more sadness when they're separated from him than from their mother.[18] There are also cases of male chimpanzees adopting a young orphan, carrying it on their backs, and taking good care of it.[19]

In general, human fathers concern themselves much less with their offspring than mothers, but there are exceptions. Among the Aka in Africa, for example, fathers look after newborns at least half the time, by day and by night. Today, in Bangladesh, in the Bedia community, or among water-dwelling gypsies living in the delta of the Sunderbans, it's mainly the fathers who stay on the boat and look after the children during the day, while the women travel the countryside to sell trinkets.[20] On average, fathers in hunter-gatherer societies spend much more time with their children than fathers in modern Western societies.[21]

Does the Faculty of Empathy Risk Diminishing Among Humans?

Specialists in evolution know that suppressing a selection factor can lead to swift evolutionary consequences. Sarah Hrdy foresees a possible atrophy of empathy, if children no longer benefit from the rich interactions associated with collaborative care. From her point of view, if empathy and the faculties of understanding others developed thanks to particular ways of taking care of children, and if an increasing proportion of humans no longer benefited from these conditions, compassion and the search for emotional connections would disappear. She questions whether such people "will be human in ways that we now think of as distinguishing our species—that is, empathic and curious about the emotions of others, shaped by our ancient heritage of communal care."[22]

One of the challenges, and sometimes tragedies, for women today is that they often have to cope alone with a task that the evolution of hominids had made communal, and for which a plethora of well-meaning people had provided in traditional societies. Daycare centers can offer a substitute to traditional communal rearing, with studies showing that good-quality daycare centers had a very positive effect on the development of children's cognitive and emotional faculties.[23] While some people recommend that women become less maternal,[24] what we should do, according to Sarah Hrdy, is revive the parental instinct among all members of society so as to foster our tendency to care for each other.

16

The Evolution of Cultures

Teaching, Accumulating, Imitating, Evolving

The notion of culture is complex, and has been defined in a number of different ways.[1] Specialists in evolution think of it as a collection of information that affects the behavior of individuals belonging to a particular culture. This information, which includes ideas, knowledge, beliefs, values, abilities, and attitudes, is acquired through teaching, imitation, and every other kind of social transmission.[2]

Cultural evolution is evident in the development of both moral values—certain values, more inspiring than others, will be more apt to be transmitted from one individual to another—and beliefs in general, insofar as certain beliefs give people greater chances of surviving or attaining a high social position.

Teaching—the voluntary, organized transmission of knowledge—is essentially an altruistic behavior that, in its non-professional iterations, consists of offering others useful information without expectation of reward. Animals teach certain kinds of expertise to their offspring—hunting, for instance—but the voluntary transmission of knowledge to non-related individuals is a specifically human phenomenon.[3]

It is important to point out that human transmission and cultural evolution are cumulative. Each generation has at its start knowledge and technological experience acquired by previous generations. Tools and behavior have a history. They become more and more complex as successive generations improve their quality and enrich their repertory.[4]

Another factor contributes considerably to the evolution of cultures: the instinct of imitation. Most human beings are inclined to conform to dominant attitudes, customs, and beliefs. Conformity to the norm will be encouraged by the community, whereas nonconformity will lead to reprobation and various forms of punishment, not very costly to the party inflicting them and sometimes disastrous to the party subjected to them. These penalties can affect an individual's reputation and even lead to his exclusion from the community.

The evolution of cultures favors the establishment of social institutions that define and supervise respect for the behavioral norms, in order to ensure the harmony of communal life. Still, these norms are not fixed: like cultures, they evolve with the acquisition of new knowledge. Different cultural groups compete with each other on the Darwinian model. Consequently, certain cultures flourish while others decline. As Robert Boyd and Peter Richerson explain:

> *In the same way that evolutionary theory explains why genes persist and spread, a sensible theory of cultural evolution will have to explain why some beliefs and attitudes spread and persist while others disappear.*[5]

Faster Than Genes

The study of the evolution of cultures is a new discipline that has led to remarkable advances over the last thirty years, particularly under the impetus of two American researchers, Robert Boyd and Peter Richerson. According to them, a twofold evolution occurs in parallel: the very slow evolution of genes, and the quicker one of cultures, which allows psychological faculties to appear which could never have evolved under the influence of genes alone. Hence the title of their book, *Not by Genes Alone*.[6]

The advent of complex societies and of civilization over the last five thousand years has actually occurred too quickly to be the result of genetic changes. But it has also occurred too slowly to be explained solely in terms of purely individual adaptation to new situations, such as war or peace, being single or married, rich or poor, which can happen in the space of a few years. Culture, on the other hand, has a rhythm of evolution that allows us to explain the growth of social complexity over the last five millennia.

Cultures and individuals shape each other mutually, just as two knife blades sharpen each other. Individuals who grow up in a new culture are different, because they acquire new habits and these habits transform their brains through neuroplasticity and the expression of their genes through epigenetics. These individuals will contribute to making their culture evolve more, and so on.

According to Boyd and Richerson, it is this cultural evolution that has allowed for the major transformations that have occurred in human societies since the appearance of our species. For example, over the last three centuries, our cultural perception of violence, wars in particular, has evolved considerably. We have gone from regarding torture as an entirely acceptable public spectacle and war as noble and glorious, to tolerating violence less and less, and increasingly regarding war as immoral and barbaric. We are progressing toward a culture of peace and respect for human rights.

Anxious Shepherds and Peaceful Farmers

Let's look at a typical example of cultural transmission. We know that murders are more frequent in the southern United States than in the northern part of the country. Sociologists who have studied this phenomenon noted that people in the South were more polite, but also more quick to react to an insult or a provocation and more attached to the Second Amendment of the Constitution, which authorizes citizens to bear arms. Southerners assign more importance to a sense of honor, and are inclined to carry out justice themselves when codes of honor are transgressed. Culture is also inscribed in their physiology: reactions to an insult, measured by the level of cortisol (a stress indicator) and testosterone (an indicator of propensity to violence), are stronger among Southerners than among Northerners.

When studying the various origins of American populations, the researchers perceived that Southerners were mostly descended from Scottish and Irish shepherds who, in their native countries, lived in sparsely populated regions. Like any shepherd, they had to supervise their herds constantly and protect the pastures from intruders. This mode of life engendered a culture more inclined to violence, in which one's word, tacit conventions (the vast, wild pasture land did not legally belong to the shepherds), swift response to provocations, and codes of honor had great importance. On the other hand, the northern part of the United States was colonized by farmers from England, Holland, and Germany, whose cultural codes are more peaceful. A farmer does not live in constant fear of someone stealing his field from him overnight.

CULTURAL DIFFERENCES ARE NOT GENETIC

All research indicates that the cultural differences present in the world are not genetic by nature. A study of a hundred Korean children adopted early on by white American families has shown that these children behave like American children, and exhibit no cultural traits reminiscent of their Korean origins. What's more, these children generally show little curiosity about their culture of origin.[7] Another study of children of European origin adopted by Native Americans after their parents were killed also showed that these children reliably adopted the behaviors and customs of the Native Americans, as well as the feeling of belonging to them.[8]

The difference in levels of violence between American Southerners and Northerners mentioned above must therefore obviously be imputed to the special systems of values and norms transmitted from generation to generation by education and example, and not to a genetic mutation.

THE MECHANISMS OF THE EVOLUTION OF CULTURES

Cultural values are often inspired by those who teach us and by prominent people in a population: charismatic leaders, scholars, celebrities. It turns out that it is the less learned and least powerful people who are the most easily swayed to conform to dominant values.

It's also worth noting the fact that cultural ideas and values are not transmitted intact, but usually undergo alterations: the transmission can be partial, and can include errors or be distorted. In some cases, this transmission can also be reliable and faithful—as in a class on grammar, physics, or math, for instance. Everything depends on the degree of intrinsic and objective invariance of the subject taught.

We have seen that cultural transmission is cumulative. Knowledge is added to other knowledge with each generation. That is the only reason why the modern world enjoys such an advance in the realm of technology. If each generation had to reinvent the way to make fire, extract metals, and produce electricity, Apple and BlackBerry would refer to nothing but a couple of fruits.

Cultures evolve more rapidly when a large amount of new information becomes available. If there is little new knowledge or if the environment is very stable, cultures have few reasons to change. On the other hand, though, if the environment is too unstable, cultures don't have the time to adapt to the constant, swift fluctuations.[9] In changing, complex conditions, it will usually be more advantageous to conform to the dominant customs of the group. For cooperation or any other value, altruism for instance, to spread through a group of individuals, they must all grant importance to the objectives of the group and be disposed to cooperate, even at a personal cost. Researchers have also shown the importance of the strength of example and the spirit of emulation that is born from observing and acting together with others.

Finally, for a process of selection to be able to operate between different cultural values, individualism or a cooperative spirit for example, these differences must have effects on the prosperity or decline of those who hold those values.

Toward a More Altruistic Culture

Knowing that emulation, inspiration, and the power of living examples—the noble aspects of conformism—are both the framework that ensures the stability and continuity of cultures, and the motivating force behind their transformation and expansion, it falls upon us to embody, in our being and our behavior, the altruism we want to encourage: the messenger must be the message.

We have seen that altruism, cooperation, and mutual aid are much more present in daily life than prevailing media and prejudices suggest. Over the last fifty years, we have seen aversion to war develop, and have witnessed the spread of the view that the earth is nothing but a "big village." The growing role of NGOs, the fact that many citizens are concerned with what is happening elsewhere in the world, especially when assistance is needed—all that indicates a change of mentalities, hence of our cultures, to be more concerned with a feeling of "global responsibility," to use an expression dear to the Dalai Lama. This evolution is underway. Perhaps it is enough to take part in it, by adding our stone to the building, our drop to the ocean. But we can also decide to actively facilitate it and amplify it, like a catalyst accelerating a chemical reaction.

17

Altruistic Behavior Among Animals

Capt. Stansbury found on a salt lake in Utah an old and completely blind pelican, which was very fat, and must have been well fed for a long time by his companions.... Mr. Blyth, as he informs me, saw Indian crows feeding two or three of their companions which were blind; and I have heard of an analogous case with the domestic cock. I have myself seen a dog, who never passed a cat who lay sick in a basket, and was a great friend of his, without giving her a few licks with his tongue, the surest sign of kind feeling in a dog.... Besides love and sympathy, animals exhibit other qualities connected with the social instincts, which in us would be called moral."[1]

Thus wrote Charles Darwin in the nineteenth century. If we observe that a hundred and fifty years earlier, Descartes and Malebranche declared confidently that animals were nothing more than "unconscious automatons, possessing neither thought, nor sensitivity, nor mental life of any kind," we can see how far we had come by Darwin's time.

Since then, studies have emerged that shed light on the wealth of animals' mental lives. As Jane Goodall, Frans de Waal, and many other ethologists have observed, the basic signals we use to express pain, fear, anger, love, joy, surprise, impatience, boredom, sexual excitement, and many other mental and emotional states are not unique to our species. Darwin devoted an entire treatise to this subject, entitled *The Expression of the Emotions in Man and Animals.*[2]

If you think about it, this shouldn't be very surprising. If intelligence, empathy, and altruism exist in humans, how could they have appeared out of nowhere? If they represent the result of millions of years of gradual evolution, one would expect to observe in animals the forerunners of all the human emotions. That was Darwin's outlook when he wrote in *The Descent of Man, and Selection in Relation to Sex:*[3]

> *With respect to animals very low in the scale, I shall give some additional facts, showing that their mental powers are much higher than might have been expected.*

An overall view of the evolution of the species allows us to understand better that evolutionary trees reflect the building up of increased levels of complexity.

WITHOUT DENYING VIOLENCE

Our intention in this chapter is to explore empathy and altruistic behavior among animals. Now, this does not entail denying the omnipresence of violence in the animal kingdom. Here, by violence, we mean all hostile and aggressive behaviors and attitudes, including the act of wounding or killing another individual and using force to exercise a constraint, to obtain something against the other's will. Most species we are going to discuss are capable of extremely violent behavior. The "chimpanzee war" that Jane Goodall observed in the Gombe Stream National Park in Tanzania, has caused a lot of ink to flow on mankind's possible warlike origins, a subject to which we will return. Jane Goodall and her collaborators were stunned to see chimpanzees killing one of their former group members, who had joined a new group that split apart from their group but was living in a shared part of the territory. We should note that they were observing this behavior for the first time, though they had been closely following the life of these chimpanzees for years. Other researchers also observed this phenomenon, the elimination of a competing group, but these cases remain relatively rare. Infanticide is also occasionally committed by males on infants of females from other communities.

We should note, too, that violence—both among animals and human beings—always attracts our attention more than peaceful behavior does. No scientific data, however, allows us yet to conclude that violence is an internal, dominant impulse among men and animals.

After forty years devoted to studying animal behavior, mainly among the great apes, one of the preeminent primatologists of our time, Frans de Waal, thinks that the focal point of his research is no longer to *prove* the existence of empathy among animals, but to study *how* it is expressed. Yet the existence of animal empathy has long been misunderstood. Frans tells about hearing a renowned psychologist[4] state that animals cooperated occasionally, but unfailingly gave priority to their own survival. And as if to prove once and for all the correctness of his point of view, he concluded: "An ape will never jump into a lake to save another."

Hearing this statement, Frans de Waal began searching through his memory and remembered Washoe, a female chimpanzee who, upon hearing cries of distress from a female friend, raced across two electric wires to reach her companion, who was struggling desperately in a moat. Wading in the slippery mud at the edge, Washoe managed to grasp her friend's outstretched hand and pull her to dry land. This is no minor feat, for chimpanzees do not know how to swim and are overcome with panic as soon as water reaches their knees. Fear of water can only be overcome by a powerful motivation; explanations involving self-interested calculations like "if I help her now, she'll help me later" don't work any better in this case than they do in the one mentioned earlier of Wesley Autrey jumping onto the tracks in the New York subway to save a passenger fallen in front of an approaching train. Only a spontaneous altruistic impulse can incite someone to abandon all caution. On other occasions, chimpanzees have been observed drowning while trying to help their young who had fallen in the water.

Among primates, examples of mutual aid abound. Chimpanzees taking care of companions wounded by leopards have been observed. They licked the blood from their wounds, delicately removed dirt from them, and chased away the flies buzzing around them. They then continued to watch over the wounded and, when they moved, they walked more slowly to keep pace with their weakened companions.[5]

At the Wisconsin National Primate Research Center, a small female rhesus macaque was suffering from such serious motor impediments that she could barely complete the ordinary functions of everyday life like walking, climbing, and eating. Far from rejecting her, the members of her family and the group took special care of her, grooming her, in fact, twice as much as the other females of the same age.[6] It should be noted that mutual grooming is one of the main forms of care and social interaction among primates. Such acts of caring for their sick or handicapped fellows are frequent among the great apes.

Animals associate with each other in various, more or less complex, ways, from simple gregariousness—the fact of being attracted by the company of their fellows—to stages of complex social organization where adults cooperate in taking care of the young, feeding them, and protecting them. As the complexity and diversity of interactions increase, it becomes useful to animals to take into account the behavior of their fellows with as much exactitude as possible. This tendency culminates with the ability to perceive the intentions of the other and to imagine what the other is thinking and feeling. That is how empathy is born.

BENEVOLENT BEHAVIOR

Before we question the "theory of mind"—the ability, mentally, to take the place of the other in order to understand the other's intentions or needs—let's first consider a series of animal behaviors that illustrate their aptitude for empathy.

Benevolent behavior can take various forms: coming to the aid of one's fellows; protecting them; rescuing them from danger; showing them sympathy and friendship, even gratitude; consoling them when they're suffering; forging ties of friendship with them not connected to reproduction or kinship; and, finally, showing signs of mourning at the death of one of their fellows.

MUTUAL AID

A number of observations show that animals are capable of spontaneously helping a fellow who is in danger, or who has specific needs he is incapable of addressing alone. Here are a few examples.

On a highway in Chile, in the middle of traffic, a dog is wandering, obviously disoriented, avoiding the passing cars as best he can. Soon, he is hit by one of them. The security cameras recording the scene show it lying on the road. Suddenly a yellow dog appears in the midst of the traffic, grips his hindquarters with its teeth, and, at the cost of great effort and after two attempts, drags his unconscious fellow to the side of the highway. Both miraculously escape the vehicles that are trying to avoid them.[7]

On a lighter note, I heard on the BBC the testimony of a kennel guard who was completely surprised one morning when he saw that three dogs had gotten out of their cages and had amply refreshed themselves in the kitchens. After that, he made sure the cages were closed, but the same scenario occurred again the next night. Intrigued, he hid in a corner of the kennel to see what was happening. Soon after the employees had left, he saw one of the dogs open the outer latch of his cage by passing his paw through the bars, which already was an impressive feat. But—surprise—instead of rushing to the kitchens, the animal first went to open the cages of two other dogs who were his friends, and only then did he and his eager companions head for the food.

Several qualities of this dog deserve to be noted: the ingenuity he showed to get out of his cage; his sense of friendship; and his ability to delay a gratification he had been waiting for all day (an expedition to the kitchens!) just in order to let other dogs consume a large part of what he could have eaten by himself.

Iain Douglas-Hamilton, who has studied elephants in the Masai Mara National Reserve in Kenya for forty years, one day saw an elephant whose trunk had been partly severed in a trap. The elephant was very agitated and couldn't feed himself. Iain then saw another elephant approach him. After touching the wound several times with his trunk, the newcomer carried reeds he had torn up from the river's edge and brought them directly to the wounded elephant's mouth. Finally, the wounded elephant was again able to feed himself, but only with these reeds that were tender enough for him to gather his stump. The most extraordinary thing is that the entire herd, so as not to abandon their injured fellow, settled near the reeds, which comprised the main source of its nourishment. This observation reveals not only a group solidarity, but also an intelligence about the specific needs of the other.

FRIENDSHIP

Primates have shown they are capable of forming lasting friendships. Frans de Waal cites the case of two female macaques, not related, who always stayed together and constantly exhibited affection for each other, kissed each other's babies warmly, and lent a helping hand in conflicts, to the point that one of them (who had a lower rank in the hierarchy) cried out to her friend in warning every time another monkey approached with a threatening attitude.[8]

Lucy was a female chimpanzee raised by humans, and for company, she was given a kitten. The first meeting was not a success. Lucy, obviously annoyed, pushed the kitten over and even tried to bite her. The second meeting wasn't much better but, during the third meeting, Lucy kept her calm. The kitten then began to follow her everywhere and, after half an hour, the female chimpanzee, forgetting her earlier reservations, took the kitten in her hands, kissed it, and completely changed her attitude. Very quickly, the two became inseparable. Lucy groomed the cat, rocked her in her arms, made her a little nest, and protected her from humans. The kitten was not inclined to climb up Lucy's flanks, as young chimpanzees do, but readily jumped onto her back and stayed there while Lucy moved. Or else Lucy would carry her in the palm of her hand. Lucy, who communicated with researchers with the help of sign language and had a relatively rich vocabulary, even gave the kitten the pet name "All Ball."[9]

The Joy of Reunion, the Sadness of Separation

In a zoo, two adult male chimpanzees who had lived in the same group, and then had lived apart for a long time, were reunited one day. The people in charge were afraid they'd fight, but the two great apes fell into each other's arms and exchanged kisses with great emotion, slapping each other on the back like old friends. They then spent a long time grooming each other.[10]

Reunions between two groups of elephant friends who haven't seen each other for a long time also give rise to exhibitions of exuberance. Cynthia Moss recounts the reunion of two herds that had spotted each other from afar (aside from trumpeting, elephants also communicate over long distances using very low frequency sounds, inaudible to the human ear). They began trumpeting as soon as they were half a kilometer away from each other, guiding each other by these calls and showing signs of cheerfulness. When they were finally within sight of each other, they began running and trumpeting loudly. The two matriarchs went straight for each other, crossing tusks, entwining their trunks, flapping their ears and rubbing against each other. All the other elephants followed suit.[11]

There have also been many cases of animal friends who, after living together for a long time, lose all interest in their usual occupations when one of their companions dies, and then let themselves die of malnutrition. J.Y. Henderson, who was a veterinarian in a circus for years, recounts the example of two horses who had long shared the same stable.[12] When one of them died, the other began moaning constantly. He barely slept or ate. They tried to put him with other horses, give him special care, and improve his diet. All to no avail; he died within two months, and the veterinarian couldn't diagnose any specific physical illness.

One also knows of a friendship between a goat and a donkey who had lived together for ten years rather neglected by their owner. When they were rescued and sent to different animal sanctuaries, the goat refused to eat for six consecutive days, lying in his stall, visibly depressed. When the new caretakers figured out that was due to his being separated from his best friend, one of them drove fourteen hours to get the donkey. As soon as he heard the donkey, the goat jumped to his feet, his behavior completely changed, and he began eating again, barely twenty minutes after his friend's arrival.[13]

The Targeted Empathy of the Great Apes

In *The Age of Empathy*, de Waal reports a number of cases of empathy among the great apes, which reveal a precise understanding of the needs of the other, along with the appropriate reactions:

> *At our primate center, we have an old female, Peony, who spends her days with other chimpanzees in a large outdoor enclosure. On bad days, when her arthritis is flaring up, she has great trouble walking and climbing. But other females help her out. For example, Peony is huffing and puffing to get up into the climbing frame in which several apes have gathered for a grooming session. An unrelated younger female moves behind her, places both hands on her ample behind, and pushes her up with quite a bit of effort, until Peony has joined the rest.*[14]

Removing someone from imminent danger is another way of protecting them. For that, one needs to anticipate and understand that the other is in danger but is not aware of that danger, and that one must intervene before it's too late.

Jane Goodall recalls observing in the Gombe National Park in Tanzania a young, nine-year-old female named Pom give an alarm call at the sight of a large snake and rush up a tree. Prof, aged three, who was following, did not hear or did not understand the alarm call and continued along the trail. As Prof was getting closer and closer to the snake, Pom's grimace of fear widened, till she rushed down to gather Prof and climbed back up the tree, bringing him to safety.[15] "Even more amazing," says Jane Goodall, "was when Gremlin, aged about the same as Pom, 'rescued' her little brother from ticks. The little brother was following his mother through a patch of tall grass, and Gremlin was following him. Suddenly she grabbed him and pulled him away—he screamed and tried to follow their mother—but she would not let go and pulled him around the grass. I went to look—and hundreds of ticks must have just hatched and were clinging to the grass stems. Later the mother sat and removed ticks!"[16]

Chimpanzees raised by humans are capable of showing empathic behavior well adapted to situations. In the former USSR, isolated from the rest of the scientific world, the Russian ethologist Nadia Kohts studied the behavior of a young chimpanzee, Yoni, for years, whom she had raised with love along with her own son. The following passage, written by Kohts and quoted by de Waal, illustrates the concern shown by Yoni for his adoptive mother:

> *If I pretend to be crying, close my eyes and weep, Yoni immediately stops his play or any other activities, quickly runs over to me, all excited and shagged, from the most remote places in the house, such as the roof or the ceiling of his cage, from where I could not drive him down despite my persistent calls and entreaties. He hastily runs around me, as if looking for the offender; looking at my face, he tenderly takes my chin in his palm, lightly touches my face with his finger, as though trying to understand what is happening, and turns around, clenching his toes into firm fists... The more sorrowful and disconsolate my crying, the warmer his sympathy.*[17]

GRATITUDE

Toward those who have taken care of them, primates often convey gratitude by mutual delousing but also by clearly showing their joy. One evening a pioneer in primatology, Wolfgang Köhler, saw that two chimpanzees had been forgotten outside under a driving rain. He hurried to their rescue, managed to open the locked door of their shelter, and stood aside to let them regain their warm, dry beds as quickly as possible. But, even though the rain continued to stream over the bodies of the chimpanzees chilled to the bone, and even as they continued to show their unhappiness and impatience, before retreating to the comfort of their shelter, they turned to Köhler and embraced him, one around his chest and the other around his legs. It was only after thus exuberantly showing their appreciation that they moved to the welcoming straw of the shelter.[18] A recent video also shows how a chimpanzee who has been brought back to health from the verge of death hugs the legendary ethologist Jane Goodall for a long time, before heading to the jungle, as she was being released into the wild.[19]

MULTIPLE FACETS OF THE EMPATHY OF ELEPHANTS

In the ecosystem of Amboseli, in southern Kenya, Cynthia Moss and her collaborators have, for thirty-five years, studied the behavior of about two thousand elephants, each of whom is identified and bears a name. The elephants have a very rich social life and possess complex auditory, olfactory, and visual systems of communication. Among those who live in the African savannahs, the females remain in the same herd all their lives, and the mothers often take care of the young of other females, which is an important factor in survival.[20] Among the mass of observations recorded over the years, the researchers have isolated over 250 significant examples of empathic reaction to a companion's distress.[21] Among these reactions are behaviors as diverse as coming to face danger together, protecting others, comforting them, helping them move, taking care of the children of other mothers, or extracting foreign objects from a companion's body.

Adult elephants often coordinate their forces when a threat presents itself in the form of a predator or a hostile elephant. When a wounded young animal or adult is in danger, another elephant usually comes to protect him. Most often, it is mothers who protect their young, by preventing them from approaching a treacherous spot, like the steep edge of a swamp, or by standing between two young elephants who are fighting, but mother friends can also intervene. When a mother has to be separated from her offspring for a few hours, the assistant mothers take over.

When an elephant has gotten stuck or has fallen and is unable to get up, often other elephants try to pull him up with their trunks, push him with their legs, or lift him with their tusks.

When a veterinarian's tranquilizer dart, or sometimes a spear, becomes stuck in an elephant's body, other elephants frequently touch the wounded spot, and sometimes manage to extract the foreign object. A mother has also been observed removing a plastic bag from her child's mouth and throwing it far away.

ALTRUISTIC BEHAVIOR AMONG DOLPHINS AND OTHER CETACEANS

Dolphins, as countless observations recorded by the ethologists Melba and David Caldwell testify, are capable of offering the same kind of targeted aid as humans, great apes and elephants.[22]

John Lilly reports the example of a young dolphin off the coast of the Antilles who had wandered away from its group. He was attacked by three sharks and uttered distress cries. Immediately, the adults in the pod who, until then, had been conversing with each other, fell silent and swam quickly toward the young dolphin in danger. Having reached the spot like torpedoes, they crashed full-speed (60 kilometers per hour) into the sharks, who were stunned and driven to escape into the depths of the sea. During this time, the females took care of the young wounded dolphin, who could no longer surface in order to breathe. Two of the females lifted him by swimming beneath him, until its head emerged from the water. From time to time, other females took over so the first pair could breathe too.[23]

In some cases, it was observed that such rescue operations could last up to two weeks, until the handicapped dolphin recovered, or else until he died. During all this time, the rescuers stopped eating, and surfaced only long enough to breathe.[24]

There are also accounts of cetaceans coming to the rescue of people. In Harbin, China, in the Polar Land theme park, the swimmer Yang Yun was participating in a free-diving competition without breathing equipment, in a twenty-three-foot-deep pool kept at temperatures near freezing for the beluga whales it contained. The swimmer was overcome with such powerful cramps in her legs that she began to sink and thought she would die. A beluga named Mila delicately took one of her legs in his mouth and brought her back to the surface, while another beluga pushed her from below with his back.[25]

In New Zealand, four swimmers were suddenly surrounded by a band of dolphins that were swimming around them in ever tighter circles, like a sheepdog herding its sheep. When one of the swimmers tried to break away, two dolphins forced him to rejoin the group. Soon after, one of the swimmers saw a great white shark pass by and realized that the dolphins had been preventing them from swimming into harm's way. The dolphins didn't let their charges go until forty minutes later.[26]

As for whales, they almost always come to the aid of a fellow whale attacked by whalers. They come between the whaler and their wounded companion, and sometimes capsize the whaling boat. Whalers often exploit this behavior. If they manage to get hold of a live baby, they know all the adults will gather around him. Then they kill the lot.[27]

Mutual aid behavior has also been observed among walruses, who create powerful social bonds, share their food, take care of the young of others, and come to the rescue of another when it is attacked.[28] For example, walruses wounded on land by a hunter's bullets are, whenever possible, dragged by others to the water's edge, and, if they have trouble swimming, other walruses carry them on their backs to keep their heads above water so they can breathe.[29]

Mutual Aid Among Animals of Different Species

Mutual aid among individuals of different species is rarer, but not unheard of. Researchers regard it as an extension of the maternal instinct and the instinct of protection.

In his memoirs, the ethologist Ralph Helfer reports a scene he witnessed in East Africa. During the rainy season, a mother rhinoceros and her baby had reached a clearing near a salt lick, when the little one got stuck in thick mud. He called for his mother, who approached, sniffed him, and then, not knowing what to do, returned to the shelter of the trees. The little one continued to emit distress calls and the mother approached again but seemed powerless. A herd of elephants arrived, also interested in the salt lick. The mother rhinoceros, fearing for her offspring, charged the elephants, who moved away and returned to the forest. A few moments later, a large elephant came back, approached the baby rhinoceros, smelled him with its trunk, knelt down, and slipped its tusks beneath him to lift him. The mother immediately rushed forward and charged the elephant, who moved away. This sequence was repeated for several hours. Each time the mother rhinoceros went back to the forest, the elephant returned to try to pull the little one out of the mud, then would give up when the mother charged. The herd of elephants ended up leaving. The next morning, Helfer and a forest ranger approached to try to free the young rhinoceros. He became frightened and in his efforts to flee managed to extract himself from the mud, and finally joined his mother, who was approaching, alerted again by his cries.[30]

Consolation

Consoling behavior has been observed among the great apes and the Canidae (dogs and wolves), but also among members of the crow family. Teresa Romero and her colleagues have recorded over 3,000 cases among chimpanzees.[31] It emerges from their study that this behavior is more frequent among individuals who are socially close, and is more usually observed among females than males (with the exception, however, of dominant males, who are generous with acts of consolation, which helps reinforce the social cohesion of the group).

Generally, a chimpanzee will come to console the loser in an altercation that didn't result in reconciliation. On the other hand, when the protagonists have reconciled after a fight,[32] this behavior is rare, which shows that the consoler is capable of evaluating the other's needs. Consolation is expressed in various ways: the victim is offered a grooming session; he is held, touched gently, or kissed. The consolation is reciprocal: those who do the consoling will often be consoled when their turn comes to lose a dispute.

The Expression of Mourning

The expression of mourning is particularly remarkable among elephants. When one of them is about to die, his fellows press around him and try to lift him up, sometimes even to feed him. Then, if they see that he has died, they go in search of branches, which they then place on and around his body, sometimes covering it up. The herd also performs rituals: elephants sometimes arrange themselves in a circle around the corpse, heads facing outwards, or file one by one past the corpse, each one touching it with his trunk or foot, and pausing in front of it before making room for the next one in line. One can't help but be reminded of the ritual of human funerals during which everyone takes turns placing a flower on the coffin. When the herd finally moves away, if the dead elephant was young, the mother often remains behind for a while and, when she has rejoined the herd, she shows signs of dejection for several days, walking behind all the others.

Elephants also seem to be systematically attracted by the bones of their fellows, which they seem to have no trouble identifying. They sometimes spend an hour turning the bones over in every direction and sniffing them, and they sometimes carry a fragment away with them. Cynthia Moss tells how she had brought back to her camp the jawbones of a female elephant to determine its age. A few weeks later, the herd to which the dead elephant had belonged was passing nearby. The elephants made a detour to examine the bones, then went away. But one young elephant, later identified as the dead female's orphan, remained for a long time after the herd had left, touching its mother's jawbone, turning it delicately over with its feet, and picking it up with its trunk.[33] There is no doubt that it had recognized where the bones had come from and that this discovery aroused in it memories and emotions. Moss also observed a female elephant named Agatha who, fifteen months after the death of her mother, often returned to the place of her death and manipulated her skull for a long time.

Chimpanzees also show signs of consternation when one of their own dies, and they sometimes linger for a long time, observing the dead body in silence.

Jane Goodall tells how an eight-year-old chimpanzee named Flint, who was very attached to his mother, Flo, fell into a deep depression when Flo died. Three days later, he climbed up to the nest of branches where his mother usually rested, contemplated it for a long time, then climbed back down and lay in the grass, prostrate, his eyes wide open, gazing into the void. He almost completely stopped eating and died three weeks later.

An intriguing case of mourning for another species has even been observed. In Zimbabwe, a young elephant had adopted a young rhinoceros as his playmate. When the rhinoceros was killed by poachers who buried him after cutting off its horn, the young elephant dug down for up to a meter to unearth his friend's body, all the while emitting cries of distress, while two older elephants surrounded him and tried to console him, supporting him with their bodies.[34]

Mourning has been observed among a number of other species, including pets. In 1858 in Scotland, a Skye terrier stayed near his master's grave for fourteen years, refusing to leave it. Neighbors fed him until he died, then buried him near his master. The villagers then made a statue of him in the little cemetery, in homage to his faithfulness.

The Phenomenon of Adoption

In both monkeys and apes, infants under six months cannot survive without a mother—unless adopted. Sisters and brothers can make good caregivers when a mother dies. But there are also cases of adoption by unrelated individuals. In *Chimps of Gombe,* Jane Goodall describes how a twelve-year-old chimpanzee adopted a three-month-old orphan, thus saving his life.[35] Christophe Boesch and his colleagues observed frequent adoptions among chimpanzees in the Taï forest in eastern Africa.[36] Out of the thirty-six young who lost their mothers followed by Boesch, eighteen were adopted. It is remarkable to note that, among those eighteen, half were adopted by males, including one by its own father, the others having no direct connection with their protégés. Usually the males do not associate with any particular female, and generally don't take care of their offspring. But the adoptive fathers carry the orphans on their backs during their daily journeys (an average of five miles a day) and share their food for years, which represents a considerable investment in the survival of the adopted chimpanzee. Researchers think that this behavior of solidarity was encouraged by the fact that these chimpanzees live in a zone where there are many leopards, an enemy of theirs.

The Transmission of Social Cultures

We have seen that elaborate cultures, implying a cumulative transmission of knowledge, have developed extensively only among humans. But that does not mean that animals are without culture. Within a species, cultural variants are observed from one group to another, variants not of genetic origin.

The chimpanzees of neighboring regions in Africa have developed grooming styles that differ from one group to another, while among the orangutans of Sumatra, it is the tools used that vary according to the region. These variations are not due to the influence of the ecological milieus, but to the diversification of social learning. In a few weeks, entire communities of monkeys, birds, dolphins, whales, wolves, and bears, to mention only a few, can adopt a new habit "discovered" by one of their members. The example is often cited of titmice in England who, a few decades ago, began piercing the aluminum caps of bottles of milk to peck at the cream floating on the surface. Over a few weeks, this behavior spread throughout the entire country. The elaborate mourning of elephants we mentioned above belongs to what humans regard as a culture.

The notion of animal culture was first introduced by Jane Goodall in her Ph.D thesis in 1963 and later elaborated by Scottish primatologist William McGrew and others.[37] As the ethologist Dominique Lestel stresses, even though animal cultures are distinguished from human cultures by the fact that they are not based on language, art, religion, or other specific aspects of human cultures, they are still cultures, since they are transmitted socially and not genetically. Nevertheless, these cultures remain much more limited than those among humans, since they do not seem to accumulate over generations.

Knowing What Others Are Thinking, or the "Theory of Mind"

Are animals capable of having some idea of what is going on in someone else's mind? They are certainly able to observe the behavior of their fellows and take it into account, but that does not imply that they are capable of envisioning the actual mental states.

We know that animals can show dissimulation and orchestrate scenes in order to deceive their fellows. When a jay, for instance, stores food and sees he is being watched by another jay, he pretends he hasn't noticed the other jay, and then, as soon as the other jay leaves, he returns to his hiding place, takes out the food and goes to hide it elsewhere. So he has understood that other jays would like to steal his food. But to what extent can he put himself in the other's place and imagine what the other is thinking? Emil Menzel[38] was one of the first ethologists to explore this question, while the concept of "theory of mind"—theory about what the other is thinking—was formulated by David Premack and Guy Woodruff.[39]

Do the observations available to us allow us to draw a precise conclusion on this? According to a study by Brian Hare on the chimpanzees in the Yerkes National Primate Research Center at Emory University, near downtown Atlanta, the apes who are at the bottom of the social hierarchy take account of what a dominant competitor knows before they approach food.[40] Thomas Bugnyar has observed similar behavior among ravens: When a raven approaches a food cache, it looks to see who is nearby. If it sees a fellow raven that might have noticed it storing the food, it hurries to the hiding place to be sure of recovering the booty before the other raven can. If it sees only individuals *whom it knows are ignorant* of where the hiding place is, it takes its time.[41] So in this case there is an awareness of *what the other knows or does not know.* Similar behavior has also been observed among capuchin monkeys, dogs and wolves, and, as we will see, dolphins.[42] According to Frans de Waal, the idea that the theory of mind applies only to humans is invalidated by all his observations.[43]

A study by Shinya Yamamoto and his colleagues has shown that not only do chimpanzees help each other, but they are also capable of evaluating precisely the needs of the other.[44] In this experiment, two chimpanzees who know each other are placed in adjoining cages. A small window allows objects to be passed from one cage to the other. The first chimpanzee receives in his cage a box containing seven objects: a stick, a drinking straw, a lasso, a chain, a piece of rope, a large flat brush, and a belt.

The second chimpanzee is then placed in a situation where he needs a specific tool, which turns out to be either a stick, or a straw, to obtain some fruit juice. The second chimpanzee signals to the first, by gestures and voice, that he needs help. The first chimpanzee looks, evaluates the situation, chooses the right tool nine times out of ten from the seven tools available, and hands it to his companion through the window. He himself receives no reward.

If the first chimpanzee's view is blocked by an opaque panel, he still wants to help when he hears the other asking for help, but since he can't evaluate his precise needs by sight, he hands over any of the seven objects at random. This experiment was repeated with several chimpanzees and, in one case, the chimpanzee with the tools went to look through a small hole he had spotted on top of the opaque panel, in order to evaluate the other's situation and hand him the correct tool!

A Clever Dolphin

At the Institute for Marine Mammal Studies in Gulfport, Mississippi, the dolphin trainers had the idea of recruiting the dolphins to help clean the pool. It wasn't long before the dolphins understood that they could exchange a piece of plastic or cardboard for a fish, and the pool soon became immaculate. But Kelly, a female, developed a stratagem to increase the yield: When she found a large piece of trash—a newspaper or a cardboard box—instead of exchanging it right away for a fish, she hid it in a rocky crevice at the bottom of the pool, then shredded it into small pieces, which she carried one after the other to her instructor to exchange for fish. A good investment, which implies at least two abilities. The first is the ability to resist the temptation of receiving a fish right away by exchanging the trash she had just found. We know, by comparison, in the famous marshmallow experiment, that more than half the time a child cannot resist the temptation of eating one marshmallow immediately, rather than two marshmallows ten minutes later.[45] The second ability the dolphin manifested is to understand that the important thing is neither the size of the paper, nor the fact of immediately giving what one has found, but that each fragment has the same value as the whole.

Kelly's ingenuity didn't stop there. She also had the idea of hiding pieces of fish (again, delaying her reward till later), which she brought from time to time to the water's surface to attract seagulls while she remained invisible below. Soon, a seagull spotted the bait and, when he was about to seize it, Kelly trapped his feet in her jaw without wounding him. Then she would wait for a trainer, who, hoping to prevent the seagull's death, would hurry over and throw a fish to Kelly, who would immediately release the bird. After noting the success of her stratagem, Kelly taught it to her calf, and soon gull-baiting became the favorite sport for all the dolphins in the pool.[46] Thus Kelly demonstrated that she was capable of reasoning, using tools, making plans, having recourse to very elaborate tricks, and teaching them to others.

A Bonobo That Tries to Help a Bird Fly

Frans de Waal tells the story of a bonobo named Kuni who, after seeing a starling stun itself against the glass wall of his enclosure, grasped it delicately and encouraged it to fly with hand gestures. After this attempt failed, Kuni brought it to the top of a tree, unfolded its wings with both hands, as if it were a miniature airplane, and threw the swallow into the air, hoping, we might assume, that it would take off flying. So Kuni had remembered what birds usually do. The bird, too ill, fell to the ground. Kuni climbed back down from the tree and, for a long time, protected the dying starling from the young chimpanzees that approached it.[47]

Do You Need an Idea of Self to Have an Idea of the Other?

This question may seem strange, but it is important with respect to the development of empathy. We know, in fact, that human children begin to display empathy between eighteen and twenty-four months, about the time they begin to recognize themselves in the mirror. The classic test consists of making a red mark on the child's forehead without his noticing: When he recognizes himself in the mirror, he touches the red spot and usually tries to erase it. Since there aren't any mirrors in the jungle or the ocean, it is all the more remarkable that many animals have passed this mirror test. The first were the great apes, as the psychologist and evolutionary specialist Gordon Gallup showed in 1970,[48] followed by dolphins, elephants, and magpies.

In 1999, a team of neuroscientists noticed that very particular neurons, the von Economo neurons (also called "VEN"), which are spindle-shaped, were, out of the twenty-eight families of primates, present only among humans and the four species of great apes.[49] These are precisely the species that passed the mirror test. Later on, the presence of VEN was also discovered among whales, dolphins, and elephants.[50]

There are correlations, then, between recognizing oneself in the mirror, the presence of von Economo neurons, and an advanced capacity for empathy. Researchers are in agreement, however, that empathy can take many different forms, and that the ability to recognize oneself in a mirror is not a necessary precondition for understanding oneself and others.

How Far Do Proofs Go?

Can one demonstrate the existence of altruism as a "motivation whose ultimate goal is the well-being of others" among animals? We have seen with Daniel Batson's experiments how hard it is to prove unambiguously the existence of this motivation among humans. One can imagine the obstacles the ethologist must face who undertakes similar experimentations among animals, with whom it is naturally much harder to communicate.

Some of the observations that have been carried out, however, clearly point to an altruistic motivation. Frans de Waal told me the following anecdote: "An old mother chimpanzee was having more and more trouble moving, especially getting to the watering hole that was far from her home. When she slowly started moving toward the watering hole, one of the young females would go ahead, fill her cheeks with water, return to the old mother, who would open her mouth wide, and the young female would spit the water into the grandmother's mouth." Christophe Boesch similarly describes a female, observed in the wild, who took water in her mouth to her old grandmother.

Daniel Batson agrees that, in this case, everything indicates the presence of real empathic concern, but that this kind of example, touching as it may be, does not constitute a proof of altruism, since we are not able to know what motivation the subject is obeying.[51] It is with this uncertainty in mind that researchers have tried to imagine experimental protocols that will allow us to answer this question convincingly.

Many of these experiments came about because of Michael Tomasello, Felix Warneken, and their colleagues at the Max Planck Institute in Leipzig. Warneken, in particular, wanted to find out if chimpanzees were capable of coming to the aid of one of their fellows gratuitously—that is, in the absence of a reward involved.[52] The scene takes place in Uganda, in a reserve where the chimpanzees spend their days on a vast enclosed terrain. At night, they are gathered into a building.

During the test, an experimenter stands against the bars separating him from the animals, pretending to want to get hold of a stick that's on the chimpanzees' side and out of his reach. Soon, one of the chimpanzees will pick up the stick and hand it to the experimenter. Then the stick is placed in a spot that is harder to reach, requiring that the chimpanzee climb up to a platform eight feet high.[53] The chimpanzee, however, still goes there. It is interesting that the fact of rewarding the chimpanzee does not increase the frequency of aid. Warneken notes that young eighteen-month-old children react spontaneously in the same way.

Did the chimpanzees want to please the humans? Nothing indicates this, since they didn't know the experimenters, who were not the same people who normally took care of them and fed them. To find out if the chimpanzees were willing to help their fellows in a disinterested way, Warneken used a second protocol.

Two chimpanzees are in adjoining enclosures separated by bars. One of them tries several times to open a door leading to a room both chimpanzees know contains food. The door is locked with a hook. This hook is arranged in such a way that it is out of reach of the chimpanzee trying to open the door, but within reach of a neighbor who cannot access the room containing the food. Will the latter give a helping hand to the former, knowing perfectly well that no reward is likely? Against all expectations, the answer is yes. Aware of the other's need and witnessing his powerlessness, the neighbor lifts the hook holding the chain, thus allowing his companion to eat his fill.

In an old film made by Meredith Crawford during one of the original studies on cooperative behavior among chimpanzees,[54] we see a tray of food placed outside two cages. A cord is passed through the two handles of the tray and one end of the cord stretches into each cage. If a single chimpanzee pulls the cord, it slips out of the handles and the tray doesn't move. One of the two chimpanzees has been amply fed, so he is not very motivated to pull on his end of the cord. But the other one is hungry and wants his neighbor to cooperate. We see him pick up his end of the cord and, with gestures, urge his fellow to pull on the other end. The latter does so unenthusiastically, pulls on the cord for a few instants, then stops. The first animal then slips an arm through the bars and encourages his colleague by tapping him on the shoulder, the way we'd say to a friend, "Come on!" The second chimpanzee, after some encouragement, ends up pulling the cord until the tray comes within reach of the hungry chimpanzee.

This observation was made public in 1937, to show that chimpanzees understood the cooperative nature of the task presented to them.[55] But it also seems to plead in favor of altruism, since the one who lent a hand to the other had nothing to gain from it except, one could no doubt object, the maintenance of mutually beneficial ties.

A similar experiment was carried out in Thailand with elephants. Joshua Plotnik and his colleagues taught elephants to pull together on the two ends of a rope to make a large wooden food-filled tray, placed thirty feet away, reach them.[56] The rope was wrapped around the tray; if one of the two elephants began to pull by itself, the rope slipped around the tray, which didn't move.

The elephants soon learned to carry out this operation, and on the second day, they succeeded eight times out of ten in bringing the tray to them by perfectly synchronizing their movements. The task was then made more complicated by bringing one elephant to the rope, then waiting a little while before the second was brought. The elephants understood there would be no point in starting all alone, and in the majority of cases, they waited (up to forty-five seconds) for the other to arrive. One of them was even cleverer and was content to block his end of the rope by putting his foot on it, letting the other one do all the hauling work! Implying that there are also free riders among elephants.

These examples concern "instrumental" collaboration. An animal can decide whether or not to cooperate. But researchers also wanted to observe prosocial choices, those that consist of choosing between two ways of acting, one beneficial to another individual, without involving cost to oneself, and the other, which does not take into account the other's situation or wishes.

To do this, Victoria Horner, Malini Suchak, and their colleagues placed two chimpanzees in neighboring cages where each could easily observe the behavior and reactions of the other. One of the two animals had thirty plastic chips in a pot: fifteen blue ones and fifteen red ones. Outside the cages, in full view of the two chimpanzees, was a tray on which two bowls of food were placed. The chimpanzee who had the chips was trained beforehand to exchange chips for food. But this time, if he gave a blue chip, he'd be the only one to eat, and if he gave a red chip, the food would be distributed to both chimpanzees.

In the beginning, the one who had the chips gave them at random, but soon the two chimpanzees realized that with the "selfish" chips, only the chip-giver would feast. In this case, the chimpanzee who received nothing showed his disappointment and appealed to his colleague with cries and body language. The experiment shows that most of the chip-owners ended up choosing mostly the "altruistic" chips.[57]

One might think that the first chimpanzee made this choice not by altruism, but in order to be able to eat calmly, without having to put up with a frantic companion expressing his disapproval noisily when the chosen chip brought him nothing. Attracting the attention of the chip-owner clearly influenced the chip-owner's choice, but when the frustrated chimpanzee expressed his desire too vehemently (by spitting at the chip-owner, aggressively passing his fingers through the bars, shaking the cage, etc.), the chip-owner chose the "altruistic" chips *less often*, as if these intemperate demands made him unwilling to share with his fellow. It was the moderate reactions, the ones that seemed simply to have the aim of attracting the other's attention without harassing him, that led to the largest number of prosocial choices.

ANTHROPOMORPHISM OR ANTHROPOCENTRISM?

Is this altruism as we understand it among humans? Although the research carried out over the last thirty years still gives rise to controversy, it does indicate that some animals are capable of empathic concern, that is, altruism. In the final analysis, that's not surprising, insofar as we expect to find among animals all the precursors of human altruism.

The scientists who have most clearly highlighted the wealth of emotions expressed by many animal species have often been accused of anthropomorphism—a cardinal sin among specialists in animal behavior. At the beginning of her career, Jane Goodall was criticized for giving names to the chimpanzees she was studying. Instead, she should simply have assigned them numbers. She was even more sternly reproached for describing their personalities and emotions, for using words like *motivation,* for saying that they could solve problems by thinking—and all the rest of it. Similarly, Frans de Waal was also reproached for using terms reserved for human behavior to describe the behavior of chimpanzees or bonobos.

To this day, a number of academics still refuse to use terms for animals that refer to mental states like anger, fear, suffering, affection, joy, or any other emotion similar to our own. Bernard Rollin,[58] professor of philosophy and animal sciences at Colorado State University, explains that researchers, in their effort not to use terms for animals that describe human emotions, speak not of fear but of "retreat behavior"; they don't describe the "suffering" of a rat placed on a burning piece of metal, but simply count the "number of its leaps or convulsions"; they don't speak of cries or moans of pain, but of "vocalizations." The vocabulary of common sense is replaced by a jargon that stems more from denial than from scientific objectivity.

As Frans de Waal notes,

> *Except for a small group of academics, basically everyone in the world believes that animals have similar emotions, similar reactions and similar decision making to those that we have. But you enter a psychology department and all of a sudden you hear "Oh, oh, I don't know that. If a dog scratches at the door and barks, you say that he wants to go out. But how do you know he wants to go out? All he has learned is that barking and scratching gets doors open."*[59]

It would obviously be absurd to attribute to an earthworm complex emotions like pride, jealousy, or romantic passion, but when an animal is obviously happy, sad, or playful, why not call a spade a spade? Such stubbornness goes against common sense and fails to recognize the very nature of evolution. "If someone wishes to violate the principle of continuity," Bernard Rollin writes, "and assert quantum jumps between animals, while remaining a proponent of evolution, the burden of proof is on him."[60] The theory of evolution implies that psychology, like anatomy, has developed gradually. So it is inconceivable that emotions, intelligence, and awareness appeared suddenly among humans. In *The Descent of Man, and Selection in Relation to Sex,*[61] Darwin cannot be more explicit:

> *If no organic being excepting man had possessed any mental power, or if his powers had been of a wholly different nature from those of the lower animals, then we should never have been able to convince ourselves that our high faculties had been gradually developed. But it can be shewn that there is no fundamental difference of this kind.*

Frans de Waal describes as *anthropodenial* the insistence on wanting to give man a monopoly over certain emotions:[62]

> *People willfully suppress knowledge most have had since childhood, which is that animals do have feelings and do care about others. How and why half the world drops this conviction once they grow beards or breasts will always baffle me, but the result is the common fallacy that we are unique in this regard. Human we are, and humane as well, but the idea that the latter may be older than the former, that our kindness is part of a much larger picture, still has to catch on.*[63]

In the West, many cultural factors contribute to this anthropocentrism; in it we can find remnants of Judeo-Christian ideology, in which only man possesses a soul; the scorn of seventeenth-century thinkers like Descartes and Malebranche, for whom animals were only "flesh-and-blood automatons"; and, in our time, the chauvinistic and prideful view that adding mankind to the continuity of the evolution of animals is an insult to human dignity and its immeasurable superiority.

There is no doubt another reason why many of us stubbornly cling to the idea of a definitive boundary between humans and animals. If we acknowledged that animals are not basically different from us, we could no longer treat them like instruments for our own pleasure. The following statement made by a researcher to Bernard Rollin testifies to this: "It makes my job as a researcher a hell of a lot easier if I just act as if animals have no awareness."[64]

The realization that all sentient beings, from the simplest to the most complex, are part of an evolving continuum, and that there is no basic rupture between the different degrees of their evolution, should naturally lead us to respect other species and to use our superior intelligence not to profit from them as if they were simple instruments in the service of our well-being, but to promote their well-being at the same time as our own.

Curiously, the study of empathy itself has come up against blockages in the framework of the study of human emotions. Many researchers in this field have shared their disappointments. Frans de Waal deplores the absence in science, until recently, of consideration for empathy: "Even with regards to our own species, it was considered to be an absurd, laughable topic classed with supernatural phenomena such as astrology and telepathy."[65] Richard Davidson had a similar experience when he began studying the neuroscience of emotions among humans. In the beginning, his scientific advisers told him that he'd be wasting his time and that this line of research had no future. But Davidson persevered and made this field of research one of the most active branches of the neurosciences.[66]

Even recently, Tania Singer, one of the major specialists in empathy and compassion in the neurosciences, confided to me that many traditional researchers regard her field of research as "light." When the two researchers quoted above, with whom I have had the privilege of collaborating for over twelve years, undertook to study the effects of meditation on the brain and on empathic capacities, they came up against the amused indulgence of many colleagues. But groundbreaking results were accumulated, and little by little, research on empathy, altruism, compassion, positive emotions, and the effects of mind-training on the brain and on our way of life has gained respectability in the scientific world.

18

Altruism Among Children

One of the big questions debated in Western civilization is whether we are born good and predisposed to cooperate with each other before society corrupts us, as Jean-Jacques Rousseau proposed, or born selfish, indisposed to help each other and only taught by society to behave in a more civil way, as Thomas Hobbes asserts.

Research carried out over the past thirty years, especially that of Michael Tomasello and Felix Warneken,[1] weighs in favor of the former hypothesis. This research established that from the age of one, when they are just beginning to learn to walk and speak, children already spontaneously exhibit behavior of mutual aid and cooperation that they were not taught by adults.

Later, after the age of five, the tendency toward cooperation and mutual aid is influenced by learning social relationships and by considerations of reciprocity, unknown by younger children, who help indiscriminately. Children then learn to be more circumspect in their choices, and progressively assimilate the cultural norms current in the society in which they are growing up.

The psychologist and pediatrician Richard Tremblay and his Canadian colleagues—authors of a longitudinal study that followed the evolution of thousands of children over several decades—have shown that it is also between seventeen and forty-two months (three and a half years) that children most often resort to physical aggression, even if this aggression remains harmless thanks to their young age.[2] For the majority of them, the incidence of this aggressive behavior diminished after about the age of four, as they learned to regulate it and as their emotional intelligence developed.

This peak of physically aggressive behavior at such a young age may seem disconcerting and contradictory to the equally numerous and spontaneous manifestations of altruistic cooperation. But, actually, the spontaneity and frequency of these two types of behavior, seemingly incompatible, are due to the fact that emotions begin to manifest fully when the cerebral systems of regulation are not yet in place. It is enough to watch small children go in a few seconds from laughter to tears, then again to laughter, to note this emotional volatility. Neurosciences confirm that around the age of four the structures of the cortex become operative, allowing the nuanced regulation of emotional episodes set off by more primitive cerebral networks linked to fear, anger, and desire. Subsequent evolution of these predispositions to altruistic behavior and violence then depends on a large number of internal and external factors.

From Birth to the Age of Twelve Months

In an oft-cited study, child psychologists Sagi and Hoffman observed that barely a day after birth, a baby who hears another infant crying also starts to cry.[3] Later, Martin and Clark showed that this reaction is greatest when the newborn is made to hear the cries of a baby its own age. On the other hand, a newborn reacts much less to the cries of an older child, and doesn't cry at all when it hears the cries of a baby chimpanzee. Finally, it stops crying when a recording of its own cries is played back![4] This seems to suggest that the small human is capable at birth of a basic distinction between "self" and "other." Other researchers attribute this reaction to a simple "emotional contagion," which, as we have seen, is a precursor to empathy.[5]

For Daniel Batson, this reaction to the cries of another newborn could be not the mark of an empathic emotion, but the expression of an innate instinct of competition to get food or attract the attention of the parents.[6] We know that as soon as a chick starts chirping in its nest when its mother approaches to feed her brood, all the other chicks immediately start chirping as loudly as they can. This reaction is interpreted as a competitive response, not an empathic one.

Babies Prefer Friendly People

Very soon, being the simple spectators they are, infants obviously prefer people who behave kindly toward other people over those who treat them with hostility. In Paul Bloom's laboratory at Yale, researchers showed six- to ten-month-old children a video in which a wooden doll with big, easily visible eyes has difficulty climbing a steep slope. Another doll enters and comes to its aid by pushing it from behind. Finally, a third doll, easily distinguishable from the second, intervenes by pushing the first doll who is trying to climb the slope, making it tumble down to the bottom. When the babies were then handed the two dolls that intervened, most of them reached for the kind doll.[7]

From One to Two Years

Between ten and fourteen months, babies react to others' distress in a much more active way: they watch the person nervously, moan, burst into tears, or else move away from the person. But they rarely try to do something directly for the victim. Some look at their mother or move over to her as if to ask for help.

At about fourteen months, children begin to show concern for people in difficulty, moving toward them, touching them gently, or kissing them. A little girl who is attentively watching a crying baby will hand her her own bottle, for instance, or a necklace she likes.[8]

Beyond eighteen months, children help in ways better adapted to the other's needs: they call an adult, hug the victim, or bring the victim not objects they themselves like, but ones they know from experience have the ability to console the victim. Hoffman reports the example of a child who began by giving its own teddy bear to a crying child. When it saw that the bear had no effect, it ran to look in the next room for the teddy bear that the crying child liked. This time the action was crowned with success: the child hugged the recovered bear in its arms and stopped crying.[9]

It's between fourteen and twenty-four months that the child becomes more aware of its own identity, becomes able to recognize itself in a mirror, and differentiates more clearly its own emotions from others'. Around the age of twenty-four months, children also become able to talk about their own emotions and those of others.[10]

From Two to Five Years

During their second year, children enter the stage described by Hoffman as "true empathy" and become capable of considering things from others' points of view and modifying their behavior to suit others' needs. The acquisition of language also allows them to extend the range of emotions with which they enter into empathic resonance. Finally, they come to experience empathy for people who are not physically present, and to extend it to larger groups, like the "poor" or the "oppressed."

Researchers filmed thirty hours of children playing. The twenty-six children, aged from two to five years, performed some 1,200 acts of sharing, consoling, and cooperation.[11] With age, concern for the other also becomes more nuanced: a three-year-old girl, for instance, will give, as a consolatory gesture, a hat to a friend she can see is in distress, knowing she lost her own favorite hat three days ago.[12]

In daily life, from their youngest age (one to three years), children spontaneously help their parents in ordinary activities.[13] It's not a question of simple imitation, since starting from the age of two and a half or three years, children often make comments like, "Can I help you?" or "I'm going to clean up." Young children help not only those close to them, but also acquaintances. It is only later, around the age of five, that they will make discriminations, reserving a different response for those who are not part of their "group."

A Series of Revealing Experiments

More recent research from the team of Michael Tomasello and Felix Warneken has shown that very young children spontaneously offered to help an experimenter complete various tasks—bringing the experimenter an object that had fallen to the floor, for instance—and they did so without the prospect of any kind of reward. As Felix Warneken notes, "The results were astonishing because these children are so young—they still wear diapers and are barely able to use language, but they already show helping behavior."[14]

Few researchers till then had experimentally studied the phenomenon of mutual aid among very young children.[15] In fact, theoreticians of child development were for a long time influenced by the hypothesis, formulated by Jean Piaget and his student Lawrence Kohlberg, that empathic behavior directed toward others did not manifest before school age, and that before that age the child was completely egocentric. Piaget studied the development of moral judgment in children, which is linked to their cognitive development. But by stressing exclusively the faculty of reasoning, he neglected the emotional aspect and came to the conclusion that young children were without empathy before the age of seven.[16] Since then, countless experimental studies have shown that quite the opposite is true, and that empathy manifests very early on in children.[17] The child begins by offering "instrumental" aid, for instance, by bringing to an adult an object he needs, which implies an understanding of the other's desires. A little later, the child manifests an "empathic" aid, for instance, by consoling a sad person.[18]

When an experimenter in the process of hanging up laundry drops a clothespin and has difficulty picking it up, almost all the eighteen-month-old children move to pick up the clothespin and hand it to him. They react on average within the five seconds following the dropping of the clothespin, which is approximately the same period of time an adult takes when placed in an equivalent situation. Similarly, the children come to open the door of a cupboard that an experimenter with his arms full of books is bumping against.[19]

Even more impressive, the children specifically recognize a situation in which the adult really needs help: if the adult deliberately throws the clothespin to the ground instead of accidentally dropping it, the children don't budge.

During these experiments, the experimenter never asks for help verbally, and most of the time, he doesn't even look in the direction of the children to convey to them that he is in difficulty. What's more, when the researchers asked the mothers, present in the room, to encourage their children to help, that didn't change anything. In fact, the children showed so much enthusiasm that, to observe differences in their willingness to help, they had to be distracted while the experimenter got back into a situation where he seemed to need help. Almost always, the children would immediately interrupt their play to help the experimenter.

It is particularly interesting to note that if children obtain a reward from the experimenter, their propensity to help is not increased. Quite the contrary: it was observed that the children who were rewarded offer their help less often than those to whom nothing was given.[20] As Warneken and Tomasello note: "This rather surprising finding provides even further evidence for the hypothesis that children's helping is driven by an intrinsic rather than an extrinsic motivation."[21]

If the child is rewarded for having done a good action, he strongly risks thinking he has acted for the reward, and not for the person who benefits from his action. He acquires an "extrinsic" motivation—he no longer acts with the aim of helping someone but in order to gain an advantage. When people stop calling on his potential for kindness, the child is inclined to behave in a less altruistic way.

PRAISE AND CRITICISM

Should we congratulate the child if he behaves well, and criticize him if not? Studies show that if children are made to understand that they are capable of altruism and that they are "kind," they will tend to behave kindly when the occasion arises.[22] When they behave in an unkind way, the best strategy seems to be to make them understand the harm they have caused, by bringing them to see the other person's point of view, and to criticize their action without telling them they are "mean." If children are persuaded they are "mean," the opposite effect will occur—namely that at the next opportunity, the child will in fact tend to behave as if he or she were really mean. And one risks making the child a pessimist inclined to think it's in his or her nature to be "bad" and that he or she can't do anything about it: the child will then tend to act in conformity with that image of him- or herself.

THE TENDENCY TO HELP OTHERS IS INNATE

In view of the research, Michael Tomasello advances a certain number of indications of how cooperation and disinterested help manifest *spontaneously* in children. *These behaviors manifest very early*—between fourteen and sixteen months—long before parents have inculcated in their children the rules of sociability, and *are not determined by any external pressure.* They are observed *at the same age* in *different cultures.* which indicates that they are indeed the result of a natural inclination in children to come to the aid of others, and are not the products of culture or parental intervention. Finally, the discovery of similar behavior among the great apes leads us to think that behavior of altruistic cooperation did not appear out of nowhere among human beings, but that it was *already present in the ancestor shared by humans and chimpanzees some six million years ago*, and that concern for our fellows is deeply anchored in our nature.[23]

Other recent experiments confirm this assertion: in Vancouver, the psychologists Lara Aknin, J. Kiley Hamlin, and Elizabeth Dunn[24] have shown that two-year-old children were happier when they gave a treat to someone else than when they received one themselves.[25]

WHEN SOCIAL NORMS TEMPER SPONTANEOUS ALTRUISM

According to Warneken and Tomasello, in order for altruistic behavior to be maintained over the course of generations, it must be associated with mechanisms that protect individuals against exploitation by each other.[26]

The psychologist Dale Hay quotes Machiavelli: "A prince must learn how not to be good."[27] Without going quite so far, we have seen that while the young child at first shows altruistic behavior toward everyone the child meets, from the age of five the child begins to make discriminations, according to degrees of kinship, reciprocal behavior, and the cultural norms inculcated in the child. The child's altruistic behavior thus becomes more selective.

These discoveries go completely against the ideas of Freud, for whom "children are completely egoistic; they feel their needs intensely and strive ruthlessly to satisfy them."[28] According to Freud, it's only when the child, around the age of five or six, internalizes the norms, constraints, and parental and social prohibitions imposed on his natural egoism that he is led to behave in a way that is acceptable to society. Yet the scientific research described above demonstrates exactly the opposite: on one hand, the child is *naturally altruistic* from the earliest age; on the other, the child learns to *moderate altruism* only after having internalized the social norms. So a wise education should consist of preserving natural inclinations to cooperate while still protecting oneself, and should do so without inculcating in the child selfish, individualistic, and narcissistic values.

MORAL SENSE AND MORAL JUDGMENTS

It emerges from research directed by psychologists—Nancy Eisenberg and Elliot Turiel especially—that moral sense is to a large extent innate. The sense of fairness, for example, appears spontaneously around the age of three and increases with time.[29] Fairness is an altruistic disposition, since it benefits the entire group. According to research published by French anthropologist Nicolas Baumard in his book *Comment nous sommes devenus moraux* (How We Became Moral): "Children in fact declare that hitting people or pulling their hair is bad, whether or not it's punished. They will even say that an action can be bad even if an adult ordered it."[30] According to the psychologist Jonathan Haidt, moral sense stems mainly from *innate intuitions* ("I just know it's bad"), to which is later added a *deliberate reasoning* resulting from conscious processes.[31] The existence of a *moral sense* is universal, even if the content of *moral judgments* varies considerably depending on contexts and cultures.[32]

It has been shown, by following the evolution of children from two to seven years of age, that the most favorable situation for the flourishing of this innate moral awareness is one in which the parents respond quickly and warmly to the efforts of their child who is inclined toward cooperation. It turns out that such cooperative children are not prone to cheat, for instance, even if they are provided with an opportunity to do so; they will continue carrying on a task their mother has given them, even if the mother leaves the room.[33]

AFTER THE AGE OF FIVE

The last phase of development, according to Martin Hoffman, corresponds to the ability to feel empathy and concern for the other by imagining, for instance, the situation of a child suffering from famine or forced labor in a distant country. Around the age of seven, the child becomes aware of the fact that one's sex and ethnicity are lasting characteristics, and that other people have histories that can arouse empathy.[34] The child also learns to put himself actively in the other's place.[35]

Between the ages of ten and twelve, the child's behavior evolves in a more abstract way, by referring to moral obligations. The child thinks more about what "being a good person" means and about how to make one's actions agree with moral sense, which the child initially apprehends intuitively. This leads the child to understand, for instance, that some sufferings result from belonging to an oppressed community, and thus to feel sympathy for such victims.

According to Nancy Eisenberg, the children who are more inclined to react with concern when others are in difficulty are those who have a good emotional intelligence and know best how to regulate their emotions. The children who react to others' suffering with anxiety and distress (rather than going to their aid) are the most self-centered and least apt to maintain good social relations.[36]

The Emergence and Regression of Aggressiveness During Childhood

Cooperative behavior among children from one to three years of age wasn't studied experimentally until recently, and it was long thought that aggressive behavior before school age did not constitute an interesting object of study. It was believed that quarrels between toddlers were inconsequential; they were more amusing than worrisome. Until Richard Tremblay and his collaborators at the University of Montreal wondered what happened before the age of five. They were surprised to find that it's between a year and a half and four years of age that the frequency of physical aggression (hitting, biting, pushing, grabbing, pulling, throwing things, etc.) turned out to be the greatest in the whole life of a human being.

They saw that the majority of children begin to engage in physical aggression between twelve and twenty-four months, that the frequency of aggressions increases rapidly, reaches a climax between the twenty-fourth and forty-eighth month, and that it then diminishes strongly until adolescence, first among girls, then among boys.[37] During adolescence, a slight rise in aggressiveness was observed among boys (who are responsible for the large majority of violent acts), but violence then continues to diminish throughout adult life. It emerges from these studies that children begin spontaneously resorting to physical aggression before *they learn not to be aggressive,* as their emotional regulation develops.

Another important discovery is that the diminution of aggressiveness occurs in a variable way depending on the child. Over 22,000 children, representative of the Canadian population, were followed from birth to adolescence, and three different evolutions of the frequency of physical aggression were noted. For half the children, this frequency increases from seventeen to forty-two months, then diminishes substantially until the age of eleven. One third of the children resort much less to physical aggression from seventeen months, and the frequency of aggression remains weak until the age of eleven. On the other hand, 17% of the children distinguish themselves clearly from the two other groups: aggressive activity is much more frequent with them starting at seventeen months, and they manifest aggressive behavior at every age.

The children of this third group encounter all sorts of difficulties whose consequences are aggravated at adolescence. At the age of twelve, they are considerably more likely than the others to have problems relating to children their own age, to experience depressive states, and to be perceived by their teachers as more unstable and more asocial. At the end of their school career, 3.3% of them continue to a higher education, as opposed to 75.8% of the boys who rarely resort to physical aggression. As teenagers, they often have run-ins with the law.

The world of early childhood, between two and five years, is thus one of rapid alternations and extremes, of both uncalculated altruism and of limitless impetuosity. It is all the more important to offer children every condition favorable to the flourishing of the best in themselves, by surrounding them with love and by offering them, by the way we ourselves act, a living example of what they could become.

Tremblay and his colleagues found that among the many variables analyzed, the most reliable predictors of violent childhood behavior are related to parental issues: having a mother who had her first child at a young age, a young single mother, a mother with no high school diploma, a mother who is depressed, a mother who drank and/or smoked during pregnancy, or an antisocial father (for the period before the end of high school).[38] Preventive interventions should therefore focus on helping families with high-risk profiles, especially mothers facing hardship. In addition, programs that teach parents to implement consistent, caring, nonviolent strategies in managing child behavior have also had positive effects in reducing child aggression.[39]

A REALIZATION OF THE INTERDEPENDENCE OF ALL THINGS

From its earliest age, a child feels as if he or she belongs to a group: he or she is one among many others, and the other is also partly himself or herself. This feeling manifests clearly in cooperative activities, during which children work toward a common aim and become aware of their interdependence, where "I" dissolves into "We."[40]

With age, this collective sense of "We" is gradually limited to certain categories of individuals, to "groups"—family, friend, and, later on, ethnic group, religion, and other factors of distinction, division, and, often, discrimination.

At adolescence and adulthood, some people again extend the circle of altruism and experience a profound feeling of "shared humanity" with other human beings, and empathy for people who are suffering. An enlightened education should highlight the interdependence that reigns between people, animals, and our natural environment, so that the child will acquire a holistic view of the world. By being taught to put more emphasis on cooperation than on competition, and on caring rather than indifference, children will be better equipped to contribute in a constructive way to the society in which they are evolving. The educative practices we make use of depend on the concept we have of childhood. If we recognize that children are born with a natural propensity for empathy and altruism, their education will serve to accompany and facilitate the development of that predisposition.

AUTHORITARIAN ASSERTION OF POWER, WITHDRAWAL OF AFFECTION, AND "INDUCTION"

Some parents tend to assert their authority in a radical way, or stop showing their affection when their child behaves badly. Neither of these attitudes yields good results. Martin Hoffman distinguishes three principal types of parental intervention: authoritarian assertion of power, withdrawal of love, and *induction*.[41]

Authoritarian assertion of power is accompanied by severe reprimands, threats, commands, privation of objects or activities the child likes, and corporal punishment. These methods produce an effect opposite to the one intended, since they engender in the child anger, fear, and chronic resentment. Punishments also tend to make the child less empathic toward his fellows and to diminish his sociability.[42] Punishments and corporal punishments, which are supposed to be educative, constitute the preferred method of intervention for abusive parents, who punish and hit their children for the smallest mistake.[43]

My sister Ève, who for over thirty-five years has taken care of underprivileged children, tells the story of parents who systematically beat their children, thinking they were educating them: "They slapped them hard," she says, "and when we told them they shouldn't hit their children, the father replied, 'But I'm not hitting them—I don't have a stick!' " The parents were themselves children of the foster care system and had been themselves mistreated.[44]

By *withdrawing love,* the parent shows his irritation and his disapproval by distancing himself from the child in two ways: emotionally, by declaring the child isn't loved and by threatening to abandon the child, and physically, by condemning the child to remain all alone ("Get in the corner!", "Go to your room!"), or by ignoring the child's presence, looking away and refusing to speak or listen to the child. The withdrawal of affection creates a feeling of insecurity in the child, who can no longer count on the love of his parents.

Research shows unanimously that the most constructive and effective attitude consists of calmly explaining to the child why it would be better for him to change his behavior. It's this approach that Hoffman calls *induction.* The child is urged to adopt the perspective of the other and especially to realize the harm he may have caused to the other. The child is also shown how to spot the harm that has been committed.[45] If the child has made fun of a playmate's physical appearance, for instance, the parents will explain how harmful words about physical appearance, the color of one's skin, or any other characteristic over which we have no control are able to make the other suffer and can have painful repercussions on a whole life. They will ask the child to imagine how it would feel to be called similar names. They will suggest the child go to his friend's side to display friendship.

Induction should be carried out with perspicacity, kindness, and fairness. Still, it is not synonymous with permissiveness and does not exclude firmness. It makes the child clearly understand that the parents disapprove of some behavior, without, however, provoking a feeling of guilt that would be lastingly harmful. It is accompanied by emotional support and avoids the authoritarian assertion of power. As the French psychologist Jacques Lecomte explains, firmness "provides the child with clear information about what the parent wants, while inviting him to assert his own autonomy. Support alone is not as effective, especially after noncompliance by the child."[46] If the parents are content to reason and appeal to the child's goodwill, the child soon understands that he or she can always have the last word. According to other studies cited by Lecomte, "a parental educative style associating love with rules usually has positive effects on the child: better personal equilibrium, good relations with those around him, and even better results at school."[47] It also turns out that children are more sensitive to calls for empathy than to reminders of abstract moral norms.[48]

One of the crucial characteristics of induction is that it presupposes the child's altruistic disposition and his desire to cooperate if the effect of behavior beneficial to others is made clearly apparent.

REGRET AND GUILT

Regret consists first of all of an awareness. It allows us to recognize our mistakes and makes us wish not to repeat them. It urges us to repair the harm committed, whenever possible. Regret is constructive, since it is accompanied by a desire for transformation and helps us regard the situation in which we find ourselves as a point of departure on the path leading to self-improvement.

On the other hand, the feeling of guilt is associated with a negative judgment about what we are fundamentally. While regret refers to particular actions and simply makes us think we have acted badly, the feeling of guilt extends to our entire being and leads us to conclude, "I am basically bad." It leads to a devaluation of oneself and engenders constant torments.

Research shows that the fact of constantly belittling a child by making him or her ashamed is harmful. The child will have the impression he or she is lacking in every quality and incapable of conforming to the ideal assigned, and will conclude that he or she will always be ill-loved. This devaluation can lead to self-hatred, violence against self, and repressed anger toward others.

Here again, the conclusions to which experimental data lead go against Freud's hypotheses, for whom the feeling of *guilt* is born from fear of parental punishment and not from *regret* at having provoked another's suffering. Completely narcissistic, the manipulative child, according to Freud, seeks by every means possible to obtain what he desires, while anxiously wavering between fear of punishment and fear of losing the protection of his parents. This somber portrayal bears no resemblance to the naturally empathic and altruistic child that recent psychological investigations describe.

FOUR ESSENTIAL ATTITUDES

Jacques Lecomte identifies four parental attitudes that, in view of all the studies carried out in this field, are the most apt to favor altruistic behavior in children:[49]

- expressing affection;
- acting in an altruistic way oneself, thereby serving as an example;
- making children aware of the impact of their actions on others;
- providing children with the opportunity to be useful to others.

As Confucius is supposed to have said, "If you teach me something, I'll forget it; if you show me something, I might remember it; if you make me do something, I will put it into practice." The living example provided by the parents at every instant of daily life, especially, is more effective than all morality lessons combined. Several studies confirm, moreover, that parents who do volunteer work are more likely to see their children act similarly when they're the same age. Generosity also seems to be transmitted from one generation to the other, as well as the predisposition to come to the aid of others.[50] On the other hand, parents who embody a selfish model will influence their children in that direction.[51]

The Tragic Consequences of Privation of Affection[52]

At one time, parents were advised not to show too much affection to young children, in order to harden them and prepare them for life. Dr. John Watson, one of the two main founders of *behaviorism,* mistrusted emotions in general. Behaviorists, who dominated behavioral research for over thirty years during the first half of the twentieth century, thought, wrongly, that everything was a question of behavioral conditioning, and that moods and emotions had almost no importance whatsoever. Watson was especially skeptical of maternal love, which he regarded as dangerous. He thought that by doting too much on their babies, mothers were harming them and causing weakness, fear, and feelings of dependence and inferiority. Society needed more structure and less human warmth. He dreamed of *baby farms,* establishments for babies without parents, where children would be raised according to scientific principles. A child could be touched only if he had behaved exceptionally well. Even then, the child would receive neither praise nor kisses, but a simple pat on the head.

As Frans de Waal remarks,

> *Unfortunately, environments like the baby farm existed, and all we can say about them is that they were deadly! This became clear when psychologists studied orphans kept in little cribs separated by white sheets, deprived of visual stimulation and body contact. As recommended by scientists, the orphans had never been cooed at, held, or tickled. They looked like zombies, with immobile faces and wide-open, expressionless eyes. Had Watson been right, these children should have been thriving, but they in fact lacked all resistance to disease. At some orphanages, mortality approached 100 percent. Watson's crusade against what he called the 'over-kissed child,' and the immense respect accorded him in the 1920s public opinion, seem incomprehensible today.*[53]

Many Romanian orphans and handicapped children (between 100,000 and 300,000) experienced the same fate under the regime of the dictator Ceauseşcu. The world remembers images of those wild-eyed children clinging like animals to the bars of their metal cribs. These children didn't know how either to laugh or cry. They spent days sitting, mechanically swaying back and forth, or clinging to each other in the fetal position. In some Chinese orphanages, as well, hundreds of children were similarly neglected, and were almost never touched by the few people who were supposed to be taking care of them. The results on the physical and psychological development of these children were catastrophic.

Professor Michael Rutter, at King's College in London, who followed for twenty years the condition of 150 Romanian orphans who had been adopted by British families, found no measurable deficit in those who came to the UK before the age of six months. However, the rate of serious, persistent disabilities, affecting health, intelligence, emotional equilibrium, and cerebral anomalies (the size of their head and brain was below average) reached 40% among the babies who left the orphanage between the age of ten months and a year.[54]

Now, it is widely accepted that infants and toddlers have a huge need for love and affection in order to grow up in the best way. But it is not rare, in early childhood, for some children to receive so little affection, and to encounter too much suffering, that they remain profoundly wounded by this. It is then very difficult for them to find a space of peace and love within themselves, and, consequently, to trust others. Researchers have established a link between the physical violence these children have undergone and a weak degree of empathy and sociability.

In the best case, often with the help of a trusted person, as Boris Cyrulnik has shown, they can show a surprising capacity for resilience, which allows them to heal their psychological wounds and to flourish in life.

Loving, Facilitating, Supporting

It is undeniable that the love and tenderness that children receive in early childhood profoundly influence the rest of their lives. Children who are victims of abuse, for instance, are twice as likely to suffer depression during adolescence or adulthood.[55] So it seems it should be a duty for adults to develop and express the best of themselves in order to show the maximum affection, kindness, and love for their own children and for children they are in charge of in the community or the educational system. It is very important to stress, however, that many people who were mistreated as children do later become loving parents. According to Jacques Lecomte, there is indeed a stronger probability of becoming an abusive person among people who have themselves been abused, but this probability remains weak (between 5% and 10%).[56] The large majority of people abused as children practice what Lecomte calls "counter-modeling," that is, they decide (usually in preadolescence or adolescence) that they will do the opposite of their parents when they have children. And, most of the time, that is indeed what happens. It goes without saying that parental support must continue throughout childhood to produce a real, lasting effect. It is a whole program, then, which begins with the transformation of self.

19

Prosocial Behavior

As was the case for research on altruism, research into prosocial behavior hardly interested early researchers; until the 1960s, ten times more studies were devoted to aggressiveness and other antisocial behavior than to help, cooperation, solidarity, and so on. According to Hans-Werner Bierhoff, author of an overview of the subject,[1]

> *One of the reasons for this lack of scientific interest in the prosocial domain may lie in the belief that prosocial behavior is realized at the cost of economic prosperity.... This may well explain the conviction of many "tough-minded" people that prosocial behavior is connected with mawkishness on the part of the helpers. However, recent theorizing and research indicate that prosocial behavior has many positive side-effects for people who are helpers, and contributes to the functioning of society at large.*[2]

Are We Generally Inclined to Help Others?

Research has shown that the majority of individuals come to the aid of others in daily life. If someone (a researcher, in this case) drops a glove while walking on the sidewalk in such a way that the person behind him can easily see it, in 72% of the cases this person calls out to the researcher and hands him the glove.[3]

In this case, the cost of intervention and the vulnerability of the interventionist are negligible. But when the two factors gain in importance, the likelihood of helping others diminishes. If you are a man in New York and you ask someone permission to use his cell phone because you've lost yours, only 15% of people will grant your request. On the other hand, if you are a woman and you make the same request in a rural area, even if you are a stranger, the reply will be favorable in almost 100% of the cases.[4]

What about emergency situations? When a volunteer student pretended to faint on a subway line in Philadelphia, in 95% of the cases he received help in the forty seconds that followed. In 60% of the cases, more than one person intervened. Here again, the rate of intervention is high when the perceived cost is low. By "cost," psychologists mean involvement in terms of time, psychological investment, the complexity of the intervention, and the foreseeable consequences. If (fake) blood was trickling from the victim's mouth, the rate of intervention fell from 95% to 65% and the interventions were less immediate (an average of a minute went by before anyone intervened)—the sight of blood frightens people and increases the psychological cost of help.[5]

The Bystander Effect

Someone faints, two individuals are about to fight in the street, a car accident has just occurred. Will I intervene, go toward the suffering person, interpose in the argument, or rush toward the accident victims? Many studies have shown that the probability that I will involve myself is inversely proportional to the number of people present. I will help much more often if I am the only witness. Bibb Latané, then at Columbia University, and John Darley, then at New York University, were among the first to show that 50% of people confronted with a realistically simulated emergency situation when alone will intervene, while this proportion falls to 22% when two witnesses are present.[6]

If several people are present during an incident, each of them will tend to pass the responsibility of intervening on to the others. This reaction is all the more pronounced when the group is large. This dilution of responsibility is also called the "bystander effect." Each individual wonders why it should be up to him to intervene, and feels relieved at the idea that someone else will take charge. And when no one intervenes, everyone hesitates to take the initiative.

This "bystander effect" had tragic consequences in the often-cited case of Kitty Genovese. On March 13, 1964, in New York, Kitty was walking toward her car when an assailant approached and stabbed her. He left, then returned a few minutes later to stab her again. She shouted, "Oh my God! He stabbed me! Help! Help!" The attacker returned a third time to kill her. During this entire time, about half an hour, thirty-eight people who lived in apartments looking out on the street heard her calls for help and witnessed these repeated assaults. Not one of them budged. It wasn't until half an hour after Kitty's death that someone finally called the police. "I didn't want to get mixed up in it," said most of the witnesses. More recently, in 2011, in China, images taken by a surveillance camera show a two-and-a-half-year-old girl getting run over by a truck, which stops at first, and then goes on its way. Then, no less than eighteen people pass by without batting an eyelid in front of the bleeding child, who is still moving.[7]

Fortunately, that is not always the case. In California one day, Bobby Green saw an incident live on TV during which a man was brutally beaten. He rushed to the site, running over half a mile, and took the victim to the hospital.[8]

If witnesses have the impression that the people arguing are related (husband and wife, for instance), they will intervene much less frequently, even if one of them is obviously being abused. In 1993, a two-year-old child, James Bulger, was killed by two ten-year-old boys. Sixty-one people acknowledged having seen the child struggling and crying while the two older boys took him from a supermarket to an empty lot where they committed the murder. Most of these witnesses said they thought they were brothers bringing their younger brother home.

The Determinants of Civic Courage

Will we intervene when we realize someone is in danger? Bibb Latané and John Darley identified five stages in this process. First of all, what is happening? I must take stock of the situation. Second, is it urgent to act? Is that person dozing on a public bench or has he fainted? Are those people about to fight or is it a simple verbal altercation between family members? Third, is it really up to me to intervene? Does the responsibility to come to someone's aid fall on me or should I count on other people present to help the person in danger? Fourth, am I capable of intervening? Do I have the requisite skill? Should I intervene directly or call for help? Fifth, I finally make a decision. Research has shown that it takes about thirty to forty seconds to pass through these five stages. After that, the dilution of the feeling of responsibility and the evaluation of the danger weigh more heavily in deciding whether to take action.[9]

CITY AND COUNTRY

Many studies have revealed that inhabitants of rural regions are more likely to help than city dwellers. For example, people's willingness to mail a stamped letter that had fallen on the street has been tested, as well as the wish to help someone who has dialed a wrong number.[10] Inhabitants of small towns are much more helpful than big-city dwellers. When a child calls out to a passerby, "I'm lost, could you call my home?" three-quarters of the adults of a small town grant his request, as opposed to less than half in a large city. According to Harold Takooshian, the author of this study, inhabitants of cities "adapt to the constant demands of city life by reducing their involvement in the lives of their fellow citizens."[11]

Confronted with an overload of social interactions, city-dwellers are forced to filter information and retain only what concerns them directly. They are more mistrustful and feel more vulnerable than their country-dwelling counterparts. The higher the crime rate is in a neighborhood, the less disposed the inhabitants are to help each other. In the United States, the crime rate is 2.7 times higher in cities than in the countryside.[12]

The city dweller is often wrapped up in various activities. He has lost the habit of establishing personal relationships with everyone he meets, since there are too many contacts, and they often seem meaningless. What's more, the city-dweller is worried about his own safety. If, in the country, it's natural to talk to the person you pass on the sidewalk and to be interested in what one's neighbors are doing, such relations are unusual in cities. We rarely talk to the person sitting next to us in the subway.

In cities, unless it is one's profession, it is impossible to take care of all the people in difficulty you meet in a single day: beggars, people who need help either because of the state of their health, their financial resources, or their homeless state. Stifling our compassion is not without its consequences. A study has shown that one's moral sense becomes diminished. At the University of North Carolina, C. Daryl Cameron and Keith Payne asked a group of volunteers to repress their compassion while they were shown photographs of crying children, homeless people, and victims of wars or famines. Soon after, they were given tests to evaluate their moral sense. Compared to another group of volunteers who had looked at the same images while letting their emotions be freely expressed, those who had repressed their compassion more readily accepted the idea of bending the rules and compromising moral values according to the circumstances.[13]

The situation in cities and places where there is a lot of suffering poses a constant challenge, then, to those who are concerned with the fate of their fellow citizens. If one puts oneself every time in the other's place, it becomes hard to look away. But if we wanted to intervene, we'd wind up doing nothing else. This laudable choice, which some make, is a full-time occupation, not something you can do now and then. Charismatic figures like Rosa Parks or the French priest Abbé Pierre,[14] who cannot bear to remain indifferent faced with so much suffering and who mobilized their fellow citizens with a great force of inspiration, can play a major role in changing social norms or organizing a system of mutual aid. But, as a general rule, studies carried out in less-populated places testify that it should be up to the community of citizens, that is, the government, town councils, and NGOs, to translate into concrete action the solidarity naturally present in most of us.

Individualists and Collectivists

Children raised in collectivist cultures, in which stress is placed on the well-being of the group and on community life, exhibit much more altruistic behavior than children raised in individualist cultures. Beatrice and John Whiting, at Harvard, observed the behavior of prosocial children aged three to ten in Kenya, Mexico, the Philippines, Japan, India, and the United States. They noted that children from community-based, nonindustrial societies were clearly more helpful than the others. For example, 100% of Kenyan children observed had a high altruism score, against only 8% of American children.[15] These children took part very early on in community activities and offering help had become second nature to them. That is also the case for children raised in Israeli kibbutzim.[16]

In general, helping behavior can vary considerably from one culture to another. One of the first studies on helping behavior was carried out by Roy Feldman in Paris, Boston, and Athens.[17] In a train station, a person who was obviously a native of that place asked a sample of passersby to mail a stamped letter for her, explaining she was about to go abroad. In Boston, 85% of people accepted; in Paris, 68%; and in Athens, 12%. Faced with a foreigner who didn't speak the language well, the readiness to help changed notably: 75% of people helped in Boston, 88% in Paris (so Parisians are friendlier than they say!), and 48% in Athens. Why are Athenians so uncooperative with their compatriots? It seems that Greeks narrowly define their social circle and consequently react distantly toward most of their fellow citizens.[18]

Men and Women

Although women and men are similar in their engagement in extensive prosocial behavior, they differ in their emphasis on particular kinds of behaviors. Women tend to engage more in prosocial behaviors that are more communal and relational, while men are more likely to engage in strength-intensive and action-oriented behavior.[19]

According to studies carried out in North America in the 1980s and 90s, in dangerous situations, men help more.[20] In one of the studies carried out in the streets of New York, 60% of those offering help during an accident were men.[21] According to the list of Americans who have received the medal from the Carnegie Hero Fund Commission (awarded for heroic actions), only 9% of the recipients are women. The interpretation offered by the researchers is that men are less hesitant to intervene in crisis situations that require physical involvement of a potentially dangerous nature.

On the other hand, women are more often rewarded (56%) than men for getting involved in humanitarian actions. And more women (58%) than men are organ donors.[22] Women provide more medical care and psychological support. In volunteer agencies in Europe, however, there are as many women as men offering their help.[23]

Mood and Circumstance

People in a good mood help more than others. It might be a temporary situation: they might just have experienced some success, heard some good news, imagined a vacation in Hawaii, or maybe shared a meal in enjoyable company.[24] But it has also been observed that people who temperamentally are usually in a good mood take part more in social activities than average people in the same society.[25]

The image we have of ourselves also influences our inclination to help others. After a personality test, half of the participants were told that the results indicated they were very attentive to others, and the other half were told that they had a high intelligence level. As they left the laboratory, each student who had just taken the test passed someone who dropped a dozen pencils, which scattered over the floor. The students who were described as kind and helpful picked up on average twice as many pencils as those whose intelligence was praised.[26]

Personal Values

As the French psychologist Jean-François Deschamps explains, consistent and planned behavior that extends over several months or years is usually inspired by personal values. According to the definition of the Israeli psychologist Shalom Schwartz, who has studied the question for three decades, values are concepts or beliefs that relate to aims or behavior we deem desirable, for ourselves as well as for others, and which guide our choices in most circumstances of daily life.[27] These values take shape in childhood and can be revised as our experience of the world and of others is enriched. Jean-François Deschamps and Rémi Finkelstein at the Parisian Laboratory of Social Psychology have shed light on a correlation between altruism regarded as a personal value and as prosocial behavior. Notably they showed that people who consider altruism an important personal value become more involved in volunteer activities.[28]

According to Shalom Schwartz, all of these studies show that kindness and "universalism" are the two values leading most often to prosocial behavior. For this author, kindness concerns mainly the well-being of those close to us and the group with which we identify, while universalism concerns the well-being of everyone. It turns out that these are also two of the three values regarded as the most important in the seventy-six cultures studied. To those is added conformism, which urges us to behave in a prosocial way in order to stay in harmony with the norms current in a society and thereby to be accepted by its members.

Among the other factors favoring prosocial behavior in general, researchers noted moral values transmitted by parents, confidence in one's ability to change things, the capacity to tolerate the unforeseeable, and openness to new experiences.[29]

Among the values that oppose prosocial behavior, Schwartz cites the feeling of insecurity, which makes us more worried about our own fate than the needs of others, and makes us try to maintain a stable, protective, and safe environment. This feeling limits openness to others and discourages risk-taking. Finally, the pursuit of power puts the stress on personal self-interest, valuing self, and dominating the competition. It leads us to justify our egocentric behavior, even to the detriment of others.

According to Vincent Jeffries at California State University at Northridge, self-restraint, strength of mind, fairness, concern for others, and discernment are among the virtues that favor prosocial behavior. These qualities allow us to master our emotions and favor the spirit of initiative, the sense of justice, compassion, and a tendency to take the long view.[30]

THE EFFECTS OF EMPATHY

Novels, films, and other media are very effective at awakening empathy for the oppressed and victims of discrimination, like slaves (*Uncle Tom's Cabin*), people interned in psychiatric asylums (*One Flew Over the Cuckoo's Nest*), people who are disfigured (*Elephant Man*), victims of colonial oppression (*Gandhi, Lagaan*), animals treated as products for consumption (*Earthlings, Food Inc.*), and the current and future victims of climate change (*An Inconvenient Truth* and *Home*).

Television news programs that portray the daily lives of female victims of spousal abuse in Mexico, or the problem of genital mutilations and the forced marriage of underage girls in Africa, have helped people to change their way of thinking in fields where governments and NGOs have long failed.

Elizabeth Paluck evaluated the impact of a TV series meant to promote reconciliation between Tutsis and Hutus in Rwanda.[31] The people portrayed are prey to dilemmas with which many Rwandans are confronted. The problem of friendships between members of the two ethnic groups is examined, as well as the difficulty of dealing with the memory of massacres, poverty, and so on. One of the scenes portrays a couple made up of a Tutsi husband and a Hutu wife who love each other despite the disapproval of their communities; they founded a youth movement for peace and reconciliation. It was observed that the viewers had closely identified with the protagonists, and according to Paluck's investigation, the effects have been very positive. Compared to a sample of viewers of other programs, those who watched the episodes of the series more readily accept mixed marriages, and want to cooperate more with members of the other community.

Empathy Facilitates Difficult Negotiations

Empathy can favor the resolution of conflicts between the negotiators of two opposing groups. Adam Galinsky and his colleagues have shown that when negotiators coldly determined their tactics by anticipating the possible reactions of the opposing party, like in a game of chess, they stuck to the position that was most advantageous for their own camp. On the other hand, when they were asked to put themselves in the place of their opponents, to imagine their situation, their difficulties, and their hopes, this reflection led them to make concessions and created a positive atmosphere leading to better results for the two parties over the long term.[32] Galinsky concluded from this that "thinking about what the other is thinking" offers a tactical advantage if you want to win at all costs, but that "feeling what the other is feeling" facilitates adopting a mutually acceptable solution that is beneficial in the long term.

EFFECT OF PROSOCIAL BEHAVIOR ON WELL-BEING

Prosocial behavior is also beneficial for the person who displays it. Meeting the people one is helping, taking part in volunteer activities, belonging to nonprofit organizations, and putting into play one's own skills in the service of others go hand-in-hand with a high level of well-being. Many studies have highlighted the link that exists between altruistic behavior and happiness.[33]

Allan Luks observed the morale of thousands of Americans who regularly took part in volunteer activities. He noted that they were generally in better health than other people of the same age, that they showed more enthusiasm and energy, and that they were less subject to depression than the average population.[34] Another study showed that teenagers who devote some of their time to a volunteer organization are less affected with drug addiction, early pregnancy, and dropping out of school.[35] Finally, people who experience depressive periods following tragic events, such as the loss of a partner, recover more quickly if they devote some time to helping others.[36]

While a large number of studies reveal *correlations* between positive psychological states and the act of helping others, they still do not show that altruism is the *cause* of these mental states. Daniel Batson and other psychologists wonder if it's altruism or the simple fact of spending more time with one's fellows that has positive effects on health. It is conceivable that the simple fact of becoming a member of a group of bird-watchers or a bridge club might produce the same effects.[37]

Aware of these methodological problems, Doug Oman reviewed six investigations that more rigorously took into account other factors likely to influence the results, and concluded that volunteer activity increases not only the quality of life of older people, but also its length.[38]

Martin Seligman, one of the pioneers of positive psychology, proposed that one group of students spend a day amusing themselves and another group take part in a volunteer activity (helping the aged, handing out food in a soup kitchen, and so on). Each group was given the same amount of money and asked to write a report for the class. The results were conclusive: the satisfaction procured by personal pleasures (eating out, going to the movies, having an ice cream, shopping, etc.)

was much less than that produced by altruistic activities. The students who had taken part in volunteer activities noted that they were more enthusiastic, attentive, easygoing, and even appreciated by others on that day.[39]

Several studies have also shown that taking care of an animal improved psychological and physical health by reducing stress and blood pressure, and also increased longevity. Taking care of a pet was also linked to notable benefits among the ill and solitary people in retirement homes, as well as among prisoners.[40]

Countless testimonies also remind us that kindness is one of the most powerful determinants of a feeling of accomplishment and contentment. Necdet Kent, the Turkish diplomat in Marseille who succeeded in persuading the German authorities to release dozens of Jews who had already been loaded onto a train, confided to French writer Marek Halter that he hadn't felt such a feeling of inner peace at any other time in his life.[41]

III

Cultivating Altruism

It's neither genius, nor glory, nor love that measures the loftiness of the human soul; it's benevolence.

—Henri Lacordaire

20

Can We Change?

One day, after a talk I had given on altruism, a person in the audience got up and said in an irritated tone: "What are you hoping for by encouraging us to cultivate altruism? Look at the history of humanity! It's always the same thing! An uninterrupted succession of wars and suffering. That's human nature, you can't change anything about that!" But is this truly the case? We have seen that cultures can evolve. But can the individual change? And if he can, does this change have an influence on society and on succeeding generations?

True, our character traits change little, so long as we do nothing to improve them. But they are not frozen in place. Our basic traits, which result from the combined contributions of our genetic heritage and the environment in which we grew up, make up only the foundation of our identity. Scientific research in the field of neuroplasticity shows that any form of training leads to a reconfiguring in the brain, on both the functional and structural levels.

Society and its institutions influence and condition individuals, but individuals can in turn make society evolve and change its institutions. As this interaction continues over the course of generations, culture and individuals mutually shape each other.

If we want to encourage a more altruistic society to develop, it is important to evaluate the respective capacities for change of both individuals and society. If humans have no ability to evolve by themselves, it would be better to concentrate all our efforts on transforming institutions and society, and not waste time encouraging individual transformation. That is the opinion of the French philosopher André Comte-Sponville. His arguments get to the heart of the debate:

> *You tell me that if we don't transform people first, we cannot transform society. We have behind us two thousand years of historic progress that prove the opposite. The Greeks were all racists and slave-owners; that was their culture. But I don't feel as if I'm better than Aristotle or Socrates simply because I'm neither a slave-owner nor a racist. So there is a progress of cultures and societies, but not of individuals as such. If someone says today, "He's a great guy because he's not a slave-owner," that's idiotic, since that person isn't that way for no reason: it's his culture that's responsible. Today, a person who is neither a slave-owner nor a racist is simply someone of his time.*
>
> *If we had waited for humans to be fair so that the poor could get medical attention, the poor would have died without any care. We didn't wait for humans to be fair, we created Social Security, taxes, a State governed by laws. So I think that the whole art of politics is to make selfish individuals more intelligent, which I call "solidarity" and which Jacques Attali calls "self-interested altruism." It's a question of making people understand it's in their own interests to take account of others' interests. It is in our own interest, for instance, to pay taxes.*
>
> *I don't at all believe in the progress of humanity, but I believe very much in the progress of society. Therefore, if you count on individual altruism to avoid economic crises, unemployment, poverty, then I won't follow you at all in that line of reasoning.*
>
> *In order to reconcile altruism and selfishness, politics were invented, which is a way to be selfish together and intelligently, rather than stupidly against each other.*
>
> *The person who best expressed the relationship between mass selfishness and the celebration we all make of love and generosity is the Dalai Lama, who said in a nicely worded phrase: "Be selfish, love each other."*[1] *This is a phrase I quote very often, because it is extremely profound, and because it links eudaemonism to altruism: "If you want to be happy, love each other."*[2]

Listening to these words, I remained perplexed and, at the time, without a convincing reply. But, upon reflection, transposed into biological language, André Comte-Sponville's argument—human beings themselves have not changed—comes down to saying that the human species has not changed genetically in two thousand years. That's true for the majority of our genes, which is not surprising if you think that it generally takes tens of thousands of years for a major genetic modification to affect a species as evolved as the human species. The genetic predispositions that influence our character traits are thus almost the same today as in Aristotle's time. The Dalai Lama agrees with this when he states that there is no basic difference between men and women today and those in the Buddha's time, no more than there is any basic difference between Easterners and Westerners: "We all share," he often says, "the same human nature, feel the same emotions of joy and sadness, benevolence or anger, and are all trying to avoid suffering. Thus as human beings we are basically the same."

But that's not all. The scientific discoveries of recent decades show that our genetic heritage, influential as it is, represents only a starting point that predisposes us to showing certain dispositions. This potential—and this is a crucial point—can then come to expression in multiple ways under the influence of our environment and by what we acquire through the efforts we make to train our minds or physical abilities. Thus, it is more appropriate to compare our genetic heritage to an architectural drawing that might be modified as the construction progresses, or else to a musical theme on which a performer improvises.

Neuronal Plasticity

The plasticity of the brain plays a large role in our capacity for individual transformation. For a long time, an almost universally accepted dogma in the neuroscience field stated that once formed and structured, the adult brain doesn't produce any more neurons and changes only through decline with age. It was thought that the organization of the brain was so complex that any important modification would cause major malfunctioning. According to one of the great specialists in neuroplasticity, Fred Gage at the Salk Institute, "It was easier to believe that there was no change. That way, the individual would remain pretty fixed."[3]

Today we know that this doctrine was completely wrong. One of the major discoveries of the last thirty years concerns "neuroplasticity," a term that takes into account the fact that the brain changes constantly when an individual is exposed to new situations. The adult brain in fact remains extraordinarily malleable. It has the ability to produce new neurons, to reinforce or diminish the activity of existing neurons, and even to attribute a new function to an area of the brain that usually carries out a completely different function.

Research carried out on people who are blind has demonstrated that the region of the brain normally dedicated to vision ("visual area") was taken over and used by hearing, in addition to the normal auditory area, which allows nonsighted people to have a much more precise perception of the spatial localization of sounds. Similarly, among the deaf, the auditory area is mobilized to refine vision, which allows them to have a peripheral vision and an ability to detect movements that are much superior to those of hearing people.[4]

In 1962, Joseph Altman at MIT showed that new neurons were constantly forming in adult rats, cats, and guinea pigs.[5] But these discoveries were so revolutionary that they were ignored or derided by the leading authorities of the time. In 1981, Fernando Nottebohm established in turn that among canaries, who create a new repertory of songs every spring, two encephalic regions linked to this learning increased respectively by 99% and 76% in volume, or neuronal mass, compared to the previous fall.[6]

In 1997, Fred Gage placed rats alone in an empty box for a month in which they had nothing to do except eat once a day. Then he transferred them to a veritable Disneyland for rats, with tunnels, wheels, pools, and various climbing elements, as well as other rats to keep them company. The repercussions of this transfer on their brain were surprising. In forty-five days, the hippocampus,[7] the area of the brain associated with learning new skills, increased 15% in volume, even among the older rats, going on average from 270,000 to 317,000 neurons.[8]

It remained to be demonstrated that such a phenomenon could occur in humans. By injecting into the brains of patients a chemical composite that allows for the tracking of the evolution of brain tumors and then examining the brains after the patients had died, Peter Eriksson, a Swedish researcher, discovered that new neurons had recently formed in the hippocampus. It became clear that, until one dies, new neurons continue to form in certain regions of the human brain (up to 1,000 a day).[9] As Fred Gage emphasizes, "This is occurring throughout life. The finding brought us an important step closer to the possibility that we have more control over our own brain capacity than we ever thought possible."[10]

In the case of Fred Gage's rats, they reacted to a new situation in which they found themselves involuntarily placed. Scientists speak of an "outer enrichment," which is semi-passive. But one can also actively and voluntarily train the mind to develop specific abilities. Here, too, research has highlighted transformations of the brain in people learning to juggle or play chess, and in athletes who train assiduously. Among violinists, the regions of the brain that control the movements of the fingering hand develop as they learn. Among musicians, those who began their training very early and continue it over many years show the greatest modifications in the brain.[11] We even know that among London taxi drivers, who have to memorize the names and locations of 14,000 streets, the hippocampus is structurally more voluminous in proportion to the number of years they have been working.[12]

Finally, we can thus envisage the possibility of an "inner enrichment" by an effort of mind. During the practice of meditation, notably, nothing changes in the outer environment. But by training one's mind, the meditator carries out a maximum inner enrichment. Research in neuroscience carried out over a dozen years in which I myself have taken part shows that attention, emotional balance, altruistic love, compassion, and other human qualities can be cultivated, and that their development is accompanied by profound functional and structural transformations of the brain.

THE IMPORTANCE OF EPIGENETIC FACTORS

Along with neuroplasticity, a second mechanism allows individuals to change: epigenetics. In order for a gene, which we have inherited from our parents, to be active, it must be "expressed," that is it must be "transcribed" in the form of a specific protein acting on the organism bearing this gene. But if a gene is not expressed, if it remains "silent," it's as if it were absent. Recent advances in genetics have revealed that environment can considerably modify the expression of genes by a process called "epigenetics." This expression of genes can be activated or deactivated under the influence not just of external conditions, but also of our mental states.

Two monozygotic twins, for instance, who have exactly the same genes, can acquire different physiological and mental characteristics if they are separated and exposed to dissimilar living conditions. In scientific terms, one would say they are genetically identical but phenotypically different. Similarly, a caterpillar and a butterfly have exactly the same genes, but they are not expressed in the same way, depending on the times of the insect's life.

These modifications in the expression of genes are more or less lasting, and in certain cases can even be transmitted from one generation to another, even though there are no changes in the DNA sequence of the genes themselves. These discoveries have truly revolutionized the field of genetics, since hitherto the very notion of transmission of acquired traits was regarded as heresy.[13] The influence of external conditions is thus considerable, and we know today that this influence has repercussions all the way down to our genes.

A series of famous experiments carried out by Michael Meaney and his colleagues at McGill University in Montreal dealt with newborn rats possessing genes that predisposed them to strong stress and anxiety. During the first ten days of their lives, these rats were given to mothers selected for being extremely caring with their young: they constantly licked them, groomed them, and were in physical contact with them as often as possible. The team established that after these ten days, the expression of the genes connected to anxiety *was blocked*, and the genes were not expressed *for the entire lives* of the rats.[14]

On the other hand, genetically identical baby rats that were given to ordinary mothers who did not give them this supplement of maternal love became fearful and anxious for the rest of their lives. The level of stress at adulthood does not depend, then, on genetic heritage, identical here for everyone, but on the way these baby rats were treated during the first ten days of their lives. Thus, our genetic fate is not engraved in stone.

Following this, Michael Meaney, Moshe Szyf, and other researchers undertook studies on human populations. We know that children who have been severely abused are 50% more likely to suffer depression at adulthood.[15] Research showed that the mistreatment to which these children were subjected set off epigenetic modifications that lasted long after the period during which they were abused. Researchers especially observed lasting modifications in the expression of genes involved in the production and regulation of cortisol, a hormone associated with stress. Among these individuals, the level of cortisol remained chronically high, even if they were in good health and no longer experiencing abuse.[16] The fact that they often suffered multiple episodes of depression could thus be explained by a persistent vulnerability associated with epigenetic modifications in their neurons at the time they were victims of this abuse.

Could training the mind to cultivate positive emotions lead to epigenetic changes? Studies undertaken at Richard Davidson's laboratory in Wisconsin, in collaboration with the Spanish geneticist Perla Kaliman, show that *within a day,* meditating for *eight hours* on mindfulness, altruistic love, and compassion already induces major epigenetic modifications.[17] We can glimpse here the possibility of an epigenetic transformation of an individual that is due not just to the influence of environment, but also to a voluntary training in cultivating basic human qualities.

Different Beings

Let's reconsider in light of the experiments described above the arguments advanced by André Comte-Sponville. It seems that a *simultaneous transformation of cultures and individuals* is possible. Children who grow up in a culture where altruistic values prevail and where society encourages cooperation will change not only in momentary behavior but also in their general attitude and mental dispositions. They will be different, not just because they will conform to new cultural norms and new rules set by institutions, but because their *brains will have been shaped differently* and because *their genes will be expressed differently.* Thus, a dynamic process of mutual influences will continue over the course of generations. As Richerson and Boyd, specialists in the evolution of cultures, stress:

> *What happens to* individuals *(for example, natural selection) affects the population's properties (for example, the frequencies of genes)....The frequency of cultural variant, a* population *property, affects its probability of being imitated by* individuals.

> *Individuals seem to be hapless prisoners of their institutions because, in the short run, individual decisions don't have much effect on institutions. But, in the long run, accumulated over many decisions, individual decisions have a profound effect on institutions.*[18]

In the final analysis, it is individuals who put totalitarian regimes in place, and other individuals who overthrow them to establish democracy. It is individuals who have perpetrated genocides when they dehumanized their fellows, and it is other individuals, sometimes the contemporaries of the former, who promulgated the Universal Declaration of Human Rights.

GIVING INDIVIDUAL TRANSFORMATION THE CREDIT IT DESERVES

Despite immense progress in the fields of democracy, women's rights, human rights in general, justice, solidarity, and the eradication of poverty and epidemics, much remains to be done. It would be regrettable to neglect the role of personal transformation in facilitating further changes. One of the tragedies of our time seems to be considerably underestimating the ability for transformation of the human mind, given that our character traits are perceived as relatively stable. It is not so common for angry people to become patient, tormented people to find inner peace, or pretentious people to become humble. It is undeniable, however, that some individuals *do* change, and the change that takes place in them shows that it is not at all an impossible thing. *Our character traits last as long as we do nothing to improve them* and we leave our attitudes and automatisms alone, or else let them be reinforced with time. But it is a mistake to believe they are fixed in place permanently.

We constantly try to improve the external conditions of our lives, and in the end it's our mind that experiences the world and that translates this perception as happiness or suffering. If we transform our way of apprehending things, we automatically transform the quality of our life. And this change is possible. It results from *training the mind*, which is also called "meditation."

21

Training the Mind:
What the Cognitive Sciences Have to Say

In 2000, an extraordinary meeting took place in Dharamsala, India. Some of the leading specialists in the study of emotions—psychologists, neuroscientists, and philosophers—spent a week in dialogue with the Dalai Lama in the privacy of his residence, among the foothills of the Himalayas. It was also the first time I had the opportunity to take part in the fascinating meetings organized by the Mind & Life Institute, founded in 1987 by Francisco Varela, an eminent neuroscientist, and Adam Engle, an American lawyer. The dialogue dealt with ways of dealing with destructive emotions.[1]

During this meeting, one morning, the Dalai Lama declared, "All these discussions are very interesting, but what can we really contribute to society?" During lunch, after an animated conversation, a proposal was made to start a research program on the short- and long-term effects of training the mind, that is, meditation. In the afternoon, in the presence of the Dalai Lama, this project was adopted with enthusiasm. This was the beginning of a series of groundbreaking research in the contemplative sciences.

A few years earlier, Francisco Varela, Richard Davidson, and Cliff Saron, assisted by Alan B. Wallace, had come to Dharamsala with a portable electroencephalograph and, encouraged by the Dalai Lama, carried out tests on some meditators. But the experimental conditions were far from ideal; we had to wait till the year 2000 for the "contemplative neurosciences" to really take off.

Studies were launched, and I was fortunate to take part in several of them, especially in the laboratories of the late Francisco Varela in France; Richard Davidson and Antoine Lutz in Madison, Wisconsin; Paul Ekman and Robert Levenson in Berkeley; Jonathan Cohen and Brent Field at Princeton; and Tania Singer in Leipzig.

THE LONG-TERM EFFECTS OF MEDITATION

It seemed logical to begin by studying subjects who had practiced meditation for many years. They were the ones, in fact, who could be expected to have the most significant brain transformations. If the results of their tests didn't reveal any change in their brain or behavior, it would have been pointless to observe other subjects who had only meditated for a few months or weeks. If, on the other hand, important changes were observed in experienced meditators, we could then ponder how they had arrived at that state, then study the way a beginner progresses over time.

In the initial phase, Antoine Lutz and Richard Davidson studied about twenty individuals—monastics and laypeople, men and women, Easterners and Westerners—who had completed between 10,000 and 60,000 hours of meditation devoted to developing altruistic love, compassion, attention, and awareness over the course of intensive retreats (often lasting several continuous years), along with fifteen to forty years of daily practice. As a point of comparison, at the time of the entrance exam for a leading music conservatory, a proficient violinist has completed about 10,000 hours of practice.

Analysis of the data very soon showed spectacular differences between meditators and untrained subjects. The former had the ability to give rise to precise, powerful, and lasting mental states. The areas of the brain associated with compassion, for example, presented a considerably greater activity in those who had meditated for a long time. What's more, each type of meditation had a different "signature" in the brain, which meant that meditation on compassion activated a series of areas in the brain (called a "neural network") different from those activated when the subject meditates, for instance, on focused attention.

In the words of Richard Davidson, "It demonstrates that the brain is capable of being trained and physically modified in ways few people can imagine."[2] The research also showed that the greater the number of hours of practice were, the greater the change in brain activity was. Since then, numerous articles published in prestigious scientific journals have reported on these studies, making research into meditation respectable, a field which, till then, had scarcely been taken seriously.

Meditators in the Lab

During the first series of experiments in Madison, a protocol was established by which the meditator would alternate between a neutral state and several specific meditative states, involving different attentive, cognitive, and emotional states. Six types of meditation were chosen: focused attention, altruistic love combined with compassion, "open presence" (see below), visualization of mental images, fearlessness, and devotion. These spiritual exercises that a Buddhist practitioner performs over many years produce meditation that is increasingly stable and clear.[3] Only the first three types of meditation were chosen for the remainder of the research, since they involved qualities that, far from being specifically Buddhist, had a universal value and could be cultivated by everyone.

In the framework of the laboratory experiments, the scientists measured the observable *differences* between the cerebral activity of a meditator at rest, called a "neutral state," and the brain activity during meditation. So that a sufficient amount of data could be gathered, the meditator alternated many times between forty-five-second periods of rest and periods of meditation that lasted one to five minutes. An entire session could last up to two hours, during which the subject had to remain completely motionless, lying in a scanner if the recording apparatus used a functional MRI, or seated more comfortably if it used an electroencephalograph. These two techniques were complementary: electroencephalography (EEG) is temporally very precise, but imagery by functional magnetic resonance imaging (fMRI) is much more precise spatially.

The scientists also added a number of behavioral and cognitive tests to measure attention, emotional balance, resilience, resistance to pain, empathy, and prosocial behavior. In particular, the research explored the changes that can occur in the six main "emotional styles" described by Richard Davidson: *resilience*, or the ability to recover from adversity; *outlook,* in the temporal sense, or how long you can sustain positive emotion; *social intuition,* how adept you are at picking up social signals from the people around you (facial expression, body language, tone of voice, etc.); *self-awareness,* how well you perceive bodily feelings that reflect emotions; *sensitivity to context,* how good you are at regulating your emotional responses according to the context you find yourself in; and finally *attention,* how sharp and clear your focus is.[4]

A Dozen Years of Experimentation

From 2000 to 2013, over a hundred men and women, monastics and laypeople practicing Buddhism, and many beginners, volunteered for these scientific experiments at about twenty renowned universities.[5] In April 2012, the first International Symposium for Contemplative Studies gathered over 700 researchers from all over the world for three days in Denver, thus marking the arrival of this field of research.

This researche has shown not only that meditation caused major changes, both functional and structural, in the brains of the volunteer practitioners, but also that a few weeks of meditation, at the rate of thirty minutes a day, already induced significant changes in cerebral activity, the immune system, one's quality of attention, and many other parameters.

Attention Can Be Improved

The practice of *concentration* consists of choosing an object on which one focuses one's attention, which one tries to maintain without letting oneself be distracted. This training aims to pass gradually from an unstable, capricious state of mind to a state of mind in which clear, stable attention prevails, along with the ability to manage emotions and inner peace. Whatever quality you wish to cultivate, it is indispensable to refine your attention; if you don't do so, the mind will not be available for the training one wants to accomplish. During this exercise, one generally focuses one's concentration on a precise element; this could be the in-and-out of the breath, a physical sensation, or an external object, a dot of light, for instance, on a laboratory screen. One then lets one's mind rest attentively on the chosen object, and one brings it back if one perceives it has strayed.

A relatively experienced person (averaging 19,000 hours of practice) can activate zones of the brain linked to attention much better than an untrained subject; on the other hand, among the most experienced subjects (averaging 44,000 hours of practice), less activation of these zones is noted, even when their attention remains stable.[6] This observation agrees with certain studies demonstrating that when someone has mastered a task, the cerebral structures put into play during the execution of this task are generally less active than when he or she was still in the learning phase.

Researchers have also established that three months of diligent training in meditation considerably improved the *stability* of attention.[7] The attention of the subjects studied required less effort, varied less from one test to another, and was less distracted by disturbing sounds, which testifies to better cognitive control.[8]

Other studies have shown that the practice of attention also allowed meditators to see clearly a complete sequence of words or images that changed rapidly, whereas people usually perceive and identify one image and then fail to identify the next two or three images due to a phenomenon called "attentional blink."[9] Usually the attention drawn by an object turns to that object, sticks to it for a while, then detaches from it. This process takes a certain amount of time, and an untrained person misses the second and third images that follow because his mind is still occupied with dealing with the first one. When an experienced meditator places himself in a state of "open presence," or full awareness of the present moment, he is completely receptive and welcomes whatever comes to him without clinging to it, which considerably reduces, or may even eliminate, attentional blink.

CULTIVATING ALTRUISTIC LOVE AND COMPASSION

To meditate on *altruistic love* and *compassion*, first you think about someone close to you; you give rise to unconditional love and kindness toward them. Then you gradually extend this love to all beings, and you continue in that way until your whole mind is filled with love. If you notice this love diminishing, you revive it, and if you become distracted, you bring your attention back to love. For *compassion,* you begin by thinking of someone close to you who is suffering, and you sincerely wish for that person to be free of suffering. Then you proceed as you did for love.

When the subjects participating in a study conducted by Richard Davidson and Antoine Lutz meditated on altruistic love and compassion, a remarkable increase was observed in the synchronization of brain wave oscillations in the *gamma* frequency, usually associated with increased connectivity and coherence between different areas of the brain.[10] The level of synchronization achieved by expert meditators was of a "magnitude that has never been reported earlier in the neuroscience literature," according to Richard Davidson, and the intensity measured in the gamma frequencies increases according to the number of hours (from 15,000 to 60,000, depending on the subject) devoted to meditation practices that give a preeminent place to cultivating altruistic love.[11]

More precise brain imagery showed that the areas strongly activated during meditation on altruistic love were already known for their association with empathy, positive emotions, maternal love, sense of affiliation, reward and a sense of wholesomeness, and preparation for action in general (the premotor cortex).

In two subsequent studies, carried out in the same laboratory, Antoine Lutz and Richard Davidson showed that when experienced meditators in a state of compassion listened to recordings alternating between that of a woman crying out in distress and of a baby laughing, activation of several areas of the brain linked to empathy was observed, including the *insula.* This zone is more activated by the distress cries than by the baby's laughter. A close correlation is also observed between the subjective intensity of meditation on compassion, the activation of the insula, and cardiac rhythm.[12] This activation is all the more intense when the meditators have more hours of training. The amygdala and the cingulate cortex are also activated, indicating increased sensitivity to others' emotional states.[13]

It seems, then, that cultivating a meditative state linked to positive emotions like altruistic love and compassion modifies the activity of brain regions and networks known to be associated with empathy.[14]

Barbara Fredrickson and her colleagues also showed that six to eight weeks of meditation on altruistic love, at a rate of thirty minutes per day, increased positive emotions and one's degree of satisfaction with existence.[15] The subjects feel more joy, kindness, gratitude, hope, and enthusiasm, and the longer their training was, the more marked were the positive effects.

At Emory University in Atlanta, Chuck Raison's team also demonstrated that meditation on altruistic love reinforces the immune system and diminishes inflammatory response. These researchers notably proved as well that reduction of the levels of a hormone linked to the inflammatory process (interleukin-6) in the blood was proportional to the time devoted to meditation.[16]

Other studies, summarized in an article by Stefan Hofmann[17] of Boston University, confirmed that meditation on altruistic love and compassion not only increases positive moods but also diminishes negative moods.

Meditation on Open Presence

Meditation on *open presence* consists of letting your mind rest in a clear state, at once vast and vivid, and free from discursive thoughts. The mind is not focused on any particular object, but remains completely present. When thoughts arise, the meditator does not try to block them, but simply lets them vanish on their own.

In this meditative state, self-centered feelings slowly fade away, thereby favoring the spontaneous blossoming of altruistic love and compassion. According to meditators who have cultivated *open presence,* without the barriers of selfishness and attachment to ego, love and compassion arise spontaneously and are free of discriminations.

It turns out that like meditation on altruistic love, the practice of *open presence* also gives rise to a notable increase of brain waves in the gamma frequencies, accompanied by increased connectivity and synchronization between various parts of the brain.

The Brain Is Structurally Modified by Meditation

What we have described up to this point shows that meditation entrains major *functional* changes in the brain—that is, modifications in the activity of certain areas of the brain due to meditation are observed during well-defined cognitive and emotional processes. It is also important to demonstrate that these changes are accompanied by modifications in the structure of the brain.

An initial study directed by Sara Lazar and her colleagues at Harvard established that among longtime meditators who had on average a dozen years of experience, the volume of the cerebral cortex had increased.[18] More recently, Britta Hölzel has shown that structural changes were already occurring after an eight-week training period of meditation on mindfulness. She observed an increase of density and thickness of gray matter in the left hippocampus (the area linked to learning and emotional control), as well as in other areas of the brain.[19]

DETECTING FACIAL EXPRESSIONS MIGHT BE LINKED TO OUR DEGREE OF EMPATHY

In Paul Ekman's laboratory, meditators took part in an experiment that measured the ability to identify correctly facial expressions that convey various emotions. A series of faces appeared on the screen, expressing joy, sadness, anger, fear, disgust, or surprise: six emotions that are universal, biologically determined, and expressed in the same way throughout the world. First a neutral face was shown, then the same face expressing an emotion and remaining on the screen for a mere thirtieth of a second. The emotive expression was again followed by a neutral expression. The images showing the emotion went by so quickly that you could miss them by just blinking your eyes. The test consisted of identifying, during that thirtieth of a second, the facial signs of the emotion just glimpsed.

These "micro-expressions," as Paul Ekman calls them, are in fact involuntary movements that occur constantly in our daily lives and that are the uncensored indicators of our inner feelings. The ability to recognize these fleeting expressions indicates an unusual aptitude for empathy.

Studying thousands of subjects taught Ekman that those most gifted at performing this task are also the most open to new experiences, the most curious about things in general, and the most reliable and efficient. The two experienced meditators who took this test did much better than the others at recognizing these fleeting emotional signs. Both obtained higher results than those of the 5,000 subjects previously tested. "They do better than policemen, lawyers, psychiatrists, customs officers, judges—even Secret Service agents," a group that till then had been shown to be more precise. "It seems that one benefit of some part of the life paths these two have followed is becoming more aware of these subtle signs of how other people feel," Ekman observed.[20]

Altruistic Behavior and Emotional Control

It is interesting to note that, according to other studies, people who have more control of their emotions behave more altruistically than those who do not. A free, serene mind is more likely to consider painful situations and the suffering of others from an altruistic point of view than a mind constantly disturbed by internal conflicts and preoccupied with its own reactions (fear, anxiety, anger, etc.).

The Benefits of Short-Term Training on Prosocial Behavior

Other scientific experiments have shown that it was not necessary to be an extremely well-trained meditator to benefit from the effects of meditation, and that twenty minutes of practice a day over a few weeks led to significant changes.

Helen Weng, a researcher at Richard Davidson's laboratory, compared two groups: in one, the participants meditated for just two weeks on altruistic love for thirty minutes a day, and in the other, they took part in "cognitive reevaluation." Weng observed in the first group an increase of prosocial behavior. What's more, in only two weeks of meditation on altruistic love, a diminution of the activation of the amygdala, an area of the brain linked to aggression, anger, and fear, was observed.[21]

By using a prosocial game created at the University of Zurich, which gives people an opportunity to help another participant surmount an obstacle at the risk of earning a lower score for oneself,

Susanne Leiberg, Olga Klimecki, and Tania Singer showed that participants who received a brief training in meditation on compassion helped more than those who had received a training to improve memory (in order to compare the effects of this meditation with another type of active training having nothing to do with altruism). These researchers showed that increase of prosocial behavior toward strangers was proportional to the period of time spent training in compassion, carried out two to five days before.[22] The fact that a relatively brief training can have a lasting effect presages good possibilities for putting such training into practice in schools and hospitals.

This was recently demonstrated by Paul Condon and Gaëlle Desbordes, who followed three groups for eight weeks. One group was trained in meditation on loving kindness, the other in meditation on mindfulness, and the third, the control group, was left without any training. After eight weeks, the altruistic behavior of the participants was put to the test by observing the probability that they would offer their seat in a waiting room to someone standing against the wall with crutches and showing signs of discomfort. Before the suffering individual enters, the participant is seated on a bench next to two other people (accomplices of the experimenter) who don't show the least bit of interest in the standing patient (which accentuates the "bystander effect" mentioned previously, known to inhibit helping behavior). Strikingly, on average, the meditators offered their seat *five times more often* than non-meditators.[23]

The Center for Compassion and Altruism Research and Education (CCARE) devised through a cooperation between scientists from Stanford University and Thubten Jinpa Langri, the main interpreter for the 14th Dalai Lama, is developing an eight-week Compassion Cultivation Training (CCT) course designed to develop compassion, empathy, and kindness for oneself and others, which combines traditional contemplative practices with contemporary research. Hooria Jazaieri and colleagues have shown that CCT resulted in significant improvements in three domains related to compassion—the capacities to generate compassion for others, to receive compassion from others (which is difficult for people who suffer from anxiety, depression, and self-criticism), and self-compassion (feelings of caring and kindness toward oneself).

Effects of Altruistic Love Meditation on Social Connections

Having social connections is a fundamental need for humans, and many studies demonstrate the benefits of social bonding on mental and physical health. In the contemporary world, however, societal changes linked to individualism, with an increasing number of people living alone, have led to greater mistrust and more alienation.

Is it possible to reinforce our feeling of belonging and our connection with those around us? We know the importance that trusting other people has on social harmony. The diminution of this trust is accompanied by prejudices against those who are not included in our close circle. Various methods have been used to reduce these prejudices. Some stress the harmful consequences of discrimination;[24] others favor positive personal contact with members of a group against which one has prejudices.[25] Researchers are now interested in methods that would not only lead to a reduction of negative attitudes, but also increase positive attitudes.

The psychologist Cendri Hutcherson, who became interested in Buddhist meditation on altruistic love, has shown that a single, seven-minute practice session increased feelings of belonging to the community, social connectedness, and kindly attitudes toward strangers.[26]

Similarly, Yoona Kang at Yale demonstrated that six weeks of meditation on altruistic love considerably reduced discrimination against certain groups (people of color, the homeless, etc.).[27]

Lessening of Unpleasant Aspects of Physical Pain

We know that anticipating what we are about to feel plays a large role in the experience of pain. In general, we can more easily bear pain whose duration and intensity are foreseeable. We can less easily endure unexpected pain, whose intensity risks increasing, and whose duration is unknown. Assessment of pain, then, depends in a large part on our mental state. For example, we accept the painful effects of a medical treatment when we have the hope of getting better, or a painful physical training in order to excel at sports. Many people are willing to donate their blood or an organ to save the life of someone close to them.

Can meditation influence our perception of pain? Several research laboratories have focused on this question. Studies carried out by David Perlman and Antoine Lutz at the University of Madison showed that when experienced meditation practitioners placed themselves in a state of *open presence* and were then subjected to intense pain, they perceived that pain with the same clarity and acuity as untrained subjects, but the unpleasant aspect of the pain was considerably diminished.[28] Moreover, trained meditators don't anticipate the pain with anxiety, whereas untrained subjects do. After the painful sensation, they return more quickly to a normal emotional state. Finally, they become more accustomed to the pain than beginners do.[29]

Fadel Zeidan and Joshua Grant at the University of North Carolina showed that after only four days of training at twenty minutes a day, the subjects who entered into a mindfulness meditation and then were exposed to pain rated this pain on average 57% less unpleasant and 40% less intense than the subjects in a control group who hadn't undertaken any training.[30]

Studies by Tania Singer's team at the Max Planck Institute that are currently under way show that when experienced practitioners undertook meditation on compassion for a suffering person and were simultaneously subjected to physical pain (an electrical shock on the wrist), compassion for others considerably attenuated the unpleasant quality of their own pain.

Meditation on Altruism, Compassion, and Focused Attention Can Slow Down the Aging of Cells

Telomeres are segments of single-strand DNA situated at the end of chromosomes. They ensure the stability of genes during cellular division but are shortened every time the cell divides. When the length of a telomere diminishes below a critical threshold, the cell stops dividing and gradually enters into a state of senescence.[31] Telomeres are nevertheless protected by an enzyme called telomerase.[32] Thus, the aging of cells in our body, our health, and our longevity are affected by the activity rate of telomerase.[33]

Cliff Saron at the University of California at Davis studied thirty meditators who had practiced meditation on focusing the mind, as well as on altruism and compassion. The meditators had practiced an average of six hours a day for three months over the course of Alan Wallace's Shamatha Project. The study revealed that telomerase activity was considerably higher after the three months of practice among meditators than among members of the control group. This study is the first to highlight a link between positive and altruistic psychological changes induced by meditation and telomerase activity.[34] The researchers also showed that the practitioners benefited from better mental health and found more meaning in their lives.

Practical Applications of These Studies

Secularized and scientifically validated, these meditation techniques could, for example, be usefully integrated into educational programs for children—a kind of mental equivalent of physical education—as well as into the therapeutic management of emotional problems in adults. When Daniel Goleman asked the Dalai Lama what he expected from these experiments, the Dalai Lama replied:

> *Through training the mind people can become more calm—especially those who suffer from too many ups and downs. That's the conclusion from these studies of Buddhist mind training. And that's my main end: I'm not thinking how to further Buddhism, but how the Buddhist tradition can make some contribution to the benefit of society. Of course, as Buddhists, we always pray for all sentient beings. But we're only human beings; the main thing you can do is train your own mind.*[35]

The practice of mindfulness, based in particular on the method of mindfulness-based stress reduction (MBSR), developed with immense success by Jon Kabat-Zinn over the last thirty years, has been gaining worldwide recognition and interest, not only in the clinical world where it was first applied, but also in educational systems and in the corporate world. Properly practiced, mindfulness meditation will naturally give rise to altruism and compassion. However, in order to avoid any risk of using mindfulness as a mere tool to increase one's concentration for achieving goals that might be ethically questionable, we feel that embedding a clear component of altruism from the start, in what could be called "caring mindfulness," might offer a very potent, purely secular way to cultivate benevolence and promote a more altruistic society.

22

How to Cultivate Altruism: Meditations on Altruistic Love, Compassion, Joy, and Impartiality

All of us, to varying degrees, have experienced profoundly altruistic love for someone dear to us, or intense compassion for someone suffering. Some of us are naturally more altruistic than others, sometimes to the point of heroism. Others are more focused on themselves, and find it hard to regard the benefit of others as an essential aim, and even harder to make it a higher priority than their own personal interest.

Generally, even if altruistic thoughts pass through our minds, they are fluctuating and soon replaced by other thoughts. If we truly want to integrate altruism and compassion into our mindstream, we have to cultivate these qualities over long periods of time, anchor them in our minds, maintain them, and reinforce them until they become a lasting part of our mental landscape.

Meditating is *familiarizing* ourselves with a new way of being and also *cultivating* qualities that otherwise remain latent if one makes no effort to develop them. Meditation is a *practice* that allows us to cultivate these qualities in the same way as other forms of training such as learning to read, to play a musical instrument, or to acquire any other ability for which we have aptitude.[1] Finally, it brings about a transformation of the way we regard others and the world around us.[2] If, for example, we perceive the world as a hostile, alien place like an enemy always ready to take advantage of us, our relationship with others will be marked by fear and mistrust. If we regard others as essential like us in their desire to be happy and not suffer, we will approach our daily lives with greater compassion.

Preparing for Meditation

The everyday circumstances of life are not always favorable for meditation. That is why it is necessary, in the beginning, to begin to meditate in a quiet place, and to arrange things so that the time we reserve for meditation, even if it is short, is not interrupted by other occupations.

Motivation

When we begin to meditate, as for any other activity we undertake, it is essential to check our motivation. It is this motivation—altruistic or selfish, vast or limited—that gives a good or bad direction to our meditation and to all our actions.

Stabilizing the Mind

In order to cultivate altruistic love and compassion, the mind should be ready, clear, and focused. To that end, we can improve our power of concentration by using a simple support that is always available: the in-and-out of our own breath.

Breathe calmly and naturally. Concentrate all your attention on the movements of the breath. Observe the sensation created by the passage of air through the nostrils when you breathe in and out. Maintain this concentration breath after breath, without tension, but also without relaxing to the point of falling into somnolence.

When you notice that you have been distracted, simply go back to observing the breath. Don't try to block the arising of thoughts; simply avoid feeding them; let them pass through the field of your awareness the way a bird passes through the sky without leaving a trace.

All training involves effort, and all change encounters resistance.

Therefore, we have to learn to overcome obstacles to meditation, including mental agitation and its opposites, laxity and lethargy, as well as lack of perseverance.

It is better to meditate regularly for multiple short periods of time than to engage from time to time in long sessions. We can, for example, devote twenty minutes a day to meditation, and profit from pauses in our daily activities to revive, even if only for a few minutes, the experience we acquired during formal practice.

Meditation on Altruistic Love

To meditate on altruistic love, you should start by realizing that deep down you want to avoid suffering, and you wish for happiness. This step is especially important for those who have a negative image of themselves and have suffered a lot, and who think they are not meant to be happy. Give rise to a welcoming, tolerant, kind attitude toward yourself; decide that from now on you wish the best for yourself.

Once you have recognized this aspiration, you then have to realize that it is shared by all beings. Acknowledge our interdependence. The shirt you wear, the glass you drink from, the house you live in—all these are possible only thanks to the activity of countless others. The simplest object in your everyday life is filled with the presence of others. Reflect on the origin of the white sheet of paper on which you write. Imagine the lumberjack who cut down the tree, the paper factory worker, the truck driver, the shopkeeper; like any of us, they all have a life, with joys and sufferings, parents and friends. They all share our humanity; none of them wants to suffer. This awareness should make us feel closer to all these beings, to feel empathy for them, to be concerned about their fate and to wish them well.

Meditate First on a Loved One

It is easier to begin training in altruistic love by thinking about someone dear to you. Imagine a smiling child coming up to us and looking at us happily, trustingly, full of innocence. You pat the child's head, look at it tenderly, and take it in your arms, as you feel unconditional love and kindness. Let yourself be completely filled with this love, which wants nothing but the happiness of this child. Remain for a few moments in full awareness of this love, without any other thoughts.

Extending to Strangers and Enemies

Then extend these loving thoughts to people you know less well and to strangers. They too want to be happy, even if they are sometimes clumsy in their attempts to escape suffering. Go further; include in this loving kindness those who have harmed you, even those who are harming humanity in general. That does not mean that you want them to succeed in their malevolent undertakings; you simply form the wish that they give up their hatred, greed, cruelty or indifference, and that they become kind and concerned for the well-being of others. Look at them the way a doctor looks at his most seriously ill patients. Finally, embrace all sentient beings in a feeling of limitless love.

Compassion

Compassion is the form that altruistic love takes when it is confronted with the suffering of others. For this, you must feel concerned by others' situations, realize their suffering, wish for them to be cured of suffering, and be ready ourselves to take action toward that aim.

To give rise to compassion, imagine that someone close to you, your mother for instance, is the victim of a car accident some night, and is lying wounded on the road, suffering terrible pain. Emergency services are late to arrive, and you don't know what to do. You feel intensely the suffering of this cherished person, and you also feel powerless and full of anguish. Experience this suffering deep down, till it becomes unbearable.

At that point, give rise to a limitless feeling of love for that person. Take her gently in your arms. Imagine that streams of love emerge from you and pour onto her. Visualize that every atom of her suffering is now replaced by an atom of love. Wish from the bottom of your heart that she survives, gets better, and suffers no more.

Then, extend this warm, loving compassion to other beings who are close to you, then, little by little, to all beings, forming this wish from the bottom of your heart: "May all beings be freed from suffering and the causes of their suffering."

Rejoicing, Celebration, and Gratitude

There are beings in this world who possess immense qualities, others who benefit humanity greatly and are crowned with success, and others who, simply, are more talented than we, or happier, or more successful. We should fully and sincerely rejoice in their accomplishments and wish that their qualities never diminish, but on the contrary persist and increase. This ability to celebrate others' good qualities is an antidote to envy and jealousy, feelings that reflect the inability to be happy at others' happiness. It is also a remedy for discouragement and a gloomy, despairing view of the world.

While rejoicing in others' merit is regarded as a cardinal virtue in Buddhism, it can also be found in the West, in David Hume, for instance, when he writes:

> *We frequently bestow praise on virtuous actions, performed in very distant ages and remote countries; where the utmost subtlety of imagination would not discover any appearance of self-interest, or find any connection of our present happiness and security with events so widely separated from us.*[3]

Such appreciation and praise are basically disinterested; we expect nothing in return, take no pride in it, and have no fear of being blamed if we don't rejoice; in short, our personal interests don't enter into the equation.

Since it is directed *toward others,* this rejoicing constitutes fertile ground for altruism. Unreserved appreciation of others' happiness also leads us to wish that this happiness persist and increase. Leibniz wrote: "To love is to find pleasure in the happiness of others. Thus the habit of loving someone is nothing other than the benevolence by which we want the good of others, not for the profit that we gain from it, but because it is agreeable to us in itself."[4] Its opposite, vexation at the thought of others' good qualities, produces nothing but disadvantages; like jealousy, it makes me unhappy and contributes nothing to my well-being, not even a fraction of the happiness, possessions, or qualities of the person I envy.

Rejoicing can be accompanied by gratitude when it is directed to those who have been kind to us. Psychologists have observed the beneficial effects of gratitude. It reinforces prosocial behavior and emotional ties; it increases well-being and diminishes envy and malevolent attitudes.[5] Buddhism encourages us to extend this gratitude to all beings, our parents first of all who have given us life, fed us, and protected us when we were incapable of taking care of ourselves, and to all those who have contributed to our education and surrounded us with affection and concern, especially the spiritual friends who have shown us the path to inner freedom.

Impartiality

Impartiality is an essential complement in the three previous meditations. The wish that all beings be freed from suffering and its causes must be universal; it should not depend on our personal preferences or on how others treat us. We should be like the doctor who rejoices when others are in good health and who is concerned with curing all his patients, however they behave.

How to Combine These Four Meditations

When we meditate on altruistic love, meditation may stray in attachment to only people who are close to you. That would be the time to move on to meditating on impartiality and extend this love to everyone—friends, strangers, and enemies.

Then it is possible that impartiality could drift into indifference: instead of being concerned for all beings, you feel distant from all of them and stop being interested in their fate. That is the time to think of all the suffering people in the world and to cultivate sincere compassion.

By thinking constantly about the sufferings afflicting others, you may become overwhelmed by a feeling of powerlessness, helplessness, or even despair, and feel overcome by the immensity of the task. You should then shift to rejoicing about all those who manifest great qualities and accomplish admirable deeds for the benefit of others.

If this joy veers into naïve euphoria, you can then go back to meditating on altruistic love. And so on.

At the end of the session, return for a few instants to your vision of the world; contemplate again the interdependence of all things and try to cultivate a fairer, less egocentric perception of reality. Understand that all phenomena are impermanent, interdependent, and thus devoid of the autonomous existence we usually attribute to them. This realization will lead to more freedom in our way of perceiving the world.

Try to remain for a few minutes in full awareness of the present moment, in a state of natural simplicity, in which the mind is free from discursive thoughts.

Before resuming your everyday activities, conclude with aspirations to bridge meditation and daily life. To do so, sincerely dedicate the merit of having meditated to all sentient beings, thinking: "May the positive energy created not just by this meditation but by all my kind actions, words, and thoughts, past, present, and future, contribute to relieving the suffering of all beings, now and for all time to come."

EXCHANGING OUR HAPPINESS FOR THE SUFFERING OF OTHERS

To develop compassion, Buddhism has recourse to a special visualization that consists of mentally exchanging, through the breath, our own happiness for the suffering of others, wishing that our suffering take the place of others' suffering. We might think that we already have enough problems, and that it's asking too much to add even more to our burden and take others' suffering onto ourselves. But it's quite the opposite that occurs. The experience shows that when we mentally take the suffering of others onto ourselves through compassion, our own suffering actually decreases. The reason for this is that altruistic love and compassion are the most powerful antidotes to our own torments. So it is a situation from which everyone benefits! On the other hand, contemplating our own sufferings, reinforced by the constant refrain of "me, me, me" that spontaneously resounds in us, saps our courage and only makes our vulnerability increase.

Begin by feeling profound love for a person who has been very kind to you. Then imagine that that person is suffering terribly. As you are filled with a feeling of sorrowful empathy faced with that suffering, give rise to a powerful feeling of love and compassion, and begin the practice of exchange, or "taking and sending" as it's called in Buddhism.

As you breathe out, think about sending all your happiness, vitality, good fortune, health, and so on, to that person with your breath, in the form of a refreshing, luminous, calming nectar. Wish that the person receive these benefits without anything held back, and think that this nectar fulfills all their needs. If her life is in danger, imagine it is prolonged; if he is destitute, that he receives everything he needs; if she is sick, that she is cured; if he is sad, that he finds happiness.

As you breathe in, think that you take into yourself, in the form of a dark, thick smoke, all the physical and mental suffering of that person, and think that this exchange relieves the pain. Imagine that their suffering returns to you like mist carried by the wind. When you have absorbed, transformed, and eliminated their pain and difficulties, feel great joy, free of any kind of clinging. Repeat this practice many times until it becomes second nature. Then gradually extend the practice of exchange to other people you know, then to all beings.

According to a variation of this practice, when you breathe out, think that your heart is a brilliant sphere of light from which rays of white light carry your happiness to all beings, all over the world. When you breathe in, take their sufferings on yourself in the form of a dense, black cloud, which penetrates your heart and dissolves into white light without leaving a trace.

Or you can imagine that you multiply into an infinity of forms that reach far out into the universe, take onto themselves the sufferings of all beings they encounter, and offer them your happiness—that you become clothing for people who are cold, food for the hungry, or refuge for the homeless. You may conclude the practice session by reading or reciting these verses by Shantideva:

May I be a guard for those who have no protector,
A guide for those who journey on the road.
For those who wish to go across the water,
May I be a boat, a raft, a bridge.

May I be an island for those who yearn for landfall,
And a lamp for those who long for light;
For those who need a resting-place, a bed;
For all who need a servant, may I be their help.

May I be the wishing jewel, the vase of plenty,
A word of power and the supreme remedy,
May I be the tree of miracles,
And for every being the cow of abundance.

Like the earth and the pervading elements,
Enduring as the sky itself endures,
For boundless multitudes of living beings,
May I be their ground and sustenance.

Thus for every thing that lives,
As far as are the limits of the sky,
May I provide their livelihood and nourishment
Until they pass beyond the bonds of suffering.[6]

This practice allows us to connect our breath with the development of compassion. It can be used any time during our daily lives, especially when we are confronted with the suffering of others or even with our own suffering.

When we suffer, we should understand that although suffering in itself is always undesirable, that does not mean we cannot make beneficial use of it when it occurs. As the Dalai Lama explains, "Profound suffering can open our hearts and minds, and open us up to others."[7] Think: "Other people besides me are afflicted by suffering comparable to mine, and often even worse. How wonderful if they could become free of it!"

The various meditations described above can be practiced in two complementary ways: over the course of regular practice sessions, and while we carry out our everyday tasks. We can especially maintain a caring mindfulness while accomplishing simple tasks, such as walking down the street, looking at everyday events and people.

In particular, to allow altruism to be more present in our thoughts, we can, at any time, look around and inwardly wish for each and every person we see that they be safe and happy, that they be free of all suffering, and that they may flourish in their lives. In this way, gradually, altruistic love, compassion, mindfulness, and other qualities developed by meditation will be fully integrated into our way of life.

IV

Contrary Forces

23

Egocentrism and Crystallization of the Ego

What are the forces that oppose altruism, and how can they be overcome? These are two important questions that we must answer if we want to contribute to the development of altruism in society.

Egocentrism is directly opposed to altruism. We will first concentrate on identifying the nature and manifestations of this egocentrism, and on tracing it back to its source, that is, to the formation of the concept of *ego* and the attachment we form to it. We will show that as egocentrism creates a chasm between self and other, the notion of belonging to a particular group (family, ethnic group, religion, village, city, country, baseball team, etc.) takes on increasing importance to the detriment of the solidarity we feel with others and the value we accord them. This process leads us to define, consciously or not, different groups of people who are close to us, or those less close.[1]

The divisions thus established are not harmless; they lead to discrimination. Many psychological studies have shown that the individual tends systematically to give preference to members of one's *own* group, neglecting any concern for fairness and care. The turning in on oneself that accompanies egocentrism naturally leads to a decline of empathy and altruism. The influence of egocentrism can culminate in violence to satisfy one's desires or to knowingly harm others.

THE FORMATION OF "ME" AND THE CRYSTALLIZATION OF THE EGO

Looking outward, we solidify the world by projecting attributes onto it—good or bad, beautiful or ugly, desirable or repulsive—which are not inherent to it at all. Looking inward, we fixate our stream of consciousness by imagining an "I" that presides in the heart of our being. We take it for granted that we perceive things as they are. We attribute permanence to what is ephemeral and perceive as autonomous entities what is actually a vast network of constantly changing relationships.

Early childhood psychology studies how a newborn learns to know the world, to situate itself in relation to others. Around the age of one, the infant comes to understand that others are distinct from him, that the world is not a simple extension of himself, and that he can act on it. We have seen that starting from the age of eighteen months, the child begins to recognize himself in a mirror and acquires self-awareness.

Although our body is undergoing transformations every instant and our mind is the theater of countless emotional and conceptual experiences, we conceive of the "self" as a *unique, constant, autonomous* entity. The simple perception of a "me" has now crystallized into a much stronger sense of identity, the ego. What's more, we feel that this ego is vulnerable, and we want to protect and satisfy it. That is how aversion for anything that threatens it and attraction for anything that pleases and comforts it manifest. These two mental states give rise to a multitude of conflicting emotions—hatred, compulsive desire, envy, and so on.

THE VARIOUS FACETS OF OUR IDENTITY

The sense of personal identity has three aspects: the *I*, the *person*, and the *ego*.[2] The *I* lives in the present; it is what thinks "I'm hungry" or "I exist." It is the site of awareness, thoughts, judgment, and will. It is the experience of our immediate condition. The *I*, especially, is nothing but the present content of our mental stream, which is changing every instant.

As the neuropsychiatrist David Galin explains,[3] the notion of *person* is broader; it's a dynamic continuum extending through time and incorporating various aspects of our corporeal, mental, and social existence. Its boundaries are more fluid: the person can refer to the body ("personal fitness"), intimate thoughts ("a very personal feeling"), character ("a nice person"), social relations ("separating one's personal from one's professional life"), or the human being in general ("respect for one's person"). Its continuity in time allows us to connect representations of ourselves that belong to the past to those that concern the future. Recourse to the notion of the *person* is entirely legitimate if we regard "person" as a practical concept allowing us to designate the history of our lived experience, that is, the ensemble of dynamic relationships between consciousness, body, and environment.[4]

There remains the *ego*. Spontaneously we think it constitutes the very core of our being. We regard it as an indivisible, permanent whole that characterizes us from birth to death. The ego is not just the sum total of "my" limbs, "my" organs, "my" skin, "my" name, "my" consciousness, but their owner. Descartes, for instance, wrote: "When I consider my mind—that is, myself, given that I am merely a thing that thinks—I can identify no distinct parts to it, but conceive of myself as a single and complete thing."[5, 6]

In Search of the Ego

If the ego existed as a distinct entity, we should be able to describe this entity clearly enough to confirm to ourselves that it is something other than simply a concept. In particular, we can ask ourselves, "Where is the ego?" It cannot be solely in my body, since when I say "I'm proud," it's my consciousness that's proud, not my body. Is it solely in my consciousness, then? That's far from obvious. When I say, "Someone pushed me," this way of speaking reveals that I sometimes locate my ego in my body. But if we pursue our investigation, we cannot say that the ego does not reside in any part of the body, no more than it is spread throughout the body. Might it simply be the sum of their parts, their structure and continuity? In that case, we can no longer speak of an entity.

We readily think that the ego is associated with consciousness. But that consciousness is also an elusive stream: the past is dead, the future hasn't yet been born, and the present doesn't last. How could the ego, regarded as a distinct entity, exist suspended between something that no longer exists and something that doesn't yet exist?

The more we try to define the ego, the more it eludes us. The only conclusion possible is that the ego is nothing but a *mental designation* affixed to a dynamic process, a useful *concept* that allows us to connect an ensemble of interdependent and ever-changing factors that incorporate perceptions of the environment, sensations, mental images, emotions, and thoughts.

We in fact have an innate tendency to simplify complex ensembles to make them into "entities" and hence to infer that these entities are lasting. It is easier to function in the world by taking for granted that the majority of our environment doesn't change from one minute to the next and by treating most things as if they were more or less constant. I would lose all concept of what "my body" is if I perceived it as a whirlwind of atoms that never remain the same even for a millionth of a second. But too quickly I forget that the ordinary perception of my body and phenomena around me is only an approximation, and that in reality *everything* is changing *at every instant*. The mistaken perception of my body as an entity that remains more or less the same and that is separate from the world is a useful simplification in our everyday experience. But it is important to realize that this is only a perception, reinforced by practical necessity, which we have then confused with reality. The same is true for the ego, the perception of which, reinforced by habit, is nothing but a mental construction.

Thus, Buddhism concludes that the ego is not nonexistent—we experience it constantly—but that it exists only as a mere concept. It's in this sense that Buddhism says that the ego (the *I* perceived as an entity) is "empty of autonomous, permanent existence." The ego is like a mirage. Examined superficially and seen from a distance, the mirage of a lake seems real, but when you approach it, you'd be hard-pressed to find water.

The Fragile Faces of Identity

The idea of our identity, our image, our status in life, is profoundly anchored in our minds and is constantly influencing our relationships with others. When a discussion goes bad, it's not so much the topic of discussion that matters to us and upsets us, but rather it's the calling into question of our identity. The slightest word that threatens the image we have of ourselves is unbearable to us, whereas the same word applied to someone else doesn't bother us. If we have a strong image of ourselves, we will constantly try to ensure that it's recognized and accepted. Nothing is more upsetting than seeing it doubted.

But what is the value of this identity? It is interesting to note that the word *personality* comes from *persona,* which means "mask" in Latin: the mask "through" (*per*) which the actor makes his role "resound" (*sonat*).[7] While the actor knows he is wearing a mask, we often forget to distinguish between the role we play in society and our true nature.

We often speak of an individual's family and social roles: the role of a mother or father, the role of a company director or an artist. In doing this, a constant and subconscious slippage occurs between the idea of a particular function—pianist, athlete, student, teacher, boss, or employee—and the identification of the person with that function, till it ends up defining the individual and distances us from our basic humanity, which we share with all our fellows.

By clinging to the confined universe of our ego, we tend to be preoccupied solely with ourselves. The slightest contradiction makes us angry or disheartened. We are obsessed with our success, our failure, our hopes and fears; as a result, happiness has every chance of eluding us. If ego is nothing but a mental construct, then freeing ourselves from it does not mean tearing our hearts out, but simply opening our eyes. Abandoning this fixation on our image leads to great inner freedom.

Out of fear of the world and other people, out of fear of suffering, we imagine that by remaining entrenched inside a bubble, that of the ego, we will be protected. For all that, we find ourselves at odds with reality, since we are *fundamentally interdependent* with other beings and with our environment.

When we stop regarding our *I* as the most important thing in the world, we become more concerned with others. Seeing their suffering more spontaneously rouses our courage and determination to work for their benefit.

What to Do with the Ego?

Unlike Buddhism, the methods of psychology aren't much concerned with lessening the importance of the ego, and even less about putting an end to the illusion of ego. In the West, calling into question the notion of ego is quite a new, almost subversive idea, since the ego is usually held as the foundational element of personality.

The idea that it is necessary to have a robust ego stems no doubt from the fact that people suffering from psychic disorders are regarded as beings who have a fragmented, fragile, deficient self. But that is confusing ego with self-confidence. The ego can procure only an artificial confidence, built on precarious attributes—power, success, beauty, physical strength, intellectual brio, the admiration of others—all the elements we believe constitute our "identity," in our eyes and those of others. When this facade crumbles, the ego is vexed or poses as a victim, and self-confidence is destroyed.

The Benevolent Strength of Non-Ego

According to Buddhism, dissipating the illusion of ego is freeing oneself from fundamental vulnerability, and thereby winning *real* self-confidence, which is one of the *natural qualities of the absence of ego.* Truly, the feeling of security procured by the illusion of ego is eminently fragile. The disappearance of this illusion goes hand in hand with the realization of our potential for an inner freedom that gives us the inner resources to deal with the ups and downs of life in an optimal way. Since we feel less vulnerable, we also become more open to others and eager to care for them.

Paul Ekman, specialist in the science of emotions, notes among people who grant little importance to their ego "an impression of kindness, a way of being that others can sense and appreciate, and, unlike so many charismatic charlatans, perfect harmony between their private and public lives."[8] But above all, Ekman says, "These people inspire others by how little they make of their status, their fame—in short, their self. They never give a second thought to whether their position or importance is recognized." Such an absence of egocentrism, he adds, "is altogether perplexing from a psychological point of view." Ekman also stresses how "people instinctively want to be in their company and how, even if they can't always explain why, they find their presence enriching. In essence, they emanate goodness."

A study that analyzes and synthesizes a number of scientific studies having to do with the psychological consequences of egocentrism, carried out by the psychologist Michaël Dambrun at the Université Clermont-Ferrand and in which I participated, showed that excessive egocentrism goes hand in hand with a search for *hedonistic* happiness, that is, happiness based on fluctuating pleasures, and with a diminution of the feeling of well-being. On the other hand, the weakening of egocentrism is accompanied by a search for *eudemonic* happiness, which is based on a way of being and is marked by a feeling of accomplishment and contentment, as well as by a more stable and deeper well-being based on openness to others.[9]

Reducing Prejudice Between Groups

A man (an actor) is lying on the lawn at the University of Manchester in England, next to a busy path. He seems to be sick. People go by. Only a few (15%) stop to see if he needs help. The same man is lying on the same lawn, but this time he is wearing a Liverpool soccer jersey (a rival club to Manchester's, but one that has many supporters among the students from Liverpool). This time, 85% of the passersby, fans of the team, approach to see if he needs a hand. At the end of the path, a team of researchers from the university questions all the passersby, regardless of whether or not they stopped.[10] This study, along with many others, confirms that the feeling of *belonging* considerably influences our readiness to cooperate and help each other.

The feeling of belonging to a group or a community in which everyone feels close to and responsible for everyone else has many virtues. It reinforces solidarity, valorizes the other, and favors the pursuit of common aims that go beyond the individual framework. It allows us, certainly, to grant more importance to *we* than to *me*.

But the strong feeling of belonging to a group also has effects that are detrimental to the harmony of human relations. Privileging members of *our* group is accompanied by a correlating de-privileging of those who do not belong to it, those who are foreigners or who belong to a rival group. This partiality leads to different forms of discrimination like racism, sexism, homophobia, and religious intolerance. And even if the group to which one is attached is the human species in general, this attachment has the corollary of "speciesism," an attitude by which other living species are regarded as intrinsically inferior.

Studies by the psychologists LeVine and Campbell on prejudice and the behavior of ethnic groups have highlighted the following characteristics: members of a group think that their values are universal and fundamentally right; they cooperate with the other members of their group but also punish them, if necessary, for their crimes (theft, murder, etc.). They want to continue to belong to the group, obey the authorities that represent it, and are ready to fight and die to defend their interests.[11]

On the other hand, they regard members of other groups as intrinsically inferior, contemptible, and immoral. They rarely cooperate with that group, do not respect the authority of its leaders, blame it for difficulties they themselves encounter, and are ready to fight against them. They fear them and do not trust them. In the education they give their children, they cite behaviors of the other group's members as examples not to follow. When the feeling of personal value linked to the group is exaggerated—the psychologist Henri Tajfel cites the examples of members of the Ku Klux Klan who dress up in white hoods and robes, or of terrorist trainees who meet in secret—it leads to the worst sectarian behavior and the most violent conflicts.[12]

Tajfel also showed that even the purely artificial creation of two groups based on whether one prefers the paintings of Klee or of Kandinsky, for example, or based on flipping a coin and choosing heads or tails, quickly leads people to prefer members of their group, to grant them more resources, and to have less confidence in the members of the other group.

THE ROBBERS CAVE EXPERIMENT

In a famous series of experiments, the psychologist Muzafer Sherif and his colleagues arranged a summer camp for boys aged twelve to fourteen. They were divided into two groups each of eleven teenagers, set up at opposite ends of a 200-acre area in Robbers Cave State Park, Oklahoma. For a week, each group thought it was alone in the park, occupying a cabin, finding swimming holes, going on hikes, and so on. The first group called itself the "Rattlesnakes."

In the beginning of the second week, each group was told of the existence of the other. This information alone quickly aroused a reciprocal feeling of hostility. The group that didn't yet have a name purposedly dubbed itself the "Eagles" (which, of course, eat snakes). The division between "us" and the "others" was thus quickly made.

Then, the experimenters announced a series of contests between the two groups (baseball games, inspection of cabins and their state of cleanliness, and so on). What's more, they were made to eat in the same cafeteria, where the prizes and trophies that were going to be distributed to the contest winners were on display. After an honorable beginning, the sporting activities quickly degenerated. The players insulted each other, and after the Eagles were defeated, their leader set fire to the Rattlesnakes' flag, which incited the latter to do the same to the Eagles' flag the next day. As the days passed, the situation got worse, tensions took on an unforeseen magnitude, and the experimenters decided to break off the experiment.[13]

A few years later, the same researchers attempted another experiment. Once a heightened level of tension had been set up between the two groups, the experimenters imagined various stratagems to reestablish peace. First they asked everyone to find and then repair a leak in the water pipe feeding the camp. During this task, hostility lessened, but soon reappeared. The experimenters then organized an evening where they took the boys of both groups to the movies. But again, peace was short-lived.

Finally, they had the idea of overturning the truck that brought food to the camp in a deep ditch, so that fixing it would require the collaboration of all the boys for an entire day, at the cost of enormous effort. One group alone could not have freed the vehicle. It was observed that ties of solidarity and then of friendship were created between the members of both groups, so that they wholeheartedly collaborated in a common aim. The enmity between the two groups stopped, and the teenagers decided to return to town together in the same bus.

For the researchers, such an experiment revealed profound insights into the development of a real culture of peace. It showed that it is not enough for two hostile groups to stop fighting or to live together. They have to work together for the common good.

Resolution of Conflicts

To reduce tension and conflicts between antagonistic groups, the establishment of personal contact between their members should be encouraged. When they learn to get to know each other by spending time together, they are much more inclined to be kind, since they grant more value to the other by perceiving the other's needs, hopes, and fears more clearly. As the Robbers Cave experiment shows, it is not enough just to put them in contact with each other, which usually tends to exacerbate hostile feelings.[14] One of the most effective techniques consists of proposing to both groups a common goal that can be attained only by joining forces.[15] The participants then learn to appreciate each other by working together toward reaching this goal.

Essentially, getting rid of attachment to ego in no way undermines our aspiration to be happy and flourish. What it does do is eliminate the excessive importance we attach to our happiness in relation to that of others. Getting rid of this attachment comes down not to devalorizing our happiness, but in revalorizing the happiness of others.

24

THE SPREAD OF INDIVIDUALISM AND NARCISSISM

Our existence, and even our survival, depends closely on our ability to construct mutually beneficial relationships with others. Human beings have a profound need to feel connected, to trust others and be trusted by them, to love and be loved in return. The psychologist Cendri Hutcherson has summarized a number of experiments showing that feeling connected to others increases our psychological well-being and physical health, and diminishes the risk of depression.[1] The feeling of connection and belonging to a wider community also increases empathy and fosters behavior based on trust and cooperation.[2] All this induces a virtuous circle, or more precisely, according to one of the founders of positive psychology, Barbara Fredrickson, an ascending "virtuous spiral," since trust and readiness to cooperate are reinforced when they are reciprocal.[3]

Despite the obvious advantages engendered by social ties, we live in a world where the individual is more and more isolated and mistrustful. Technological, economic, and social upheavals have led to a weakening of the social bond, along with an erosion of mutual trust.[4] In 1950, a poll revealed that 60% of North Americans and Europeans trusted a stranger at first sight. In 1998, the percentage dropped to 30%.[5] In the West, the individual is withdrawing more and more into himself, and this tendency constitutes an obstacle to the expansion of altruism. Individual freedom and our search for autonomy comes with many benefits, but they cannot flourish without being balanced by an appropriate sense of responsibility toward and solidarity with others.

The Two Faces of Individualism

Societies and cultures can differ in the extent to which they are based upon predominantly "self-regarding," individualistic, and self-centered values, or upon "other-regarding," group-oriented, community-centered, and state-respectful values.

In English, the word *individualism* was first used in a derogative way in the late 1830s by followers of the social Utopian Robert Owen, who was a precursor of the cooperative movement, and in a positive way by Christian writer James Elishama Smith, who argued that without individualism people cannot prosper, amass property, or increase their happiness.[6]

Individualism is a philosophical, moral, social, and political stance that affirms that the interests of the individual should take precedence over those of the community and the state. It encourages independence and self-reliance. It demands that the individual has the right to promote his own interests, without having to take the interests of society into consideration. It also calls for freedom from any kind of obligations imposed by religious, ethnic, social, or governmental institutions.

From this perspective, individualism comes close to "ethical egoism," which considers that people have no obligation to help and serve others, although they may choose to do so if they please and if it contributes to the promotion of their own interest. It contrasts with "ethical utilitarianism," which holds that one should not elevate self-interest and the individual himself to a status not granted to others. It is the direct opposite of "ethical altruism," which considers that one has a duty to care for others, even if it might sometimes be at the cost of one's selfish interests. It could be argued that someone who does not care for others, cannot expect, much less demand, that others care for him.

Individualism can lead to a reductionist approach to human beings by regarding them as autonomous entities, instead of as belonging to a vast, interdependent network, thus ignoring the complexity of human relations. Science has thought us to identify and analyze the most basic components of phenomena, as well as their immediate causes. However, if one limits oneself to a reductionist approach, one will underestimate the importance of overall relationships between phenomena and between the systems they comprise. One-sided reductionism also ignores emergent phenomena, where the whole is qualitatively different from the sum of its parts.

In essence, individualism has two main aspects. It first designates a perfectly legitimate way of thinking that commands respect for the individual, and insists that the individual should not be used as a simple instrument in the service of society. This way of thinking gave birth to the essential concept of human rights, without denying the importance of the duties of the citizen, of the interdependence of the members of the human community, or of solidarity. Such an individualism is thus in no way synonymous with selfishness to the extent that the former confers on the individual a moral autonomy and allows the individual to exercise his choice in full freedom. Acknowledging individual talents is also a desirable way to build viable collective organizations. This constructive aspect of individualism is far from being detrimental to the interest of the community.

However, there exists another aspect of individualism, one whose increasing influence in our era should be deplored. This is an egocentric aspiration to be free of any kind of collective responsibility and to give priority to the idea of "everyone for himself." It encourages the individual to do whatever his immediate feelings, desires, and impulses dictate, regardless of others and of his responsibility to society.

It is to the latter aspect that for instance the Merriam-Webster's dictionary refers to when defining individualism as "the belief that the needs of each person are more important than the needs of the whole society or group." In the midnineteenth century, the historian Alexis de Tocqueville saw in individualism a withdrawal into the private sphere and an abandonment of the public sphere and of participation in the life of the city. Similarly, at the end of the nineteenth century, the sociologist Émile Durkheim was concerned with the decline of shared values and norms, and about the emerging aversion for anything that stood in the way of personal and individual preferences.

The English economist and sociologist Richard Layard thinks that this decline is a matter of an excess of individualism, and that "individuals will never live satisfying lives except in a society where people care for each other and promote others' good as well as their own. The pursuit of personal success relative to others cannot create a happy society, since one person's success necessarily involves another's failure.... [Today] the balance has tilted too far towards the individual pursuit of private interest and success. So it is excessive individualism, we believe, that is causing a whole range of problems."[7]

TRUE FREEDOM

Individualism is often associated with the notion of individual freedom. "For me, happiness would be doing anything I want with no one having to say anything about it," declared a young Englishwoman questioned on the BBC. A twenty-year-old American named Melissa explains, "I don't care at all about how society views me. I live my life according to the morals, views, and criteria I created myself."[8]

Freeing oneself from the dogmas and constraints imposed by a rigid and oppressive society is a victory, but this freedom is merely an illusion if it leads to our falling into the meshes of our own individualistic mental fabrications. To want to do everything that occurs to us is to have a strange concept of freedom, since in that way we become the slave of all the thoughts that agitate our minds. For individuals caught up in this way of thinking, individual freedom ends up not only harming them, but also destroying the social fabric. The French essayist Pascal Bruckner deplores "this disease of individualism that consists of wanting to escape the consequences of one's actions, this attempt to enjoy the benefits of freedom without suffering any of its inconveniences."[9]

The individualist confuses freedom to do anything that comes to mind with true freedom, which consists of being master of oneself. Spontaneity is a precious quality, provided it isn't confused with mental agitation. Being free internally is first of all freeing oneself from the dictatorship of egocentrism and the negative emotions that accompany it: craving, hatred, jealousy, and so on. It's taking control of one's life, with joy and enthusiasm, instead of abandoning it to tendencies forged by our habits and conditioning. Let's take the example of a sailor on his boat: his freedom does not consist in letting his boat drift at the mercy of the winds and currents—in that case, he wouldn't be navigating, but drifting—but in being master of his boat, taking the tiller, trimming his sails, and navigating in the direction he has chosen.

The idea that I am free to do anything I want in my own little world, so long as it doesn't harm anyone, is based on an overly narrow view of human relations. "Such freedom is based not on relations between humans, but on separation," Karl Marx writes. By limiting oneself to abstaining from doing harm, one risks harming others by renouncing the possibility of doing good to the other: "Man's inhumanity to man is not only perpetrated by the vitriolic actions of those who are bad. It is also perpetrated by the vitiating inaction of those who are good," said Martin Luther King Jr. A harmonious society is one in which the freedom to accomplish one's own benefit is joined with the responsibility to accomplish the benefit of others.

THE DOWNWARD SPIRAL OF INDIVIDUALISM

Individualism pushed to its extreme has led to the cult of appearances, of aestheticism, of performance, which publicity—that weapon of consumer society—is constantly pushing forward. Priority is given to hedonism, to the desire to be "different," to the cult of personal expression and personal freedom. People want to be "real" while "having fun" every second. We have to "have a great time" and "get the most" out of life.[10]

In politics, especially in the United States, individualism goes hand in hand with a mistrust of the government, which is regarded at best as a necessary evil, and at worst as a real enemy of individual liberties. The founding fathers of American individualist society were inspired by Rousseau's idea that the first humans were without any social bonds and lived freely and independently.[11] According to such an idea, it was only later that humans became linked by a "social contract" according to which they gave up some of their liberties to benefit from communal life. Rousseau's views do not correspond to reality since human beings descend from a long line of primates who lived in groups, with a high degree of interdependence. The more vulnerable the species is to predators and adverse conditions, the more important is the tendency to form communities. Humans are obviously social animals.[12]

Individualism can also be expressed by a desire for insularity: "Do whatever you have to do, but stay where you are and leave me alone." Maurice Barrès describes the individualism of the inhabitants of a village in the Lorraine in this way: "They are well aware of what's happening in their neighbor's home, they observe him, but they take care to show that they don't need him."[13] This desire for making one's life private can lead to isolation and solitude within society. Already, in Western Europe and North America, 40% of the elderly live alone, as opposed to only 3% in Hong Kong, where extended families still comprise several generations. In Manhattan and Washington, DC, for example, according to the latest United States census in 2013, about half of all households have single occupants, and in some neighborhoods the proportion is two-thirds.

Individualism also leads to thinking that we are entities that are fundamentally separate from each other. The Spanish philosopher Ortega y Gasset expressed this idea in this way: "Since human life in the strict sense is untransferable, it is essentially solitude, radical solitude."[14] Such views are a far cry from taking into account the interdependence of all things.

The individualist thinks he is protecting himself, but by reducing himself to an autonomous entity, he is diminishing himself and becoming vulnerable, since he feels threatened by others instead of benefiting from their cooperation. Speaking about the fragmentation of society, the sociologist Louis Dumont wrote, "The whole has become a heap."[15] Instead of an interdependent ensemble that functions as such, we have become a "heap" of individualities that make do, each on his own.

The Deforming Mirror of Narcissism: Everyone Is Above Average

The main risk of individualism is that it can degenerate into narcissism, which is characterized notably by an overestimation of oneself in relation to others. Studies carried out in the United States have shown that 85% of students think, for example, that they are more sociable than average, and 90% think that they are among the 10% most talented.[16] No less than 96% of university professors think they are better pedagogues than their colleagues, and 90% of motorists (even those who recently caused an accident!) are convinced they drive better than others.[17]

These same studies show that the majority of people think they are more popular, nicer, more fair-minded, and more intelligent than average. They also think they are more logical and funnier. The problem being obviously that, by definition, the majority of people cannot be above the average. And, amazingly, most think their ability to think objectively about themselves is also higher than normal![18]

Narcissism Goes Against Altruism

Narcissism is described in psychology as "a pervasive pattern of grandiosity, need for admiration, and a lack of empathy."[19] The narcissist is an unconditional admirer of his own image, the only one that interests him, and nourishes constant fantasies of success, power, beauty, intelligence, and everything that can reinforce this flattering image. He has little regard for others, who are for him only instruments useful to enhance his own image. He clearly lacks the attribute of neighborly love.

Those who suffer from excessive self-love describe themselves as being nicer, more attractive, and more popular. Obviously they are deluding themselves, and according to their friends, their relationship abilities are simply average.[20] Narcissists, then, don't simply have a good opinion of themselves; they grossly overestimate themselves. Disappointments begin for them when they are objectively evaluated, on exams, for instance, or when they turn out to be no better than others on the average.

It has often been asserted that by having a very high opinion of themselves, people with narcissistic personalities increase their chances of success in exams and professional activities, but that is not true: research has shown that in the final analysis, they fail on average more often than their peers.

Some psychologists have long believed that deep within, narcissists hate themselves and overestimate their image in order to remedy a feeling of insecurity. All the research, summarized by psychologist Jean Twenge in *The Narcissism Epidemic,* has shown that this hypothesis is false in the vast majority of cases.[21] In particular, Keith Campbell and his colleagues at the University of Georgia conceived of a way of evaluating unconscious attitudes with the help of the Implicit Association Test. By recording the response time to questions on a computer keyboard, they showed that narcissists associate more quickly than others the word *me* with adjectives of praise like "wonderful," and less quickly than average with deprecatory adjectives like "awful," which conveys excessive self-esteem.[22] The results unequivocally established that narcissistic individuals indeed suffer from a superiority complex.[23] Trying to help a narcissist by advising him to increase his self-esteem comes down to pouring oil on fire.

The Fall of Narcissus

When the narcissist is finally confronted with reality, depending on the situation, he may adopt two different attitudes: anger against himself or anger at others. In the first case, he blames himself for not being able to be better, and he takes the energy he used till then to promote his ego and turns it against himself, in the form of aggression, anxiety, or suppressed anger. The fall of the narcissist can lead to depression, even suicide.

It can also express itself through animosity toward others.[24] During one study, some students were told that their results in intelligence tests were lower than average. Those who had been identified as having the highest opinion of themselves compensated for this bad news by disparaging the other participants, while those who had a modest opinion of themselves tended to react in a friendlier way and to compliment the others on their good results. By blaming others for their own failures, narcissists do not draw lessons from their mistakes and do not bother to remedy their weaknesses.[25]

The psychiatrist Otto Kernberg, who has studied cases of students who shoot classmates to death in American schools, speaks of "malignant narcissism." Since they are unable to make themselves stand out by the positive qualities they lack, narcissistic personalities want to coerce respect from others by harming them. Eric Harris and Dylan Klebold, the two students who carried out the massacre at Columbine High School, killing twelve students and a teacher, reacted in an extreme way to the relatively mild insults of their classmates. But to the oversized egos of these two teenagers, their classmates were losers who deserved to be taught a lesson. In a video recorded before they took action, Eric and Dylan wondered which director, Spielberg or Tarantino, would make a movie about their story. We see them say to themselves, laughing: "Isn't it fun to get the respect we're going to deserve?"[26] Narcissism is a dominant character trait among psychopaths, who are totally without empathy for those they manipulate and make suffer—sometimes gleefully.

The Madness of Greatness

Dictators are often both narcissists and psychopaths. They are also megalomaniacs, as demonstrated in the mythical dimension with which they embellish their biographies, their propensity to have monumental statues of themselves erected, and the spectacular parades organized in their honor in front of immense crowds.

Kim Jong-il, the late "dear leader" of North Korea, is a prime example of the megalomaniac psychopath. According to his official biography, he was born at the top of Paektu Mountain, the highest mountain in Korea. The glacier supposedly emitted a mysterious sound at the time of his birth, and opened up to disclose a double rainbow. Kim Jong-il supposedly walked at the age of three weeks and began speaking at the age of eight weeks. During his university studies, he is supposed to have written no less than 1,500 books! The first time he tried golf, he is supposed to have gotten an astronomical score, including five holes-in-one (a world record). As icing on the cake, according to the North Korean newspaper *Minju Joson*, he is supposedly also the inventor of the foot-long hamburger.[27] Of course, no mention is made of the chronic famine that affects his people, the pitiless repression of all dissidence, or the countless citizens who were locked up and killed in concentration camps.

The Epidemic of Narcissism

According to studies by Jean Twenge and her colleagues, North America has for over twenty years been suffering from a real epidemic of narcissism, which is, for the time being, mostly sparing Europe and the East.[28]

In 1951, 12% of young people between fourteen and sixteen agreed with the statement, "I am an important person." In 1989, this percentage rose to 80%![29] The analysis of tens of thousands of questionnaires showed that 93% of high school students had a considerably higher narcissism score in 2000 than in 1980.[30] In the United States, in 2006, one student out of four fulfilled the conditions for being qualified as narcissistic, and one out of ten suffered from narcissistic personality disorder.[31]

Young Americans themselves admit to this change. A survey carried out with a thousand students shows that two-thirds of them agree with the statement, "My generation of young people is more self-promoting, narcissistic, overconfident, and attention-seeking than previous generations." Most think that one of the main reasons for this egocentrism stems from using social media sites like MySpace, Facebook, and Twitter,[32] which are, for the most part, devoted to self-promotion. In fact, narcissism mainly affects the young. In a study involving 35,000 people, researchers from the National Institutes of Health (NIH) showed that 10% of twenty- to thirty-year-olds suffered from narcissistic personality disorder, against only 3.5% of those over sixty-five.[33]

When in 2007 the media published the results of Twenge's research, many students, far from questioning this growth of narcissism, replied that it was entirely justified. One of them wrote to a newspaper, "This extremely high opinion of oneself is justified, since this generation will be remembered as the best ever." Another protested, "But we are special. There is nothing wrong with knowing this. It is not vanity that this generation exhibits—it's pride."[34]

The psychologist Brittany Gentile and her colleagues at the University of Georgia wondered if networks like MySpace were content to attract narcissistic personalities or if, even worse, they meant to induce narcissistic tendencies. They randomly divided into two groups a number of students. They asked the students in the first group to spend some time updating their MySpace page, and the students in the second group to spend the same time drawing up an itinerary between two places with the help of Google Maps. They then asked the students to answer a questionnaire to measure their degree of narcissism. They weren't entirely surprised to note that 75% of the students who had spent as little as thirty-five minutes on MySpace had reached a higher level of narcissism than the average of the group that had spent the same time on Google Maps.[35] Some even said, "I like to be the center of attention," or "Everyone likes to hear my stories," or "I am a born leader."

According to French psychologist Christophe André, in traditional societies where everyone knew each other and where everyone had his place (regardless of whether or not he was satisfied with it), it was hardly useful to project any kind of image of oneself, since one only risked ridicule. But these days, were are constantly dealing with strangers who know nothing of our identity, qualities, and defects. So it is tempting, and sometimes useful, to broadcast as ostentatiously as possible the image of ourselves that we would like to see recognized by those around us. [36]

One of the champions of narcissism, the American entrepreneur Donald Trump, who exhibits his name in huge gilded letters on all the buildings and skyscrapers he owns, on his private jet, on his university buildings, and elsewhere, declared, "Show me someone without an ego, and I'll show you a loser."[37] But this is wrong. It was observed that high school students who have a too-high opinion of themselves have grades that decline from year to year, and the percentage of those among them who abandon their studies is higher than average. An excess of self-confidence leads them to think that they know everything. Consequently, they are neither motivated nor persevering.[38]

According to a survey carried out in 2006, becoming famous is the main ambition for young people in the United States (51% of twenty-five-year-olds). A teenager who was asked, "What do you want to be when you're older?" replied, "Famous." "For what?" "It doesn't matter, I just want to be famous." I myself recently heard a twenty-three-year-old man ask a Tibetan lama to pray that his name appear, it didn't matter how, in the credits to a movie.

SELF-ADORATION

An ad on NBC proclaims, "You may not realize it, but everyone is born with their one true love—themselves. If you like you, everyone else will, too."[39]

One of the bestsellers in the United States in 2003 was entitled *The Girl's Guide To Loving Yourself: A Book about Falling in Love with the One Person who Matters Most... YOU!*[40]

Modern parents readily comply with the whims of their children. North American parents in particular will even accept the fact that their children don't want to do their homework. Thus, a mother decided to excuse her son from doing his homework because it made him "unhappy"; another let her ten-year-old son decide whether or not he wanted to go to school. [41] In traditional societies, children eat what the family eats and are dressed by their parents according to the climate and the circumstance, and not according to what they prefer. Many American parents, far from inspiring a healthy dose of modesty in their children, constantly call their daughters "little princesses" and describe their sons as "the best in the world." In kindergarten, they are made to sing, "I am special! Look at me!"

At school, children's sensitivity and pride must be carefully treated. Again in the United States, some schools have eliminated the worst grade (F). A study revealed that in 2004, 48% of high school students had received an A average, whereas only 18% had received such a high average in 1968. It is common for students to complain to teachers about not receiving an A, and to demand their grade be raised.[42] They also challenge comments and assessments by their teachers, arguing that they're "just opinions." So it is not surprising that American students think they're the best and the brightest in the world, even when they score lower than students in many other countries, according to almost all evaluations of academic success.[43] American schools also practice inflation of school prizes and distinctions, both in classwork and in games and sports. Even those who come in last are awarded a trophy for "Excellence in Participation."[44] A primary school in New York decreed that September is "All About Me Month," and the first week is called "Focus on the Individual."

To satisfy the desire to be unique and different, everything has to be personalized, all the way down to a cup of coffee. In the United States, someone had fun by calculating all the possible combinations of coffee that fast-food chains offer, like an extra-large café latte with cinnamon and dark chocolate with cane sugar. He arrived at the sum: 18,000. A Burger King wrapper proclaims, "You are special and you deserve a sandwich that's just as special." And we all know the L'Oréal TV ad that says you should buy their products "because you're worth it."

Although generally the rate of narcissism remains not as high in Europe as in the United States, it is still tending to increase even in countries where it has been till now very rare—in Scandinavian countries, for example. A study carried out in Norway analyzed the print media to observe the frequency of one set of words reflecting community-based views (*common, mutual, duty, equality*) against another set denoting individualist values (*I, me, rights, individual, entitlement, preferences*). It turned out that between 1984 and 2005, in the same body of texts, the total for words in the first series fell from 60,000 to 40,000, and that of words in the second series went from 10,000 to 20,000.[45] The epidemic of narcissism is quickly spreading through China and Russia among the nouveaux riches who have emerged in the last dozen years.

According to Twenge, the focus on self-admiration is causing "a flight from reality to the land of grandiose fantasy. We have phony rich people (with interest-only mortgages and piles of debt), phony beauty (with plastic surgery and cosmetic procedures), phony athletes (with performance-enhancing drugs), phony celebrities (via reality TV and YouTube), phony genius students (with grade inflation)."[46] It is important to try to understand the reasons and motivations for this epidemic of narcissism, because its comes with a decline of empathy ("I don't have time to worry about your problems") and an increase in aggression ("And if you insult me, you will pay"), which are both destructive to society.

Good and Bad Self-Esteem

Promoting self-esteem is fashionable, but many studies have confirmed that it is counterproductive when it results not just in providing self-confidence, which is an excellent thing, but in fabricating a deformed image of oneself, as has most often been the case, especially in the United States. The psychologist Roy Baumeister, who has made the most complete synthesis of all research having to do with self-esteem, concludes, "It is very questionable whether [the few benefits] justify the effort and expense that schools, parents, and therapists have put into raising self-esteem.... After all these years, I'm sorry to say, my recommendation is this: forget about self-esteem and concentrate more on self-control and self-discipline."[47] In fact, research shows that favoring the development of self-control allows children to persevere in their efforts, maintain their motivation in the long run, and succeed at school—all objectives that were pursued in vain by pedagogy centered on self-esteem. Students who have better self-control have a greater chance of completing their studies and less risk of abusing alcohol and drugs and, for girls, of becoming pregnant during adolescence.[48]

It is important, however, to stress that a "good," healthy self-esteem is indispensable to flourish in life, and that an unhealthy devaluation of self can lead to serious psychological troubles and to great suffering. According to Christophe André, good self-esteem facilitates resilience and allows us to preserve our inner strength and serenity when faced with adverse life conditions. It also allows us to recognize and tolerate our imperfections and limitations without feeling diminished by them. William James, the founder of modern psychology, wrote in 1892: "Strangely, one feels extremely lighthearted once one has accepted in good faith one's incompetence in a particular field."[49]

Self-esteem built on a swollen ego can procure only an artificial, fragile confidence. When the disconnect with reality becomes too great, the ego becomes irritated and tense, and vacillates. Self-confidence evaporates, and nothing remains except frustration, depression, and anger. Self-confidence worthy of the name is naturally free of infatuation and does not depend on promoting an artificial image of oneself. Authentic self-confidence is born from a feeling of balance with oneself, based on a peaceful strength that is not threatened by external circumstances or inner fears, a freedom beyond fascination with image and fear of losing it. Christophe André concludes, "There is nothing further from good self-esteem than pride.... On the other hand, humility is more than simply favorable to good self-esteem: it is its very essence."[50]

The Solitude of Hyperconnectivity

According to the American sociologist Sherry Turkle, so-called social media in fact constitute for the individual a way to be alone while still being connected to many people.[51] Young people have gone from conversation to connection. Electronic conversations are terse, fast, and sometimes brutal. Human conversations, face-to-face, are of a different nature: they evolve more slowly, are more nuanced, and teach patience. In conversation, we are called upon to see things from another point of view, which is a necessary condition for empathy and altruism.

Many people today are ready to talk to machines, which seem to care about them. Various research institutes have conceived of social robots meant to serve as companions to the elderly and to autistic children. Paro, the best-known therapeutic companion robot, is a baby seal developed at the Division of Intelligent System Engineering at the Research Institute for Science and Technology, Tokyo University of Science. It is meant for the elderly, especially those with Alzheimer's disease. These people are often deprived of social connections (in the hospital or a nursing home), and this companion, which responds to touch by movements, little cries, and smiles, offers them a kind of presence. Sherry Turkle tells about having seen an elderly person confide to one of these baby seal robots and speak to it about the loss of her child. The robot seemed to be looking her in the eyes and following the conversation. The woman said she was comforted by it.

Might individualism lead to an impoverishing of human relations and to a solitude such that one can only find compassion or love from a robot? We risk having sympathy only for ourselves and managing the joys and sufferings of existence only in the bubble of our ego.

God Did Not Create You So You'd Be Like Everyone Else

All major religions promote humility. A verse in Proverbs reads, "The Lord will destroy the house of the proud." The Sermon on the Mount notes that the meek "shall inherit the earth." Saint Francis of Assisi constantly preached and embodied humility. Christianity also stresses forgiveness, which requires a degree of humility. Christians insist on "self-emptying" (*kenosis*), and the writer and religious scholar C. S. Lewis writes, "Most profound religious experiences obliterate the self. They involve self-forgetting and surrender." St. Benedict's rule, which inspires the life of the Benedictine monks, describes the twelve levels of humility that the monk has to put into practice.

Similarly, we read in the Bhagavad Gita, one of the great Hindu texts, "Humility, modesty, nonviolence, forgiveness,... self-control;... absence of ego;—this is said to be knowledge. That which is contrary to this is ignorance."[52]

Buddhism regards humility as one of the cardinal virtues on the spiritual path. Many maxims urge the practitioner to rid himself of pride; for example: "The water of qualities does not remain on the rock of pride," or "Humility is like a cup placed on the ground, ready to receive the rain of qualities." Westerners are usually surprised to hear great Eastern scholars or contemplatives say, "I'm nothing special and don't know much." They wrongly think it's a question of false modesty.

But, in our day, many are tempted by à la carte religions, which owe their success in part to their inclination to flatter the ego, instead of helping to unmask it. In the past thirty years, Japan has experienced an explosion of cults and a great diversity of religious trends. According to the governmental Agency for Cultural Affairs, 182,000 different religious associations are registered in the country, and at least 500 new religions are represented by these associations.[53] In California, a woman named Sheila founded Sheilaism, of which she is the sole follower. When she was asked what the religion constituted, she replied, "It's just—try to love yourself and be gentle with yourself."[54]

In the United States, the faithful are not much inclined to go to churches that preach humility, and some evangelical churches expressly flatter narcissistic tendencies. They sell T-shirts that say "Jesus Loves Me." Others state that "God wants you to be rich." This tendency is not just evidence of a clergy sometimes more interested in monetary gain than in spiritual progress, but of the predominant ideology of the most popular evangelical churches in the United States.

Effort, perseverance, altruism, and training one's own mind have given way to impulses of the moment and to constant promotion of ego—what the Tibetan master Trungpa Rinpoche called "spiritual materialism."[55]

The Virtues of Humility

Humility is sometimes scorned, regarded as a weakness. The writer Ayn Rand proclaims, "Discard the protective rags of that vice which you called a virtue: humility."[56] Pride, however, the narcissistic exaggeration of the self, closes the door to all personal progress, since in order to learn, you must first realize that you don't know. Humility is a forgotten quality of the contemporary world, the theater of seeming. Magazines are constantly giving advice about how to "affirm" yourself, "make an impression," "be beautiful"—to *seem* instead of *be*. This obsession with the favorable image one wants to present is such that we no longer even ask ourselves anymore the question of the groundlessness of seeming, but only how we can appear most positively. However, as La Rochefoucauld wrote, "We should gain more by letting the world see what we are than by trying to seem what we are not."[57]

Most people associate humility with a lack of self-esteem, a lack of confidence in one's own abilities, and an inferiority complex. They don't recognize the benefits of humility, for if "self-importance is the privilege of the fool," humility is the virtue of one who has taken the measure of all that's left for him to learn and the path he still has to travel. Humble people are not beautiful, intelligent people who take pride in convincing themselves they're ugly and stupid; they are people who don't make much of their ego. Not thinking of themselves as the center of the universe, they open up more easily to others and are especially aware of the interconnection between all beings.

A humble person has nothing to lose or to gain. If he is praised, he thinks it's for what he has been able to accomplish, not for himself as an individual. If he is criticized, he thinks that bringing his faults out into the open is the best service anyone could do him. "Few are sufficiently wise to prefer censure, which is useful, to praise, which is treacherous," wrote La Rochefoucauld,[58] as if echoing Tibetan sages who remind us that "the best teaching is one that reveals our hidden faults." Free from hope and fear, the humble person remains carefree and without affectation. Paradoxically, humility also favors strength of character: the humble person makes decisions according to what he thinks is fair and holds to them, without worrying about either his image or what people will say about him.

Humility is a quality that is invariably found in the wise person who has acquired many qualities, for, they say, it's when the tree is loaded with fruit that the branches bend to the ground, whereas the proud person is like the tree whose bare branches point up to the sky. While traveling with His Holiness the Dalai Lama, I often noted his great humility laden with kindness. He is always attentive to people of modest means and never poses as an important person. One day, after greeting François Mitterrand, who had just accompanied him to the front steps of the Élysée palace, the Dalai Lama, before getting into his car, went over to shake the hand of one of the guards standing at the side, beneath the stunned gaze of the president of the republic.

Humility is a component of altruism, since the humble person is naturally concerned about others and attentive to their well-being. Social psychology studies, on the other hand, have shown that those who overestimate themselves show a tendency to aggression that is greater than average.[59] A link has also been highlighted between humility and the ability to forgive, whereas people who think they're superior judge the faults of others more harshly and regard them as less forgivable.[60]

25

The Champions of Selfishness

As we have seen in detail, studies carried out by various teams of psychologists have established that truly altruistic actions are abundant on a daily basis, disproving the thesis that human motivation is systematically selfish by nature.

Another school of thought argues not that altruism is nonexistent, but that it is pernicious, immoral, or unhealthy. These thinkers assert what psychologists and philosophers call "ethical selfishness," a doctrine according to which selfishness is a virtue that is the foundation of a personal morality.

Machiavelli justified selfishness in some respects. He was convinced that evil was necessary in order to govern, and that altruism constituted a weakness. "A prince," he wrote, "and especially a new prince, cannot possibly exercise all those virtues for which men are called 'good.' To preserve the state, he often has to do things against his word, against charity, against humanity, against religion. Thus he has to have a mind ready to shift as the winds of fortune and the varying circumstances of life may dictate. And as I said above, he should not depart from the good if he can hold to it, but he should be ready to enter on evil if he has to."[1]

A more radical position would be taken by the German philosophers Max Stirner and Friedrich Nietzsche, who denounced altruism as a regrettable sign of impotence. Max Stirner exercised some influence over Karl Marx's intellectual development and over the German anarchist movement. He rejected the idea of any duty or responsibility toward others. In his eyes, selfishness represents the symbol of an advanced civilization. He thus sings its praises:

> *Here, egoism, selfishness must decide, not the principle of love, not love motives like mercy, gentleness, goodnature, or even justice and equity.*[2]

Nietzsche too had little regard for neighborly love, a notion he regarded as an attitude promoted *by the weak for the weak,* inhibiting the pursuit of personal development and creativity. According to him, we should feel under no obligation to help others, no more than we should feel any guilt at not intervening in their favor. "You shall seek your advantage even at the expense of everything,"[3] he advises, and adds, "You crowd together with your neighbours and have beautiful words for it. But I tell you: Your love of your neighbour is your bad love for yourself."[4] By speaking thus, Nietzsche violently censures Christianity and all those who preach subjection of the individual to an external authority. He concludes in *Ecce Homo,* written not long before he lost his sanity: "Morality, the Circe of mankind, has falsified everything psychological, from beginning to end; it has demoralized everything, even to the terrible nonsense of making love 'altruistic.' "[5]

After these philosophers, the twentieth century knew two figures who symbolized selfishness. One is the American writer Ayn Rand. Almost unknown in Europe, she is an icon among libertarian thinkers in the United States. The other is Sigmund Freud, still very influential in France, Argentina, and Brazil, but on the way to being forgotten everywhere else in the world where university-level teaching of psychology scarcely makes a case for psychoanalysis.[6] Ayn Rand proclaims that being selfish is the best way to be happy. Freud asserts that endeavoring to adopt an altruistic attitude leads to a neurotic imbalance, and so it is healthier to accept fully one's natural selfishness.

The Ayn Rand Phenomenon

The case of the writer Ayn Rand,[7] who went so far as to assert that altruism is "immoral," is particularly interesting, since she continues to enjoy considerable influence in American society, especially in ultraconservative circles.[8] It is hard to understand the rift that divides the United States today, between Republicans and Democrats, between supporters and opponents of social solidarity and an active role of the government in the lives of citizens, without measuring the influence of Ayn Rand's thinking. Born in Russia at the beginning of the twentieth century and naturalized as an American, Rand died in 1982 at the beginning of the Reagan era; she is one of the most popular authors across the Atlantic. In 1991, according to a poll carried out by the Library of Congress, Americans cited *Atlas Shrugged*, her main work, as the book that influenced them the most, after the Bible! Published in 1957, this 1,400-page saga, which defines the vision of Ayn Rand's world—was printed in a run of 24 million copies. Even today it sells several hundred thousand copies a year. Two other novels, *Anthem* and *The Fountainhead*, published in 1938 and 1943, respectively, were also huge bestsellers.

The vogue for this author and philosopher was so great that in the United States, almost everyone of a certain age had "an Ayn Rand phase." President Ronald Reagan was one of her fervent admirers. Alan Greenspan, former head of the Federal Reserve, which controls the American economy, declared she had profoundly shaped his thinking, and that "our values are congruent."[9] Ayn Rand was at Greenspan's side when he took the oath before President Ford. She is also a heroine for the Tea Party and political movements that derive from her their urge to reduce the role of government in the lives of citizens to a strict minimum. Paul Ryan, who was a candidate for the American vice presidency in 2012 as Mitt Romney's running mate, requires his coworkers to read the writings of Ayn Rand; he asserts it was she who inspired his political career. The bulk of Paul Ryan's economic and social program consisted of reducing taxes for the rich while reducing subsidies for the poor.[10]

Ayn Rand was very aware of her influence and "modestly" spoke of the three A's that counted in the history of philosophy: Aristotle, St. Augustine, and herself.[11] In France, *Atlas Shrugged* was published only recently, at the urging and with the financial contribution of an American admirer.

Rand does not claim that we are all fundamentally selfish: she deplores the fact that we are not selfish enough. For her, altruism is nothing but a masochistic vice that threatens our survival and leads us to neglect our own happiness in favor of the happiness of others, and to behave like "sacrificial animals." "Altruism means that you place the welfare of others above your own, that you live for others for the sake of helping them, and that justifies your life. That is immoral, according to my morality," she declared on TV in 1979. On the other hand, Rand says, "And here, over the portals of my fort, I shall cut in the stone the word which is to be my beacon and my banner. The word which will not die, should we all perish in battle. The word which can never die on this earth, for it is the heart of it and the meaning and the glory. The sacred word: EGO."[12]

According to Rand, altruism is not only detrimental; it is "a monstrous notion" that represents "the morality of cannibals." It is also a failing: "You owe your love to those who don't deserve it.... Such is your morality of sacrifice and such are the twin ideals it offers: to refashion the life of your body in the image of a human stockyard, and the life of your spirit in the image of a dump."[13]

Rand doesn't mince her words. In 1959, during a televised interview, she declared, "I consider altruism as evil.... Man must have self-esteem.... Altruism is immoral...because...you are asked to love everybody indiscriminately...you only love those who deserve it." When the interviewer remarks, "There are very few in this world who are worthy of your love," Rand replies, "Unfortunately, yes.... Nobody has ever given a reason why man should be his brother's keeper. You see examples everywhere of man perishing by attempting to be their brother's keeper."[14] In one of her novels, *The Fountainhead,* Rand writes, "Has any act of selfishness ever equaled the carnage perpetrated by disciples of altruism?"[15]

Ayn Rand thinks that human relations should be based on the business principles. Concerning these statements, in the same interview, the journalist questions her about her personal life: "You are helping your husband financially. Is there any contradiction here?" "No, because you see, I am in love with him selfishly. It is in my own interest to help him. If he ever needed it, I would not call it a sacrifice, because I take selfish pleasure in him." She expands on this by asserting that in the presence of a drowning person, it is morally acceptable to risk saving him only if it's someone close to you whose death would make your life unbearable. In any other case, it would be immoral to try to save him from drowning if the danger to yourself is high; that would show a lack of self-esteem.[16]

It would be tempting to brush Ayn Rand aside and regard her as a sinister anomaly who claimed to rebuild the world from almost nothing on the basis of selfishness (she tolerated Aristotle, whom she regarded as her sole philosophical inspiration, even though she "disagreed strongly with many of his positions"). Still, the fact that she made such a mark on American culture, which in turn exercises great influence over the rest of the world, forces us to consider this phenomenon, embarrassing as it may be.

REDUCING THE ROLE OF THE GOVERNMENT TO A STRICT MINIMUM

Ayn Rand greatly contributed to the extreme individualism that is spreading throughout the United States. She provided a doctrine for all those who argue that the government should confine itself to watching over the protection of individual liberties and should not intervene in any way whatsoever in the personal affairs of citizens, especially not in the functioning of the economy. Neither the government nor anyone else should force us to concern ourselves with the poor, the elderly, or the sick, or compel us to pay taxes to help the unfortunate. That would be imposing on individuals the unacceptable obligation to share resources they earned from the sweat of their brows with people they don't even know, without any advantage in return. In short, in a libertarian economy, the poor are regarded as killers of growth, beings who harm entrepreneurs. Only the individual creates growth; society is predatory, and the welfare state, a concept that prevails in Europe, constitutes "the most evil national psychology ever described," and those who benefit from it are nothing but a gang of looters.[17] For Rand, it's the poor who exploit the rich.

This follower of selfishness is thus against Social Security and subsidies of any kind, the guaranteed minimum wage, and so on. According to her, citizens should pay only minimal, voluntary taxes solely to allow the government to protect their personal interests and ensure their safety by preserving a monopoly on the legal use of force (police and army). The government should not intervene in the functioning of the economy and should abstain from any kind of regulation. This apology for laissez-faire capitalism gave birth to the extreme forms of deregulated economy whose unfortunate consequences we see today.[18]

AYN RAND'S MORAL AND INTELLECTUAL MISTAKES

When a political-economic system is such that society abandons people who are old, alone, and without resources; children whose parents don't have the means to offer them an education; or sick people who die for lack of care, not only is the system not fulfilling its role, but the human values that should regulate society are degraded.

According to the economist Joseph Stiglitz, it is above all the wealthy who are distressed by a strong government, since it "could use its power to adjust the imbalances in our society by taking some of their wealth and devoting it to public investments that would contribute to the common good or that would help those at the bottom."[19] But in reality, continues Stiglitz, "The fact of the matter is that there has been no successful large economy in which the government has not played an important role."[20] That is the case notably in Scandinavian countries where taxes are high—which would horrify Ayn Rand—and the inequality between rich and poor is less. Ayn Rand's ideas, then, are a recipe for the unbridled promotion of individualism and inequality in society, an inequality whose harmful effects on quality of life, prosperity, justice, even health, are well-known.[21] Today, as the economist Daniel Cohen stresses in *The Prosperity of Vice,* "A world left to the sole forces of 'every man for himself' is a mirage that must have been forgotten.... The role of the state is being restored to its former glory."[22]

Ayn Rand developed her main argument in the following way: man's most precious possession is his life. This is an end in itself and cannot be used as a means to accomplish the benefit of others. According to objectivist ethics, taking care of oneself and pursuing one's own happiness by every means available constitute man's highest moral rationale.[23]

Up to that point, the reasoning is not very original, and we can readily acknowledge that humans' most cherished aspiration is to live their lives to the end and to experience more joy than suffering.

Then Rand clumsily sets in place the cornerstone of her intellectual building: man's basic desire is to remain alive and to be happy; *therefore he must be selfish.*

That is where the logical fault lies. Rand reasons in the abstract and loses contact with lived experience. The latter shows that a selfishness as extreme as the one she advocates is much more likely to make the individual unhappy than to favor his or her prosperity. And that was, apparently, the case for Rand herself, according to the testimony of those who knew her for a long time. Haughty, narcissistic, curt, manipulative, and devoid of empathy, bordering on the psychopathic, she maintained vindictive and conflicted relationships with many of her friends and collaborators. She scorned the common run of people, whom she regarded as "mediocre, stupid, and irrational."

Lost in the sphere of mental constructs, Rand ignored the fact that in reality—that reality she claimed to love above everything—altruism is neither sacrificial nor a cause of frustration, but constitutes one of the main sources of happiness and fulfillment among humans. As Luca and Francesco Cavalli-Sforza, father and son, one a renowned geneticist and the other a philosopher, write, "Ethics arose as the science of happiness. In order to be happy, is it better to take care of others than to think exclusively of oneself."[24] Research in social psychology has shown that the satisfaction produced by egocentric activities is less than that engendered by altruistic activities.[25]

The American philosopher James Rachels provides an additional argument to demonstrate the incoherence of Rand's theses:

> *What is the difference between me and everyone else that justifies placing myself in this special category? Am I more intelligent? Do I enjoy my life more? Are my accomplishments greater? Do I have needs or abilities that are so different from the needs or abilities of others? In short,* what makes me so special? *Failing an answer, it turns out that Ethical Egoism is an arbitrary doctrine in the same way that racism is arbitrary. And this, in addition to explaining why Ethical Egoism is unacceptable, also sheds some light on the question of why we should care for others. We should care for the interest of other people*

for the same reason *we care for our own interests; for their needs and desires are comparable to our own.*[26]

FREUD AND HIS SUCCESSORS

Freud's position on altruism, less dogmatic than Rand's, is more based on intuition than on reasoning, but it turns out to be just as removed from reality. Freud paints a degrading picture of the human being, starting in early childhood: "Children are completely egoistic; they feel their needs intensely and strive ruthlessly to satisfy them."[27] Yet all studies based on the objective and systematic observation of many children, especially the studies carried out by Tomasello and Warneken that we described previously, have clearly demonstrated that Freud's assertion is wrong, and that empathy and kind behavior count among the very first spontaneous behavior patterns of young children.

What's more, if we believe what Freud wrote in a letter to the clergyman Pfister, things don't get any better in adulthood: "I don't rack my brains much over the subject of good and evil, but, on average, I haven't discovered much 'good' in men. Based on what I know of them, they are for the most part nothing but scoundrels...."[28]

According to Freud, society and its members are important to the individual only insofar as they favor or stand in the way of the satisfaction of his instincts. This disposition embraces all aspects of our existence, even dreams, which are "all completely egoistic." Freud even asserts, "If a dream seems to have been provoked by an altruistic interest, we are only being deceived by appearances."[29]

Freud alludes only rarely to altruism,[30] notably when he declares, "Individual development seems to us a product of the interplay of two trends, the striving for happiness, generally called 'egoistic,' and the impulse toward merging with others in the community, which we call 'altruistic.'"[31] He adds, however, that altruistic and social tendencies are acquired under external constraints, and that "one should not overestimate human aptitude for social life."[32] Above all, the definition Freud gives of altruism as "aspiration for union with other members of the community" is inappropriate: one can unite with others to do good but also to harm, to promote racism, to belong to a gang of criminals, or to perpetrate genocide.[33]

Darwin and many others, however, haven't stopped stressing the natural propensity of humans and other animals who live in society to cooperate and to display social instincts that, according to Darwin, "are always present and persistent," as well as to give aid and assistance to their fellows, adding: "They feel at times, without the stimulus of any special passion or desire, some degree of love and sympathy for them; they are unhappy if long separated from them, and always happy to be again in their company. So it is with ourselves."[34] Darwin concludes, "Thus the reproach is removed of laying the foundation of the noblest part of our nature in the base principle of selfishness."[35]

Freud frequently uses the term *Einfühlung*, which, as we have seen, gave birth to the term "empathy," without regarding it as a step toward altruism. As Jacques Hochmann explains in his *History of Empathy*,[36] Freud speaks of empathy as a way we compare our state of mind to that of others, and thus have a better understanding, for example, of the involuntary comic effect produced by a naïve or stupid remark. "Our laughter," writes Freud, "expresses a pleasant feeling of superiority."[37]

In *Why War?*, Freud formulates the hypothesis of the existence of a "death wish" that would initially be exercised against the individual himself before it is turned toward others:

> *Everything truly happens as if we were forced to destroy people and things, so that we don't destroy ourselves, and so that we can protect ourselves against the tendency for self-destruction.*[38]

This devastating depiction of human nature didn't fail to impress contemporary thought, even though it has been profoundly called into question and revealed to be without any scientific basis. The theses of Freud and of the ethologist Konrad Lorenz, according to which the tendency to aggression is a primary and autonomous impulse among humans and animals, have been invalidated by many research studies.[39]

Carl Gustav Jung, another founding figure of psychoanalysis, has a similarly somber view of human nature:

> *Evil is of gigantic proportions, so that for the Church to talk of original sin and to trace it back to Adam's relatively innocent*

slip-up with Eve is almost a euphemism. The case is far graver and is grossly underestimated.... Evil is human nature itself.[40]

Thus Freud and Jung created a secular version of original sin in the modern world.

ALTRUISM IS SUPPOSEDLY AN UNHEALTHY COMPENSATION FOR OUR DESIRE TO HARM

According to Freud and his disciples, humans show very little inclination to do good, and if perchance they come to nourish altruistic thoughts and behave kindly, that's not real altruism, but rather a way to try to contain aggressive tendencies constantly lurking in their minds. Freud in fact describes aggressiveness as an "ineffaceable feature of human nature."[41] In "Drives and Their Fates," Freud writes:

As an object relation, hate is older than love, its source being the narcissistic ego's primal rejection of the stimuli of the outside world.[42]

For Freud, morality and prosocial behavior are born solely from a feeling of guilt and from defense mechanisms used by the ego to handle the restrictions that society imposes on the innate aggressive impulses of the individual, as well as the irrational demands of the superego.

According to the ethologist Frans de Waal, the reasoning of those who think that humans are naturally malevolent and aggressive is usually the following: "(1) natural selection is a selfish, nasty process, (2) this automatically produces selfish and nasty individuals, and (3) only romantics with flowers in their hair would think otherwise."[43] As for Darwin, he was, on the contrary, convinced that moral sense was innate and acquired over the course of evolution. Various studies presented by the psychologist Jonathan Haidt in his book *The Righteous Mind* have shown that moral sense appears spontaneously in young children and is not attributable to the parents' influence, social norms, or "demands imposed by society," as Freud asserted.[44] The psychologist Elliot Turiel had already observed that, from infancy, children have a sense of fairness, and think that harming others is wrong.[45]

For psychoanalysis, on the other hand, altruism is only a defense mechanism meant to protect oneself from aggressive impulses that are hard to suppress. One must above all not try to be altruistic. According to Freud:

> *All who wish to be more noble minded than their constitution allows fall victims to neurosis; they would have been more healthy if it could have been possible for them to be less good.*[46]

For Anna, Freud's daughter, altruism fits into the framework of defense mechanisms against internal conflicts.[47] Notably, according to the *International Dictionary of Psychoanalysis,* altruism is "an outlet for aggressiveness," which instead of being repressed is redirected toward "noble" aims. Altruism is also supposedly "a vicarious enjoyment where conflict becomes attached to a pleasure that one refuses for oneself, but that one helps others to obtain." Finally, altruism is defined as "a manifestation of masochism," since it's supposedly the sacrifices linked to altruism that are above all sought by the person who practices altruism.[48] According to research in psychology, however, there is no indication proving that kindness stems from negative or masochistic motivations.

Enhancing Selfishness

Psychoanalysis often describes itself as a way to know oneself, rather than a therapy. It is opposed to any overall evaluation of the effectiveness of its methods, deeming this approach too simplistic (the French psychoanalyst Jacques Lacan even speaks of "the subversion of the role of the doctor by the rise of science"). But, as a report by INSERM[49] (the French National Institute for Medical Research) shows, when this effectiveness was evaluated by taking into account a sufficient number of cases, the therapeutic benefits were deemed almost nonexistent when compared with cognitive behavior therapy, which was proven effective for many disorders.

It even seems that the fact of following a psychoanalytic therapy often leads to an increase of egocentrism and a diminution of empathy. Following an investigation into the image and effects of psychoanalysis practiced on a large sample of the population, the social psychologist

Serge Moscovici concluded that in most cases "the psychoanalyzed person—arrogant, secretive, given to introspection—always withdraws from communication with the group."[50] And the French psychiatrist Henri Baruk reproaches analytical practice with reinforcing interpersonal conflicts, insofar as the psychoanalyzed subject "often views with bitterness his friends, his parents, his spouse, all of whom he holds responsible for his ills." Baruk also notes that some psychoanalyzed subjects become extraordinarily aggressive, and are extremely severe toward others whom they constantly accuse, behaving like antisocial individuals.[51] Psychoanalytic practice, then, seems to make our tendencies toward altruism atrophy.

Some psychoanalysts, far from denying this selfish orientation, seem to endorse it. Jacques Lacan affirms that "well-intentioned people are much worse than those who are ill-intentioned."[52] Pierre Rey, former director of the magazine *Marie Claire,* had daily sessions with Lacan to try to cure himself of social phobia, which he said never diminished over the course of ten years of treatment.[53] He asserts that he learned a lot from his analysis, among other things the fact that "all human relations are articulated around depreciation of the other: in order to exist, the other must be less."[54]

It is undeniable that many psychoanalysts treat their patients kindly, and that patients testify to having benefited from psychoanalytic treatment, but there is no choice but to note, in light of the writings and words of the founders, that, overall, psychoanalytic theory seems to encourage selfishness and leaves little place for altruism.

Freeing the Emotions or Freeing Yourself from Emotions?

Pierre Rey's testimony, along with those of others, shows that psychoanalysis can't readily be viewed as a science of the emotions. Otherwise, how could its outcome be such an inability to handle destructive emotions? Rey reports, "A terrifying upwelling of cries blocked behind my shell of polite friendliness gushed forth from me. From then on, everyone knew where they stood with the feelings I had for him. When I loved, I loved passionately, for this life and the next. When I hated, for this life and the next, and people soon knew it."[55]

There is a confusion here, with grave consequences, between *freeing* the emotions, the way a pack of wild dogs is set free, and *freeing oneself* from the burden of destructive, conflicting emotions, in the sense of no longer being a slave to them. In the first instance, one gives up all control of negative emotions and lets them explode at the slightest opportunity, to the detriment of the well-being of others and of one's own mental health. In the second instance, one learns to free oneself of their power, without either repressing them or letting them destroy our equilibrium.

Psychoanalysis does not resort to methods that permit one to gradually free oneself from the mental poisons of hatred, compulsive desire, jealousy, pride, and a lack of discernment, and to cultivate the qualities of altruistic love, empathy, compassion, mindfulness, and focus.

If psychoanalysis were limited to the realm of ideas, it would be one thing, but the fact that it has become a therapeutic practice has led to harmful consequences for many patients. A typical example is that of autism. In the 1950s, psychoanalysts, with Bruno Bettelheim in the lead, held mothers responsible for the autism of their children. "I believe," wrote Bettelheim, "the initial cause of withdrawal is rather the child's correct interpretation of the negative emotions with which the most significant figures in his environment approach him."[56] Psychoanalysts then spent the next forty years trying to "treat" these mothers (thus adding to their suffering in having an autistic child by making them feel guilty for the illness), all the while abandoning the child to his fate.

In fact, according to psychoanalysis, "the psychosis of the child is caused by a defense mechanism stemming from the attitude of an incestuous mother who is urged by the absence of a phallus to destroy the substitute for the missing phallus represented by her offspring."[57] Try to imagine anything more absurd.

In France, according to Franck Ramus, research director at CNRS (a national organization for scientific research), psychoanalysts continue to blame the parents, especially the mother, for their child's illness. A psychiatrist with thirty years' experience recalls witnessing "bizarre scenes" when he was training in the field of child psychiatry in consultation centers for autistic children: "Blaming the parents is a reality. During the interviews, they were interested only in the parents, whom they bombarded with questions. During the debriefing sessions, they were all qualified as psychotic, and the children's problems were the exclusive consequence of paternal or maternal toxicity."[58]

These theories have been abandoned for decades by all researchers and scientists, for whom autism is a neurodevelopmental disorder with a strong genetic component.[59] There are many different forms of autism, and according to studies synthesized by Martha Herbert at Harvard, it is possible that the increase of the incidence of autism over the last fifty years might partly be linked to the globalized use of pesticides and fertilizers.[60] What is certain is that this illness is in no way caused by the psychological influence of the mother.

Freud's Successors Have Continued to Evolve in the Sphere of Egocentrism

Many emulators of Freud have preserved the orthodoxy of his doctrine to this day. Others have gone back to certain key points and have questioned, for example, the violence instinct or the postulate according to which all our desires are dictated by sexuality—what about, for example, the desire to walk in the woods, or visit an elderly friend? But, while trying to give their therapies a more human aspect, they have usually only promoted the more attractive forms of egocentrism. As the psychologists Michael and Lise Wallach have shown,[61] in most of the adaptations of Freudian theories, like those suggested by Harry Sullivan, Karen Horney, and, on certain points, Erich Fromm, egocentrism continues to rule supreme

These psychologists argue notably that all forms of restrictions and obligations, dictated by society or by our internal norms, hinder our personal realization and distance us from our true identity.[62] The unconstrained gratification of our impulses seems to them to be a priority. But in that case, it would be impossible to take part in collective activities and live in society. How could one play music or sports without conforming to the rules or sticking to a discipline? Imagine an orchestra in which every musician played however he liked, ignoring the conductor and the score. Nothing would distinguish the music from any kind of cacophony.[63]

In practice, expressing oneself free of any constraints seems more destined to hinder the good of society than to accomplish it.[64] I met a young American woman who told me, "To be really myself, to be free, I have to be faithful to what I feel, and spontaneously express whatever I like and whatever suits me." True freedom, however, does not consist in doing whatever comes to mind, but in being master of oneself. Gandhi agreed with this when he said, "The outward freedom that we shall attain will only be in exact proportion to the inward freedom to which we may have grown at a given moment. And if this is a correct view of freedom, our chief energy must be concentrated on achieving reform from within." This transformation, if we want to thwart the debilitating views of the champions of selfishness, consists precisely of diminishing our egocentrism and cultivating altruism and compassion.

26

Having Hatred or Compassion for Yourself

Of all diseases, the most ferocious is despising one's own being.

—Montaigne

The ability to love others is often associated with that of loving oneself. The golden rule found in almost identical formulations in all great religions is: "Love others as you love yourself." So it seems that the fact of wanting good for oneself is an indispensable precursor to altruism. If one regards one's own well-being as valueless, or, worse, if one wants to harm oneself, it will be very difficult to desire good for anyone else. On the other hand, if one truly wants to do oneself good, and if one recognizes the value and legitimacy of this aspiration, one can extend it to others. In fact, clinical studies show that those who hate themselves and want to harm themselves, and who sometimes inflict physical suffering on themselves, admit that they find it very difficult to conceive of love and compassion for others.[1] We should also remember that the simple fact of wishing good for oneself is in no way selfish, since it is compatible with a wish for the good of others.

Can You Truly Hate Yourself?

During one of his many meetings with scientists, the Dalai Lama heard a psychologist talking about "self-hatred." He turned to his translator, thinking he hadn't understood correctly, then to the psychologist, asking him, "You did say *self-hatred?* But that's impossible. One can't want to harm oneself." Although Buddhist psychology is of a great richness and abounds in nuances, it does not envisage the possibility that any individual would wish himself ill. The psychologist explained to the Dalai Lama that self-hatred was unfortunately a frequent affliction in the West. A long conversation ensued, and after listening to the scientists' explanations, the Dalai Lama responded, "I understand a little better now. It's like a state of profound unease, a disease of the self. People don't really want to suffer, but they blame themselves for not being as talented or as happy as they'd like." The psychologist explained that that was only one dimension of the problem, and that certain people had undergone repeated abuse and violence until they thought that if they had suffered so much, it was because they were basically bad or without any value. The scientists also explained to the Dalai Lama that some people went so far as to wound themselves voluntarily, and that self-mutilation was practiced by 10% to 15% of European adolescents. The Dalai Lama remained silent for some time, visibly moved.

To remedy self-hatred, Western clinical psychologists have emphasized the necessity of helping their patients develop more kindness toward themselves; they have created therapies based on the concept of *self-compassion*. Initially, I felt a certain unease about this concept, which I had heard a lot about in the West. I wondered in fact if by focusing too much attention on oneself, such a therapy risked reinforcing egocentric and narcissistic tendencies, to the detriment of openness to others. I later grew aware of the benefits of self-compassion for mental health after some fruitful conversations with Paul Gilbert, an English researcher and clinical psychologist, who for thirty years has been taking care of people who suffer from self-aggression, and with the American psychologist Kristin Neff, whose research has shown that in general the development of self-compassion and the benefits it leads to are not accompanied by an increase of narcissism.

So this is how I tried to connect this concept of self-compassion with Buddhist teachings. Basically, kindness and compassion for oneself comes down to asking oneself, "What is really good for me?" If one asks oneself this question in all honesty, one should be led to conclude, "Yes, if it were possible, I would rather not suffer, and I'd rather feel happy."

The main obstacle, for many people who have a very negative image of themselves and who adopt self-destructive behavior, also comes from the fact that, too often, the possibility of happiness has long been denied them. Simply wishing to be happy only makes memories of traumatic events arise. These people then come to *turn this violence against themselves,* instead of hoping for a happiness that has constantly eluded them.

Still, as soon as they accept the mere *idea* that it is preferable not to suffer, which is often a difficult step for them, they are ready to adopt ways of being and acting that allow them to escape the vicious circle of suffering. This attitude also becomes a platform for generating compassion for others, since it facilitates the understanding that others, like me, would rather avoid suffering.

In fact, many scientists who study self-compassion and therapists who use it as a tool to help their patients have drawn inspiration from Buddhist teachings. At the same time, the research on self-compassion has also motivated those who conduct programs, both Buddhist and secular, aimed at cultivating altruism and compassion, to include training in self-compassion as a preliminary step.

Another essential point seems to be the realization of a *potential for change.* Often, those who harm themselves think they are basically guilty ("It's my fault") and that they are condemned to be what they are ("It's part of myself"). If their unhappiness were truly unavoidable, we would only be adding to their torments by telling them they can get better. If we cannot choose what we are—namely the result of a multitude of factors independent of our will (such as how we were treated in childhood)—we can actually act on our present and our future.

The Feeling of Having No Value

It is not rare for some people to be tormented by the feeling that they are unworthy of being loved, that they lack any qualities, and that they are not made for happiness. These feelings are usually the result of the scorn or repeated criticism of parents or relatives. Added to this is a feeling of guilt: such people judge themselves responsible for the imperfections attributed to them.[2] Besieged by these negative thoughts, they constantly blame themselves and feel cut off from other people.

According to Paul Gilbert, in this pathological self-criticism that constitutes a kind of inner harassment, one part of the self constantly accuses another part, which it hates and despises.[3] You think it's better to blame yourself than to provoke the anger of those who abuse you, and risk a redoubling of violence." According to Neff:

> *The best way to counteract self-criticism, therefore, is to understand it, have compassion for it, and then replace it with a kinder response. By letting ourselves be moved by the suffering we have experienced at the hands of our own self-criticism, we strengthen our desire to heal. Eventually, after banging our heads against the wall long enough, we'll decide that enough is enough and demand an end to our self-inflicted pain.*[4]

In order for these people to go from despair to the desire to recover in life, we must help them establish a warmer relationship with themselves, and to feel compassion for their own suffering instead of judging themselves harshly. From there, they will also be able to improve their relations with others.

VIOLENCE DIRECTED AGAINST YOURSELF

As we said above, self-mutilating behavior affects 10 to 15% of adolescents in Western Europe, especially girls, a great number of whom experienced traumatic childhoods (abuse, rape, incest, systematic denigration by the parents, etc.). Among those who present severe personality disorders, self-mutilation occurs in 70% to 80% of cases. By inflicting major physical damage on themselves, they are trying to put an end to a painful emotional state. Most of them assert that self-mutilation provides them with a sensation of *relief* and reduces the high physical and psychological tension that is oppressing them. Two-thirds assert that they don't feel any pain during self-mutilation.[5] Self-mutilation in fact provokes a release of endorphins in the brain, substances that procure a fleeting sensation of calmness.

These practices are not a specifically cultural phenomenon, but rather a universal signal of extreme distress when the pain becomes overwhelming and is not acknowledged. They are so clearly forewarnings of a possible suicide attempt.[6]

ESTABLISHING A WARM RELATIONSHIP WITH YOURSELF

Paul Gilbert has for thirty years been treating people suffering from self-aggression. He has developed a therapeutic method of training in compassion (Compassionate Mind Training, or CMT).[7] He tries to have his patients discover a zone of security and human warmth and, little by little, to substitute kindness toward oneself for self-hatred. Clinical studies carried out on a large number of patients have shown that CMT considerably reduced depressive states, self-mutilation, and feelings of inferiority and guilt.

According to Gilbert, one of the problems of those who criticize themselves excessively is that they do not have any soothing memories to evoke when they feel bad—memories of kind, affectionate treatment. They can easily imagine the critical part of themselves, the part that tends to control and dominate them, but they have trouble calling to mind and visualizing kind, compassionate images. One of the therapist's roles is thus to help them establish a warmer relationship with themselves.[8] Kristin Neff's research has led her to identify three essential components of compassion for oneself:

- *self-kindness*, that we be gentle and understanding with ourselves rather than harshly critical and judgmental;
- recognition of our *common humanity,* feeling connected with others in the experience of life rather than feeling isolated and alienated by our suffering;
- *mindfulness*: that we hold our experience in balanced awareness, rather than ignoring our pain or exaggerating it.[9]

According to Kristin Neff, individuals who have acquired habits of extreme self-criticism don't realize that they are in fact capable of kindness toward themselves. To help them, they are asked to begin by identifying such a possibility, even if they feel it very weakly, and then to make it stronger.[10]

From there, they will feel increasingly safer to open up to others, feel less threatened by empathic distress, and feel more concerned by others' fate as well.

Understanding We Are Part of Humanity

It is important to realize the interdependence of all beings and of the world around us. The psychologist Heinz Kohut insisted on the idea that to feel that one belongs is one of the main aspirations of human beings. One of the major causes for mental health problems is the feeling of being cut off from others, even when they are just a few inches away.[11] The feeling of having no self-worth, however, goes hand in hand with feeling separated from others, and hence being vulnerable. That is why, according to Neff: "Recognition of the common humanity embedded in self-compassion is such a powerful healing force.... Our humanity can never be taken away from us, no matter how far we fall."[12]

To allow them to reinforce the feeling of being connected to the world and to all beings, Paul Gilbert suggests to his patients visualizations like this:

> *I would like you to imagine a sea in front of you that is a beautiful blue, is warm and calm, lapping on a sandy shore. Imagine that you are standing just in the water with the water lapping gently at your feet. Now as you look out over the sea to the horizon imagine that this sea has been here for millions of years, was a source of life. It has seen many things in the history of life and knows many things. Now imagine the sea has complete acceptance for you, that it knows of your struggles and pain. Allow yourself to feel connected to the sea, its power and wisdom in complete acceptance of you.*[13]

Practicing Mindfulness

This technique has its origin in Buddhism. It allows us to handle disturbing thoughts and emotions. A secular version was developed by Jon Kabat-Zinn, who has used it for thirty years with great success in hospitals under the name Mindfulness-Based Stress Reduction, or MBSR.

Since then, Kabat-Zinn's methods have been applied in hundreds of hospitals throughout the world, mainly to resolve physical and mental difficulties and pain associated with serious illnesses, postoperative convalescence, chemotherapy and other cancer treatments, as well as chronic pain.[14]

Many studies have established that among patients who follow mindfulness training for eight weeks according to the MBSR method[15] for thirty minutes a day, the immune system is reinforced, and positive emotions (joy, optimism, openness to others) are more frequent.[16] In the case of self-hatred, a study by Shauna Shapiro and her colleagues found that a six-week training in MBSR considerably increased the participants' level of self-compassion.[17] In *Mindful Compassion,* Paul Gilbert and Choden explored how to join meditation on altruistic love and compassion with mindfulness meditation.[18]

SELF-ESTEEM AND KINDNESS TOWARD ONESELF

Kristin Neff's research has clearly highlighted the differences between *self-compassion* and *self-esteem.*[19] We might wonder, in fact, if people who criticize themselves should try above all to acquire a higher opinion of themselves. But, as we have seen, one can also fear a reinforcement of the individual's narcissism. In fact, research has shown that acquiring an excessively high opinion of self has many disadvantages, including a tendency to overestimate one's abilities, to demand things of oneself of which one is not capable, and to blame others when things go badly.[20]

Kristin Neff has made clear the fact that unlike self-esteem, an increase of compassion for oneself is not accompanied by an increase of narcissism.[21] On the contrary, it is accompanied by a serene acceptance of our own weaknesses and faults, an acceptance that preserves us from the temptation to blame ourselves for what we are, an acceptance that is not synonymous with resignation.[22] Neff in fact states:

> *One reason that self-compassion may be more beneficial than self-esteem is that it tends to be available precisely when self-esteem fails. Personal flaws and shortcomings can be approached in a kind and balanced manner that recognizes that imperfec-*

tion is part of the human condition, even when self-evaluations are negative. This means that self-compassion can lessen feelings of self-loathing without requiring that one adopt an unrealistically positive view of oneself—a major reason why self-esteem enhancement programs often fail.[23]

The healing effect on anxiety, depression, shame, and mental suffering that was long attributed to the development of higher self-esteem turns out actually to be more closely related to self-compassion.[24]

Compassion for Oneself, Compassion for Others

According to the observations of Paul Gilbert and his colleagues, among patients who suffer from self-aggression, any mention of love for others or compassion for sufferers usually arouses a reaction of rejection. No doubt it's too much to demand of people who already have so much trouble loving themselves. There are of course notable exceptions: people who suffered considerably in their youth at the hands of adults, and who then reconstructed themselves and spent the rest of their lives helping people in difficulty. Once one has established a better relationship with oneself, it becomes easier to feel kindness and compassion for others.

27

The Shortfall of Empathy

We have seen that affective resonance with others—empathy—was one of the factors that, combined with valuing the other and concern for the other's fate, would engender altruistic attitude and behavior. But it is also possible that empathy could be lacking. The causes for such a shortfall and its effects are many. In some cases, lack of empathy is caused by an emotional erosion linked to external situations of increased tension, which results in professional fatigue, or burnout, especially among doctors and nurses. In other cases, that of psychopaths, a complete lack of empathy and of caring feelings manifests from childhood. Linked to genetic heritage, this lack is associated with dysfunctions of certain regions of the brain. In all cases, these defects produce major negative effects in people who suffer from them, and in everyone those people affect, because their cold insensitivity leads them to harm others and sometimes even to commit atrocities.

Burnout: Emotional Exhaustion

Medical personnel are confronted daily with the suffering of others. When they experience empathy, they suffer from their patients' suffering. This suffering set off by empathy is real, and studies in neuroscience have shown that regions of the brain for pain or distress are activated.[1] What will the consequences be in the long run? The sufferings of a patient will not always last. In the best case, the patient gets better, and in the worst case, dies. Fortunately, it is very rare for patients to suffer intensely for years. Patients come and go, but the burden of empathic suffering of the medical staff is renewed day after day. In many cases, the doctor or nurse will end up suffering from burnout. Their capacity for resilience when repeatedly faced with the sufferings of others becomes exhausted. They can no longer bear this situation. Those who suffer from this type of exhaustion are generally forced to discontinue their practice.

One study has shown that in the United States, 60% of practicing doctors have reported symptoms of burnout, including emotional exhaustion and feelings of powerlessness and ineffectiveness, even uselessness. Those who are subject to burnout also tend to depersonalize the patients: the patients are then treated less well, and the frequency of medical errors increases.[2]

Some doctors adopt a strategy. They say to themselves, "In order to take care of my patients, I must avoid reacting emotionally to their suffering." They understand that excessive sensitivity and emotional reactions can affect the quality of care or disturb a surgeon who needs all his calm to carry out perfectly precise actions and make difficult decisions. But creating a distance and establishing an emotional barrier between oneself and the patient is likely not the best way to approach the patient's suffering. Such an attitude can quickly degenerate into cold indifference.

On the other hand, a large number of nurses and doctors evince great human warmth, which is a source of powerful comfort for the sick person. It turns out that people who are thus naturally gifted with kindness and compassion are less often affected by empathic exhaustion. Isn't it the ability to feel and show kindness that makes the difference? One of the essential factors of burnout could be the progressive fatigue of empathy when it is not regenerated or transformed by altruistic love.

People sometimes talk about *compassion fatigue*. It would probably be more appropriate to talk about *empathy fatigue*, as we have seen in chapter 4. Empathy is limited to an affective resonance with the one who is suffering. Having accumulated, it can easily end up in exhaustion and distress. But altruistic love is a constructive state of mind that helps both the one who feels it and the one who benefits from it. Cultivating altruistic love and kindness, therefore, can remedy the difficulties posed by burnout.

REGENERATING COMPASSION IN MEDICAL PRACTICE

A friend of mine, Dr. David Shlim, who has long lived in Nepal and practiced meditation for years, has, since the year 2000, organized seminars in the United States that gather together about a hundred doctors who want to feature compassion more in their practices.[3] During these seminars, doctors have noticed that despite the fact that kindness and compassion are integral parts of the ideal of medicine, the Hippocratic oath, and the medical code of ethics, the curriculum at medical schools did not even mention the word *compassion,* let alone methods to cultivate it. A doctor present at the seminar remarked, "I think I've never heard the words *medicine* and *compassion* in the same sentence in all my time at medical school." Medical students and young doctors who begin to practice in hospitals are the ones most often tested by unforgiving schedules that can require twenty-four hours' uninterrupted presence with patients. This "training" is so exhausting that, according to the doctors themselves, it leaves hardly any room for compassion.

David confided to me that as a young doctor he sometimes was on call for thirty-six hours in a row. One day, at four o'clock in the morning, he had just dozed off in the staff room when he was awakened by the intercom: a patient, his seventh that night, had just been admitted to the emergency room. As he dragged himself there like a boxer half-stunned by his opponent, he was surprised to catch himself thinking that if the sick person died before he arrived, he could go back to sleep instead of spending the next few hours taking care of her. David had not lost his compassion, but he no longer had enough energy to put it into practice.

For many interns in training, exhaustion causes irritability, resentment, and bitterness rather than kindness, compassion, and empathy. Medical students are selected more for their ability than for their desire to help others. Without offering these young doctors some appropriate training for kindness, how can we expect them to show readiness and compassion, when, in the circumstances they must face, would constitute a challenge even for those who have cultivated these qualities for years? As Harvey Fineberg, president of the Institute of Medicine of the National Academies in America, writes: "Every doctor knows what it takes to become technically *competent:* learn more about scientific advances and the latest successful drugs and procedures. How many physicians, however, have any sense of how to become more compassionate?"[4]

In his preface to *Medicine and Compassion,* David Shlim writes, "Training in compassion, however, does require some effort. Most people agree that doctors are more skillful at treating people after twenty years of practice than they are when they first start out. Like the study of medicine itself, the cultivation of compassion can become a lifelong pursuit, with continued improvement throughout."[5]

All over the world there are countless doctors, nurses, and nurse's aides who tirelessly devote themselves to the well-being of others with admirable devotion. But in order to reduce the burnout that affects health professionals, and not dehumanize a profession whose very essence is humanity, it would be useful to offer medical practitioners ways to develop the inner qualities they need in order to help others better. If health care professionals had the possibility to cultivate compassion and introduce it to the very heart of current practices at hospitals, patients would feel better taken care of and doctors and nurses would draw more satisfaction and emotional equilibrium from it. Further, by granting more importance to compassion, the people who administer or reform health systems would be inclined to stress the way patients are treated rather than only the reduction of costs and of the time spent with each patient.

The Factors That Contribute to Burnout

The phenomenon of burnout not only affects the people who take care of the suffering. It is a vaster syndrome that afflicts people in all lines of work. The psychologist Christina Maslach, a professor at the University of Berkeley in California, has devoted herself to studying the causes and symptoms of burnout. She defines it as a syndrome of emotional exhaustion, which results from an accumulation of stress linked to difficult human interactions during our daily activities.[6] She identifies three main consequences of burnout: emotional exhaustion, cynicism, and a feeling of ineffectiveness.

Emotional exhaustion is the feeling of being "worn out," "at the end of one's tether," of no longer having the necessary energy or pleasure in oneself to face the next day. Those who find themselves in that case cut down on their relationships with others. Even if they continue to work, they withdraw behind professionalism and bureaucracy to manage their social relationships in a purely formal way, devoid of any personal or emotional involvement. They set up an emotional barrier between themselves and others. A New York policeman confided to Christina Maslach, "You change when you become a cop—you become tough and hard and cynical. You have to condition yourself to be that way in order to survive this job. And sometimes, without realizing it, you act that way all the time, even with your wife and kids. But it's something you have to do, because if you start getting emotionally involved with what happens at work, you'll wind up in Bellevue."[7]

The second major symptom of burnout is cynicism and insensitivity to those one encounters professionally. One depersonalizes them and regards them with a cold, distant attitude, and one avoids engaging in overly personal relations with them. One even gives up one's ideals. One social worker confided to Maslach, "I began to despise everyone and could not conceal my contempt," while another reports, "I find myself caring less and possessing an extremely negative attitude. I just don't give a damn anymore." Yet another even wanted other people to "get out of my life and just leave me alone."

These symptoms are also accompanied by a feeling of guilt, with health care professionals feeling distress at the thought that they aren't taking care of their patients as they should, and that they're becoming cold and insensitive.

The third aspect of burnout manifests in the form of a loss of feeling of personal accomplishment and self-realization, which causes a feeling of failure. Loss of self-confidence and any sense of the value of what one has accomplished leads to profound discouragement and, often, depression, loss of sleep, chronic fatigue, headaches, gastrointestinal disorders, and high blood pressure. A study carried out in the countries of the European Union showed that 50% to 60% of all work days lost are linked more or less directly to stress.[8]

Empathic Exhaustion Linked to an Unfavorable Environment

Most people suffering from burnout underestimate the influence of their environment and overestimate their share of personal responsibility. [9]

The feeling of powerlessness and frustration can in particular affect social workers and members of other professions who *know what they could do but cannot do it.* Eve Ekman, daughter of the psychologist Paul Ekman, takes care of homeless people in San Francisco needing urgent medical or psychological assistance. She told me that the most difficult part of her work, in addition to the strong emotional charge linked to the state of the patients themselves, was the feeling of powerlessness in remedying the roots of the problem: the municipality didn't provide a budget anymore, the shelters were closed, and, once the immediate emergency was taken care of, she had no other choice but to put the poor people back on the street, knowing full well they would soon face new difficulties. "I can't take them home with me; I can't do anything else, and I feel as if what I'm doing is pointless and meaningless. Discouragement can unfortunately lead to depersonalizing the poor and rejecting them." Eve concludes, "So it is important to prepare yourself for such tasks and to maintain full awareness of your inner state so as not to succumb to burnout."

Men and Women Faced with Burnout

Research shows that men and women are equally vulnerable to burnout.[10] Some minor differences have been observed, though: women are more vulnerable to emotional exhaustion, while men have a tendency to depersonalize the people they work with and to seem disdainfully cold to them. That might be due in part to the fact that women work more often than men in the care profession (nurses, social workers, psychological counselors), while men form the majority among doctors, psychiatrists, police officers, and service professionals. Nonetheless, in light of her studies, Christina Maslach thinks that this is not enough to explain the differences observed, and that the differences are linked more to differences of temperament between the two sexes.

Moreover, in the United States, Asian immigrants suffer as much from burnout as the white population, but black and Hispanic immigrants are clearly less affected.[11] The latter are much less subject to emotional exhaustion or depersonalization of the other, perhaps because the black and Hispanic communities place more stress on family and friendship ties and on the importance of personalized relationships with others.

Can Compassion Be Pathological?

Taking care of others and devoting oneself to alleviating their sufferings stems in principle from altruism. But, in certain cases, the motivations of those who serve others are ambiguous, even selfish. Some throw themselves headlong into charitable activities because they have a profound need for approbation or affection.[12] Some help others in order to raise low self-esteem or because they hope to fill a need for intimacy and human contact that remains unsatisfied in their daily lives.

On another register, some psychologists, like Michael McGrath, at the University of Rochester, speak of pathological altruism, defined as "the willingness of an individual to place the needs of others above him- or herself to the point of causing harm, whether physical, psychological, or both, to the purported altruist."[13] We should note, however, that this definition is ambiguous, and does not allow us to distinguish between egocentric motivations and truly altruistic motivations. Does a mother who sacrifices herself to save her child suffer from pathological compassion? One could say that compassion is unhealthy or inappropriate in situations where the difficulties and sufferings one is ready to take on are much greater than the good one can bring to the other. Sacrificing one's quality of life in order to satisfy the whims of someone else makes no sense. Letting one's health deteriorate in order to offer nonvital help to others, or help that others can procure for themselves, when one is at the end of one's physical or psychological strength is not a reasonable thing to do. On the other hand, when the inconveniences for ourselves are the same order of magnitude as the advantages for the other, the choice depends on our degree of altruism, but should not be regarded as unhealthy. Remember the example of Maximilien Kolbe, a Franciscan friar who, in the

Auschwitz extermination camp, offered to take the place of a father when, in revenge for a prisoner's escape, ten men were chosen to die of hunger and thirst.

NARCISSISM AND PERSONALITY DISORDERS LINKED WITH A LACK OF EMPATHY

Whereas burnout leads to a lack of empathy after a slow wearing-down of emotional equilibrium, other shortfalls of empathy correspond to traits and dispositions sometimes due to hereditary causes, sometimes to the influence of external conditions. They are then associated with brain dysfunctions that have been studied by the neurosciences.

In narcissism, personality disorders, psychopathy, and certain forms of autism, different components of the chain of affective reactions involved in social life do not function normally, and lead to lack of empathy and of consideration for others.

Narcissists think only of themselves and are not really interested in others' fate, even if they have no difficulty imagining what others are thinking. Still, they are not necessarily manipulative or harmful, like psychopaths.

Those who suffer from personality disorders are also excessively self-centered. Overly emotional, excitable and troubled, they have difficulty correctly inferring others' feelings. They need love, but are full of resentment and anger, usually because they were neglected or abused when they were children (40% to 70% of them were victims of abuse).[14] Because of this, while still needing others, they reject them and suffer from an inner void, a painful emotional life, and recurrent depression. Among them, 10% end up committing suicide, and 90% attempt suicide.

As for autistic people, they suffer from a defect of cognitive perspective. They have trouble imagining what others think and feel. According to Richard Davidson, they also have difficulty regulating their emotions, and hence they fear being exposed to situations that would set off emotional storms in them; this probably explains why they avoid other people's eyes, gazes which for them are too emotionally charged and hard to decipher.[15] Some autistic individuals show little empathy, while others are not only capable of empathy, but feel it more than ordinary people.

It is among psychopaths that empathy is most cruelly lacking. The suffering of others doesn't move them at all, and they use their intelligence to manipulate and harm others.

Full Head, Empty Heart: The Case of Psychopaths

Psychopaths (also called "sociopaths" or "antisocial personalities") are almost entirely devoid of empathy. Usually, as children they already show a lack of interest in the wishes and rights of others, and constantly violate social norms.[16] Before they start harming humans, they are often cruel to animals, which they like to torture.

The sight of suffering, terrified or happy people causes no affective reaction among psychopaths. Because they experience no unpleasant feelings when they see their victims suffer, they commit the worst atrocities without either hesitation, fear of punishment or remorse. In particular, they have trouble feeling and imagining emotions of sadness and fear, their own as well as others'. When they are asked to try, their attempts cause very few subjective, psychological, or brain reactions.[17] In his book *Without Conscience,* Hare cites the case of a psychopath who was trying to explain why he felt no empathy for the women he had raped: "They are frightened, right? But, you see, I don't really understand it. I've been frightened myself, and it wasn't unpleasant."

Psychopaths lack the whole chain of reactions that begins with emotional contagion, is continued by empathy, and culminates as empathic concern, or compassion. With psychopaths, lacking any feeling in favor of the other, everything occurs on the cognitive level and they excel in mentally imagining what is happening in their heads. They have no other aim but to promote their own interests. Psychologists and criminologists who have worked with psychopaths have been struck by their extreme egocentrism: narcissistic, they think they are superior to others and endowed with innate rights and prerogatives that transcend those of others.[18] In brief, according to Robert Hare, professor emeritus at the University of British Columbia, and one of the pioneers in this field of research, a psychopath is "a self-centered, callous, and remorseless person profoundly lacking empathy."[19] According to

Hare, author of a checklist of characteristics that allow a psychopath to be identified,[20] "trying to explain a psychopath's feelings is like describing colors to a color-blind person."[21]

Psychopaths can be hard to spot, since they operate under a mask of normality and use their calculating intelligence, often combined with a superficial charm, to deceive and manipulate their victims.

Adrian Raine at the University of Pennsylvania has also shown that when psychopaths are asked to read out loud, in front of witnesses, a description of all the crimes they have committed—a task which in normal subjects sets off pronounced feelings of shame and guilt—the areas of the brain linked to those states of mind were not activated in these individuals.[22]

A serial killer-rapist maintained he was "kind and gentle" with his victims, five women he had kidnapped at gunpoint, raped, and stabbed to death. As proof of his kindness, he asserted that when he stabbed his victims "the killing was always sudden, so they wouldn't know what was coming."[23]

In a normal population, there are an average of 3% psychopaths among men and 1% among women. But among prisoners, 50% of men and 25% of women reveal personality disorders, and about 20% of men are psychopaths.[24] When psychopaths are freed after serving their time in prison, they are three times more likely than other released felons to commit a second offense in the following year.[25] In fact, a diagnosis of psychopathy provides the best prognosis for recidivism.

In an overview, James Blair, chief of the Unit on Affective Cognitive Neuroscience at NIMH (National Institute of Mental Health), is of the opinion that the emotional dysfunction linked to psychopathy has a significant genetic component of about 50%.[26] He notes that external circumstances, like sexual abuse, which lead to serious personality disorders, are generally accompanied by increased reactivity to emotional disturbances and events perceived as threatening, whereas the opposite is true for psychopaths, who underreact to these events. The emotional nonreactivity of psychopaths is linked to a diminution of functional activity in two areas of the brain linked to the expression and regulation of emotions (the amygdala and the ventrolateral cortex).

Psychopathy Induced by Practicing Violence

If most psychopaths are that way from early childhood, others can become so in extreme circumstances. Forcing people to kill can desensitize them to others' suffering to the point of making them into psychopaths. John Muhammad was an American soldier who, before being sent to Iraq, was regarded as a likeable person and had an active social life. He was married and had three children. His wife, Mildred, says that everything changed when he came back from Iraq.[27] John was a broken man; he hardly spoke at all and no longer wanted people to come near him, his wife included. She ended up asking for a divorce, after which he threatened her with death several times. She took these threats very seriously, since John was someone who weighed his words carefully.

In 2002, five people were killed in a single day, in Maryland, each by a single bullet shot from a distance. In two weeks, as an atmosphere of terror reigned over the region, thirteen people were killed. Many of these murders occurred in the neighborhood of Mildred's house. When John was finally identified and arrested, the elements of the investigation indicated that the goal of these crimes seemed to be to kill Mildred. By including the murder of his wife in a series of crimes perpetrated seemingly randomly in public places, John could have killed his wife without any suspicion pointing at him. Only the mysterious "beltway sniper" would have been incriminated.

Tragically, John's syndrome was induced by a system that places other humans in situations where they *are forced* to kill other humans they don't know, about whom they are completely ignorant, and toward whom they have on the face of it no reason to show any personal hatred. This process, which leads people to regard anyone on "the other side" as someone to be killed, ends up dehumanizing a normal human being.

Psychopaths in Suits

Psychopaths are not all violent, and some of them are very successful in modern society, especially in the world of finance and business, as shown in the book by the labor psychologist Paul Babiak, in collaboration with Robert Hare, *Snakes in Suits: When Psychopaths Go to Work*.[28] These are "successful psychopaths," in contrast to "psychopaths who fail," who, impulsive and violent, quickly find themselves in prison. According to Babiak, psychopaths in suits and ties lack empathy, but in the business world, that's not necessarily seen as a bad thing, especially when there are difficult decisions to make, such as laying off employees or closing a factory.

Eloquent speakers, charming and charismatic but without any scruples, convincing at job interviews, virtuosi of managing their image, and unsurpassed manipulators, they regard their colleagues in a strictly utilitarian way and use them to climb the ladders of business. In a world where the economic environment is more and more competitive, many psychopaths have thus inserted themselves into the upper levels of business and finance. The sadly infamous Bernard Madoff, as well as Jeff Skilling, former president of the Texas company Enron and condemned to twenty-four years of prison for fraud in 2006, are notorious examples.

Two British researchers at the University of Surrey, Belina Board and Katarina Fritzon, used Robert Hare's evaluation inventory to study the personality traits of thirty-nine high-ranking business executives and compared them to patients at Broadmoor psychiatric hospital: "The results were definitive. The character disorders of the business managers blended together with those of the criminals and mental patients," Belina Board reported in the *New York Times*, concluding that the executives in question had become "successful psychopaths" who, like patients suffering from psychotic personality disorders, lacked empathy, tended to exploit others, were narcissistic, dictatorial, and excessively devoted to work.[29] They even surpassed psychiatric patients and psychopaths in certain areas such as egocentrism, superficial charm, lack of sincerity, and manipulative tendencies. They were, however, less inclined to physical aggression, impulsiveness, and lack of remorse.

The Brain of Psychopaths

Kent Kiehl, at the University of New Mexico at Albuquerque, started a multimillion-dollar research program, financed by the National Institute of Mental Health, to collect the records, brain scans, genetic information, and interviews of a thousand psychopaths, with the aim of compiling a database that would be useable for all researchers. Kiehl notes that the cost of legal prosecution and incarceration of psychopaths, added to the tragedies they cause, amounts in the United States to between 250 and 400 billion dollars a year. No other mental disorder of such magnitude has been so neglected.[30]

One of the main studies of this team, carried out by Carla Harenski, showed that when one exposed psychopaths to emotionally disturbing stimuli (images representing serious moral transgressions—a man pressing a knife against a woman's throat, or terrified faces), the regions of the brain that react strongly in normal subjects were notably inactive in psychopaths. That is particularly the case for the amygdala, the orbitofrontal cortex, and the superior temporal plane.[31] A physical reduction of the size of the amygdala was also observed in psychopathic criminals.[32]

This points to a link with altruism and compassion, since other studies have shown that meditating on compassion can change the activity and, after a certain amount of practice, the structure of the amygdala.[33]

In Kiehl's opinion, it's the entire paralimbic network (interconnected brain structures involved in the management of emotions—anger and fear, in particular—the pursuit of goals, the respect for or violation of moral norms, decision-making, motivations, and self-control) that is affected.[34] His hypothesis is supported by fMRI data, which reveal in psychopaths a thinning of the paralimbic tissue, indicating that this brain region is underdeveloped.[35]

Adrian Raine has observed major deterioration of gray matter in the prefrontal cortex in personalities with psychopathic tendencies who manifest neurological disorders.[36] But, as Raine notes, it is still difficult to distinguish unambiguously the sequence of causes and effects: "Is it the fact of living the violent life of a psychopath that leads to structural and functional modifications of the brain, or is it the other way round?"[37]

Treatment of Psychopaths

For a long time, following opinions going back to the 1940s and to an oft-cited but not very convincing study carried out in the 1970s, it was taken for granted that these illnesses were incurable and believed that interventions could even aggravate psychopathic tendencies.[38] But, more recently, innovative research carried out by the psychologist Michael Caldwell at the Mendota Juvenile Treatment Center in Madison, Wisconsin, has given rise to renewed optimism by showing that certain correctly targeted interventions, including cognitive therapy and psychological assistance for families (in the case of juvenile delinquents exhibiting psychopathic features), could prove effective.[39]

Caldwell used a therapy called decompression, which aims to interrupt the vicious circle of crime and punishment, a cycle that often leads psychopaths to take part in even more reprehensible behavior. In addition, he utilized successful interventions that created more human relationships between guards and inmates.[40] Previously, guards saw inmates as nothing but dangerous delinquents who had to be kept under control by any means possible. On their side, the psychopaths, in Caldwell's words, "don't make any difference between a human being and a Kleenex"—that is, they regard others as instruments, useful or threatening. By working patiently with everyone, Caldwell managed to help psychopaths see the guards as human beings and to make the guards understand that they could treat psychopaths more humanely in their daily interactions while still being careful to ensure their security.

The results were remarkable: a sample of over 150 young psychopaths treated by Caldwell showed a probability that was twice less likely to commit a crime than an equivalent group serving time in a classic detention and rehabilitation center. In the latter group, the juvenile delinquents studied went on to commit sixteen murders in the four years that followed their release from prison. The same number of those who followed Caldwell's program committed no murders.

The economic advantages of successful intervention are considerable: every time American society spends $10,000 in treatment, it saves $70,000 that would have been necessary to keep delinquents for a long time in prison.[41] Unfortunately, psychopathy is often ignored by health care systems, possibly because nonspecialists have difficulty diagnosing psychopaths, who lie convincingly during interviews with psychologists.

Instead of thinking that psychopaths *are monsters,* it is important to understand that they are human beings who, because of their empathic and emotional limitations, may be led to *behave monstrously.* As always, it is necessary to distinguish the illness from the person affected.

Regenerating Empathy, Amplifying Kindness

As a little girl, Sheila Hernandez always felt alone. "My mother gave me away when I was three to some strangers," she said, "a man and a lady, and the man molested me when I was around fourteen. A lot of painful things happened to me, and I just wanted to forget. I would wake up in the morning and just be angry that I woke up. I felt like there wasn't any help for me, 'cause I was just on this earth wasting space. I lived to use drugs and used drugs to live, and since the drugs made me even more depressed, I just wanted to be dead."[42]

At the end of her tether, Hernandez was admitted to Johns Hopkins Hospital. She had HIV, endocarditis, and pneumonia. Her constant use of drugs had affected her circulation so much that she could no longer use her legs. According to one doctor, Sheila Hernandez was "virtually dead." When Glenn Treisman, who for twelve years has been treating depression in HIV-positive and drug-addicted poor people, came to see her, she told him she didn't want to speak with him because she would die soon and leave the hospital sooner. "Oh no you're not," Treisman said. "You're not heading out of this place to go and die a stupid, useless death out on the streets. That's a crazy idea you have. That's the nuttiest thing I ever heard. You're going to stay and get off those drugs and get over all these infections of yours, and if the only way I can keep you in here is to declare you dangerously insane, that's what I'll do." Sheila stayed.

After thirty-two days of attentive care, her perceptions completely changed: "It turned out that all what I felt before I went in, I found it was wrong. These doctors told me I had this to offer and that to offer, I was worth something after all. It was like being born all over again.... I came alive for the first time. The day I left, I heard birds singing, and do you know I'd never heard them before? I didn't know until that day that birds sang. For the first time I smelled the grass and the flowers, and even the sky was new. I had never paid attention to the clouds, you know."

Sheila Hernandez never took drugs again. A few months later, she returned to Johns Hopkins, where she was employed in hospital administration. She did advocacy work during a clinical study of tuberculosis, and she secured permanent housing for the study's participants. "My life is so different. I do these things to help other people all the time, and you know I really enjoy that."

Many people like Sheila never emerge from the abyss. Those who do get out are rare, not because their situation is hopeless, but because no one has come to their aid. The example of Sheila and many others shows that manifesting kindness and love can allow the other to be reborn in a surprising way. The potential for this rebirth was present, so close, but for so long denied or blocked out. The greatest lesson here is the strength of love and the tragic consequences of its absence.

We know that people who have suffered from abuse in early childhood often show self-destructive behavior or violence against others. In their case, it's not because they were *dehumanized,* but because, tragically, they weren't *humanized* enough by affection, care, presence, and the contact of loving parents or people who showed them human warmth at one stage in their life, that of early childhood, when it is absolutely necessary for a human being's normal development. We know that meeting or being in the presence of sincerely kind people can make a vital difference.

Other studies suggest that empathy can be an important antidote to prevent physical and sexual abuse and neglect of children. J. S. Milner and his collaborators have shown that mothers who exhibited increased empathy when they watched a video of a crying child presented almost no risk for their own children, while those who showed no discernable change of empathy, whether the child laughed, cried, or simply looked around, presented a high risk of abusing their children. These mothers also testified to feeling personal distress and increased hostility when they watched their child cry.[43]

As for sexual abuse, it has been proven that certain clinical interventions aiming to increase empathy reduce the probability of abuse, rape, and sexual harassment in men identified as presenting a high risk of committing sexual assault.[44]

Various research studies have also shown that altruism, induced by amplifying empathy, can inhibit aggression. Research on forgiveness in particular has shown that an important stage in the process of forgiveness consisted of replacing anger with empathy.[45] Harmon-Jones and his neuroscientist colleagues have highlighted the fact that empathy directly inhibits the activity of regions of the brain linked to aggression.[46]

The main lesson to draw from all this information is that empathy is a vital component of our humanity. Without it, we have difficulty giving meaning to our existence, connecting to others, and finding emotional balance. We can also drift toward indifference, coldness, and cruelty. So it is essential to recognize its importance and cultivate it. Moreover, in order to avoid sinking into an excess of affective resonance, which can lead to empathic distress and burnout, we must, as we mentioned in a previous chapter, embed empathy in the vaster emotional and cognitive sphere of altruistic love and compassion, which serves as an anditote to empathy fatigue. We will thus have the necessary qualities to accomplish the benefit of others while at the same time fostering our own fulfillment.

28

At the Origin of Violence: Devaluing the Other

The ultimate weakness of violence is that it is a descending spiral, begetting the very thing it seeks to destroy. Instead of diminishing evil, it multiplies it.

—Martin Luther King Jr.

At the root of all forms of violence there is a lack of altruism and a devaluing of the other. Not granting enough value to the other's fate, we knowingly harm him, physically or morally.

By "violence" we mean here the ensemble of actions and hostile, aggressive attitudes between individuals, including use of constraint and force in order to obtain something against the other's will, or in order to harm his physical or mental integrity. Violence is often used by humans and animals to obtain food, reproduce, defend themselves, conquer or protect a territory, or assert one's authority or hierarchical rank. One can also considerably harm another by torturing him mentally and making his life unbearable, without resorting to physical violence.

Why violence? The attitudes that incite us to harm others are linked in part to our *dispositions* and our character traits, but they are also strongly influenced by our transient *emotions* and by *situations* in which we find ourselves. Violent behavior can arise in the heat of the moment or be premeditated.

LACK OF EMPATHY

When we enter into affective resonance with someone else, if he is suffering, we feel uneasy, while if we do not feel empathy, this suffering doesn't move us. The extreme case is that of psychopaths. When a psychopath who was in prison for rape and kidnapping was questioned, he replied, "Do I feel bad if I have hurt someone? Yeah, sometimes. But mostly it is like… uh…[laughing]…how did you feel the last time you squashed a bug?"[1]

A breeder who was concerned exclusively with the swiftness, effectiveness, and profitability of his stable and who castrated his horses by crushing their testicles between two bricks, replied when asked if it was very painful, "No, if you watch out for your thumbs."[2]

HATRED AND ANIMOSITY

Hatred makes us see the other in an entirely unfavorable light. It leads us to amplify his defects and ignore his qualities. These cognitive distortions result in a deformed perception of reality. The psychologist Aaron Beck said that when one is under the influence of violent anger, something like three-quarters of our perceptions of the other are mental fabrications.[3] The aggression that comes from hatred thus involves a rigid categorization that makes us see the opponent as being basically evil, and oneself as being right and good.[4] The mind shuts itself up in illusion and convinces one that the source of dissatisfaction lies entirely outside oneself. Actually, even if the resentment was set off by an external object, the resentment itself is nowhere else but in our own mind.

The harmful effects of animosity are obvious. The Dalai Lama describes it thus:

> *By giving in to animosity, we do not always harm others, but we unfailingly harm ourselves. We lose our inner peace, we no longer do anything right, we have poor digestion, we can't sleep, we make people who come to see us run away, we glare furiously at anyone who dares to stand in our path. We make life impossible for those who live with us and we even distance ourselves from our closest friends. And since those who want to share our company become rarer and rarer, we become more*

> *and more alone.... So long as we harbor within us this inner enemy that is anger or hatred, even if we destroy our external enemies today, others will appear tomorrow.*[5]

The Thirst for Revenge

"An eye for an eye, a tooth for a tooth." The desire for revenge is a major cause of violence. Blood vengeance is approved in many cultures. Wherever there are tribal wars, revenge constitutes one of the main motives.[6] An inhabitant of New Guinea describes his feelings when he learns that the person who had killed his uncle was paralyzed by a poisoned arrow: "I feel as if I am developing wings, I feel as if I am about to fly off, and I am very happy."[7]

The feeling of revenge is closely linked to egocentrism, notably when one has not just been wronged, but also humiliated, especially in public. Wounded pride is willing to make great sacrifices to avenge itself. This is the case for individuals, but also for nations that enter into war to avenge attacks on their national pride. When someone violently avenges himself for some criticism that attacked his image, the act of punishing this affront does not, however, prove the criticism was unjustified. Hitting someone who has called you a liar does not prove you told the truth.[8]

The existence of "honor codes" considerably increases the risks of violent confrontations. One study showed that young men who attach great importance to such codes, and who are always ready to avenge an insult, are the most likely to commit a violent act in the following year.[9]

Goodwill, forgiveness, and an effort to understand the aggressor's motives are often regarded as generous but optional choices. It is hard to bear in mind that the desire for revenge stems essentially from an emotion similar to the one that led the aggressor to do harm in the first place. It is even rarer for victims to be capable of regarding a criminal as being himself a victim of his own hatred. However, so long as hatred of one person engenders that of the other, the cycle of resentment and reprisals is endless. History is full of examples of hatred between families, clans, tribes, ethnic groups, and nations, which have been perpetuated from generation to generation. What's more, revenge is usually disproportionate to the gravity of the wrong it means to avenge. There are many examples of excessive reprisals for minor attacks on someone's honor. A cowboy's gravestone in Colorado reads, "He Called Big Smith a Liar."[10]

In some cultures and religions, revenge is not only tolerated but exalted in the founding texts. Although the New Testament urges forgiveness—"Forgive us our sins; as we also forgive every one that is indebted to us"—the Old Testament puts these words in God's mouth:

> *I will render vengeance to mine enemies, and will reward them that hate me. I will make mine arrows drunk with blood, and my sword shall devour flesh; and that with the blood of the slain and of the captives, from the beginning of revenges upon the enemy. Rejoice, O ye nations, with his people: for he will avenge the blood of his servants, and will render vengeance to his adversaries, and will be merciful unto his land, and to his people.*[11]

The Therapist's Point of View

It is important to stress that one can feel profound aversion to injustice, cruelty, oppression, fanaticism, and harmful actions, and do everything one can to thwart them, without succumbing to hatred. When one looks at an individual prey to hatred, one should regard him more as a sick person to be cured than as an enemy to subdue. It is important not to confuse the sick person with his illness, or a feeling of repulsion for an abominable *action* with definitive condemnation of a *person*. Even the most cruel torturer was not born cruel, and who can assert he will not change? If people either undergo a genuine transformation or become harmless because of old age or any other reason, there is no justification to continue punishing them, by keeping them in jail, for instance. As the Dalai Lama says, "It might be necessary to neutralize a vicious dog that bites everyone around it, but what's the point of chaining it up or shooting it in the head when it's just an old, toothless mutt that can barely stand on its legs?"[12]

As Gandhi says, "If we practice an eye for an eye and a tooth for a tooth, soon the whole world will be blind and toothless." Rather than follow the law of an eye for an eye, isn't it preferable to rid one's mind of the resentment that's eating away at it and, if one has the strength, to wish that the murderer change radically, renounce harm, and make reparation for the harm he has committed as much as he can? In 1998, in South Africa, an American teenager was raped and killed in the street by five young men. During the trial, the victim's parents, both lawyers, said to the principal attackers: "We do not want to do to you what you did to our daughter."

A few months before she died in Auschwitz, Etty Hillesum wrote:

> *I can see no way around it. Each of us must look inside himself and excise and destroy everything he finds there which he believes should be excised and destroyed in others. We may be quite certain that the least iota of hatred that we bring into the world will make it even more inhospitable to us than it already is.*[13]

That is particularly true for the death penalty, which is still practiced in many countries, although the number of executions continues to decrease over the years. In the eighteenth century, in England, a seventeen-year-old girl was hanged for having stolen a petticoat. In China, not so long ago, one could be condemned to death for having stolen a bicycle. China remains by far the country where most executions are performed. Amnesty International gave up establishing a precise number of executions because of the opacity of the Chinese judicial system, but believes there are several thousand a year. According to the estimations of the Dui Hua Foundation, about 5,000 people were executed in 2009.[14, 15] In Saudi Arabia, innocent people are regularly condemned to death following accusations of witchcraft made by their neighbors.

We know, however, that the death penalty does not have any preventative value. Its suppression throughout the European Union did not give rise to an increase of criminality, and its reestablishment in certain states in North America, where it had been temporarily suppressed, did not diminish the crimes committed. Since life in prison is enough to prevent a murderer from committing a second offense, the death penalty amounts to legalized revenge. "If crime is a transgression of the law, revenge is what hides behind the law to commit a crime," writes the essayist Bertrand Vergely.[16] Thus, the death penalty is nothing but the law of an eye for an eye disguised in a judge's gown. As Arianna Ballotta, president of the Italian Coalition to Abolish the Death Penalty, notes, "As a society, we cannot kill in order to show that killing is evil."

Wilbert Rideau: Spared to Do Good

The *New York Times* called Wilbert Rideau "the most rehabilitated man in America."

Born in Louisiana to a poor family, Rideau grew up in a heavily racist environment. He was abandoned first by a brutal father and then by his mother, who worked as a maid, before going on welfare. In 1961, when he was nineteen, Wilbert held up a bank, hoping to steal enough money to begin a new life in California. He took three bank employees hostage, but when they panicked and tried to escape, he fired his gun, killing one woman and gravely wounding two other people. Wilbert was black, and the hostages were white. When he was arrested and taken to the local prison, several hundred people were waiting there to lynch him. He barely escaped being executed right on the spot.

After a biased trial during which the defense did not call a single witness, Wilbert was imprisoned in Angola prison, one of the most infamous in the United States. He spent twenty years on death row. His sentence was then commuted to life in prison, and after forty-four years, following a retrial, his crime was reduced from first degree murder to manslaughter. He was then freed, since he had served twenty years more than the required sentence.

He never denied his crimes, which still haunt him. Even the most peaceful times in his life revive the painful memory of the irreparable harm he caused. "No matter how much I say I am sorry, that is not going to bring my victims back to life. I have to live for two and do as much good as I can."

In Angola prison, Wilbert began to read, then to write. He finally became the first black editor of a prison magazine in America, *The Angolite,* which was, thanks to the support of a few enlightened wardens, the first prison magazine that was practically uncensored.

What brought Wilbert to change? In his own words, "If you just hate yourself, you end up committing suicide. People don't change because of a magic touch. They grow. First I realized how much my actions had impacted my mother. Then it was just an extension of that to feel sorry for the family of the victim and then others. I knew I was better than the crime I had committed. In America no one is trying to rehabilitate anybody. You have to do it on your own. I don't know of any more powerful way to change people than education."

Wilbert learned to turn away from violence completely: "I was in one of the most violent prisons in the USA, but I managed to go through all these years without a single fist fight. There are a few simple rules: you don't deal with dope and you don't get into activities that are ruled by violence."

One day he was interviewed by a journalist from the BBC.

"Do you ever feel violence in you?"

"No."

"Angry?"

"I get pissed off, but not really angry."

Those are qualities that would be welcome in most so-called ordinary people.

Violence and Narcissism

According to a long-standing opinion among psychologists, people who have a poor opinion of themselves are inclined to resort to violence in order to compensate for their feeling of inferiority, and to show others what they are capable of. If this theory were true, in order for these individuals to renounce violence, it would be enough to provide them with other means of constructing a better image of themselves. However, as the psychologist Roy Baumeister at the University of Florida has shown, all serious studies have concluded that this theory is false. On the contrary, it turns out that most violent people have a high opinion of themselves. Rarely humble or self-effacing, most of them are arrogant and vain.[17] All the people who came in contact with the dictators of the twentieth century—Stalin, Mao Tse-tung, Hitler, Idi Amin, or Saddam Hussein—confirm that they were definitely suffering from a superiority complex, not an inferiority complex. Many psychopathic criminals and convicted rapists think of themselves as exceptional beings, endowed with manifold talents.[18]

THE EGO THREATENED

A person who is endowed with real humility is scarcely concerned with his own image. A person who possesses undeniable qualities and justified self-confidence will have few opportunities to be damaged by criticism. On the other hand, a person who considerably overestimates his qualities sees his ego constantly threatened by the opinion of others, and is quick to react with anger and indignation.[19] The psychologist Michael Kernis and his collaborators have shown that the most reactive and most hostile individuals are those who have a high but unstable opinion of themselves.[20] So it is those equipped with an oversized ego and who feel vulnerable who are the most dangerous. Any interlocutor who doesn't show them enough respect or offends them, even superficially, is sure to receive immediately a hostile response.[21] A series of interviews conducted by the psychologist Leonard Berkowitz with English criminals imprisoned for violent acts also confirmed that these delinquents had an abnormally enlarged but fragile ego, causing them to react to the slightest provocation.[22]

The same is true for dictators and totalitarian regimes. Despite appearances, they are aware of the illegitimacy of the oppression they exercise over their own people or over others, and are particularly intolerant and prompt to crush any dissidence. The political historian Franklin Ford notes that "ancient history—and later history as well—suggests that official terror is usually the mark of a regime that may appear brutally self-confident but is in fact insecure."[23]

When one is confronted with criticism, one can react in two ways. Either one thinks the criticism is justified and one thus revises the opinion one has of oneself, or else one does not value the criticism at all and rejects it—one thinks the other is ill-intentioned, stupid, or somehow prejudiced. The most usual reaction then is anger.

THE IMPRUDENCE OF MEGALOMANIACS

Positive illusions about oneself usually lead to overestimation of one's ability to conquer an opponent; this can sometimes end up causing confrontations with catastrophic outcomes. The most serious mistakes of nations waging war come from gross overestimation of their forces. On certain occasions, an intimidating maneuver stemming from pure boastfulness can trick the opponent, but most often it ends in crushing defeat.

The political scientist Dominic Johnson studied this phenomenon in the field of video games, and showed that the more certain a player was of himself, the more often he lost. In a game where the participants assume the role of state leaders who enter into conflict, the players who were overconfident launched rash attacks and set off a cascade of reprisals devastating for both camps. Since women are less prone to this failing, the worst possible combination was a woman that opposed two men suffering from excessive self-confidence.[24]

In certain cases, a firm attitude can be an effective signal that one is not about to let oneself be manipulated, and to dissuade potential attackers. This explains in part the bragging matches and intimidating behavior that the males of both the human and animal species indulge in. These ritualized behaviors can substitute for violent confrontations.

The Mechanisms of Violence

Regardless of whether or not the protagonists are right or wrong, if we want to remedy violence, we must understand what is going on in people's heads. To do this, it is indispensable to listen not only to the victim's testimony, but also to the aggressor's. In most cases, those who have made use of violence do not regard themselves as guilty; they present themselves as victims, asserting that they have been treated unfairly and should be shown tolerance. In *Prisoners of Hate,* Aaron Beck explains that aggressors are firmly entrenched behind the belief that their cause is just and that their rights have been violated. The object of their anger (who, to the eyes of neutral observers, seems to be the victim) is perceived by them as the offender.[25] Bosnian Serbs, for example—perpetrators of merciless ethnic cleansing—regarded themselves as one of the most wronged peoples in the world. Even when these assertions grossly misrepresent reality, it is important to analyze the motives of aggressors if we want to prevent new eruptions of violence.

Studies show that perpetrators of violence present the facts in such a way as to minimize their fault, while victims almost always exaggerate the harm they have undergone.[26] Victims and perpetrators of violent acts tend to experience them in different chronological contexts. For example, an abused woman will describe the years of abuse she underwent, while the violent man who has just committed abuse will try to explain his despicable action by invoking the immediate events that set it off.

Based on study of domestic violence in North America, the sociologist Murray Straus has shown that mutual hostility is the norm rather than the exception. Even when a single spouse is violent, he will assert he was reacting to an injustice committed by the other.[27] This of course refers to mild domestic violence, not to cases of rape, and not to the chronic abuse and domestic violence suffered by women, and often children, in many countries and cultures throughout the world.

Many crimes are committed "in the name of justice": reprisals inspired by jealousy or a feeling of betrayal, crimes of honor, settling of accounts, reactions to insults, family conflicts that fester, and actions of self-defense. According to the lawyer and sociologist Donald Black, only 10% of homicides have a "pragmatic" aim (murder of a police officer during an arrest, of a homeowner during a break-in that goes bad, or of a rape victim so that she won't talk). In the majority of cases, criminals claim the "morality" of their actions.[28]

Several criminologists[29] have shown that murder is usually the outcome of a series of quarrels and violent acts between family members, neighbors, or acquaintances; one person insults another, who returns the insult instead of trying to put a stop to the conflict, and things go from bad to worse.[30]

An overview of a number of published studies led Roy Baumeister to note that the majority of murders occur in two types of situations. In the first case, two people who know each other argue, the conflict escalates, and insults and threats are exchanged, until one of the protagonists takes out a knife or a gun and kills the other. Most people regret these murders committed in the heat of the moment. In the second case, murder results from an armed holdup during which the criminals encounter unexpected resistance and resort to violence in order to reach their goal, eliminate witnesses, or escape.[31]

These studies instruct us about what occurs in most documented murders, but they do not include the less frequent existence of premeditated murders and frightening killings like those that occurred in the past few years in the United States at Columbine and, more recently, at Sandy Hook in Connecticut, which are made possible by the open access to powerful, deadly weapons.

The Fiction of Absolute Evil

Even those who have committed the worst atrocities—including the bloodiest dictators—claim they acted to defend themselves against the forces of evil, and they are often actually convinced of this. Their interpretation of reality, as aberrant and repugnant as it may be, still leads to the observation that none of them seemed to be moved initially by the sole desire to do *evil for evil's sake*.[32]

Media and works of fiction like to evoke evil in its pure state. They portray monsters, fundamentally evil mutants who wish to harm for harm's sake and rejoice in doing so. Most horror films open with happy scenes that are soon turned upside down by the intrusion of evil—a gratuitous evil, or an evil motivated solely by the sadistic pleasure of making people suffer.[33] Evil comes from the "other," the stranger, the person who is not one of us. These are not kind people who have temporarily gone bad: the evil person has always been evil, and will always be so; he is implacable, profoundly selfish, sure of himself, and subject to uncontrollable fits of rage. He is the enemy of peace and stability.

What Baumeister denounces as a myth is the idea that certain people can be evil by nature and have no other aim than doing harm. If the crimes that appear as the manifestation of absolute, gratuitous evil are widely diffused in the media, it is precisely because they are rare and aberrant.[34]

The Pleasure of Doing Evil

Some serial killers have acknowledged that they took pleasure in killing.[35] The murderer Arthur Shawcross spoke of his time serving in Vietnam as one of the best times in his life. He had free rein to kill men, women, and children. He not only killed, but also tortured and mutilated his victims.[36] Back in the United States, he committed fourteen murders before he was arrested. In Cambodia, the Khmer Rouge would torture their victims before killing them. This is true in most wars.

Sometimes gang members sadistically torture their victims before killing them. But the American sociologist Martin Sanchez Jankowski, who lived for ten years among California gangs, reports that, even among these criminals, they represent only a tiny minority.[37] Unfortunately, for that minority, this pleasure quickly becomes an addiction.[38] The social psychologist Hans Toch estimates that about 6% of men inclined to violence become chronically violent and take pleasure in it.[39] There again, we see that we are not far from the percentage of the 3% of psychopaths present in every population.

How can we understand people taking pleasure in making others suffer? Roy Baumeister has suggested that the pleasure linked to sadism does not come from the act itself, but from the moment that follows it. He compares it to the pleasure procured by extreme sports. In the case of bungee jumping, for example, one jumps into the void from a bridge or the top of a cliff, attached by a harness to an elastic cord that makes you rebound just before you hit the ground. According to Baumeister, when, after this terrifying experience, one comes back to normal, this return is accompanied by a euphoric sensation. After a certain number of times, the terrifying aspect of the act diminishes, while the pleasure it arouses remains just as strong, which creates a phenomenon of dependence. Baumeister thinks the same is true for sadistic violence. By inflicting violence on others—a behavior that begins by being unpleasant, shocking and revolting, but to which one becomes accustomed—the moment that follows the violent act is experienced as euphoric relief. Later, disgust for the violence itself gradually diminishes, and the person kills without the slightest hesitation.[40]

VIOLENCE AS AN EASY SOLUTION

People who repeatedly enact violence tend to become desensitized to the suffering of others, whether it's in war, during genocide, or, to a lesser degree, by playing violent video games. With time, they feel less and less restraint about committing their crimes and become capable of ever-increasing violence. Murder can then become an occupation like any other. Nathan McCall, a black American journalist for the *Washington Post* who grew up in a gang in Portsmouth, explained that the first time he took part in a gang rape, he felt horrible, distressed: he felt pity for the victim and disgust for his actions. But afterwards, gang rape became routine. McCall ended up in prison, where he educated himself and began a new life, that of a writer devoting his efforts to the improvement of interracial relations in the United States.

According to the criminologists Gottfredson and Hirschi, one of the reasons why people sometimes resort to using violence to reach their goals stems from the fact that most crimes require little or no skill, patience, work, or effort. Shoplifting in supermarkets, robbing a shop, or grabbing a handbag from an old lady in the street is easier than earning one's living by learning a profession and acquiring skills that involve years of training. A pistol is enough to rob the cash register in a store; you don't even have to be a good shot, since taking out the weapon and threatening the cashier is usually enough.[41] Terrorists are also convinced that violence is the best and simplest of methods to impose their will, since they think they don't have much chance to succeed by legal methods.[42] Similarly, criminals settle conflicts between themselves with violence: two drug dealers can't resort to the court or the police to settle their differences. So they create a parallel, expeditious justice.

The force of example is also a factor in major violence. We know that children who have long seen their parents arguing and physically attacking each other are more likely to practice domestic violence when they in turn live as part of a married couple.[43] They are used to thinking that violence is an acceptable way to resolve a conflict or impose one's will. Many (but not all) battered children become abusive parents in turn.

Yet, sociological studies have shown that in the long run, for the great majority of criminals, crime does not pay: 80% of bank robbers get arrested, and those who practice organized crime have a much shorter life expectancy than the rest of the population.[44]

Respect for Authority

When one submits to an authority, it is that authority that decides what is good and what is bad. If an officer orders a soldier to execute war prisoners, he knows that violates international conventions, but the soldier is not in the position to question the orders of a superior. And he says to himself that the prisoners might have killed some of his comrades.

Many studies, including one by the American psychologist Stanley Milgram,[45] revealed how much we are willing to bend to the orders of an individual in a position of authority, even if it's in contradiction to our own system of values. In a series of experiments that have since become famous, carried out between 1960 and 1963, Milgram made volunteers (600 subjects recruited by ads) believe they were taking part in an experiment on memory, and that scientists wanted to evaluate the effects of punishment on the training process. He asked the participants to teach various word combinations to a student (actually an accomplice of the experimenter). If the student gave a wrong reply, the participant was supposed to administer an electric shock whose intensity increased by 15 volts with each mistake made. The participant had a range of buttons indicating the voltages, from 15 to 450 volts, and accompanied by indications that went from "Slight Shock" to "Very Strong Shock," culminating, at 450 volts, with the warning, "Danger, Severe Shock." Actually, the actor student received no shock at all, but simulated pain with shouts whose intensity was proportional to the power of the shocks inflicted.

The scientist in charge of the experiment wore a white smock and looked like a respectable authority. He only gave a few instructions, using a firm, terse tone and saying things like "The experiment requires you to continue."

Before undertaking this experiment at Yale, Milgram had done a survey among his psychiatrist and sociologist colleagues and among graduates, asking them to predict the outcome of the tests. They unanimously answered that the vast majority of the subjects would refuse to administer the shocks as soon as they became painful. Only a few psychopathic cases, 2% or 3% of the subjects, would normally remain indifferent to the suffering they were inflicting.

The reality was quite otherwise. Kept on the "straight path" by the injunctions of the experimenter, 65% of the participants ended up administering the maximum dose, which they knew could potentially be deadly. The average of the strongest shock administered was 360 volts! This experiment has been reproduced many times in other laboratories and has led every time to the same results.

According to Milgram and those who analyzed these experiments, the individual who takes part in a system of authority no longer regards himself as an *actor responsible* for unmoral actions, but rather as an *agent* executing the will of another person. He shifts his responsibility onto the possessor of authority. Only a handful of participants rebelled, and when the experimenter said to one of them, "You don't have a choice," he crossed his arms over his chest and replied defiantly, "Yes, I have many choices, and the one I'm making is to stop." The participants in this experiment were neither sadistic nor indifferent. As they administered the shocks in increasing intensity, their hands and voices trembled, and sweat pearled on their foreheads. Raised like many others in respect for the authority of their parents and educators, they were obviously disturbed by a moral conflict. When one is thus divided between one's personal ethics and the moral obligation to conform to authority, and when one doesn't have much opportunity to take a step back to assess the situation, most of the time one follows orders. These days, nonconformism and rebellion against any hindrance to individual liberties are much more widespread, but the fact remains that in 2010, a repetition of Milgram's experiment as a TV show gave identical results.[46]

The False Prison at Stanford, or the Power of Situations

In 1971, the psychologist Philip Zimbardo imagined an unusual experiment to evaluate the influence of circumstances and situations on human behavior, malevolent behavior in particular. He had a replica of an actual prison built in the basement of Stanford University, with some cells and quarters for guards. Then he recruited volunteers willing to become either prisoners or guards. In the beginning, none of the students had a natural affinity with either of these groups. Yet within the space of a week, they would undergo a radical transformation.

The setting was extremely realistic, since actual policemen, who had agreed to take part in the experiment, came to arrest the volunteers chosen by lot to become prisoners. The prisoners were transferred, blindfolded, to the "prison" at the university and duly imprisoned. At first, the prisoners, dressed as inmates with a number on their chest, joked around and had trouble taking the situation seriously.

The leader of the volunteer guards read out loud the prison rules, as the scientists filmed most of the events with a hidden camera. In a few days, the situation degraded considerably. The guards tolerated neither dissension nor any breaking of the rules, and imagined all sorts of humiliating punishments for the prisoners. They made them do many push-ups, swore at them, and called them only by their number. Soon, some prisoners adopted a submissive, resigned attitude, while others showed a rebellious inclination. The guards increased pressure and began to wake up the prisoners several times a night. "Get up, you bums!" they shouted to the sound of shrill whistles. Bullying, some of which became obscene, occurred more frequently; violent actions were committed; some prisoners began cracking under pressure, and one of them started a hunger strike. The situation degenerated so far that the scientists were forced to abort the experiment prematurely after six days, instead of the fifteen days initially planned.

One of the guards later testified: "I had to intentionally shut off all feelings I had toward any of the prisoners, to lose sympathy and any respect for them. I began to treat them as coldly and harshly as possible verbally. I would not let show any feelings they might like to see, like anger or despair." Little by little, his feeling of belonging to the group became stronger. "I saw the guards as a group of pleasant guys charged with the necessity of maintaining order among a group of persons unworthy of trust or sympathy—the prisoners."

For Philip Zimbardo, "Evil consists in intentionally behaving in ways that harm, abuse, demean, dehumanize, or destroy innocent others—or using one's authority and systemic power to encourage or permit others to do so on your behalf."[47] In light of this research, he came to realize that almost all of us tend to overestimate the importance of character traits linked to our habitual tendencies and, on the other hand, to underestimate the influence that situations can exercise over our behavior.[48]

The Stanford experiment is rich with teachings; it shows us how individuals who in principle are kind can be led to make others suffer entirely gratuitously, to the detriment of the moral values they themselves possess. This reversal occurs under the insidious pressure formed by a given framework whose logic is implied to all, to the point of substituting its norms for each person's individual values.[49]

This experiment lets us better understand the case of Abu Ghraib, the Iraqi prison where American guards, both men and women, obscenely humiliated their prisoners. On the video images that were released, we see a woman in uniform leading one of the prisoners by a leash, naked and on all fours, as if he were a dog. President Bush asserted it was just a case of a few "bad apples" in an otherwise healthy army. But Zimbardo argued that this wasn't a case of a few bad apples, but rather of a rotten barrel, and that the army and its system as a whole was to blame.

Violence Born from Thirst for Wealth and Power

Appropriating others' property and overcoming and despoiling one's rivals have always been major sources of violence, as much for individuals as for nations. It is a utilitarian, predatory, calculating, and generally merciless violence. A criminal who was asked why he robbed from banks replied coldly, "Because that's where the money is."[50] It's also usually for practical reasons—from fear of being denounced or because a holdup goes wrong—that criminals kill the witnesses of their crime, without any premeditation.

This pragmatic violence is illustrated on an entirely different scale by the conquests of Genghis Khan in the thirteenth century. It was mainly his desire to seize the wealth of the conquered peoples and increase his power that pushed this Mongolian conqueror to become most likely the worst murderer in history. His invasions caused about 40 million deaths. On the scale of today's world population, that would be the equivalent of 700 million individuals.[51] His troops massacred 1.3 million inhabitants of the city of Merv and the 800,000 inhabitants of Baghdad, where his armies laid waste for days, leaving no survivors.[52]

It was not a genocide. Genghis Khan wanted two things: to impose his power and to appropriate the wealth of other peoples. He had established a very simple rule: either the cities agreed to open their gates to him and acknowledge his sovereignty, and he spared them; or they resisted, and he destroyed them and massacred their population.

On the individual level, the desire to establish one's domination over others is also a powerful motive for violent behavior. According to the philosopher Frantz Fanon, those who practiced torture confess that even if they didn't manage to make the most resistant speak, the simple fact of making them scream in pain was already a victory.[53] Similarly, according to Baumeister, men who engage in domestic abuse generally do so in order to establish their power as the head of the family.[54]

IDEOLOGICAL DOGMATISM: DOING EVIL IN THE NAME OF GOOD

When a religious or political ideology declares it is acceptable to kill in the name of a superior cause, those who have adopted it set aside their scruples and kill for that "good cause" anyone who doesn't conform to the views promulgated by the dominant group. Political purges violently suppress the slightest dissension and designate the scapegoats held responsible for problems that the leaders were unable to solve. This was the case for the Khmer Rouge, which never admitted a single "mistake" and savagely eliminated anyone they regarded as responsible for the failures of their political ideology, torturing and executing over a million innocent people.

This violence committed by a political regime finds its religious counterpart in the example of the Crusades. In Antioch, crusaders decapitated their enemies and threw their heads with catapults over the walls of the besieged city. In Jerusalem, they massacred Muslims, even those who didn't actively resist them. They gathered together a community of Jews, locked them up in a synagogue, and set fire to it. Convinced of working in the service of their God, crusaders performed evil in the name of good.[55] Between the eleventh and thirteenth centuries, the Crusades caused more than a million deaths. If this number is compared to the world population at the time (about 400 million), that is the equivalent of 6 million dead in the twentieth century, which numerically equals the Jews slaughtered in the Holocaust.[56]

DOES A "VIOLENT INSTINCT" EXIST?

Some of the most influential thinkers and researchers in the twentieth century, notably Sigmund Freud and Konrad Lorenz, have asserted that humans and animals possess an innate instinct for violence which they have trouble repressing. According to Freud, the biblical commandment "Thou shalt not kill" is the very proof that "we are descended from an endlessly long chain of generations of murderers, whose love of murder was in their blood as it is perhaps also in ours."[57] According to Freud and Lorenz, appeasing this aggressive instinct, just as one satisfies sexual impulses and the desire for food, is supposed to procure a certain satisfaction. In *Civilization and Its Discontents,* Freud writes, "I take the view that the tendency to aggression is an original, autonomous disposition in man."[58] Aggression was thought to build up in humans like pressure in a pressure cooker, and needed to be vented and released from time to time.

But neither physiologists nor psychologists have been able to demonstrate the existence of such a spontaneous impulse for hostility. Aggression does not manifest as a natural motivation comparable to that of hunger, thirst, or the need for activity and social contact.[59] The need for social contact is a tendency that regularly arouses specific behavior in everyone, even in the absence of stimulation from the external environment. According to the psychologist Jacques Van Rillaer, "Aggressivity is not a kind of substance produced by the organism, which the individual must externalize under penalty of destroying himself. To understand defense and attack behaviors, it is infinitely more useful to wonder about the relations of the subject with others, and with himself, than to invoke the action of a mysterious death impulse.... This Freudian theory is nothing but a myth."[60]

The hypothesis of an omnipresent aggressiveness in the animal kingdom as a fundamental part of its nature was also popularized by Konrad Lorenz, one of the founders of modern ethology, in his book for the layman, *On Aggression,*[61] in which the author sets out to demonstrate the basically violent nature of the animal kingdom. He states that aggression is an "indispensable way to attain man's highest goals."[62] According to him, the misfortune of humans stems from the fact that they are "without those safety mechanisms that prevent carnivorous animals and predators from killing members of their own species."[63] When two wolves fight for domination of the pack, if one of them decides to give up the fight, it lies on its back, thus presenting its carotid to its opponent, an extremely dangerous situation, but one that causes its opponent's aggressivity to vanish instantly. According to Lorenz, because we descend from vegetarian ancestors and not from predators, "during human prehistory, there was no selective pressure likely to produce a mechanism that would inhibit murdering one's fellows." For Lorenz, when man began making weapons, there were no safety mechanisms in place: "We tremble at the idea of a creature as irascible as all the pre-human primates are, now brandishing a very sharp hand-axe." In short, humans supposedly suffer from a "harmful dose of aggression whose unhealthy heredity still penetrates mankind to the marrow,"[64] and makes humans born killers. Actually, as we will see in a later chapter, the large majority of humans feel profound repugnance about killing other human beings.

Early on in his career, the primatologist and ethologist Frans de Waal was concerned with the emphasis placed up to that point in time on violent behavior, especially by Lorenz. He set out to study the behavior of the long-tailed macaque, a species that was reputedly particularly aggressive. But after long periods of observation, he noted that in the end these monkeys rarely fought each other.[65] After several decades devoted to the study of primates, de Waal concluded that aggression depended essentially on external conditions and on the style of relations established between individuals, and not on a universal instinct for violence that was shared by all beings, as Lorenz argued.

Several other ethologists have also contradicted Lorenz's theories, including Irenäus Eibl-Eibesfeldt, who[66] offers numerous arguments refuting these theories, and argues that "man's aggressive impulses are counterbalanced by his equally deep-rooted social tendencies. It is not only conditioning that programs us to be good—we are good by inclination." The psychologist Alfie Kohn reached a similar observation: "Freud and Lorenz notwithstanding, there is absolutely no evidence from animal behavior or human psychology to suggest that individuals of any species fight because of spontaneous internal stimulation."[67]

What's more, psychologists regard chronic and impulsive violence as pathological, and acknowledge that anger and aggressivity are harmful to the health.[68] In a study carried out by Williams and Barefoot, 255 medical students passed a personality test measuring their degree of aggressiveness. Twenty-five years later, it turned out that the most aggressive ones had five times more heart attacks than those who were less hostile.[69]

Here, as in the case of the wicked-world syndrome we discussed earlier, it seems that the fascination the spectacle of violence exercises over us makes us forget that it does not constitute the norm in animal behavior. It is indeed more exciting to show wild animals hunting than sleeping most of the day, but it's comparable to showing only images of a man spending his leisure time hunting deer, and not showing those of the family man, farmer, or doctor that he also is. The sad reality of hunting for pleasure is undeniable, but it alone does not define the man.

The idea that murderers are completely incapable of controlling their violent impulses has also been dismissed by specialists, except with regards to a few pathological cases. According to the FBI expert John Douglas, who studied the cases of hundreds of murderers, it is impossible to believe that these criminals temporarily lost total control of their actions. He notes, for example, that none of these murderers committed a murder in the presence of a uniformed policeman. If their killer's rage had truly been uncontrollable, such a factor should not have prevented them from killing.[70]

This also applies to collective violence. In January 1993, according to the historian Gérard Prunier, an international human rights commission arrived in Rwanda before the genocide had reached its extreme, but at a time when members of the Hutu community had begun killing many Tutsis and burning their houses. When this commission arrived, though, the crimes instantly stopped, and as soon as it left, the murders resumed.[71] So humans are generally capable of checking their desire to harm when they know it's not the time to give it free rein.

The Perspective of the Neurosciences on Violence

A study revealed that when certain regions of a rat's or cat's brain are activated, these animals immediately enter into an uncontrollable rage, and furiously attack anyone in reach.[72] The same study showed that stimulation of other regions of the brain activates the cat's hunting behavior, causing the cat to chase a phantom prey in a crazed way. However, with the hunting behavior stimulated, the cat did not violently or indiscriminately attack anyone who appeared that did not resemble prey. So hunting and violence are two distinct behaviors, and the neural networks of violent aggression and predation are also different. Moreover, the areas of the brain linked to aggression are organized in a structured way. When a certain number of these areas are activated, the cat hisses and arches his back, but the experimenter can still touch him. When certain additional areas are activated, the cat becomes enraged and lunges at the experimenter's face.[73] The amygdala especially is one of the brain areas closely implicated in the impulsive behaviors of fear and aggression in superior animals and humans. It is activated notably when danger is perceived, which induces a reaction of fight or flight.

Charles Whitman killed several people from the top of a tower on the campus of the University of Texas at Austin, before shooting himself in the head. He left a note saying he felt incapable of resisting the rage that was overwhelming him, and asked that his brain be examined after his death. The autopsy revealed that a tumor was compressing his amygdala.[74] It is clear that our emotional world can be considerably disturbed by such brain pathologies.

Other studies in the neurosciences shed light on the differences between the various types of violence. Adrian Raine, at the University of Pennsylvania, compared the brains of murderers who acted impulsively with those of murderers who premeditated their crimes. Only the former showed a dysfunction in a section of the brain (the orbital cortex), which plays an essential role in regulating emotions and controlling violence.

The Influence of the Media

Almost 3,500 scientific studies and the overviews published in the last decade have shown that the spectacle of violence acts as an incitement to further violence. For the American Academy of Pediatrics, the evidence is clear and convincing: "Significant exposure to media violence increases the risk of aggressive behavior in certain children and adolescents, desensitizes them to violence, and makes them believe that the world is a 'meaner and scarier' place than it is."[75] These effects are measurable and lasting. Children are particularly vulnerable, but we are all affected.[76]

These studies have also made it possible to refute the hypothesis (inspired in part by Freudian theories) by which the spectacle of violence allows the individual to purge himself of the aggressive impulses he is supposed to have. It has now been established that on the contrary, this spectacle aggravates violent attitudes and behaviors.[77] Yet despite these scientific observations, the idea of a liberating catharsis continues to be regularly invoked.

According to Michel Desmurget, research director at the National Institute of Health and Medical Research (INSERM) at the Center for Cognitive Neurosciences in Lyon, violent images operate according to three principal mechanisms. First, they increase the propensity to act with violence or aggression, acting as the *priming mechanism*. Second, they raise our threshold of tolerance for violence—the *habituation mechanism*. Third, they exasperate our feelings of fear and insecurity—the *wicked-world syndrome*. It is the convergence of these influences that, in the end, explains the impact of audiovisual violence.[78] It has also been established that violent images reduce emotional reactivity to violence, lower one's propensity to come to the aid of an unknown victim of aggression, and weaken the capacity for empathy.

After two decades of studies on the influence of television, researchers at the University of Pennsylvania have demonstrated that TV viewers who constantly watch negative actions show an increased tendency to act in the same way, and that the more one watches television, the more inclined one is to think that people are selfish and would deceive us at the first opportunity.[79] Long before the audiovisual age, Cicero observed:

> *If we are forced, at every hour, to watch or listen to horrible events, this constant stream of ghastly impressions will deprive even the most delicate among us of all respect for humanity.*[80]

On the other hand, when the media take the trouble to highlight the generous aspects of human nature, spectators easily enter into resonance with this positive outlook. The recent series entitled *CNN Heroes* met with great success in the United States. This show broadcasts portraits and testimonials about individuals, often quite humble and unknown, who undertook innovative, beneficial social projects, or who have become wholeheartedly involved in defending just causes.

The most revealing studies are those that have measured increase of violence following the introduction of television in regions where it hadn't existed previously. One of these studies, carried out in isolated rural communities in Canada, showed that two years after the arrival of television, verbal violence (insults and threats) observed in elementary schools had doubled, and physical violence had tripled. Another study revealed a spectacular increase of violence in children after the introduction of English-language television shows (which contained a high proportion of violent images) in South Africa. Keeping in mind the magnitude of the effects observed, Brandon Centerwall, at the University of Washington in Seattle, estimated that there would be, in the United States alone, 10,000 fewer homicides, 70,000 fewer rapes, and 700,000 fewer physical, injury-producing attacks each year if television did not exist.

In France, according to the Conseil supérieur de l'audiovisuel (Higher Audiovisual Council), a TV viewer watches television an average of three hours and thirty minutes per day, which exposes him, more or less, to two murders and a dozen violent actions every hour, or almost 2,600 murders and 13,000 violent acts each year. In the United States, a twelve-year-old has already seen some 12,000 murders on television. Research analyzing 10,000 hours of programs selected at random showed that 60% of American shows contain violent actions, at a rate of six scenes per hour. The most frightening thing is that in programs meant for young people, this percentage reaches 70%, with fourteen violent scenes every hour. We can see the benefits a reduction in the number of violent images could lead to. In fact, one study has revealed that, among nine-year-old children, this reduction had the direct consequence of a diminution of the level of violence at school. What's more, as the psychologists Mares and Woodard have shown,[81] TV programs with prosocial tendencies lead to an increase of corresponding behavior, diminish aggressiveness, and encourage viewers to be more tolerant.

The most worrisome aspect of the harmful effects of audiovisual violence is its lasting impact. Dimitri Christakis and Frederick Zimmerman, at the University of Washington in Seattle, have studied almost 200 boys aged two to five for five years. These psychologists discovered that one hour of violent programs a day *quadrupled* the probability of behavioral disorders in the following five years.[82]

The same effects have been observed in adults: subjects who watched television for between one and three hours per day when they were twenty-two manifested, at the age of thirty, one and a half times more risk of attacking a third party physically or verbally, and two and a half times more risk of being involved in a fight than individuals who had watched less than one hour.[83]

The psychologist Bruce Bartholow, at the University of Missouri, has shown that the brains of people exposed regularly to violent images become almost insensitive to these images when they are projected in front of them. These individuals are shown to be more aggressive than others during a test measuring their aggressiveness after projection of the images.[84]

According to Michel Desmurget,

> *scientific data show today, without the slightest doubt, that by lessening our exposure to violent material, we can contribute to creating a less violent world. Of course, that does not mean that television is responsible for all the evils of our society. Nor does it mean that all viewers will become dangerous murderers if they watch too many violent films on television. It simply means that the television screen represents a notable vector of fear, anxiety, aggressiveness, and violence. It would be wrong not to act on this causal lever mechanism, so much more amenable to change than other social determinants, such as poverty, education, abuse in early childhood, etc. Instead of criticizing (and even reviling) the scientific community when it denounces the effects of this televisual violence, it would no doubt be legitimate to demand an accounting from the audiovisual companies that make such great use of it.*[85]

The desire of television networks to increase their audience by constantly diffusing violent images is not only regrettable, considering their effects on society, but also stems from a misguided assumption about their viewers. This foregrounding of violence is supposed to answer the public's taste, but research does not confirm this opinion. The psychologists Ed Diener and Darlene DeFour showed fifty students a detective film that depicted frequent scenes of violence; fifty other students were shown the same film in which these scenes had been cut, while the plotline was preserved. It turned out that the students who saw the nonviolent version enjoyed the film just as much as the others. The researchers concluded that the fact of considerably reducing the frequency of violent scenes in television programs and in films would not lead to any loss of viewers.[86] This point of view is also confirmed by the popularity of films that present human nature in a positive light, like *The Tiger and the Snow, Groundhog Day, Amélie, Forrest Gump,* and so on, far from the usual cynical view of existence.

The Case of Video Games

Video games have become one of the favorite pastimes of children and teenagers all over the modern world. In the United States, 99% of boys and 94% of girls have played video games, and the time they devote to them is constantly increasing.[87]

An overview carried out by Craig Anderson and his colleagues dealing with 136 research studies measuring the effects produced on 130,000 people by playing violent video games established that these games unquestionably furthered the development of aggressive thoughts and behavior, and lessened prosocial behavior. These effects are important and have been observed in both children and adults, in boys and in girls.[88] Douglas Gentile and his colleagues at the University of Iowa, for example, established that the more teenagers are exposed to violence in video games, the more hostile they are to others, the more they argue with their teachers and are involved in fights, and the less they succeed at school.[89] The degree of hostility and densensitivization of subjects who played violent games is clearly higher than that of those who played games neutral from the point of view of violence—a motorcycle racing game, for instance.

To measure the long-term effects of video games, Douglas Gentile and his colleagues questioned twice (a year apart) over 400 children aged nine to eleven along with their peers and teachers. It turned out that those who played more violent video games during the first test attributed more hostile intentions to people they met, were more verbally and physically violent, and were less inclined to altruism when questioned again a year later.[90]

Analyses of video games show that 89% contain violence, and 50% contain acts of extreme violence toward the characters in the game.[91] The more realistic the game is and the more blood one sees flowing, the more its effect on the viewer's aggressiveness is accentuated.[92] As Laurent Bègue, professor of social psychology at the University of Grenoble, reports,[93] the video game that sold the most in the whole world in 2008, Grand Theft Auto IV, is incredibly violent. The player can, for example, drive on the sidewalks and crush pedestrians, whose blood stains the bumpers and windshields of the SUV the player has just hijacked. Since actions in video games are controlled by the player himself, his identification with the character who performs the violence is potentially stronger than when passively watching violent images on a TV or film screen. To that is added the repetitive aspect, which can make the player addicted. For we know that, in any learning activity, changes at the level of the brain and temperament are more marked when one practices an activity regularly.

The psychologists L. Kutner and C. Olson have distinguished four aspects of virtual games that are especially sought out by children: excitement and pleasure (they play to win, to reach a certain score, or to meet the challenge posed); socialization (they like playing with friends); the effect on their emotions (they play to calm their anger, forget their problems, feel less alone); and dispelling boredom (they play to kill time).[94]

From the point of view of the American military authority and instructor Dave Grossman, the conditioning effected by violent video games in which enemies appear suddenly and frequently, and must immediately be pulverized in a bloody and realistic manner, is a way to become desensitized to the act of killing, the effectiveness of which has been proven in the armed forces. But there is a crucial difference: children and other video game adepts are not subject to any authority that defines the rules and limits their actions. Soldiers are at least subject to the orders of their superiors and are supposed to shoot only when they have been ordered to do so.[95]

What's more, children associate violent games not with heartrending tragedies, but with amusement and fun, their favorite beverage or food, and the friends they play with. Thus, a whole section of the population is ready to accept as models brutal superheroes endowed with supernatural powers who have no mission other than killing, for no reason, the largest possible number of people.[96] "Not to speak," writes the psychologist Laurent Bègue, "of the hypocrisy of the gaming industry that, with profits that are far from virtual (70 billion euros in 2011), continues to stigmatize parents (who are supposed to do a better job of controlling which games their offspring have access to) and lead us to believe that if there is a problem, it stems not from their software, but from people who have psychiatric problems, who spoil the atmosphere at the shooting gallery!"[97]

It is undeniable that video games can also be used for educative purposes, provided they are conceived with that purpose in mind. Otherwise, it has been established that their use harms performance at school.[98] It has been observed that playing video games can increase visual alertness.[99] But one can imagine other ways to increase attention than by killing people all the time. So we can neither simply say that video games are bad nor that they're not as harmful as most scientists claim. Everything depends on their content, and it is precisely that content that produces beneficial or harmful effects. John Wright, eminent observer of media influence, liked to say: "The medium is not the message. It's the message itself that's the message."

BENEFICIAL VIDEO GAMES

"I like video games," said American comedian Demetri Martin, "but they're really violent. I'd like to play a video game where you help the people who were shot in all the other games. It'd be called Really Busy Hospital." Until recently, little attention was paid to the creation of prosocial, nonviolent video games in which the characters cooperate and help each other, instead of kill each other. Things are about to change.

For two years, under the inspiration of the science adviser to President Obama, a group of researchers including psychologists, educators, and neuroscientists have gathered several times in Washington to consider the best way to use the keen interest of youth in video games for constructive goals.

Richard Davidson, director of the Laboratories for Affective Neuroscience and Brain Imaging and Behavior at the University of Wisconsin, has now teamed with Kurt Squire, associate professor at the UW–Madison School of Education and director of the Games Learning Society Initiative. Their project was awarded a 1.4-million-dollar grant by the Bill and Melinda Gates Foundation, with a mission of inventing and rigorously testing two educational games meant to help high school students cultivate their social and emotional skills.[100]

The first game will help cultivate attention and calm the mind. According to Davidson, "If you can learn to focus your attention more skillfully and concentrate, that will have ripple effects on all kinds of learning." The second will stress empathy, altruism, compassion, and prosocial cooperation. "Empathy," said Davidson, "is actually a better predictor of life success than cognitive intelligence."

There are good reasons to think that if these games are presented in an attractive way to young people who enjoy video games, they will have positive effects on the players. Saleem, Anderson and Gentile carried out the first study, which clearly showed that prosocial video games[101] reduce the general level of hostility and malevolent feelings in players, while simultaneously increasing positive emotions, compared to violent or simply neutral games, and this is true in the long term.[102] When they checked the players' motivation, they noted that the lessening of aggression and the increase of positive emotions were especially marked in those who showed altruistic motivation. On the other hand, among players who stated they had taken part in prosocial games mostly for selfish reasons, to diminish their empathic distress, the level of hostility increased as they played.[103]

The Sight of Weapons

It has been shown that by their presence alone, weapons set off psychological processes that activate aggression. The American social psychologist Leonard Berkowitz gave volunteers the opportunity to avenge themselves for insults made by someone (an accomplice of the experimenter) by administering electric shocks to him (actually nonexistent). In half the cases, the experimenter also placed a revolver on the table (with the explanation that it was for another study). The subjects placed in the presence of this weapon administered, as revenge, more electric shocks than the others. More recently, a study by Christopher Barlett, at the University of Iowa, showed that people playing a violent video game with a joystick in the form of a pistol were more aggressive after the experiment than those who had played the same game with a classic joystick.[104]

Women and Children, First Victims of Violence

A report by Amnesty International, entitled "Broken bodies, shattered minds: Torture and ill-treatment of women," indicates that one woman out of five in the world is a victim of serious abuse on a daily basis, and that "torture of women is rooted in a global culture which denies women equal rights with men, and which legitimizes the violent appropriation of women's bodies for individual gratification or political ends."[105] In India, the proportion of women suffering from domestic abuse rises to 40%, and in Egypt, to 35%. The organization, which cites numerous testimonials by women and girls who have been beaten and raped, adds that "without exception, women's greatest risk of violence comes not from 'stranger danger' but from the men they know, often male family members or husbands.... What is striking is how similar the problem is around the world."[106]

The existence of "crimes of honor," which can go as far as homicide, has been observed in several countries, including Iraq, Jordan, Pakistan, Afghanistan, and Turkey. The mere presentiment that a woman may have damaged the family honor can lead to torture and murder. In November 2012, Pakistani parents killed their fifteen-year-old daughter, Anusha, by spraying her with acid simply because she had looked at a boy who had stopped in front of their house on a moped, when they had forbidden her to look at boys (she was supposed to lower her eyes); they then let her suffer on the ground for hours because "that was her fate" (said her mother) after such a dishonor.[107]

Women who have been bought and sold for forced labor, sexual exploitation, or forced marriage are also exposed to torture. After drugs and weapons, the slave trade in human beings represents the third highest source of profit for international organized crime. Women who are victims of it are vulnerable to physical violence, especially rape, illicit imprisonment, confiscation of their identity papers, and slavery.

In armed conflicts, women are often torture victims because of their role as educators, and as symbols for their community. Thus, during the genocide carried out in Rwanda in 1994 and the conflict in ex-Yugoslavia, Tutsi, Muslim, Serbian, Croatian, and Kosovar women were tortured simply because they belonged to a particular ethnic, national or religious group.

Women who have been torture victims can encounter numerous obstacles when they try to obtain reparation, especially the indifference or mockery of the police, the absence of appropriate provisions in criminal law, sexist prejudice in the judicial system, and criminal procedures that violate the fairness of legal process.

In some countries, women are not allowed to appear in court: it is the men of their family who are supposed to represent their interests. The police regularly abstain from investigating cases of violence alleged by women and often leave them to their sorry fate instead of registering their complaints. In Pakistan, women who are rape victims can themselves be accused of *zina* (fornication), a crime punishable by death by stoning or public flagellation. As the Amnesty International report stresses:

> *In the past, violence against women in the home was viewed as a private matter, not an issue of civil and political rights. Today, the international community has explicitly recognized violence against women as a human rights issue involving state responsibility.... States have a duty to ensure that no one is subjected to torture or ill-treatment, whether inflicted by agents of the state or by private individuals. Yet far from protecting women, states all around the world have allowed beatings, rape, and other acts of torture to continue unchecked. When a state fails to take effective measures to protect women from torture, it shares responsibility for the suffering these women endure.*

Moral Violence

In some cases, the mental suffering inflicted by others is harsher and more difficult to endure than physical violence. The sufferings are set off by a multiplicity of causes over which we sometimes have no control, but in the end, it is our mind that translates into happiness or misery the external circumstances with which we are confronted. Consequently, any kind of violence that destroys our inner peace seriously affects our perception of the world and of others. Some forms of violence, including rape and other forms of sexual abuse, combine physical violence with devastating effects on mental integrity. Other attitudes, like scorn, indifference, wounding words or attitudes, and malevolence in general, can destroy our inner well-being.

Harassment is one of the most common forms of mental cruelty, different facets of which the Swedish psychologist Heinz Leymann has catalogued. It can consist of refusing someone any possibility of expressing themselves; constantly interrupting them; insulting them; criticizing their work and private life; ridiculing them; making fun of their physical aspect; mimicking their gestures; attacking their personal, political, or religious convictions; and even threatening them. It can also consist of ignoring someone's presence; avoiding any eye contact with them; not talking to them and thereby giving them the impression that they are being rejected; giving them a task that isolates them from their colleagues; forbidding colleagues to speak to them; forcing them to do tasks that are either below or above their abilities; assigning them useless or absurd tasks; or else making them perform humiliating jobs or jobs that are harmful to their health. Harassment can culminate in physical aggression, especially that of a sexual nature.[108]

In schools, bullying incidents are forms of harassment that are sometimes cruel and that can have long-term effects on those who are its victims. One way of remedying this is to establish a mentoring system in which students tutor younger peers. This way of making older children responsible not only benefits progress at school—for both the elder and the younger student—but also helps to diminish bullying.

How to Reduce Violence

Three main factors counteract the desire to harm others: *altruism,* or kindness, which will cause us to be sincerely concerned with the fate of others; *control of our emotions,* which allows us not to give in to sudden impulses; and *moral scruples,* which make us hesitate at the idea of harming others, or regret having harmed them. We discussed the characteristics of kindness and consideration of others at length in earlier parts of this book.

As for control of emotions, it turns out that a number of criminals share the characteristic of being very impulsive and suffering from a lack of emotional control. They are more vulnerable than average individuals to various addictions and very quickly squander the spoils of their criminal activities. Several studies have proven that being easy prey to intense, fleeting emotions, and not taking a step back to assess the situation, favors giving in to violent behavior. In general, any emotional tension that escapes our control leads us to make irrational, instinctive choices that seem the easiest solution to, or way out of, an emotionally charged situation.[109]

Experience shows that appropriate training and sustained attention allow us to identify and manage emotions and mental events as they occur. This training also includes the development of healthy emotions like empathy, altruistic love and compassion.

The first stage of this training consists of identifying how emotions arise. This step requires one to cultivate a vigilant attention to the unfolding of mental activities, accompanied by an awareness that allows us to distinguish afflictive emotions from emotions that contribute to our well-being.

Experience also shows that like an untreated infection, afflictive emotions gain power when given free rein. Failing to control them, one forms habits to which one will again be prey as soon as one's emotional charge reaches a critical threshold. What's more, this threshold will get lower and lower, and one will grow more and more excitable.

Conclusions of psychological studies contradict the general belief that by letting anger explode one temporarily lowers the accumulated pressure.[110] Actually, it's quite the opposite that occurs. If one avoids letting anger openly manifest itself, blood pressure diminishes (and it diminishes even more if one adopts a friendly attitude), whereas it increases if one lets anger burst out.[111]

In addition, it serves no purpose to merely suppress the emotions. That would come down to preventing them from expressing themselves while still leaving them intact, which amounts to nothing but a temporary, unhealthy solution. Psychologists assert that a suppressed emotion can provoke serious mental and physical disorders, and that we must at all costs avoid turning our emotions against ourselves. Still, uncontrolled expression of emotions can also have disastrous consequences. One can die of a stroke in a fit of rage or be consumed by obsessive desire. What matters above all is to know how to establish an intelligent dialogue with one's emotions.

To do this, one of the methods used most often consists of neutralizing disturbing emotions with the help of specific antidotes. In fact, two diametrically opposed mental processes cannot occur simultaneously. One can alternate quickly between love and hate, but one can cannot feel at the same instant of consciousness the desire to harm someone and that of doing him good. As the philosopher Alain remarked, "One movement excludes another; if you hold out your hand in a friendly way, no fist punches are possible."[112] Similarly, by training one's mind in altruistic love, one eliminates animosity little by little, since these two states of mind are mutually exclusive. These antidotes are to the psyche what antibodies are to the organism.

Since altruistic love acts like a direct antidote to hatred, the more one develops it, the more the desire to harm will dwindle and finally disappear. So it is not a question of suppressing our hatred, but of turning the mind to something entirely contrary to it: love and compassion. Little by little, altruism will end up impregnating our mind more and more, until it becomes second nature.

A second way of confronting disturbing emotions consists of mentally dissociating ourselves from the emotion afflicting us. Usually, we completely identify with our emotions. When we are caught in a fit of anger, it is omnipresent in our mind and leaves little room for other mental states such as patience or taking anything into consideration that could calm our discontent. But even at that moment, the mind remains capable of examining what is going on inside it. To do this, all it has to do is observe its emotions, the way we would observe an external event taking place in front of our eyes. The part of our mind that is aware of anger is simply aware: it is not angry. In other words, mindfulness is not affected by the emotion it observes, in the same way that a ray of light may shine on a face disfigured by hatred or on a smiling face, without the light itself becoming mean or kind. Understanding that allows us to keep our distance and to give anger enough space for it to dissolve on its own.

By doing this, we avoid two equally detrimental extremes: suppressing emotion, which will remain somewhere in a dark corner of our consciousness, like a delayed-action bomb, or letting emotion explode, to the detriment of those around us and our own inner peace.

Societies that try to promote a high opinion of the individual, as well as narcissism, deem the feeling of shame unhealthy and undesirable.[113] However, feelings of unease and regret experienced when one recognizes having committed an action that goes against moral values stems from a lucid discernment and constitutes a driving force for transformation: by acknowledging our mistakes, we intend not to repeat them and, whenever possible, to repair the wrong done. Regret differs from feeling guilt;

instead of concentrating on a particular action, guilt overflows into the whole being, making us think "I'm a horrible person," and may translate into a devaluing of self and into doubts about our ability to transform.

Psychological studies show that the fact of experiencing a feeling of shame while thinking about the sufferings one has inflicted on others or while contemplating the possibility of harming them, associated with an empathic awareness of these sufferings, serves as an antidote to violence. These scruples lead the individual to see reason—and also annihilate the sensation of pleasure that some criminals associate with their harmful actions.[114]

The Courage of Nonviolence

It is relatively easy to shoot at a crowd. It certainly requires more courage to confront, with bare feet and without any weapons, armed troops, as Burmese monks did during the 2008 insurrection to show their disapproval of the dictatorial regime that was still in power. Nonviolence is not a sign of weakness, but of courage and determination. It does not consist of letting oneself be oppressed, but of acting in a just way, without being blinded by hatred or a desire for revenge that clouds over all faculty of judgment. As the Dalai Lama often says, nonviolence and tolerance do not come down to saying "Go on, hurt me!" They are neither submission nor giving up; they are accompanied by strength of mind and an intelligence that spare us from useless mental sufferings and prevent us from falling into malevolence. We know that violence usually leads to a chain reaction that is disastrous for everyone. So we must avoid it by all means possible and resolve conflicts through negotiation and dialogue.

When we are the victims of an abuse or an injustice, it is legitimate to use the appropriate means and the necessary vigor to remedy it, but *never* with hatred and always with the hope of reaching a more just, constructive situation. This is what Gandhi did in India, during the nonviolent movement of Satyagraha ("the power of truth"), and what Martin Luther King Jr. did in all his actions, based on these words:

> *Nonviolence is a powerful and just weapon, which cuts without wounding and ennobles the man who wields it. It is a sword that heals.*[115]

29

The Natural Repugnance to Kill

Research carried out by the American General S. L. A. Marshall on the behavior of soldiers during the Second World War showed, to the great surprise of his general staff, that only 10% to 15% of soldiers in combat situations had used their weapons to shoot at the enemy. The others showed bravery nevertheless: they debarked on the beaches of Normandy, came to the aid of their wounded comrades, provided others with ammunition, but did not use their weapons. They didn't hide or run away, but they did not fire at the enemy, even when they were attacked and their lives were in danger. General Marshall concludes:

> *It is therefore reasonable to believe that the average and normally healthy individual—the man who can endure the mental and physical stresses of combat—still has such an inner and usually unrealized resistance toward killing a fellow man that he will not of his own volition take life if it is possible to turn away from that responsibility.*[1]

The conclusions of his study were challenged for some time, so unexpected were they, but analysis of the Napoleonic wars, the Civil War in the United Sates, the Falkland Islands war, and other conflicts leads to the same conclusions.[2] These facts concern traditional wars, during which conscripts and professional soldiers fight in an army. Things are different in the case of massacres and genocides during which individuals, by various means, including dehumanizing the other and desensitization, annihilate their natural repugnance to kill.

Avoiding Shooting at the Other

During the Second World War, it turned out that, most often, soldiers fired only when they were forced to do so by their superiors, and stopped as soon as those superiors left. According to Colonel Albert J. Brown, "Squad leaders and platoon sergeants had to move up and down the firing line kicking men to get them to fire. We felt like we were doing good to get two or three men out of a squad to fire."[3]

The majority of soldiers avoid obeying orders: some hold their rifle at their shoulder and pretend to fire, while others fire above or to the side of their target. There are even some who explain with pride and satisfaction how they managed to disobey the order to kill. According to the American Lieutenant Colonel Dave Grossman, who explores this question in his book *On Killing,* "At the decisive moment, each soldier found that, in his heart, he could not bring himself to kill the man standing before him."[4]

Repugnance to kill increases as physical proximity between combatants increases: one then realizes that one is facing a human being like oneself. The historian John Keegan noted with surprise the almost complete absence of sword injuries during massive bayonet charges in Waterloo and during the Battle of the Somme. When soldiers came to hand-to-hand combat, the aversion to use the bayonet to pierce the other's body was so great that they usually turned their weapons around and fought with the butts of their rifles.[5]

We can imagine different explanations for this natural repugnance. If, for instance, I perceive the other as my fellow, I realize he has children, a family, life plans, the closer I feel to him, the more concerned I am by his fate. As soon as the other has a face, I naturally grant value to his existence, and it becomes difficult for me to inflict suffering on him, even more so to kill him. "Up to that time, a man I was going to kill had always seemed my direct opposite. This time I was kneeling on a mirror,"[6] says the Trojan hero Hector from the pen of Jean Giraudoux.

FEAR OF DYING IS LESS TRAUMATIC THAN THE COMPULSION TO KILL

It is during close combat that trauma caused by the conditioning to kill is at its worst. By gaze and by physical contact, one finds oneself closely and intensely confronted with the other's humanity, without any way to escape the stages of the death one is inflicting. The soldier who directly confronts the enemy knows that he has killed and knows who he has killed.

He thus finds himself confronted with a hopeless dilemma: either he overcomes his repugnance to kill, but acts against his conscience, or he does not fire at the enemy, but then feels guilty for abandoning his companions in arms, especially if some of them have not survived. As Glenn Gray, an American writer and veteran of the Second World War, writes, "Consciousness of failure to act in response to conscience can lead to the greatest revulsion, not only for oneself, but for the human species."[7] By killing another person, one kills a part of oneself.

CREATING A DISTANCE

To prevent the soldier from thinking of the enemy as his fellow, the idea is drilled into him that the opponent is despicable, hateful, different in every way from him. The enemy becomes a repugnant being, a "rat," "vermin," an inferior being who does not deserve to live and who threatens the soldier's relatives, his country, all of humanity. When "the other" appears with such abject features, the process of identification is rendered very difficult, and it becomes desirable to eliminate him. Dave Grossman distinguishes several types of distance between the killer and his victims: cultural, moral, social, physical, and semantic.[8]

Cultural distance is based on ethnic, racial or religious differences that permit the killer to dehumanize the other by asserting he is fundamentally different from himself.

Moral distance stresses belief in the moral legitimacy of the soldier and his desire for vengeance. According to studies by Samuel Stouffer, 44% of GIs in the Second World War wanted to kill a Japanese soldier, whereas only 6% of them expressed this desire with regard to German soldiers.[9] This difference was attributed to the desire to avenge the attack on Pearl Harbor.

Moral distance increases when the soldier reassures himself, saying that he is only doing his duty and faithfully carrying out the orders of his superiors. According to Grossman, the soldier "must assure himself the world is not mad, that his victims are less than animals, that they are evil vermin, and that what his nation and his leaders have told him to do is right.... The killer must violently suppress any dissonant thought that he has done anything wrong. Further, he must violently attack anyone or anything that would threaten his beliefs. His mental health is totally invested in believing that what he has done is good and right."[10]

Social distance grows with the conviction that certain social classes are inferior to others from any perspective, and that they are made up of subhumans whose lives are a negligible quantity. During feudal wars, for example, massacres were not the work of serfs or peasants, but of the aristocratic elite, who pursued their adversaries on horseback. In India, the Dalits (literally "the crushed"), previously called "untouchables," are victims of numerous crimes committed by caste members who think they are superior. The court very rarely rules in favor of untouchables, even when there is flagrante delicto: the massacre of fourteen untouchables perpetrated in 1982 in the village of Kestara, for example, resulted in all the accused, who had acted in broad daylight, being acquitted.

Physical distance makes the act of killing more abstract. As the psychologist and military instructor Richard Strozzi-Heckler writes, "The combatants in modern warfare pitch bombs from 20,000 feet in the morning, causing untold suffering to a civilian population, and then eat hamburgers for dinner hundreds of miles away from the drop zone." He will not have "to live his days remembering the man's eyes whose skull he crushed."[11] André Malraux said one cannot kill an enemy who looks you in the eyes. A Hutu who took part in the Rwandan genocide testifies:

> *Still I do remember the first person who looked at me at the moment of the deadly blow. Now that was something. The eyes of someone you kill are immortal, if they face you at the fatal*

> *instant. They have a terrible black color. They shake you more than the streams of blood and the death rattles, even in a great turmoil of dying. The eyes of the killed, for the killer, are his calamity if he looks into them. They are the blame of the person he kills.*[12]

Mechanical distance separates the operator from his future victims, reduced to being only simple virtual targets on a screen. The Gulf War was nicknamed the "Nintendo War." The enemy has become an echo on a radar screen, a thermic image at night, a simple pair of geographic coordinates on a GPS.

The use of drones, guided from command posts situated at the other end of the world, is a contemporary example of this virtual distance. Still, new techniques allow the operator to see the effects of his actions with much more realism, and many drone operators, revolted by their task, develop serious psychological disorders.

Brandon Bryant was a drone pilot for six years.[13] He just had to press a button in New Mexico for a man to die on the other end of the planet. Brandon remembers his first missile firing: on his screen, he clearly saw two men die immediately, and he witnessed the slow death of a third. The man lost a leg; he held the stump as his hot blood streamed onto the asphalt. After returning home, Brandon called his mother, crying. "I felt disconnected from humanity for almost a week," he said. For six years, Brandon saw men, women and children die in real time. "I never thought I would kill that many people," he writes. "In fact, I thought I couldn't kill anyone at all."

One day, after firing a missile at a house that supposedly was sheltering Taliban fighters, suddenly he saw a child walk around the corner. Then a flash filled the screen—the explosion. Sections of the building collapsed. The child had disappeared. Brandon felt sick to his stomach. He couldn't bear anymore to watch people explode on his screen: "I wish my eyes would rot," he confided. He collapsed, bent double, and spat blood. The doctors diagnosed post-traumatic stress syndrome. Brandon quit the Air Force and is now trying to reconstruct his vision of the world.

Semantic distance is also created. One does not speak of "killing" the enemy; rather, the enemy is "neutralized" or "liquidated." The enemy's humanity is negated; he becomes a strange beast called a "Kraut," a "Jap," a "Reb." Even weapons of war receive benign nicknames. The most monstrous bomb the United States used in Vietnam and Afghanistan weighed 6.8 tons, razed everything for hundreds of feet around, and was called "Daisy Cutter." One of the most terrible defoliants, 80 million liters of which were poured over Vietnam and which still causes numerous cancers and birth defects, bears the harmless name "Agent Orange." All kinds of euphemisms are used according to the situation; a zone is "zapped" or "treated," and a "pocket of resistance is liquidated." One does not say that a man was killed trying to kill other men, but that he died "on mission" or in the "field of honor"; one isn't killed by one's own troops, but is a "victim of friendly fire," and so on.

Avoidance Rituals

In order to avoid killing, ancient cultures and, more recently, urban gangs have developed codes and rituals that allow them to perform simulacra of battles, victories, and submissions. This recourse to symbolic acts allows them to display their strength and show their resentment while avoiding actual violence. As the social psychologist Peter Marsh explains, the protagonists thus create a perfect facade of aggression and power, but the actual level of violence remains very low.[14] Gwynne Dyer concludes that while one can certainly find "the occasional psychopath who really wants to slice people open," most of the participants are more interested in "status, display, profit, and damage limitation."

Who Kills?

Another point revealed by these studies is equally disturbing: in armed conflicts, a tiny percentage of men is responsible for most enemy losses. That is true both for the land army and the air forces. It has been shown that during the Second World War only 1% of American fighter pilots were responsible for 30% to 40% of in-flight destruction of enemy planes, not because they were better or bolder pilots than the others, but, according to R. A. Gabriel, because "most fighter pilots never shot anyone down or even tried to"; they looked in the cockpit at another man, a pilot, a flier, one of the "brotherhood in the air," a man frighteningly like them.[15]

Who, then, are these soldiers who feel no inhibitions about killing? There is such a thing as a "natural soldier," according to the Canadian military historian Gwynne Dyer; "he will have no objections [to killing] if it occurs within a moral framework that gives him justification—like war—and if it is the price of gaining admission to the kind of environment he craves."[16] Most of these soldiers "end up in armies (and many move on again to become mercenaries, because regular army life in peacetime is too routine and boring)." But such men are so rare, Dyer writes, that they form "only a modest fraction of small professional armies, mostly congregating in the commando-type special forces."

A study by Swank and Marchand,[17] still concerning the Second World War, revealed that the 2% of the soldiers who were capable of enduring uninterrupted combat for long periods of time presented the profiles of aggressive psychopaths. It became apparent that these men felt no remorse about their actions. As for the others, after sixty days of continuous combat, 98% of the survivors suffered from various psychiatric disorders.

Certain individuals go even further. Dave Grossman cites the case of a Vietnam veteran, R. B. Anderson, who, in a testimonial entitled *Parting Shot: Vietnam Was Fun,* writes:

> *The fact is that it was fun.... It was so great that I went back for a second helping. Think about it.... Where else could you divide your time between hunting the ultimate big game and partying at "the ville"? Where else could you sit on the side of a hill and watch an airstrike destroy a regimental base camp?... I was a warrior in war. Only a veteran can know the thrill of the kill and the bitterness of losing a friend who is closer to you than your own family.*[18]

Other veterans admit having felt a certain euphoria when they hit the bull's-eye and killed an enemy. But most often this euphoria is quickly overcome by a profound feeling of guilt.

Stifling Empathy by Conditioning

In order to be capable of killing, one must manage to stifle any feeling of empathy for, closeness to, or resemblance to the other. A psychopath naturally lacks empathy. He is capable of coldly inflicting the worst tortures on others without being moved by it.

So it is not surprising that the training of soldiers in modern armies integrates techniques aiming specifically at making this natural repugnance to kill disappear. Since only few people are psychopaths (about 1 to 2% of the population), armies try to annihilate empathy in the others. To do this, they have the soldier simulate the act of killing numerous times, in order to make this action commonplace and gradually to desensitize the doer.

After the Second World War, military instructors realized that in order for this conditioning to be effective, they had to give the targets human forms and make them appear suddenly in a given environment—which forces the soldier to shoot very quickly, without thinking. The figures fall backwards when the shooter hits a bull's-eye, which provokes a feeling of satisfaction in him. Thus he undergoes a conditioning that is reinforced by a reward. By imitating a credible environment in a realistic way, the soldier is led to stop feeling the slightest hesitation or emotional reaction when he aims at living beings. When an enemy suddenly appears, soldiers who have gone through this intensive conditioning phase assert they shoot automatically, as if they were still training in aiming at moving targets.

American soldiers have had recourse to various other techniques of extreme conditioning to root the act of killing in the deepest part of the recruits' psyches. An American sergeant in the Marines, a Vietnam vet, testifies, "We'd run PT in the morning and every time your left foot hit the deck you'd have to chant 'Kill, kill, kill, kill.' It was drilled into your mind so much that it seemed like when it actually came down to it, it didn't bother you, you know?"[19] This conditioning was imposed repetitively for thousands of hours, under the direction of a strict authority, under the constant threat of punishment for anyone who failed. So it is not surprising that many authors, including Gwynne Dyer, speak of a Pavlovian conditioning to kill, rather than training.[20] These methods have allowed the number of soldiers ready to kill to be considerably increased. During the Korean War, the percentage of combatants who fired at the enemy went from 15% to over 50%, and reached 90% to 95% during the Vietnam War, an unprecedented circumstance in the history of warfare.

Today, things have changed. A new code has been adopted among American Marines, urging soldiers to regard every adversary as a human being just like them and to avoid any violence not indispensable to the success of their mission.

LEARNING TO KILL BEFORE THE AGE OF TWENTY

The American military also observed that this training had few effects on adult recruits, and that it was between the ages of seventeen and twenty that men had to be trained to kill. After twenty, there wasn't much point, since it then becomes difficult to overcome the repugnance to kill. Young recruits, on the other hand, readily participate in the conditioning, motivated by their confidence in their hierarchical superiors. According to Grossman, they are forced to "internalize the horrors of combat during one of the most vulnerable and susceptible stages of life."[21] The Vietnam War was nicknamed the "teenagers' war," since the average age of combatants was under twenty.

Research in the neurosciences has shown that the brain is the theater for major modifications mainly during the first two periods of life: an initial spike in brain activity occurs just after birth, when the newborn is exposed to all the wealth and variety of sensorial stimulation from the outside world. Then this process slows down until puberty.

Recent studies have revealed that a second period of major modification occurs at adolescence. Between the ages of sixteen and twenty, a large number of neural networks formed during childhood come undone. New networks are formed, more specialized and more stable, which will be preserved into adulthood.[22]

What's more, before the age of twenty, the prefrontal cortex, which ensures the regulation of emotions engendered by other brain regions, is not completely developed. This explains the emotional instability of adolescents, their hypersensitivity, and their taste for danger and novelty. This stage is necessary, but it is accompanied by great vulnerability.

Thus, with the sole aim of increasing their effectiveness in combat, the ability to kill their fellows has been profoundly, lastingly, drilled into young people who, in Vietnam for example, were drafted by their government and not volunteers. Their most profound mental dispositions were manipulated, and the image they had of their fellows was radically modified. Such a conditioning requires time, and an equal amount of time, if not more, would be required to undo it. However, not much action is taken in that direction. After having served their time in war, the veterans are often left to themselves in society, without anyone worrying about compensating for the dehumanizing conditioning they underwent with any adequate antidote. Today, many psychologists and neurobiologists, among them Amishi Jha at the University of Miami and Richard Davidson at the University of Madison, have undertaken to help these veterans.

Nothing but Victims

It goes without saying that the main victims of war are those who undergo this violence. But there are no victims without aggressors, and it is essential to understand better the mechanisms of aggression. When, for various reasons, soldiers overcome their repugnance to kill, the psychological aftereffects are profound. William Manchester, who enlisted in the American navy during the Second World War, tells in his memoirs that when he shot an elite Japanese marksman he had furtively approached, he whispered, as if in a daze, "I'm sorry," and began vomiting uncontrollably. "It was a betrayal of what I'd been taught since a child," he writes.[23]

The price to pay to force men to overcome their repugnance to kill is thus very high. According to various estimates, almost 90% of American soldiers in the Vietnam and Iraq wars have subsequently suffered from post-traumatic stress syndrome, PTSD, which manifests as crises of extreme anxiety, terror, recurrent nightmares; phenomena of dissociation from reality; obsessive, depressive, and asocial behavior; and, too often, suicide: there were more suicides among veterans who returned from Iraq and Afghanistan than deaths in combat.[24]

A study carried out at Columbia University on 6,810 veterans showed that only those who had taken part in intensive combat were affected by this syndrome.[25] Compared to the rest of the American population, they are far above the national average when it comes to the use of tranquilizers, number of divorces, unemployment rate, alcoholism, suicide, hypertension, heart disease, and ulcers. On the other hand, Vietnam veterans who were not in combat situations present characteristics similar to those of draftees who served in the United States.

What Lessons Can We Draw from This?

We have seen how the conditioning to kill can profoundly modify the behavior and self-esteem of young soldiers. However, the malleability of temperament and the plasticity of the brain allow us to envisage the possibility for transformations that are just as substantial, but this time toward kindness.

Collaboration between the neurosciences and meditators who for millennia have refined effective methods has shown that the fact of cultivating altruistic love also has profound and lasting effects. It would seem that the mind training suggested by Buddhist contemplatives is diametrically opposed to that of young recruits. It consists of reviving, amplifying, and stabilizing our natural tendency to feel empathy and grant importance to others, regardless of who they are. This training also differs from conditioning, since it is associated with profound reflection on the reasons that make altruism a virtue useful for every human being.

The Point of View of Religions

Since they claim to convey a message of love, we expect from religions a clear, unequivocal condemnation of all acts of killing. But stances are sometimes, to say the least, ambiguous, especially on the question of war. A young soldier stationed in Iraq read one day, above the door of the military chaplaincy, "We are doing the work of God." That seemed so aberrant to him that he lost his faith.[26] As the Dalai Lama remarked, "God must be very confused. Both sides kill each other and in the meantime they pray to God."[27]

Anthony Swofford, a former US Marine who fought during the second Gulf War, says very justly in his book *Jarhead:*

I recognized the incompatibility of religion and the military. The opposite of this assertion seems true when one considers the high number of fiercely religious military people, but they are missing something. They're forgetting the mission of the military: to extinguish the lives and livelihood of other humans. What do you they think all those bombs are for?[28]

We often hear that the commandment "Thou shalt not kill" means "Thou shalt not commit murder," but that the Bible does not forbid killing altogether, since many eminent characters in the Bible killed their enemies for reasons that seemed justified to them.

In fact, the Old Testament and the Torah exonerate the act of killing in the case of a so-called just war, a concept that has given rise to numerous interpretations.[29] The Torah also accepts capital punishment in the case of murder, incest, adultery, and idolatry.[30] In his *Large Catechism,* Martin Luther also explains that God and governments are not bound by that commandment, since they must punish criminals. The Koran adopts a similar position: "And do not take any human being's life—that God willed to be sacred—other than in [the pursuit of] justice." However, the Koran does forbid attacking first.[31]

Thus, exempting war and the death penalty from the biblical commandment has often, by widening the limits of what is regarded as just and acceptable, led to the perpetration of massacres and genocides in the name of "good." During the Second World War, for example, religious authorities, both Catholic and Protestant, forbade priests and pastors from being conscientious objectors. That did not prevent the pastor André Trocmé, who saved several thousand Jews with the villagers of Chambon-sur-Lignon, from militating for nonviolence. In the will he drafted during the war, when his activities as a rescuer of Jews constantly placed him in danger, he wrote about being a conscientious objector: "I can neither kill nor take part in this work of death that is war."[32]

This point of view seems more in keeping with the words of Saint Paul: "For all the law is fulfilled in one word, even in this; thou shalt love thy neighbor as thyself. Love worketh no ill to his neighbor: therefore love is the fulfilling of the law."[33]

Archbishop Desmond Tutu, winner of the Nobel Peace Prize,

sums it up clearly: "I know no religion that states it is permissible to kill."[34] When he uttered these words at a meeting between representatives of several religions in which I took part at the World Economic Forum in Davos, I suggested that the religious leaders issue a common declaration on the basis of Tutu's statement. The question was evaded under the pretext that there were "a variety of points of view on this subject."

For Buddhism, there is no difference between killing in peacetime and killing in wartime. A soldier is responsible for the murders he has committed; a general is responsible for the murders committed under his orders. A sincere Buddhist can do nothing but refuse to take part in acts of war. The same is true for Jainism, which preaches strict nonviolence, *ahimsa*. Followers of Jainism are models in the matter of carrying this ideal into everyday life. These two nontheistic religions base their understanding of the world on the laws of cause and effect. According to these laws, ignorance, hatred, animosity, and desire are the first causes of violence. Malevolence is always counterproductive because it gives rise to or perpetuates hatred.

It is no less possible to carry out a firm, determined action without feeling the slightest hatred, in order to prevent a dangerous being from doing harm. One day the Dalai Lama was asked what the best conduct would be to follow if a criminal entered a room and threatened its occupants with a revolver. He replied in a half-serious, half-teasing tone, "I would shoot him in the legs to neutralize him, then I'd go over to him to stroke his head and take care of him." He was quite aware that reality is not always so simple, but wanted to get it across that an energetic action was enough, and that it was not only useless but harmful to add hatred to it.

Such a position immediately rouses questions: "Are you going to give up defending yourself or defending your country faced with an attack? Do we have to let dictators oppress their people and massacre their opponents? Don't we have to intervene to interrupt a genocide?" These questions asked out of context imply obvious answers: "Yes, we have to defend ourselves against an attack. Yes, a dictator should be eliminated, if that's the only way to avoid countless sufferings. Yes, genocide must be prevented at all costs." But one should also ask the right questions. If one finds oneself driven to such extremes, it is because one has, often for a long time, turned a blind eye on causes of discontent or neglected to undertake everything that could have prevented the attacker from attacking us and a genocide from occurring. We know too well that the warning signs of practically all genocides have been ignored, when it could have been possible to remedy them in due course.

If I want to avoid getting dysentery in a tropical country, I'm not content just with bringing a bag of antibiotics: I find out about the quality of the water. I filter it and boil it. I dig a healthy well in the village, respect the rules of hygiene, and teach them to others. Similarly, whoever wants to avoid killing at all costs is not content with saying to himself, "If it turns bad, I'll take my rifle and settle the question." He will be constantly attentive to all the possible causes of the other's discontent and resentment, and will try to remedy them before animosity flares up and inflames tempers irremediably. Too often, violence is regarded as the most effective and quickest way to settle a conflict. But as the Buddha taught, "If hatred answers hatred, hatred will never cease."

30

Dehumanizing the Other: Massacres and Genocides

We have shown that humans have a profound repugnance toward killing their fellow humans. But, powerful as it may be, this resistance is overcome in certain particular situations and leads to behavior that counts among the most sinister in human history, causing persecutions, massacres, and genocides. The sheer repetition of these atrocities requires us to question the processes that lead to breaking down the barriers that usually restrain us from killing.

The factors that erode this aversion are many and bring into play powerful emotions, among them hatred, fear and disgust. These factors also include devaluing, dehumanizing, and demonizing the other; desensitization of the torturer, who becomes indifferent to the suffering he inflicts; an affective and moral dissociation from the victims; a dilution of responsibilities; and an establishment of ideological systems that justify violence. Individuals are thus dragged into an often irreversible trap.

As the psychologist Aaron Beck explains in *Prisoners of Hate,* the members of a group that has been designated as the enemy are first of all *homogenized;* they lose their identities as individuals, and victims become interchangeable. They are then *dehumanized* and no longer perceived as being able to inspire empathy: "They could just as easily be inanimate objects, like mechanical ducks in a shooting gallery or targets in a computer game. Finally, they are *demonized*.... Killing them is no longer optional; they *must* be exterminated.... We attack the projected image, but harm or kill real people."[1]

When the value of a group of individuals is degraded in the minds of members of another group, each individual in the devalued group becomes a negligible quantity. He is henceforth perceived as an abstract unit regarded as harmful or exploitable at will. A slogan of the Khmer Rouge announced to those they eliminated en masse: "To keep you is no benefit, to destroy you is no loss."[2] Aside from persecution, this process of devaluing can also lead to individuals being instrumentalized: humans become slaves, and animals become food products.

During the conquest of the Philippines by the United States, at the end of the nineteenth century, a soldier from the American Washington regiment declared, "Shooting human beings is a 'hot game' and beats rabbit killing all to pieces. We charged them and such a slaughter you never saw. We killed them like rabbits; hundreds, yes thousands of them.... No cruelty is too severe for these brainless monkeys."[3]

Pio, who took part in the Rwandan genocide, testified, "The hunt was savage, the hunters were savage, the prey was savage—savagery took over the mind."[4] In the early twentieth century, in the rubber plantations of Argentina, British company officials would celebrate Easter Sunday by dousing the Indians with kerosene and then setting them on fire, "to enjoy their agony," while others burst out laughing, speaking of "Indian hunting."[5]

In a book published in Germany in 1920 entitled *Die Freigabe der Vernichtung Lebensunwerten Lebens* (*The Permission to Destroy Life Unworthy of Life*), Karl Binding, a retired law professor, and Alfred Hoche, a professor of psychiatry, defended the notion that a large percentage of sick people and mentally handicapped people did not deserve to live.[6] They described them as unworthy of life: to destroy them was a form of healing. They spoke of "mental death," "human ballast," and "empty shells of human beings." Putting such people to death was an "allowable, useful act."[7] Binding and Hoche detailed in their book what they regarded as a legal, medical justification of euthanasia, which inspired the Aktion T4 plan in the Third Reich, during which almost 250,000 sick and handicapped people were killed in gas chambers.[8] Almost 10,000 infants afflicted with malformations were also killed by lethal injection.

According to the historians Frank Chalk and Kurt Jonassohn, massacres have always existed, but hardly any written trace of these massacres exists, since the fate of the exterminated populations did not concern ancient historians. The destruction of Melos by the Athenians, of Carthage by the Romans, and of numerous cities by the Mongols caused millions of victims, as did the Crusades.[9]

THE DE-INDIVIDUALIZATION OF THE ACTORS AS WELL AS THE VICTIMS

Within a group that perpetrates mass acts of violence, the individual is only a member of a group, one among so many others. Having lost his individual specificities, he stops thinking autonomously, stops examining the morality of his actions, and no longer feels guilt.

In his eyes, victims are no longer people who have a history, with wives and children, aspirations in life, but are only "one of them," one of those beings designated as despicable and hateful. An "other" who no longer has a name, just a number.

Such a de-individualization can even occur with people we know. After the Rwandan genocide, during which the actors of massacres almost always knew their victims, who had been their neighbors and often their friends, one participant declared, "In our condition, it meant nothing to us to think we were busy cutting our neighbors down to the last one.... *They were no longer what they were before, and neither were we.* We weren't bothered by them, or by the past, since we weren't bothered by anything."[10]

The de-individualization of the victims is aggravated when they are also *dehumanized.* Perpetrators of massacres use the same metaphors all over the world. The objects of their hatred become so many rats, cockroaches, monkeys, or dogs. Impure and repulsive—since "bad blood" flows through their veins—the victims contaminate the rest of the population and therefore must be eliminated as quickly as possible. A Californian settler responsible for the deaths of 241 Yuki Indians because one of them had killed a horse belonging to him justified his actions by comparing Indians to nits and said that "a nit would make a louse,"[11] a common metaphor among the invaders of North America.

During the Nanking massacre in 1937, Japanese generals said to their troops, "You must not consider the Chinese as a human being, but only as something of rather less value than a dog or cat."[12] Closer to us, during the first Gulf War, in 1991, American pilots compared their strafing of retreating Iraqi soldiers to a "turkey shoot" and called civilians who ran for cover "cockroaches."[13]

During the Bosnian War, armed with a megaphone, the Serbian paramilitary Milan Lukic urged Muslims to leave the city with these words: "Muslims, Muslims, you yellow ants, black days have come!"[14] In February 2011, the Libyan dictator Muammar Kaddafi summoned his faithful to take to the streets to "eliminate all the cockroaches who opposed his regime," even as he was causing his own people to be massacred.

Native peoples of the American continent aroused the same scorn and were also dehumanized before being massacred. As the philosopher Thomas Hobbes wrote about the Indians of North America, they were a "savage people" who lived in a "brutish manner," keeping the company of "hound-dogs, apes, asses, lions, barbarians, and hogs."[15] Oliver Wendell Holmes, professor of anatomy and physiology at Harvard in the nineteenth century, found it natural for white people to hate the Indians and "hunt him down like the wild beasts of the forest," so that "the red-crayon sketch is rubbed out, and the canvas is ready for a picture of manhood a little more like God's own image."[16] Even the American president Theodore Roosevelt declared in 1886, "I don't go so far as to think that the only good Indians are the Dead Indians, but I believe nine out of ten are, and I shouldn't like to inquire too closely in the case of the tenth."[17]

For centuries, whites systematically devalued blacks, resorting to the same process of comparing them to animals. In his *History of Jamaica,* Edward Long wrote that the orangutan was closer to the negro than the negro was to the white man,[18] and at the end of the nineteenth century, the eminent brain specialist Paul Broca asserted that "the conformation of the Negro, in this respect as in many others, tends to approach that of the monkey."[19]

As a survivor of the concentration camps, Primo Levi thought that the most important tool of violence is to compare victims to animals in order to facilitate the task of executing them.[20]

Debasing Jews by comparing them to animals is a tendency that goes back to the beginnings of Christian history. The patriarch of Constantinople, Saint John Chrysostom, described the synagogue as a "den of wild animals." Gregory of Nyssa, also a Church father, called the Jewish people a "race of vipers."[21] In sixteenth-century Europe, Luther, leader of the Reformation, reviled the Jews who refused to convert to Protestantism, asserting they would have to be expelled like "rabid dogs." He went so far as to declare that if he were ever asked to baptize a Jew, he would rather drown him like a venomous snake. He compared their synagogues to "evil pigpens." To "clean" them, he suggested an eight-point purification method—a kind of Final Solution before the fact. "We must not show them any pity, or any kindness. We are at fault if we do not kill them!" he wrote in his treatise *The Jews and Their Lies*.[22]

Jacques Sémelin, a scholar of mass violence and genocide, thinks the need to dehumanize the enemy is the reason why the killer often disfigures his victims: by cutting off their nose or ears, the killer makes sure they no longer have a human face, creating a psychological distance that allows him to convince himself that the victims of his atrocities are not human beings, or have ceased being so.[23]

DISGUST

Disgust is an emotional reaction of atavistic defense against external agents that could contaminate us: bodily secretions (mucus, vomiting, excrement), parasites (worms, lice, etc.), decomposing bodies and vectors of contagious diseases (plague victims, lepers). Disgust leads to a reaction of rejection, even destruction, of the potentially contaminating substances or individuals. This emotion, the evolution of which has equipped us to preserve ourselves from biological threats, is often transposed onto a moral level. It then leads people to reject those they regard as "impure" and harmful, and who constitute, they think, a source of contamination for society on ethnic, religious, or ideological levels. Those who set themselves up as representatives of "purity" then make it their duty to execute a "cleansing." Contagious agents remain dangerous even in small numbers—hence the necessity, in the eyes of the persecutors, to get rid of them down to the last one.

We know that Hitler and Nazi propaganda compared Jews to cancers, typhus, and plague-carrying rats who threatened to contaminate the purity of the Aryans. This image of illness produced among the Germans a phobic reaction, a quasi-paranoia.[24]

Desensitization

We have seen that as individuals give in to violence, they become insensitive to the suffering of the other. Their capacity for empathy diminishes until it disappears. They are then capable of even more extreme violence, and murder becomes a job like any other for them.

Based on her interviews with former combatants in Bosnia, the historian Natalija Basic has highlighted the different stages of this process of desensitization. "At first, there is a phase of cumulative radicalization during which the perpetrator learns to kill. In the second phase, the violence carried out is reinterpreted as being a 'moral' action. Then comes the phase of habituation to homicide. Finally, the act of killing is defined as 'work,' a profession in its own right."[25]

As Jacques Sémelin also explains, after the first shock, killers get used to killing. They acquire reflexes, technique, and become professionals of collective murder. A participant in the Rwandan genocide testified, "At first, the people who had already killed chickens, goats especially, had an advantage. That's easily understandable. Later, everyone got used to this new activity and caught up."[26]

A Hutu militant, Leopold, whose statements were gathered by the journalist and writer Jean Hatzfeld, testified, after the genocide during which 800,000 Tutsis were killed in three months: "Since I was killing often, I began to feel it did not mean anything to me.... I want to make clear that from the first gentleman I killed to the last, I was not sorry about a single one."[27]

A clerk in the Austrian police recruited into a German *Einsatzkommando,* Walter Mattner wrote to his wife while stationed in Belorussia in 1941: "I also took part in the day before yesterday's huge mass killing (*Massensterben*). When the first truckload [of victims] arrived my hand was slightly trembling when shooting, but one gets used to this. When the tenth load arrived I was already aiming more calmly and shot securely at the many women, children, and infants.... Infants were flying in a wide circle through the air and we shot them still in flight, before they fell into the pit and into the water. Let's get rid of this scum that tossed all of Europe into the war."[28]

Rudolf Höss, the commandant of Auschwitz, who supervised the extermination of 2.9 million people, confessed in his autobiography that the sufferings he inflicted on his victims caused great emotional turmoil in him, but that for the greater good of National Socialism, he had "stifled all softer emotions."[29]

The Case of the 101st Battalion

In Ordinary Men,[30] the historian Christopher Browning recounts in minute detail the history of the 101st reserve battalion of the regular Hamburg police. This battalion was made up of Hamburg citizens, two-thirds from the working class and one-third from the lower middle-class—mature men who were drafted into the police because they were deemed too old to serve in the army. They had never taken part in any killing actions, and nothing predisposed them to become pitiless murderers. They had to join the German army that was occupying Poland, at the height of the persecutions that the Hitler regime was directing against Jewish communities. At dawn on July 23, 1942, the battalion was sent to the village of Jozefow, which counted 1,800 Jews among its inhabitants. Only the commandant, Wilhelm Trapp, fifty-three, who had begun his career as a simple soldier and whom his men affectionately called "Papa Trapp," knew about the mission.

"Pale and nervous, with choking voice and tears in his eyes," report the documents and testimonials collected by Browning, Trapp explained to his men that they had to perform a terribly unpleasant task. This mission was not to his liking, he said, but the orders came from the highest authorities. The battalion was to gather together all the Jews of Jozefow. The men of working age would be sent to a camp. All the others—old men, women, and children—would be shot by the battalion. Trapp ended with a proposition: those of his men who didn't feel up to taking part in this mission could step out and be excused. One man took a step forward, followed by a dozen others. Already the day before, Lieutenant Buchmann, who had been informed of the mission before the men, had refused to take part in the operation, explaining that "he could not shoot defenseless women and children."[31] The others, almost 500 policemen, didn't budge.

Once his men were sent to carry out their mission, the distress of Trapp, who led operations from his HQ set up in a classroom, was obvious to everyone. According to one witness, he "began to run around again and wept like a child." During this time, the roundup began. Three hundred men of working age were separated from their families and gathered on the public square, and all the others were led into a forest, where the massacre began. It would last until nightfall. Not used to killing, the policemen took time carrying out their task. A considerable number of slow deaths ensued. Some men, revolted, left the forest after killing one person, on the excuse of searching the houses, or they busied themselves with some other task. One of them, who went almost mad, wandered alone into the woods, shouting for hours. Others, incapable of continuing the vile mission, asked their sergeant to dismiss them and were sent to the village. Others willfully misfired. But most continued to kill. Alcohol was handed out to them. By nightfall, seventeen hours after their arrival in Jozefow, there was only one Jew left alive, except for a little girl who emerged from the forest, wounded in the head, whom Trapp took under his protection. The men returned to the barracks in town, "gruesomely besmirched with blood, brains, and bone splinters," silent, haunted by shame.

Why did so few men seize the occasion to refuse to take part in this disastrous mission? According to Browning, one reason was the surprise effect. Caught off-guard, the policemen had no time to reflect. Just as important was the *esprit de corps*—the identification of a man in uniform with his companions in arms, and the extreme difficulty he felt in standing out from the group. Leaving the ranks that morning meant abandoning his comrades; it came down to admitting that you were "weak," even "cowardly." Another man, aware of what is implied by real courage—the courage of refusing—said simply, "I was a coward."

If only a dozen policemen bowed out right away from the imminent massacre, many more sought to escape it by resorting to less obvious stratagems, or asking to be relieved from the execution squads once the killing began. It is estimated that 10% to 20% of the men refused to take part in the execution squads. That means that at least 80% killed without pause the 1,500 Jews of Jozefow, down to the last one. Those who resisted spoke mostly of a purely physical kind of revulsion, and not of moral or political principles.

A few days later, the battalion went to another village and arrested some Jews. All of them, including the policemen, feared that another killing was being prepared, and Trapp decided to free the Jews and send them back home.

But the men would soon become hardened to murder. A month later, part of the battalion was sent to Lomazy. There, assisted by *travnikis,* prisoners of war from Soviet regions commanded by the SS, a third of the men of the battalion, most of them drunk (since this time they were plied with alcohol before the action) exterminated 1,700 Jews, who were then piled into mass graves, in half the time it took in Jozefow. The recalcitrant ones were now less numerous.

As Jacques Sémelin explains, "Experience gained in the field is ultimately considered to be the most important causal factor in the descent into mass murder.... It is war that makes warriors, and it is through the act of killing that men become mass killers."[32]

Mass murders occurred one after the other, and the battalion also took part in deporting thousands of Jews to the camp in Treblinka, and finally to the huge massacre of the "harvest festival," which claimed 42,000 victims on November 3, 1943, in the region of Lublin. When the fall of the Third Reich began in early 1944, most of the battalion returned to Germany: the 500 men of the 101st battalion were responsible for the direct or indirect deaths of at least 83,000 Jews and hundreds of Polish civilians.

Moral Compartmentalization

According to the psychologist Albert Bandura, our ability to selectively activate and deactivate our moral norms explains why people can be cruel at a given moment and compassionate the next.[33] This deactivation occurs in several ways, and its effects can be cumulative. The person will associate objectives presented as praiseworthy (defending the homeland, extracting important information by torture, getting rid of those who threaten society, etc.) with reprehensible acts; the person will obscure his own involvement as agent by shifting responsibility for what he has done onto his group, or by displacing it onto authority figures; he will close his eyes to the sufferings inflicted on the other; he will accuse those he mistreats of every evil. In this way, the same individual can succeed in showing tenderness to his children, who are fully worthy of it in his eyes, and the greatest cruelty to those he sees as "cockroaches" and whom he has been ordered to exterminate.

In *Facing the Extreme*,[34] the philosopher Tzvetan Todorov cites the case of Josef Kramer, former bookseller and commandant of the Bergen-Belsen camp, who cried when he listened to Schumann but who was just as capable of smashing with his truncheon the skull of a prisoner who wasn't marching quickly enough. "Why did music make him weep, but not the deaths of other human beings?" Todorov wonders. At his trial, Kramer declared: "I felt no emotion when I carried out these actions."[35] That didn't prevent him from being an affectionate father, as his wife testified: "The children were everything to my husband."[36]

Studying the case of five Nazi doctors, the psychiatrist Robert Jay Lifton showed that their double role, of doctor *and* persecutor, was made possible by a process of psychological dichotomizing, or compartmentalization, which allowed them to assume one identity or the other according to the circumstance.[37] This compartmentalization, Lifton explains, allows the "normal" part of oneself to evade guilty feelings, while the other, disavowed by the former, does the "dirty work." That is how a former *Gauleiter* could declare that "only his 'official soul'" committed the crimes that led to his hanging in 1946. His "private soul" had always disapproved of them.[38] This process is for the killer a question of self-preservation, without which he could not bear committing atrocities day after day.

Cognitive Dissonance and Rationalization

The expression "cognitive dissonance" was conceived by the psychologist Leon Festinger; it designates in the killer a subconscious doubling of himself to get around the internal conflict between the inhuman actions he's carrying out and his own self-image. In fact, killers find themselves plunged into an intense situation of cognitive dissonance.[39] They experience an acute conflict between their practice as killers and their self-images. In order to avoid regarding themselves as base individuals and to sustain themselves in the process of committing massacres, they must fabricate representations of their victims that allow them to justify their conduct and find themselves in conformity with an image of themselves that is, if not good, then at least acceptable. Managing to assign meaning to their actions allows them to continue killing with a good conscience.

In order to reconcile themselves with the horror of their crimes and to discharge themselves of a responsibility too heavy to bear, killers often call on a sense of duty, or the necessity of committing a repugnant but salutary task. Instead of thinking, "How many horrible things I've done!" they say to themselves, "How many horrible things I have *had* to do!"[40]

In interviews that Franz Stangl, director of the Treblinka camp, gave to the journalist and historian Gitta Sereny, he explains, "The only way I could live was by compartmentalizing my thinking."[41] Stangl clings to the idea that he himself didn't light the fires in the crematorium ovens: "There were hundreds of ways to take one's mind off it; I used them all.... I made myself concentrate on work, work, and again work."[42] He admits he did horrible things, but they weren't of his own free will, and even went against his conscience. He dissociated his conscience from his actions: "No one asked for my opinion. It wasn't me who did that."[43]

Executioners also rationalize their crimes by trying to see them as a last resort. Mukankwaya, a thirty-five-year-old Hutu, mother of six children, describes how, with other women, they had beaten to death with cudgels children from the neighboring houses. The young victims looked at them with eyes wide open in terror: they had been friends and neighbors all their lives! She justified this killing by arguing she had done these children a "favor," since they would have become penniless orphans, their parents having already been killed.[44]

One of the forms of cognitive dissonance also consists of trivializing massacres by using macabre humor that willfully makes use of innocuous vocabulary. In Croatia, Serbian groups penetrating Vukovar shouted, "Slobodan, send us some salad to go with the meat from Croats whose throats we've cut."[45] Similarly, on July 14, 1995, the Bosnian Serb Colonel Ljubisa Beara informed his superior that in

Srebrenica, he still had "3,500 parcels to deliver," i.e., execute.[46] In Nazi vocabulary, *re-installing* or *evacuating* meant "to send to a concentration camp" some "parcels" that had to undergo "special treatment," the code name for mass gassing.[47]

The Cohesion of the Group

As Sémelin reminds us, conformity and loyalty to the group perpetuate two other excuses for drifting toward mass crimes. The group constitutes a source of power over the individual, a grip ensured by the fear of being rejected and regarded as a traitor.[48] During the French Revolution and the Terror that followed, more "traitors" to the cause were guillotined than enemies of the revolution. While an enemy reinforces the group's determination to continue battle, the presence of a renegade calls into question the validity of the accepted ideology, and because of this, is regarded as an intolerable threat. To that is added the necessity to implicate the greatest possible number of individuals in the massacre, so that responsibility for the killings is widely shared.[49]

In order to create a real team spirit, the group sometimes utilizes initiation rites requiring the newcomer to prove his loyalty by killing a victim for the first time, with everyone looking on. In Rwanda, the Hutus who hadn't yet killed Tutsis were treated as trainees. The organizers of bands of *Interahamwe* Hutus would capture a Tutsi and order the suspect to kill him in order to show he was really with them.[50]

Authority and Situations

"I deeply wish to draw the attention of those in authority to the tragic ease with which 'brave men' can become killers without even realizing it,"[51] wrote Germaine Tillon, an ethnologist and great moral figure who escaped from the Ravensbrück camp. The psychologist Philip Zimbardo reminds us how much we underestimate our vulnerability to the influence of external situations, and are not sufficiently vigilant about them:[52] "Any deed that any human being has ever committed, however horrible, is possible for any of us—under the right or wrong situational circumstances. That knowledge does not excuse evil; rather, it democratizes it, sharing its blame among ordinary actors rather than declaring it the province only of deviants and despots—of Them but not Us."[53] Thus, when we try to understand the causes for inhuman and aberrant behavior, we should begin by analyzing the situation before we bring in individual dispositions (character traits, pathologies, genetic influence, etc.).

Zimbardo finds a certain number of factors that, generally, allow those in power to lead an ordinary person to resort to violence against his moral convictions. The representative of authority must first present an acceptable justification so that others will carry out an action normally regarded as inadmissible, such as torture, under the pretext of concern for national security or serving the country. The instructions and rules to be observed must seem sensible on the face of it. Later, they will be used to require blind obedience, even if what is happening has become senseless. The authority figure must also appear respectable at first sight, and his transformation into an abusive and unreasonable figure occurs in stages. Any possibility of evasion must then be made difficult. In the case of dictatorships, those who were ordered to afflict the persecuted populations were threatened with being subjected to the same fate as their victims if they didn't obey.

However, as the historian Christopher Browning noted in the case of Nazi Germany: "In the past forty-five years no defense attorney or defendant in any of the hundreds of postwar trials has been able to document a single case in which refusal to obey an order to kill unarmed civilians resulted in the allegedly inevitable dire punishment."[54] According to Ervin Staub, when the Bulgarians refused to hand over the Jewish populations and demonstrated in the streets against this diktat, the Nazis did not continue their efforts.[55]

THE ESTABLISHMENT OF A SYSTEM

Killing a large number of people in not much time requires the establishment of a system, sometimes a sophisticated one, as in the case of the gas chambers and crematorium ovens, sometimes one that is terribly simple, like the general use of machetes in Rwanda or certain methods used by the Tutsis against the Hutus during the Burundi massacres in 1972. As one of the participants of that massacre explains:

> *Several techniques, several, several. One can gather two thousand persons in a house—in a prison, let us say. There are some halls that are large. The house is locked. The men are left there for fifteen days without eating, without drinking. Then one opens. One finds cadavers. Not beaten, not anything. Dead.*[56]

It has been demonstrated that most massacres and genocides are the work of merciless minorities, organized according to a highly repressive hierarchy that allows it to impose its authority by terror on the majority of the population. The population is generally resigned, faced with a repressive, efficient, omnipresent system: individual risks linked to resistance are too great and often pointless.

Concerning Rwanda, the American researcher Scott Straus came to the conclusion that the number of Hutu killers, in 1994, was between 14% and 17% of the adult male population.[57] What's more, only 25% of these killers were responsible for almost 75% of the massacres. In short, "It seems clear that the main momentum of the killings was carried out by a relatively small number of specially trained Hutus who, allying themselves with often-drunken criminal and hooligan opportunists, went on a murderous rampage coordinated by local officials acting on orders from above." Equipped with this knowledge, the American political scientist John Mueller thinks that ethnic war is more the result of small bands of gangsters and criminals who manage to sow terror in a region, and who profit from this by robbing from their victims.[58] Similarly, as Benedikt Kautsky, a survivor of Auschwitz, explains, "Nothing could be more mistaken than to see the SS as a sadistic horde driven to abuse and torture... by instinct, passion, or some thirst for pleasure. Those who acted in this way were [in the] minority."[59]

Even if instigators of massacres and serial killers represented only a small percentage of the population, as during any genocide, in hundreds of regions of Rwanda, the killing madness and group spirit incited almost the entire male population to take part in the killings, although to quite varying degrees. According to the writer Jean Hatzfeld, in the neighboring hills of the commune of Nyamata, for example, 50,000 of the 59,000 Tutsi inhabitants were killed by machete in the space of one month, whether in their homes, in churches where they had taken refuge, or in the forests and swamps where they were trying to hide.[60]

BEYOND HUMAN CONDITIONS

In *Facing the Extreme,* Tzvetan Todorov imagines what happens to people when they are subjected to conditions so inhumane that they come to lose their humanity. We have seen how, in the case of the Stanford experiment directed by Philip Zimbardo, the establishment of external situations that change normal relationships between human beings could quickly lead a group of ordinary students to behave with a cruelty and sadism that they would never have thought themselves capable of before.[61] In the unbearable conditions of concentration camps, the feelings and moral values that comprise the foundations of human existence were often annihilated. As Tadeusz Borowski, a survivor of Auschwitz, testifies, "Morality, national solidarity, patriotism and the ideals of freedom, justice and human dignity had all slid off man like a rotten rag."[62]

The privations were so great, writes Primo Levi, another survivor of Auschwitz, that moral behavior seemed impossible: "Here the struggle to survive is without respite, because everyone is desperately and ferociously alone."[63] In order to survive, one must "throttle all dignity and kill all conscience, climb down into the arena as a beast against other beasts, let oneself be guided by those unsuspected subterranean forces which sustain families and individuals in cruel times."[64]

The experience that prisoners in Communist camps have come away with is the same. Varlam Shalamov, who spent 25 years in a gulag, asserts, "The camp conditions did not permit men to remain men; that is not what camps were created for."[65] This observation was echoed by Eugenia Ginzburg, an inmate in the Kolyma gulag for twenty years: "A human being pushed too far by the forms of inhuman life...gradually loses all hold on normal notions of good and evil....Perhaps we ourselves were morally dead."[66]

The threshold of resistance is often reached after prolonged hunger, or the imminent threat of death: "Hunger proves an insuperable ordeal. When he reaches this ultimate degree of degradation, a man is prepared for anything," writes Anatoly Marchenko, a Soviet dissident and writer who was interned in one of the gulags that subsisted after Stalin's death.[67] "But what is the meaning of this observation?" wonders Todorov. "Does it mean that this is where the truth of human nature lies, and that morality is only a superficial convention, abandoned at the first opportunity? Not at all; what it proves, on the contrary, is that moral reactions are spontaneous and omnipresent, and that it is necessary to use the most violent means to eradicate them."[68] He shares the opinion of Gustav Herling, a writer who escaped from a gulag:

> *I became convinced that a man can be human only under human conditions and I believe it is fantastic nonsense to judge him by actions that he commits under inhuman conditions.*

But Todorov points out that upon reading the testimonials of survivors, he had no choice but to observe that certain people did show a moral sense, even extraordinary heroism. Primo Levi, notably, who, while stressing the climate of mistrust and rivalry between prisoners, speaks affectionately of his friend Alberto, who died during the forced marches when the camps were evacuated, and who, while struggling for survival, was able to remain strong and gentle at the same time. He also mentions another friend, Jean Samuel, whom he nicknamed Pikolo, and who "did not neglect human relationships with less privileged comrades."[69]

Testimonials from Auschwitz survivors show that, without help, survival was impossible. Simon Laks confirms he owed his own survival to "a few countrymen with a human face and a human heart."[70] Eugenia Ginzburg also reports countless gestures of solidarity, proof that in the final analysis, not everyone was "morally dead."[71] Powerful as it may be, the constraint of external circumstances can never be total and, according to Viktor Frankl, an Austrian psychiatrist, philosopher, and camp survivor: "Everything can be taken from a man but one thing, the last of the human freedoms—to choose one's attitude in any given set of circumstances, to choose one's own way."[72]

There are rules in the camps, but different from those of ordinary society. As Todorov explains, stealing from camp administrators is not only allowed but admired. On the other hand, stealing, especially bread, from fellow inmates is scorned and, most of the time, severely punished. Informers are detested and punished. Killing can be a moral action, if that is the only way to prevent a killer from continuing to take lives. Bearing false witness can become a virtuous action if it saves human lives. Loving one's neighbor like oneself is, in such extreme conditions, an excessive demand, but avoiding harming him is not.

Tadeusz Borowski, whose story about life in Auschwitz is one of the most harrowing, concludes, however: "I think that man will never cease to rediscover man—through love. And that is the most important and most lasting thing."[73] Borowski himself behaved in Auschwitz in a completely different way from the characters in his stories, and his devotion to others bordered on heroism.

A Deadly Snowball Effect

People who take a step on the path of barbarism are not always fully aware of crossing an unacceptable boundary, since they don't clearly apprehend the outcome of this path, and think that a minor infringement of their sense of morality will not have any consequences. This initial base action is usually only the first stage of a cumulative snowball effect that becomes difficult to escape and that leads the individual to perpetrate increasingly serious violent acts.

That is how, because of external influences they don't dare or don't know how to resist, out of fear or weakness, these individuals commit actions they would have refused to carry out if they had been asked to do so in another context.

As the psychologist Roy Baumeister explains, "Once the members of the group are waist-deep in blood, it is too late for them to question the group's project as a whole, and so they are all the more likely to wade even deeper."[74]

In *Un si fragile vernis d'humanité* (Such a Fragile Shell of Humanity), the philosopher Michel Terestchenko demonstrates how one can let oneself get caught up in the snowballing of evil or, on the contrary, avoid engaging in it.[75] He gives the example of Franz Stangl who, stage by stage, becomes commandant of the Sobibor concentration camp, then of the Treblinka camp in Poland. His mind weak, at each new appointment that advanced him further on the path of ignominy,

Stangl hesitated and tried to evade the new responsibilities that would be his. But fear of reprisals for himself and his family, his submission to authority, and his lack of courage made it so that every time he gave in, sinking ever further into barbarism.

After the war, Franz Stangl found refuge in Brazil, where he was finally arrested in 1967 and condemned in 1970 to life in prison for murdering 900,000 people. In 1971, he granted seventy hours of interviews to the historian Gitta Sereny.[76] The second day of their conversation, discussing the arrest of one of his former chiefs who was tortured by the Germans, he suddenly declared, "I hate the Germans for what they pulled me into.... I should have killed myself in 1938. That's when it started for me. I must acknowledge my guilt."[77] It was only at the end of their interviews that Stangl again acknowledged his responsibility and said to Sereny, "I have never intentionally hurt anyone, myself." Then, after a long silence: "But I was there...So, yes, in reality I share the guilt...My guilt is that I am still here. I should have died." Then he motioned to Sereny that he had nothing more to say. Stangl, who was kept in solitary confinement, died nineteen hours later of a heart attack.

How had he gotten to that point? A simple police officer, he was swiftly promoted to the Department of Criminal Investigations in a small Austrian town. In 1938, the Nazis asked him to renounce Catholicism and sign a declaration to that effect. In his eyes, that was an important stage toward his degeneration. He felt as if he had sold his soul.[78] He was transferred to the town's Gestapo headquarters, then appointed, in Berlin, Director of Security of the Institute for the Aktion T412 plan, dedicated, as we've seen, to performing euthanasia on the mentally and physically impaired. This program allowed the Nazis to test and perfect the techniques of mass elimination they would use in the concentration camps. When Stangl learned of the nature of the work they expected of him, he tried to escape from it: "I was...I was speechless. And then I finally said that I didn't really feel I was suited for this assignment."[79] But his superior made him understand that his nomination was the proof of the exceptional trust they had placed in him and that he would not have to practice euthanasia himself. If he accepted, the disciplinary actions underway against him would be suspended. The chief of operations, Christian Wirth, nicknamed "Christian the Savage," who would himself become director of the Belzec camp, declared scornfully that they had to "do away with these useless mouths."

With one thing leading to another, in 1942, Stangl was sent to Poland and was entrusted with the construction of the Sobibor camp. One day, his superiors brought him to the Belzec camp, which was already active. He discovered the horror of the situation: there were trenches filled with decomposing bodies. Christian Wirth then told him that that was what Sobibor was going to become and that he, Stangl, had been appointed director of it. Stangl replied again that he wasn't made for such a task, but there was no way out. With a friend, he discussed deserting and running away, but abandoned that idea out of fear of failing, and of the fate that would then fall upon him and his wife and children, whom he loved above all else.

During a visit to Sobibor, his wife ended up discovering what was going on in the camp. Horrified, she confronted her husband, who stated he wasn't involved in the atrocities being committed. "How can you *be* there and have nothing to do with this?" she retorted, "You mean you don't see it happening?" To which, trying to calm her, he replied: "Oh yes, I see it, but I don't *do* anything to anybody," adding that his work was purely administrative.[80] Finally, he was appointed to the management of Treblinka: "Treblinka was the most awful thing I saw during all of the Third Reich," he confided to Gitta Sereny, burying his face in his hands. "It was straight out of Dante's Inferno."[81]

He went to find General Globocnik, chief of operations in Warsaw, and attempted, unsuccessfully, once again to withdraw, stating he could not carry out orders.[82] He then went to see the new chief of police and begged to be transferred. In vain. Eventually, he got used to his macabre work, began drinking like most of his comrades, so as not to think too much about it, and carried out his task to the end.

What lesson can we draw from this tragic example? Michel Terestchenko emphasizes this: "the radical importance of refusing *from the beginning*, of not giving in to the slightest demand." Only this uncompromising refusal "allows the moral integrity of the individual to be preserved as well as his freedom."[83] Refusal does not imply that *any particular order* is called into question, but rather the authority from which it emanates.

This is not indeed an easy thing to do and, as Terestchenko writes, "everyone easily dons the knight's armor when it costs only the price of a dream. But, having returned to reality, the weight of things, the constraint of situations, the concerns of self-interest again make themselves felt, bogging us down in torpor and docile passivity. Rare are those who find in themselves the courage to extract themselves from it."[84] Varlam Shalamov, who spent seventeen years in a gulag, warns us:

> *If we leave the tops of our mountains, if we look for compromises, arrangements, pardons, it will all be over; if our conscience falls silent, we won't be able to resist the slippery slope.*[85]

There have, however, been people who were able to say no.

MORAL STRENGTH: REFUSING TO COLLUDE WITH THE OPPRESSOR

The case of Pastor Trocmé and the inhabitants of Chambon-sur-Lignon, in Haute-Loire, who saved thousands of Jews from Nazi persecution, offers a striking contrast—of people who, from the beginning, firmly determined that they would not compromise with what they thought was right and who, at peril of their lives, went so far as to say openly to the representative of the Vichy government that they were protecting Jewish families and had no intention to stop doing so, whatever the price they had to pay.[86] For them, it was immoral not to protect Jews, and they would never call that principle into question, deciding that there are lines that must not be crossed.

In *Good People in an Evil Time,* Svetlana Broz, granddaughter of Marshal Tito, recounts different examples of mutual aid and collective resistance during the Bosnian War, as in Baljvine, a mountain village where the Serbs steadily blocked the passage of the paramilitaries who persecuted Muslims, who had themselves protected the Serbs of that village during the Second World War.[87]

On the first day of the Srebrenica massacre, Drazen Erdemovic, a Croat married to a Serb, decided to run away so as to take no part in the massacre. He told his colleagues: "Are you sane? Do you know what you're doing?" They answered that if he didn't want to be one of them, he could hand in his rifle and go over to the Muslims. Over the course of that day, he estimates he took part under compulsion in the execution of some hundred prisoners. But when they summoned him elsewhere to kill another five hundred people, he refused and even received the support of part of his unit.[88]

In Rwanda, in Kigali itself, in certain places of refuge, some men refused to take part in the killing, as in the Hôtel des Milles Collines where the director, Paul Rusesabagina, offered beer and money to soldiers and militiamen coming to look for the Tutsis he was protecting. Similarly, Bishop Joseph Sibomana, of the diocese of Kivungo, gave all his money to some militiamen to keep them from massacring the Tutsis who had taken refuge in his church.[89]

NON-INTERVENTION IN RESPONSE TO THE GRADUAL INTENSIFICATION OF GENOCIDE

Genocide usually proceeds in stages. It is first tested several times during short periods on samples of the population, then extended to a larger number. The Armenian genocide, for example, began with limited massacres. Then, faced with the passivity of other nations, there was an escalation: 200,000 Armenians were killed in 1905. The international community barely protested. Encouraged by this indifference, in 1915, the Turks undertook the methodical extermination of half a million Armenians.[90] Later on, Hitler drew lessons from the non-intervention of neighboring powers and, on the dawn of the invasion of Poland, declared, "After all, who talks nowadays about the extermination of the Armenians?"[91]

After Kristallnacht (November 9, 1938), many pogroms were set off by a call for murder and looting by Goebbels on government radio. A large part of the population was shocked by this wave of violence. However, as Jacques Sémelin stresses, spontaneous reactions against the inexcusable schemes of the government in power have a chance of influencing the government provided spokespeople dare openly to voice this disapproval. "In fact, no spiritual or moral authority inside Germany openly echoed this popular emotion. This incredible outbreak of hatred was therefore followed by a deafening silence that could be interpreted as a kind of assent, or even satisfaction."[92]

Everything happened as if the population's capacity for collective reaction had been progressively stifled. German society let itself be carried away in a process of destruction that it tolerated without reacting. Even worse, "this increase in passive involvement simultaneously turned into an active increase of many areas of activity that collaborated with the 'final solution.' "[93]

Becoming Aware of the Reality of a Genocide

According to Sémelin, this awareness has three phases. The first is the *incredulity* of other countries and their resistance to information. In the case of the extermination of the Jews, the enormity of the massacre reported by some informants made it literally unbelievable to the leaders of the allied nations and their citizens; everyone thought the reports were exaggerated. There was a collective denial that was terribly painful for the survivors, who were not only forced by the authorities to keep silent, but even suspected of giving doubtful testimony.

In a second phase, the news *begins to become believable* to an increasing number of individuals, thanks to the dissemination of a multitude of pieces of information and rumors.

After a period of latency or incubation comes the third phase, that of actually *becoming aware,* during which mental defenses break down so the horror of the reality can be absorbed.[94] This latency period often turns out to be fatal to the targeted populations, as was the case in Rwanda, as this absence of reaction by the international community encourages the planners of massacres to pursue their program of extermination to its end.

Unfortunately, this awareness is rarely translated into an intervention. People pretend to act; responsibilities are shifted onto other people; negotiations doomed to failure—since the persecutors have no intention to give up their project—are attempted; and, very often, people prevaricate until the tragedy reaches irreversible proportions.

Regardless of factors, over half the genocidal episodes of the last fifty years have been ideological genocides (Cambodia), or punitive "politicides" during which a regime punished a rebel minority (the massacre of the Kurds by Saddam Hussein's regime).[96]

"Certainly, the greatest responsibility lies with the system, the very

WARNING SIGNS OF GENOCIDES AND POLITICIDES

After the Rwandan genocide in 1998, President Clinton, haunted by the inability of nations, his own in particular, to intervene in time, asked the political scientist Barbara Harff to analyze the indicators of a high risk of genocide. Harff and her colleagues studied 36 genocidal episodes among the 129 civil wars and regime collapses that occurred between 1955 and 2004. They isolated 8 factors that could have permitted 90% of these genocides to be predicted.[95] These are the eight factors:

- the existence of genocidal antecedents (since the conditions that already led to genocides may be ever-present);
- the amplitude of political upheavals (since the despotic elite are always ready to resort to any means necessary to stay in power or seize power again);
- the ethnic nature of the governing elite (if the leaders come from an ethnic minority, they react with violent repression when they feel threatened);
- the ideological nature of that governing elite (an extreme ideological system justifies its efforts in restraining, persecuting, or eliminating certain categories of people);
- the type of regime (autocratic regimes are much more inclined to engage in repression of opposition groups);
- limited openness to commercial exchanges (openness, on the contrary, indicates a readiness of the government and its leaders to maintain the primacy of law and fair economic practices);
- severe political, economic, or religious discriminations against minorities;
- the efforts of a group motivated by an ideology of exclusion in order to seize power when the central authority has collapsed (as was the case for the Serbs in Bosnia).

structure of the totalitarian state,"[97] wrote Primo Levi. Totalitarian regimes despise reason and assign no value whatsoever to human life. They despise intellectual freedom and the growth of knowledge, and have no respect for justice. Goering proclaimed in March 1933: "Here, I don't need to worry about justice; my sole mission is to destroy and exterminate, nothing else." Mao Tse-Tung didn't hesitate to say that the life of his citizens didn't matter, so long as he reached his goal:

> *Of our total population of six hundred million people, thirty million are only one out of twenty. So what is there to be afraid of?... We have so many people. We can afford to lose a few. What difference does it make?*[98]

Mao caused the death of 50 million people.

The Responsibility to Protect

Instead of maintaining the "duty to intervene,"[99] which risks antagonizing governments anxious to defend their sovereignty, the political scientists Gareth Evans and Mohamed Sahnoun prefer to speak to the responsibility that falls on governments to protect their citizens. But, they stress, if governments are not in a position to protect their citizens from large-scale massacres, famines or other calamities, or if they are not disposed to do so, such a responsibility must be assured by the "community of nations," mainly by the UN and intergovernmental and regional organizations. Such a responsibility implies three obligations: that of *preventing,* by eliminating the latent and immediate causes of internal conflicts; that of *reacting* with appropriate measures, coercive if necessary, to situations where the protection of citizens is a pressing necessity; and that of *reconstructing,* by providing assistance at every level in order to facilitate the resumption of commerce, reconstruction, and reconciliation.

31

Has War Always Existed?

Is war inevitable? For the English philosopher Thomas Hobbes: "For where there is no Commonwealth, there is, as hath been already shown, a perpetual war of every man against his neighbour; and therefore everything is his that getteth it and keepeth it by force; which is neither propriety nor community, but uncertainty."[1]

Hobbes presents man as a basically selfish being, inclined to violence and competition, ready to do anything to make his own interests triumph over others'. He was one of those who think that, left to themselves, men quickly end up killing each other.

Winston Churchill goes further: "The story of the human race is war. Except for brief periods and precarious interludes, there has never been peace in the world; and long before history began, murderous strife was universal and unending."[2] All throughout our academic education, we have been taught that the history of humanity is nothing but one long, uninterrupted series of wars.

Shaped by this intellectual heritage, the first paleontologists who studied the history of the human species systematically interpreted the marks of breaks or crushing on prehistoric human remains as signs of violent death caused by their fellows. As we will see, it turned out that, in most cases, that was only the fruit of their imagination.

In the same vein, an evolutionary psychology manual explains that human history "reveals coalitions of warring males omnipresent throughout all cultures."[3] The founder of sociobiology, Edward O.

Wilson, shares this view of humankind and its evolution: "Are human beings innately aggressive?... The answer to it is yes. Throughout history, warfare, representing only the most organized technique of aggression, has been endemic to every form of society, from hunter-gatherer bands to industrial states."[4] Such assertions are countless in the fields of anthropology, archeology and paleontology.

But over the past twenty years an increasing number of researchers has been defending very different theses. In his book *Beyond War: The Human Potential for Peace,* the anthropologist Douglas Fry has gathered together the discoveries of researchers, after re-examining a vast collection of archeological and ethnographic studies.[5] The debate about our origins, violent or peaceful, seems not to be about to die out, but as the eminent ethologist Robert Sapolsky stresses in his preface to Fry's book: "A thorough review of the evidence leads, first, to a critique of the status quo picture of war and human nature—here dubbed the 'man the warrior' perspective—and, second, to the construction of a new interpretation of human aggression. The book argues that warfare is not inevitable and that humans have a substantial capacity for dealing with conflicts nonviolently."

In fact, the majority of the history of *Homo sapiens* unfurled before the phenomenon of war appeared about ten thousand years ago.

Are We the Descendants of Killer Apes?

According to two influential anthropologists, Richard Wrangham and Dale Peterson, authors of a book with the explicit title *Demonic Males: Apes and the Origins of Human Violence,* we are "the dazed survivors of a continuous, 5-million-year habit of lethal aggression."[6] According to them, humans are the descendants of "killer apes" and inherit from their ancestors an innate predisposition to violence.

Similarly, in his bestseller *African Genesis,* the popularizer of science Robert Ardrey proclaims, "We are Cain's children. The union of the enlarging brain and the carnivorous way produced man as a genetic possibility. The tightly packed weapons of the predator form the highest, final and most immediate foundation on which we stand.... Man is a predator whose natural instinct is to kill with a weapon."[7]

These assertions rest on two hypotheses: one, that violence predominates among certain great apes; and two, that this condition was true for our common ancestor and for the first hominids.

A Relatively Peaceful Social Life

The first point rests mainly on the observation of violent behavior among chimpanzees, especially on the episode of the "chimpanzee war" in the Gombe reserve in Tanzania as described by Jane Goodall. Actually, as we have seen in a previous chapter, elimination of one group of chimpanzees by a rival band remains a relatively rare phenomenon. In everyday life, disputes are infrequent, and are generally resolved by reconciliations between protagonists who groom each other. Observations in the field carried out by Jane Goodall and other researchers in fact show that, if chimpanzees devote 25% of their time to social interactions, for a given individual, the frequency of aggressive interactions does not exceed an average of two disputes per week.[8] What's more, among chimpanzees, it is not unusual for a dominant male to intervene during an argument and hold the arguers apart from each other until they calm down.

What about other primates? After reviewing a large number of studies of over sixty species, Robert Sussman and Paul Garber concluded that the vast majority of interactions are friendly and cooperative (preening, sharing food, etc.).[9] By contrast, antagonistic interactions—mild spats, forcible ejections, threats and fighting—constitute barely 1% of social interactions. These authors conclude that, "Taken together, these data may help to explain observations that nonhuman primates live in relatively stable, cohesive social groups and solve the problems of everyday life in a generally cooperative fashion."[10] Similarly, after having observed baboons for fifteen years, Shirley Strum concludes, "aggression was not as pervasive or important an influence in evolution as had been thought, and social strategies and social reciprocity were extremely important."[11]

From Whom Do We Descend?

We are genetically quite close to chimpanzees and bonobos (our DNA is 99.5% identical with theirs), but we do not descend from either one of them. According to the data at our disposal, the evolutionary lineage of early humans separated from that of the great apes six million years ago, long before the scission between bonobos and chimpanzees. So there is no reason to think a priori that our common ancestor resembled chimpanzees more than the more peaceful bonobos. As Frans de Waal remarks:

> *Had bonobos been known earlier, reconstructions of human evolution might have emphasized sexual relations, equality between males and females, and the origin of the family, instead of war, hunting, tool technology, and other masculine fortes. Bonobo society seems ruled by the "Make Love, Not War" slogan of the 1960s rather than the myth of a bloodthirsty killer ape that has dominated textbooks for at least three decades.*[12]

VIOLENCE AMONG PREHISTORIC MAN

In 1925, a young anatomy professor, Raymond Dart, discovered the fossilized skull of a young two- or three-year-old primate in a quarry in South Africa. The skull of the "Taung child," from the name of the site, was extraordinarily well-preserved and presented a mixture of simian and human characteristics. Dart named the species *Australopithecus africanus* ("the southern monkey from Africa") and asserted it was an ancestor of the human species. His hypothesis was first rejected by the scientific community and then, as new specimens of Australopithecus came to light, the importance of his discovery was acknowledged, and australopithecines classified among our ancestors, the hominids.

But Dart also had a fertile imagination. Although he was not a specialist in the processes of fossilization, after he had discovered several Australopithecus specimens, he saw in the presence of fractured skulls and broken bones proofs that these ancestors of man were not only hunters, but also that they killed each other and practiced cannibalism.[13] The many baboon skulls and the few skulls of australopithecines that were crushed or had holes in them and that had been found on the same site signified to Dart that the individuals had been killed with clubs made from shinbones whose protuberances had produced the marks observed on the skulls. Similarly, based on the observation of regularly spaced holes on one skull, he decided it was a ritual murder. When a colleague asked Dart what percentage of the australopithecines he thought had been murdered, he replied, "Why, all of them, of course." In Dart's highly colored prose, our ancestors were "confirmed killers: carnivorous creatures that seized living quarries by violence, battered them to death, tore apart their broken bodies, dismembered them limb for limb, slaking their ravenous thirst with the hot blood of victims and greedily devouring livid writhing flesh."[14]

Dart's interpretations—which in the meantime inspired an entire literature on man's ancestral barbarism, including *The Children of Cain* we cited earlier—have not held up under the investigations carried out by his successors. Minute examination of fossil remains led specialists in physical anthropology to conclude that the breakage in bones and skulls was the result of compression applied to the specimens by rocks and soil during the millennia of their fossilization.[15]

Another paleontologist, C. K. Brain, concluded that those holes observed in skullcaps were very likely perforations produced by the teeth of an extinct species of leopard whose remains were found in the same geological layer as the australopithecines.[16] So we can agree with Douglas Fry's conclusions: "The murderous, cannibalistic killer apes that Dart so vividly portrayed in fact turned out to have been merely lunch for leopards. Dart's gruesome reconstructions were a fantasy."[17]

As for the marks found on the skull of the Taung child, it was later shown that they resembled in every detail—size and distribution, outline of the scratches, forms of the fractures, etc.—the marks still made today by modern crowned eagles on the Ivory Coast on the skulls of the young baboons on which they feed.[18]

Thus, the main discoveries that led the first researchers to assert that our prehistoric ancestors were very violent toward each other, turned out to be, one after the other, explicable more plausibly by natural phenomena or by violence inflicted by non-human predators.

Has War Always Existed?

War is defined as an aggression carried out in a group by members of one *community* against members of *another community*. In almost every case it causes the deaths of non-specific members of the enemy community. So war should be distinguished from the *personal* violence characteristic of homicides and acts of vengeance, which aim at one or several individuals in particular.[19]

War leaves identifiable traces: fortifications built around villages; weapons intended for combat (which differ from hunting weapons); representations of scenes of war in art; burial places containing a large number of skeletons with points of projectiles or other artifacts embedded in the bones or other sites of the body; as well as a reduction of the number of males buried near villages (suggesting they died elsewhere). The simultaneous presence of several of these indications and their repetition in the same region constitute a proof of warlike activities.

The examination of a number of archeological documents has led many researchers, including the anthropologist Leslie Sponsel, to note:

> *During the hunter-gatherer stage of cultural evolution, which dominated 99 percent of human existence on the planet... lack of archaeological evidence for warfare suggests that it was rare or absent for most of human prehistory.*[20]

During millions of years hominids, our ancestors, had immense spaces at their disposal. According to the survey carried out by the United States Census Bureau, ten thousand years ago, just before the development of agriculture, the population of the planet numbered between 1 million and 10 million individuals.[21] Until that time, vestiges were indeed found indicating that certain individuals were probably victims of murder, but no trace of war *between groups* has been found. According to the anthropologist Jonathan Haas: "Archaeologically, there is negligible evidence for any kind of warfare anywhere in the world before about 10,000 years ago."[22] That seems plausible if we think, along with Frans de Waal, that the first human societies lived in small scattered bands, far from each other, and had no reason to wage war. They were much more concerned with surviving and escaping the predators prevalent at the time.[23]

THE FIRST SIGNS OF WAR

The study of hunter-gatherer societies that still exist today also shows that they are comprised of small egalitarian communities, without leaders or marked hierarchy, which, because of their great mobility, could not own many goods or stockpile provisions.[24] According to the evolutionary specialist Bruce Knauft: "With emphasis on egalitarian access to resources, cooperation, and diffuse affiliative networks, contrary emphasis on intergroup rivalry and collective violence is minimal."[25] The ethnologist Christopher Boehm, well-known for his encyclopedic knowledge, and who has studied hundreds of diverse societies, summarizes the image that emerges from the data he has analyzed in this way:

> *The data do leave us with some ambiguities, but I believe that as of 40,000 years ago, with the advent of anatomically modern humans who continued to live in small groups and had not yet domesticated plants and animals, it is very likely that all human societies practiced egalitarian behavior and that most of the time they did so very successfully.*[26]

Even today, the Paliyan of South India, studied by the British ethnographer Peter Gardner, greatly value respect for the other, as well as autonomy and equality among all members of the community, men and women alike. The Paliyan avoid any form of competition and even abstain from making comparisons between people. They seek no form of prestige and have no leader. They prefer to resolve conflicts by mediation or avoidance rather than by confrontation.[27] The same is true for the Kung of the Kalahari. When a skilled hunter brings back a particularly fruitful hunt, he is welcomed cheerfully but also, so that he won't take himself too seriously, with jokes like "What a useless heap of skin and bones!" If anyone tries to impose himself as leader, he is subjected to general ostracism.[28]

Many cultures also have customs that work to prevent the emergence of a hierarchy within the group. According to Boehm, among the Hazda, "when a would-be 'chief' tried to persuade other Hazda to work for him, people openly made it clear that his efforts amused them." Among the Iban, "if a chief tries to command, no one listens."[29]

It's when some hunter-gatherers began to become sedentary around 10,000 years ago that inequalities, hierarchical stratifications, and hereditary transmissions of wealth began.[30] These sedentary populations began to cultivate the land and domesticate animals; they could thus accumulate wealth, which conferred power, attracted envy, and had to be protected. This new situation created hitherto nonexistent reasons to attack a *group* of people in order to seize their wealth, their land, or their herds. These raids were no longer directed against any particular individual, but against communities. Little by little they transformed into wars of conquest. Triumphant minorities governed. Aristocracy, clergy, and other hierarchical structures appeared, marking the end of equality within a society.

About ten thousand years ago, then, we detect the first signs of war. In the Near East, hunting and gathering gave way to an economy based on agriculture and animal husbandry. Archeological digs indicate scattered traces of war going back to about nine thousand five hundred years ago, followed by a geographical propagation and intensification of war over the centuries. Fortifications, absent till then, appear about seven thousand years ago along trade routes.[31] The first signs of massacres and mass burials of adult males were also found.[32]

The famous walls of Jericho, which are over nine thousand years old, were long thought of—wrongly—as the first known military fortifications. A closer examination of the situation led the archeologist Marilyn Roper to conclude that no sign of war could be found there. What's more, five other sites contemporary with that region are without surrounding walls.[33] The moats of Jericho were dug only on three sides, thus leaving one side open, which scarcely makes sense for a defensive structure. The archeologist Bar-Yosef suggested a plausible alternative: The Neolithic walls of Jericho seem to have been built in order to form a rampart against floods and mudslides.[34]

On the American continent, the first signs of war appear four thousand years ago in Peru and three thousand years ago in Mexico. In his study of the coastal regions of North America, the archeologist Herbert Mashchner notes that before two thousand years ago, we find only a small number of traces of trauma attributable to blows, for instance, among skeletal remains. Then about 1,500 or possibly 1,800 years ago, the signs characteristic of warlike activities become evident. Defensive structures and larger villages, built in strategic positions that facilitate their defense, are encountered. Further, a decline in population, attributable to warfare, can be seen.[35]

So it seems that the assertions of the anthropologists Wrangham and Peterson, according to which "neither in history nor around the globe today is there evidence of a truly peaceful society," are supported by no tangible proof.[36] These authors argue that the existence of war goes back millions of years, without backing up their assertions by the use of archeological data. For Fry, one of the methodological errors of these authors consists of likening violent deaths (an ambiguous term) and homicides to acts of war.[37] They speak, as the American archeologist Lawrence Keeley also does, of "prehistoric wars," for circumstances that have nothing in common with what we today call "war."[38] As Fry remarks, it's a little as if one spoke of war when an Englishwoman poisons her husband or South American bandits rob and kill travelers on a deserted road.[39]

VIOLENCE IN PRIMITIVE SOCIETIES

Anthropologists teach us that human beings have spent over 99% of their existence on the planet in nomad bands surviving on hunting and gathering. Here again, we find at work the same prejudices, well-illustrated, for example, by the evolutionary psychology manual called *The Dark Side of Man: Tracing the Origins of Male Violence,* in which Michael Ghiglieri declares, "Human recorded history, including hundreds of ethnographies of tribal cultures around the globe, reveals male coalitional warfare to be pervasive across cultures worldwide."[40] The same author concludes: "We live in a world in which cheaters, robbers, rapists, murderers, and warmongers lurk in every human landscape."

One of the anthropologists who has contributed greatly to this somber view of things is Napoleon Chagnon, author of a publication—which became instantly famous—on the Yanomami Indians of the Amazonian forest.[41] In this article and the book that followed, *Yanomamo: The Fierce People,*[42] Chagnon asserts that men who had committed murders during raids on neighboring tribes had more wives and three times more children than those who had never killed anyone. Thus, since killers have a reproductive advantage over their less violent fellows, they would more likely transmit their genes to the following generations, and should thus have been favored by evolution. Chagnon deduced from this that violence might be the main force acting behind the evolution of culture. His book sold millions of copies worldwide, contributing widely to propagating the image of violent primitive man.

But it turned out that his study erred on a number of points, especially in the selection of different age groups: the sample of killers that Chagnon had selected was on average ten years older than that of the non-killers. It is obvious that, regardless of their quality as "killers" or "non-killers," men of thirty-five will have had, on average, more children than those of twenty-five. Chagnon's study is marred with many other methodological errors that invalidate his conclusions.

The French psychologist Jacques Lecomte searched for other anthropological studies on this theme and found only two, one conducted among the Cheyenne, the other among the Waorani, in Ecuador.[43] Both are methodologically more rigorous than Chagnon's study, and lead to the opposite conclusion: men involved in murderous activity have on average fewer children than men not involved in this type of activity.[44]

The anthropologist Kenneth Good, a student of Chagnon's, expected the worst when he first traveled to the site. In the end, he spent many years among the Yanomami and even married a woman from the group. He discovered an entirely different reality:[45]

> *To my great surprise I had found among them a way of life that, while dangerous and harsh, was also filled with camaraderie, compassion, a thousand daily lessons in communal harmony.*[46] *As I passed my first year with the Yanomama, I found that little by little I was growing to like their normal way of life, the harmony and cohesion of their group.... I liked the familial mutual aid, the way people took care of children, without ever being separated from them, pampering them or constantly educating them. I liked the respect they had for each other.... Despite raids, fits of anger and fighting, in the end they are a happy people, living in a harmonious society.*[47]

Kenneth Good remains clear about the potential for violence of the Yanomami and acknowledges the existence of raids to avenge a murder or to seize women belonging to neighboring tribes but, according to him, by attributing to an entire people the behavior of a few individuals, Chagnon deformed reality as much as a sociologist who described New Yorkers as "a people of thieves and criminals" would do. In summary, among the Yanomami, violence is the deed of only a minority of individuals and, even among them, it is rare.[48]

We can wonder if the popularity of Chagnon's book might partly be due to the fact that it seems to give scientific support to beliefs about man's violent nature. How can we form a more nuanced idea of the incidence of violence in primitive cultures? In their introduction to the *Cambridge Encyclopedia of Hunters and Gatherers,* Richard Lee and Richard Daly summarize the conclusions of a number of up-to-date studies:

> *Hunter-gatherers are generally peoples who have lived until recently without the overarching discipline imposed by the state.... The evidence indicates that they have lived together surprisingly well, solving their problems among themselves largely without recourse to authority figures and without a particular propensity for violence. It was not the situation that Thomas Hobbes, the great seventeenth-century philosopher, described in a famous phrase as "the war of all against all."*[49]

Even today, the Batek and Semai of Malaysia, for example, avoid violence and systematically choose to distance themselves from their potential enemies, going so far as to take flight in order to avoid any kind of conflict. They are however far from cowardly, and show great courage in their daily lives. The anthropologist Kirk Endicott once asked a Batek why his ancestors had not used their blowpipes with poison arrows to shoot at the Malais, who were launching raids to capture Batek and reduce them to slavery. The man was shocked by the question and replied, "Because it would kill them!"[50] When disputes arise within their community or with another group, they find a way to settle them through mediation. As one Semai explained, "We're very careful not to hurt others.... We really hate being involved in conflicts. We want to live in peace and security."[51] Nonviolence is ingrained in their children starting in infancy.

There do exist dissident voices, like the anthropologist Carole

Ember, but she too commits the mistake of including under the term "war" any kind of hostile behavior, including individual murders.[52] Using more realistic criteria, other researchers have counted over seventy traditional cultures that are mainly exempt from violence.[53] That does not mean that violence and murder are absent from these cultures, but that it's a question of personal disputes and not conflicts between groups.

HURL THE SPEARS, BUT BE CAREFUL NOT TO WOUND ANYONE!

In Arnhem Land in Australia, a number of cave art sites have been discovered that are 10,000 years old, where animals, humans and mythical creatures are represented. Most scenes evoke daily life, and some of them show people hurling spears and boomerangs.

The archeologists Paul Tacon and Christopher Chippindale interpreted these latter images as scenes of war. In an article entitled "Ancient Warriors of Australia," they explain that "Some of the paintings depict fighting, warriors, aspects or the results of warfare, and even elaborate, detailed battle scenes."[54]

Yet well-documented studies have established that war was unknown among the aborigines.[55] But, above all, ethnologists have described an ancestral custom, known as *makarata,* still practiced until recently, that strongly resembles what was represented in the cave paintings. When the members of two tribes had accumulated grievances and complaints against each other—seduction of women or promises not kept—having gone beyond a certain limit of tolerance, one of the tribes would set out on an expedition and camp near the other.

The first night was spent in reciprocal visits, carried out by individuals who knew each other well and hadn't seen each other for a long time. Then, the next morning, a few dozen men from each camp would stand face to face. An elder from one of the tribes would open the hostilities by haranguing an individual from the other tribe, pouring all his detailed recriminations onto him. When he was out of breath and arguments, the accused would retort with just as much verve, for as long as he liked. Then came the turn of a second member of the first tribe to reel off his speech, to which the person targeted would reply by expressing his own grievances. It is remarkable to note that these vehement reproaches were always addressed to individuals, never to the group itself. As we have seen, we know that mass violence, massacres as well as genocides, always begin by demonizing a particular group.

After endless talk, finally, the throwing of spears began. It was always one individual that aimed at another, and it was mainly practiced by the elders. Whenever some young men threw the weapon, the elders would always remind them, "Be careful, don't wound anyone!" The exchanges of throws calculated to miss their target would continue, until, inadvertently, a person was injured. Then, everything would stop. After a last torrent of verbal dispute, in which this time all the relatives of the victim would join in, who were usually distributed among *both camps* because of marriages between groups, the meeting was over.

We can see how the possibility was theatrically provided for each of the members of the two tribes, who usually entertained good relations, to "get things off their chest" when too many grudges had been accumulated. A much more serious conflict was thus avoided. By piercing the abscess, the illness is cured and good relations resume. Far from being an act of war, these ceremonial battles served to calm tensions and to *avoid* actual conflicts. However, despite the fact that in twenty years of observations, W. Lloyd Warner never observed a single death resulting from these *makarata,* he made this ritual, which he himself defined as a "ceremonial combat to make peace," one of the "six categories of war" that he listed.[56] It is, to say the least, paradoxical to call "war" a ritual meant to make peace and which causes no deaths.[57]

NEITHER ANGELS NOR DEMONS: PUTTING VIOLENCE IN PERSPECTIVE

It was important, then, when considering the overviews of Douglas Fry and other anthropologists, to dissipate the belief in a humanity that has always been brutal, bloodthirsty and instinctively given to violence. Nevertheless, once a vision closer to reality has been re-established—namely that most primitive tribes stressed cooperation and peaceful cohabitation more than exploitation and aggressiveness—it would be just as wrong to give an idyllic vision of our ancestors. The image of Rousseau's "noble savage" is no more plausible than that of the "martial man." Individual violence was part of the existence of our ancestors and resulted in murders, themselves followed by reprisals. Although the method attempting to establish a count lends itself to controversy, it seems that the rate of violent death (including death due to non-human predators) varies from 1% or 2% to 15% in prehistoric societies and in contemporary societies of hunter-gatherers, with extremes that have naturally drawn attention, like the Waorani of the Amazon, for example, among whom up to 60% of violent deaths among men has been registered.[58]

On the other hand, today, the homicide rate in Europe is only 1 per 100,000 inhabitants (.001%) per year. Despite all the alarmist news widely spread in the media, we live in incomparably greater safety than in the past.

Though war did not exist during the first 98% of human history, it has soared, starting about 10,000 years ago, to reach catastrophic dimensions for several millennia. But over the course of the last few centuries, especially since the second half of the twentieth century, as the following chapter illustrates, the number of conflicts and their gravity have continued to diminish.[59]

32

The Decline of Violence

Every moment, acts of extreme violence are committed at one place or another on the planet, and we are informed of them almost instantaneously. Statisticians also tell us sometimes that violence is increasing in one part or another of the world. But what about the overall evolution of violence across the centuries?

To answer this question, it is indispensable, on the one hand, to envisage the evolution of violence over long periods of time and, on the other, not to take into account solely events or conflicts that strike our conscience the most, but to analyze the greatest amount of data possible.

The answer is surprising and disproves currently held ideas: individual and collective violence has continued to diminish for a millennium, especially in the last sixty years. This conclusion is the fruit of detailed, large-scale investigations carried out by several teams of researchers over the last three decades.

One of the reasons this assertion startles us stems from ignorance or forgetfulness of the level of violence that characterized past centuries. One survey, conducted by Steven Pinker, a Harvard professor and author of a scholarly, 800-page book on the decline of violence, shows that people are systematically mistaken in their evaluation of the level of violence that prevailed at different times in history. According to this survey, the English people questioned believe that the twentieth century was overall slightly more violent than the fourteenth century in terms of homicides, whereas in reality it was twenty to fifty times less so, depending on the nation in question. The same is true for almost all the other parameters taken into account to measure violence over the centuries.

The Decline of Individual Violence

In the fourteenth century, a European was on average fifty times more at risk of being victim of a homicide than today. By using the archives in English courts and municipalities, the political scientist Robert Gurr has discovered that at Oxford, in 1350, the yearly homicide rate was 110 per 100,000 inhabitants. This rate fell to 10 in the sixteenth century and to 1 today.[1] As the figure below shows, the same is true throughout all of Europe.

Homicides of non-related individuals have diminished more than family murders, while men have remained responsible for 92% of murders. At the end of the 1820s, infanticide represented 15% of homicides in Europe. Today, it represents no more than 2%, and homicides in general have diminished by half since 1820.[2]

According to the most complete World Health Organization statistics in this field, the yearly rate of homicides throughout the world fell to 8.8 per 100,000 people in 2009.[3] In all the countries of Western Europe, this rate fell to 1, whereas it remains high in countries where the forces of order and justice are corrupt or under the thumb of major

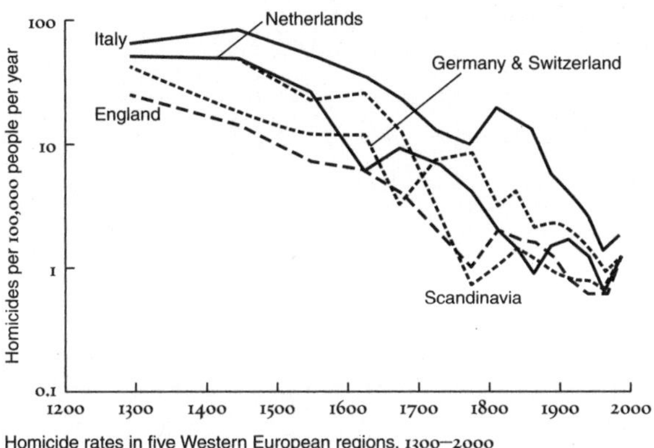

Homicide rates in five Western European regions, 1300–2000

drug traffickers (34 per 100,000 in Jamaica, 30 in Colombia and 55 in Venezuela). Other nations like Russia (30) and South Africa (69) have trouble transitioning between a totalitarian regime and a democracy.[4]

Sometimes violence increases temporarily in certain countries or cities, due to particular situations stemming typically from conflicts and political instability, but it is over the long term that we should judge the decline of violence. In the United States, for example, at the end of the 1960s violence increased, doubling in the early 1990s (while it remained stable in Canada). Then, after the introduction of new city safety policies, the rate of attacks, thefts, rapes and other crimes again fell by half.

Corporal punishment was still common when I was in public school in Île-de-France in the 1950s. Until recently, it was regarded as an effective pedagogical method, and resorting to it was encouraged both at school and at home. During the last few decades, it has sharply diminished. A Prussian teacher in the eighteenth century, obviously keen on statistics, reports in his memoirs having inflicted 154,000 whip blows and 911,527 blows with a stick on his students in his fifty-one-year career![5] Eighty-one percent of Germans still slapped their children in 1992, but in 2002 this number fell to 14%, while the percentage of those who beat them until bruises appeared fell from 31% to 4% — all following a national ban on corporal punishment. Still, corporal punishment remains frequent in certain countries in Asia and Africa.[6]

More generally, child abuse has diminished considerably in most

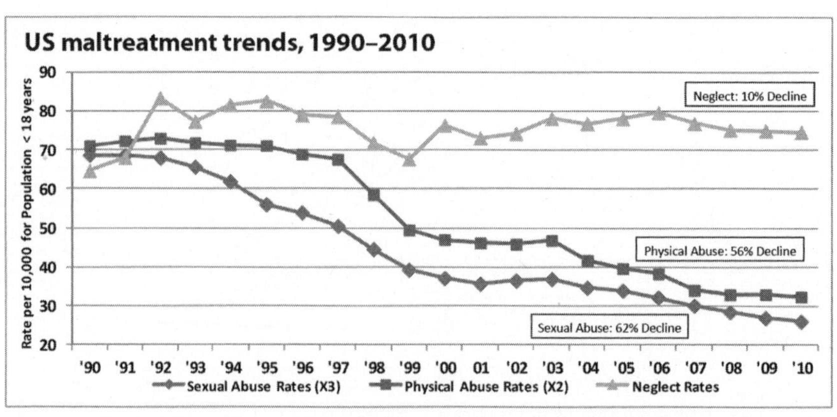

Note: Trend estimates represent total change from 1992 to 2010. Annual rates for physical abuse and sexual abuse have been multiplied by 2 and 3 respectively so that trend comparisons can be highlighted.

countries. Thus, as the graphic above shows, it went down over 50% in the United States between 1990 and 2010.[7]

Domestic violence has also diminished considerably in Western countries—in the United States, the frequency of rapes went down 85% between 1979 and 2006—although it remains a serious problem in many countries.

The Decline of Institutionalized Violence

By "institutionalized violence" we mean any form of suffering one individual inflicts on another that is regarded as "legitimate" by the dominant powers in a society, which encourage it and support it.

For several millennia, human sacrifices were frequent in many civilizations—among the Hebrews, the Greeks, the Hindus and the Celts, for example; they took extreme forms among the Khonds of India (an Indian tribal group living in the districts of Orissa and Madhya Pradesh), or in the tribes of Benin and Dahomey, who sacrificed their fellows by the thousands. The peak was attained by the Aztecs who, according to the historian Matthew Price, sacrificed up to forty people a day, which corresponds to 1.4 million individuals between 1440 and 1524.[9] In the upper castes of India, widows were sometimes burned alive on the pyre of their late husband. It is estimated that this ritual, called *sati,* cost the lives of 200,000 Indian widows from the fourteenth to the nineteenth centuries, until the British forbade the practice.

In the Middle Ages, torture was practiced openly, and didn't seem to shock anyone. Hanging, breaking on the wheel, impaling, being torn apart by horses, and torture by being burned alive were all common practice.[10] Condemned men—sometimes innocent ones—were hanged from a beam, their legs spread apart, head down, to be cut in half beginning at the crotch, all in the presence of a crowd of onlookers, including children. Those who inflicted these tortures were experts in anatomy, and strove to prolong the suffering of the victims. Torture was authorized by Pope Innocent IV (c. 1195–1254) in the framework of religious persecution, and was widely practiced by the Dominicans of the Inquisition, who put to death about 350,000 people. Pope Paul IV (1476–1559), the Grand Inquisitor, was a fervent promoter of torture, which did not prevent him from being canonized in 1712.[11]

Just 250 years ago, in France, the president of the Academy of Sciences complacently observed the torture of a man torn-and-quartered in public for having attacked Louis XV with a penknife.[12] Samuel Pepys, member of the English Parliament and author of a diary describing life in London in the seventeenth century, recounts going for a stroll in Charing Cross where a pillory was set up for public executions. That day, Pepys witnessed the hanging of Major General Harrison, whose body was then taken apart so that his head and heart could be exhibited to the public, who shouted for joy. Pepys noted that Harrison looked "as cheerful as any man could do in that condition." Pepys then went to eat oysters with some friends.[13]

In the sixteenth and seventeenth centuries, between 60,000 and 100,000 people (85% of them women) were executed for witchcraft, usually burned on a stake after having confessed under torture to the most unlikely crimes (such as having devoured babies, caused shipwrecks, or having sexual relations with the devil). The last of the "witches" to be publicly burned alive in Switzerland was Anna Göldin, in 1782, in the canton of Glarus.

During the Spanish Inquisition, auto-da-fés were announced far ahead of time so that the populace could come watch them; as during a soccer match these days, the night before the torture all the hotels in the city were full. The condemned man was brought in procession to the place of execution, with the public chanting religious songs; the sentence was proclaimed loudly and clearly, and the execution took place. Sometimes those who were to be burned at the stake were strangled first, but the crowd protested if this favor was done too often for the condemned, since they wanted to see at least some of them burned alive.[14] The historian Barbara Tuchman recounts that sometimes the inhabitants of a small French town bought a condemned man from a neighboring town, to be able to enjoy a public execution.[15]

Violence was present even in amusements, beginning with the circus games of ancient Rome. Barbara Tuchman describes two popular sports in fourteenth-century Europe:

> *Players with hands tied behind them competed to kill a cat nailed to a post by battering it to death with their heads, at the risk of cheeks ripped open or eyes scratched out by the frantic*

> *animal's claws... Or a pig enclosed in a wide pen was chased by men with clubs to the laughter of spectators as he ran squealing from the blows until beaten lifeless.*[16]

In the sixteenth century, in Paris, a stage spectacle that was much appreciated by the crowds consisted of slowly lowering into a fire cats hanging from ropes, and watching them struggle with horrible cries until they were reduced to ashes.

REJECTION OF VIOLENCE: A CULTURAL EVOLUTION

We can see how far we've come since then. Attitudes began to evolve in the seventeenth and especially the eighteenth centuries. With the philosophers of the Enlightenment, people began to talk more often of sympathy for one's fellow beings, human rights, legitimate aspirations toward happiness, and justice for all. The sufferings of others began to be regarded with more empathy.

In 1764, a twenty-six-year-old Milanese named Cesare Beccaria published a treatise, *On Crimes and Punishments,* in which he advocated abolishing torture and the death penalty. Beccaria also suggested that governments and courts should try above all to prevent crimes and to reform criminals instead of punishing them. This pamphlet was well-received in Europe, and its ideas were taken up by Voltaire, d'Alembert, and Thomas Jefferson.[17] But it was also placed on the Church's Index of Forbidden Books and ridiculed by Muyard de Vouglans, a lawyer and specialist in religious affairs, who accused its author of being soft-hearted and wanting to call practices—torture, mainly—into question that had survived the test of time.

In 1762, in Toulouse, Jean Calas was wrongly accused of having killed his son. Condemned, he was publicly subjected to breaking on the wheel. Attached by his outstretched arms and legs to a wheel, his bones were broken one by one with a sledgehammer while he proclaimed his innocence. After two hours, they ended up strangling him. It was following this case, which had a particular repercussion, that Voltaire wrote his *Treatise on Tolerance* and obtained a review of the trial and the rehabilitation of Calas. Today, in most countries, the norms have changed and lean more toward respect for life, human rights, and justice.

Slavery, which cost the lives of millions of Africans and inhabitants of the Middle East—the estimated range is anywhere between 17 and 65 million[18]—has been progressively abolished, mainly starting at the end of the eighteenth century (the first country to abolish slavery was Sweden, in 1335, and the latest, Mauritania in 1981). Even though it has been officially suppressed throughout the world, slavery remains endemic in certain countries (outright slavery in Mauritania, forced and "bonded" labor in India—10 million people—China, North Korea, Russia, Pakistan, the Gulf States, Brazil, and quite a few other countries), and takes new forms, especially through the trafficking of children and women for prostitution and forced begging. But it is today the work of Mafia-like traffickers and corrupt functionaries, and not, as had been the case for centuries, of governments and the general population.

After the Second World War, for the first time in human history, the idea of universal principles applicable everywhere and for everyone began to take shape. On December 10, 1948, the Universal Declaration of Human Rights was signed in Paris, the first article of which stipulates: "All human beings are born free and equal in dignity and rights. They are endowed with reason and conscience and should act towards one another in a spirit of brotherhood," while the third recalls that "Everyone has the right to life, liberty and security of person."[19]

In 1983, the European Convention on Human Rights forbade the death penalty, except in wartime. In 2002, protocol number 13 forbade it in all circumstances, even wartime, and has now been ratified by 45 of the 47 countries that signed the Convention.

The death penalty was abolished in 140 of the 192 member countries of the United Nations. According to Amnesty International, in 2013, only 22 of the 198 countries around the world continued capital punishment,[20] including China (several thousand executions a year), Iran (369), Iraq (169), Saudi Arabia (79), North Korea (70+), the United States (39), Somalia (34), the Sudan (21), and Yemen (14).

Most modern governments signed the International Convention against Torture adopted by the United Nations in 1984. Things are far from perfect—in Saudi Arabia, for example, they still execute people accused of witchcraft—but that shouldn't stop us from remembering that norms do continue to improve.

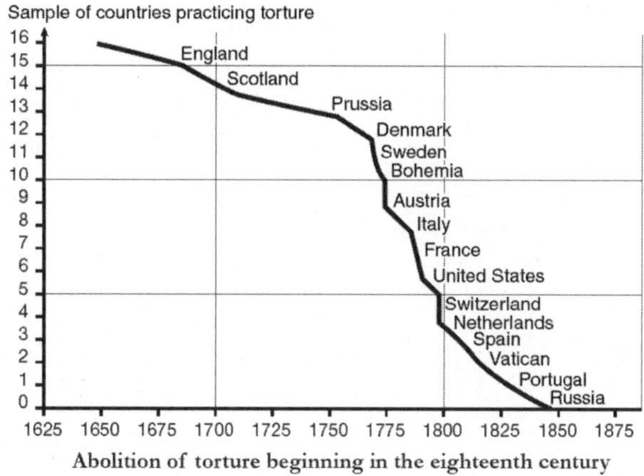

Abolition of torture beginning in the eighteenth century

According to studies carried out in the United States, acceptance of difference is progressing. The number of individuals lynched—almost always people of color—went from 150 a year in the 1880s to zero in the 1960s.[21] The number of murders directly motivated solely by racial hatred in that same country where 17,000 homicides were perpetrated every year has fallen to one per year, even though racial bias obviously continues to play a role in murder, death sentences, etc. Today, racial violence represents no more than 0.5% of all forms of aggression. According to a Gallup survey, 95% of Americans disapproved of interracial marriage in 1955. This percentage has fallen today to 20%, while the number of those who think that white and black students should attend separate schools has gone from 70% in 1942 to 3% today.

The Decline of Wars and Conflicts

From the fifteenth to the seventeenth centuries, two to three wars broke out in Europe every year.[22] The knights, counts, dukes and princes of Europe constantly attacked each other and avenged past attacks by trying to ruin their opponents, killing and mutilating peasants, burning villages, and destroying harvests.

Teams of researchers have analyzed thousands of conflicts, many of which had fallen into oblivion and been rediscovered thanks to the

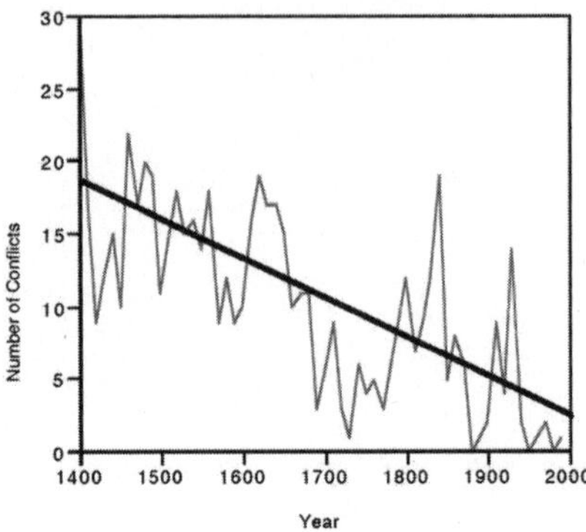

methodical consultation of historical archives in many countries. Studies carried out based on these researches allow us to spot general tendencies. The political scientist Peter Brecke, notably, analyzed 4,560 conflicts that occurred since 1400.[23] He took into account any conflict, whether between countries or within countries (civil wars, settling of accounts between clans and tribes, etc.)—which led to at least fifty deaths. In a book that includes over 1,000 bibliographical references, Steven Pinker summarizes the broad outlines of these researches: the frequency of wars between nations has regularly diminished over the centuries, as well as the average number of victims per conflict. What's more, 2% of wars (the "great wars") are responsible for 80% of the deaths. Finally, it seems that wars don't follow any regular cycle, but can break out at any time, according to particular circumstances.[24] The table above illustrates the phenomenon of the general diminution of the number of conflicts in Europe from the year 1400 to the present (the main peaks correspond to the wars of religion, the Napoleonic Wars, and to the two World Wars of the twentieth century). The number of conflicts has, however, increased in Africa.

Was the Twentieth Century the Bloodiest in History?

The Second World War was the deadliest in history, with 63 million dead, while the First World War caused 15 million. In absolute numbers, the twentieth century has indeed been the bloodiest in history. But if we take into account the direct and indirect consequences of conflicts on the population, the number of persons killed as well as the number of civilians decimated by famines and diseases, for example, and if we look at the *proportion between the number of dead and the worldwide population at the time,* it turns out that many wars caused much greater ravages than the Second World War.

What is closer to us—in time and place—concerns us more, and we tend to forget historical events that are remote. Who, aside from historians, has heard of the revolt of An Lushan, in China, in the eighth century? This civil war, though, which lasted for eight years, caused 10 million deaths, the equivalent of 325 million deaths today.[25] If we evaluate the impact of past wars by measuring the proportion of the world population that died in them, the Second World War ranks only eleventh in terms of deadliest conflicts. If the 63 million deaths between 1939 and 1945 are equivalent to 173 million compared to the world population in 2011, then the Mongolian conquests by Genghis Khan in the thirteenth century, which caused 40 million deaths, are seen to be equivalent to *770 million deaths* today. That makes them, in relative numbers, the bloodiest act of war in all history—measured by the number of victims compared to the world population.[26]

Matthew White, a scholarly librarian who devoted twenty years of his life to compiling every available source, calculated the number of deaths provoked by other atrocities in history. The conflicts under the Chinese Xin Dynasty in the first century caused 10 million deaths, or the equivalent of 368 million today; Tamerlane's invasions in the fourteenth and fifteenth centuries caused 17 million deaths (340 million today), the fall of the Ming Dynasty, in the seventeenth century, caused over 25 million (321 million today), the fall of Rome between the third and fifth centuries resulted in 8 million deaths (294 million today), the Muslim conquests of India from the eleventh to the seventeenth century 13 million (260 million today), and the conquest of the Americas, which caused the extermination of the local populations (due to massacres and especially illnesses brought by the colonizers) from the fifteenth to the nineteenth centuries caused 15 million deaths (192 million today).[27]

These calculations might seem artificial to those who think that the important thing is the number of human lives sacrificed, but the adjusted numbers are a more representative index of the level of violence and measure the impact of this violence on those populations in terms of risk and insecurity. We can see that our own experience and quality of life in society are very different if each of us has one chance out of a hundred or one chance out of ten thousand of being killed within the year. In fact, it is less dangerous to live on Earth in our era than at any other time in history since the appearance of wars ten thousand years ago.

For almost sixty years, none of the major world powers have entered into war against another. Military service has been reduced or abolished in most democratic countries, as well the size of armies, even though arms sales by wealthy countries to the rest of the world remains a major factor in violence. Under the aegis of the United Nations, national borders are now recognized as sacrosanct, and the number of wars leading to redistribution of territories has fallen sharply since 1950. Brazil, surrounded by ten other countries, has not been at war for 150 years, Sweden for 170 years, and Switzerland for 200 years. Costa Rica gave up its army in 1948. Since 1950, it is only conflicts involving an Islamic country or group that have not significantly diminished.[28] This seems to result from the aggregation of several factors that, as explained below, foster violence in a country: absence of a functional democracy and of respect for human rights, mistreatment of women, lack of education, living in isolation with minimal exchanges of ideas, services, and goods with other countries.

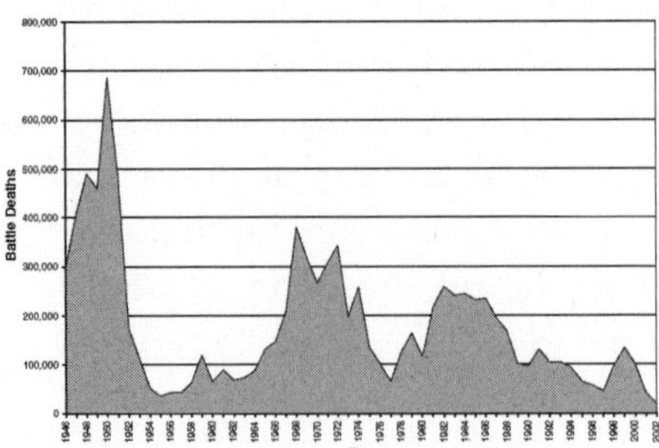

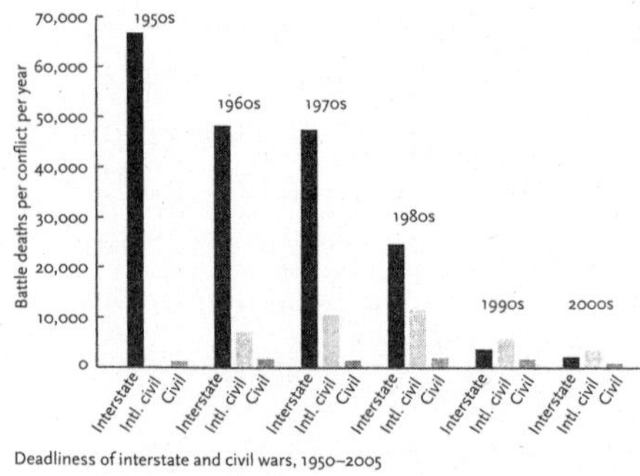

Deadliness of interstate and civil wars, 1950–2005

The average number of victims per conflict has fallen from 30,000 in 1950 to 800 in 2005.[29] This statistic goes against received ideas, since everyone remembers bloody conflicts like the Iran-Iraq War of the 1990s, which caused almost a million deaths. But they are numbers that emerge from analysis of all conflicts of every size, including both wars between nations and civil wars, conflicts between communities involving militias, mercenaries and other paramilitary organizations, as well as unilateral violence, that is, massacres of unarmed civilian populations, perpetrated by militias or governments. This tendency is illustrated by the graphs above, the work especially of Bethany Lacina and Nils Petter Gleditsch at the Peace Research Institute of Oslo, who deal with all conflicts except for genocides (which they analyze separately).

Concerning genocides, the analyses of the political scientists Rudolph Rummel and Barbara Harff, as well as researchers who compiled the database on conflicts at Uppsala University in Sweden (Uppsala Conflict Data Program, UCDP), have been summarized by Steven Pinker in the graph below. Note that the number of victims here too has been decreasing since 1950, despite tragic peaks—Bosnia with 250,000 deaths, Rwanda with 700,000 deaths, and Darfur with 373,000 deaths (evaluated in 2008).

Moreover, according to the political scientist John Mueller, most recent genocides could have been prevented by an appropriate

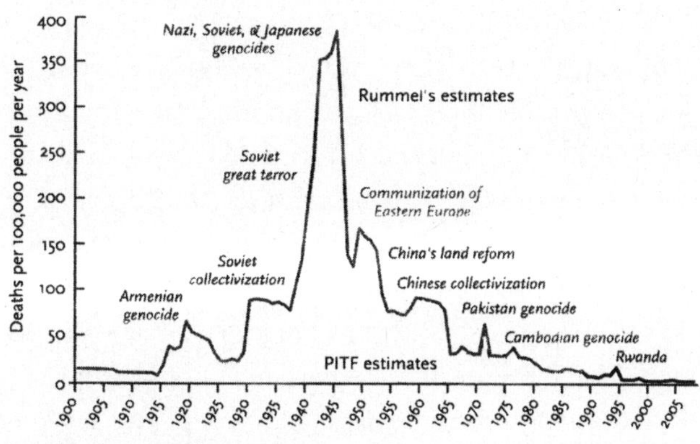

Rate of deaths in genocides, 1900–2008

intervention of peacekeeping forces. The deaths of the 700,000 Tutsis in the Rwandan genocide were, for the greater part, caused by about 10,000 men recruited by Hutu leaders from the most violent segments of the population—criminal gangs, mercenaries, alcoholics, and drug addicts[30]—and the United Nations and the world powers could easily have neutralized them.

In summary, despite the emergence of a certain number of tragic wars and massacres, the world has experienced, over the last sixty years, the most peaceful period in its history in 10,000 years. Worldwide, despite major variations depending on the region, a citizen of the world of today is much less likely to be killed or attacked than a century ago, and even less than a thousand years ago.

ACTS OF TERRORISM

Media reverberation of acts of terrorism is immense. But the numbers from the largest available database, the Global Terrorism Database, show that the number of deaths imputable to terrorism is tiny compared to that of other causes of violent death.[31] According to the observation agency that keeps this database up to date, since 9/11, terrorism has caused the death of 30 American citizens (11 on American soil), or 3 per year, whereas, during the same period, there were 18,000 homicides, 191 youngsters were killed by firearms in schools[32] and auto accidents caused 40,000 deaths. As John Mueller emphasizes, an average American has a greater risk of being killed by lightning, a peanut allergy, or wasp sting than by an act of terrorism.[33] Finally, experts have shown that fear of terrorism has caused six times as many deaths in the United States as terrorism itself. They estimate that 1,500 Americans, preferring to take their car instead of a plane for a journey from fear the flight could be hijacked or attacked, have died in road accidents. They were probably not aware that the probability of dying from a plane accident during a 4,000 kilometer flight is equivalent to the risk run by traveling 20 kilometers in a car.[34] The results of a questionnaire submitted to users of air transport testify to this distorted fear of specific rare events like terrorism: people were ready to pay fourteen dollars for a premium that covered for "any act of terrorism," but only twelve dollars for one that covered for "any reason." Yet the latter, by definition, includes the former![35]

Throughout the world, about 7,000 people are killed yearly in terrorist attacks (including in countries at war like Afghanistan). Sunni Islamist militants are responsible for two-thirds of these deaths.[36] According to a Gallup survey, 38% of Muslims questioned in numerous countries partially approve of the 9/11 attack, but only 7% approve of it completely.[37] This indicates that, as during a genocide, it is a minority of committed extremists who perpetrate the vast majority of crimes.

Factors Responsible for the Decline of Violence

Before the aforementioned global studies were undertaken to measure the decline of violence, in the 1940s, the philosopher Norbert Elias foretold this decline and attributed it to the increased interdependence of world citizens.[38] The more dependent people are on each other, the less likely they are to harm each other. Consensual life in society requires an increased control of emotions and a respect for civility. When our existence depends on a larger number of people, we tend to be less violent toward them. In brief, all the studies show that we find a lower homicide rate in urban, secular, commercial societies that are strongly connected socially.[39]

The sense of civic responsibility is also correlated to the level of violence. The American sociologist Robert Putnam has shown, for example, that the civic sense is more marked in the north of Italy than in the south, where violence is more frequent (6 to 15 homicides a year per 100,000 inhabitants in the south, compared to 1 to 2 in the north). He has also shown that the civic sense is linked to the quality of social services, especially educational services.[40]

The Existence of a Stable Government

Populations that live in an established nation-state have on average a rate of violent death that's four times lower than populations that do not enjoy the existence of a government equipped with functioning institutions.[41] Europe counted no less than 5,000 politically independent units (baronies, duchies, principalities, etc.) in the fifteenth century, 200 in the Napoleonic era, 34 in the 1960s, and 50 today.[42] As we have emphasized, the countless little political entities of the fifteenth century were constantly in conflict with each other.

As large kingdoms, then countries and finally democracies, formed, kings and then nations assumed the monopoly on violence. Any other form of violence linked to conflicts between rival clans, private militias or citizens settling accounts between themselves, became illegal and was repressed by the authorities, which now had much more powerful methods of intervention to impose and then maintain peace. In a state of law, citizens ultimately respect authority and laws if they recognize their benefits and acknowledge their fairness, which in turn leads to diminished violence.

Over the past few centuries, European nations have little by little disarmed citizens, militias and other armed bands. According to some analysts, if in the United States the number of homicides—especially in the southern states—is ten to fifteen times higher than in Europe, it's because democracy was established there before the nation disarmed the citizens, who maintained the right to bear arms. Initially, the state authorized the formation of armed citizen militias to maintain order where state forces weren't yet present. During the settling of the Far West, in which the central government played a negligible role, homicide rates reached record highs: 229 homicides per 100,000 in Fort Griffith, Texas, 1,500 in Wichita, and up to 24,000 a year (1 person out of 4!) in Benton, Wyoming. Cowboys killed each other at the slightest provocation.

This tolerance for bearing arms has persisted, although it no longer has a reason for existence, since the state is now responsible for the safety of citizens throughout the entire territory. The right to bear arms is deeply embedded in American culture. As the CNN commentator Fareed Zakaria has written, "The United States stands out from the rest of the world not because it has more nutcases—I think we can assume that those people are sprinkled throughout every society equally—but because it has more guns." America is in fact the only country in the world where there are over 90 guns per 100 inhabitants. (Serbia follows with 58 and Yemen in third place with 54. At the other end of the spectrum one finds Singapore, a pretty safe place, with

0.5 guns per 100 inhabitants.)[43] Over 310 types of firearm circulate in the civilian population, and it's just as easy to buy a semi-automatic rifle that fires up to 50 shots a second as it is to buy a coffee grinder. A reload of 600 bullets costs only 20 euros. After another massacre in December 2012 at Sandy Hook Elementary School, in Newtown, Connecticut, during which 20 children and 8 adults were killed with an automatic weapon, Larry Pratt, executive director of the Gun Owners of America, basically declared on CNN that if *everyone* carried a gun, at least people could defend themselves, and suggested that teachers be armed.[44]

Despite these tragic events, and although homicides remain considerably more numerous than in Europe, since the stabilization of the state their number has been reduced tenfold. Similarly, among the African Kungs, reputedly peaceful and described as a "harmless people" in the title of a book devoted to them, we can observe that the homicide rate, already low, was diminished threefold when the region came under the authority of the government of Botswana.[45]

The Rise of Democracy

The leaders of democratic nations who can be ousted from their posts by popular vote are less inclined to engage in absurd and harmful wars. Democracy has turned out to be the form of government most likely to favor peace both inside a country and between countries. Democracies engage less often in war than dictatorial regimes or countries in which democratic institutions are not respected.[46] Civil wars are also less frequent in democracies and, when they occur, they result in fewer victims than in autocracies. Using a "democracy score" from 0 to 10 assigned to each country and assessing a number of variables that are expected to affect the occurrence of military conflicts, political scientists Bruce Russet and John Oneal have examined all possible ways of pairing the countries of the world. It appeared that when one of the two countries paired was a full autocracy, it doubled the probability that they would enter into a conflict, compared to an average pair of countries. This probability is the lowest if both are democracies, but it is already significantly reduced when a single one of the countries is a democracy.[47] Even more, a community of democratic states, like the

European Union, is the form of global governance most likely to favor peace between its members. Two democratic countries that belong to such a community or to a federation are 83% less likely to enter into war with each other as two other nations paired by chance.[48]

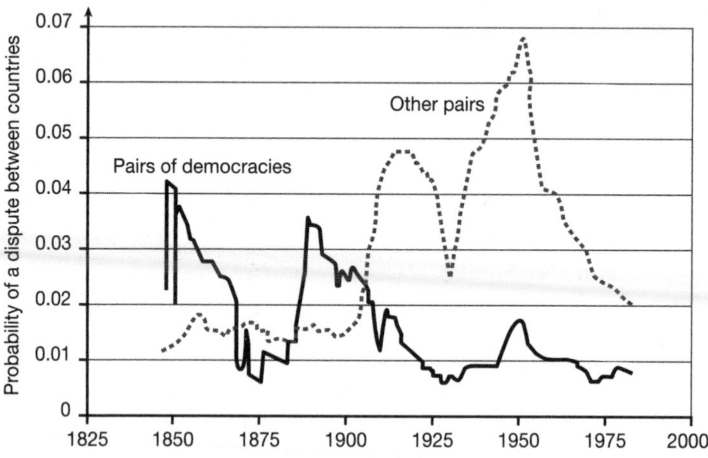

Probability of militarized disputes between pairs of democracies and other pairs of countries, 1825–1992

Over time, the continued increase in the number of democracies compared to autocracies can only strengthen peace in the world.

INTERDEPENDENCE AND COMMERCE

The economy in the Middle Ages was mainly based on the possession and exploitation of land. One of the swiftest ways to get rich was, then, to conquer one's neighbor's lands. Economic and technological revolutions in the nineteenth and twentieth centuries led to an increase in exchanges of services and merchandise. Because of this, mutual dependence of populations increased. As Steven Pinker emphasizes, "If you are trading favors and surplus with someone, your trading partner is more valuable to you alive than dead."[49] So it turns out that open countries that maintain extensive commercial relations with other countries have a reduced probability of entering into conflict with each other.

That speaks for globalization which, as we know, doesn't enjoy unanimous support among the various currents of thought about the future of the human community. On the face of it, an increase of *freely given* exchanges, in a world that is more *open* (to education, health reform, tolerance, the right not to be mistreated, etc.) takes into account the natural interdependence of all the inhabitants on the Earth and, if correctly understood and used, should lead to a greater respect for the other and to the propagation of a feeling of universal responsibility. Progress like this seems to lead to a diminution of violence and its causes.

But *openness* and *freedom* must be linked with altruistic motivation if we hope for them to result in social justice and in reducing inequalities instead of aggravating them. In the absence of altruism, open borders and general freedom risk leading to exploitation of the weakest. Some affluent nations and multinational corporations replace military and political colonialism with economic colonialism and use free exchange and the openness of customs barriers to exploit the poorest populations—their cheap labor, their lands and the resources of their country. That is notably the case with mining resources in Africa. But the increasing discrepancy between the wealthiest and the poorest is not only immoral; it is also a factor for increasing resentment and, in the end, for violence. Like democracy, globalization should be learned and be accompanied by an increased maturity of citizens and governments, inspired not by thirst for gain, but by the spirit of cooperation and concern for the other's fate.

For the effects of commerce between countries to be fully beneficial, it seems indispensable to stress the development of a truly equitable commerce. Well-thought-out regulation should, without hampering freedom, or limiting the openness of borders, permit profiteers and speculators to be controlled, and ensure that multinational enterprises don't succumb to the temptation of transforming themselves into clever systems of exploitation of the poor.

Twice during the 1990s, Luiz Inacio Lula da Silva was on the point of being elected president of Brazil. Each time, Wall Street caused the election to derail by threatening to withdraw capital invested in the country and sharply increasing interest rates—measures that would have thrown Brazil into crisis. Goldman Sachs was at the top of the list of those who tried to intimidate Brazilian voters in this way. As the economist Joseph Stiglitz remarks, "The markets are shortsighted and have a political and economic agenda that seeks the advancement of the well-being of financiers rather than that of the country as a whole."[50] In 2002, however, the Brazilians finally refused to let their choices be ruled by international financiers and elected Lula. He performed great benefit for his country, considerably reducing inequality—even though much remains to be done—while stimulating growth and education and reducing violence.

PEACE MISSIONS AND MEMBERSHIP IN INTERNATIONAL ORGANIZATIONS

According to the political scientist Virginia Fortna, the answer to the title of her book *Does Peacekeeping Work?* is a "clear and resounding yes."[51] Fortna examined data relative to 115 ceasefires in civil wars waged between 1944 and 1997. It emerged that peacekeeping missions deployed by the United Nations, NATO, the African Union, or any such adequate entity reduce by 80% the risk of a conflict reopening. Even though certain peace missions fail—as the Rwandan genocide and the ethnic cleansing in Bosnia testify—their presence considerably reduces the risk of a resumption of hostilities. One of the most important positive effects of these missions is to reassure the participants in a conflict that they no longer risk being attacked at any time by their opponent. Moreover, accepting the presence of a peace mission favors negotiations. The presence of these missions also prevents minor incidents from quickly degenerating into major confrontations. Finally, thanks to the improvement of humanitarian aid in countries at war (Doctors Without Borders, Doctors of the World, UNICEF, the International Red Cross, and other NGOs), the number of people who die of hunger and disease because of war has diminished over the last thirty years.[52]

Membership in international organizations has undeniably contributed to the decline of violence, even if the enforcing power of these institutions, especially the United Nations and the International Court of Law, and international treaties still remains limited (the Anti-personnel Mine Ban Convention for instance has yet to be signed by the United

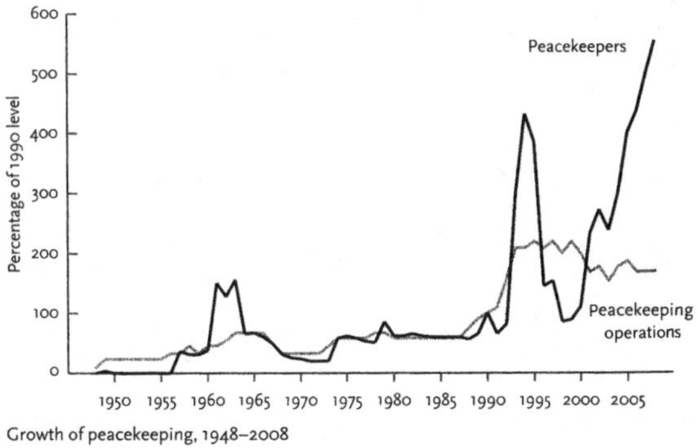

Growth of peacekeeping, 1948–2008

States, Russia and China, even though 162 other states have signed it). The European Commission, the European Parliament and the European Court of Law are institutions that permit conflicts to be resolved by legal means, hence transcending the self-interests of individual nations. It has been said that "peace is the main accomplishment of the process of European integration,"[53] and it is on those grounds that the European Union was awarded the Nobel Prize for Peace in 2012.

War No Longer Arouses Admiration

Attitudes toward war have also changed. In the past, only few voices were raised to discredit war, like Voltaire's who spoke, in *Candide,* of "millions of murderers in uniform." Wars were mostly considered to be a necessary evil with positive outcomes. In the nineteenth century, Hegel wrote: "Wars are terrible, but necessary, for they save the nation from social petrification and stagnation." Alexander de Tocqueville affirmed, "War almost always enlarges the spirit of a people and raises its character."[54]

Until the First World War, patriotic heroism was the order of the day, and pacifism was reduced to unforgivable cowardliness. Soldiers were accompanied by bands on their departure, and cannons were blessed. "At school, we sang 'Die for the Homeland!' It was the most beautiful song,"[55] recounts the French farmer Ephraïm Grenadou, veteran of the First World War. Authors at the time glorified war. A few strong voices were raised in favor of pacifism, including that of the Socialist Internationale, which strongly opposed war and was supported especially by Jean Jaurès who, on the verge of the 1914–18 war, fought till his last breath for peace, proclaiming, "The affirmation of peace is the greatest of fights." Hated by nationalists, he was assassinated in July 1914 by a nationalist, who was then acquitted in 1919.

Over the course of the twentieth century, the attitude of our contemporaries faced with war has evolved considerably. Patriotic enthusiasm belongs to a time gone by, and today, as the political scientist John Mueller stresses, war is no longer perceived as a heroic, holy, virile, or purifying enterprise, but as an immoral, repulsive, barbaric, futile, stupid operation, and a source of enormous waste.[56] Conquerors no longer arouse admiration, while the conquered are no longer regarded as humiliated populations, but as victims. Just before the second Iraq war, no one wanted to see Saddam Hussein continue his deadly dictatorship, but millions of demonstrators took to the streets around the world to proclaim, "Anything except one more war." This evolution contributes to favoring the development of a feeling of "universal responsibility" that the Dalai Lama and many other great moral figures of our time—including Gandhi, Nelson Mandela, Desmond Tutu, and Martin Luther King Jr.—have wished for.

The Rise of Respect for Human Rights, for Women, for Children, and for Animal Rights

An analysis of the content of hundreds of thousands of books of all kinds published in English has shown that the frequency of references to civic rights has doubled since 1960; references to women's rights have quintupled; and references to children's rights have increased tenfold.[57]

In Western democratic countries, violence against women is less and less accepted, and the abuse that's still rampant in many countries revolts the public opinion of societies where greater equality between the sexes reigns. In 1976, in the United States, domestic violence was ranked only ninety-first in importance on a list of 140 crimes. Most people questioned in that country thought that violence was unacceptable between individuals who didn't know each other, but tolerable between spouses.

This investigation also revealed that at that time, Americans thought that the sale of LSD was a more reprehensible crime than the rape of a woman in a park! Since then, things have changed. In 1995, another survey showed that 80% of people questioned saw domestic violence as "a social and legal problem of great importance." Remember that in the United States, rapes fell 85% between 1979 and 2006.

The fact still remains that violence against women remains a major problem in many countries around the world. A report by the World Health Organization studying 48 countries established that, depending on the country, from 10% to 50% of women have been victims of severe domestic violence—50% of them in Peru and Ethiopia compared to 10% in Japan, Brazil, and Serbia.[58] Disparities remain great. Only 1% of New Zealanders think that it is permissible to beat a wife when she disobeys her husband, against 78% of Egyptians in rural areas, and 50% of Indians in the northern districts of India. The list of atrocities committed against women is long, from genital mutilation to forced prostitution, and includes "crimes of honor" in which women were murdered by some relatives after being accused of tarnishing the "honor" of the family, even though these women were often victims of abuse by other men.[59]

Child abuse is also less and less tolerated and, as we have seen, its frequency has considerably diminished. According to surveys, in 1976, only 10% of people questioned in the United States were of the opinion that child abuse should be considered a serious problem. In 1999, this percentage went up to 90%.[60]

Attitudes toward animals, too, have changed greatly since the 1970s, mainly following publication of *Animal Liberation*, the book by the philosopher Peter Singer that launched the movement of the same name.[61] Throughout the world, the way we treat animals in many slaughterhouses is abominable; the public has begun to become aware of this incontrovertible moral problem. Under the pressure of public opinion, rules have been passed that forbid the most barbaric torture and impose some measures for improvement in the treatment of animals before and during slaughter, even though this is still a hell for animals.

In research laboratories, researchers have long had carte blanche to conduct the most improbable and useless experiments (like making hundreds of cats die of heat in order to study their resistance to high temperatures). Increasingly stricter rules have been put in place (in Europe especially), and a recent survey showed that most researchers now acknowledge that animals feel pain—a fact that, surprisingly, has long been disputed. Software for virtual dissection (V-Frog) allows people today to study the anatomy and physiology of a frog in a much more precise and instructive way than the archaic and barbaric methods of vivisection.[62] Other substitutes to experimenting on live animals are being developed, such as carrying out toxicity tests on cell cultures, using computer simulations and modeling (*in silico* testing), etc. These days, researchers who are indifferent to the fate of laboratory animals are scorned by their colleagues.

What's more, aside from regions in the world that number many vegetarians (400 to 500 million in India, or about 40% of the population), in many countries, the number of people who become vegetarian out of concern for the fate of animals is regularly increasing. At the same time, the number of hunters is diminishing, and their average age increasing.

THE DECLINE OF RELIGIOUS INTOLERANCE

A study of the inhabitants of North America indicates that in 1924, 91% of American secondary school students thought that "the Christian religion is the only true religion, and all populations should be converted to it." In 1980, this number fell to 38%, despite the power of Evangelical movements in the United States. In 1990, 62% of American Protestants and 74% of Catholics agreed with the statement, "All religions deserve respect."[63] It has been shown that greater tolerance goes hand in hand with a lessening of violence.

Religious intolerance still remains a major factor for violence throughout the world. In numerous societies, religion is manipulated for political ends and used as a rallying flag to revive sectarian, tribal, or nationalist passions, and to increase hatred. Intolerance is also a characteristic of practitioners so profoundly convinced of the truth of their beliefs that they think anything is permitted for the sake of imposing them on others. Inability to respect the religious and intellectual traditions of others, including, of course, those of non-believers, leads people to ignore the diversity of human beings and their legitimate aspirations. As the Dalai Lama often says, "The deep conviction people have when they follow their own path should be coupled with absolute respect for the path of others."

THE MARGINALIZATION OF VIOLENCE

According to the lawyer Donald Black, in developed countries, most crimes are committed by members of the poorest sectors of the population, who derive little security from the government that is supposed to protect them. They mistrust the authorities, scorn them and are scorned by them in return. According to the criminologist Mark Cooney, they are stateless people within the state; they function outside of the state system, often thanks to illegal activities. Without recourse to the justice system and unable to call the police for help, they institute a parallel system of justice that is particular to them, and usually settle their differences by resorting to violence.[64] Most homicides thus stem from capital punishment applied by private individuals. According to Steven Pinker, the process of the "civilization of customs" has considerably reduced violence in our societies, but it has not eliminated it: it has relegated it to people on the outer fringes of society and the economy.[65]

EDUCATION AND READING, CATALYSTS FOR EMPATHY

At the end of the eighteenth century, over half of French citizens knew how to read and write. In England, the number of books published by decade went from a few hundred in the fifteenth century to 80,000 in the early nineteenth century.[66] It seems that, to a certain extent, when people began to read stories and novels that advocated tolerance and portrayed the suffering linked to violence, people became more used to putting themselves in the place of others, envisaging their point of view, and imagining their feelings, which favored the development of empathy and the decline of violence. *Uncle Tom's Cabin*, for example, in which the novelist Harriet Beecher Stowe movingly describes a slave's condition, was the highest-selling novel in the nineteenth century, and had a major impact on the emergence and success of the abolitionist cause.[67]

THE INCREASED INFLUENCE OF WOMEN

Despite progress still to be made, Western countries are evolving more toward respect and increased acknowledgment of the role of women in society. With a few rare exceptions, war is planned, decided upon, and perpetrated by men, and 99.9% of soldiers who take part in combat are also men (even in countries like Israel, which recruit a large number of women, women are rarely on the front lines). Men are also the most intransigent during negotiations. Swanee Hunt, former American ambassador and activist against exploitation of women throughout the world, told me that one day she met a group of African officials engaged in peace negotiations that seemed stymied by two parties. Having noted that both delegations were made up exclusively of men, Hunt asked, "Why aren't there any women in your group?" They replied: "Because they'd make concessions." Swanee Hunt remembers thinking at that point: "Bingo! That's why this negotiation, like so many others, isn't successful!"[68] In fact, how can a solution acceptable to the various participants be found at all without making mutual concessions?

A collection of ethnographic studies shows that every society that treats women better is less prone to war. In the Middle East especially, a survey revealed that individuals who were most in favor of equality between men and women were also the most in favor of a nonviolent resolution to the Israeli-Arab conflict.[69] Steven Pinker concludes:

> *Biology and history suggest that all else being equal, a world in which women have more influence will be a world with fewer wars.*[70]

Tsutomu Yamaguchi, a survivor of the two nuclear attacks on Hiroshima and Nagasaki (whither he fled after the explosion in Hiroshima, thinking to find refuge there) gave this ultimate piece of advice before dying at the age of ninety-three: "The only people who should be allowed to govern countries with nuclear weapons are mothers, those who are still breast-feeding their babies."[71] Women and children are the first victims in wars, and the more their voices can be heard in society, the lower the risk will be for conflict. It is not a question of simply giving more power to women, but of moving away from cultural models that celebrate virile strength, glorify war, and justify violence as a quick and effective way to resolve problems.[72] In *Sex and War*, the biologist Malcolm Potts and his co-authors think that giving women complete control over their reproduction (by allowing free access to contraception and the choice of their spouse) is a crucial factor in fighting violence.[73] Refusing to treat women as mere reproductive vessels is the best way to prevent an excessive portion of the population being made up of young men who often find themselves jobless and marginalized. In fact, it has been demonstrated that, in societies that grant more autonomy to women, there are fewer gangs of rootless young men who become troublemakers.[74]

Desmond Tutu, the Gandhi activist Ela Bhatt, the former US president Jimmy Carter, and other members of the Global Elders have launched a movement called "Girls, Not Brides."[75] Archbishop Desmond Tutu especially militates passionately against girls being married in childhood or puberty, a phenomenon that's still widespread in Africa and Asia (every day, 25,000 girls are married too young and without their consent). A teenaged girl under fifteen is five times more likely to die in labor than a young woman in her twenties. This scourge could prevent the realization of six of the eight Objectives for the Millennium for Development pursued by the United Nations: reducing poverty and hunger, ensuring basic education for all, promoting the equality of the sexes and the autonomy of women, reducing infant mortality, improving maternal health, and fighting AIDS, malaria and other diseases. Only two objectives, the preservation of the environment and the establishment of a global partnership for development, are not directly linked to the problem of early marriages of girls. Compulsory education of girls could contribute to thwarting this practice.

It's Better to Restore Peace and Cure Wounds than to Avenge Affronts

Most peace processes have been crowned with success when one of the parties has, of its own free will, taken an innovative, risky, and irrevocable step. This kind of initiative reassures the opponent and produces confidence in the fact that the other has no intention of resuming hostilities. Concerning civilian conflicts, it turns out that it is better to calm resentments and facilitate reconciliation than to insist that "justice be done" at all costs. I recently heard the testimony of women from Liberia stating they'd rather restore peace in the community than revive hatred by pursuing all those who had committed atrocities. This wish to turn the page while being satisfied with incomplete justice and granting general amnesty (except for a few military leaders) perplexed the representatives of the International Court of Law, who were divided between their engagement in not letting these crimes against humanity go unpunished and the opinion of concerned citizens, for whom reconciliation was more important than punitive justice.

One of the best examples of this attitude is that of the Commission for Truth and Reconciliation created in 1995 by Nelson Mandela and presided over by Archbishop Desmond Tutu, both winners of the Nobel Peace Prize. This commission was charged with taking note of violations of human rights and crimes committed, during the last fifteen years of apartheid, by the South African government and by liberation movements, in order to allow for national reconciliation between victims and perpetrators of violent acts.

An important point in this process consisted of encouraging public confession of crimes committed, often linked to a request for forgiveness, in the presence of the victims, and offering amnesty in exchange. It was important in the eyes of all to reveal the truth and acknowledge all crimes committed without dissimulation, so as not to leave anything in the shadows that could perpetuate resentments, and then deciding by common accord to renounce the application of the law of an eye for an eye. "To forgive, not to forget" was the motto of this healing undertaking.[76]

THE CHALLENGES STILL TO BE OVERCOME

There is still a lot to do, and immense financial resources are still wasted in waging wars. Two billion dollars a day get devoted worldwide to military expenses—but these colossal sums could be used to meet all kinds of urgent needs of humanity and of the planet. To give only a recent example, the cost of the war in Iraq has risen to three trillion dollars, and the cost of the Afghanistan war, since its beginning in 2001 until its end in 2011, amounted to 557 billion dollars.[77]

Today, 95% of weapons that feed conflicts throughout the world are made and sold by the five permanent members of the Security Council of the United Nations. As the Dalai Lama declared during a visit to France, "A country that sells weapons sells its soul."

But a reduction of weapons would not be enough in and of itself. Weapons are only the tools of war, and historical studies show that an increase of the destructive power of weapons does not necessarily lead to an increase of the number of victims in conflicts. The absolute weapon, the atomic bomb, has fortunately not been used since Hiroshima and Nagasaki. So it is the factors that lead to war that should as a matter of urgency be addressed.

A lack of natural resources does not lead people into war. Senegal and Malawi, two countries with few resources other than agricultural, ranked "high" (respectively 72 and 77 in the world) in the Global Peace Index (GPI) 2014 report, higher than the United States, which ranks 101 ("medium")[78]. In fact, many countries in Africa have major mining resources that can turn out to be a curse since they are often ravaged by armed conflict over control of these resources, as is the case with the Democratic Republic of Congo (which ranks 155, among the last ten countries with "low" level of peace).[79] As we have seen, recurrent causes of conflicts are linked more to the absence of a stable democratic government, to corruption, to repression, and to intolerant ideologies.

The poverty of citizens, especially when it quickly worsens, represents a major cause for instability and violence. Deprivation of food, degradation of health services, education, and security services are frequent causes of conflicts. Half of the wars occur today in countries where the billion poorest people live (this was not always the case, since in the past wealthy countries were often busy with conquest of colonies or fought among themselves). The countries whose GNP was $250 per inhabitant in 2003 have, on average, entered five times more often into war (15% compared to 3%) in the last five years than the countries whose average GNP was $1,500. Neglecting poverty in the world maintains a major source of insecurity and violence.[80]

If poverty can lead to war, war leads in turn to poverty by resulting in the devastation of infrastructures (roads, factories, and so forth) and agricultural resources, the dispersion of qualified people, and institutional chaos. As for dictators, they pay scant attention to reason or human lives. So a stable, democratic government is indispensable for emerging from both poverty and war. Transitions are always long and difficult, as the present state of countries of the former Soviet bloc attests, since establishing democracy demands time, and requires a profound transformation of cultures.

As for religions, they should make special efforts in favor of peace. Historically, they have rarely been instruments for that peace that their ideals advocate. They have often become ferments of division and not of union. It is all the more important that religious leaders meet and learn to know each other better, as the Dalai Lama constantly recommends, so that they can act together toward peace when unrest and dissension appear.

In summary, wars bring more suffering to victims of an attack than they do well-being to the aggressors. But as long as the aggressor draws advantages from war, limited as they may be, it will be hard to prevent wars from occurring. Those who resort to violence should therefore be punished, so that they no longer benefit from it.

The Age of Reason

As more and more children have access to education and develop their intelligence and knowledge, the citizens of the world become aware of the necessity for living in peace. It has been observed that the faculty of reasoning, degree of intelligence, and level of emotional equilibrium of ten-year-old children were signs of their subsequent acceptance of democratic, pacifist, anti-racist, and egalitarian points of view.[81]

In conclusion to his 800-page book on the decline of violence, Steven Pinker counts on reason to reduce violence. He thinks reason alone can let us extend the reach of empathy and moral sense beyond the circle of our relatives and members of our "group"—nation, religion, ethnic group or any other particularism apt to undermine the perception of our common humanity.[82]

33

The Instrumentalization of Animals: A Moral Aberration

The notion of altruism is severely tested by the way we treat animals. When a society accepts as a given the outright use of other sentient beings for its own ends, and grants almost no consideration to the fate of those it instrumentalizes, then we can only speak of institutionalized selfishness.

The massive exploitation of animals is accompanied by a degree of additional devaluation: they are reduced to the state of products for consumption, meat-making machines, living playthings whose suffering amuses or fascinates the crowds. We knowingly ignore their nature as sentient beings and rank them among objects.

This ruthless point of view was expressed by Émile Baudement, holder of the first chair of animal husbandry at the Agronomical Institute at Versailles in the mid-nineteenth century:

> *Animals are living machines, not in the accepted sense of the word, but in its most rigorous sense as used in mechanics and industry.... They give milk, meat, strength: they are machines producing a return for a given expense.*[1]

In the same line of thinking, a century later, the commentator in a televised report devoted to the establishment of industrial breeding in France announced with a certain pride in his voice: "Every action of their biological lives should correspond to our needs and our schedule....The bovine becomes what we had hoped: an industrial product."[2] Even more cynical, a manager of the American company Wall's Meat recently declared:

> *The breeding sow should be thought of, and treated as, a valuable piece of machinery whose function is to pump out baby pigs like a sausage machine.*[3]

The vision of the system is summarized by the president of an American poultry company with 225,000 laying hens, Fred C. Haley: "The object of producing eggs is to make money. When we forget this objective, we have forgotten what it is all about."[4]

Is it conceivable to desire the advent of a more altruistic society while closing our eyes to the fate we inflict on the billions of animals killed every year for our consumption?

In the system of industrial production, the lifespan of animals is only a fraction of their natural expectancy, 1/60th for poultry. It is as if a human's life expectancy were only a year and four months.[5] Animals are confined to cubicles where they can't even turn around; castrated; separated at birth from their mothers; made to suffer for our amusement (bull fights, dogfights, cockfights); caught in traps that crush their limbs in steel jaws; skinned alive,[6] crushed alive in giant screws (the fate reserved for hundreds of millions of male chicks every year).

In short, we decide when, where and how they are to die, without the slightest concern for what they feel.

The Extent of the Suffering We Inflict on Animals

Humans have always exploited animals, first by hunting them, then by domesticating them. But it wasn't until the beginning of the twentieth century that this exploitation took on an amplitude hitherto unequaled. At the same time, violence against animals disappeared from our daily lives, for it began to be deliberately practiced far from our gaze. Advertisements and children's books show us images of cows frolicking in flowering fields, but the reality is quite otherwise. In wealthy parts of the world—North America, Europe and increasingly elsewhere around the globe, especially China—99% of the animals we eat are "produced" in industrial breeding grounds where their brief lives are nothing but a succession of sufferings. All that is made possible the instant we think of other sentient beings as objects for consumption, reserves of meat, "agricultural products" or "movable property"[7] that we can treat however we please.

In the early twentieth century, the first major American slaughterhouses were, according to the testimony of James Barrett, "dominated by the sight, sound and smell of death on a monumental scale."[8] The sounds emanating from the killing machines and the slaughtered animals constantly assailed the ears.

In *The Jungle*,[9] a book that provoked a veritable outcry in 1906, Upton Sinclair described the situation in the Chicago slaughterhouses, where animals were killed en masse by poor workers, usually immigrants exploited by the big corporations of the time:

> *They brought about ten thousand head of cattle every day, and as many hogs, and half as many sheep—which meant some eight or ten million live creatures turned into food every year. One stood and watched, and little by little caught the drift of the tide, as it set in the direction of the packing houses. There were groups of cattle being driven to the chutes, which were roadways about fifteen feet wide, raised high above the pens. In these chutes the stream of animals was continuous; it was quite uncanny to watch them, pressing on to their fate, all unsuspicious a very river of death. Our friends were not poetical, and the sight suggested to them no metaphors of human destiny; they thought only of the wonderful efficiency of it all. The chutes into which the hogs went climbed high up—to the very top of the distant buildings; and Jokubas explained that the hogs went up by the power of their own legs, and then their weight carried them back through all the processes necessary to make them into pork. "They don't waste anything here," said the guide, and then he laughed and added a witticism, which he was pleased that his unsophisticated friends should take to be his own: "They use everything about the hog except the squeal."*[10]

Sinclair continues:

At the head there was a great iron wheel, about twenty feet in circumference, with rings here and there along its edge. Upon both sides of this wheel there was a narrow space, into which came the hogs at the end of their journey; in the midst of them stood a great burly Negro, bare-armed and bare-chested. He was resting for the moment, for the wheel had stopped while men were cleaning up. In a minute or two, however, it began slowly to revolve, and then the men upon each side of it sprang to work. They had chains which they fastened about the leg of the nearest hog, and the other end of the chain they hooked into one of the rings upon the wheel. So, as the wheel turned, a hog was suddenly jerked off his feet and borne aloft.... The shriek was followed by another, louder and yet more agonizing—for once started upon that journey, the hog never came back; at the top of the wheel he was shunted off upon a trolley, and went sailing down the room. And meantime another was swung up, and then another, and another, until there was a double line of them, each dangling by a foot and kicking in frenzy—and squealing. The uproar was appalling, perilous to the eardrums.... There would come a momentary lull, and then a fresh outburst, louder than ever, surging up to a deafening climax. It was too much for some of the visitors—the men would look at each other, laughing nervously, and the women would stand with hands clenched, and the blood rushing to their faces, and the tears starting in their eyes. Meantime, heedless of all these things, the men upon the floor were going about their work. Neither squeals of hogs nor tears of visitors made any difference to them; one by one they hooked up the hogs, and one by one with a swift stroke they slit their throats. There was a long line of hogs, with squeals and lifeblood ebbing away together; until at last each started again, and vanished with a splash into a huge vat of boiling water.... This slaughtering machine ran on, visitors or no visitors. It was like some horrible crime committed in a dungeon, all unseen and unheeded, buried out of sight and of memory.[11]

Profit Above Everything

These days, in the United States alone, more animals are killed *in a single day* than in a year across all the slaughterhouses in Sinclair's time. According to David Cantor, founder of a study group dedicated to responsible policies for animals, it's a "cruel, fast, tightly run, profit-driven system of torture and murder in which animals are hardly thought of as living beings and are presumed not to matter in terms of their suffering and deaths."[12]

In the last decades of the twentieth century, the drive for "efficiency" and profit on an ever bigger scale brought about major changes in the meat industry. Slaughterhouses became less numerous, but much larger, capable of slaughtering *several million* animals a year each. In the countries of the European Union, new rules aim to reduce suffering somewhat in industrial breeding houses. Although welcome, these are but tiny improvements in the face of the constant suffering of the animals. In the United States, recent testimony, including that by the writer Jonathan Safran Foer,[13] shows that the only thing that's really changed is that we now kill more animals, more quickly, more efficiently, and less expensively.

Industrial animal production systems almost everywhere escape the laws protecting animals from abuse: "The Common Farming Exemptions make any breeding method legal so long as it's current practice in the sector," Foer notes. In other words, "commercial companies have the power to define what cruelty is. If the industry adopts a practice, that of amputating an undesired limb without analgesic, for example—you can give free rein to your imagination on this—this operation automatically becomes legal."[14]

Since it would cost money to take care of or even euthanize animals that are weak or in poor health who fall down and are unable to get up again to follow the others on the "staircase to Heaven" (the name given to the ramp leading to the slaughterhouse), in the majority of American states, it is legal to let these weak animals die of hunger and thirst for days, or to throw them, still living, into garbage trucks. That occurs every day.

Workers are constantly kept under pressure so that the chain of slaughter continues to go full-speed ahead: "They don't slow that line down for nothing or nobody," confided an employee to Gail Eisnitz, investigator for the Humane Farming Association:

> *As long as that chain is running, they don't give a shit what you have to do to get that hog on the line. You got to get a hog on each hook or you got a foreman on your ass.... All the drivers use pipes to kill hogs that can't go through the chutes. Or if you get a hog that refuses to go into the chutes and is stopping production, you beat him to death. Then push him off to the side and hang him up later.*[15]

Economic competition makes it so that each slaughterhouse tries to kill more animals per hour than its competitors. The speed of the conveyer belts in slaughterhouses allows 1,100 animals to be dealt with per hour, which means that a worker has to kill an animal every few seconds. Accidents are common.

In England, Dr. Alan Long, who goes to slaughterhouses regularly as a researcher, noticed a certain reserve among workers about killing young animals. They told him that the hardest thing in the work was to kill lambs and calves, because "they're just babies." It's a poignant moment, says Dr. Long, "when a bewildered little calf, just torn from its mother, sucks the slaughterman's fingers in the hope of drawing milk and gets the milk of human unkindness." He calls what goes on in slaughterhouses "a relentless, merciless, remorseless business."[16]

THE HYPOCRISY OF "CARE"

If professionals sometimes advise breeders to avoid some cruel practice or other, it's because of its negative repercussions on the fattening of animals; if they are urged to treat the animals led to slaughter less harshly, it's mostly because wounds cause the carcass to lose value: they seldom think the animals shouldn't be mistreated because it's immoral in and of itself.[17]

As for veterinarians employed by the industry, their role is not to watch over the health of the animals for their own sake, but to contribute to the maximization of profit. Breeders' main purpose is to prevent animals from dying too early, before they've turned a profit.[18] Hence, animals are filled with antibiotics and growth hormones. Eighty percent of the antibiotics produced in the United States are used by the animal industry. As the philosopher Élisabeth de Fontenay notes:

> *The worst is hidden in the formidable hypocrisy that consists of advocating and putting into play a so-called ethics of well-being, as if it were a constraint imposed out of respect for the animal on the demands of the industrial breeding industry, whereas it necessarily profits from the smooth functioning and profitability of the enterprise.*[19]

Once they've used the animals, they destroy whatever's left over as cumbersome objects and throw them out like trash.

A Hidden Reality

In the 1990s, the painter Sue Coe deployed considerable ingenuity in getting into the slaughterhouses of various countries. She constantly had to face marked hostility, ranging from vituperation like "You have no right to be here!" to death threats if she published the name of the slaughterhouse visited. She was never authorized to use her camera; only her sketches were, at best, tolerated: "Slaughterhouses, especially the larger ones, are guarded like military compounds, and it is almost impossible to gain access. I usually got in by knowing someone, who knew someone else, who had a business relationship with the plant or slaughterhouse." In her book *Dead Meat*, she describes her visit to a slaughterhouse in Pennsylvania:

> *The floor is extremely slick... The walls, floors, everything, everywhere are covered with blood. The chains are caked with dried blood... I definitely do not want to fall in all the blood and intestines... The workers are wearing nonslip boots, yellow aprons, and hard hats. It is a scene of controlled, mechanized chaos.* [20]

Like most slaughterhouses, "This place is dirty—filthy in fact—flies swarm everywhere." According to another testimony, the cold storage rooms are full of rats and, at night, they run over the meat and gnaw it.[21]

At lunch time, the workers disperse. Sue stayed alone with six decapitated bodies that gushed blood. The walls were splattered and there were drops of blood on her sketchbook. She sensed something moving to her right and went over to the knocking pen to investigate. Inside, there was a cow. She wasn't stunned; she slipped in the blood and fell. The men went to lunch and left her there. Time passed. From time to time she struggled, kicking the walls of the steel enclosure with her hooves. At one point she lifted her head enough to look out and fell back. Sue could hear the blood dripping, and music coming from a loudspeaker.

Sue began to draw...

One man, Danny, returned from his lunch. He gave the wounded cow three or four violent kicks to make her get up, but she couldn't. He leaned over the metal stall and tried to stun her with his compression stunner, which shot a 5-inch bolt into her brain.

Danny attached a chain to one of the cow's rear legs and lifted her. But the cow was not dead. She struggled, her feet kicking as she was raised, head down. Sue noted that some cows were completely stunned but not all. "They struggle like crazy while Danny is cutting their throats." Danny speaks to the ones still conscious: "Come on girl, take it easy." Sue watches the blood gush out "as though all living beings are soft containers, waiting to be pierced."

Sue then visited a horse slaughterhouse in Texas:

> *The horses await slaughter. They are in terrible shape, with crippled legs and hair matted with blood. A horse, with a broken jaw hanging down, obviously can't eat. There is a lot of whipping. The sound is crack-crack, and as the whip hits, there is a smell of burning. We heard the sound of horses being whipped a long way from the slaughter-house. It sounds like gunshots. The horses try to stampede away from the kill floor, and two men beat them in the face until they turn back.... My companion sees a white mare giving birth to a foal in front of the restraining pen. Two workers use a six-foot whip on the horse as she gives birth, to get her to speed up and go onto the*

kill floor. The foal is thrown into the spare parts bucket. The boss in his cowboy hat observes from the overhead walkway.[22]

As she leaves another slaughterhouse that reminded her of Dante's inferno, Sue sees a cow with a broken back lying in the hot sun. She walks toward her, but security guards block her way and escort her off the premises: "The Holocaust keeps coming into my mind...."[23] writes Coe.

A Global Enterprise

The fate of other animals raised for consumption is scarcely any better. In America, every year 150 times more chickens are killed now than eighty years ago, thanks to the development of mass breeding factories. Tyson Foods, the largest chicken-rearing company in the world, slaughters over 10 million *each week*. Fifty billion chickens are killed every year throughout the world.

During its brief lifetime, each chicken is allotted the space of a piece of paper. The air it breathes is laden with ammonia, dust and bacteria.[24] Overcrowding is the cause for many different kinds of abnormal behavior—plucking out its own feathers, aggressive pecking and cannibalism. "The battery becomes a gallinaceous madhouse," remarks the Texan naturalist Roy Bedichek.[25] Artificially accelerated growth of chickens can be likened to that of a child who reaches 330 pounds at the age of ten.

In order to reduce behavior that costs them money, breeders keep chickens in semi-darkness, which reduces their tendency to fight each other because of the narrow space in which they are kept. To prevent them from wounding or killing each other, they clip off their beaks. In the 1940s, their beaks were burned off with a blowtorch. Today, breeders use a guillotine armed with heating blades. The stumps that result from this hasty amputation often form painful neuromas.[26]

At an American farm where 2 million laying hens were packed together into hangars that each held 90,000 of them, a manager explained to journalists from *National Geographic:* "When production drops to the uneconomic point, all 90,000 birds are sold to processors for potpies or chicken soup. It doesn't pay to keep track of every row in the house, let alone individual hens; with 2 million birds on hand you have to rely on statistical samplings."[27] And then they start again from square one.

Transportation is also a source of long periods of suffering. In the United States, it is estimated that 10% to 15% of chickens die during the journey. Among those who arrive at the slaughterhouses, one third have recent fractures due to the way they were manipulated and transported en masse.

Slaughterhouses are supposed to stun the chickens in an electrified bath. But to save money they usually use a voltage that's too weak (1/10th the dose required to stun). Consequently, many chickens—at least 4 million a year in America, according to a government estimate—arrive still conscious at the scalding tank.[28]

Male chicks of laying hens are destroyed—250 million in the United States every year. "'*Destroyed?*' notes Foer. "That seems like a word worth knowing more about. Most male layers are destroyed by being sucked through a series of pipes onto an electrified plate.... Others are sent fully conscious through macerators (picture a wood chipper filled with chicks). Cruel? Depends on your definition of cruelty."[29]

As for pigs, in order to prevent them from biting each other's tails, the tails are cut off with an instrument that crushes the stump at the same time in order to reduce bleeding. Sows are confined in steel stalls barely larger than their bodies where they are attached for two or three months by a leash that prevents them from turning around or taking more than one step forwards or backwards. When the sow is ready to be slaughtered, she is placed in a mechanism called a "steel virgin," a metal box that prevents all freedom of movement. Males are castrated without anesthesia. The skin of their testicles is cut open with a knife, their testicles stripped bare, and they are pulled on until the cord holding them up is broken.[30]

According to Foer, "Piglets that don't grow fast enough—the runts—are a drain on resources and so have no place on the farm. Picked up by their hind legs, they are swung and then bashed headfirst onto the concrete floor. This common practice is called 'thumping.' 'We've thumped as many as 120 in one day,' said a worker from a Missouri farm."[31]

Calves suffer from being separated from their mothers and are locked in stalls that prevent them from adopting their natural sleeping position, head tucked under. The stalls are also too narrow to allow the calf to turn around or lick itself. Food for calves is deliberately low in iron, since consumers like "pale" meat whose color is due to the fact that the animals were rendered anemic.[32] Therefore, the calves lick any iron piece present in their stall. That's why the stalls are made of wood in order to keep any iron piece out of their reach.[33]

Every Day, All Year Long...

Jonathan Safran Foer gives us a harrowing description of the complete slaughtering procedure. We should not forget that this is happening today, every day, all year long, in almost all the slaughterhouses in so-called civilized countries:

> *At a typical slaughter facility, cattle are led through a chute into a knocking box.... The stun operator, or "knocker," presses a large pneumatic gun between the cow's eyes. A steel bolt shoots into the cow's skull and then retracts back into the gun, usually rendering the animal unconscious or causing death. Sometimes the bolt only dazes the animal, which either remains conscious or later wakes up as it is being "processed."... The effectiveness of knocking is also reduced because some plant managers believe that animals can become "too dead" and therefore, because their hearts are not pumping, bleed out too slowly or insufficiently.... As a result, some plants deliberately choose less-effective knocking methods. The side effect is that a higher percentage of animals require multiple knocks, remain conscious, or wake up in processing.... Let's say what we mean: animals are bled, skinned, and dismembered while conscious. It happens all the time, and the industry and the government know it. Several plants cited for bleeding or skinning or dismembering live animals have defended their actions as common in the industry and asked, perhaps rightly, why they were being singled out.*[34]

When Temple Grandin, professor of animal science at the University of Colorado, carried out an audit of the entire profession in 1996, she concluded that one bovine slaughterhouse out of four is unable to render the animals unconscious at the first try in a reliable way. The speed of the assembly line has increased by almost 800% in a century and the staff, often hastily trained, work in nightmarish conditions: mistakes are inevitable.

Thus, it is common for animals not to be stunned at all. In one slaughterhouse, outraged employees secretly filmed a video that they sent to the *Washington Post*. Over twenty workers signed declarations under oath asserting that the violations denounced in the film are frequent and that the managers are perfectly aware of them. One of the workers testifies: "I've seen thousands and thousands of cows go through the slaughter process alive. The cows can get seven minutes down the line and still be alive. I've been in the side puller where they're still alive. All the hide is stripped out down the neck there." And when workers who complain are listened to at all, they often get fired.[35]

After the head-skinner, the carcass (or cow) proceeds to the "leggers," who cut off the lower portions of the animal's legs. "As far as the ones that come back to life," says a line worker, "it looks like they're trying to climb the walls." When the cows reach the leggers, the leggers don't have time to wait for their colleague to come stun the cow again. So they simply cut off the bottom part of the leg with their clippers: "When they do that, the cattle go wild, just kicking in every direction."[36]

One hundred million animals are also killed each year for their fur. On a documentary filmed with a hidden camera by a team of Swiss investigators,[37] we see Chinese breeders who stun minks by spinning them around, held by their rear legs, and banging their heads on the ground. Then they skin them alive, and once all the skin is removed with the fur, they throw the animals, whose skin is stripped bare, onto a pile of their fellows. The eyes of these minks who are slowly dying, silent and motionless, is unbearable to anyone with even an ounce of pity. The contrast is all the more striking since, while continuing to "peel" these animals like eggplants, the breeders are chatting among themselves, smoking cigarettes, as if nothing were wrong.

All these descriptions and, even more, the spectacle of documentaries showing this sad reality might be unbearable for many of us. But it would be good to ask ourselves why it bothers us so much. Might it be because we know that we are directly or indirectly contributing to the perpetuation of this violence?

Unfortunately, these are not just a few horror scenes blown out of proportion. The numbers surpass the imagination. Every year, over 1 billion land animals are killed in France, 15 billion in the United States, and approximately 70 billion in the world.[38] More recently, China, India, and many other emerging countries have intensified industrial breeding. In many countries, especially within the European Union, new laws should put an end to the worst of these treatments, but they are still practiced in many industrial breeding factories elsewhere in the world.

As for fish, crustaceans and "seafood," a study using data provided by several international organizations concerning yearly catches, a study that takes into account the tonnage of catches and an evaluation of the average weight of each species, ended up at the astronomical number of about 1 trillion, or *1,000 billion,* fish killed yearly.[39]

This estimation does not include either the numerous catches that are not officially recorded, which would at least double that number, or the immense amount of marine species that are gravely affected by the fishing industry. In France, the number of fish and crustaceans killed each year is about 2 billion.

As Foer remarks, "No fish gets a good death. Not a single one. You never have to wonder if the fish on your plate had to suffer. It did. Whether we're talking about fish species, pigs, or some other eaten animal, is such suffering the most important thing in the world? Obviously not. But that's not the question. Is it more important than sushi, bacon, or chicken nuggets? That's the question."[40]

KILLING HUMANELY?

It is true that here or there some improvements have occurred. In the United States, where industrial breeding has long been exempted from the application of all the laws on animal protection, the situation has improved a tiny bit thanks to the work of Temple Grandin, who redesigned plans for slaughterhouses so that the animals would be less overcome with panic as death approached. It is indeed unquestionably desirable to attenuate all the sufferings of animals, in any way possible, but there is something terrible in the attitude that consists of reassuring ourselves by telling ourselves that now 70 billion animals will be "killed humanely" every year.

The French lawyer David Chauvet says about this: "For most people, the fact of killing animals is not a problem, so long as they're killed without suffering. We talk then about 'killing humanely.' Of course, no one would accept being 'killed humanely,' unless perhaps if it's out of self-interest, in order to shorten one's own suffering, for example. But it is certainly not in the interest of animals to be killed to end up in separate pieces in supermarket aisles."[41]

In December 2006, the governor of Florida, Jeb Bush, brother of the former president, temporarily suspended the execution of death row inmates because it took twenty minutes for one of them to succumb to a lethal injection that was supposed to kill him in four minutes. Bush said he was acting out of "humanitarian concerns." I personally see very little humanity in killing someone in four minutes instead of twenty. Condemned inmates are also served their favorite meal before execution. That's better than torturing the condemned man for hours before killing him, but the death penalty remains what it is, an act of legal revenge: "If the crime is a transgression of the law, revenge is what is hiding behind the law against committing a crime," writes Bertrand Vergely.[42] The exploitation of billions of animals can be regarded as a permanent massacre that hides behind indifference.

This point has not escaped some defenders of animal rights: being content with making life and death conditions more "humane," as the "welfarists" do, is only a dodge to give ourselves a better conscience while we continue massacring animals. They demand that we bring to an end our exploitation and killing of animals. They argue that attempts to make slavery more "humane" in fact only contributed to prolonging it, whereas it was its abolition that was necessary.

Most of the sufferings we inflict on others have nothing unavoidable about them. They are made possible by our way of viewing others. If we liken an ethnic group, for example, to vermin, we'll have no scruples about taking measures to eliminate it. If we regard certain people as sworn enemies, we will rejoice in their suffering. From the moment other sentient beings become inferior beings whose fate is negligible to us, we won't hesitate to use them as instruments to serve our own well-being.

Some people will object: "After all, that's life. Why so much sentimentality about behavior that is the way we've always acted? Animals themselves are always eating each other. Those are the laws of nature. What's the point in wanting to change them?" We can quickly reply that we are supposed to have evolved from the times regarded as barbaric, by becoming more peaceful and more human. Otherwise why marvel at the progress of civilization? Even today, aren't people who systematically use brutality and violence called "barbaric"?

It would probably be enough for most of us to be better informed, and to be aware of what is happening every day in industrial breeding factories and slaughterhouses, so that we would naturally change our minds, and even our mode of life. Regular TV programs, for instance, hardly ever show what is going on behind the doors of slaughterhouses—even though they are not shy to broadcast war and horror movies—and they often convey the views of the livestock industry. In any case it practically would be impossible for reporters to investigate freely in slaughterhouses. We can find, however, on the Internet especially, reports showing the reality of the places from which the meat we eat comes. As an example we can cite the documentary called *Earthlings*,[43] which clearly shows how we treat animals.

Is it still possible to keep our eyes closed? One day, perhaps, the futuristic vision of H. G. Wells will become reality:

> *In all the round world of Utopia there is no meat. There used to be. But now we cannot stand the thought of slaughterhouses.... I can still remember as... a boy the rejoicings over the closing of the last slaughterhouse.*[44]

It only depends on us.

34

Backfire:
Effects of the Meat Industry on Poverty, Environment, and Health

In the previous chapter, we examined the serious ethical concerns about how we treat animals. But that is not the whole story. If we are concerned with poverty and the increasing inequalities between rich and poor, if we are concerned about the environment and human health, and if we accept the conclusions of scientific studies presented by reports like those of the Intergovernmental Panel on Climate Change (IPPC, established by the UN), the Food and Agriculture Organization (FAO), the Worldwatch Institute and others, then we can't help but question the excessive practices of animal breeding and wonder about the negative impacts that consuming meat has for humans and for our environment. You be the judge, given these few statistics:

- Industrial breeding contributes to 14.5% of greenhouse gas emissions linked to human activities, in second place after buildings and before transportation;[1]
- To produce 1 kilo of meat, 10 kilos of food that could feed poor countries must be used;[2]
- 60% of land available in the world is devoted to the breeding industry;
- The breeding industry alone consumes 45% of all the water destined for production of food;

- By reducing meat consumption, we could prevent 14% of deaths in the world.

THE MEAT OF WEALTHY COUNTRIES IS COSTLY TO POOR COUNTRIES

The equation is simple: 1 hectare of land can feed 50 vegetarians or 2 carnivores. To produce 1 kilo of meat, you need the same surface of land as to cultivate 200 kilos of tomatoes, 160 kilos of potatoes, or 80 kilos of apples.[3]

In *Diet for a Small Planet*, Frances Moore Lappé stresses that 1 acre of grains produces five times more protein than the same acre used to produce meat and 1 acre of legumes produces ten times more.[4]

The breeding industry consumes 750 million tons of wheat and corn every year that would be enough to feed adequately the 1.4 billion poorest human beings. Over 90% of the 225 million tons of soy harvested in the world also serve to feed animals in the meat industry.[5]

Almost two-thirds of all the land available is used for the meat industry (30% for pasture and 30% to produce the food for the animals that are bred for meat).[6]

To obtain 1 calorie of beef by intensive breeding, 8 to 26 calories of plant food are required, which could have been consumed directly by humans.[7] In weight, 7 kilos of grains are necessary to produce 1 kilo of beef. *The ratios are deplorable.* It's not surprising that Frances Moore Lappé described this kind of agriculture as "a protein factory in reverse."[8]

Eating meat is a privilege of wealthy countries, one that is practiced to the detriment of poor countries. As the figure on the following page shows, the wealthier populations become, the more meat they consume. An American eats 120 kilos of meat per year, as opposed to only 2.5 kilos for an Indian. On average, wealthy countries consume ten times more meat than poor countries.[9] Worldwide meat consumption increased five times between 1950 and 2006, a growth rate that's twice as high as that of the world population and, if the current tendency continues, this consumption will double again between now and 2050.[10]

A little over a third of the world production of grains is destined for animals in the meat industry every year, along with a quarter of the worldwide production of fish.[11] As Éric Lambin, professor at the

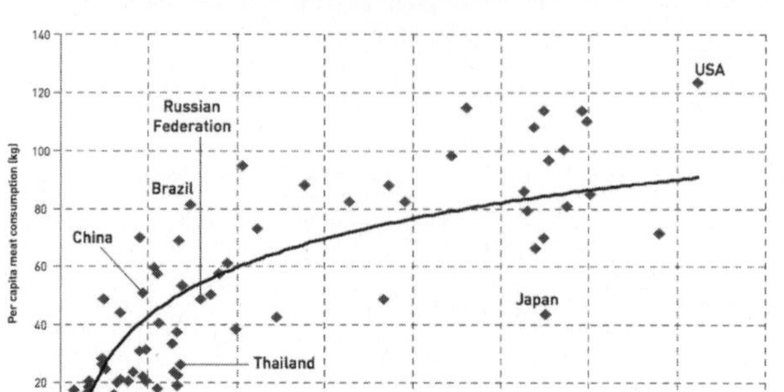

Note: National per capita based on purchasing power parity (PPP).
Source: World Bank (2006) and FAO (2006b).

universities of Louvain and Stanford, remarks, "this competition between man and livestock for the consumption of grains is accompanied by an increase of the price of grains, which has tragic consequences for the poorest populations."[12]

The fact that a quarter of the 2.8 billion people who live with less than two dollars a day depend on the breeding industry for their subsistence and that the breeding industry in general contributes largely to economic development should be taken into account, but does not weaken the point of view we have just expressed. In fact, it is not these small farmers who contribute to the massive production of meat (an Indian, we have seen, consumes sixty times less meat than an American) and, consequently, to the diversion to the production of meat of cereal resources that could directly feed poor populations.[13] It is the large, quasi-industrial enterprises destined for intensive breeding, as well as monocultures destined for these enterprises, that create this imbalance and injustice. Despite everything, even the small farmers of poor populations participate in the degradation of the land on which these populations live. In the long run, their subsistence would be better assured by the development of agro-ecological methods that regulate the quality of the soil and vegetation.[14]

According to estimates by the Worldwatch Institute, in order to produce a beef hamburger in Central America, 17 square meters of virgin forest are transformed into pasture, and 75 kilos of plants and animals are destroyed. The United States imports 100,000 tons of beef from Central America every year.[15] If all the grains destined for American livestock were consumed directly, they could feed 800 million humans.[16] In 1985, during the famine in Ethiopia, as the population was dying of hunger, that country exported grains for English livestock.[17]

Humid tropical forests cover about 720 million hectares and are home to some 50% of the biodiversity of the planet. Over 200 million hectares of these forests have been destroyed since 1950, notably to make room for pasturage or cattle farms.[18] A report by Greenpeace published at the end of January 2009 estimates that 80% of the deforestation of the Amazon is caused by the increase of the number of cattle.[19]

As for devoting 100 million tons of wheat and corn to the production of ethanol for cars, an envoy for the Food and Agriculture Organization of the UN estimated that this diversion constituted a "crime against humanity." Feeding cars when almost 1 billion people can't get enough to eat...

THE IMPACT ON FRESHWATER RESERVES

Fresh water is a rare, precious resource. Only 2.5% of the planet's water is fresh water, almost three-quarters of which is contained in glaciers and permanent snow cover.[20] In many poor countries, access to water is very limited. Populations, usually women and children, often have to travel many miles on foot to reach a water source and bring it back to their homes.

Lack of drinking water is a threat of worldwide proportions: Forty percent of the world's population, dwelling in 24 countries, suffers from a lack of water, both in quantity and quality.[21]

Over 3 million children under five years of age die every year from diarrhea caused essentially by contaminated water and pathogenic germs transmitted through food. Presently, 70% of freshwater resources are degraded or polluted.[22]

Yet the production of 1 kilo of meat requires fifty times more water than that of 1 kilo of wheat.[23] *Newsweek* described this volume of water imagistically: "The water that goes into a 1,000 pound steer would float a destroyer."[24] It is estimated that half the consumption of drinking water worldwide is destined for the production of meat and milk products. In Europe, over 50% of water pollution comes from the intensive breeding of animals, including fish farms. In the United States, 80% of drinking water is used for breeding animals. The demands of animal production are exhausting vast aquifers on which countless dry regions throughout the world depend. At the current rate, the quantity of water used for industrial animal breeding should increase by 50% between now and 2050.[25]

INDUSTRIAL BREEDING AND CLIMATE CHANGE

The environmental impacts of meat production are particularly severe in the case of intensive breeding.

The production of 1 kilo of beef produces fifty times more greenhouse gas emissions than that of 1 kilo of wheat.[26] Worldwide production of meat contributes around 14.5% to greenhouse gas emissions responsible for climate change.[27]

This number includes the gases emitted during the various stages of the production cycle of meat: deforestation to create pastures, production and transportation of fertilizer, fuel used by agricultural machines, fabrication of growth hormones and food additives, gas emissions from the livestock's digestive system, transportation of livestock to the slaughterhouses, mechanization of the slaughtering process, treatment and packaging of meat, and transportation to points of sale. In total, livestock breeding for meat production contributes more to global warming than the entire transportation sector (which represents 13% of greenhouse gas emissions) and is surpassed only by the construction industry and the worldwide energy consumption by human habitations.

The greenhouse effect is due mainly to three gases: methane, carbon dioxide, and nitrous oxide. Methane is particularly active since one molecule of that gas contributes twenty times more to the greenhouse effect than one molecule of carbon dioxide. Between 15% and 20% of methane emissions worldwide are linked to livestock breeding. In two centuries, the concentration of methane in the atmosphere has more than doubled.

Ruminants—steer, cows, buffalo, sheep, goats, and camels—constitute one of the largest sources of methane production. Methane results from microbial fermentation in the digestive system of ruminants: it is exhaled during respiration by eructation, or in the form of flatulence. It is also emitted by the solid waste these animals produce, by the decomposition of manure, and by fermentation of animal feces in storage pits.[28] A dairy cow produces over 130 kilos of methane per year, which corresponds to 500 liters of gas per day![29]

As for carbon dioxide, the expansion of the meat industry has contributed largely to the 30% increase of its atmospheric concentration in two years. The industrial production of meat in fact depends on the mechanization of agriculture (in order to produce the enormous quantity of food for animals it needs), on the fabrication and use of petroleum-based chemical fertilizers, and on deforestation and other elements that are sources of CO_2 emissions.

As for nitrous oxide, it is the most aggressive of greenhouse gases: 320 times more active than carbon dioxide. It is also a stable composite that has a lifecycle in the atmosphere of 120 years. The main emission sources of this gas are the spreading of nitrogenous fertilizer, the degradation process of these fertilizers in the soil, and waste from livestock breeding. Sixty-five percent of nitrous oxide emissions humans produce comes from livestock breeding. Nitrous oxide represents about 6% of all greenhouse gases.[30]

ANIMAL WASTE

A bovine produces on average 23 tons of waste per year.[31] In the United States alone, livestock animals produce 130 times more excrement than humans. Animal waste pollutes the waters more than all other industrial sources combined.[32] The Smithfield Company alone kills 31 million pigs every year, which produce the equivalent of 130 kilos of excrement per citizen in North America. This company has immensely polluted the rivers of North Carolina.

Animal excrement produces huge quantities of ammonia, which pollutes waterways and seashores and causes algae invasions that stifle aquatic life. Immense zones of Western Europe, the northeastern United States, and coastal regions of Southeast Asia, as well as vast plains in China, today receive considerable surpluses of nitrogen that can range from 200 to 1,000 kilos of nitrogen per hectare per year.[33]

Surpluses of nitrogen and phosphorous also infiltrate the soil by leaching or runoff, polluting aquifers, aquatic ecosystems, and humid zones.[34]

THE EFFECTS OF FISHING

Intensive fishing is leading progressively to the extinction of numerous species of fish, and has an enormous impact on biodiversity. After exhausting the species that live close to the surface, trawlers are plunging their nets deeper into the sea, and are now scraping the oceans' floors. Trawling the oceans' depths is devastating a fragile biodiversity that has taken tens of thousands of years to form. Ten deep-water trawlers could destroy the surface area of a city the size of Paris in two days.[35] What's more, it is estimated that the quantity of fish harvested worldwide is vastly higher than the catches that are legally declared. To give only one example, according to estimates by the marine biologist Daniel Pauly and his colleagues at the University of British Columbia in Vancouver, each year China captures 4.5 million tons of fish, much of it along African coasts, but it only declares 368,000 tons to the FAO.[36] Countless pirate craft ignore altogether the quotas (which are devised to slow down the exhaustion of marine populations) imposed on authorized fishermen.

Because of purely commercial considerations and ignored regulations, industrial fishing is also accompanied by an immense waste of lives. A shrimp trawling operation, for instance, throws overboard, dead or dying, between 80 and 90% of sea creatures gathered during each deep-sea trawl. What's more, many of these "bycatches" are comprised of threatened species. Shrimp represent only 2% by weight of the quantity of marine food consumed in the world, but 33% of the bycatch worldwide. As Jonathan Safran Foer notes in *Eating Animals,* "We tend not to think about this because we tend not to know about it. What if there were labeling on our food letting us know how many animals were killed to bring our desired animal to our plate? So, with trawled shrimp from Indonesia, for example, the label might read: 26 POUNDS OF OTHER SEA ANIMALS WERE KILLED AND

TOSSED BACK INTO THE OCEAN FOR EVERY 1 POUND OF THIS SHRIMP."[37] In the case of the tuna fishery, 145 other species are regularly killed while catching tuna.

Meat Consumption and Human Health

Many epidemiological studies have established that eating meat, especially red meat and processed meats, increases the risk for colon and stomach cancers, as well as cardiovascular diseases.

A study carried out in 2005 by the European Prospective Investigation into Cancer and Nutrition (EPIC) under the direction of Elio Riboli involving 521,000 individuals showed that participants in the test who ate the most red meat had 35% higher risk of developing colon cancer than those who consumed less.

A study published in the *Archives of Internal Medicine* involving 500,000 people shows that 11% of deaths among men and 16% among women could be avoided by a reduction in red meat consumption.[38]

According to a UN Human Development report (2007–2008), the risk of colorectal cancer diminishes by about 30% whenever you reduce the daily consumption of red meat by 100 grams. The countries that consume the most red meat, like Argentina and Uruguay, are also the countries where the colon cancer rates are highest in the world.[39] As for consumption of processed meat (like hot dogs, bologna, and sausages), it has been linked to an increased risk of stomach cancer.

According to another study published at Harvard in 2012 by An Pan, Frank Hu, and their colleagues, involving more than 100,000 people followed over many years, daily meat consumption is linked to a risk that's increased by 18% among men and 21% among women for death from cardiovascular disease, and by respectively 10% and 16% for death from cancer.[40]

Among major red meat consumers, the simple fact of replacing meat with whole grains or other sources of vegetable protein diminishes the risk for early death by 14%. During the period of this same study, 9.3% of deaths among men and 7.6% among women could have been prevented if all the participants had consumed less than 40 grams of red meat a day.

Because of the phenomenon of bioconcentration, meat contains about fourteen times—and milk products, 5.5 times—more pesticide residue than vegetables.[41] Persistent organic pollutants accumulate in the fatty tissues of animals, thereby entering the human food chain. These persistent organic pollutants are also found in the flesh of farmed fish, which are fed with concentrated food made notably from animal proteins. These molecules are carcinogenic and toxic for the development of the nervous system of the fetus and of young children.[42]

As we said in the previous chapter, in the United States, 80% of antibiotics employed are used with the sole aim of keeping industrially bred animals alive until they are killed. Since big industrial farms don't treat sick animals individually, massive amounts of antibiotics are added to their food. From 25% to 75% of these antibiotics can be found in rivers, the soil, and drinking water, producing resistance to these treatments in humans, and causing other undesirable effects.

The Good News

Methane, as we've seen, is twenty times more active than CO_2 in the production of the greenhouse effect. But there is some good news: its lifecycle in the atmosphere is only ten years, compared to a century in the case of CO_2. So reducing the production of meat would quickly reduce a major factor in climate change.

Another piece of good news is that, as we have mentioned, the world could feed 1.5 billion poor people by providing them with the billion tons of grains that feed livestock raised for slaughter. If, for example, all the inhabitants of North America abstained from eating meat for a single day, that would allow, indirectly, 25 million poor people to be fed every day for an entire year! It would also effectively contribute to the fight against climate change. That is why, according to R.K. Pachauri, winner of the Nobel Peace Prize and director of the UN's Intergovernmental Panel on Climate Change, a worldwide tendency toward a vegetarian diet is essential to fight hunger in the world as well as a deficit of energy and the worst impacts of climate change: "In terms of immediacy of action and the feasibility of bringing about reductions in a short period of time, it clearly is the most attractive opportunity,"[43] he concludes.

These statements are confirmed by the March 2014 report by the

IPCC. "We have shown that reducing consumption of meat and dairy products is key to be able to bring agricultural climate pollution down to safe levels," explains Fredrik Hedenus, one of the report's authors. "Major diet changes take time; so we should think starting now of how we could make our food more respectful of the climate."[44]

According to a co-author of the report, Stefan Wirsenius, greenhouse gas emissions "can certainly be reduced by increasing the effectiveness of meat production and dairy products and by making use of new technologies. But if consumption continues to increase, the diminutions these measures can lead to will probably be insufficient to contain climate change within tolerable limits."

The excellent news, then, is that we can all take part in an effective, easy, quick approach to slowing down global warming and eradicating poverty. To do this, it is not necessary to stop traveling or heating the house (although we should of course also moderate these factors), only one thing is necessary: to decide, here and now, to stop eating meat, or, if that's too difficult, at least to reduce its consumption.

35

Institutionalized Selfishness

Those who believe and have confidence in the emergence of a more altruistic society should not be discouraged when faced with manifestations of selfishness. The mere existence of real altruism does not make selfishness disappear from society.

We can see that selfishness is the rule in totalitarian regimes that assign little value to the individual. But it also manifests in free and democratic countries, when cynical interest groups make their own profit an absolute priority, ignoring the harmful consequences of their activities on the population. When these groups knowingly resort to all kinds of manipulations to preserve their interests, it is legitimate to speak of *institutionalized selfishness.*

This is the case for industries, companies, or financial entities that with their considerable means have been able to influence governments to modify laws and regulations to serve their own special interests. These organizations devote fortunes to ad campaigns promoting harmful products, or to hide the deleterious effects of their activities, whatever the price paid by humans and the planet. Their financial clout also allows them recourse to high-ranking lawyers so as to prolong indefinitely court cases brought against them and thereby discourage the victims of their activities, who often have only modest resources.

When these groups can thus concentrate their wealth, pass environmental costs onto society, exploit workers and maintain poverty to use cheap labor—all in the name of an "economic growth" that isn't even a reality—while their contribution to society is, when all is said and done, a negative one, the responsibility for letting all this happen lies, as Joseph Stiglitz stresses, in uncaring economic and political systems: "Much of what has gone on can only be described by the words 'moral deprivation.' Something wrong happened to the moral compass of so many of the people working in the financial sector and elsewhere."[1]

Examples of institutionalized selfishness abound, and the aim of this book is not to draw up a list of them. A few particularly emblematic examples will suffice to demonstrate how such practices have been able to arise and continue with impunity.

THE MERCHANTS OF DOUBT

That is the name of the book by Naomi Oreskes and Erik Conway, historians of science, which describes the machinations of the tobacco industry, mainly in the United States, and of interest groups that deny the reality of global warming and the effect of human activities on the climate.[2] One of the most disturbing aspects of their investigation is the role played by scientists close to the extreme right in America who, for several decades, have led effective disinformation campaigns allowing them to trick public opinion into doubting well-established scientific facts.

The physicists Frederick Seitz and Fred Singer, among others, took part in the industry's campaigns. The former was active in the creation of the atomic bomb during the Second World War, the latter in the development of rockets and observation satellites. Seitz also became president of the American Academy of Sciences.[3] Nothing in their scientific training, however, gave them the competence required to proclaim, as they did for years, that the links between tobacco and cancer were not proven, that acid rain was not caused by the fumes from the coal industry (but rather by volcanoes, which is false), and that CFC gases (chlorofluorocarbons) had no effect on the destruction of the ozone layer. Joined by the physicists William "Bill" Nierenberg and Robert Jastrow, they also strove for thirty years to deny the planet's global warming. They began by stating it didn't exist, then that it was natural, and, finally, that even if it continued to increase, we just had to adapt. They questioned the results of serious studies on global warming and claimed that the scientific community was deeply divided on these questions.

Their tactics were all the more perverse since they presented themselves as defenders of "good science," accusing their colleagues of manipulating the data and conclusions of their research in the service of anti-capitalist, anti-libertarian, even Communist political trends. Armed with their notoriety and the unconditional support of the industries that feared any regulation of their activities, they managed to influence several American presidents, Ronald Reagan and Bush Senior and Bush Junior in particular (George Bush Sr. called them "my scholars").[4] They also duped media as respectable as the *New York Times*, the *Washington Post*, and *Newsweek*, who readily made themselves the mouthpieces for these disinformation campaigns, in the aim of "giving equal space to diverse opinions," placing scrupulous scientific researchers on equal footing with biased, unsubstantiated opinions. These experts acquired by financial lobbies all had in common an anti-Soviet obsession dating back to the Cold War and an avowed sympathy for neoconservative capitalism.[5]

100 Million Deaths in the Twentieth Century: The History of Tobacco

In the 1930s, German researchers had demonstrated that tobacco leads to lung cancer. But, because of their association with the Nazi regime, their research was ignored. It was in 1953 that Ernest Wynder and his colleagues at the Sloan-Kettering Institute in New York discovered that cigarette tar applied to the skin of mice led to deadly cancers.[6] This news came like a bomb in the media, and the tobacco industry panicked.

In December 1953, the presidents of the four main American cigarette brands[7] gathered around John Hill, the head of the leading advertising agency in the United States, in order to devise a media campaign to convince the population that there was "no sound scientific basis for the charges," and that they were "sensational accusations" concocted by researchers greedy for publicity and subsidies for their laboratories.[8] This campaign would later be considered by the courts as the first of many stages of a conspiracy organized to hide the toxic effects of tobacco.

Hill and his accomplices began by forming the Tobacco Industry

Research Committee, with Hill insisting on including the word "research" in order, he said, to "spread and maintain doubt" about the validity of the scientists' discoveries in the mind of the public. This committee distributed to doctors, politicians, and journalists hundreds of thousands of pamphlets that claimed to demonstrate that there was no reason to be alarmed about the harmfulness of tobacco.[9] By doing this, they managed to sow discord in public opinion.

"Doubt is our 'product', since it's the best way to fight all the facts that are now known to the public," declared an internal memo from the director of a large tobacco company in 1957.[10] *Doubt Is Their Product* is also the title of the book by the scientist David Michaels, Assistant Secretary of Energy for Environment, Safety and Health under the Clinton administration and who, like Oreskes and Conway, shows how the tobacco industry very quickly recruited "experts" charged with providing their communications services with material that would "keep the debate open" where research studies had unequivocally established that tobacco is the cause of millions of premature deaths.[11]

In 1957, the American Public Health Service ruled that tobacco was "the main cause of increased frequency of lung cancer." In Europe, other public health organizations made similar declarations.

In 1964, on the basis of over 7,000 studies demonstrating the harmfulness of tobacco, the Surgeon General established in a report entitled "Tobacco and Health" that a smoker was "twenty times more likely to die of lung cancer than a non-smoker," that tobacco led to a decided increase in other lung and heart diseases, and that the more someone smoked, the more harmful the effect was on the smoker's health.[12]

The industry realized it was facing a grave crisis but didn't concede defeat, and gathered its forces together. The tobacco firm Brown and Williamson chose to act as if nothing had happened and announced, in 1967, that "There is no scientific evidence that cigarette smoking causes lung cancer or any other disease." In court, the tobacco industry always managed to coax a few scientists over to its side to assert that the scientific data remained inconclusive.

It came to light only later that those scientists working for the industry had actually reached the same conclusion as the others. Even more: they had also noted that nicotine was habit-forming among smokers, two conclusions the industry chose first to hide, then to deny until the 1990s, when it was charged with deception. As a preventative tactic, in the 1960s the industry introduced cigarette brands that were marketed as "better for your health." If we think of the 5 million people dying at that time all over the world and still dying every year because of cigarettes, we can get some idea of the cynicism of this description.

A new wind of panic blew through the industry in the 1980s, when the Surgeon General concluded that passive smoking was also harmful to the health, and recommended measures limiting the use of tobacco inside buildings. The tobacco industry again united with Fred Singer to discredit not only the EPA (Environmental Protection Agency), which had compiled the scientific studies, but also the researchers themselves, accusing them of doing "bad science."

Here again, as early as the 1970s, the tobacco industry knew that the smoke floating in the air contained more toxic products than the smoke inhaled by smokers.[13] The main reason for this is that the combustion of this "lateral" smoke occurs at a lower temperature and in an incomplete way.[14]

The most convincing study came from Japan in 1981. Takeshi Hirayama, at the Cancer Research Institute, demonstrated that the wives of smokers died from lung cancer twice as often as the wives of nonsmokers. The study involved over 540 women who were followed for fourteen years. The more the husband smoked, the more the mortality rate of the wives increased.[15]

The tobacco industry then turned to a famous statistician, Nathan Mantel, who declared that Hirayama's results had been incorrectly analyzed. PR firms then took over, with newspapers displaying front-page headlines denying the risks of passive smoking, while full-page ads announcing the good news were financed by cigarette companies. As another duplicity, internal memos, found later on, confirm they knew very well what the truth was. One of them notes: "Hirayama was right. TI (Tobacco Industry) knew it and attacked Hirayama, knowing all the while that his results were correct."[16]

Smoking, then, was not just a question of personal risk. Putting one's friends, colleagues, and one's own children in danger was a whole other matter, which public opinion would surely not swallow so easily.

And yet, the tobacco companies persisted in their lying campaign: Sylvester Stallone was paid $500,000 to smoke cigarettes in five of his movies, in order to associate smoking with strength and good health. Philip Morris financed a project called *Whitecoat,* enrolling European scientists to "reverse the erroneous scientific and popular concept that ETS [environmental tobacco smoke] is harmful to health."[17] Sixteen million dollars were spent with the sole aim of maintaining doubt in the public's mind. Fred Singer, predictably, sent many articles to the press, denouncing the new scientific reports, which he described as "junk science." In 1999, analyzing the articles published in the press on passive smoking, two researchers at the University of California, Gail Kennedy and Lisa Bero, established that 62% of articles published in newspapers and non-specialized magazines between 1992 and 1994 continued to assert that the studies concluding on the harmful effects of passive smoking were "subject to controversy," whereas *all* the serious scientific studies had confirmed this harmfulness.[18]

Another stratagem consisted of creating pseudo-scientific journals in which the tobacco industry published articles that would never have passed the threshold of the editorial committees of serious scientific journals. They also organized conferences where it presented scientists won over to its cause, whose opinions were then repeated in "reports." All these strategies ended up constituting a number of references that, although lacking any scientific value, had the aim of contradicting serious research.[19]

Finally, in 2006, an American court ruled that "the tobacco industry had developed and applied strategies meant to deceive consumers about the dangers of cigarettes, dangers of which it has been aware since the 1950s, as the internal documents of the tobacco companies themselves proved."

In November 2012, an American federal judge ordered tobacco companies to publish corrective declarations stating clearly they had lied about the dangers of smoking. These declarations must describe without dissimulation the effects of tobacco on smokers' health, and mention the fact that smoking kills on average over 1,200 Americans a day, more than murders, AIDS, suicide, drugs, alcohol, and car accidents combined.[20]

Even today, according to the World Health Organization (WHO),[21] tobacco kills almost 6 million people every year. Five million of them are smokers or former smokers, and over 600,000 are nonsmokers involuntarily exposed to smoke.[22] Passive smoking, then, is dangerous, even in small doses.[23]

Tobacco caused 100 million deaths in the twentieth century, more than both World Wars combined. If the present tendency continues, it will lead to up to 1 billion victims in the twenty-first century. Eighty percent of these deaths will occur in countries with low or average incomes.

Despite all that, the tobacco industry has still not thrown in the towel. It is now targeting developing countries, and is prospering in Africa and Asia (which is home to 60% of the billion smokers on the planet, 350 million of them in China alone). In Indonesia, for example, it offers young people a reward if they agree to transform their cars into ads for their brands. On morning television, there are up to 15 ads per hour to promote tobacco consumption. In that country, with 11 million workers, the tobacco industry is the second largest national employer, and 63% of the male population are smokers.[24] In India, 50,000 children work in tobacco farms and factories. In China, Marlboro even sponsors school uniforms (with their logo, of course.)[25] Worldwide, according to WHO, tax revenue on tobacco sales is on average 154 times higher than the sums spent on the anti-tobacco fight.[26] The long-term effects of disinformation campaigns continue to make themselves felt, since 25% of Americans still think today that there is no solid evidence proving that smoking kills.[27]

ANY SOLUTIONS?

According to WHO, gruesome anti-tobacco ads and photos on cigarette packs contribute to reducing the number of young people who begin smoking, and increases the number of smokers who decide to stop smoking. We also know that banning advertising lowers cigarette consumption. So the first thing to do would be to *ban all ads*.

The studies show that most smokers aware of the dangers of tobacco want to stop smoking. Still, in many countries, few people know the specific risks of tobacco consumption (only 37% in China, where people smoke freely in crowded trains or buses). So governments should start out by *correctly informing* the population.

We know that a therapeutic regimen, counseling, and taking certain medications can at least double one's chances of successfully stopping smoking. So consumers need *help to break the habit*. But only 19 countries, representing 14% of the world population, have national health services offering help with giving up smoking.

The WHO thinks a ban is impracticable in the context of globalization. But we can imagine an organization like the European Union taking the initiative and setting the example. Countries like Finland, Australia and New Zealand have already taken the path of eradication with two initiatives: removing any positive image of tobacco by making all cigarette packs the same, and banning smoking in the streets to put an end to the phenomenon of imitation.

A group of English medical experts also thinks the prospect of a worldwide ban is unrealistic; instead, it is encouraging governments to have the public health bill systematically paid by the tobacco companies, since they are responsible for all these diseases and deaths.[28] In Canada, a class action suit is underway, representing 45,000 Quebecois who are demanding 27 billion dollars in damages from these companies. In the United States, the big cigarette companies signed the Master Settlement Agreement in 1998, by which they agreed to pay the record sum of 246 billion dollars over twenty-five years. Obviously, the American legal system has not struck hard enough despite everything, since the tobacco industry continues to do well, unlike those who smoke its products.

DENIAL OF CLIMATE CHANGE

In 1965, Roger Revelle, scientific adviser to President Johnson, was ordered to prepare a report on the increase of carbon dioxide in the atmosphere. His conclusions, presented to the Congress, determined: "The present generation has altered the composition of the atmosphere at a global level by regularly emitting a quantity of carbon dioxide from the burning of fossil fuels."[29] But that was the Vietnam War era, and the government had other priorities. As for climatologists, they had already come up with models predicting, under the effect of the increase of CO_2, an increase of the temperature of the surface of the globe, with major consequences from every point of view—biodiversity, human migrations, diseases, and so on.

The American government then asked two groups of experts to study the question further.[30] They too reached the same conclusion. This observation made politicians feel very uneasy: intervening effectively would have required considerable changes in the field of energy. So they chose to put the problem aside. One of the scientists recounts that, when the leaders in Washington were told that the rate of CO_2 in the atmosphere would double in fifty years, they replied: "Come back in forty-nine years."[31] The American government adopted the strategy of "wait and see" and claimed that in any case humanity could adapt. So why was it necessary to pass regulations to diminish the rate of CO_2 in the atmosphere?

As scientists continue to accumulate studies and try to alert those in authority and public opinion, American magnates finance media campaigns to deny global warming, supported by a few laboratories ready to defend this argument. According to the calculations presented in an investigative report by Greenpeace, the brothers David and Charles Koch, two oil industry magnates with ultra-conservative opinions, who are respectively the fifth and sixth wealthiest men in the world, have contributed over 60 million dollars to this campaign since 1997.[32] The journalist Chris Mooney showed that Exxon Mobil had, in a few years, paid 8 million dollars to no less than 40 organizations that denigrate scientific research that proves global warming.[33] In 2009, there were over 2,300 lobbyists in Congress focused on questions linked to climate change, in the aim of protecting the interests of big industry.[34]

A researcher with impeccable qualifications, Benjamin Santer works at the Lawrence Livermore National Laboratory, connected with the University of California. He was the one who, in an article in *Nature* in 1996, offered the decisive proof that global warming was due to human activities and not to variations of solar activity. His studies demonstrated that the troposphere (the area of space closest to us) was getting warmer, while the stratosphere (the space outside the troposphere) was getting colder. It should have been the opposite if the warming of our climate were caused by the sun: since the stratosphere receives the sun's rays first, it should have begun to get warmer.[35]

Santer was then put in charge of coordinating writing the eighth chapter of the UN's IPPC report, dealing with climate changes. This institution received the Nobel Peace Prize in 2007, along with Al Gore.

Confronted with the conclusion stemming from the evidence presented by Santer and unable to challenge it scientifically, Seitz, Singer, Bill Nierenberg, and their stooges proclaimed that the researcher had deliberately falsified his results. They also tried to have him fired from his university. Seitz wrote an article in the *Wall Street Journal* entitled "A Major Deception on Global Warming," as well as other articles of the same sort accusing Santer of suppressing certain parts of that eighth chapter of the IPPC report, passages that cast doubt on global warming and its causes.

Actually, Ben Santer had only made a certain number of revisions following the recommendations of his colleagues. When a researcher submits an article to a scientific journal or presents a review, it is in fact normal for data, analyses, and conclusions to be sifted through by a group of experts. As usual, these experts had asked for details and additional information.

Fred Seitz obviously knew about this process. But he asserted, without the slightest foundation, that the modifications made by the researcher were meant to "deceive policy makers and the public"[36] in order to make them believe that scientific proof existed showing that human activities were causing global warming.

Over the years, then, the American media were bombarded with fallacious information meant to provide the most conservative politicians with the arguments they needed. The journal of the American Academy of Sciences, the *PNAS*, published a study showing that 97% of researchers specializing in climate in the United States attributed to human activity the responsibility for global warming and its predicted consequences. This unanimity of the scientific community was not enough to impress the senator from Oklahoma, James Inhofe, who retorted: "This 97% doesn't mean anything."[37] In other circumstances, that same senator had described global warming as "the greatest hoax ever perpetrated on the American people;"[38] earlier, he had said, "There is substantial scientific evidence that increases in atmospheric carbon dioxide produce many beneficial effects upon the natural plant and animal environments of the Earth."[39] All the Republican presidential candidates for 2012 vocalized their skepticism about climate change, and refused to consider industrial emissions of carbon dioxide as being the main cause of global warming.[40] Sixty-four percent of Americans continue to think the scientific community is deeply divided on the subject.[41]

"Spreading doubt," and "keeping the controversy open," the objectives of interest groups, were crowned with success. But here the interest of a few is being made to triumph over the common good. Making this kind of denial serve special interests does indeed qualify as institutionalized selfishness.

The Pharmaceutical Industry: A Challenge for Public Health

For a century, pharmaceutical companies all over the world have produced medications, antibiotics in particular, that have saved countless lives, and have contributed to increasing life expectancy in the United States from forty-seven in 1900 to almost seventy-nine today. However, these inarguable successes are no excuse for indulging in a series of practices that are certainly not in the interest of patients or of society at large.

It is alarming to note, as the British doctor Ben Goldacre demonstrated in his book *Bad Pharma*,[42] that the private interests of pharmaceutical companies have often been privileged over those of public health. Under pretext of protecting their investments in research, these companies cover up the data from studies they cite to assert a new medicine is effective. In particular, they communicate to the medical and scientific community only the results of studies that are favorable to their products. If we add to that the exaggerations and distortions inherent to every advertising campaign, which boasts of merchandise in a way disproportionate with its actual benefits, doctors don't have the necessary information that would allow them to choose the best treatments for their patients with full knowledge of the facts. The transparency of the pharmaceutical industry stops where its financial interests begin.

A Distortion of Scientific Research

It would be perfectly possible to know unambiguously the effectiveness of medicines sold on the market. But because of a systematic lack of transparency of pharmaceutical companies and a lack of will on the part of regulatory organizations, that is not the case. Why?

Medicines are tested by the same people that make them, and not by independent scientific laboratories. The comparison between the experimental protocols used in rigorous scientific studies and those used in pharmaceutical laboratories shows that, in the latter, they are often ill-conceived, tested on an insufficient number of patients, and over too short a period of time. What's more, these results are interpreted in such a way as to exaggerate the benefits of the product. When tests produce results that don't satisfy the companies, the companies are content to ignore them, thus depriving independent investigators of information indispensable to a fair evaluation of the medicine in question.

In 2007, Lisa Bero and other researchers at the University of San Francisco examined all the published tests on the benefits of statins, anti-cholesterol medications that reduce the risk of heart attacks and are widely prescribed. They analyzed 192 tests comparing a specific statin to another or to a different kind of medication, and they observed that studies financed by the industry gave *favorable results twenty times more often* about their own products than studies carried out by independent scientific laboratories. This example is the rule rather than the exception.

Unfortunately, there are many ways to bias these experimental procedures. One might select patients more likely to react favorably to the treatment. Or, one could be content to look at the results halfway through the study and interrupt the study prematurely to avoid obtaining worse results at the end of the same test. Pharmaceutical companies that use the services of researchers reserve, contractually, the prerogative to interrupt a study at any time if they think it's not headed in the right direction, which obviously affects the objective evaluation of the medication being tested. Once the study is over, the company has complete control over publishing or silencing the results, depending on what suits it.

Pharmaceutical Companies Completely Lack Transparency

An article published in *JAMA (Journal of the American Medical Association)*, the main American medical journal, reveals that out of a sample of 44 studies carried out by pharmaceutical companies, in 40 cases, the researchers had to sign a confidentiality contract.[43] This confidentiality has nothing to do with the protection of the laboratories' rights over the product they have produced. It aims solely at disseminating only the tests that show that their products are effective, and to silence with impunity the tests that give negative results. To take an example from the European Union, half of all tests carried out on medical products are never published. But a knowledge of *all* studies carried out on a new product and comparison with already existent medications are indispensable for doctors to be able to prescribe the most effective medicine. Today, doctors have only results that are pre-selected by laboratories. In fact, the few systematic studies, long and costly, that have been carried out indicate that the majority of new medications placed on the market are no more effective than those that exist already. And, sometimes, they are even less effective.

We'll cite a revealing example, that of Tamiflu. In 2005, fearing an avian flu pandemic, governments all over the world spent billions of dollars to buy and store this medication purported to reduce complications from flu, which can be fatal. In England, there was enough to treat 80% of the population. However, to date, Roche, the manufacturer, has published no data showing that Tamiflu effectively reduced the rate of pneumonia and death. Roche's Internet site, however, announces that this medication reduces complications by 67%.

In December 2009, Cochrane Collaboration, a nonprofit organization that aims to facilitate collaboration between scientists all over the world, decided to check what the state of things actually was. Every year this organization carries out and publishes hundreds of systematic, detailed analyses of medical research. Cochrane contacted Roche, which declared it was ready to communicate the data provided it remained confidential, which made no sense for an organization whose goal was to inform the scientific community. What's more, Cochrane had to agree not to reveal either the conditions imposed by Roche, or the results of their investigation, or even the fact that these investigations existed! All that about a medication that had already been consumed by hundreds of thousands of people and had cost governments and citizens billions of dollars. Cochrane asked for clarifications and Roche didn't reply.[44] In January 2011, Roche announced that all its data had been transmitted to Cochrane, which was false, and, in February, that it had been published, which was also false. In October 2012, the editor in chief of the prestigious *British Medical Journal,* Fiona Godlee, published an open letter to Roche, asking it to make public the results of a dozen unpublished tests, since Roche had made public only the results of two tests that were favorable to its medication.[45] Still in vain.

So Cochrane carried out an analysis on the little data available, and it became clear that the methods described in the articles that were supposed to prove the benefits of Tamiflu were far from optimal: the type of people chosen to be tested, especially, was not random, but determined by the positive result the company wanted to obtain. What's more, a lot of major data was missing. To date, there is no "double blind," placebo-comparing study carried out demonstrating the effectiveness of Tamiflu on serious forms of flu. The most that has been observed is a slight reduction of the duration of symptoms on commonplace forms of flu.

After an investigation published in 2008, it turned out that GlaxoSmithKline (GSK) had neglected to make public the data from nine studies showing not only the ineffectiveness on children of its paroxetine-based antidepressant, but also revealing serious undesirable effects, namely an increase of a risk of suicide among those children.[46] GSK made no effort to inform anyone, and an internal memo asserts, "It would be commercially unacceptable to include a declaration in the instructions indicating that effectiveness has not been demonstrated, since that would harm the profile of paroxetine." In the year following that confidential memo, in the United Kingdom alone, 32,000 prescriptions for paroxetine were written for children.

Vioxx (rofecoxib) was placed on the market by Merck mainly to relieve the pain of osteoarthritis. Merck continued to lead aggressive marketing campaigns to promote the sales of Vioxx even when the laboratory had known since 2000 of the serious cardiovascular dangers of this product. The firm didn't decide to withdraw it from the market until 2004, after tens of thousands of cardiovascular accidents, often mortal, had been registered.[47]

During a trial, a group of independent experts showed that Merck had covered up the comparatively high death rate due to rofecoxib, although it had been observed during clinical trials aiming to explore its action on Alzheimer's disease. Under cover of confidentiality,

Merck had provided only partial information and incorrect analyses. According to two unpublished clinical trials, however, mortality was three times higher under rofecoxib as compared to a placebo.[48] In the two published articles, the authors, several of whom were employed by Merck, had asserted that rofecoxib was "well-tolerated."[49] By the survivors, perhaps?

During the last decade, various measures and resolutions concerning medications have been made by national and international organizations, as well as by editors of medical journals, but none has been put into practice.[50] In 2007, it was decided that the results of all studies, positive or negative, had to be put online on a site created for the purpose. There again, an audit published in the *British Medical Journal* revealed that only 1 study out of 5 was thus made available to the medical community. Another sham.

REGULATORS AREN'T DOING THEIR DUTY

The same is true for government regulators who are supposed to verify the quality of the research from laboratories producing medications, and on that basis authorize them to market the medications. They don't always have access to all the data from the pharmaceutical companies; according to Goldacre, the British doctor and author of *Bad Pharma,* it is sometimes just as difficult to obtain the data they have as "to squeeze blood from a rock."

He gives the example of researchers at the Cochrane Center who worked in 2007 on a systematic study of two medications widely used for weight loss, Orlistat and Rimonabant. Such a study requires access to all existing data: if any are missing, especially data that gave negative results, the researchers can only come up with a deformed picture of the situation.

In June 2007, Cochrane asked the EMA (European Medicines Agency), the organization that approves of and supervises medications for all of Europe, to provide it with the experimental protocols and reports on the studies in question. Two months later, the EMA replied it had decided not to provide these reports, invoking the protection of commercial interests and the intellectual property of pharmaceutical companies. The researchers replied by return mail that there was absolutely nothing, in an objective report on the harmlessness and effectiveness of a medication, that could harm the protection of such commercial interests. And even if there were, could the EMA explain why the commercial interests of pharmaceutical companies should be more important than patients' health?[51]

As a last resort, the Cochrane researchers turned to the European Ombudsman. "This was the beginning of a battle for data that would shame the EMA, and would last more than three years," reports Goldacre.[52] In 2009, in a dramatic turn of events, one of the two medications, Rimonabant, was withdrawn from the market because it increases the risk of serious psychiatric problems and suicide. The EMA was then forced by the European Ombudsman to provide all the data in its possession. In 2010, the conclusions of the Ombudsman were overwhelming: the EMA had failed to do its duty and to reply to the serious accusation that its withholding of information went against patients' interest. For all those years, patients had suffered from a lack of transparency on the part of the pharmaceutical companies and of government regulators.

With great fanfare, the European Agency of Medicines created a list of medical tests called EudraCT, and the European legislation requires all studies to be registered with it. But, according to all competent opinions, transparency continues to be lacking, and the WHO, among others, declared that the EudraCT list was practically unusable because it is almost impossible to navigate through the mass of crude, poorly organized data that have been put online.[53]

The Cost of Research Is Greatly Inferior to That of Advertising Expenses

Drug companies spend astronomical sums each year on advertising to influence the therapeutic decisions of doctors—60 billion dollars a year in the United States alone, the equivalent of the GDP of Bolivia or Kenya, and three times that of Laos.[54]

When a pharmaceutical company refuses to let a developing country use a new medication for AIDS at an affordable price, it is, it says, because it needs income to finance costly research. This argument loses all credibility when we learn that the company, like all other pharmaceutical companies, spends twice as much on marketing its products as on research.

It is unacceptable to think of a medication the way we would a product of ordinary consumption, cosmetics or a box of detergent, for example. Medications should have no other reason for existing than their usefulness in the service of public health. Consequently, only strictly scientific criteria should be applied to them, and we should begin by banning all forms of advertising concerning them.

The money spent on advertising, moreover, is entirely paid for by the patients themselves, or by public funding if they are reimbursed by social welfare, or else by the insurance companies that finance patients' costs. About 25% of the sale price of a medication serves to cover advertising expenses.

Medical advertising does more than draw the attention of doctors to one medication rather than another; it is often deceptive. To check this, you just have to gather the assertions found in medical advertisements and compare them to the data available on the medications in question.

Such a study was carried out in 2010 by a group of Dutch researchers who sorted through the main medical journals throughout the world between 2003 and 2005.[55] The results were astonishing: only half the therapeutic effects described by the advertisements were corroborated by scientific studies. What's more, only half the studies themselves were of good quality.

The largest medical journals worldwide, *JAMA* and *NEJM (New England Journal of Medicine)*, for example, each receive between 10 and 20 million dollars of income from advertisements paid for by pharmaceutical companies.[56]

The promotional strategies of pharmaceutical firms encompass the medical press, medical representatives, the various institutions for medical training, and the opinion formers in the field of health.

MEDICAL VISITORS UNDULY INFLUENCE DOCTORS

There are a number of reasons why doctors should stop receiving representatives of pharmaceutical businesses and companies.[57] These representatives, called "medical visitors," come regularly to sing the praises of products manufactured by their laboratory.

Medical visitors certainly do their work conscientiously, and it would be unfair to criticize them on a personal level. Moreover, in the present situation, they facilitate the task of doctors, whose long hours often make it impossible for them to read all the scientific literature published every month in their specialty.

It is the system that is deficient and ethically unacceptable, since we know that drug companies, and by extension those who represent them, offer a deformed image of their products. The general interest would be served if the new medications vaunted by laboratories were more effective than those that exist already, but often, as we shall see, that is not the case.

Most doctors say they keep their critical wits. Studies carried out on this question show that quite the opposite is the case. One of these studies followed, in the United States, a group of doctors before and after a trip paid for by a drug company to a fashionable holiday spot.[58] Before they left, most of the doctors had declared they didn't think this kind of event would change their prescription habits. But it turned out that upon their return they tripled the prescriptions of the products from the company in question. How do we know that? In the United States, it's easy to find out, since pharmacies are authorized to sell their prescription archives to commercial companies that analyze them for pharmaceutical companies.[59] Patients' names are omitted, but not doctors' names. So companies can find out which medications the doctors prescribe, and adjust the sales pitch of their representatives. And, unlike in Europe, nothing forbids them from granting favors to the doctors who most prescribe their products.

According to Ben Goldacre and many other experts, doctors should simply refuse to receive medical visitors, and they should be forbidden access to clinics, hospitals, and medical schools.[60] Moreover, pharmacists should not under any condition be authorized to divulge information about their prescriptions.

Much Research Serves Only to Produce a Copy of What Already Exists

Of course sometimes a drug company discovers and manufactures a new medication that saves hundreds of thousands of lives. But, these days, most new medications contribute no tangible therapeutic progress, while they are sold much more expensively than previous ones. A real improvement would consist of better effectiveness, less frequent dosage, a diminution of risks, or else a simpler or safer administration of treatment.

But a large number of "new" medications belong to two categories known in English by the nickname *me-too* and *me-again,* and nothing justifies putting them on the market.

"Me-too" drugs are copies of existent medications sold under different names. "Me-again" drugs are medications whose patent is ending (the legal period of protection is twenty years) and will soon fall into public domain. The manufacturers, anxiously seeing the day when other companies will be free to commercialize generic versions of products that had till then brought them a fortune, hurry to come out with a new version whose chemical formula is slightly modified, without it leading to the slightest therapeutic difference. Renamed and much-publicized, the "me-again" drugs will be sold two or three times more expensively than the patent-defunct product. That isn't difficult, since, as we've seen, in order to obtain authorization to commercialize a medication, you just have to demonstrate that it is slightly better than a placebo, which is the case for 30% of new medications approved by health authorities. What patients need is not a more expensive duplicate, but a more effective medication.

According to an analysis by Adrian Hollis published by the WHO, the main problem with the "me-too" and "me-again" drugs is that they discourage innovation. So before authorizing a new medication for sale, proofs should be required that it is actually *superior* to those that exist already.[61]

The ALLHAT study (Antihypertensive and Lipid-Lowering Treatment to Prevent Heart Attack Trial),[62] which began in 1994 and cost 125 million dollars, studied high blood pressure, a disease that affects about a quarter of the adult population. The study compared chlorthalidone, an old, inexpensive compound, to amlodipine (Pfizer's Norvasc), a new, very expensive compound that is abundantly prescribed. They knew both remedies were equally effective in controlling blood pressure. The goal was to find out the number of heart attacks affecting patients treated by these two medications. At the end of the study, in 2002, it was observed—to the great surprise of all—that the old medication was clearly better. What's more, the savings for patients and social services if this remedy was used would have greatly exceeded the cost of the study itself. Unfortunately that study did not prevent the sale of amlodipine at top price, highly publicized to doctors and pharmacists.[63]

SERIOUS ETHICAL MISTAKES CONCERNING HUMAN GUINEA PIGS

For decades in the United States, many new medications were tested on prisoners. Today, it's the poor people in wealthy countries and populations in developing countries that undergo these tests. Indeed, they are paid, sometimes with enticing sums, but the subcontractors are poorly supervised and often unscrupulous, accidents are frequent, and help for the victims nonexistent in case of accident. Sometimes, people who make it a profession on which their lives depend to act as guinea pigs suffer so much from constantly taking new substances that they end up pretending to swallow the pills. One of these "professionals" describes his ordeal as "a mild torture economy."[64]

These tests also have the defect of being carried out on ethnic groups other than the populations to which the medications will finally be administered. It is far from certain that poor inhabitants of rural communities in China, Russia, or India will react to the substances given them in the same way as an inhabitant of New York. If, for example, you give a new medication for blood pressure to people who have never taken it, it is very likely that the effects will be much more encouraging than for someone who has already followed various treatments. In that way the results are distorted. Finally, those who volunteer for these studies will rarely be the beneficiaries of these new medications, which are meant mainly for wealthy countries.

POSSIBLE SOLUTIONS

Faced with such indifference to the good of others, faced with such serious offenses, it is important to conceive of possible remedies. We have seen that the drug industry provides only incomplete, biased information. This situation has until recently widely escaped the media and the public, despite the warnings given occasionally by responsible scientists.

So it is indispensable for the regulatory health authorities, independent of the industry, to be the ones to inform practitioners clearly of the virtues and dangers of existing medications, and to ensure continual training of doctors. Independent scientific committees should also judge the validity of studies carried out by laboratories. For that, the indispensable preliminary condition is access to *all the experimental data* concerning the efficacy of tests of medicinal products. This arrangement would indeed be an onerous one, but in the end, there would be huge savings for governments.

Pharmaceutical companies should also be penalized if it is revealed that they have hidden the results of studies unfavorable to their product, which is common practice today. In *Bad Pharma,* Ben Goldacre argues that devoting resources to improving the system of medication production would be more important and useful to society than carrying out more research.

Monsanto, Extreme Example of Institutionalized Selfishness

Monsanto has embodied institutionalized selfishness for almost a century, and because of that deserves special mention. Established in forty-six countries, this company is known above all to the public as the worldwide leader in GMOs, and one of the main firms responsible for the massive expansion of monocultures. It exercises draconian control over the farmers to whom it sells seeds; they are not authorized to reuse them from one year to the next.

What we are not so familiar with is that, since its creation in 1901 by a self-taught chemist named John Francis Queeny, the firm has been one of the largest producers of toxic products, including PCBs[65] and the sadly famous Agent Orange used during the Vietnam War. Thousands of people died because of these products, which contained dioxins. For dozens of years, Monsanto covered up, then denied, the harmful effects of these products on health, until a series of trials revealed its criminal actions. Monsanto presents itself today as a company of the "life sciences," a sudden convert to the virtues of sustainable development.

In her book *The World According to Monsanto,* Marie-Monique Robin, a journalist who won the Albert-Londres Prize and a documentary filmmaker, reports the results of a detailed investigation she carried out on every continent.

A Poisoned City

Anniston is a small city in Alabama, which today numbers 23,000 inhabitants, 25% of whom, mainly African-Americans, live below poverty level. Anniston was for a time one of the most polluted cities in the United States. It was there, in fact, that between 1929 and 1971, Monsanto produced PCBs and for forty years dumped with impunity highly toxic waste from that production into Snow Creek, a canal that flows through the city. "It was poisoned water. Monsanto knew it but never said anything," recounts David Baker, a survivor.[66] Today, the most polluted neighborhoods have been abandoned, and look like ghost towns.

PCBs served as lubricants and insulation in machines; they entered into the composition of paint and products for the treatment of metal, welding, adhesives, and so on. They were everywhere. They are now classified among "persistent organic pollutants" (POP), very dangerous substances since they resist natural degradation and accumulate in living tissues throughout the food chain.

Near the end of the 1960s, public information began to circulate about the dangers that PCB cause humans. Monsanto began to get worried...about its own business. An internal memo written in 1970 explains to sales personnel: "You can give verbal answers; no answers should be given in writing.... We can't afford to lose one dollar of business."[67]

In the 1990s, in Anniston, the rate of deaths accelerated, women had miscarriages, and a high proportion of children showed signs of mental retardation. Monsanto offered to buy the houses of poor inhabitants at a good price in exchange for the promise not to sue them. Then the company offered one million dollars to the inhabitants of affected neighborhoods to buy their silence and settle the question once and for all. Before this strategy took shape, a lawyer from Anniston, Donald

Stewart, sided with the population and ended up obtaining court authorization to consult Monsanto's internal archives, a mountain of documents that the company had refused to make accessible before then.

Examination of these archives revealed that, beginning in 1937, the company knew that PCBs presented grave health risks, workers had died after being exposed to PCB vapors containing dioxins, and that others had contracted a skin disease that had disfigured them. This disease, which was named "chloracne," is characterized by an eruption of pustules all over the body and a browning of the skin, and can last several years, or in some cases never entirely disappear.

In 1955, a researcher from Monsanto based in London suggested that rigorous research be carried out to evaluate the toxic effects of Aroclor. Dr. Kelly, director of Monsanto's medical service, curtly replied: "I don't know how you would get any particular advantage in doing more work."[68]

But pressure mounted. In November 1966, Dr. Denzel Ferguson, biologist at the University of Mississippi, and his team plunged twenty-five caged fish into the water of the creek that goes through Anniston: "All 25 fish lost equilibrium... and all were dead in 3½ minutes and... blood issues from the gills after 3 minutes exposure."[69] In certain places, the water is so polluted that it kills all fish, even if it's diluted 300 times. The expert concluded: "Snow Creek is a potential source of legal problems.... Monsanto needs to monitor the biological effects of its effluents as a protection against future accusations."[70]

PCBs Spread All Over the World

PCBs have contaminated the entire planet, from the Arctic to the Antarctic.[71] In 1966, a Swedish researcher, Søren Jensen, discovered an unusual toxic substance in samples of human blood: PCB. As one thing led to another, he saw that PCBs have extensively contaminated the environment, even though they are not manufactured in Sweden. He found large quantities in salmon caught along the coasts and even in the hair of his own children.[72] He concluded that PCBs accumulate throughout the food chain in the organs and fatty tissues of animals, and that they are at least as toxic as DDT.

"And yet," comments Marie-Monique Robin, "Monsanto management did not change its attitude: one year later it allocated an additional $2.9 million to further development of Aroclor products in Anniston and Sauget."[73]

PROTECTING BUSINESS, SAYING NOTHING

For *forty years,* Monsanto acted as if nothing was wrong, all the way up to the definitive ban of PCBs in the United States in 1977. "The company's irresponsibility was staggering," said Ken Cook, director of the Environmental Working Group, a Washington-based NGO that houses on its Internet site the "mountain" of Monsanto's internal documents:[74] "It had all the data at its fingertips, but it did nothing. That's why I say it was guilty of criminal conduct."

Monsanto ended up asking a private laboratory to perform studies whose results indicate that PCBs "are exhibiting a greater degree of toxicity than we had anticipated."[75] Still, in 1976, the St. Louis offices, the company's headquarters, sent a letter to Monsanto Europe, warning them that if questions were asked about PCB's carcinogenic effects, they should reply that "preliminary health studies conducted on our workers making PCBs, as well as long-term studies carried out on animals, do not lead us to think that PCBs are carcinogenic."[76]

A WEIGHTY CONDEMNATION, SOON FORGOTTEN

A trial finally took place, in 2002, thanks to a big law firm from New York entering the scene. Monsanto and its subsidiary company Solutia were judged guilty of having polluted the territory of Anniston and the blood of its population with PCBs. The grounds for the verdict were "negligence, wantonness, fraud, trespass, nuisance, and outrage." The verdict was accompanied with a severe judgment that deemed Monsanto's behavior went "beyond all possible bounds of decency, so as to be regarded as atrocious and utterly intolerable in civilized society."[77] Monsanto and its subsidiaries were ordered to pay 700 million dollars in damages.

Despite that, "They never showed the slightest compassion for the victims," Ken Cook, who followed the entire trial, confirmed to

Robin, "not a word of excuse or a sign of regret, just denial now and forever!"[78]

"Integrity, transparency, dialogue, sharing and respect," proclaimed Monsanto's Pledge in 2005. Today, the company's website goes further:

> *Integrity is the foundation for all that we do. It includes honesty, decency, consistency, and courage.... We will ensure that information is available, accessible, and understandable.... The safety of our employees, the communities where we operate, our customers, consumers, and the environment will be our highest priority.*[79]

Safety, a high priority for Monsanto? It certainly has not been so in the past, and nothing yet shows it will be so in the future.

Agent Orange

In 1959, Monsanto launched into production of the herbicide Lasso, better known under the nickname "Agent Orange," which would be sold to the American army to defoliate the Vietnamese jungle from 1962 to 1971.[80] Agent Orange caused many cases of cancer in Vietnam, as well as the birth of 150,000 children afflicted with severe birth defects and serious illnesses.[81] Many American soldiers also suffered from it.

Declassified documents have revealed that the two main manufacturers, Monsanto and Dow Chemicals, had deliberately covered up the data from their own research, so as not to lose a very profitable market, which at the time gave rise to the signing of the largest contract ever entered into by the American army.[82] In 1983, Raymond Suskind, of the University of Cincinnati, published a study, ordered by Monsanto, concluding that the dioxins emanating from 2,4,5-trichlorophenol, the main substance in Agent Orange, had no harmful effects on health.[83] His study would be cited often to reassure the public when the American army used Agent Orange in Vietnam. During a suit against Monsanto, it turned out, too late for the victims, that Suskind had manipulated the data with the aim of demonstrating the harmlessness of a highly carcinogenic product.[84]

After a file compiled by Greenpeace and a report on Monsanto's frauds written by Cate Jenkins and the Environmental Protection Agency (EPA)—which Monsanto tried by every means possible to silence[85]—and finally after the decisive intervention of Admiral Elmo Zumwalt, former commander of the American fleet in Vietnam whose son had died after being exposed to Agent Orange, Congress ended up asking the National Academy of Sciences to draw up a list of illnesses attributable to dioxin exposure.[86] This list, delivered sixteen years later, included thirteen serious pathologies, which permitted the Dept. of Veterans Affairs to compensate and cover the medical charges of the thousands of veterans who served during the Vietnam War.[87] Nothing, however, was provided for the Vietnamese children.

ROUNDUP

Roundup was Monsanto's miracle weed killer, possessing every virtue, no harmful effect for humans, and, what's more, certified biodegradable, hence respectful of the environment. "Roundup can be used where kids and pets'll play and breaks down into natural material,"[88] Monsanto boasted. The company was later condemned in several countries for deceptive advertising.

In Argentina, where Roundup is currently sprayed by plane on vast soy plantations, many cases of poisoning, some of them fatal, have been recorded. In the United States, declassified documents have shown that laboratories working under the aegis of Monsanto had covered up reports establishing the toxicity of glyphosate-4 (the chemical component of Roundup) on animals.[89] Since then, several studies have linked its usage to an increase of certain cancers in the United States, Canada and Sweden.[90]

GMOs

In 1972, Paul Berg, a geneticist at Stanford, managed to recombine two DNA strands from different species in a single hybrid molecule; Stanley Cohen, another Stanford geneticist, managed to introduce a gene taken from a toad's chromosome into the DNA of a bacterium.[91]

That same year, Monsanto asked the geneticist Ernest Jaworski, assisted by a group of thirty researchers, to try to manipulate the genetic makeup of plants to make them resistant to herbicides. After many tries, the Monsanto researchers, as well as those from two other laboratories, announced they had managed to introduce an antibiotic resistance gene into tobacco and petunia, by using as vector a bacterium that often infects those two plants.

The three laboratories in question, including Monsanto, registered patents. This was the beginning of the "patenting of life," with the Supreme Court ruling that "Anything under the sun that is made by man can be patented." The European Patent Office in Munich followed their lead and granted patents for microorganisms, then for plants (1985), animals (1988), and finally human embryos (2000).[92] Today, the Patent Office in Washington grants about 15,000 patents concerning living organisms every year.

The Monsanto researchers then began a frantic race to develop plants that would be resistant to their star herbicide, Roundup. The project was as follows: farmers would plant Roundup-resistant soy, then would spray enough herbicide to kill all the weeds and any other form of vegetation. Only the resistant soy would be spared, and would grow alone in the midst of a biological desert.[93]

The Monsanto researchers finally succeeded at inserting into the cells of soy a Roundup-resistant gene, found among microorganisms in decontamination pools at a glyphosate factory. In 1993, Monsanto launched Roundup Ready soy. As the Japanese biologist Masaharu Kawata of Nagoya University remarked about the combination of foreign genes inserted into the soy, "The 'Roundup tolerant soybean gene cassette' is a completely artificial one that never existed in natural life and could not have evolved naturally."[94]

In 1994, Monsanto filed a request to market its Roundup Ready (RR) soy, the first industrially manufactured GMO. The American regulatory institution, the Food and Drug Administration (FDA), decreed that "food...derived from plant varieties developed by the new methods of genetic modification are regulated within the existing framework, utilizing an approach identical to that applied to foods developed by traditional plant breeding."[95]

Claiming that GMOs are "quasi-identical" to their natural homologues (which is called the "principle of substantial equivalence," a concept without any scientific foundation) comes down to likening them to normal food products, and allows biotechnology companies to evade the toxicological tests ordained by law for food additives and other synthetic products, as well as to avoid labeling their products in the United States.[96]

MONSANTO CONVERTS

Monsanto realized that, in order to maximize its profits, it also had to own the seeds. So the firm acquired a large number of seed companies, and its stocks went up.

"Improving agriculture, improving life" is the motto on Monsanto's website, which describes itself today as a "relatively new company" whose main goal is to help farmers all over the world. It's as if Monsanto's weighty chemical past, going back to 1901, had never existed.

In the late 1990s, the company changed its tactics and concentrated on agriculture, spurred on by a new president, Robert B. Shapiro, nicknamed the "guru of Monsanto." Under the heading "Food, Health and Hope," it promises the moon—factories that manufacture biodegradable plastics, corn producing antibodies against cancer, canola oil that protects against heart disease, and more.

In the United States, over 90% of corn, soy and cotton is grown from genetically modified seeds, for which Monsanto holds the majority of patents, and GMO-derived products appear in about 70% of manufactured foodstuffs.

Monsanto controls its seeds with an iron fist, and institutes countless legal proceedings against farmers and small businesses. Usually, investigators from Monsanto introduce themselves to the farmer and tell him he has violated technological conventions (Monsanto requires new seeds to be bought from it every year).[97] According to Bill Freese, analyst for the Center for Food Safety in Washington, the investigators say, "Monsanto knows that you are saving Roundup Ready seeds, and if you don't sign these information-release forms, Monsanto is going to come after you and take your farm or take you for all you're worth." Most farmers give in and pay the damages. The ones that resist have to face the legal wrath of Monsanto. The heaviest sentence passed on a farmer was as high as $3 million, and the average penalty is $380,000, enough to ruin a farmer. But these sentences are only the tip of the iceberg. The number of cases settled out of court is twenty to forty times higher than the number of cases that go to trial.

To top it all off, if you own a farm situated next to another farm on which seeds from Monsanto are used, and if by misfortune some of the other farm's seeds migrate to your land, carried by the wind or by birds, Monsanto can sue you, claim damages, and sometimes ruin you.

"As an agricultural and technology company committed to human rights, we have a unique opportunity to protect and advance human rights." Those are the words of the current president of Monsanto, Hugh Grant, who prudently adds, "We have a responsibility to consider not only how our business can benefit consumers, farmers, and food processors, but how it can protect the human rights of both Monsanto's employees and our business partners' employees." As Auguste Detoeuf, a graduate of the École Polytechnique and a humorist, wrote, "The worker just sells his body; the technician just sells his brain; the businessman sells his soul."[98]

THE SPREAD OF GMOs OVER EVERY CONTINENT

In 1998, African scientists strongly opposed Monsanto's GMO promotional campaign, which featured starving African children with the caption, "Let the Harvest Begin!" These scientists, who represented most of the countries affected by poverty and hunger, stated that the genetic technologies would undermine the ability of the various nations to feed themselves by destroying biodiversity, local technologies, and sustainable agricultural methods.[99]

That is what has already happened in South America. As Walter Pengue, an agricultural engineer at the University of Buenos Aires, told Marie-Monique Robin, "Roundup Ready soybeans spread through Argentina at an absolutely unprecedented speed in the history of agriculture: an average of over two million acres a year. We now have a veritable green desert devouring one of the world's breadbaskets."[100] Before the arrival of GMOs, Argentina grew a large number of grains (corn, wheat, sorghum), oleaginous plants (sunflower, peanut, soy), and vegetables and fruits, and the production of milk was so far developed it was described as the "milk basin." Some regions of Argentina, like the province of Santiago del Estero, have one of the highest deforestation rates in the world. Forests of rich biodiversity are giving way to monocultures of soy. Local labor is losing its source of employment and income. Large companies often evict farmers from their land by force.

Over the short term, intensive culture of GMO soy has bailed out of bankruptcy the Argentine government, for which agricultural levies represent 30% of the national budget. But the long-term damages are of such great magnitude they are barely conceivable. The intensive use of Roundup tends to make the earth sterile, since it kills everything except GMO soy. The thousands of species of microorganisms that give life to the earth are disappearing. In the area of health, local doctors have observed a significant increase of fertility anomalies, like miscarriages or stillbirths, and many other problems in the villages that are most often under massive aerial spraying of insecticide.[101]

India is staggering beneath the high price of transgenic cotton seeds from Monsanto (a variety known by the initials Bt) and the fertilizer that has to go with them, plunging farmers into debt. And when the sale price of their harvests goes down, many heads of families are pushed to suicide, often by swallowing an insecticide or fertilizer, the same poison that caused their ruin. "They lied to us," a village leader said to Marie-Monique Robin. "They had said that these magic seeds would help us make money, but we're all in debt and the harvest is nonexistent!" "What will become of us? Tell the world that Bt cotton is a disaster!" another farmer exclaimed.[102] The *Hindu Times* reports 270,940 suicides of Indian farmers since 1995. Monsanto denies any link between these suicides and the introduction of Bt cotton, but Indian farmers and NGOs on site don't seem to agree.

Vandana Shiva, recipient of the Right Livelihood Award (the "alternative Nobel Prize") in 2003 and named by *The Guardian* one of the 100 most remarkable women in the world, fights against the practices that are at the root of so many acts of despair in India. She explains that the region of India that has the highest suicide rate of farmers is Vidharbha, in Maharashtra (10 suicides per day). That is also the region that comprises the largest acreage of Monsanto GMO Bt cotton.

Monsanto GMO seeds have turned the seed market upside-down. The cotton seeds that reproduced naturally ad infinitum cost 7 rupees a kilo. Bt cotton seeds, however, cost up to 17,000 rupees a kilo.[103] In August 2012, the state of Maharashtra banned the sale of Monsanto transgenic cotton seeds, commercialized by its Indian branch Mahyco Monsanto Biotech because of the inferior quality of the seeds, sold at exorbitant prices.[104]

In 1987, Navdanya, Vandana Shiva's foundation, launched a campaign called "Seeds of Hope," in counterpoint to the title of the book that Shiva would later publish, *Seeds of Suicide*.[105] It called for a transition that would include a return to organic, renewable seeds and to open-pollination varieties of seeds that farmers can keep and share. A transition began then from chemical agriculture to organic agriculture, and from iniquitous trade based on artificial prices to fair trade, based on real prices. According to her experience in the field, she thinks that farmers who have adopted this change earn ten times more than farmers growing Bt cotton.

To those who call her a naïve idealist and claim that organic agriculture will never be able to respond to the food needs of the planet, Vandana Shiva replies that the power of agro-industry will lead to a domination of genetically homogeneous seeds, catastrophically harming biodiversity, which will end up forcing farmers to use increasing quantities of chemical fertilizers, pesticides and water. Farmers in developing countries will not receive fair economic benefits from their harvests, which will go to a handful of multinationals that will hold all the power and the future of food safety.

A Few Victories

For the consumer who shops in a supermarket, the only way to know if a product contains GMOs, or has come from them, is the label. Legislations are different, however, in Europe and the United States. Europe is more protected than the United States against the abuse of firms like Monsanto. European law stipulates that labeling is obligatory for any product containing more than 0.9% ingredients of transgenic origin. In the United States, however, no rule like this has to this date been imposed for all the states. California was still fighting in November 2012 for food containing GMOs to be labeled and transgenic ingredients mentioned. If this new Californian law proposal, called "Proposition 37," passes, that fight would constitute a precedent in a country where 88% of corn and 94% of soy come from genetically modified seeds.[106]

The French government pleaded in October 2012 for "an overhaul of the European system of evaluation, authorization and control of GMOs and pesticides." It stated it was mobilizing to support independent, scientific studies on the long-term effects of consumption of GMO foods linked to pesticides. A new report of the National Federation of Friends of the Earth reveals that the growing of GMO plants continues to decrease in Europe, and that the surface cultivated with GMOs is also diminishing.[107]

In 2012, Germany, along with five other European countries, suspended the growing of genetically modified corn; this decision was made against the advice of the European Commission.

Greenpeace continues to alert the public to the potential dangers of agriculture based on genetically modified seeds and on manipulations by the agro-food industry.

To remedy hunger throughout the world and to feed 9 billion people by 2050, it is wiser to invest in green agriculture, and not in the use of costly genetic manipulations that threaten biodiversity and leave farmers at the mercy of the greed of multinationals. We must also stop the practice of "patenting of life." Governments have shown too much indulgence toward the opaque manipulations of these multinationals that use globalization as a mere tool to turn out profit by basically exploiting poorer populations, while an enlightened globalization, based on solidarity and the understanding of the interdependence of sentient beings and their ecosystem, could on the contrary be a source of cooperation for the good of all.

The United Nations Special Rapporteur on the Right to Food, Olivier De Schutter, has urged that the needs for smallholder farmers should be at the center of food security strategies, and has urged nations to reinvest in their agricultural sectors rather than rely on imports from volatile world markets. He has also been critical of large-scale land acquisitions and biofuel production in food-insecure countries, and is encouraging agro-ecology to provide solutions to our planet's food crisis.

In his report, "AgroEcology and the Right to Food,"[108] which he presented before the UN Human Rights Council in Geneva, De Schutter explores how governments can and must achieve a reorientation of their agricultural systems toward modes of production that are highly productive, highly sustainable, and that contribute to the progressive realization of the human right to adequate food.

Drawing on an extensive review of the published scientific literature, the Special Reporter identifies agro-ecology as a mode of agricultural development that not only shows strong conceptual connections with the right to food, but has proven results for quick progress in the concretization of this human right for many vulnerable groups in various countries and environments. He concludes that "the scaling up of these experiences is the main challenge today." The report demonstrates that agro-ecology, if sufficiently supported, can double food production in entire regions within 10 years while mitigating climate change and alleviating rural poverty.

In conclusion, institutionalized selfishness, a few examples of which we have presented, might lead us to think that altruism is not a fundamental component of human nature, and might discourage those who try to cultivate it and promote solidarity with society. But all the facts presented in this book should not lead us to call into question either the existence or the importance of altruism in our lives. What this chapter shows above all is the power a minority of determined and unscrupulous egotists have to throw the proper functioning of society off-kilter and divert everything for the sake of their profit. So it is up to civil society to denounce the machinations of those who practice institutionalized selfishness, and upon government organizations to neutralize them.

V

Building a More Altruistic Society

Utopia signifies not the unrealizable, but the unrealized. Yesterday's utopia could turn into today's reality.

—Théodore Monod

36

The Virtues of Cooperation

Cooperation and partnership are the only route that offers any hope of a better future for all humanity.

—Kofi Annan[1]

As Joël Candau, of the Department of Anthropology and Sociology at the University of Nice, points out: "Ours is the only species where one observes cooperation that is strong, regular, diverse, risky, extensive, and which involve punishments, often costly, between individuals who share no familial ties."[2] Mutual aid, reciprocal gifts, sharing, exchanges, collaboration, alliances, associations, and participation are all forms of the cooperation found throughout human society. Cooperation is not only the creative force that drives evolution—we have already seen that evolution *needs* cooperation to be capable of constructing increasingly complex levels of organization—but it also lies at the heart of the human species' unprecedented accomplishments. It allows society to accomplish tasks that one person would not be able to accomplish by himself. When the great inventor Thomas Edison was asked why he had twenty-one assistants, he replied: "If I could solve all the problems myself, I would."

Cooperation can seem paradoxical. As far as selfishness is concerned, the most attractive strategy is that of the "free rider" who benefits from the efforts of others to achieve his aims while expending the minimum of effort. Yet plenty of research shows that it is preferable—for oneself as well as for others—to trust one another and to cooperate rather than acting as a lone ranger. Although human beings have a certain tendency toward the "closed" cooperation linked to tribal instinct, they are also gifted with a unique aptitude for "open" cooperation, which goes well beyond an individual's kin or social group.[3]

"As such," Candau goes on, "human cooperation constitutes just as great a challenge to the most orthodox theory of evolution, underpinned as it is by the notion that competition between individuals who are concerned with their own reproduction alone, as it does to traditional economic theory founded on the existence of "selfish" agents devoted exclusively to the maximization of their own interests. Here we see an anthropological fact which demands explanations."[4]

The Advantages of Cooperation

One beautiful morning in the fall, I met with my friend Paul Ekman, one of the preeminent psychologists of our time, who has dedicated his life to the study of emotions. We first met in India in 2000, at a Mind & Life Institute conference organized around the Dalai Lama on the theme of destructive emotions, and we have been working together ever since.[5]

We had planned to spend a day together discussing the issue of altruism. As a result of his many meetings and conversations with the Dalai Lama, Paul too has become convinced that we must do all that is humanly possible to usher in a more altruistic, united and cooperative society, that is to say, a "global compassion."[6]

He began by telling me how, in small communities and villages, the more the inhabitants cooperate, the more prosperous they become and the greater the chances their children have of survival. Among the tribes of New Guinea, where Paul worked in the 1960s, everyone has to muck in together, from preparing meals to assisting with childbirth or defending against predators. In these villages, no one wants to work with those who are prone to pick fights, and if somebody attempts to exploit another, his reputation will not go unscathed, leaving him with little chance of survival in the community. In a village, you can't get away with exploiting others for long and you can't run away from a bad reputation either. This is why over the course of time our genetic development has directed us toward cooperation. Furthermore, there is an inherent satisfaction in working together to achieve a common goal. As a result of natural diversity, there will always be people who are fundamentally selfish, but they only represent a margin of society. Unfortunately, as we saw in the chapter on institutionalized selfishness, they can, in certain circumstances, succeed in forming highly powerful oligarchies.

In a small community, if someone suffers, the others immediately feel concern and tend to help that person. Ephraïm Grenadou, a French farmer at the start of the twentieth century, recalls: "When we raised the alarm by ringing the village clock, if there was a fire or something, everybody would come very, very quickly. They would run from the fields, from their houses, from all over. Within a few minutes the village square would be heaving with people."[7] In our modern society, the media present us with more suffering in a single day than we would ever be able to alleviate in our whole life, a unique situation in the history of humankind. This is why, according to Paul Ekman: "If we are to bring about change that results in an increase in altruism, it must be selective, focused on specific goals, and linked to actions which have impacts and which form part of a social movement."[8]

To what extent can cooperation and benevolence extend beyond our innermost circles? Nothing is set in stone: our education and cultural environment are at least as important as our genetic inheritance. The environment of the first five years of our lives has a particularly major influence on our motivations and emotions, which then go on to act as a filter for our perception of other people's emotions. According to Paul Ekman, talking in evolutionary terms, appropriate emotions (i.e., emotions that have been adapted to a given situation and which are expressed constructively) favor cooperation. In other words, without cooperation, we cannot survive.

Human beings, by virtue of their language, their capacity for empathy, and their vast range of emotions, are gifted with a profound sociability that is rarely taken into account by public policy and is neglected by most economists. If we continue regarding ourselves as individuals driven chiefly by self-interest, greed and antisocial motives, we may keep in place systems based on reward and punishment, thus perpetuating a distorted and wretched version of the kind of humanity we aspire to. On the individual level, competition poisons emotional and social links.

In strongly competitive societies, individuals do not trust one another, they worry about their safety, and they constantly seek to promote their own interests and social status without much concern for others. On the other hand, in cooperative societies, individuals trust one another and are prepared to devote time and resources to others. This sets in motion a virtuous cycle of solidarity and reciprocity that nurtures harmonious relationships.

If cooperation benefits everybody, how do we promote it? For Joël Candau, choosing an "open" cooperation, which transcends social groups, is above all a moral choice, which necessarily means that we overcome the doubt inherent in the challenges faced by all members of society: must cooperation be confined to the members of a community or rather opened up to other groups? What balance can be struck between cooperation and competition? What happens to those who take advantage of a cooperative system in order to promote their interests alone?[9]

COOPERATION WITHIN A COMPANY, AND COMPETITION BETWEEN COMPANIES

According to Richard Layard, professor at the London School of Economics, cooperation is an indispensable contributing factor to prosperity within a company. For some time we have seen the idea gain traction that it is desirable to promote ruthless competition between the employees of the same company—or, in the case of education, the students in a class—since everyone's performance would improve as a result. In reality, this competition is harmful, since it damages human relationships and working conditions. When all is said and done, as the economist Jeffrey Carpenter has shown, it is counter-productive and decreases the company's prosperity.[10]

Teamwork is particularly undermined by *individual* incentives and bonus schemes. On the other hand, rewarding the performance of the *team as a whole* encourages cooperation and improves results.[11] Managers and heads of business must therefore try to instill trust, solidarity and cooperation.

According to Layard, competition is only healthy and useful *between* companies. Placing companies in open competition stimulates innovation and research into ways of improving services and products.

It also leads to a reduction in prices, to the benefit of everyone. The opposite occurs in heavily bureaucratic, centralized, state-owned economies, which more often than not result in stagnation and inefficiency.[12]

As we will see below, for cooperation to be more efficient than competition, a number of factors must come together, including the frequent practice of reciprocal services and the mutual appreciation of the services given. In traditional economic analysis, if cooperation is most efficient, then cooperative firms should be the ones that survive best in the long term.

The Cooperative Movement

As the historian Joel Mokyr observes, a company's success lies less in having exceptional, multi-talented employees, and more in the fruitful cooperation between people with a good reason to trust each other.[13] According to the International Cooperative Alliance, an NGO which represents cooperatives from across the world, a cooperative is "an autonomous association of persons united voluntarily to meet their common economic, social and cultural needs and aspirations through a jointly-owned and democratically-controlled enterprise." There is evidence to show that employees who have part-ownership of the business, and have their own say on the distribution of income, are more satisfied with their working conditions, enjoy better physical and mental health, and even have a lower mortality rate.[14]

As such, cooperatives like mutual funds and NGOs fall under the so-called social or caring economy. According to the ICA (International Year of Cooperatives, 2012), more than 1 billion people worldwide are members of cooperatives.[15]

Mutual Trust Solves the Problem of the Commons

In an article that appeared in 1968 in the journal *Science*, one that would go on to be cited widely, Garrett Hardin discussed the "tragedy of the commons."[16] Taking the example of a rural village in England where each farmer can graze his sheep on a piece of land that does not belong to anybody, he put forward the hypothesis that, in such a situation, it is in the interest of each farmer to graze the maximum number of animals on an area which is available to everyone but where the resources are limited. This inevitably leads to overexploitation and, ultimately, land degradation. In the end, he thought, everyone loses out.

Hardin presented this as an inevitable outcome, without really basing his conclusions on solid historical data. Since his article was published, the "tragedy of the commons" has been a hot topic of discussion among economists. Hardin also cited the example of ocean exploitation, which threatened—one by one—to push various species of fish and marine mammals to the verge of extinction. On this point, his 1968 article was prophetic, since today 90% of large fish stocks have been destroyed.

On the other hand, in the case of the example cited by Hardin—the practice of using "common land" for grazing, which was standard for a long time in many European countries and is still carried out in some parts of the world, historical research has shown him to be mistaken. First, it is false to state that the land did not belong to anybody: it was unofficially the property of the community, which was well aware of its value. The members of this community had established a balanced system for regulating the use of commons that generally worked satisfactorily. As the historian Susan Buck Cox notes: "Perhaps what existed in fact was not 'a tragedy of the commons' but rather a triumph: that for hundreds of years—and perhaps thousands—...land was managed successfully by communities."[17]

The ecologist Ian Angus[18] agrees wholeheartedly, noting that Friedrich Engels had described the existence of this custom in pre-capitalist Germany. Communities which shared the use of land in this way were called "marks":

"The use of arable and meadowlands was under the supervision and direction of the community....The nature of this use was determined by the members of the community as a whole....At fixed times and, if necessary, more frequently, they met in the open air to discuss the affairs of the mark and to sit in judgment upon breaches of regulations and disputes concerning the mark."[19]

In the end this system succumbed to the Industrial Revolution and land reform, which granted supremacy to private property, big landowners, monoculture, and industrial farming. Land privatization has often had an adverse effect on prosperity. It has, for example, allowed landowners with an appetite for quick profit to destroy forests. Similarly it is big landowners, and not small communities, who have over-exploited the land and caused soil erosion and depletion, excessive use of fertilizers and pesticides, and of monocultures.

Like many others, Hardin assumed that human nature was selfish and that society was made up exclusively of individuals who were indifferent to the consequences of their actions on society. In fact, his article has often been used to endorse land privatization. This was apparent, for example, in Canada, in 2007, when the conservative government proposed the privatization of the indigenous population's land, with the so-called aim of facilitating their "development."

A more realistic vision was put forward by Elinor Ostrom, the first woman to receive the Nobel Prize in economics, who spent most of her scientific career investigating this very issue. Her work *Governing the Commons*[20] teems with examples of populations forming constructive agreements based on cooperative strategies. Indeed farmers, fishers, and other local communities the world over have created their own institutions and regulations aimed at preserving their common resources, ensuring that they last in the good years as well as the bad.

In Spain, in regions where water is scarce, the irrigation system used in the *huertas* has worked efficiently for more than five centuries, maybe as many as ten.[21] The users of these irrigation networks meet regularly in order to modify their community management regulations, nominate officers, and resolve any occasional conflicts. Here cooperation works perfectly well and, in the Valencia region, for example, the illegal water withdrawal rate lies at a mere 0.008%. In Murcia, the water tribunal even goes by the name of the "Council of Wise Men."[22]

In Ethiopia, Devesh Rustagi and his colleagues have studied the exploitation of communal forestry reserves by 49 groups in the Bale region in the province of Oromia. They noticed that the groups who managed their forestry resources the best were those with the most cooperative members. The putting in place of sanctions and the implementation of patrols to prevent stealing were essential to the success of this cooperative system.[23]

Ostrom has shown that the effective running of such communities depends on a number of criteria. First, the groups must have clearly defined borders. If they are too big, the members do not know each other and cooperation becomes a challenge for them. There must also be rules which govern the use of collective goods, but which can be modified according to any given circumstances to respond to specific local needs. Members must not only respect these rules, but also have in place a series of measures for cases of conflict and be willing to accept the fact that settling disputes can be costly. Ostrom's work does not claim to prove that people are altruistic, but that they are able to devise institutions, based on reciprocity, which give them incentives to achieve socially desirable outcomes.[24]

Praising Ostrom's work, French academic Hervé Le Crosnier drew the following conclusion: "Fundamentally, his message is that people who day in, day out face the need to guarantee the sustainability of the common resources which underpin their lives have a great deal more imagination and creativity than economists and theorists are willing to give them credit for."[25] The Internet offers countless examples of benevolent work that is valuable to the common good. The operating system Linux, for example, is an open source, non-commercial system whose codes are available to everyone, meaning it can be improved by programmers the world over.

COOPERATION AND "ALTRUISTIC PUNISHMENT"

In order for cooperation to prevail in society, it is essential to be able to identify and neutralize those people who profit from the good will of others, thus usurping the primary goal of cooperation. In a small community where everyone knows each other, free riders are swiftly detected and banished. On the other hand, when it is easier for them to go unnoticed, such as in towns or cities, it is crucial to promote cooperation by means of education and the transformation of social norms and by putting in place institutions that keep a check upon these free riders. In April 2010, a meeting entitled "Is altruism compatible with modern economic systems?" was organized in Zurich under the auspices of the Mind & Life Institute and the Department of Economics at the University of Zurich (UZH).[26] Eminent psychologists, cognitive science specialists, and social entrepreneurs gathered around the Dalai Lama.

While there I had the chance to talk to Ernst Fehr, a very highly regarded Swiss economist, who challenged the paradigm that individuals have no consideration for anything beyond their own interests. His studies have shown that, to the contrary, the majority of people are inclined to trust others, to cooperate, and to behave altruistically. He concluded that it was unrealistic and counter-productive to develop economic theories based on the principle of universal selfishness.[27]

Ernst Fehr and his colleagues have on multiple occasions placed groups of people in situations where mutual trust plays a central role. For example, they asked them to take part in an economic game, with real losses or earnings at stake.

Typically the experiment would play out as follows. Ten people are given 20 euros. They can either keep the sum for themselves or put it toward a shared project. When one person has invested his 20 euros in the project, the researcher doubles his stake to 40 euros. Once the ten participants have decided on their strategy, the total amount invested in the project is distributed evenly between the members of the group.

It is clear that if everyone cooperates, everyone profits. Essentially, the 200 euros invested by the group, increased by the other 200 euros from the researchers, pays out 40 euros to each participant, or double their investment. This ideal outcome presupposes that each member of the group trusts the other or cares for the other. Indeed, all that is required for every member to benefit is for just over half the group to cooperate.

On the other hand, if mistrust prevails and nine people keep their 20 euros and just one invests his money in the shared project, when this meager sum is divided among everybody, the nine participants who refused to cooperate end up with 22 euros (their original 20 euros plus the 2 euros yielded from the sum shared out from the one person who invested in the project), while the single cooperator is left with a mere 2 euros (since his 20 euro investment has been shared out among all ten people), representing a loss of 18 euros. Traditional economic theory has it that, in a society of selfish people who are mistrustful of everyone else, cooperation is in no one's interests.

Yet Ernst Fehr's team observed in the course of multiple experiments repeated many times over that, contrary to received wisdom, 60% to 70% of people trust each other from the outset and collaborate spontaneously.

Across any population, however, there is always a certain portion of individuals who prefer not to cooperate (around 30%). What trend is observed here? Second time around, the cooperators, having noted that there were some bad players in the group, nevertheless carry on cooperating. As the game is repeated, however, they grow weary of those who are exploiting the trust seen elsewhere in the group to turn a profit without taking any risks. By the tenth round, cooperation, that is conditional to some form of fair reciprocity, breaks down and becomes practically nonexistent.

As such, the majority's trust and goodwill erodes when a minority abuses the system for its own profit, harming the community as a whole. This is unfortunately what happens in an economic system that grants total freedom to unscrupulous speculators. It is also the consequence of wholesale deregulation of financial systems. The problem therefore is not that people are unwilling to collaborate and that altruism has no place in economics, but that profiteers prevent the majority's readiness to cooperate from asserting itself. In other words, the selfish derail the system. This would not happen if our cultures were more oriented toward "caring" economics.

Can we prevent the breakdown of cooperation? Ernst Fehr had the idea of continuing the experiment by introducing a new parameter: the possibility of punishing the bad collaborators. Every participant could therefore make an anonymous payment of 1 euro so that a fine of 3 euros would be imposed on the profiteers by the researcher. This is what Ernst Fehr refers to as "altruistic punishment," since it is costly to the person who imposes it and does not bring him an immediate return.[28] Why should somebody act in this way? It seems absurd from the point of view of one's personal interests, but the experiment shows that most people have a strong sense of fairness and are willing to spend a certain amount to ensure that justice is respected.

The impact of this new measure was spectacular. The cooperation rate skyrocketed and leveled off at almost 100%. It is important to note that this new protocol took place with the same participants as beforehand. The lone rangers, who had never contributed to the group's profits, started to cooperate and invested all of their money in the communal project.

In the first phase of the test, the selfish members had undermined the group dynamic. In the second, the altruists succeeded not in turning the selfish members into altruists—unfortunately a utopian ideal—but rather in creating a system where the selfish had a vested interest in behaving *as if they were altruists.*

In the end, everyone benefits from this, to the extent that if after a few rounds of the game the group is given the option of repealing the altruistic punishment, all of the participants express their desire to keep it in place, including the 30% of free riders, who realized that the group was functioning much better and that they themselves were reaping the rewards. Altruistic punishment is a very ancient method by which primitive societies managed to sustain efficient cooperative systems for tens of thousands of years.[29] In fact, even if everyone was selfish, the players could still use punishment or establish rules that make cooperation desirable to promote their individualistic self-interest. But societies can do better since wise altruists can establish rules and institutions that encourage a caring economy to flourish, while keeping in check the hard-core free riders with proper safeguards.[30]

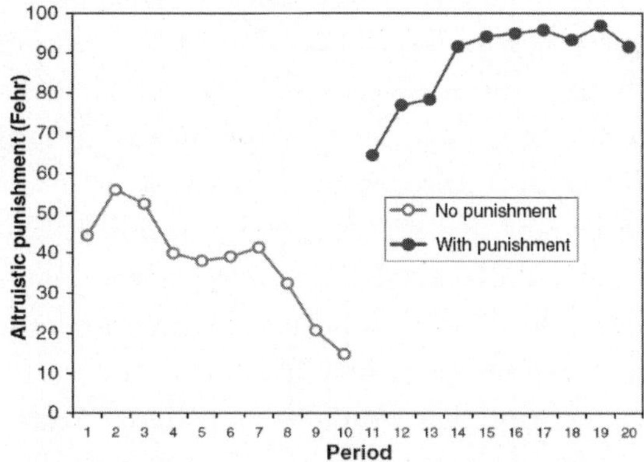

A graph showing the decline in cooperation under the influence of the profiteers, and the spectacular increase in cooperation following the introduction of altruistic punishment

Research shows that in the absence of rules a breakdown in cooperation occurs no matter the culture. However, the effects of altruistic punishment differ considerably from one culture to the next. In some cultures, the majority of people do not appreciate their upholders of justice, and take revenge by punishing them on their own. Unable to identify individual cooperators, they decide to punish them randomly to make them realize that they would do better not to get mixed up in other people's business. An *antisocial punishment* therefore replaces the *altruistic punishment*.

This trend is strong in cultures with little sense of civic duty, where the state is inefficient, there is scant respect for justice, and people do not trust their corrupt law enforcement agencies. In these countries, fraud is not just accepted but considered a means of survival. One can measure the strength of a culture's sense of civic duty by assessing, for example, the percentage of the population that considers it acceptable to dodge fares on public transport.

Benedikt Hermann and his colleagues studied the behavior of the inhabitants of sixteen towns across the world.[31] They observed that antisocial punishments—which seek to undermine this sense of civic duty rather than encourage it—were practically nonexistent in Scandinavian countries, Switzerland, the United Kingdom, and other countries where there is an emphasis on cooperation and community values. By contrast, they are found in abundance in countries with a weak sense of civic duty and where cooperation is restricted to between close relations or friends. In these circumstances, antisocial punishment is predominant. This can be observed, for example, in Greece, Pakistan and Somalia, three countries that score very poorly in the Corruption Perceptions Index (CPI) published each year by Transparency International.[32]

It is also apparent that societies with established altruistic standards flourish more and manage the problem of the commons better. If Danish people can leave an unsupervised baby to take some air in its stroller outside a restaurant at lunchtime without fearing it might be kidnapped—something that would be considered madness in Mexico or New York—it is because they have a certain value system programmed into them.[33] If the inhabitants of Taipei and Zurich automatically pay their bus or tram fare even in the absence of anyone to check whether they do so or not, it does not show that they are natural-born profiteers forced to conform to regulations through fear of being punished: they pay for their ticket voluntarily and are shocked if they see someone break the law. In countries where illegal practices are culturally accepted, profiteers always find ways of fulfilling their goals, regardless of the number of inspectors.

It is therefore important to bring together several strategies: putting in place appropriate institutions which allow altruists to cooperate without obstruction, to channel selfish behavior into prosocial behavior by establishing sensible and fair regulations, improving norms through education and helping the caring potential of human beings to be fully expressed and become the predominant attitude in our cultures.

Better Than Punishment: Reward and Appreciation

The evolutionists Martin Nowak and Drew Fudenberg, from Harvard University, have noted how, in real life, interactions between individuals are generally not anonymous and rarely occur in isolation. When people know who has cooperated, who has cheated, and who has punished them, the dynamic of these interactions changes. What's more, people worry about their reputations and do not want to run the risk of being ostracized by their peers for behaving antisocially.[34]

Studying the behavior of very young children shows that they are capable of noticing how an individual cooperates with others, and deducing from that whether or not he will cooperate well with them. In fact, from the age of one, they prefer people who behave in a cooperative manner.[35]

In this context, Nowak and his colleagues wondered whether, in real life, rewarding good cooperators would be more efficient than punishing the bad ones. Punishments deemed "altruistic" by economists do not in truth say anything about their motivations. A punishment is genuinely altruistic if, say, a parent corrects his or her children to prevent them from picking up bad habits. Punishments can also be motivated by the feeling that it is important to maintain a sense of fairness in society. Often, however, they boil down to a form of vengeance. The neuroscientist Tania Singer showed that men are particularly willing to part with a certain amount of money solely for the pleasure of taking revenge after being wronged in a trust game.[36] In circumstances where the persons involved can be identified, there is a strong risk that revenge will trigger a vicious cycle of reprisals in which everyone gets hurt.

In a series of experiments conducted by David Rand and other researchers under the direction of Nowak and Fudenberg, it emerged that over the course of repeat interactions in a trust game which allowed individual cooperators and free riders to be identified (thus altering the terms of Ernst Fehr's experiment, where the participants were anonymous), the strategy which produced the best long-term results involved continuing to cooperate no matter what happened.[37] In a group of two hundred students, those who saw the most significant success were the persistent cooperators. Those who engaged exclusively in vengeful behavior generally found themselves locked in a cycle of reprisals that made them crash to the bottom of the leader board.

Costly punishments are therefore just an effective stopgap, even if they are far more worthwhile than taking a laissez-faire approach. The best way of increasing the level of cooperation, however, is clearly to give favor and encouragement to positive interaction—fair exchanges, cooperation, and the strengthening of mutual trust. A system centered on *rewards* and encouragement that is linked to the safeguarding of rules

---

In Praise of Fraternity

May all men remember that they are brothers.

—Voltaire

In 1843, Jean-Charles Dupont, a lawyer from France's Society of the Rights of Man, wrote in the *Revue républicaine:* "Man aspires to liberty and equality, but he cannot attain them without the help of other men, without fraternity."[38] A century later, the Universal Declaration of Human Rights (adopted in 1948) stipulates in its first article: "All human beings are born free and equal in dignity and rights. They are endowed with reason and conscience and should act towards one another in a spirit of brotherhood."

The twin sister of altruism, fraternity represents a desire for greater mutual respect and reciprocity; it strengthens social cohesion by favoring solidarity and cooperation. In the words of the French economist, writer and senior civil servant Jacques Attali, fraternity is "today the main driving force pushing the world's vanguard forward."[39] According to him, it is a rejection of solitude, placing value on relationships with others, encouraging us to mingle, to learn how to get to know other people, and how to give and receive. It also shows us that, in our interdependent world, each of us needs other people to succeed. On the other hand, when people only take an interest in their own fortune, almost everyone ends up losing out. "Fraternity," Attali goes on to say, "lies in the pleasure of giving, even when there is no personal interest involved. When people gain pleasure from furnishing another's solitude, in showing compassion for another's suffering, in giving without expecting anything in return, in adopting children for the simple joy of seeing them happy, in taking care of handicapped people or the frail, in short in behaving with humanity, without expecting any acknowledgement or reward."[40]

It is manifest in the prodigious work done by charities, the proliferation of NGOs which help, nourish, save, care, and repair, and the mobilization which follows natural disasters; in the growing will to go above and beyond, and in globalization which does not involve the economic exploitation of poor countries by multinationals, but the sharing of knowledge, technology, and cultural and artistic wealth.[41]

Although, still in the words of Attali, "most nineteenth- and twentieth-century revolutionaries considered it to be a weak, naive concept, of value only to Christians, Freemasons or imbeciles," fraternity lives on: "It was there in the Russian gulags and the German camps (and their successors), where it became a mode of survival. It was also there in India when Mahatma Gandhi used it as a force for dignity.... And finally it is there every time somebody has the truly revolutionary courage to articulate the simple point that each of us stands to benefit from the happiness of other people. It can even be heard when called by other names: altruism or responsibility, compassion or generosity, love or tolerance."[42]

To sum up in one sentence, as Martin Luther King Jr. told us: "We must learn to live together as brothers or perish together as fools."[43]

and punishments which let one be protected against free riders does seem, therefore, the most apt way of promoting a fair and benevolent society. In a company, in particular, it is more constructive to create a pleasant working environment, to honor good and loyal service in various ways, and to redistribute a share of the profits to employees, than it is to penalize them if they grumble about carrying out their tasks. Once again we see that cooperation is more effective than punishment.

FAVORABLE CONDITIONS FOR COOPERATION

In his work *Why We Cooperate*, the psychologist Michael Tomasello explains that mankind's cooperative actions are founded in the existence of a shared objective, the attainment of which requires participants to assume different roles coordinated by concerted attention.[44] Collaborators must be receptive to others' intentions and react to them in appropriate fashion. In addition to a shared objective, collaborative action requires a certain division of the workload and an understanding, guaranteed by good communication, of each individual's role. Cooperation demands tolerance, trust and fairness.

It is also reinforced by social norms, which have varied enormously over the ages. The philosopher Elliott Sober and the evolutionist David Sloan Wilson have reviewed a large number of societies from across the world and observed that in the vast majority of them, behaviors deemed acceptable are defined by social norms. The important thing about these norms is that it does not cost much to uphold them, whereas punishments can, by contrast, be very costly to those on the receiving end—exclusion from the community, for example.[45] Thankfully we live in a time where social norms tend more toward respect for life, human rights, equality between men and women, solidarity, nonviolence, and fair justice systems.

Martin Nowak, for his part, describes five favorable factors for cooperation. The first is the regular practice of reciprocal services, as is the case, for example, with farmers who help each other at harvest-time, or villagers who all join in to build a neighbor's house. The second factor is the importance of reputation in communities: those who cooperate willingly are appreciated by everyone, while poor cooperators are badly regarded. The third factor involves population structure and social networks, which either facilitate or thwart the formation of cooperating communities. The fourth factor is the influence of family ties, with greater cooperation seen among related individuals. The fifth and final one is linked to the fact that natural selection operates on multiple levels: in certain circumstances, selection occurs solely on the individual level, while elsewhere it influences the fortunes of a group of individuals taken as a whole. In this second case, a group of cooperators can also have more success than a group of bad cooperators who are constantly in competition with one another.[46]

For generations, human beings have developed a web of reciprocity and cooperation in villages, towns, states, and, nowadays, across the whole world. Through the connectivity of global networks, information and knowledge can spread around the entire planet in a matter of seconds. If a stimulating idea, an innovative product, or a solution to a vitally important issue is circulated in this way, it can be used to benefit the whole world. There exist, therefore, countless methods that are conducive to developing cooperation. Looking to the future, we need to cooperate more than ever, and to do so on a global scale.

37

An Enlightened Education

Education is the kindling of a flame, not the filling of a vessel.

—Aristophanes

Martin Seligman, one of the founders of "positive psychology" (according to which, in order to gain enjoyment from existence, one cannot merely neutralize negative and afflictive emotions—one must also promote the birth of positive emotions), asked thousands of parents the following question: "What is the thing you want most for your children?" For the most part, their responses were: happiness, self-confidence, joy, pleasure, thriving, equilibrium, kindness, health, satisfaction, love, balanced behavior, and a life full of meaning. In summary, well-being is the first thing that comes to parents' minds for their children.[1]

Seligman's next question to the same parents is "What do we teach at school?" to which the response came: the ability to think, the ability to fit into a mold, language and math skills, work ethic, the capacity to pass examinations, discipline and success. The answers to these two questions barely overlap at all. The qualities taught at school are undeniably useful and for the most part necessary, but school could also teach ways of achieving well-being and self-fulfillment; in short, what Seligman calls a "positive education," an education which also teaches every student how to become a better human being.

In most of his public talks, the Dalai Lama insists on the fact that intelligence, however important it might be, is simply a tool which can be used for good as well as for evil. Indeed how we use our intelligence depends entirely on the human values which inspire our existence. According to the Dalai Lama, and he is adamant about this point, intelligence must be dedicated to the service of altruistic values. In the past, these values were instilled through a religious education, sometimes in a positive manner, but too often in a normative, dogmatic fashion which barely left children any chance of exploring their personal potential. Today, education can only be secular, so respecting each individual's freedom. But in doing so, modern education, too often focused on "success," individualism and competition, allows hardly any scope for encouraging children to appreciate the importance of human values, of emotional intelligence and of working together. As the Dalai Lama explains:

> *Education is much more than a matter of imparting the knowledge and skills by which narrow goals are achieved. It is also about opening the child's eyes to the needs and rights of others. We must show them that their actions have a universal dimension. And we must somehow find a way to build on their natural feelings of empathy in such a way that they come to have of sense of responsibility towards others. For it is this which stirs us into action. Indeed, if we had to choose between learning and virtue, the latter is definitely more valuable. The good heart which is the fruit of virtue is by itself a great benefit to humanity. Mere knowledge is not.*[2]

He goes on to say that it is therefore essential that the teaching of these fundamental values is reintroduced into education, based on a foundation of scientific findings acquired over the course of the last few decades pertaining to psychology, child development, brain plasticity, attention and emotional balance, the virtues of benevolence, solidarity, cooperation and understanding the interdependence of all beings.

Without attempting to provide an exhaustive analysis, let us now look at some initiatives likely to facilitate the blossoming of these altruistic values.

Neutrality Leads Nowhere

Afraid of imposing particular values, many educators would rather adopt a morally neutral approach, thinking that it is not the role of a school to influence students' moral preferences. We can certainly dismiss any form of prescriptive moral teaching that reflects the specific worldview of the educator him or herself. But who could decry the act of inspiring in children a constructive appreciation of benevolence, cooperation, honesty, and tolerance? Indeed moral neutrality is a delusion, since children will develop a value system regardless. Yet without the guidance of wise teachers, they risk finding it in the media, with all its violence and its focus on consumerism and individualism as promoted by advertising, or in the company of other children whose moral compass is as uninformed as theirs. In order for a society—and the education system underpinning it—to be harmonious and fair, it cannot stray from a consensus on the deleterious nature of violence and discrimination, as well as on the advantages of benevolence, fairness, and tolerance. Indeed, many teachers act as a reference point against which young people are able to find guidance throughout their lives, not to mention universally accepted sources of inspiration.[3]

Many initiatives are going in this direction. In Canada, for example, in British Columbia, influenced by Clyde Herzman and other researchers, emotional intelligence is now taught in most schools. In Quebec, a new program for teaching secular ethics has been launched, and, in 2010, the Dalai Lama held a conference on this subject before an audience of hundreds of trainee teachers. In India, in January 2013, still on the Dalai Lama's initiative, the University of Delhi decided to incorporate courses in "secular human values" in all its training programs. In the United States, at the instigation of the educationalist and psychologist Mark Greenberg, several hundred schools teach their students how better to recognize and manage their (and others') emotions, something which is contributing to a decrease in the number of classroom conflicts.[4]

A Quiet Revolution

Kidlington Primary School is located in a poor suburb of Oxford, England. In 1993, the head teacher, Neil Hawkes, decided to introduce the teaching of basic human values into the education of five hundred students at the school.[5] One of the methods used there involves establishing a list of words representing the values deemed to be the most important by teachers and students, such as respect, benevolence, responsibility, cooperation, trust, tolerance, openness, patience, peace, courage, honesty, humility, gratitude, hope, love, generosity, etc. According to Hawkes: "I cannot stress enough how important it is to ensure that everyone has the chance to be involved in the process of identifying the values that the school is going to teach. If they are, then each person feels ownership of the values."[6] Each word takes it in turn to be "Word of the Month" and is placed in a conspicuous position on the school's walls. The word then becomes the object of group discussions and represents the focal point around which different subjects are taught. It also serves as a basis for resolving disputes.

Rather than teaching such values peripherally to other subjects, they have become the starting platform from which the entire school curriculum is formed, along with any other administrative or educational decisions taken.

With students, the awareness that they can manage their emotions and behavior transforms the classroom environment, giving rise to a more sustained level of engagement and increasing the enjoyment of studying. Over the years, reports of this method have shown that the environment created by a values-based educational approach is conducive not only to students' personal development and the quality of their social relations, but also their learning progress. Since the program's introduction, Kidlington School's results have consistently been above national average, and far higher than other schools located—as in the case of Kidlington—in disadvantaged areas.[7]

Frances Farrer, the author of one such report, observed an improvement in emotional stability, general behavior, and a heightened sense of belonging in the community. Kidlington School is now visited by educators from across the world seeking to gain inspiration from its model. Farrer also noted that short periods of silent reflection at the beginning of morning and afternoon classes have a long-term pacifying effect on students and decrease incidences of fighting.

In 2003, in Australia, under the aegis of the Ministry of Education, Professor Terence Lovat used the Kidlington values-based education system to launch a similar program in 316 schools with a combined total of more than 100,000 students. Conclusions drawn from evaluating their results, carried out by Lovat and his colleagues at the University of Newcastle, confirmed that in a values-based environment learning improves, teachers and students are more satisfied, and the school is calmer. According to Lovat's report, the school therefore became "a better place to teach and a better place to learn."[8]

A SPECTACULAR SUCCESS

It's morning in the classroom of a nursery school in Madison, Wisconsin. Children aged four or five, born largely to disadvantaged backgrounds, are lying on their backs learning how to focus on the in-out motion of their breathing, and on the movements of a pebble or a cuddly little bear sitting on their tummies. After some minutes, at the ding of a triangle, they stand up and head off together to check the progress of the "seeds of peace" that each of them has planted in pots that line the classroom windows. The teacher asks them to reflect on the care that the plants require and, by association, the care that friendship requires too. He then helps them realize that what is making them feel calm is something that allows other children to feel calm also. At the start of each session, the children recite out loud the motto that is to inspire their day: "May all that I think, all that I say, and all that I do cause no wrong to others, but rather help them."

These are just a few of the elements of a ten-week program begun by the Center for Investigating Healthy Minds, founded by the psychologist and neurologist Richard Davidson. Although his colleague Laura Pinger and their other partners only teach on this program for three thirty-minute sessions per week, it has a remarkable effect on the children, who enjoy those sessions very much and ask their instructors why they don't come every day.[9]

Over the weeks, the children are naturally encouraged to carry out acts of kindness, to realize that the things that upset them make others feel upset too, to better identify their emotions and those of their classmates, to demonstrate gratitude, and make benevolent wishes for themselves and those around them. When they are worried, they are shown that they are very much able to solve their problems by working on external factors, but also by working on their own emotions.

After five weeks the time comes for each child to give away to another child one or more plants that they have grown. The kids are then made to realize that they are linked to all the children, all the schools, and all the people in the world, and that everyone wants peace and depends on one another. This leads them to feel a sort of gratitude toward nature, animals, trees, lakes, oceans, and the air we breathe, and to gain awareness that it is important to take care of our world.

Some might consider it somewhat naive to think that such a program, interesting though it may seem, could have a real effect on such young kids. This is why the researchers went further than mere subjective observations, assessing the program's effects by questioning the teachers and parents in great detail about the behavior and attitudes of the children before and after taking part. This assessment revealed an overall improvement in prosocial behaviors and a decrease in the emotional issues and aggression among those who underwent the experiment.

But the scientists added one last test, known as the "stickers" test. On two occasions, at the start and the end, they gave each of the children a certain number of those adhesive figurines they adore so much, along with four envelopes containing respectively a photo of their best friend, their least favorite child, an unknown child, and a visibly ill child wearing a bandage on his forehead. They then asked each child to distribute the figurines across the four envelopes, which would then be handed out to their classmates. At the start of the program, the children gave almost all of their stickers to their best friend, and very few to the others.

One would hope that, after ten weeks of practicing benevolence, a change would come about. As it turned out, the difference was spectacular: in the second test at the end of the program, the kids gave an *almost equal number* of stickers to the four groups of children: they no longer made any distinction between their favorite classmate and the one they liked least. The significance of this outcome can be measured by considering what we know about the extent to which in-group out-group discriminations are typically long-term and marked, and about the toxic effect those discriminations have on society.

In light of the remarkable results of this method, its simplicity, and the effect it could have on a child's subsequent development—something which is currently the object of further study—it seems a shame not to implement it throughout the world. Indeed, Madison city

---

DISCOVERING INTERDEPENDENCE

We are in a class of around twenty students aged six to seven living in foster care at the Paideia School in Atlanta. An instructor visiting from Emory University says: "Look at this pullover. I love it. It's comfortable and keeps me warm. My father gave it me and, when I wear it, I think of him. But it hasn't come from nowhere. Where's it come from? What's had to happen for me to be able to wear this pullover?"

The kids' answers come flying. "You!" "Yes, of course," replies the instructor, a bit put out, "but what else?" "You need your father," says another. "Yes, of course. But my father doesn't make pullovers."

"He bought it in a shop!" someone pipes up. "Okay, but the shop assistant doesn't knit sweaters either." Slowly but surely, the kids start talking about knitting, wool, sheep, farms, transport, roads, and all the people involved in the creation of this pullover, all of whom must also have parents, grandparents, a house, food, etc.

"Where does it finish?" the instructor asks. Without hesitation, one child gleefully exclaims: "It doesn't finish anywhere! You need the whole world!"

The conclusion leaves the kids deep in thought, until one of them—a little perplexed—asks: "Even children?" The instructor nods his head. "Yes, even children."

---

council has now asked Richard Davidson and his team to roll out the program in several schools across the city. When the Dalai Lama was made aware of these results, he made the following comment: "One school, ten schools, a hundred schools, and then—through the United Nations—all the schools in the world..."

EDUCATING THE HEART AND MIND

The realization that all beings are interdependent forms part of a program developed by Emory University in Atlanta. This program aims to teach a form of analytic meditation on altruism and compassion (Cognitive Based Compassion Therapy, or CBCT) to kids taken into foster care after suffering traumas linked to neglect and separation from their biological parents. There is a very high probability that these children's formal education has been interrupted.[10] As part of the program, they participate in twenty-five- to thirty-minute sessions twice a week during the normal school day.

Emotional intelligence, compassion for oneself and for others, awareness of interdependence, empathy, non-discrimination: these are the principal qualities that the program seeks to promote. On a wider scale, the CBCT program's objective is to work simultaneously in the school community, with teachers, school administrators, parents and even the system for placing children, always with an emphasis on compassion.

This program lasts eight weeks and comprises: 1) developing attention and stability of mind; 2) observing the inner nature of thoughts, feelings, and emotions; 3) exploring self-compassion—recognizing our desire for happiness, the mental states that lead to personal fulfillment, and willingness to free oneself from emotional states that detract from happiness; 4) developing impartiality toward other beings, be they friends, enemies, or strangers, and at the same time questioning the value—fixed, or superficial and changing—of this categorization, and identifying a shared desire in everyone to be happy and to avoid suffering; 5) developing gratitude toward others, with no one able to survive without the support of countless other people; 6) developing benevolence and empathy; 7) developing compassion for those who are suffering, and a desire that they be freed from that suffering; 8) implementing altruism and compassion into everyday life.

Children are very receptive to this sort of education. When one of the instructors compared anger to a spark in a forest, which at the start can easily be extinguished but which rapidly becomes a huge, destructive, out-of-control inferno, a little five-year-old girl said: "There are a lot of forest fires in my life."

Cooperative Learning

Learning with others, by others, for others, rather than alone against others: cooperative learning is about making students work together in small groups where they give each other mutual assistance and encouragement, praising one another's success and effort. When a difficult task must be completed, the efforts of each group member are necessary for the overall success of the project, something that requires them not only to work together, but also to think about how best to utilize each member's skills.

In schools, cooperative education involves forming groups of children at different levels, with a view to letting the most advanced help those having difficulties. In these circumstances, one sees how the children who find learning easy, rather than feeling superior to the others (as is the case in a system driven by constant testing and assessed written work) are filled with a sense of responsibility to help those struggling to understand. What's more, the spirit of group camaraderie and the absence of intimidating, judgmental influences from others bring confidence to the kids and inspire them to give their very best.

In cases of cooperation groups comprising children at the same level who were experiencing difficulties studying, it was observed that solidarity helped them come up with new ways of resolving their difficulties, something which before they felt was out of reach and led them to be marginalized in the class. In his book *Cooperative Learning*, Robert Pléty, math teacher and researcher at the University of Lyon, France, explains his approach in class as follows: he gives his math lesson followed by an exercise to establish which students have understood and which have not. He then divides them into groups of ten, three or four, with some made up solely of students who haven't understood, others made up of students who understood everything, and then others with a mixture of the two. He then observes what happens when he gives them the same exercise again (which is important in the case of the students who didn't understand) or a new one (to see whether cooperation also improves the better students' results). Pléty continued his study for seven years, accumulating a large amount of data.

The results are impressive: in the case of the mixed groups, the success rate increases by a full 75%. The groups of better students remain, in the majority of cases, at the highest level. The surprise comes with the groups who failed first time around: after being put together, 24% of them managed to do the exercise. The learning dynamic therefore changed. Less good students succeed in making progress together by adopting the trial-and-error method, which serves them well in the end. In addition, Pléty observed that "interest and satisfaction seemed to be etched on the faces of students whose brows had before been constantly frowning during math classes."[11]

The idea of cooperative learning is nothing new. In the seventeenth century, Johann Amos Comenius, a Czech educator who was a forerunner to Rousseau, highly influential in his day and now considered by some to be the father of modern education, was convinced that students could benefit from reciprocal teaching.

Later, in the nineteenth century, in Quincy, Massachusetts, a passionate educator by the name of Francis Parker made cooperative learning widespread in all the area's schools. Thousands of people came each year to visit his schools, and his cooperative learning methods spread across the whole of North America's education system. Unfortunately, in the 1930s, competition became increasingly popular in public schools. In the 1940s, however, cooperative learning became the order of the day once more thanks to the sociologist Morton Deutsch, and then championed from the 1980s to the present day by David and Roger Johnson and many other educators. It is now practiced successfully more or less all over the world, even if it does remain a minority approach.

The Johnsons created a method that they have implemented in numerous schools, the results of which they have already assessed. Along with Mary Beth Stanne at the University of Arizona, they have also processed the data from 164 research studies on different cooperative teaching methods, observing that the best results come about when small groups of two to five students who, after receiving instructions from the teacher, work together until they have understood everything and completed the task given them. They then celebrate their joint success. The best results arise from groups that are mixed in terms of skills, sex, cultural background, and motivation levels.[12]

Compared with competitive teaching, cooperative learning has many advantages related to memorizing lessons, the desire to learn, the time taken to complete a task, and the transfer of knowledge between students. What's more, there is evidence of an increase in emotional intelligence, moral awareness, friendships, altruistic behaviors, and relations with teachers. Children enjoy better psychological health, greater self-confidence, and greater enjoyment from learning. With regard to behavior, cooperative learning goes hand in hand with lower levels of discrimination (racist and sexist), delinquency, bullying, and drug addiction. Sixty-one percent of classes practicing cooperative learning received higher results than those following traditional methods.[13]

The Johnsons describe competition as "negative interdependence" whereby students work against each other to achieve a goal that only a few of them can attain.[14]

THE BENEFITS OF MENTORING

Bringing together children with different aptitudes can also be done in the context of mentoring. Here, a child is entrusted with giving a younger kid one-to-one classes for a few hours a week under the supervision of a teacher, who helps the tutor prepare the sessions. There are multiple benefits to this arrangement, as shown in a report carried out by Peter Cohen with James and Chen-Lin Kulik of the Center for Research on Learning and Teaching at the University of Michigan, which analyzed sixty-five studies.[15]

A somewhat unexpected finding has been that not only does the child on the receiving end of the teaching make progress, but so does the tutor. When the tutor is not at a high academic level, there is a reasonable fear that spending time worrying about someone else's studies might aggravate their own difficulties. What surprised the researchers was that the precise opposite occurred: the tutor, feeling a sense of responsibility toward his pupil, made an effort to revise the subjects that he had studied one or two years previously, while also taking greater care of his own studies. As such, the struggling child is sometimes the one who receives the help, and at other times the one who does the helping—so the mentoring grows the tutors' capacity for learning while simultaneously developing their capacity for teaching. At the end of the year, the children placed in tutor-pupil pairs had, on average, higher results than those children who had not taken part in the program.[16] One-to-one mentoring is practiced today in the USA, the UK, Australia, New Zealand, Israel, and several hundred schools in French-speaking Belgium, and to some extent throughout the world.

Another form of mentoring is that which occurs when an adult supports a child who is going through difficulties. In 1991, philanthropist and humanitarian Ray Chambers[17] founded the Points of Light Foundation in the United States, with the aim of enrolling appropriate people to work as mentors for children from disadvantaged areas. This program now has more than five million mentors and is producing remarkable results.

The Rights Respecting Schools Initiative

This initiative from the Canadian branch of UNICEF helps schools transform their learning environment by adopting an approach based on respecting rights, which promotes an understanding of universal values toward others and oneself within the school community. It has now been applied to several other countries, including the United Kingdom.[18]

A studied performed in the United Kingdom in over 1,600 Rights Respecting Schools revealed an improvement in learning, a decrease in absence, prejudice, and bullying, as well as an improvement in pro-social behaviors and a more positive attitude regarding diversity. What's more, students attending these schools are motivated and know how to express their own opinions, participate in decision-making processes, resolve disputes in a peaceful manner, and better understand the global challenges relating to social justice.

Philosophy with Eight-Year-Old Children

In the small village of Tursac, in the Dordogne region of France, the teacher Claude Diologent decided to run philosophy workshops with his elementary students. Over their heads? Not a bit of it. The children love it. Sometimes it's the teacher who introduces a topic, sometimes the students pick an issue that interests them—happiness, honesty, fairness, kindness, etc.—and, with the teacher's help, they discuss it together. They sit in a circle and pass each other a baton to give them the floor. The child who receives the baton can speak calmly without fear of interruption. When the baton has gone full circle, a debate opens up between the children, guided by the teacher. Every Friday afternoon, the students gather around the person who, for that month, is "Speaker" of the children's assembly, and they discuss any issues that have arisen over the week. If, for example, a student has insulted a classmate, the Speaker asks him why he acted in such a way and if he realizes that he has hurt someone's feelings. The student willingly accepts that that is the case, explains himself, and says he is sorry, and the other one forgives him.

These philosophical workshops aimed at very young pupils have been rolled out in several parts of the world. Keith Topping, of the University of Dundee, and Steve Trickey, an educational psychologist, have carried out a review of ten studies which have shown an improvement in creative thinking, cognitive skills, emotional intelligence, logical reasoning, reading, mathematical skills, and self-confidence. In light of their findings, Topping and Trickey found themselves wondering why philosophy among young children wasn't systematically integrated into the education system.[19]

The Jigsaw Classroom

The Jigsaw Classroom is a teaching technique developed in 1971 by the American psychologist Elliot Aronson.[20] Based on the principle of cooperative learning, this method encourages schoolchildren to listen, interact, and share by allocating each one an essential role to carry out: learning cannot take place without the cooperation of each pupil, and—just like a jigsaw—each piece is indispensable to the whole.

The students are split into groups of six and the lessons are divided into six parts, with each child having just one of these set aside for studying alone for a period of about ten minutes. The students of each group who received the same lesson then join together and confer, checking that they have fully understood their part. After that the groups of six reconvene and spend half an hour exchanging what they have learned with the other members of the group. Finally all of them are questioned on the overall lesson. In this way, the students quickly learn how to share their knowledge and become aware that each of them cannot pass the test without the help of all the others.

Jigsaw classrooms reduce hostility and bullying among students. They have been shown to be particularly effective in eliminating racial prejudice and other forms of discrimination, and in improving academic results in children from ethnic minorities.[21] The best results are obtained when this method is applied from an early stage. It has also been observed that this technique improves results in schoolchildren even if it is implemented for only 20% of classes. It can therefore be used in conjunction with any other pedagogic approaches.

BAREFOOT COLLEGE, THE SHEPHERDS' SCHOOL, AND THE CHILDREN'S PARLIAMENT

It's 7 p.m. on one evening in the month of February. Near Tilonia, a small village in Rajasthan, India, we enter a room, four meters by six, in a house located at the edge of a marsh. Two hurricane lamps, recharged during the day by solar panels, light up the space. In a few minutes, about thirty girls aged from six to fourteen, along with four or five boys, sit down on the clay floor.

The schoolmistress is barely any older than the most senior of the children. The class begins with a wonderful hubbub. She has laid out a series of white sheets of cardboard in a circle, on which are written various syllables in the Hindi language. As soon as one of the pupils puts together two syllables to form a word, she pounces onto one of the sheets, shows it to the others, and explains the meaning of the word. Then a long sentence is written in a circle using the cardboard, and the students have to, each in turn, go around the circle reading it aloud. After that, in pairs, the children sing little rhymes about rain (in Rajasthan, rain is so scarce that everyone prays for it to come), the harvest, and farm animals, animating their songs with gestures reflecting the subjects. This playful approach continues into the evening until 10 p.m., during which time the children seize every opportunity to answer the schoolmistress's questions. Not even the slightest sign of boredom or distraction can be read on their faces.

These girls are not like the others. All day long, they tend to cows or goats. In the area around Tilonia, the team at Barefoot College, founded almost forty years ago by Bunker Roy,[22] have year after year created 150 evening schools for the children of people living in the countryside throughout the whole region. In each classroom (a space made available by the village), the schoolmistress gives five levels of lessons.

Sita is fourteen. The schoolmistress asks her how many liters of milk her cow produces each day. "Four." "How many cows do you look after?" "Three." "How many liters of milk does that make every two weeks?" Sita heads over to the blackboard, made especially for Barefoot College by the local women, takes from her pocket a piece of chalk made by young handicapped children from the College, and does the multiplication. Three girls join her, checking the numbers that she is lining up and whispering their opinions. Here, no one is punished for helping their classmates when their teacher asks a question. It's a normal reaction. Their entire education, related like this to everyday life, is based along the lines of cooperation.

Under the aegis of Barefoot College, the children of these 150 evening schools have also formed a "Children's Parliament," forty members strong, the majority girls, which operates all year round, electing ministers and gathering once a month to discuss issues relating to the children's lives. From this, the children gain awareness of their rights, and do not hold back from addressing even the most delicate matters when injustices or abuses are committed against any of their members. Parents and village leaders take this very seriously and send a delegation to attend, in silence, the Parliament's deliberations. The children also campaign in the villages during their elections, held every two years, and so learn the central tenets of democracy. The Rajasthan Children's Parliament allows them to become equal, responsible members of society, irrespective of their caste, sex, or economic situation. Members regularly inspect the 150 evening schools placed under their jurisdiction.

The children put pressure on local village authorities to improve living conditions in villages, for example by installing solar energy or water pumps. They also organize cultural activities and festivals for children, designed to bring a welcome reprieve from their tough daily routines. Health authorities have observed, remarkably, an overall improvement in the health situation of the region's villages that are covered by the Children's Parliament.

Bunker Roy tells how when the Parliament received a prize in Sweden, one thirteen-year-old girl, who then held the rank of prime minister, met the queen of Sweden. The queen was so impressed by the poise and composure which the young village girl displayed before the gathering of adult dignitaries that she asked her: "How is it that you manage to be so self-assured?" To which the young girl replied: "I am prime minister, Your Majesty."

A Teacher's Empathy

According to the American educator Mark Greenberg, in the eyes of students a good teacher is someone who is not only able to give a good lesson, but who also shows a range of human qualities (listening, benevolence, availability, etc.). In addition, it has also been observed that when teachers show signs of empathy, students' academic performance goes up, while violence and vandalism go down.[23]

As the French psychologist Jacques Lecomte explains in an article on humane education, it is effectively essential that teachers establish a personal relationship with their students and do not settle for transmitting knowledge in a cold, detached manner.[24] To kindle the flame of which Aristophanes speaks, the teacher must be genuinely concerned with the pupil's fortune. He must in particular display three vitally important qualities: authenticity, solicitude, and empathy.

In their book *Kids Don't Learn from People They Don't Like,* David Aspy and Flora Roebuck, of the National Consortium for Humanizing Education, in Washington, noted how teachers who most exhibit these three qualities help their students' progress more on average than other students in an establishment over the course of the academic year.[25] Aspy and Roebuck cited a program aimed at improving the three qualities among teachers in a school located in a very socioeconomically poor neighborhood. The results were conclusive: the school climbed nine places in the reading competency scale. On average, pupils aged seven to ten made more progress in math than all other students in the same zone. The school saw its rate of absenteeism reach its lowest level in all the forty-five years since its creation. There was an overall decrease in vandalism and brawling between students. And the benefits were mutual: the resignation rate among teachers fell from 80% to 0. Once the news had spread, many teachers from other educational establishments asked for a transfer to the school.

In Nepal, Uttam Sanjel, founder of the Samata Shiksha Niketan schools—which are built entirely from bamboo, each one home to as many as two thousand children[26]—uses a somewhat unusual method for recruiting teachers. When he needed to hire a hundred new teachers for a newly built school in Pokhara, he placed an advertisement in the newspaper, for which he received almost a thousand applications. Along with his team, he made an initial selection of around three hundred (the majority women), then he gave a trial to three teachers per class, each one for a week. He then asked the children to decide which teacher they found most inspiring and understood the best, and with whom they most wanted to study. I imagine that there would be quite some resistance from teachers' unions in Western countries toward introducing such ways of recruiting teachers, but in this case the results seem to have been highly successful. The classes are very dynamic and the students are in constant discussion with their teachers. In the yearly national exams, the pupils at Samata schools have an above-average pass rate.

A Baby in the Classroom

In a class reserved for difficult children with a frequent tendency to violent behavior, a mother brings in her young baby and places it on the ground on top of a blanket, around which the students form a circle. They observe the baby closely for a while before being offered to take the infant in their arms. The students hesitate, but eventually a few of them go for it and pick up the baby with great care. They are then asked to describe what they imagine the baby's experience to have been, as well as their own emotions.

This is the Roots of Empathy project conceived by Mary Gordon who, along with her team, works in Canada and Australia to increase solicitude and mutual respect among schoolchildren. This organization now has over 1,100 programs numbering 70,000. Mary Gordon regards this original form of intervention as a way of building, "child by child," a more attentive, peaceful, and civil society.[27]

Once a month, the mother returns with her baby and the students chart its development, its new ways of interacting with those around it, etc. At each session, the students talk among themselves and with their teachers.

Evaluations of the effectiveness of the Roots of Empathy project, carried out by Kimberly Schonert-Reichl of the University of British Columbia, show that the program has a positive effect on the students' emotional development. A more benevolent atmosphere in classes is noted, as well as better emotional intelligence, an increase in altruistic behavior (in 78% of students), in the ability to adopt another person's perspective (71%), and in sharing (69%), and a decrease in aggressive behavior in 39% of pupils.[28] What's more, these improvements were sustained or enhanced over the three years following the program.[29] According to Mary Gordon, the answer to bullying and other antisocial behaviors lies in the benevolence and compassion that occur naturally in each of us.

The children, guided by the Roots of Empathy instructor, observe the parent-child relationship and the ways in which the child develops, and by the same token they learn how to better understand parental love as well as their own temperament and that of their classmates.

Darren, a fifteen-year-old student, had already been sent twice to a reform school. His mother had been murdered in front of him when he was four, and ever since he had lived in foster care. He would always act in a threatening manner to establish his authority. He had a shaved head, with the exception of a ponytail, and a large tattoo on the back of his head. That day, a young mother was visiting class with Evan, her six-month-old baby. At the end of the class, the mother asked if anyone wanted to hold the baby. To everyone's surprise, Darren raised his hand. The mother seemed a little apprehensive, but nevertheless handed him the baby. Darren put him in the harness, turned toward his chest, and the baby snuggled there peacefully. He carried him over to a quiet corner of the room and rocked him back and forth for several minutes. Eventually he returned to where the mother and instructor were waiting and asked: "If no one has ever loved you, do you think you can be a good father?" A seed had been sown. Thanks to those few moments of contact with a baby's unconditional affection, a teenager whose life had been marked by tragedy and neglect began to build a different image of himself and the relationships possible between humans.

Reconnecting with Nature

Recently I was in Franche-Comté, France, at the house of a friend whose parents were the last independent farmers in the region. As we were wandering around the countryside, my friend said to me: "Once upon a time, during cherry season, we would all be up in the trees filling our boots. Nowadays the cherries stay on the branches. The children don't climb trees anymore."

Several studies have shown that children in urban areas in Europe and North America play ten times less in public places, especially the street, than thirty years ago.[30] Contact with nature is often restricted to a background image on a computer screen, and games have become increasingly solitary, violent, stripped of beauty, wonder, and any notion of camaraderie. Between 1997 and 2003, the percentage of children aged nine to twelve who spent time playing together outside, going hiking, or gardening fell by half.[31] This phenomenon is linked to a number of factors: that more and more people are living in urban areas, that "the street" has become more dangerous in parents' minds—traffic, potentially dangerous encounters, etc.

In his book *Last Child in the Woods,* the American author and journalist Richard Louv writes that we are raising a generation of young people who are suffering from "nature deficit disorder" as a result of having lost virtually all contact or interaction with their natural surroundings. Louv cites this remark from a young student: "I prefer playing at home because that's where I have all my electronic stuff."[32] There is a lot of research to suggest that intensification in contact with nature has a major impact on a child's cognitive and emotional development.[33]

For years, Finland has had the reputation for being the European country with the best education. Several factors have contributed to this, including the fact that the teaching profession is very highly regarded there, and that teachers are given a lot of latitude for choosing the pedagogic techniques that seem most appropriate to their pupils. The Finns also take care to attain a balance between hard work in the classroom and group play outdoors, which improves the children's faculties for empathy and their emotional intelligence. Finland's Ministry of Social Affairs and Health summarize the country's educational philosophy as follows: "The most important aspect of knowledge acquisition is not regurgitating information...that has come from outside, but in a child's interaction with his or her environment."[34]

POSITIVE EDUCATION

Very often success is measured simply by the passing of school examinations and the securing of a well-paid job. In today's world there is considerable pressure placed on children to succeed. Martin Seligman and other psychologists are of the opinion that this pressure and the vulnerability it can activate in the event of failure are among the factors contributing to the sharp increase—ten times greater than in the 1960s—in depression and suicide among teenagers in developed countries. Fifty years ago, the average age of someone suffering from depression for the first time in the United States and Western Europe was around twenty-seven; nowadays, it is below fifteen.[35]

Under the banner of what has been named "positive education," where the aim is to teach well-being to children, Seligman and his colleagues from the University of Pennsylvania, Karen Reivich and Jane Gillham, have developed two main programs targeting schools. These are the Penn Resiliency Program (PRP) and the Strath Haven Positive Psychology Curriculum. The objective of the first is to improve students' ability to deal with the day-to-day problems faced by all teenagers. It promotes optimism and teaches children to reflect on their problems with greater flexibility. It also teaches them stress management techniques.[36] Over the course of the last twenty years, 21 studies centered on 3,000 young people aged eight to twenty-one have shown that this program is particularly effective in lowering the risk of depression.

In 2008, a school in Australia, Geelong Grammar School, invited Martin Seligman and his family, along with about fifteen of his colleagues, to spend several months implementing their positive education methods at all levels of the school, from the principal to the cooks via all students and faculty. The teachers at Geelong have integrated positive education into all theoretical subjects, on the sports fields, in class councils, and even in music lessons.

Empathy and benevolence are important parts of the program, and students are encouraged to integrate them into their everyday lives. "You feel better when you do something for someone else," declared one of the students, "when you're playing, even with video games."

One year later, the school had, in everyone's opinion, changed profoundly. Not one of the two hundred teachers left Geelong at the end of the school year, and admissions and applications were on the rise.

The majority of initiatives underpinning positive and cooperative education are founded in reports that have widely shown the benefits they have for children. It is also apparent that human values, particularly the various aspects of altruism, cooperation, and mentoring, can play a very positive role in education.

38

Fighting Inequality

An imbalance between rich and poor is the oldest and most fatal ailment of all republics.

—Plutarch

Inequality exists everywhere in nature, both between different species of the animal kingdom and between individual animals from the same species, and human beings are no exception. If we are unequal in terms of physical strength, intellectual capacity, or the wealth into which we are born, we are, on the other hand, equal in our desire to avoid suffering and enjoy life. Society cannot impose a made-to-measure happiness on everyone. It does have a duty, however, not to neglect those who are suffering. We cannot prevent inequality from arising, but we must nevertheless do all in our power not to let it persist. An individualist society will make little effort to stave it off, while a society that places the utmost importance on the value of altruism and the fortunes of others will ensure that inequality, which is at the source of so much suffering and discrimination, is redressed, along with lack of opportunities in life and reduced access to education and health care.

Inequality, as the French sociologist and philosopher Edgar Morin explains, can occur on several different levels: territorial (poor regions and rich regions), economic (extreme wealth and extreme poverty in a single region), sociological (ways of life), or in health (those who enjoy advances in medicine and technology, and those who do not). We must also distinguish between inequality linked to education and working conditions (between those who gain pleasure from their profession and those who endure theirs with the sole goal of making ends meet; inequality in how justice is administered (in certain countries the majority of legal authorities are corrupt); inequality in taxation (capital flight into tax havens); and inequality between those who struggle through life and those who are able to enjoy it. Morin continues:

> *These inequalities are not measured merely by the amount of money one has. Wealth does not necessarily bring happiness. But poverty does bring unhappiness.... The mission of a politics of humanity is not to make everything equal—which would result in destroying diversity—but to envisage the paths to reform which would bring about a gradual reduction in the worst forms of inequality.*[1]

Economic Inequality on the Increase Almost Everywhere in the World

We have already seen how in the United States the richest 1% of the population currently owns 40% of the country's wealth, compared with just 13% of it twenty-five years ago.[2] This symbolic figure relating to inequality was taken up by the "Occupy Wall Street" movement[3] and gave rise to its slogan: "We are the 99%." Such a level of inequality is morally unjustifiable and is a scourge on society. What's more, contrary to the claims of neo-liberals, the wealth at the top of the ladder remains there, and does not "trickle down" to the bottom to create a more dynamic society for all.

As Joseph Stiglitz explains, inequality is both the cause and consequence of the failure of the political system, and it contributes to the instability of our financial system, which in turn contributes to increased inequality. It is this vicious cycle that has thrown us into the abyss, and we will only be able to emerge from it by reforming the system.[4]

The most equal societies strive constantly to uphold social justice, while in the most unequal societies, financial and political institutions are engaged just as energetically in maintaining an unequal status quo that favors the ruling minority.[5]

Inequality hinders those that suffer from it the most, since they consider themselves to be treated unjustly. Breakdown of trust and disillusionment are not conducive either to productivity or quality of life at work.

In the years 1880–1890, the banker John Pierpont Morgan announced that he would never agree to invest in a company where the directors were paid over six times the average wage.[6] In the United States, in 2011 a boss took home on average 253 times more than a normal employee (compared with thirty times more fifty years ago, and sixteen times nowadays in Japan).[7]

Like Andrew Sheng, Chief Adviser to the China Banking Regulatory Commission, we may well ask ourselves the following question: "Why should a financial engineer be paid four to a hundred times more than a real engineer? A real engineer builds bridges. A financial engineer builds dreams and, when those dreams turn out to be nightmares, other people pay for it."[8]

The divide in the United States is widening faster and faster. For thirty years, 90% of Americans saw their income increase by just 15%, while those who make up the wealthiest 1% experienced a leap of 150%. Between 2002 and 2007, this 1% of the population monopolized over 65% of national income gains.[9] While the best-off became considerably richer, the situation for the majority of Americans got worse.

In Europe, although income inequality is overall lower than it is in the United States, it is on the rise. The most equal countries are those in Scandinavia, where the richest 10% earn just six times more than the poorest 10%.[10]

Research carried out by economists at the IMF[11] suggests that almost everywhere in the world income inequality slows growth and triggers financial crises. A recent report by the Asian Development Bank claimed that if inequality in income distribution in developing countries in Asia had not worsened over the course of the last twenty years, the region's rapid economic growth would have lifted a further 240 million people out of extreme poverty.[12] The 2014 report from the OECD concludes that the gap between rich and poor is at its highest level in 30 years in most OECD countries. Today, the richest 10% of the population in the OECD area earn 9.5 times more than the poorest 10%. By contrast, in the 1980s the ratio stood at 7:1.[13] This long-term trend increase in income inequality has curbed economic growth significantly, chiefly because of families with lower incomes slipping behind and not being able to invest in their education.

A notable exception is China, since despite its having maintained an oppressive totalitarian regime—notably, and unusually, at the same time as being a capitalist state since the 1990s—it has lifted more people out of poverty in the last few decades than any other country in history. According to an OECD report, the number of people living below the poverty line (a little over 1 dollar per day) decreased by 150 million between 2000 and 2010 and now represents just 6% of the rural population. In the same period, across the whole country, the poorest people's wages increased proportionately even more than those of the richest. Yet immense fortunes have been amassed among the wealthiest, often thanks to nepotism within the leadership and due to wholesale corruption, with such inequality causing social unrest and ever-increasing protest.[14] The lack of transparency in the system also allows many scandals to be covered up, with those implicated escaping any kind of punishment.

In India, since the introduction of neo-liberal reforms in the 1980s, the economy has flourished greatly and the GDP has increased on average by 6% per year. But this national prosperity has been accompanied by a considerable increase in inequality. While the richest 20% display ever more signs of their wealth, the poor have become ever more vulnerable and their situation ever more precarious.

Studies by the statistician Abhijit Sen of Jawaharlal Nehru University, New Delhi, show that while the purchasing power of the richest 20% went up by 40% in the years 1989 to 2004, that of the poorest 80%—representing 600 million people, mainly from rural areas—*went down.*

Worldwide income inequality, according to a survey of 70 countries published by the International Labour Organization under the auspices of the United Nations, has continued to increase in most parts of the globe since the start of the 1900s. Workers have only seen a tiny part of the fruits of global economic growth, which has ended up accumulating among the wealthiest minority.

What's more, in all the countries studied, in times of economic crisis, the elite classes almost always come out alright, while people with low incomes are affected disproportionately. The wealthiest also benefit much more than anyone else when the economy recovers.[15] In summary, in 51 of the 73 countries in the study, the gap between rich and poor had increased.[16]

Women, for their part, earn just 10% of global income, despite carrying out two-thirds of humankind's work.

Tax and social protection schemes, which play a major role in easing the levels of inequality brought about by free market capitalism, have in many countries ceased to be effective over the last fifteen years, since libertarian capitalism aims at reducing the role of government and at reducing social welfare as much as possible. Another factor has been the cutting of the top tax rate for people with the highest incomes in most countries. The OECD highlights the need for governments to revise their fiscal policy so that the best-off play an equal role in shouldering the tax burden. In the words of Warren Buffet: "There's been class warfare going on for the last 20 years and my class has won."

An inquiry carried out by the World Economic Forum at Davos by over a thousand experts concluded that inequality should be considered the most urgent problem facing the world in the coming decade.[17]

THE SOUTH AMERICAN EXCEPTION

In Latin America, the number of people living in poverty has fallen by 30% over the last ten years. According to Nora Lustig, an economist at Tulane University, this shift is owed to education, wage equalization, and the social advantages granted to the poorest families provided they send their children to school.[18] The minimum wage across the entire continent has skyrocketed since 2003, especially in Brazil, where it has gone up by 50%. The same goes for pensions, which are index-linked to wages.

According to Karla Breceda, Jamele Rigolini and Jaime Saavedra, three economists from the World Bank, Latin American government spending on education for children belonging to the poorest 20% now forms a markedly higher share of their GDP than it does in the United States.[19] In some Latin American countries, the proportion of children completing their secondary studies has risen by 20%, while several countries have also become champions of preschool education. The government of the city of Rio de Janeiro, for example, has considerably

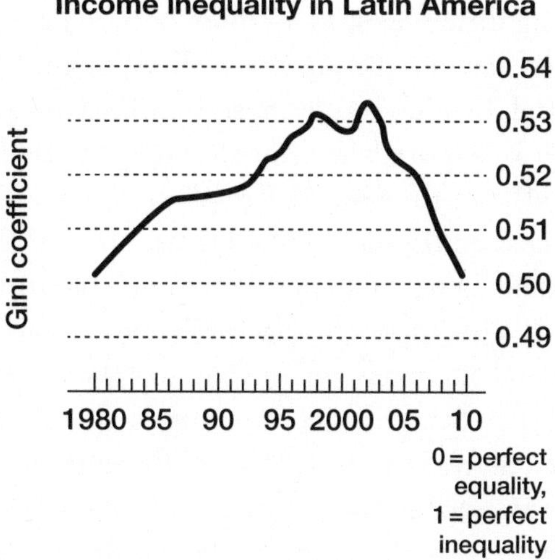

increased its network of kindergartens since 2009. All children born into families below the poverty line are guaranteed to have a free place at a kindergarten from the age of six months. A report by the World Bank points out that the current generation of children in Latin America are much better educated than their parents.

The Price of Inequality

Richard Wilkinson, an epidemiologist at the University of Nottingham, England, and Kate Pickett of the University of York, have between them spent fifty years studying the effects of inequality on society. The conclusions of these studies are recorded in their book *The Spirit Level,* which argues that greater equality produces a healthier society, where greater harmony and prosperity prevail.[20]

Based on a mass of scientific research and data drawn from major international organizations, including the United Nations, the authors show that for each health care or social indicator (physical health, mental health, school success rates, the status of women, trusting others, obesity, drug addiction, violence and murder, the rate of imprisonment, the chance of escaping poverty, early or unwanted pregnancy, infant mortality, and the well-being of children in general) the results are significantly worse in countries where inequality is highest.

Even if we were only to take developed countries into consideration, there are striking differences, as a group, between countries in which there is the least income inequality, such as Japan, Scandinavia, the Netherlands, and Belgium, and those in which inequalities are the largest, such as Singapore, the United States, South Africa, Mexico, Russia, Portugal, and the United Kingdom. Even within the United States, in the most equal state, New Hampshire, all the factors cited above are markedly better than in the country's other states.

With regard to life expectancy at birth in developed countries, it is still the most equal countries with strong social cohesion (Japan, Sweden, and the other Scandinavian countries) that come out on top, while the United States is at the bottom of the rankings.

The same goes for international aid contributions as a percentage of GDP: the rate is highest by far in the Scandinavian countries (between 0.8% and 1% of GDP), while it is four times less in the United States, Australia, and Portugal (all around 0.2%), which are also leaders in inequality. In both this and in international aid, France finds itself roughly in the middle of the table (0.5% of GDP).

Mutual trust plays a particularly important role in ensuring that a society functions well. Its absence translates into a sharpened anxiety, a feeling of insecurity, and even violence, isolation, and mental disorders. Trust boosts altruism and cooperation, and is closely linked to the level of equality. If one were to ask the following: "Do you think that you can trust most people?" the answer is positive almost 70% of the time in Scandinavia, dropping to 40% in the United States, 35% in the United Kingdom, 20% in Singapore, and 17% in Portugal. If we look at how this develops over time, the fall in the level of trust in the United States, which went from 60% in 1960 to 40% in 2004 (the date of the latest survey), corresponds with the increase in inequality.[21]

A report headed up by epidemiologists at the University of Yamanashi, Japan, and the Harvard School of Public Health demonstrated that, in thirty of the world's richest countries, the mortality rate in the 15–60-year age group could be lowered by almost 10% by reducing income inequality. In the United States alone, 900,000 deaths could be prevented each year if the inequality rate were to decrease by 7%.[22]

In several countries, it can be observed that if the poor enjoy worse health than the rich, and if they live less long, it is not because of the absolute amount of their wage, but because of the difference in wages between the richest and the most disadvantaged. The life expectancy of a black American in 1996 was 66.1 years, whereas for a man in Costa Rica with the same purchasing power—taking into account discrepancies in the cost of living—it was 75 years. This difference is explained by the fact that in Costa Rica there is little racial discrimination, while black Americans are victims of racism, have on average fewer opportunities in education than their white counterparts, and live in deprived areas isolated from the rest of society.[23]

Inequality is a source of disdain and rejection, not to mention something that is flagrantly linked to the stigmatization of certain groups (blacks in North America, immigrants in Europe, foreigners more or less everywhere in the world, etc.). One of the consequences of this stigmatization is the widespread opinion that it is individuals themselves, and not society, who are responsible for poverty, and we even go so far as to condemn them for it. As Tocqueville said: "Thus the same man who is full of humanity towards his fellow-creatures when they are at the same time his equals, becomes insensible to their afflictions as soon as that equality ceases."[24]

Large gaps between rich and poor produce violent societies where there is much conflict, since wealth is not measurable by sheer volume of possessions alone, but by the quality of relationships. They also lead, where the poorest elements of society are concerned, to a withdrawal from public life and a high rate of apathy at elections.

Conversely, solidarity benefits the poor when cooperation prevails over competition, but it also benefits the middle and wealthy classes, who fare better when disparity in all its forms is reduced. The most equal democratic societies are also the most prosperous in the long term. Sweden, for example, far more equal than the United States, has experienced growth of 0.5 point year on year since 2000. In a report published in 2011, two economists with the IMF, Andrew Berg and Jonathan Ostry, found that growth was more consistent in more equal countries and that, throughout these periods of growth, income distribution has had a greater effect than the extent of trade liberalization.[25]

In Finland and Belgium, not only is the school success rate among the most disadvantaged much higher than in very unequal countries like the United States, but it is also better, albeit by a small proportion, among children with the wealthiest parents. As such, the benefits of social equality spread throughout the whole of society. In a document released by the World Bank, Ezequiel Molina, Jaime Saavedra, and Amber Narayan observe that countries with the highest rate of educational inequality develop more slowly.[26]

These observations absolutely decimate the argument endlessly rolled out by American conservatives which states that too much equality would stifle growth. For those diehard supporters of the market economy and free competition, the notion is that the rich getting richer stimulates the economy and benefits everyone, something that we have shown to be false. Wilkinson and Pickett show the precise opposite is true: for all to benefit, the rich included, it is the poor who must get richer.

One of the characteristics of the most equal societies is "social mobility," in other words where the poor have the chance to get rich, and the rich do not stay as rich over the course of their lives, or from one generation to the next. The example of Sweden again shows that only 20% of wealth (or poverty) is passed down from one generation to the next, while in China, a far less equal country, this rate is 60%.[27]

How to Reduce Inequality

In his book *The Path to Hope,* Edgar Morin sets out a series of proposals for reducing inequality, for example by revising downwards (or canceling altogether) the debts of poorer countries and providing them with, at a feasible price, renewable energy sources, medicine, and free treatment for fighting pandemics, as well as, in times of famine, the food they require. Food self-sufficiency must be re-established in those countries where it is lacking, in addition to the implementation of mechanisms for economic regulation capable of checking financial speculation, the source of artificial fluctuations in the price of staple products, which are themselves the frequent cause of the ruin of small producers. Furthermore, international controls must be put in place to ensure that corruption does not divert aid sent to poor countries, increasing inequality even further.[28]

In *The Path to Hope,* Edgar Morin and Stéphane Hessel propose the creation—at the international level—of a Permanent Council to fight inequality, which would monitor both the fundamental causes and symptoms of inequality, at the same time as control excesses at the top and find remedies for the shortages, insecurity, and dependencies at the root of poverty.[29]

At the international level, adds Morin, a permanent watchdog would also need to be established to monitor inequality, charting its developments and offering tangible measures to reduce it gradually.

In Scandinavia, the primary source of equality is the redistribution of resources by the state. Taxation levels are high, but there are substantial social services. The Swedish government in particular has worked more vigorously than others to strengthen the efficiency of public services created to protect the poor. This has not prevented Scandinavia, the most equal group of nations in the world, from remaining among the countries where growth is highest and most stable.

A summary of proposals from several experts published in *The Economist* presents a series of reforms that would bring about a reduction in inequality around the world. This would firstly involve clamping down on corruption, nepotism, and influence peddling, all of which allow those in positions of power or at multinationals to exercise undue pressure on governments and to enjoy monopolies through which they can maintain a stranglehold on the markets. Nepotism is especially widespread in China and other emerging countries, while in developed countries, industrial monopolies are a strong factor in perpetuating inequality and concentrating wealth in the hands of a select few. Banks and big business put pressure on the state at times of crisis under the pretext that they are "too big to fail without causing catastrophes on a national scale," allowing them to escape punishment for their woeful, sometimes dishonest, management. Other priorities include reducing exploitation and wastage, and the establishment of an effective social welfare system that would provide, in particular, for the needs of the poorest and youngest at the same time as demanding greater financial support from the rich and adult population. Latin America has shown this to be possible by associating social support with enrolling citizens into professional apprenticeship schemes and encouraging them to attach greater importance to their children's education.

Income tax and wealth tax must be considered a means of financing the state and reducing inequality, and not as a punitive measure against the rich. Many experts are in agreement that it would be preferable not to increase the top tax rate by much, but to ensure that taxation is genuinely progressive—the billionaire Warren Buffet became the talk of the town in 2012 when he announced that his secretary paid proportionately more tax than he did, and that he would be willing to pay more tax—and that the tax system becomes fairer and more efficient, especially by abolishing tax havens. The wealthiest people can afford skillful lawyers who show them various ways to avoid taxes and deduct considerable sums from their tax returns, ways that are not available to the middle classes or the poor, thus further increasing injustice and inequality.

According to the 2014 OECD report "Focus on Inequality and Growth," not only cash transfers to the poor, but also increased access to public services, such as high-quality education, training and health care, constitute long-term social investment that can create greater equality of opportunities in the long run.[30] The most direct policy tool to reduce inequality is redistribution through taxes and benefits. Contrary to what politicians and economists who hold libertarian views argue, the OECD analysis shows that tackling inequality through tax and other redistribution policies does not harm growth, provided these policies are well designed and implemented.

Since income inequality undermines education opportunities for disadvantaged individuals, lowers social mobility and hampers skills development, redistribution efforts should focus on families with children and youth and include improving job-related training and education for the low-skilled, over the whole working life.

Essentially, an unequal society is a broken society. Political leaders must repair this breakdown and heal the inequality that has, with the exception of Latin America and Scandinavia, been a continual scourge in the world since the 1970s. To achieve this end we require a political will that must not draw its inspiration from the laissez-faire attitude of the free market, and which promotes an economic policy founded on the common good, solidarity, reciprocity, and social justice, otherwise known as the "Positive Economy," a term coined by the group BeCitizen to denote an altruistic economy which focuses on instituting social well-being and ecological capital.

39

Toward a Caring Economy

The world has enough for everyone's need, but not enough for everyone's greed.

—Gandhi

The economy must exist to serve society, not to be served by society. It must also benefit society *as a whole.*

Without condoning the imposition of sterilizing constraints on the spirit of enterprise, innovation, and prosperity, economic regulation must prevent those driven solely by self-interest from taking advantage of the intricacies of the financial system to siphon off a disproportionate amount of resources. As the French writer Daniel Pennac said: "Individual happiness must have collective results, failing which society is just a predator's dream."[1] The state must protect the weak, guarantee that everyone's work is fairly remunerated, and ensure that the privileged and the wealthiest do not exert their power to influence political decisions in their favor.

An economy becomes dysfunctional when those who have made a negative contribution to society are those who reap the most reward. An example would be the autocrat who becomes immeasurably rich by seizing ownership of his country's natural resources, or even the banker who receives colossal bonuses even though his actions have placed society in a precarious situation.

A healthy economy must not give way to disproportionate

inequality. This does not refer to the natural forms of disparity that are manifest in any human community, but rather extreme inequality that derives not from people's actual dispositions, but from the economic and political systems which are skewed to promote this iniquity.

None of this is inevitable, and it is entirely possible to set things on a different course, provided there is a popular and political will to do so. Even in the world of economics, the respect for human values exemplified by altruism is not an idealistic dream but a pragmatic expression of the best way to achieve a fair economy and long-term harmony. To be harmonious, the pursuit of prosperity must accommodate an aspiration for the well-being of all citizens and respect for the environment. Economists might argue that it is not their job to be altruistic or compassionate, but if they say that they don't "care" for society, it is not acceptable. This is why we need a more caring economy.

Homo Economicus, Rational, Calculating, and Selfish

The concept of the "economic human," *Homo economicus*, appeared at the end of the nineteenth century as a critical response to John Stuart Mill's writings[2] on political economics, and was widely adopted by the founders of so-called "neoclassical" economic theory, in particular Francis Edgeworth and Vilfredo Pareto. This involves a theoretical representation of the relationships between humans, identifying them as selfish agents capable of making rational choices that optimize their chances of satisfying their own preferences and promoting their own interests.[3] This theory stands in opposition to the notion of *Homo reciprocans,* which states that humans are motivated by a desire to cooperate and take into consideration the benefits to the community.

The underlying idea is that if everyone were to behave in this way, and the supply-and-demand market remains free of any constraint, said market will work out best for each party. Neoclassical theory has been taught to millions of students since the start of the twentieth century. In *Economics,* one of the most influential textbooks on economics, Paul Samuelson and William Nordhaus explain that *Homo economicus* represents an idealized vision of rational man, in which the population would be made up of two types of persons: "consumers who are endowed with sets of tastes that they try their utmost to satisfy, and entrepreneurs who are only trying to maximize their profits."[4] Yet as Philippe Kourilsky, professor at the Collège de France in Paris, explains: "*Homo economicus* is a caricature of real mankind. In truth, it is a dehumanized version that contributes to the dehumanization of a section of economic science."[5]

As one might suspect, *Homo economicus* is not altruistic: "The first principle of Economics is that every agent is actuated only by self-interest,"[6] wrote Francis Edgeworth, one of the founding fathers of modern economics.[7] Many others have echoed his views, among them William Landes and Richard Posner, an economist and lawyer respectively, who state: "Altruism is not a trait with a particularly strong survival rate in the competitive markets."[8]

According to this reductive view of humankind, even if we do each other mutually beneficial favors, it is always in the service of our own needs, and we only seek to gain profit from any human relationships we maintain.[9] Here we see again the notion of universal selfishness discussed earlier. Even the idea of fairness, which economists call upon frequently, does not escape this fate. The psychologist Elaine Walster and her co-authors assure us that "equity theory, too, rests on the simple, but eminently safe, assumption that humans are selfish."[10] All these statements are based not on scientific evidence but on dogmatic beliefs.

This conception of economics is at once simplistic and erroneous. As the Nobel laureate and Harvard professor Amartya Sen writes:

> *It strikes me as absolutely extraordinary that people can dismiss any attitude as irrational other than that of the maximization of self-interest. [Such a position] necessarily implies that we reject the role of ethics in our real decision-making.... Taking universal selfishness as read may well be delusional, but to turn it into a standard for rationality is utterly absurd.*[11]

Homo economicus's most serious flaw, continues Kourilsky, is his fundamental amorality: "In classic economics, one supposes that this moral deficit is compensated for by the rather mystical notion of the 'invisible hand,' which would re-establish—somewhat mysteriously—a balance of sorts."[12] According to the metaphor used by Adam Smith, the "invisible hand" describes a spontaneous phenomenon that guides the markets when reasonable individuals governed by self-interest alone are placed in free competition. Smith argues that in trying to maximize their own well-being, individuals contribute to the good of society as a whole. According to him, the intervention of the state is useless, since the invisible hand is the best way of regulating the economy. Passionate advocates of the market economy are therefore of the opinion that, since the invisible hand is taking care of everything, they have no duty whatsoever toward society.[13] The truth is that the invisible hand of blind selfishness cannot build a better world: freedom without duty leads only to an exacerbation of individualism. Adam Smith himself readily recognized this: "People of the same trade seldom meet together, even for merriment and diversion, but the conversation ends in a conspiracy against the public, or in some contrivance to raise prices."[14]

Nowadays, many founders of companies are aware that the notion of *Homo economicus* is nothing but a caricature of human nature, and have themselves introduced far more complex value systems in which altruistic qualities play a vital role.

Milton Friedman, the famous champion of libertarianism and deregulation, stated: "Few trends could so thoroughly undermine the very foundations of our free society as the acceptance by corporate officials of a social responsibility other than to make as much money for their stockholders as possible."[15] Over the last ten years, observes Frans de Waal in *The Age of Empathy:* "every advanced nation has had major business scandals, and in every case executives have managed to shake the foundations of their society precisely by following Friedman's advice.... All too often it leads to exploitation, injustice, and rampant dishonesty. Given its colossal fraud, the Enron Corporation's sixty-four-page 'Code of Ethics' now seems as fictional as the safety manual of the *Titanic.*"[16]

It is clear, emphasizes the French economist Serge-Christophe Kolm, that "an economic system does not simply produce goods and services. It also produces human beings and the relationships between them. The way in which a society produces and consumes has a major influence on personalities, characters, knowledge, desires, happiness, and types of interpersonal relationships."[17] So many things that are essential to happiness have nothing to do with economic transactions.

Adam Smith himself, the father of the market economy, was not nearly so extreme as his successors and, in a work too often overlooked by economists, his *Theory of Moral Sentiments,* he stated: "To restrain our selfish, and to indulge our benevolent affections, constitutes the perfection of human nature; and can alone produce among mankind that harmony of sentiments and passions in which consists their whole grace and propriety."[18]

Any theory of economics that excludes altruism is fundamentally incomplete and diminished. Most of all it is at odds with reality, and as such is bound to fail. Essentially the complex mathematical models created by neoclassical economists to try to explain human behaviors are based on presuppositions that are for the most part false, since the majority of people are not entirely selfish, are not fully informed (concealing information is one of the strategies used by those who manipulate the markets), and are far from making rational choices all the time.

Even though we are generally convinced that we are rational, our decisions, economic or otherwise, are very often irrational and strongly influenced by our immediate gut feelings and emotions. Intuition is a highly adaptable faculty that allows us to make fast decisions in complex situations, but it also lures us into thinking that we have made a rational choice, which takes more time and deliberation. This has been widely evidenced in behavioral psychology, chiefly by Amos Tversky and Daniel Kahneman. Their findings won them the first-ever Nobel Prize in Economics to be awarded to a psychologist, in this case Kahneman, who recently painted a revealing picture of these traits we have in his much acclaimed book *Thinking, Fast and Slow.*[19] Similarly the neuroscientist Brian Knutson and his team at Stanford University have shown the extent to which economic decisions, especially risk-taking, are strongly influenced by emotions, impulses, and personal preferences. They indicate that the parts of the brain associated with the limbic system, which is linked to the emotions that govern primitive behaviors such as searching for food and evading predators, also play an important role in our reactions to monetary rewards and punishments.[20] What's more, at the point when investors make financial decisions, observations of their cerebral activity reveal heightened states of excitement that facilitate risk-taking and influence the degree of objectivity in their decision-making.

The context of a situation also influences decisions that are supposed to be rational without our realization: the psychologist Dan

Ariely asked participants in a study to note down the last two digits of their Social Security number on a piece of paper, then asked them to take part in an auction. The people whose Social Security number ended with a high figure, i.e., between 80 and 99, bid an average of fifty-six dollars for a computer keyboard, while those whose number ended in a lower figure, i.e., between 1 and 20, only bid sixteen dollars for the same keyboard.[21] There is nothing remotely rational about this economic (yet perfectly ordinary) decision.

Emotions, motivations, and value systems undeniably influence economic decision-making. Since this is the case, it is best for these emotions to be positive and their motivations to be altruistic. Why not then introduce the voice of care into the economy, instead of satisfying ourselves with the voice of reason, a necessary but insufficient voice on which economists place too much importance?

THE DOWNWARD SLIDE OF THE FREE MARKET

The billionaire investor and philanthropist George Soros uses the term "free market fundamentalism" to describe the belief that the free market is not only the best but the *only* way of managing an economic system and preserving civil liberties. "The doctrine of laissez-faire capitalism holds that the common good is best served by the uninhibited pursuit of self-interest,"[22] he writes. If the laissez-faire attitude of an entirely deregulated free market were based on the laws of nature and had some scientific value, if it were anything other than an act of faith pronounced by the champions of ultraliberalism, it would have stood the test of time. But it hasn't, since its unpredictability and the abuses it has permitted have led to the financial crises with which we are only too familiar. For Soros, if the doctrine of economic laissez-faire—a term dear to philosopher Ayn Rand—had been submitted to the rigors of scientific and empirical research, it would have been rejected a long time ago.[23]

The free market facilitates the creation of businesses; innovation across many fields, for example in new technology, health, the Internet, and renewable energy; and affords undeniable opportunities to young entrepreneurs wishing to start up business activities that will further society. We have also seen, in the chapter on the decline of violence, that commercial exchange between democratic nations considerably reduces the risk of armed conflict between them. Yet, in the absence of any safeguard, the free market permits a predatory use of financial systems, giving rise to an increase in oligarchies, inequality, exploitation of the poorest producers, and the monetization of several aspects of human life whose value derives from anything other than money.

The Price of Everything, the Value of Nothing

In his book *What Money Can't Buy: The Moral Limits of Markets,*[24] Michael Sandel, one of the United States' most high-profile philosophers and an adviser to President Obama, says that neo-liberal economists understand the price of everything and the value of nothing.

In 1997, he ruffled a lot of feathers when he questioned the morality of the Kyoto Protocol on global warming, the agreement that removed the moral stigma attached to environmentally harmful activities by simply introducing the concept of buying the "right to pollute." In his view, China and the United States are the least receptive countries to his outspoken objections to free market fundamentalism: "In other parts of east Asia, Europe and the UK, and India and Brazil, it goes without arguing that there are moral limits to markets, and the question is where to locate them."[25] He gives some examples of the commercialization of values which in his view should not be monetized:

- For $8,000, Western couples can buy the services of an Indian surrogate mother;
- For $250,000, a rich hunter can pay for the right to kill a black rhinoceros in South Africa, a protected species in danger of extinction;
- For $1,500 to $25,000 per year, an increasing number of doctors in the United States are offering a "concierge" service, granting permanent access to their mobile telephone and the opportunity for same-day appointments;

- An online casino "gave" $10,000 to a single mother from Utah desperate to raise money to pay her son's school fees, on the condition that she had to have their Internet domain name permanently tattooed across her forehead.

Can we monetize everything? Would there be any sense in letting someone buy a Nobel Prize if they had not deserved it? As for slavery, it continues to exist, just in different forms: trafficking women and children for prostitution the world over; Bangladeshi, Nepalese and Pakistani workers harshly exploited in the Gulf states; entire families in India shackled by debts spanning several generations to employers who deprive them of any freedom (more than ten million children from such families are subjected to forced labor in this way).

The only question the economist asks is: "How much?" Markets make no distinction between worthy and unworthy choices: it is only the parties concerned who can confer value on any of the things or services exchanged. This can apply to anything, even hiring a hit man.

Do we want a market economy or a market society? According to Sandel, even if the market economy is an effective tool for organizing productive activities, from a moral point of view, it should not invade all sectors of human life.

It therefore is not free trade in itself that must be called into question, but the fact that all freedom can only be implemented in a manner that is responsible toward those around you. These responsibilities are governed by moral values and by an ethical code that is respectful of the well-being of the community as a whole, starting with the obligation not to harm others when pursuing self-interest. By virtue of the fact that the unscrupulous and profit-hungry miss no opportunity to take advantage of unconditional freedom for their own profit and to the detriment of others, it is essential to establish regulations, which are nothing more than protective measures for society. This is, however, not what has happened, as Amartya Sen explains:

> *The apparatus of regulation was dismantled year after year by the Reagan administration until George W. Bush's time in office. But the success of the liberal economy has always certainly depended not only on the dynamism of the market itself, but also on regulatory mechanisms and controls to ensure that speculation and profit-seeking do not lead to excessive risk-taking.... If you are concerned about freedom or happiness, you must try to organize the economy in such a way that they are possible.*[26]

According to Stiglitz, "well-designed regulations did succeed in ensuring the stability of our financial system for decades, so regulations can work. Moreover, this period of tight financial regulation was also one of rapid economic growth, a period in which the fruits of that growth were more widely shared than they are today.... By contrast, in the period of 'liberalization' the growth of a typical citizen's income was far lower than in the period of regulation.... There is a simple reason for the failure of liberalization: when social returns and private rewards are misaligned, all economic activity gets distorted, including innovation. The innovation of the financial sector was directed not at improving the well-being of Americans but at improving the well-being of bankers."[27]

The reality is that the free market economy does not work as well as its supporters claim. They say that it leads to greater stability, but successive global crashes have shown that it can be very unstable and have devastating consequences. What's more, all the evidence points to the markets being far less effective than they maintain, and that the fairness of supply and demand, so dear to classical economists, is nothing but a myth, since we live in a world where a vast number of needs remain unsatisfied, and in particular where the investment required to eradicate poverty and respond to the challenges of global warming is lacking. For Stiglitz, unemployment, which prevents countless workers from contributing to the economy to their full potential, is the worst failing of the deregulated market, the greatest source of inefficiency, and one of the major drivers of inequality. Poverty, as Amartya Sen explains, is a deprivation of freedom, and not just any freedom: the freedom to express the potential that each person has in life.[28]

The politicians and economists who have dominated the US

political establishment since the Reagan administration thought we had to do away with all regulation pertaining to the free market and give free rein to the laissez-faire philosophy. They thought it was the best way to create equal opportunities for all: the most enterprising and the hardest working would be those who would succeed the most. The American Dream glorifies the shoe shiner who becomes a millionaire through sheer force of ingenuity and perseverance. Yet studies show that in the United States, with the odd exception, the wealthiest people, who lest we forget make up 1% of the population, as well as their descendants, have the greatest chance of preserving their level of wealth in the long term. Stiglitz summarizes the situation as follows: "America had created a marvelous economic machine, but evidently one that worked only for those at the top."[29]

According to the champions of deregulation, the rich's accumulation of wealth is supposed to benefit the poor due to the fact that they create jobs, stimulate the economy, and let wealth "trickle down" to the bottom. We must therefore not kill the goose that lays the golden egg. The problems start when the goose keeps all its eggs. The reality is that nowadays there is a minimal amount of trickling down, and it no more quenches the thirst of the poor than the water of a mirage.

In collaboration with economists from various countries, French economist Thomas Piketty has analyzed hundreds of years of tax records from thirty countries across Europe, the US and Japan. The conclusion of his fifteen years of painstaking analysis from this unprecedented mass of data is that the rich are getting richer and that their wealth doesn't trickle down. In fact it trickles up. These findings, presented in *Capital in the Twenty-first Century*,[30] flatly contradict the claim, repeated over and again by libertarian economists, that the accumulation of wealth at the top of the pyramid benefits everyone by filtering down to the middle classes and the poor. This is simply not true.

One of the main features of Piketty's findings is that when people obtain most of their wealth through inheritance and from subsequently investing it, they invariably grow richer and richer, while those who earn wages and salaries for their productive work grow relatively poorer. This goes plainly against the idea that a small government and a deregulated economy made the USA a land of opportunity for all. The current system resembles a game of Monopoly with one player having one set of dice and the other three. The latter can only get richer and richer. His success has nothing to do with his hard work and personal skills. The three sets of dice represent inherited wealth, earnings made on financial investment and assets (such as property, art collections, etc., which generate non-taxable passive income), and proportionately less taxation on the rich. One set of dice stands for productive work based on personal skills.

Piketty has also shown that the only times when inequality decreased in the USA was when the government directly intervened to promote growth, during the New Deal in the 1930s and the Marshall Plan after World War II. Then the working person could hope to gain equal footing with the financiers through his or her own merit and hard work. Based to some extent on altruism, a Keynesian style of economics is aimed at achieving prosperity for both present and future generations, not at ensuring the selfish, short-term gain of a minority. Thoughtful regulation allowed the creation of a balance in society by applying an incremental wealth tax rate. People were more concerned for their fellow man and the social contract had a stronger element of coöperation instead of barefaced competition. From the 1980s on, the American Dream ended with the likes of Ronald Reagan, Milton Friedman, and Ayn Rand, as social solidarity waned and inequality continued to grow thanks to major tax cuts granted to the rich.

If more and more citizens across the world are feeling outrage toward the current economic system it is because, as Stiglitz says, following the 2008 crisis: "It was rightly perceived to be grossly unfair that many in the financial sector (which, for shorthand, I will often refer to as 'the bankers') walked off with outsize bonuses, while those who suffered from the crisis brought on by these bankers went without a job.... What happened in the midst of the crisis made clear that it was not contribution to society that determined relative pay, but something else: bankers received large rewards, though their contribution to society—and even to their firms—had been negative. The wealth given to the elites and to the bankers seemed to arise out of their ability and willingness to take advantage of others."[31]

To illustrate this, let us remember that at the onset of the crisis, Goldman Sachs highly recommended that its customers invest in Infospace,[32] a start-up selling various online services that had grown rapidly and been given the highest possible rating, even though it was dismissed by an analyst as a "piece of junk." Excite, a similar business that also had a strong rating, was dismissed as "such a piece of crap."[33] In 2008, after 9 million poor Americans had lost their houses, often their sole asset, the heads of Goldman Sachs received 16 billion dollars in bonuses. Similarly, the five most senior people at Lehman Brothers, one of the biggest sellers of risky mortgage loans, pocketed over 1 billion dollars in bonuses between 2000 and 2007.[34] When the company went bankrupt and their customers were ruined, they held on to the entirety of this money. As Stiglitz remarks: "Something has happened to our sense of values, when the ends of making more money justifies the means, which in the US subprime crisis meant exploiting the poorest and least-educated among us."[35]

SAFEGUARDS FOR THE GOOD OF ALL

In 1982, President Ronald Reagan, with the support of Chicago School economists in favor of a laissez-faire system, ushered in a period of thirty years of financial deregulation by lifting regulations on bank deposits, thus allowing bankers to make risky investments with their customers' savings. By the end of that decade, hundreds of savings and credit organizations had filed for bankruptcy, costing the American taxpayer 124 billion dollars and gobbling up the savings of those who had placed their trust in the system.[36] In 2004, Henry Paulson, CEO of Goldman Sachs, manipulated the core political establishment into deregulating the banks' debt limits, allowing them to increase their borrowing immeasurably without any guarantee whatsoever that they could pay it back.

According to Nouriel Roubini,[37] a professor at the New York University School of Business, the financial sector, step by step, seized control of the political system. Between 1998 and 2008, it spent 5 billion dollars lobbying politicians.

In Washington, there's an average of six lobbyists for each Congress representative or Senator. Since the 2008 crisis, even more money has been spent on lobbying. In Europe, according to figures presented by Siim Kallas, European Commissioner for Administrative Affairs, there were 15,000 lobbyists representing 2,600 interest groups in Brussels.[38]

The economist James K. Galbraith (son of the famous economist

John K. Galbraith) summed it up by saying, about the wealthiest elite, that "the members of this new class have set out to take over the state and to run it—not for any ideological project but simply in the way that would bring to them, individually and as a group, the most money, the least disturbed power, and the greatest chance of rescue should something go wrong. That is, they set out to prey on the existing systems."[39]

The freedom provided by deregulation ought to have been used to stimulate creativity as well as healthy, fair competition, but too often it has allowed investors to make use of new technologies to circumvent the few remaining regulations, charge predatory rates, and cheat people with increasingly opaque financial schemes. In 2009, Lord Turner, head of the Financial Services Authority in the UK, described much of the City's[40] activities as "socially useless." They help the rich to become richer, but do not help the middle class and the poor, who constitute the largest part of society, to become better off.[41]

The only regulations in force in the United States, for example, were created under the influence of major financial groups to wipe out any potential competitors and return to the age of monopolization. Patents on living organisms, plants, and seeds, and the shares of firms like Monsanto and big pharmaceutical companies, are prime examples of this.[42] The financial powers-that-be are especially resistant to any form of regulation that aims to protect consumers and the environment.

George Soros has said that—considering their inherent instability—regulation is indispensable to the markets in the same way that watertight compartments are to a large tanker: if one financial sector takes on water, the others remain unharmed, thus preventing the entire thing from sinking.[43] One of the ways of limiting market volatility would be to apply the Tobin tax, proposed in 1972 by the Nobel Economics Prize winner James Tobin, which involves a tax on international currency transactions. The rate of taxation would be minimal, between 0.05% and 0.2%, but it would help to control the unstable nature of transactions. Such a tax would also be an effective tool against speculation. It is now being seriously considered by several governments and the European Parliament.[44]

Regulations must be devised by experts with the requisite skills who have the interests of society at large in mind, who wish to uphold fairness, reduce inequality, crack down on free riders, and give the majority of the population—who support cooperation and benevolent mutual aid (as we have already seen in the experiments carried out by Ernst Fehr and Martin Nowak detailed in chapter 36—the option not to be held hostage by a small number of unscrupulous speculators.

According to Harvard professor Michael Porter and economic consultant Mark Kramer, good regulation encourages social objectives and investment, generates shared benefits, and stimulates innovation, rather than promoting the pursuit of short-term profit that only benefits the few, as is the case in a deregulated economy. Such regulation must, according to them, state clearly defined social goals regarding, for example, the use of energy resources, as well as matters of health and security. It must also prompt producers to factor the environmental effects of their products and activities into their accounts and cost price analysis (e.g., waste management, environmental degradation, depletion of natural resources, etc). But regulation must also sustain companies' innovation potential by giving them freedom of choice regarding the measures they implement to achieve the social and environmental goals set by regulators. It must not undermine the progress it seeks to encourage.

In all circumstances, regulation must foster transparency, root out malpractice, and serve as an antidote to markets subjected to harmful monopolization by big multinationals.

Porter and Kramer advocate a form of capitalism that is nourished by social goals, creating shared value and engendering mutual benefits. They cite the example of Yara, a Norwegian mineral fertilizer company which realized that many African farmers did not have access to fertilizers and other agricultural commodities because of a lack of port and road infrastructure. With the help of the Norwegian government, Yara launched a 60-million-dollar program in Mozambique and Tanzania aimed at improving port and road facilities, creating "corridors of growth" that sought to improve the situation of 200,000 farmers and generate 350,000 new jobs.[45]

THE BEGINNING OF THE END OF EXORBITANT BONUSES: THE SWISS LEAD THE WAY

Current trends illustrate what happens when we cease to let ourselves be governed by ethics or even common sense, the original basis of "protestant liberalism." A British banker explained to a friend of mine that the employment contract he signed when he was hired in the City of London stated that "obviously no bonus will be paid if the bank has not made an overall profit." If such contracts—which were the rule back in the 1970s—had remained in force, many scandals would have been averted. "It was madness. People lost their souls—it was all about earning more, more, more than other people. Why? They weren't even sure," says Henri Philippi, former boss of HSBC France in *L'Argent sans maître* (Money Without a Master).[46] When things are going well, financiers receive *incentive pay*, which aims to encourage good performance, and when the results are poor, they receive so-called *retention pay* (no longer any mention of the "incentive" word) urging them to stay at the company.[47] Some companies even go so far as to pay off their outgoing executives so that they promise not to join a competing firm.

In a referendum on March 3, 2013, 67.9% of people in Switzerland approved a law curbing the "excessive pay packages" for Swiss company bosses. In particular, this law forbids bonuses for executives when they join or leave a company (the notorious "golden handshakes"). Indeed many big companies attract senior executives by offering them a starting bonus that can be as much 5 or 10 million euros. In addition, the Swiss decided that board and management salaries must now be approved at annual general meetings for shareholders. Penalties for breaching these rules range from a fine equivalent to six years' salary to three years in prison.

In February 2014, the European Union followed suit as the EU's two legislative bodies, the European Parliament (EP) and the European Council (Council), agreed to restrict retail asset managers' bonuses and are now trying to enforce this measure while bankers are devising new type of allowances to circumvent this European Union's bonus cap.

Uniting the Voice of Care with the Voice of Reason

There are two types of problems that free economic market activity and individualistic selfishness will never be able to resolve: *collective goods* and poverty in the midst of plenty. To solve these problems we need to bring about the voice of care and altruism. This is the opinion of Dennis Snower, economics professor at Kiel and founder of the Global Economic Symposium (GES), which was held in Rio de Janeiro in October 2012, and which I attended at his invitation along with the neuroscientist Tania Singer.

Making such a declaration in an opening speech, in front of an audience of some six hundred financiers, statesmen, social entrepreneurs, and journalists, required audacity. Indeed, for traditional economists, it is unthinkable to talk of motivation (beyond that of self-interest) and emotions (although they influence all the decisions we make), let alone altruism and solidarity. As we have already seen, economics is not supposed to use any language other than that of *reason*. Snower was therefore somewhat anxious before his speech, just as he was in dedicating three plenary sessions to a neuroscientist discussing empathy, and—worse still—a Buddhist monk explaining that altruism, inextricably linked as it is to happiness, is the concept that provides the most effective response to the challenges of our times.

Much to his relief, things went extremely well and, three days later, when participants had to vote for ten proposals that the GES would then endeavor to support, two of our projects were included. These involved "compassion gymnasia" aimed at fostering altruism within companies, and compassion training from preschool level, based around a hugely successful program led by the psychologist and neurobiologist Richard Davidson in Madison. Snower's gamble had paid off: those in attendance were open to his vision.

His question was as follows: how do we promote the cooperation required to solve the world's most serious problems? We are faced with two particular types of problem, that of "collective goods" or "public goods," and that of poverty in the midst of plenty.

A collective good exists in a social group in so far as it can be used by all members of the group, irrespective of their contribution to it. Social services, fundamental science and medical research, and parks and gardens for the enjoyment of everybody, are examples of this. Democratic freedoms are among the most important collective goods, even if they are often not regarded as such. In numerous countries, citizens have fought for these freedoms and they have often had to pay a high price to institute them. But once these freedoms are in place, everyone benefits from them, even those who have not fought for them.

The problem with collective goods is that those who make no contribution to them can nonetheless continue to draw advantage from them. As such there is a strong temptation to behave like a free rider. Those who contribute to collective goods are acting in a truly altruistic manner, because they are making sacrifices that will benefit others. This is the case, for example, when someone writes an article on Wikipedia, makes a Social Security contribution, or takes the effort to prevent global warming, overexploitation of our oceans, or any other environmentally harmful activity.

The state of the environment in particular is one of the most vitally important public goods, in which one person's benefit does not reduce another's. Everyone wins, for example, when greenhouse gas emissions are reduced. If everyone contributed to the efforts and costs required to reduce these gases, we would all benefit. But if this contribution is made only by some, they will pay dearly for their actions without collectively gaining much, since a few isolated efforts will not be sufficient. On a totally different level, any attempts to establish global regulations to clean up the dysfunctional financial system also have an impact on the collective good, while giving free rein to the selfish and to free riders can result only in the deterioration of the environment and society.

Natural resources—forests, open farmland, water, biodiversity—of course enter into the idea of collective goods. Each hectare of forest destroyed on behalf of a private individual or a small group reduces the overall area of forest available to everyone on the planet. If everyone were to act selfishly, the effect would be catastrophic.

In Dennis Snower's words, "*Homo economicus*—the individualistic, self-interested, rational person on whom economics and much economic policymaking focuses—will not contribute sufficiently to the provision of collective goods. The reason is that free economic market activity does not compensate this person for the full social benefits." In other words, if an individual acting in isolation makes the wise decision not to destroy too many trees, the market economy couldn't care less.

Snower goes on to ask how this situation can be remedied. His answer is clear: "It is the willingness to contribute to the common good, even though the individual cost exceeds the individual benefit."

The second issue is that of poverty in the midst of plenty, another problem that *Homo economicus* will clearly never be disposed to solving. In his eyes, if a single mother who has not had the chance of an education is in poverty, the only option is for her to work more. The process of globalization and rising wealth have marginalized many countries and trapped them in poverty, ill health, food insecurity, corruption, conflict, and a poor level of education.

To break this vicious cycle, the privileged must not only accept the need to fix inequality, but also want to achieve this without hoping for anything other than improving the lives of other people. For Snower, this is something that the free market cannot ever automatically engender, and here again the solution lies in the will of the privileged to make a concerted effort to render better services to those most in need.

Traditional economists came to the conclusion that to do this meant finding ways of encouraging people to face up to the problems of poverty and shared wealth. The government can, for example, raise taxes and subsidize the most disadvantaged; it can also reconsider property laws, redistribute income and wealth, or directly supply the population with collective goods.

But in a world where politicians aim only to be elected or re-elected, where financial interest groups wield a disproportionate influence on policymakers, where the well-being of future generations is often ignored since their representatives do not have a seat at the negotiating table, where governments pursue national economic policies that are to the detriment of the global interest, decision-makers have barely any inclination to create institutions whose goal would be to encourage citizens to contribute to collective wealth, which would serve to eradicate poverty.

In this context, how do we go about persuading different countries and cultures to enrich collective goods? There are two foreseeable responses: one is the voice of reason; the other is the voice of care.

The voice of reason is what urges us to consider things objectively. It allows us above all to reflect on how perspectives are interchangeable, and makes us understand that if we want others to behave responsibly, we must start by doing so ourselves by favoring cooperation. This rational step has undoubtedly been a significant factor in promoting the rights of women, minorities, and other sets of individuals whose rights have been trampled upon. In addition, it drives us to take into account the long-term consequences of our actions. According to Snower, even what we just attributed to reason might actually result from our instinct for reciprocity, through which we expect people to reciprocate our beneficial and responsible actions.

In fact, Dennis Snower states, no one has been able to show convincingly that reason alone, without the help of some prosocial motivation, is enough to persuade individuals to widen their sphere of responsibility to include all those who are affected by their actions. What's more, if the balance of power tips in your favor, nothing will stop you from serving yourself shamelessly at the expense of others. Devoid of care and spurred on by selfishness, reason can lead to deplorable behavior, to manipulation, exploitation, and merciless opportunism.

This is why we need the voice of care. It is founded on a different interpretation of human nature and can naturally accommodate empathy in economics, as we do in life, not to mention the capacity to put ourselves in others' places, compassion for those who are suffering, and the altruism that encompasses all these qualities. Combined with the voice of reason, the voice of care can fundamentally change our will to contribute to collective goods. Such ideas echo the Buddhist teachings on uniting wisdom and compassion: without wisdom, compassion can be blind; without compassion, wisdom becomes sterile.

For anyone who holds that it is more rational to be selfish than altruistic, on the basis that it is the most realistic and effective way of guaranteeing their prosperity and survival, and that altruists are utopian and irrational idealists ripe for exploitation, Robert Frank of Cornell University has this to say: "Altruists are neither more nor less rational than non-altruists. They are simply pursuing different goals."[48] It is even probable that, in many situations, the altruist will act in a more realistic manner than the egotist, whose judgments will be tarnished by the pursuit for self-interest. The altruist pictures everything with a more open perspective. He will find it easier to view situations from different angles, and to take the most appropriate decisions. Lacking consideration for the interests of other people is not rational—it is just inhumane.

In addition, while the voice of reason alone does not provide a sufficiently compelling rationale for the selfish to eliminate poverty in the midst of plenty, the voice of care does many times over. As such, it deserves our attention and must guide us in our efforts to resolve the world's problems.

In this spirit, Dennis Snower concluded his opening address to

GES 2014 with this remark: "When mainstream economics tells us that people cooperate only to exploit economic synergies, it blinds us to our innate capacities for care, reciprocity, fairness and moral concern. We must work toward a society and polity that gives emphasis to our most inclusive moral values—such as the Golden Rule, central to all the great religions—and give dignity to those artists, employers, and public servants who devote themselves to widening our horizons of compassion. In building social affiliations that match our needs for economic cooperation, we will help lay the groundwork for a peaceful, fulfilling future for all."[49]

EXTENDING RECIPROCITY

Altruism is contagious, and imitation, or inspiration, plays an important role in human societies. Numerous studies have shown that the mere fact of seeing someone help a stranger increases the probability of the onlooker doing likewise. This trend is cumulative: the more one sees others acting generously and taking care of others, the more likely one is to follow suit. Conversely, the more selfish others are, the more one tends to be too.

The combination of the voice of care with reciprocity is a powerful force for achieving social good. In the 1980s, the French economist Serge-Christophe Kolm, former professor at Stanford and director of studies at the École des Hautes Études en Sciences Sociales in Paris, investigated, in his book *La Bonne économie. La réciprocité générale* (The Good Economy. General Reciprocity), how to achieve a sufficiently altruistic and united society in the modern world. Expressing a markedly different stance from Francis Edgeworth's cited above, and unusually for an economist, Kolm is of the opinion that:

> *Good society is made of good people.... Goodness is the prioritization of altruism, voluntary solidarity, reciprocal giving, generosity, sharing amongst brothers, free community, loving one's neighbour and loving charity, benevolence and friendship, sympathy and compassion.*[50]

According to him, two economic systems prevailed in the twentieth century: "Capitalism and totalitarianism, each founded on selfishness, the objectification of others, hostility, conflict and competition between people, domination, exploitation, alienation." But there is an alternative: "Another system is possible, founded on drawing out the best in people and the best in social relations, and on reinforcing them." This system is the economics of reciprocity, an economics which engenders interpersonal relationships that are "infinitely more gratifying and humane, which produce better people."[51] According to Kolm, general reciprocity is the process by which each individual gives to society (time, resources, skills) and, reciprocally, benefits from everyone else's contributions, without being entirely sure about from whom they come – a spirit of "all for one, one for all."[52] On the other hand, we could talk of *negative reciprocity,* where goods and services are exchanged in the hope that one will benefit from that exchange more than others. So, positive reciprocity is also a form of fairness.

For anyone who fears that such an economy cannot function and would lead us into recession, Kolm shows—with equations to back him up—that the opposite would happen. Reciprocity "brings about a much more efficient and productive economy."[53]

What's more, this efficiency, and the resulting prosperity, cannot be reduced to some abstract "global prosperity" calculated by indiscriminately adding up everyone's fortunes, which would give a deceptive image of the situation of different segments of the population. What matters is the real prosperity that benefits the population *at every level*, including the middle classes and the poorest. For those stuck in poverty, it makes no difference if the country's wealth doubles, whether that country is the United States, where 1% of the population has 40% of national wealth, or an African country whose oil or mineral riches go directly into the coffers of the ruling elite. In the United States, prosperity has not even benefited the middle classes, whose incomes have been flat-lining for twenty years. As the French engineer and humorist Auguste Detœuf wrote: "Capital is an accumulation of work, but since we can't all do everything, there are those who do the work and others who do the accumulating."[54]

According to Kolm, there are multiple advantages to reciprocity. It promotes efficiency, productivity, and transparency, by virtue of the fact that information is naturally shared instead of monopolized or concealed—the case, as we have seen, in most big companies. Altruistic

Mondragon: A Successful Alternative

Modern societies have for the most part opted for a capitalist structure when it comes to production. With capitalism, private individuals set up companies, choose their staff, and decide what they want to produce, where to produce it, and what to do with any profit. A handful of people make these decisions in the name of a majority of employees who provide the bulk of the production work. These employees must accept the consequences of the decisions made by the management and the major shareholders or leave their job to work somewhere else. The exemplary success of Mondragon in the Basque Country in Spain, and of many other cooperatives throughout the world, demonstrates that there can be other successful ways to operate that are more caring for all those involved.

The Mondragon Corporation (MC), the biggest cooperative group in the world today, is the fruit of the vision of a young Basque priest, Don José María Arizmendiarrieta Madariaga. In 1941, he became vicar of the parish of Mondragon, a small village that had suffered greatly during the Spanish Civil War. In response to mass unemployment, Don José María decided to strive for economic development in the town by implementing the theories that underpin mutual benefit companies.[56] In 1943, he set up a democratically run professional training college. In 1956, five young graduates from that college founded a workshop dedicated to manufacturing paraffin cookers and stoves. Little by little, the combined efforts of these associates turned this modest workshop into an industrial group that would become the biggest in the Basque Country and the seventh-biggest in Spain.

Still under Don José María's guidance, these young entrepreneurs also founded the *Caja Laboral Popular Coopérativa de Crédito,* a credit union that provides workers with the necessary financial backing to launch new cooperative enterprises. In 2010, the *Caja Laboral* had over 20 billion euros of deposits.

Today, MC is comprised of more than 250 companies (half of which are still cooperatives) across six areas of activity: industry, finance, retail, learning (the University of Mondragon), research, and training. In 2010, MC numbered 85,000 members, of which 43% were women. Power equality between men and women has a very positive influence on relationships at the heart of the business, unlike large capitalist firms, which are all too often dominated by men. Overall revenue reaches 30 billion euros per year, but Mondragon has never been listed on the stock exchange, giving it total independence and freedom in its decision-making.

Everything about the way Mondragon is organized is different. In each company, the members of the cooperative (on average 80%–85% of the total number of workers at each company) collectively own and manage the company. At the annual general meeting, the partner-employees democratically elect, hire, or lay off their executives. They nominate a general manager, but retain the power to make fundamental decisions: what to do, where and how to do it, and how to apportion profit.

The best-paid employee can only earn six times more than the lowest-paid—as opposed to four hundred times in many American companies. As a result, in the Basque Country, the salaries of MC employees are 15% higher than the local average, while executive pay is overall lower than it is in the private sector.

Mondragon also supports job security thanks to a system that allows workers at MC companies requiring fewer employees to transfer to others in greater need, all in an open and transparent fashion according to democratic rules linked to subsidies that allow the costs of the moves to be subsidized.

A part of each company's revenue is fed into a fund for research, leading to astonishing results in new product development. The MC also founded the University of Mondragon, home to over 4,000 students.

When speaking to a visiting British journalist from the *Guardian*, an MC employee said: "We are not some paradise, but rather a family of co-operative enterprises struggling to build a different kind of life around a different way of working."[57] Worker-owned and worker-managed firms have not been successful to the point of driving manager-run firms out of business, but they certainly offer an inspiring alternative for those who wish to bring about a more caring economic system.

As the journalist, Richard Wolff, remarks, "given the performance of Spanish capitalism these days—25% unemployment, a broken banking system, and government-imposed austerity (as if there were no alternative to that either)—MC seems a welcome oasis in a capitalist desert."

---

motivations promote cooperation, which boosts efficiency. Reciprocity brings about greater fairness in the distribution of resources and benefits. Fairness, by its token, promotes reciprocity, and a virtuous cycle is set in motion. Reciprocity leads to cooperation, which has always been at the heart of the evolution of species, creativity, and progress. It is strengthened as individuals gain awareness of its possibilities and advantages. In particular it leads to a decrease in the spending normally apportioned to competition, and a considerable increase in working relations, which bolsters creativity.[55] But how do we inspire this dynamic shift?

Toward a Positive Caring Economy

According to Edgar Morin, we are today witnessing a renaissance of the social and solidarity-based economy in different countries, including France. This development is based on cooperatives and mutual funds, microfinance (so long as it does not get diverted from its original intention by the quest for financial gain), and on fair commerce, which promotes small producers in developing countries by protecting prices from the brutal fluctuations of the markets, and by supporting local associations that cut out rapacious intermediaries. It also encourages local food production and supply, as with the *Associations pour le maintien d'une agriculture paysanne (AMAP)*, a community-supported agricultural association in France, which allows market gardeners to deliver their products to individuals in towns. Organic production and agroecology are further contributors to this development.

Here again we see a will to move away from the single way of thinking that is the markets, instead favoring mutual assistance and using social networks that leverage different financial, bonding or guarantee instruments based on trust between members.[58]

An economy that prioritizes the common good must promote social justice and equal opportunities so that every human being can fully reach their potential. At the World Economic Forum in Davos in January 2010, during a session called "Rethinking Values in the Post-Crisis World," Muhammad Yunus, winner of the Nobel Peace Prize and pioneer of the concept of microfinance, which lets poor entrepreneurs escape poverty, said:

> *We do not have to change the way business is done, we simply need to change its goals. There is* selfish business, *the purpose of which is just profit for a few people. It reduces humanity to a single dimension, money, and thus ignores our humanity. Then there is* selfless business, *the goal of which is primarily to serve society. This is also known as* social business. *Charity is a one-time giving that can be very helpful, but does not have sustainable effects.* Social business *can help society in a sustainable way.*[59]

Social business is viable and can be as profitable as selfish business, but the direct beneficiary is society. You may, for instance, start a business for the very purpose of creating one hundred jobs, or to provide many communities with cheap and clean water. These are your direct goals, rather than making money just for the sake of it. If you succeed in creating these jobs or in providing the water required, this is your success indicator on your end-of-year balance sheet. According to Yunus: "Today, most of technology is put at the service of selfish business. But the same technology could be used for selfless business. We could also create a social business stock market, functioning like any other stock exchange, which would give people the choice to invest in the selfless economy. The goal is not to replace or compete with the traditional economy, but to provide an alternative, so that the selfless economy can have an opportunity to do more good in this world."[60]

Muhammad Yunus, or How Not to Underestimate Humankind

"Today's crisis is a man-made crisis, not a tsunami, not a natural disaster. How did we cause it? We converted the financial market into a kind of casino. The system today is driven by greed and speculation—betting—rather than real production. When you move away from a real economy toward a speculative economy, this is what happens.[61]

"We have to think again about everything. When all we do is pursue money and maximize profit, it becomes first a passion and then a habit. It absorbs all our attention and we become like moneymaking robots. We need to remember that we are human beings and a human being is a much bigger entity than a moneymaking entity. We have forgotten our purpose. Making money cannot solve everything and it narrows us down, reducing us to profit-hungry automata.

"When I see a problem, I want to create a business that will solve that problem. Charity money will do the job only once. In social business the profit does not go to the investor, but to society. Social business can have an endless life and be fully sustainable. It becomes independent and can stand on its feet. A social business is a non-dividend sustainable company designed to solve human problems. Social business has to be efficient, not to make money but to get things done. In conventional business profit is the objective. In social business, accomplishing the project for the benefit of the community is the object. Business is just a vehicle that can be driven to places where it helps others.

"To give an example, there are 160 million people living in Bangladesh, and 70% used to have no electricity. It made me think that this was a good opportunity for us to do something useful. So we founded Grameen Energy to bring renewable, solar energy to the villages. At the start, we sold barely a dozen panels a day, at a price slightly above the cost, simply to keep our operation going. Sixteen years later, we were selling 1,000 solar-panel systems per day and in November 2012, we crossed the 1 million mark of homes equipped with solar-panel systems.

"As a consequence, the cost of manufacturing solar panels went down. Since at the same time the price of kerosene was skyrocketing, it became and remains all the more attractive for poor people to get renewable energy. It took us 16 years to reach 1 million homes, but it will take fewer than three years to get to the second million. We did this not to make money, but to achieve a social goal. Using kerosene to cook inside homes and light these homes creates a lot of health problems as well as fire hazards. Renewable energy is good for the environment, good for health, good for people's livelihoods.

"Two thirds of the population has nothing to do with banks and are stuck in poverty. With empty hands, you can't start anything. Microcredit fills the gaps left open by banks. When we started the big financial authorities said it couldn't be done. We have shown that it works very well.

"Grameen Bank takes no money from any external source. We only take deposits for people, mostly women, who borrowed microcredit from us and securely deposit their savings when they make a little. People should not have to come to the bank. The bank should go to the people. We have to propose schemes that can be understood by the women to whom we lend. They should be simple and attractive. We currently have 8.5 million borrowers in 80,000 villages. They don't have to come to our office. Grameen Bank goes to their doorstep every week.

"I have never bought or owned a single share of Grameen Bank. I am not interested in money. I am not against making profit, but we should always ask, "Profit for whom"? Now, after 37 years of existence, we lend 1.5 billion dollars per year. Over 99% is reimbursed.

"Many large companies have charitable foundations. These could easily be converted into social business activities and become much more powerful tools. They will not be writing a check. In social business you have to get involved and bring your creative power into it. When you create a social business, employees can use the whole spectrum of their human qualities, such as care, in addition to their professional skills. As such it becomes much more attractive and rewarding for people.

"Science fiction is always ahead of science. But then a lot of what was science fiction yesterday becomes science today. We should also write "social fiction" and inspire people who will think "Why not?" Real change will not happen just by making predictions. These are notoriously bad at envisioning the future. Nobody predicted the fall of the Berlin Wall, or of the Soviet Union, but these happened very fast. So we should imagine the future and then make it happen."

THE RISE OF FAIR TRADE

In his book *Le Commerce équitable* (Fair Trade), the French social entrepreneur Tristan Lecomte talks about the tragedy of small producers who, because of their chronic poverty and isolation, and their inability to group together to offer a sufficient level of production, are incapable of trading with buyers and powerful multinationals that dictate their prices to a large number of dispersed and disorganized small producers. To have direct access to the markets, these small producers must be incorporated into a group which respects their interests and guarantees them a decent income.[62]

What's more, there are many intermediary organizations that seize the bulk of the profit. In Thailand, for example, husked rice is bought from small producers at just *10 euro cents* per kilo. Thai buyers have come to form an almost mafia-style network that keeps prices as low as possible before selling it on at a much higher rate.[63] In addition, world prices fluctuate greatly. The price of coffee, for example, fell by 45% in a year between 1998 and 1999.

A Madagascan worker who sews T-shirts in a textile factory, for his part, makes 2.5 euro cents per T-shirt, or fifty times less than what a French worker would earn for the same job.[64]

The United Nations Conference on Trade and Development (UNCTAD) advocates fairer trade between countries from both sides of the so-called North-South divide, but just like the International

Labour Organization (ILO), whose aim is to protect workers in developing countries, it has no legal power. This is not the case with the World Trade Organization (WTO), which has the power to punish countries that do not respect their obligations, but unfortunately hampers producers in poor nations from gaining access to markets in richer countries. As regards IMF loans for countries experiencing hardship, these are linked to demands for structural adjustments that have often let the countries in question avoid economic collapse (as was the case in Argentina), but they almost never go toward serving the interests of the most destitute or to small producers, by virtue of the fact that they favor hegemonic multinationals.

In order to promote sustainable development and fair trade, it is therefore essential to help production centers in poorer countries make progress by improving the social and environmental conditions that are key to their production activity. Without this support, the challenge of protecting the environment could become an additional burden for small producers, who are shackled with paralyzing obligations at the same time as pitiful prices for their products.

Unlike aid in the form of charitable giving, fair trade establishes a trade system that allows small producers to prosper and, over time, to self-finance.[65] Charity is thus replaced with a solidarity-based economy.

The year 1988 saw the creation of the International Federation for Alternative Trade (IFAT) and the launch in the Netherlands, initially through products with the Max Havelaar label, of fair-trade products in major retail outlets. In 1997, the three main international fair-trade labels—Max Havelaar, Transfair, and Fairtrade—grouped together as the Fairtrade Labelling Organization (FLO). The British association Oxfam is another pioneer in this field, having coupled aid programs with the purchasing of products from small producers and selling them via a broad network of shops, mainly in England.

The "Max Havelaar" logo guarantees that the sales channel of a product is fair trade, and now numbers over 800,000 producers in 46 countries, all the while improving the living conditions of some 5 million people.

In short, according to the charter of the French fair-trade organization *Plate-Forme pour le Commerce Équitable (PFCE)*, this form of trade must be based on solidarity and prioritize engaging the most disadvantaged producers in order to achieve a sustainable collaboration. Their products must be bought as directly as possible and at a price that allows the producer to live properly. Fair trade must also be transparent by providing the buyer with all necessary information on the product itself and its distribution channels. It must support the environment and free and democratic dealings between producers and buyers, cutting out the exploitation and abuse of child labor and encouraging autonomy among producers.

In *80 Hommes pour Changer le Monde* (80 Humans to Change the World), the entrepreneurs Sylvain Darnil and Mathieu Le Roux cite several examples of successful fair-trade businesses.[66] In Laos, for example, Sisaliao Svengsuka has founded Laos Farmers Products, the first non-collectivist cooperative in that now peaceful country, albeit one under an authoritarian communist government. This company gathers the harvests from 10,000 families and distributes their products via fair-trade retail outlets in Europe and the United States.

In Japan, Yusuke Saraya founded Saraya Limited, a prosperous company selling 99.9% biodegradable detergents. In 2003, the company generated sales of 150 million euros. Saraya has managed to reduce its use of energy, water, and packaging by 5% to 10% per year, maintaining growth throughout.

In India, Elaben Bhatt founded the first trade union for women, originally itinerant vendors, in the region of Gujarat. Dubbed the Self-Employed Women's Association (SEWA), it has allowed women excluded from official workplaces and who are victims of bullying by the authorities to be recognized and respected. Elaben fought to gain them licenses and also created a microcredit bank modeled on Muhammad Yunus's Grameen Bank. It is now possible for the union's 700,000 members to secure loans at favorable rates to invest in their business activities. As with Grameen Bank, the loans are repaid in as many as 98% of cases.[67]

Ethical Funds

Even though they now only represent a few percent of the financial market, ethical funds are today expanding rapidly.

Various qualifying criteria remain: child labor is forbidden, while educational support, health care, development aid for people in third-world countries, preserving the environment, and advantageous employment policies for workers are all encouraged. What's more, ethical funds attract good long-term investment because they are, by virtue of their altruistic missions, less subject to the sort of immoral or reckless conduct that plagues the selfish economy.

Socially responsible investing (SRI) applies the principles of sustainable development to financial investment. Financial managers practicing SRI select companies exhibiting best practice in environmental, social, and governance issues, and exclude those whose founding values are morally deficient and that do not adhere to international standards, as well as some broad business sectors such as the tobacco or arms industries. In 2012, following an in-depth study of fourteen European countries, SRI accounts for as much as 6,760 billion dollars, or 14%, of financial assets.[68] It ought to be noted, however, that the SRI tag is often attributed to funds content to avoid investing in certain industries, such as those mentioned above, but which are prepared to invest in, for example, the oil and gas or pharmaceutical industries, where ethical standards are very poor. There are, on the other hand, a small number of SRI funds that actively seek out companies with a truly positive social and environmental impact, as is the case, for example, with Triodos Bank in the Netherlands, where investments are made with complete transparency, as well as Calvert Investments in the United States.[69]

For his part, former United States vice president Al Gore has, along with the financier David Blood, launched an investment fund called General Investment Management (GIM), aimed at projects and services promoting long-term change and environmental protection. This fund has already raised several hundred million pounds sterling.

Global Alliance for Banking on Values (GABV) is a consortium that brings together twenty or so alternative (microfinance, community banks, sustainable development banks, etc.) or ethical banks from all five continents, all of whom have sworn to serve local communities while also seeking viable solutions to global problems. Each takes into account in a balanced fashion the "triple bottom line" notion frequently used by economists, i.e., profit, individuals, and the planet. This rapidly expanding consortium aims to encompass a billion people by 2020.

CREATING A POSITIVE ECONOMY STOCK EXCHANGE

One useful initiative would be to create *positive economy stock exchanges* across the world that would bring together investment linked to economic business activities targeting the common good and that include an altruistic element. The idea behind such stock exchanges would not be for them to enter into competition with the prevailing financial system, but to offer a trustworthy and effective alternative to anyone wishing to join in the effort already under way in the various sectors of the positive economy:

- the *social and solidarity-based economy,* which gathers together cooperatives, mutual funds, mutual savings banks, microfinance enterprises, crowdfunding initiatives, impact investment funds, and solidarity-based careers;
- *ethical funds,* which only pursue socially and ecologically responsible investment, as well as investing in areas conforming to a comprehensive range of ethical criteria;
- *fair trade,* which safeguards the interests of small producers, and allows them to organize themselves better and enjoy a more visible status;
- the *green economy* and the generation of renewable energy (with states providing subsidies to enable it to replace energy generated by hydrocarbons). It also includes investment in fighting pollution in towns and natural spaces (rivers, oceans, etc.), as well as the production of forms of vegetable protein, and curbing industrial farming and the exploitation of animals;
- *impact investing* is a new investment model whose primary objective is to respond to a social or environmental need, with the potential promise of a "moderate" financial return. According to some financial experts, this method represents a new type of financial asset that is set to grow considerably. A study by J.P. Morgan and the Rockefeller Foundation published in 2010 estimates that this form of investment will reach as much as 500 billion dollars in the ten years to come.[70]
- *cooperative banks,* which have no shareholders but rather "cooperative members." Such banks often propose investing in social ventures and sustainable development.

Some initiatives have already been launched. In London, the Social Stock Exchange (SSE), in the works since 2007, finally opened in 2013 after a few setbacks. Its aim is to be a gateway for social enterprises looking to raise capital and for investors who wish to find businesses reflecting their ethical values.

In Brazil, the social entrepreneur Celso Grecco founded the *Bolsa de Valores Sociais (BVS)*, another sort of social stock exchange, which operates within Brazil's largest stock market, Bovespa, and offers investors a portfolio of socially responsible investment opportunities with an efficiency and transparency that is sometimes lacking in philanthropic organizations, especially those in Brazil. In 2006, the BVS model was replicated in South Africa by the social entrepreneur Tamzin Ratcliffe, founder of the GreaterGood trust, whose partnership with the Johannesburg Stock Exchange is creating new socially responsible investment channels.

Official Development Aid

According to OECD figures on official development aid (ODA) given to developing countries, the United States comes out on top in terms of total spending, with 30.7 billion dollars in 2011, ahead of Germany (14.5), the United Kingdom (13.7), France (13.9), and Japan (10.6). Yet if we look at this contribution as a proportion of GDP, of the countries featured in the study, just Sweden, Norway, and Luxembourg reach 1%, and along with Denmark (0.86%) and the Netherlands (0.75%) they represent the only five countries attaining the 0.7% target stipulated by the United Nations. These are well ahead of the United States (0.2%), South Korea (0.12%), and Greece (0.11%).[71]

Giving Back to Society: Philanthropy on a Global Level

Andrew Carnegie stands as one of the great philanthropists of the nineteenth and twentieth centuries. He was an American industrialist who, at the start of the twentieth century, donated what in today's terms would be 7 billion dollars to various foundations, and in particular funded some 2,500 free public libraries in the United States. Bill

Gates, founder of Microsoft, has devoted 95% of his fortune to fighting disease and illiteracy in developing countries. His foundation, the Bill & Melinda Gates Foundation, set up in 2000, has already spent almost 10 billion dollars on vaccinating 55 million children, and has a spending power equivalent to that of the World Health Organization (WHO).[72]

As for Warren Buffett, he has pledged the equivalent of 28 billion euros to charities directed by Bill and Melinda Gates and by members of his own family. This decision, which accounts for over 80% of his fortune, represents the largest individual donation in history.

Chuck Feeney, an Irish-American philanthropist, was for a long time one of the greatest anonymous philanthropists in history. He secretly donated 6 billion dollars to various causes across the world before finally being identified in 1997 (see box below).[73] Then there is Pierre Omidyar, the founder of eBay, and his wife Pam, whose Omidyar Network foundation has been involved in microfinance projects in Bangladesh, improving opportunities for women in India, and promoting government transparency in numerous countries.

Giving Pledge, a campaign launched in 2010 by Warren Buffett and Bill Gates, aims to encourage the world's richest people to give the majority of their wealth to philanthropic causes. In April 2013, 105 billionaires had already committed to the pledge.[74] These philanthropists comment that it is good to leave enough money to their inheritors so that they can get by, but not so much that they are tempted to do nothing.

In the United States, private philanthropy represents 1% of the country's GDP, more than double the European average.

At the Philanthropy for the 21st Century conference held in Great Britain in February 2012,[77] participants raised the fact that philanthropy is not granted the respect and status it deserves in the United States. Yet the fact that a growing proportion of the world's wealth is found in the hands of private individuals shows that one of the best ways to create a social benefit is to donate to a fund serving to promote the common good. What's more, a growing number of companies have become aware that social engagement is not only good for their image, but also improves the motivation and satisfaction of their employees.

According to Antoine Vaccaro, president of the philanthropic research center CerPhi,[78] in a world where we can no longer rely exclusively on the state to safeguard the general interest, new forms of

The Invisible Philanthropist

Over the course of the last thirty years, Chuck Feeney, with a 7.5 billion dollar fortune behind him built up from his duty-free shopping empire, has traveled the globe ensuring the successful operation of the various secret charitable projects under his foundation The Atlantic Philanthropies. From the United States to Australia, Ireland to Vietnam, the foundation has spent 6.2 billion dollars on education, science, health, and human rights. Nobody this wealthy has ever given away so much of his fortune in his lifetime. Overall, 1.3 billion dollars will be spent between now and 2016. While most titans of the business world are busy feverishly hoarding and multiplying their wealth, Feeney does all he can to live a frugal life.

During the first fifteen years of his mission, which began in 1984, he hid his generosity in almost obsessive fashion. Most of the organizations that benefited from his donations had no idea about the source of the considerable sums they were receiving through the intermediary Atlantic Philanthropies. Those who did know were sworn to secrecy.

In the end, when he was trying to sell his company and found himself suspected of illegally siphoning off large sums of money, Feeney had to reveal his philanthropic activities. He then had to prove that he had *given away* the money. "I'm happy," he declared in a rare interview, "when what I'm doing is helping people and unhappy when what I'm doing isn't helping people."[75]

So in 1997 Feeney reluctantly withdrew his anonymity. Yet this transition proved positive since two of the world's richest men, the aforementioned Bill Gates and Warren Buffett, have both cited him as a major source of inspiration.

Throughout his travels, Chuck Feeney continues to live frugally and reside in modest abodes. He has flown millions of kilometers in economy class, claiming that business class won't help him get to his destination any quicker; he wears a rubber Casio watch which, he says, shows the times just as well as a Rolex. His message to philanthropists is simple: "Don't wait to give your money away when you're old or, even worse, dead. Instead, make substantial donations while you still have the energy, connections and influence to make waves."[76]

---

foundation and the multiple pathways between generosity and social or solidarity-based economies are now recognized as having the capacity to make a significant contribution to taking responsibility for the general interest alongside the state.

THE COMING OF GLOBAL SOLIDARITY

In France, the 1970s witnessed the associative sector boom; almost 30,000 associations were created in 1975 alone. There are now estimated to be around 1.2 million associations in France.

The online crowdfunding movement has also seen a spectacular rise in recent years. Around 2.7 billion dollars were invested in this way in 2012 (1.6 in North America), an 80% leap compared with 2011 figures. In 2013, this form of financing had surpassed the 5 billion dollar mark.[79]

On the site GlobalGiving, between 2002 and May 2013, some 321,644 donors gave almost 85 million dollars to 7,830 projects. One of the projects current in May 2013, Kranti (Revolution), received $165,342 from 1,142 donors to offer education to girls from India who had been victims of human trafficking and forced into prostitution.

Kiva was founded in 2005 with the conviction that "people are naturally generous and will help others if they get the chance to do it in a transparent and responsible way."[80] Via its microfinance site, Kiva encourages relationships based on partnership rather than charity. According to figures from May 2013, *every week* more than 1.5 million dollars are lent to over 3,200 borrowers by 21,600 lenders; the equivalent of one loan every twelve seconds. Since Kiva's launch in 2005, 98.99% of loans have been duly repaid.

On Kickstarter, one of the best-known online platforms in this field, around 30% of investments in 2012 went toward social or philanthropic projects, versus 17% to small businesses, 12% to film or performing arts, and 7.5% to music. A single donor contributed to over 750 projects himself.

Since its creation in 2006, the crowdfunding site Razoo has already raised 150 million dollars and allowed over 15,000 NGOs to accomplish countless socially responsible projects. The Australian site StartSomeGood hosted, among others, a project by the Place in the Sun Foundation, which aimed to organize a seven-week summer camp in the middle of rural Mali to run a pilot primary education program with five local teachers. In Mali, only 33% of adults can read or write—the lowest literacy rate in the world. Some $9,600 were needed, and after nine days 43 donors had given as much as $7,800, and the project was ultimately successful with $10,700 of funding.

Edgar Morin and Stéphane Hessel proposed to create *maisons de la fraternité* (fraternity houses), bringing together existing solidarity-based public and private institutions, adding new emergency services aimed at people suffering from moral or material distress, "victims of overdoses not just of the narcotic kind, but also of unhappiness and sorrow." These centers would provide friendship, outreach, support, information, initiatives, and volunteering opportunities.[81]

The Rise of Free Access to Knowledge

The some 18.6 million registered contributors to the online encyclopedia Wikipedia have voluntarily dedicated over 41,019,000 hours to the collaborative project, versus just 12,000 hours of work for the first edition of the (chargeable) *Encyclopædia Britannica,* which has for a long time been the leading light in this area. In France alone, over 1 million rubrics are edited every quarter and, from Wikipedia's launch in 2001 until April 2013, 1.29 billion edits were carried out in the various languages on offer.[82]

Anywhere in the world where there is an Internet connection, it is now possible to follow university courses from prestigious colleges for free. This practice was inspired by the Massachusetts Institute of

The Teacher with the World's Biggest Class

In August 2004, Salman Khan, then a hedge fund manager in Boston, began giving his cousin, Nadia, lessons over the telephone. She had been struggling with her math homework. With Nadia making rapid progress, other cousins started asking "Sal" for help, hoping to reap similar rewards. To make things easier, in 2006 Sal started posting ten-minute educational videos on YouTube so that everyone could watch them at their leisure. In 2010, Sal quit his job managing the hedge fund to work full-time on his vocation to offer a "free, world-class education for anyone, anywhere," helped by a few collaborators (between 10 and 30 people depending on the need). Today, the "Khan Academy" hosts over 4,300 free videos on arithmetic, physics, chemistry, biology, history, and finance, which have been watched by over 260 million students, with 6 million new students joining every month.

Technology (MIT), the famous American university which opened up this new concept over twenty years ago. Nowadays, many of the world's major universities are following suit. The website Coursera (www.coursera.org) already offers 370 free courses from 33 universities to 3.5 million subscribers, while EDX (www.edx.org) has made available courses from 28 of the world's most distinguished institutions, including Harvard University, MIT, the *École polytechnique de Lausanne,* Australian National University, etc.

These sites let users pick the best courses available at the same time as raising the profile of teachers, who can now reach a very large audience. The teachers for their part have to supply well presented, attractive, and regularly updated courses.

The success of these altruistic schemes dispels the preconceptions of traditional economics and shows that systems based around cooperation, openness, and trust ultimately work better. This is highlighted by Gilles Babinet, an expert in digital economic matters:

> *The digital transition will never be complete unless we move from a culture of mistrust and division to a culture of collaboration and sharing. Indeed the success of the digital transformation has hinged on values of openness, free access to information, and worthwhile co-creation. More often than not its success stems from cross-fertilization between content generated by multiple collaborators for free. Public spheres or big business, which favor compartmentalization, the culture of secrecy, the principle of hierarchy, and vertical channels of communication, are having real difficulty adapting.*[83]

Innovation in the Service of the Common Good

In many developing countries, affordable mobile telephones offer banking services to millions of small farmers and producers, letting them sell their products directly at more favorable prices without going through multiple intermediaries who take their share of the profit at each phase. In Kenya, Vodafone M-pesa serves 10 million small producers, and transactions made through them account for 11% of the country's GDP. In India, Thomson Reuters has implemented, for a cost equivalent to a four-euro quarterly subscription, a mobile messaging service that keeps people living in the countryside updated on the progress of their agricultural products, along with weather forecasts and other bits of advice. An initial assessment of this service showed that it had increased the income of its 2 million subscribers by a factor of 60%.[84]

Johnson & Johnson, a company which, since its foundation in 1886, has emphasized social values, has for example helped its employees quit smoking, resulting in a two-thirds decrease in the number of smokers. The company ultimately saved 250 million dollars in health care bills, almost 3 dollars for each dollar invested in the detoxification programs run from 2002 to 2008.[85] Johnson & Johnson was ranked third in a survey conducted by the weekly magazine *Newsweek* on the "greenest" companies in America in 2012.[86] Here we see the shared benefits for the employer and the employee, the producer and the consumer.

The Man Who Changed Bangladesh's Landscape

The first time I met Fazle Abed, having a cup of tea in Vancouver at a peace conference with the Dalai Lama, I knew nothing about him. He asked me what I did and I answered that I oversaw a humanitarian organization that had built around thirty schools and fifteen medical clinics. Without the least showiness, he then stated: "I've built 35,000 schools." It made me feel very humble. On another occasion, in Delhi, he told me: "It's quite simple—all you need to do is multiply what you do by a hundred."

This is, effectively, what he had done. Born in East Pakistan, which would become Bangladesh, Fazle first studied naval architecture at the University of Glasgow. Given that there were virtually no shipyards in East Pakistan, he decided to complete his accountancy training in London. On returning to his homeland, Fazle got a job with the oil company Shell, his skills allowing him to move up the ladder quickly. In 1970, he was working at the company's headquarters in London when a devastating cyclone took the lives of 300,000 of his fellow countrymen and women. Fazle decided to quit his well-paid job and leave again for East Pakistan where, with a few friends, he set up HELP, an organization whose objective was to help those most severely affected on the island of Manpura, where three-quarters of the population had been killed. Once again he was forced to leave East Pakistan due to the fighting that ultimately led to the partition with West Pakistan. He created an NGO aimed at garnering support from European countries for the independence cause in his homeland.

When the independence war finished at the end of 1971, Fazle sold his apartment in London and left, taking all his belongings, to see what he could do for his country. The newly created Bangladesh was emerging from a traumatic war, and the 10 million refugees who had fled to India had returned. Fazle chose to begin his activities in a far-flung rural area in the northeast of the country. It was here he founded the Bangladesh Rural Advancement Committee (BRAC). Thanks to his organizational genius and his vision, BRAC is now the world's largest NGO. So far this organization has helped 70 million women, and a total of 110 million people, in 69,000 villages. It employs 80,000 volunteers and 120,000 paid staff in an ever-increasing number of countries, particularly in Africa. Here, it has been noted that the BRAC model for intervening on multiple levels—microfinance (80 million people have benefited from the NGO's scheme), education, drinking-water management, improving health, etc.—has been entirely appropriate and effective in regions where very few other programs have registered success. It is no exaggeration to say that BRAC has changed Bangladesh's landscape. There isn't a school, training center for women, or family planning clinic anywhere in the countryside that does not bear the NGO's logo.

Fazle Abed's gamble paid off. He did not multiply his activities by a factor of a hundred, but by a hundred thousand, retaining the same efficiency and quality throughout. At the World Economic Forum in Davos, a good number of participants tend to arrive by private jet into Milan Airport, then take a helicopter or a limo to the famous resort. One morning, at 5 a.m., I came across Fazle, sitting alone in the darkness of a bus that would take us to the airport in Zurich. For me, this said a lot about the simplicity and modesty behind which hides the indomitable determination that drove him to accomplish so great a task.

40

VOLUNTARY, JOYOUS SIMPLICITY

Civilization, in the real sense of the term, consists not in the multiplication, but in the deliberate and voluntary reduction of wants. This alone promotes real happiness and contentment, and increases the capacity for service.

—GANDHI[1]

Austerity" is not a nice word to hear. In the minds of most people, it alludes to the smothering of daily pleasures, making one's existence joyless and imposing restrictions that forbid the free enjoyment of life. What's more, according to some economists, history shows that austerity programs are generally inefficient, by virtue of the fact that they lead to underemployment, joblessness, and recession.[2]

"Voluntary simplicity" is a whole other concept. It does not involve depriving us of what makes us happy—that would be absurd—but coming to a better understanding of how to achieve genuine satisfaction, and to stop being addicted to the causes of our suffering rather than prioritizing our happiness. Simplicity goes hand in hand with contentment.

According to the American social activist Duane Elgin, "voluntary simplicity is a way of life that is outwardly simple and inwardly rich."[3] In his view, this simplicity does not necessitate a "return to nature" for those who have already left it behind, but can rather be practiced in any situation. Simplifying our lives means having the intelligence to examine what we usually consider to be indispensable pleasures and to check whether they do indeed genuinely improve our well-being. Voluntary simplicity could be seen as an act of liberation. It therefore does not involve living in poverty, but in moderation. It is not the solution to all our problems, but it can certainly contribute to helping them. Nor is voluntary simplicity solely the privilege of primitive tribes with no other choice: a survey carried out in Norway showed that 74% of the people asked would prefer a simpler life, centered on what is essential and indispensable, to an opulent one based on numerous material benefits that come at a high cost to one's stress levels.[4] In addition, voluntary simplicity is not a trend born in rich countries. This way of living, once associated with wisdom, has been praised across the ages and across cultures.

The writer and thinker Pierre Rabhi, one of the pioneers of agroecology, argues that the time has come to establish a policy and culture, entered into on a free and consensual basis, that is founded on the power of "happy moderation"—making the decision to curb our needs, break from the cannibalistic tensions of consumer culture, and to return humanity to the forefront of our preoccupations. Such a choice should be profoundly liberating.[5]

We are free to accumulate goods constantly, to live in a pretty, stylishly decorated house, to eat increasingly sophisticated food—but at what cost? At the cost of our time, our energy, our attention and, ultimately, our well-being. As the Taoist wise man Zhuang Zhou said: "He who has gained some insight into the meaning of life will no longer bother to care about that which does not contribute to life."

The current situation effectively has two sides. The first is a human tragedy, that of the poorest populations suffering great hardship from financial crises and rising inequality, while the rich are little affected and even take advantage of the situation to increase their wealth. The second is linked to the insatiable pursuit of the superfluous. Recently, in the middle of the lobby in a large hotel in Singapore, I saw these immense marble columns, two-meters wide, stretching up to the ceiling five floors above. This ostentatious decoration must have cost a fortune despite being perfectly unnecessary.

Voluntary simplicity is at once joyous and altruistic. Joyous because it is not permanently plagued by the hunger for "more";

altruistic because it does not encourage the disproportionate concentration of resources in the hands of a few, resources which—were they to be spread evenly—would significantly improve the lives of those deprived of basic needs.

Voluntary simplicity also goes hand in hand with wisdom: by not aspiring to the unreasonable, we remain constantly aware of the fortunes of those in need today, as well as the well-being of future generations.

What Can We Hope for from Consumerism?

In 1955, an American retail specialist by the name of Victor Lebow described what unbridled capitalism meant for us:

> *Our enormously productive economy demands that we make consumption our way of life, that we convert the buying and use of goods into rituals, that we seek our spiritual satisfaction, our ego satisfaction, in consumption. The economy needs things consumed, burned, worn out, replaced, and discarded at an ever-increasing rate.*[6]

At the time of the 2008 financial crisis, one of George W. Bush's first public reactions was to ask American citizens to start consuming as much as possible again. The more they consumed, the faster the country would recover from the crisis and the happier people would be.

The least we can say about this logic is that it does not correspond with the findings of scientific research. The multiple effects of consumerism have been studied over long periods by psychosociologists, most notably by Tim Kasser (author of *The High Price of Materialism*) and his colleagues. Their studies, spanning two decades and involving samples from thousands of participants representing the entire population, have established that people most prone to consuming all manner of goods and services—those who place great importance on wealth, image, social status, and various other material values promoted by so-called consumer societies—are overall less satisfied with their lives than those who focus on the more fundamental values in life, such as friendship, happiness, the quality of life experiences, and concern for others, as well as feeling responsible toward society and the environment.

Compared to the rest of the population, those inclined to search for satisfaction in consuming any kind of good, and who have an attachment to material values, feel fewer positive emotions. When asked to record their day-to-day emotions in a private journal, it was clear that they experience less joy, enthusiasm, gratitude, and peace of mind than those less given to consumer culture.

Furthermore, according to Kasser's study, big consumers are more anxious and depressed, and more subject to headaches and stomach pains. They have less vitality and report having difficulties when it comes to adapting to life in general. Their health is worse off than the national average. They drink more alcohol and smoke more cigarettes. They spend more time watching television. When they feel a bit depressed, they tend to go out shopping. Obsessed with their possessions, they get more upset than the average person when they lose them. They are often tormented by dreams of death. They admire the rich and consider them to be "intelligent, cultured, and successful in everything." According to the Dalai Lama, "this explains why it is a mistake to place too much hope in material development. The problem is not materialism in and of itself. It is rather the underlying idea that says that perfect happiness can stem from satisfying the senses alone."[7]

Consumption and Altruism

It is particularly common for dyed-in-the-wool materialists to show below-average levels of empathy and compassion toward those who are suffering; they are manipulative and tend to exploit others to their advantage. Kasser's research has also demonstrated that they do not like mentally putting themselves "in another person's place."[8] Little interested in solutions that require an overarching perspective on things, they prefer competition to cooperation.[9] They contribute less to the common good and are barely concerned at all with environmental issues. Their social ties are weak: they have workmates, but very few real friends. Their friendships and relationships are more superficial and less longstanding than those of the rest of the population. They feel the pain of solitude more acutely, and are detached from their environment.

In short, according to Kasser, it would appear that "materialistic values lead people to view being close to and caring for others as a profitless pursuit, one that will not gain them anything of worth.... These values may orient individuals to see other people primarily as a means to their own materialistic ends."[10]

The psychologist Barry Schwartz calls these "instrumental friendships," writing that in capitalist, consumer societies "all that is required is that each 'friend' can provide something useful to the other. Instrumental friendships come very close to being market-like, contractual relations."[11]

This negative correlation between consumerist tendencies and well-being has been observed in a wide variety of settings in North and South America, Europe, and Asia. Throughout, where there is much importance attributed to wealth and social status, a lower level of concern for the environment in general is apparent.[12]

All in all, the research carried out by Kasser and his colleagues shows that a preference for consumption and materialistic values increases personal suffering and forms an obstacle to the establishment of harmonious and caring human interactions. Sheldon and Kasser have also shown that achieving goals linked to humane values leads to much greater levels of satisfaction than the realization of material objectives.[13]

The consumer society is based on the cult of desire. Influenced by Sigmund Freud's nephew, Edward Bernays (who was in charge of President Woodrow Wilson's propaganda machine and one of the pioneers of the advertising industry), Paul Mazur, a Wall Street banker in the 1930s, explained his goals as follows:

> *We must shift America from a needs- to a desire-culture. People must be trained to desire, to want new things even before the old have been consumed.... We must shape a new mentality in America. Man's desire must overshadow his needs.*[14]

These fine words remind me of the reflection of a Tibetan lama contemplating the hundreds of neon advertisements lighting up Times Square in New York: "They are trying to steal my mind."

Kasser's main suggestion for fixing this inclination toward consumption is to ban any advertising aimed at children, as has happened in Sweden and Norway.[15] He cites the revealing words of Wayne Chilicki, chief executive of General Mills, one of the world's biggest food companies: "When it comes to targeting kid consumers, we at General Mills follow the Procter & Gamble model of 'cradle to grave.' We believe in getting them early and having them for life."[16]

Kasser concludes that by focusing on external rather than internal values we look for happiness where it isn't, thus creating our own feeling of dissatisfaction. He comments that, in the current economic landscape, selfishness and materialism are no longer considered to be moral problems, but rather life's primary objectives. In the words of Pierre Rabhi: "The consumer becomes a cog in a machine that is always producing more so that we can always consume more."[17]

Renting and Repairing Instead of Buying

Barely half a century ago, we had one watch or one camera for life. We took care of these objects, with one of their primary qualities being that they needed to last. Nowadays, the life cycle of consumer products is increasingly short, something which is greatly increasing quantities of industrial pollution. One solution put forward by the politician Anders Wijkman and the ecologist Johan Rockström is, instead of buying manufactured products, to introduce a system of renting them along with a maintenance and quality renewal service. Consumers will enjoy the best products available, while it will be in the interests of manufacturers to keep their products in service for as long as possible and recycle them efficiently.

Maintenance services would also create many jobs, which is not the case when products are simply thrown onto the scrapheap. In this way, we would strengthen the circular and recyclable side of consumption, avoiding the interminable wastage that has become the norm in today's society. In 2010, 65 billion tons of raw materials were extracted from the earth and injected into the world economy. This figure is expected to reach 82 billion in 2020.[18]

There are some initiatives working toward this goal. The firm Xerox rents out its machines rather than selling them. In the same way, Michelin rents tires for heavy goods vehicles, keeps them in good condition, and recycles them at the end of their life. Rolls Royce has stopped selling its jet engines to airlines, renting them out instead and taking charge of their maintenance.[19]

In France, the Green senator Jean-Vincent Placé has spoken out against planned obsolescence, in other words the fact that many manufacturers deliberately plan their products' life spans to only just outlast their warranty. The moment they malfunction, the products are deemed irreparable and so you have to buy a brand-new one.

Jean-Vincent Placé denounces this process as an "ecological and social aberration," and introduced a bill in April 2013 forcing manufacturers to extend the legal compliance period of their products. This new guarantee will oblige manufacturers to take responsibility for defective products for longer (two to five years). The bill also demands that spare parts be made available for repairs for a period of ten years from a product's time of purchase. Manufacturers who deliberately reduce the life span of a product will be sentenced to two years in prison and receive a fine of up to 37,500 euros.[20]

In the United Kingdom, numerous groups of volunteer mechanics and DIY enthusiasts have also formed, with the new motto being "We don't throw away anymore, we fix." In France, the site commentreparer.com (howtorepair.com) offers consumers explanatory help sheets so that they can fix their appliances themselves.

MONEY DOESN'T MAKE YOU HAPPY . . . UNLESS YOU GIVE IT AWAY

The mind is enriched by what it receives, the heart by what it gives.

—VICTOR HUGO

It is obvious that, for those deprived of basic means of subsistence and who struggle to feed their children, the act of doubling or tripling the resources available to them could change everything and provide them with an undreamt-of feeling of satisfaction. But, once the threshold of material comfort has been crossed, increasing wealth does not lead to a corresponding increase in quality of life.[21] The "Easterlin Paradox" (see graph below) owes its name to the researcher who directed attention to this phenomenon.

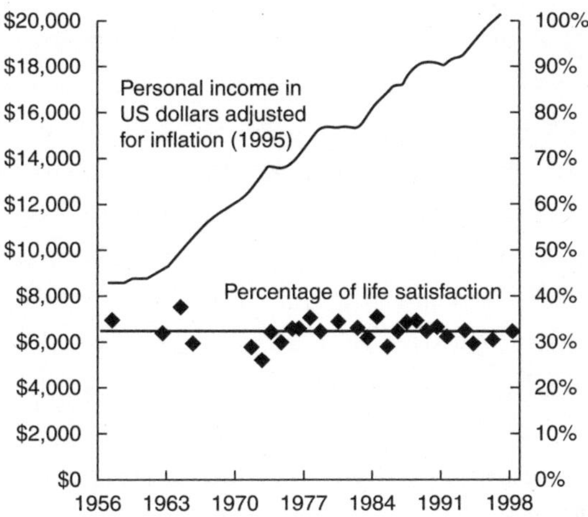

Economic growth and life satisfaction in the United States

This graph perfectly illustrates that the United States' significant economic growth has not led to any increase in life satisfaction.[22]

People in Nigeria consider themselves as happy as people in Japan, despite their GDP per capita being twenty-five times lower.[23] According to Richard Layard, professor at London School of Economics: "This paradox applies just as well to the United States as it does to England and Japan.... We have more food, more clothes, more cars, bigger houses, more central heating, more foreign holidays, a shorter working week, nice work, and, above all, better health. Yet we are not happier...If we want people to be happier, we really have to know what conditions generate happiness and how to cultivate them."[24]

Plenty of other factors are as, if not more, important than wealth. Trust in all its various forms is one of them. Denmark is, according to numerous studies, one of the countries where people are most satisfied with their living conditions. It is not one of the world's wealthiest countries, but there is very little poverty and inequality. This satisfaction can be explained, among other things, by the high level of trust that people feel toward each other, including toward strangers and institutions: people's natural instinct is to think that a stranger is kind. This trust goes hand in hand with a very low level of corruption.

As with anything, wealth can be destructive or constructive. It can provide a powerful way of doing good for others, but it can also drive us to wrong others.

What can you do with 4 billion dollars that you cannot do with 2? Very little for yourself, but a great deal for others. Even if your own needs are largely satisfied, many people are in desperate need of help.

Jules Renard, the acerbic and somewhat pessimistic writer, was only too right when he exclaimed: "If money doesn't make you happy, give it away!" He might have added: "And you will be satisfied." Indeed it is proven that giving is better for you emotionally than receiving. This has been demonstrated in research carried out by the Canadian psychologist Elizabeth Dunn when she compared the level of well-being among people who had spent money on themselves with those who had spent it on other people: "We found that people who reported spending more money on others were happier."[25] This phenomenon has been noted both in large-scale philanthropy and small 5-dollar donations, thanks to a study carried out in 136 countries, where each time an average of 1,300 people have been investigated.[26]

There is therefore a very poor correlation between money and happiness, which can, according to Dunn and fellow psychologists Daniel Gilbert and Timothy Wilson, in part be explained by the way in which people spend their money. Leaning on quantitative research, they suggest that, in order to find happiness, compulsive consumers would be better off pursuing experiences rather than material goods, using their money to benefit others instead of themselves, ceasing comparing themselves to others on a material level (which only feeds envy or vanity), and paying very close attention to the happiness of others.[27]

Simplify, Simplify, Simplify

"Our life is frittered away by detail... Simplify, simplify, simplify!" said the American moralist Henry David Thoreau. To simplify in word, thought and deed is to refuse to let yourself be monopolized by time-consuming activities and ambitions that bring only minor feelings of contentment; rather it is to find satisfaction in what is useful and necessary to living a good life without coveting the superfluous.

In 2005, Kirk Brown and Tim Kasser ran a comparative study between two hundred adherents of voluntary simplicity and two hundred normal Americans. Several interesting differences emerged: the voluntary simplicity devotees had a much higher level of life satisfaction, and were overall more likely to act in a way that has a positive impact on the environment and to lower their carbon footprint.[28]

THE PRESIDENT OF SIMPLICITY

The Uruguayan José Mujica, better known as Pepe, is not only the poorest president in the world, he is also among the most popular. The French weekly *Courrier international* selected a story about him as their "favorite article" of 2012.[29] Much to people's astonishment, he explains that: "My lifestyle is not remotely revolutionary, I am not poor, I just live simply. I may appear to be an eccentric old man, but this is a free, deliberate choice."[30]

Prior to his presidency, he had spent fifteen years in prison, nine of which were in solitary confinement, paying a dear price for his involvement with the left-wing Tupamaros group that fought against the country's dictatorship. Tortured throughout his imprisonment, he was almost driven mad. He explains that reading and writing saved his life. When democracy was restored in 1985, Pepe Mujica threw himself into politics and was elected president in 2009.

No luxurious presidential palace for Pepe. The president has instead chosen to live in a poor suburb of Montevideo in a run-down, $45m^2$ farm with a zinc roof, where he draws water from a well in the garden. He has lived there for twenty years with his wife Lucia, a senator, and his dog, a three-legged mongrel called Manuela. The house is not even his—it's his wife's. Both of them tend to the garden themselves and they sell flowers grown there.

José Mujica donates over 90% of his presidential salary (around 9,400 euros per month) to NGOs, in particular to a shelter program for the country's poorest people. He lives off the remainder, which is not far from the average wage in Uruguay. Mujica rejects consumer society, citing the wise words of the Ancients: "The poor are those who always want more and more."

His only possession is a Volkswagen Beetle he bought in 1987 for around 1,400 euros. He spent his last holidays with Lucia on the terraces of various cafés in his town, without a bodyguard in sight.

"I want to have time for the things that inspire me.... That's what real freedom is: moderation, not consuming much, a small house that lets me have the time to enjoy the things I really love.... If I had lots of things, I would only focus on them not getting stolen. The old girl and I both do the sweeping, which saves us a lot of time—that's what really motivates me."

In September 2012, at the age of seventy seven, he arrived at a major Latin American Mercosur conference with a broken nose: he explained that he had been wounded helping a neighbor fix his house that had been destroyed by storms. He is straight-talking, and hasn't held back from labeling the Kirchners, Argentina's ruling couple, "delinquent Peronists," and the former Argentine president Carlos Menem as a "mafioso" and "burglar." Uruguay is the least corrupt country in South America, and one of the happiest.

Pepe Mujica accuses the majority of world leaders of nurturing a "blind obsession to achieve growth with consumption, as if the contrary would mean the end of the world."[31]

An Appeal for Simplicity

In June 2012, at "Rio + 20," the United Nations Conference on Sustainable Development, Mujica made a memorable speech on simplicity:[32]

> *We cannot go on being ruled by the market forever; on the contrary, we have to rule the market.... The ancient thinkers—Epicurus, Seneca, and even the Aymara—put it this way: "A poor person is not someone who has little but one who always needs more, and more and more."*
>
> *My compatriots fought hard for the eight-hour workday. And now they are making that six hours. But the person who*

works six hours gets two jobs, so he ends up working longer than before. But why? Because he needs to make monthly payments for his motorcycle, his car, more and more payments, and when he's done with that, he realizes he is a rheumatic old man, like me, and his life is already over. And I ask you this: is this really what life is about?

What I am telling you is very basic: development does not have to go against happiness. It has to work in favor of human happiness, of love on Earth, human relationships, caring for children, having friends, covering our basic needs. Precisely because this is the most precious treasure we have: happiness. When we fight for the environment, we must remember that the essential element of the environment is human happiness.

41

Altruism for the Sake of Future Generations

The Holocene: An Exceptional Period for Human Prosperity

For the last twelve thousand years, we have been living in a geological epoch known as the "Holocene," a period characterized by extraordinary climate stability that has allowed the expansion of human civilization as we know it (see graphs below). These temperate conditions have provided the ideal environment for the development of agriculture and complex societies. It took just one thousand years or so for the majority of our semi-nomadic hunter-gatherer ancestors to settle ten thousand years ago.[1]

Before the Holocene, humans had great difficulty surviving. At one point they were even on the verge of extinction: DNA analysis of populations from around the world show that we probably descend from just two thousand individuals, the sole survivors of particularly harsh conditions in the sub-Saharan region around one hundred thousand years ago.[2] We are the surviving members of an endangered species, and we owe that survival in large part to the unprecedented climate stability of the last ten thousand years. Before this, glacial periods and major climate instability limited population growth. Twelve thousand years ago, Earth was home to between 1 to 10 million human beings, and about 15 million five thousand years ago. It was only two thousand five hundred years ago that the 100 million threshold was crossed.[3]

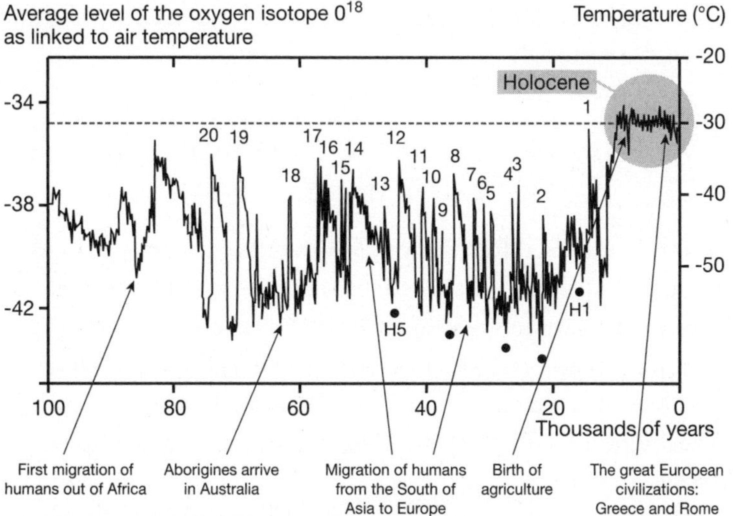

The numbers above the peaks in temperature (20, 19, etc.) represent the number of large and sudden fluctuations in average temperature during the period in question (Heinrich events).

During the ice age that preceded the Holocene, much of the Northern Hemisphere was covered in glaciers several kilometers thick, preventing the formation of any major human society and agricultural practice. Yet average temperatures were just 4 to 5 °C lower than they are today, which goes to show how temperature fluctuations that at first seem minimal are capable of bringing about radically different living conditions.

There have certainly been some minor climate variations during the Holocene—the warming in the year 1000 CE and the Little Ice Age at the start of the seventeenth century—but each time Earth has quickly restored balance.

The most likely reason for this exceptional climate stability of the past ten thousand years is that Earth's orbit around the Sun has stayed especially constant—more or less circular—for twelve thousand years. Indeed variations in its orbit are considered to be a major cause of climate changes that have occurred in the past.[4] This stability would persevere for at least twenty thousand years were it not threatened nowadays by humankind, which has triggered the most rapid climate change the planet has ever known. According to Will Steffen, director of the Climate Change Institute at the Australian National University: "The expanding human enterprise could undermine the resilience of the Holocene state, which would otherwise continue for thousands of years into the future."[5]

We Have Everything to Gain By Preserving This Favorable Situation

Up until the Industrial Revolution, Man's influence on the environment was limited and easily absorbed by nature, which recycled the by-products of human activity on its own. The rise of agriculture was the main man-made transformation experienced by the planet. Yet it was inconceivable that any living species issued from the natural process of evolution could have the capacity to create major upheaval on a global scale.

But things have changed. Toward the middle of the eighteenth century, we acquired the ability to transform fossil fuels into cheap and effective energy sources, an innovation that led to unprecedented economic and social development. The capture and processing of nitrogen from the atmosphere into chemical products, fertilizers in particular, was also made possible by the use of energy from fossil fuels. Immense progress was made in the fields of health care, medicine, and living conditions in urban areas, leading to a population boom: 1 billion people inhabited the planet in 1800, compared with 7 billion today.

These new energy sources let man develop and exploit vast areas that had hitherto been wild, triggering in particular unprecedented deforestation. By 2011, half of Earth's forest had been cut down, most of it in the last fifty years. Since 1990, half of the world's tropical rainforest has been destroyed, and there is every possibility that it will disappear entirely in the next forty years.[6]

For the first time, a geological epoch's characteristics are closely linked to human activity. Since 1950, we have effectively entered a new era that has become known as the Anthropocene, or "the human epoch," the first in which the actions of humankind have been the primary factor shaping the planet, in a manner equivalent to the most severe forces of nature.

Why 1950? If we look at growth charts plotting various factors that have had an impact on the environment, it is clear that the 1950s represent what scientists have termed "the Great Acceleration."[7]

The graphs below are telling: water consumption, the number of cars, deforestation, exploitation of marine resources, the use of chemical fertilizers, the level of CO_2 and methane in the atmosphere, etc. are all increasing at a virtually exponential rate. You do not need to be a mathematical genius to grasp that it is inconceivable that this rate of growth can be sustained without creating major turmoil.

Sea levels are rising by a little over 3 millimeters per year, twice as quickly as in the twentieth century; the average temperature is threatening to increase by between 2°C (according to the most optimistic predictions) and 8°C (according to the least optimistic) before the end of this century. The 2014 synthesis from the UN Intergovernmental Panel on Climate Change (IPCC) concludes that unless drastic measures are taken, the increase of temperature is estimated to reach 3.7°C, which will make our planet a very different place to live. Ninety-five percent of the surface area of the world's glaciers is reducing each year;[8] deforestation is showing no sign of abating;[9] and the oceans are getting warmer and more acidic as a result of excessive atmospheric levels of carbon dioxide, affecting sea life that has not experienced such pronounced change at any point in the last twenty-five million years. Nowadays, according to politician Anders Wijkman and executive director of the Stockholm Resilience Centre, Johan Rockström: "Anthropogenic pressures on the Earth System have reached a scale where abrupt global environmental change can no longer be excluded."[10]

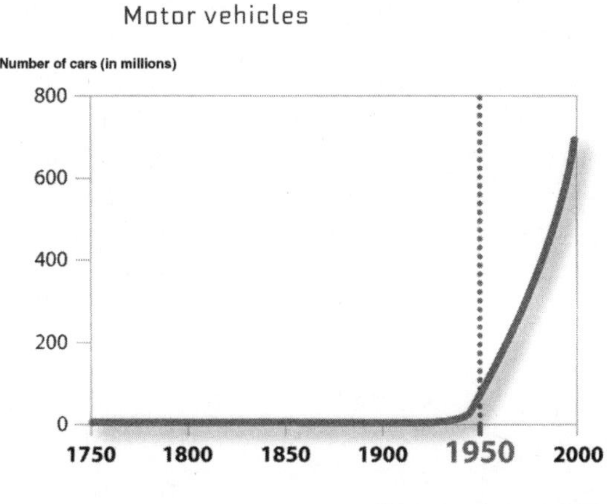

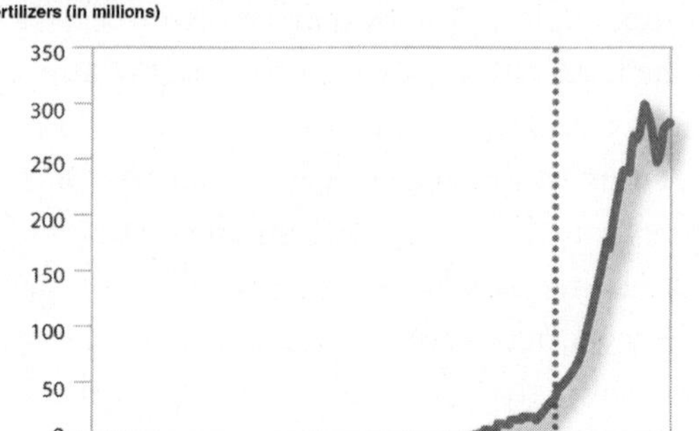

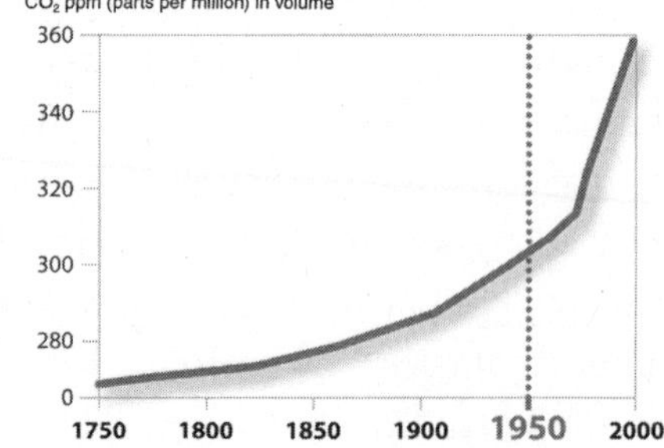

For the first time in history, in May 2013, CO_2 levels reached 400 ppm.

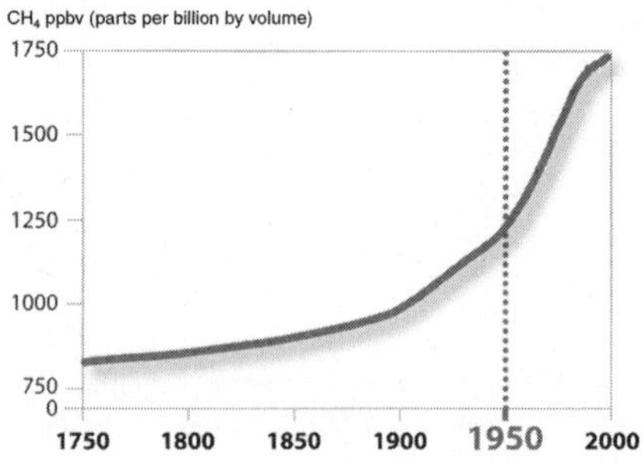

Freshwater usage

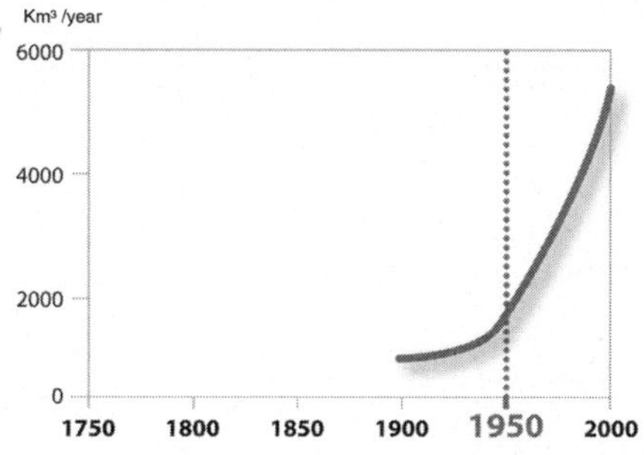

Shiklomanov (1990) Global Water Resources

Exploitation of marine resources (fishing)

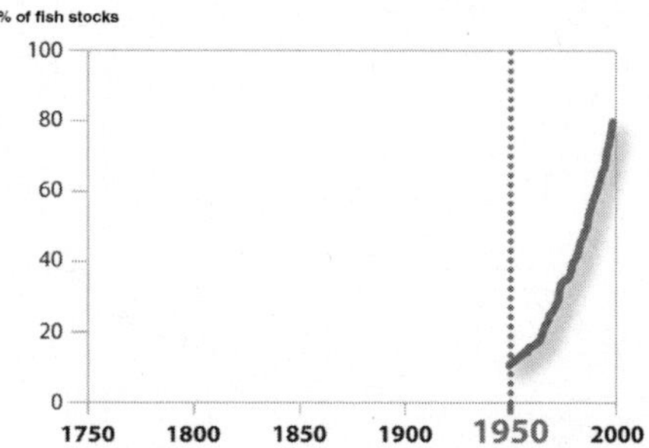

Percentage of global fisheries either fully exploited, overfished or collapsed. Source: FAOSTAT (2002) Statistical databases

Pollution of coastal waters by nitrogen fertilizers

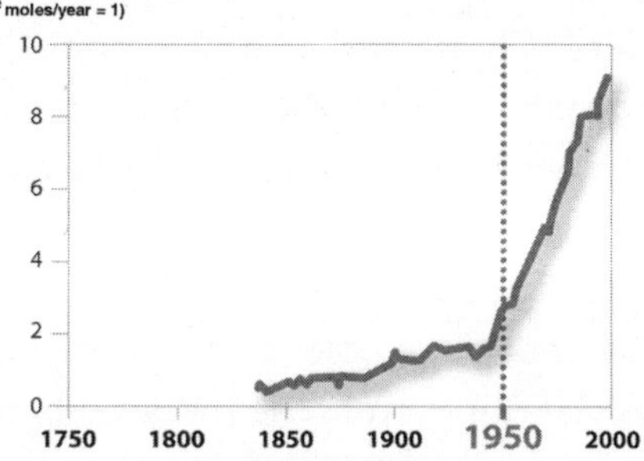

Model-calculated partitioning of the human-induced nitrogen perturbation fluxes in the global coastal margin for the period since 1850. Source: Mackenzie et al. (2002) Chem. Geology 190:13-32

Loss of biodiversity and extinction of species

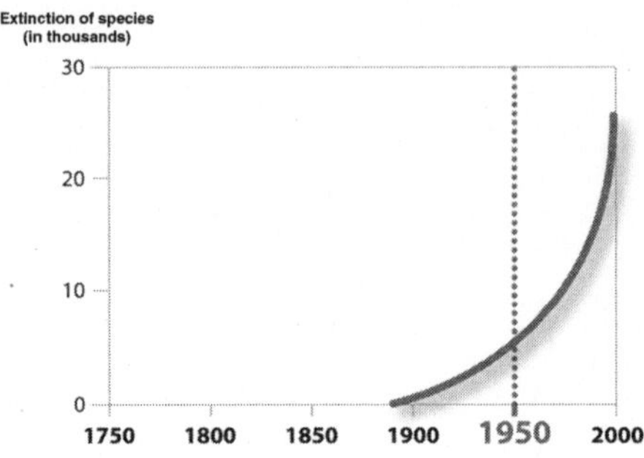

Mathematically calculated rate of extinction. Source: Wilson (1992) The diversity of life, the Penguin Press.

Human population growth

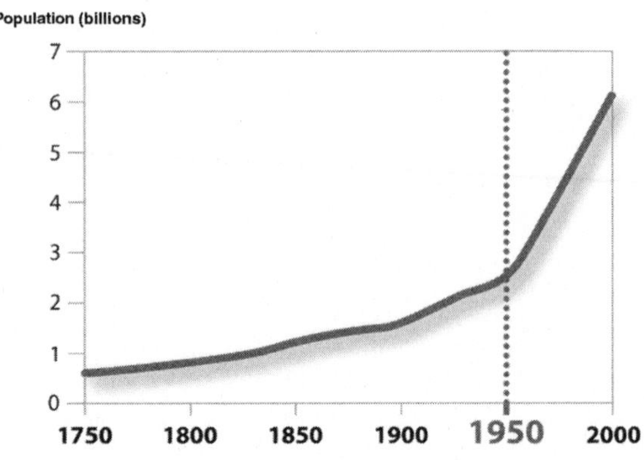

US Bureau of the Census (2000) International database

In 2007, in just a few months, the Arctic lost 30% of its sea ice cover in the summer, initiating what Mark Serreze, director of the National Snow and Ice Center, has called a "death spiral."[11] Generally speaking, the Arctic has warmed at least twice as quickly as the rest of the planet. This is because the ice *reflects* 85% of the light (and the resulting heat) it receives back into the atmosphere. By consequence, the more the ice melts, the faster the remaining ice melts. The same is true in the glaciers of the Himalayas, the "third pole" that has been tarnished by dust pollution and industrial fumes from the Indian subcontinent.

Thousands of scientists (97% of them) are united in expressing the view that if humankind does not quickly change its way of life, and if its response continues to be lacking, the planet risks reaching a "point of no return" that we will no longer be able to contain, destabilizing our climate and plunging our species into conditions that are not conducive to our survival. There are still some climate change skeptics (some 3% of scientists) who make a lot of noise in the media, but their arguments are devoid of substance, as we have already seen in chapter 35.

THE PLANETARY BOUNDARIES WITHIN WHICH HUMANITY CAN CONTINUE TO PROSPER

The concept of "planetary boundaries" was introduced and expounded in an article appearing in the journal *Nature* in 2009, signed by the Swede Johan Rockström and twenty-seven other internationally renowned scientists, among them the Nobel laureate Paul Crutzen, who was the first to rechristen our era the "Anthropocene."[12]

According to Rockström: "Transgressing planetary boundaries would be devastating for humanity, but if we respect them we have a bright future for centuries to come."[13]

If we remain within these boundaries, we can maintain a safety zone in which humanity can continue to prosper.

The study of Earth's resilience, its complex dynamics, and its mechanisms for self-regulating living systems, has allowed the identification of "thresholds" which, if crossed, risk the advent of potentially irreversible "tips."

There is of course a degree of uncertainty in the assessment of these boundaries, but what is certain is that the biosphere has entered a danger zone, like a motorist who, driving along a road in the fog toward a precipice, does not know the exact distance at which it will be too late to brake.

What's more, these boundaries are closely interdependent, and if one were to be crossed it could trigger a domino effect that would accelerate the toppling of the others. Ocean acidification, for example, is closely linked to climate change, by virtue of the fact that a quarter of the additional carbon dioxide generated by humans dissolves in the ocean, where it forms carbonic acid that inhibits the ability of coral, mollusks, crustaceans, and plankton to build their shells and skeletons. The acidification of the ocean's surface has increased by 30% since the start of the Industrial Revolution. It is now happening one hundred times faster than it has at any point in the last twenty million years, causing severe damage to coral reefs.[14]

The impoverishment of biodiversity is particularly severe. At the rate things are going, as much as 30% of mammals, birds, and amphibians are at risk of extinction before the end of the twenty-first century.[15] According to the WWF, there has been a 52% decline in wildlife populations worldwide between 1970 and 2010. Freshwater animals, like frogs, showed an average decline of 79%, marine species of 39%

In order to avoid major environmental changes, boundaries in the following areas have been identified and, for the most part, precisely quantified:

- climate change;
- depletion of the ozone layer;
- soil usage (agriculture, livestock farming, exploitation of forests);
- freshwater usage;
- impoverishment of biodiversity;
- ocean acidification;
- infiltration of nitrates and phosphates into the biosphere and ocean (two distinct factors);
- aerosol content in the atmosphere;[16]
- chemical pollution.

These nine factors must be kept within secure levels, otherwise we risk reaching the aforementioned point of no return. As we see in the figures below, all the factors measured were insignificant in 1900, and were still easily within previously set boundaries in 1950. Today, three major factors—climate change, the loss of biodiversity (where the safety level has been exceeded by a factor of ten to a hundred[17]), and pollution by nitrates (where the safety level has been exceeded by a factor of three)—have crossed their respective boundaries, and the other six are approaching them rapidly.

(especially among marine turtles, many shark species, and large migratory seabirds such as the wandering albatross), and land-dwellers, like the African elephant, of 30%.[18] The extinction rate has sped up by a factor of 100 to 1,000 because of human activity in the twentieth century, compared to the average rate (not counting major catastrophes, such as the one that led to the extinction of the dinosaurs). In the twenty-first century, this rate is expected to multiply by tenfold again. These are not things that can be fixed.

Evolution of ten factors for which planetary safety limits have been defined

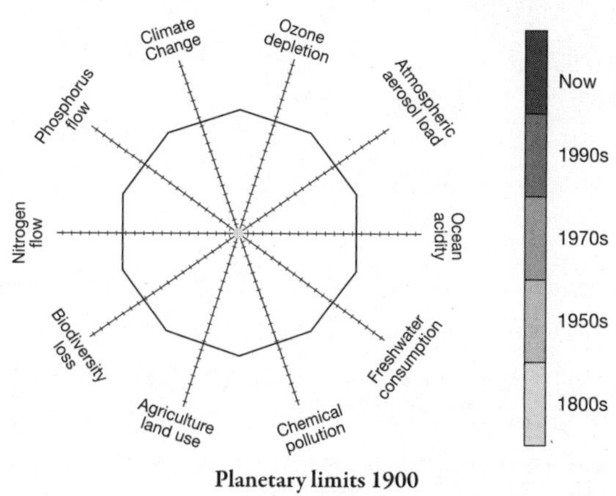

Planetary limits 1900

Evolution of ten factors for which planetary safety limits have been defined

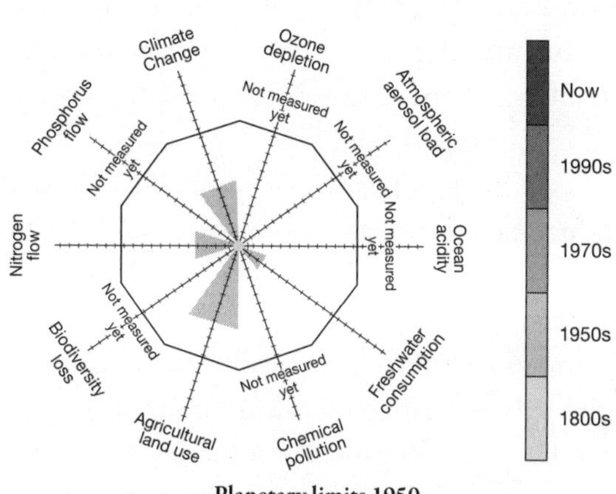

Planetary limits 1950

Evolution of ten factors for which planetary safety limits have been defined

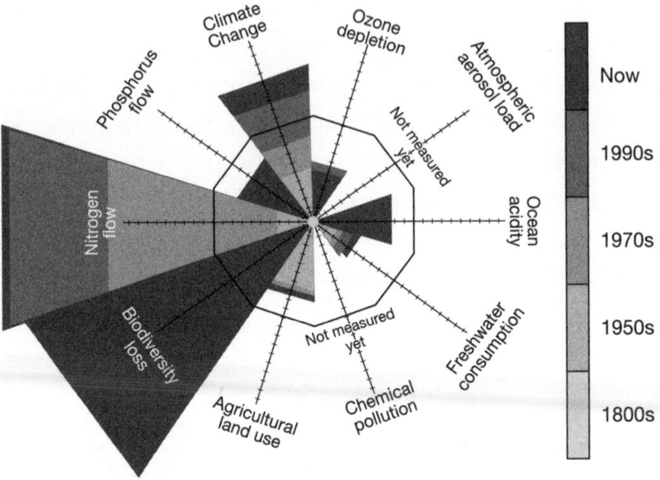

Planetary limits 2010

As for chemical products, "persistent organic pollutants," heavy metals, and radioactive material, all of them have harmful and cumulative effects on biological organisms, reducing fertility and causing permanent genetic damage. These pollutants have already caused the decline of several animal species, sea birds, and an especially large proportion of mammals. Humans themselves are not spared. In 2004, ministers from thirteen European Union countries agreed to have their blood tested. Fifty-five chemical products were detected, ranging from products used on non-stick pans to plastics and perfumes, and even some pesticides that are illegal in Europe. All the ministers had traces of PCB in their blood, a toxic substance manufactured by Monsanto that was banned in Europe in the 1970s.[19]

This planet is resilient, in so far as it is capable of reacting to upsets, just like a mammal can, for example, regulate and maintain its body temperature, even if the temperature outside is fluctuating. Nevertheless, it has its limits. The nitrogen and phosphorous cycles have been profoundly disrupted. Modern agricultural techniques and the inadequate handling of urban waste now release more nitrogen into the biosphere than all of Earth's processes combined. Only a small number of the pesticides used in farming are made from plants; as such, most nitrogen and phosphorous ends up in rivers, lakes, and the sea, where they disrupt aquatic ecosystems.[20]

THE FUTURE'S NOT SO BAD . . . FOR NOW

The vast majority of Tibetans I know have never heard of global warming; they all know, however, that the winter ice is less thick than it was in the past, and that temperatures are rising. Elsewhere in the world, in places with free access to information, a good number of us are aware of the dangers posed by global warming, but we hold back from taking any of the necessary measures to curb it.

Evolution has endowed us with ways of reacting energetically to imminent threats, but it is harder for us to feel concern for a problem that will come about in ten or twenty years. We tend to take the "we'll see when we get there" attitude.

We are even less inclined to take into account the environmental effects of our way of life on future generations. We often refuse to consider going without instant pleasures since it means envisaging disastrous consequences that will most likely happen in the long term. Diana Liverman, a respected environmental scientist, has lamented that CO_2 isn't pink in color. If everyone could see the sky getting pinker and pinker with the more CO_2 we emitted, we would in all likelihood feel increasingly alarmed at the effect it was having.[21]

American Indians used to say that, before making an important decision, one had to imagine the effects that decision would have on the people not just of their generation but seven generations down the line. Nowadays, it is hard enough to persuade decision-makers to take an interest in the threats facing the next generation. As for ultraliberal economists, they are only interested in the relationships between producers and consumers, and remain willfully blind to the fact that unbridled access to energy and natural resources cannot continue forever. Today, two-thirds of the world's most important ecosystems are overexploited,[22] and, according to Pavan Sukhdev, the Indian banker and leader of the study called The Economics of Ecosystems and Biodiversity, or TEEB: "We are consuming the past, present and future of the biosphere in an unthinking rush that we call progress and GDP."[23]

THE SCALE OF THE CHALLENGE

In 2013, concentrations of carbon dioxide increased at their fastest rate for 30 years. Between 1990 and 2013 there was a 34% increase in "radiative forcing," the warming effect on our climate due to long-lived greenhouse gases such as carbon dioxide, methane and nitrous oxide.[24]

Despite the protestations of the skeptic camp, average temperatures have also been continually on the increase, as we will see below.[25] At the rate things are going, in Africa in 2050 there will be a 50% to 80% probability that the following summer will be the hottest on record (since measurements began in 1900), and this probability will approach 100% by the end of the twenty-first century.[26]

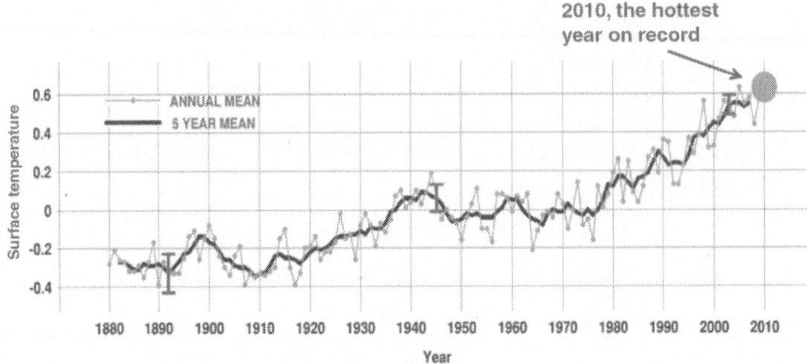

A large part of the uncertainty surrounding the extent of this warming is founded on the possibility that this sudden acceleration has been brought about by a combination of different factors. A study published in 2010 by Natalia Shakhova and her colleagues at the International Arctic Research Center shows, for example, that methane emissions due to the melting of the Siberian tundra's permafrost are much greater than previously estimated.[27]

But a warming of the climate by just 1.5°C would lead to major changes affecting human societies. Food resources would diminish, several contagious diseases sensitive to temperature would increase, and population migrations triggered by climate change would bring about much conflict. The number of refugees would be around the 200 million mark.

Sea levels, which have been measured since 1993 by satellite, are rising by 3.3 millimeters per year, and, because of this acceleration, could go up by 80 centimeters by 2100, forcing entire populations to emigrate.[28] Over 200 million people will be at risk. Fourteen of the world's megalopolises, including New York, Shanghai, and Mumbai, are today situated at sea level. Their coastlines would move further inland.

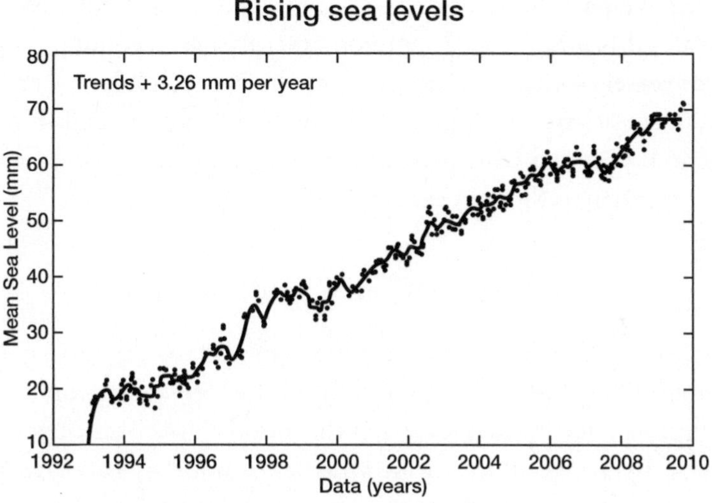

An Immense Violation of Human Rights?

Let's imagine that a few thousand individuals decide on the fate of 7 billion others, without consulting them or worrying about their aspirations. It is not hard to conceive of the howls of indignation that such a situation would provoke. There would be talk of a flagrant violation of human rights. Yet is this not what we are doing now in deciding the fate of future generations?

This attitude is reflective of the narrow notion of altruism held by a certain number of us. They are concerned about the fate of their children and grandchildren, but it is difficult for them to think about future generations with the same sense of responsibility. Groucho

Marx wonderfully illustrates this egocentric attitude with his famous quip: "Why should I care about future generations? What have they ever done for me?"

The point of view bound up in Groucho Marx's joke is unfortunately taken seriously by many philosophers, who note that our relationship with future beings is one-way, since none of them will be in a position to pay us back or to punish us for our current actions. Norman Care, former professor at Oberlin College in Ohio, for example, asserts that we can have no bonds of love or anxiety for indefinite future persons: "their interests cannot interest us."[29] He is of the view that we have no community bond with the humans of tomorrow, nor any sense of belonging to a common enterprise or a common humanity. Conversely, other thinkers, such as the British philosopher Derek Parfit, do not share this highly individualistic opinion, and think that it is morally unjustifiable to attach greater importance to the present generation than to those of the future.[30]

Do Future Beings Have Rights?

It is undoubtedly tricky for us to picture these generations to come: in our minds, they are nothing but a multitude of vague people. Moreover, philosophers have questioned the moral status of beings who do not yet exist, above all by asking whether or not they can have rights. The question may seem strange since, however virtual and anonymous they may seem to us today, it is certain that an incalculable number of them will come into the world.

According to the philosopher Clare Palmer, with whom I discussed this issue, philosophers trip up here due to the fact that theories dealing with the rights of the individual were designed to resolve ethical issues among people living in our own time.[31] Richard Degeorge, from the University of Kansas, is among those who consider that a future being can only have rights once they have come into the world.[32]

Ernest Partridge, an American philosopher specializing in environmental ethics, believes that this argument is valid for "active rights," namely the rights to do something, but that "passive rights," such as the right not to be denied the chance of living a healthy life, are entirely applicable to people in the future.[33]

In addition, many philosophers consider that rights and duties can only concern specific people, and that we do not have to feel responsible for the suffering or happiness of beings in general. To escape this impasse, all one needs to do, instead of arguing about "rights," is to speak the language of altruism and compassion. If the extension of altruism to all our fellow beings is a faculty unique to the human species, then its extension to future generations is but a logical consequence.

Not knowing who these people will be takes nothing away from the fact that, like us, they will aspire to evade suffering and be happy. We therefore cannot exempt ourselves from asking about the consequences of our actions and our way of life. It is perfectly normal for us not to ransack the house that we intend to bequeath to our grandchildren. Why not grant the same attention to the future inhabitants of the planet? This is the view of Edith Brown Weiss, professor of international and environmental law at Georgetown University, who talks of the "principle of intergenerational equity," which states that each generation leaves its successor a planet that is in at least as good a condition as that generation had inherited it.[34]

How Are Our Contemporaries Reacting?

According to research by Robert Kurzban and Daniel Houser, the former a psychologist at the University of Pennsylvania, the latter an economist, around 20% of people are altruists who bear the fortunes of future generations in mind and are disposed to altering their ways of consumption to avoid destroying the environment. Among them, some are motivated principally by respect for nature, while others are most preoccupied by human well-being, with yet more thinking that the two issues are one and the same.[35]

Around 60% of people follow prevailing trends and opinion leaders, something that highlights the power of the herd instinct in humans. These "followers" are also "conditional cooperators": they are ready to contribute to the public good on the condition that everyone else does likewise.

The final 20% are not at all inclined to cooperate and want more than anything to take advantage of all the opportunities available to them. They are not opposed to other people's happiness in principle, but it is not their business. They assert the right to be happy without any sense of duty or responsibility toward others in return. Preferring competition over cooperation, they are dedicated to promoting their own personal prosperity.

These deep-down individualists who act like lone rangers are sometimes described by the less charitable term "free riders," by virtue of the fact that they seek to gain as much as possible from their fellow beings and from the planet, considered in both cases to be instruments of their own well-being. Feeling little responsibility toward their peers, they are even less worried about the people of tomorrow. Here we again see that libertarian attitude promulgated by followers of Ayn Rand, which boils down to "me, more me, and me again," and we recall the words of the billionaire Steven Forbes about the expected rise in sea levels: "To change what we do because something is going to happen in one hundred years is, I would say, profoundly weird."[36] In other words, *après moi le déluge*…

Ecological Footprint

The way of life of this individualist minority—often the most rich—is such that its ecological footprint is disproportionately large compared to the rest of the population. A person's ecological footprint is defined as the area of land required to supply him with food and habitat, the energy required for his movements. These movements are linked to an individual's consumption and waste management, as well as the emissions (greenhouse gases and pollutants) for which he is responsible. If one were to divide the total area of Earth's biologically productive land by the number of its inhabitants, each person would have around 1.8 hectares. Yet the average ecological footprint is currently 2.7 hectares per person in the world, proof that we are living beyond our global means. These ecological footprints vary according to living standards: the average American's is 8 hectares; it is 6 hectares in Sweden; 1.8 hectares in most parts of Africa; and 0.4 hectares in India.[37] Stephen Pacala of Princeton University has calculated that the best-off, those who represent 7% of the global population, are responsible for half the world's CO_2 emissions, while the poorest 50% only emit 7%, a negligible amount for 3.5 billion people. The richest 7%, who moreover enjoy the best means for protecting themselves against pollution, benefit at the expense of the rest of the world.[38]

There certainly exist, among those with great fortunes, people who are generous and determined to strive for a better world, but they remain the minority. Today, the lifestyle of the wealthiest compromises the future prosperity of humanity and the well-being of the biosphere.

We must act, but it is not enough to economize by simply insulating our homes better, employing solar or geothermic energy, using appliances that consume less electricity, etc. It appears that people who make these kinds of savings often end up spending more money traveling, for example, or enjoying other activities and purchases that bring about—directly or indirectly—greenhouse gas emissions and various other forms of pollution. We must therefore not only save energy, but also live more modestly and stop associating moderation with dissatisfaction.[39]

Some countries have succeeded in meeting this challenge. Japan, for example, consumes half as much energy per capita than European Union countries, and three times less than the United States. This is due to the fact that it has to import a great deal of its energy, making it more expensive. High energy prices have had a salutary effect on consumption, without doing any harm to the country's prosperity or competitiveness at the international level. To the contrary, these limitations have stimulated innovation and the development of businesses that are less energy-intensive, particularly in the field of new technology.[40]

Close Collaboration Between Science and Government Is Essential

According to recent findings, limiting global warming to 2°C would appear to require an 80% reduction in CO_2 emissions between now and 2050. The public's willingness to do what is necessary to meet this objective remains very weak, particularly at times of recession, while leaders think of nothing but stimulating consumption.[41] Scientists, who produce the most reliable data, are regarded more often as spoilsports rather than holders of the knowledge needed to lead to the best decision-making.[42] Those in power never stop negotiating compromises, which are inherently harmful since they are less effective than the solutions being recommended. It's the equivalent of a severely ill person asking his doctor for permission to take only half the dosage of the medication required for his recovery.

For thirty years now, governments have signed over 500 international agreements to protect the environment. But, with the exception of the Montreal Protocol in 1987, which led to efficient measures to slow down the depletion of the ozone layer, most of these have been relatively ineffectual because of a lack of coordination, political will, and, above all, the absence of sanctions for those contravening the terms of the agreements.

In his book *Collapse: How Societies Choose to Fail or Succeed*, Jared Diamond calculated that the billion inhabitants living in rich countries enjoy thirty-two times more resources per person than the other 6 billion in the world.[43] If this 6 billion consumed as much as the wealthier billion, we would need three planets to provide for their needs. To look at China alone, where the income per capita is still just a tenth of that of the average American, the planet's demand for natural resources would double. Or if China had the same number of cars per person as the United States, it would use up the world's entire petrol production.[44] Yet China is *moving in that direction.* The situation therefore simply isn't tenable.

It is high time we established an atmosphere of trust between scientists, decision-makers, economists, business, and the media so that the latter parties listen to and understand the scientific consensus and realize that they are working toward a common purpose in a spirit of cooperation and solidarity. As H. G. Wells said: "history is a race between education and catastrophe."

Contemporary society is built on the myth of unlimited growth that very few economists and politicians are willing to question. No previous generation has mortgaged the future to this extent. These debts will be repaid in the form of ecological disasters when we have overstepped our planet's safe boundaries. At the start, those countries that have contributed the least in terms of wastage will suffer more than others, but ultimately no one will be spared. As Martin Luther King Jr. said: "We may have all come on different ships, but we're in the same boat now."

FEEDING 9 BILLION HUMANS

The human population will continue to grow until about 2050, probably stabilizing at around the 9 billion mark. This growth will take place predominantly in poorer countries.[45] By consequence, food production will have to increase by 70% between now and 2050. Lifting 1 billion human beings out of poverty and feeding 2 or 3 more billion constitutes an enormous challenge, made all the more acute by the weakening of the ecosystem occasioned by the production of the additional food required. Indeed the expansion of agriculture and livestock farming contributes greatly to crossing five of the nine planetary boundaries required to safeguard humanity.[46] It is therefore essential to implement measures for producing more food for human beings without further depleting our ecosystems.

Agriculture alone accounts for as much as 17% of greenhouse gas emissions. According to a Food and Agriculture Organization (FAO) report, in all the world's tropical areas, harvest yields could fall by between 25% and 50% in the next fifty years, due to a decrease in annual rainfall.[47] The warming will lead to a temporary increase in agricultural production in temperate areas, but this increase soon risks being compromised by the proliferation of diseases and parasites that threaten harvests.

However, according to the "Agroecology and the Right to Food" report published in 2011 by Olivier De Schutter, who was the United Nations Special Rapporteur on the Right to Food from 2007 to 2014, agroecology could double the food production of entire regions in ten years' time while simultaneously reducing poverty in rural areas and providing solutions to climate change. This Belgian law professor's proposals could transform the international trade system that has been built up by the World Trade Organization (WTO) since the Second World War.[48]

For those who argue that agricultural production would plummet by 40% if we were to abolish pesticides, preventing us from feeding the world, De Schutter's response is as follows: "These figures suppose that we would not compensate for the rejection of pesticides by improving our production techniques, for example with the biological control methods promoted by agroecology.... In addition, agroecology lowers production costs, since it reduces the use of pesticides and chemical fertilizers. The price of these products has risen faster in the last four or five years than the price of the foodstuffs themselves. Agroecology is particularly beneficial to small producers in developing countries wishing to operate at low cost."[49]

Agroecology is a cutting-edge science that combines ecology, biology, and traditional knowledge. Research in this field is not yet sufficiently developed since it is not patentable, so is still relatively unattractive to big business. It also suffers from people's inability to consider agricultural modernization from any point of view other than increased mechanization and industrialization.

THE INJUSTICE OF ENVIRONMENTAL CHANGE

I met Jonathan Patz for the first time with our mutual friend the neuroscientist Richard Davidson in a small Nepalese restaurant in Madison, Wisconsin. Jonathan arrived by bicycle, the simplicity of his appearance belying his status as a preeminent academic. He is now director of the Global Health Institute at the University of Wisconsin–Madison, and one of the main authors of the reports published by the UN's Intergovernmental Panel on Climate Change, the co-winner of the Nobel Peace Prize with Al Gore in 2007. He has specialized in, among other things, the study of the health effects of environmental change.

He explained to us why global environmental change is at the source of one of the most serious ethical crises of our time, namely the unequal manner in which this change affects populations. This inequality exists between nations (poor countries suffering much more than the richest), generations (future generations will be more affected than the current one), species (some will be endangered to the point of extinction), and social classes within a single country (once again, the most disadvantaged will suffer more than the rich; children and the elderly more than the middle-aged; and those living on the street more than those in housing).[50]

Regions that are already experiencing the serious consequences, and will go on to suffer the worst effects, of global warming and other major changes to our ecosystems bear the least responsibility for this change. Jonathan showed us two maps of the world. On the first, the size of the countries is proportionate to their share of responsibility for global CO_2 emissions into the atmosphere. We can see that the rich northern hemisphere countries (the United States, Europe, Russia) are swollen like balloons, while Africa practically disappears off the map. On the second one, the size of the countries represents the number of deaths caused by recent spikes in temperature and other phenomena linked with climate change. This time, it is the rich countries that become virtually invisible, while Africa and India invade the globe.[51] The risk of climate-related disease will have more than doubled by 2030.[52] In short, those who suffer from these calamities are not those who have caused them.

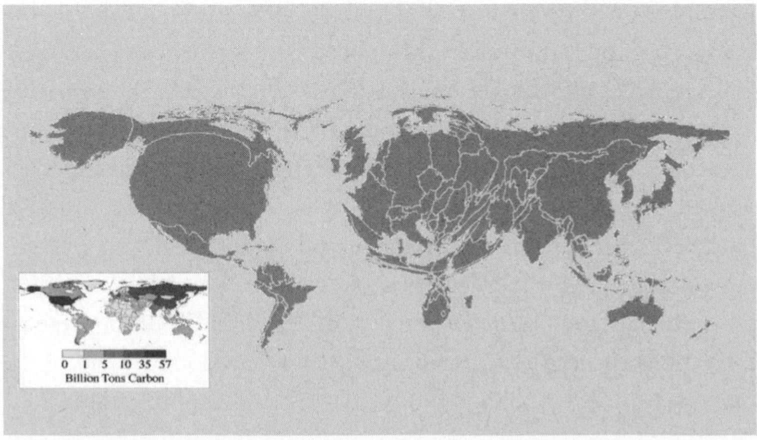

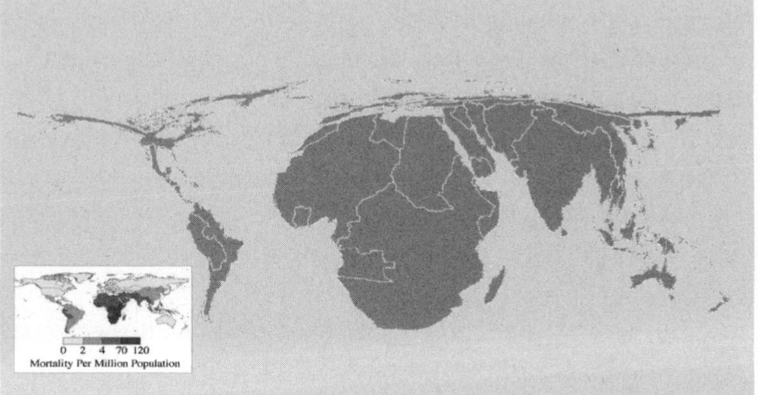

In the top map, the size of the countries is proportional to their responsibility in volume of global emissions of CO_2. In the bottom map, the size of the countries is proportional to the number of deaths due to recent extremes in temperature.

It is also these countries that will suffer disproportionately from the rise of several diseases whose incidence rates vary with climate. According to the WHO, 88% of disease attributable to climate change affects children below the age of five. This involves several diseases, including malaria, dengue fever, yellow fever, cholera, diarrhea, river blindness (onchocerciasis), leishmaniasis, Lyme disease, and respiratory diseases, especially asthma. Each year, 800,000 deaths are caused by air pollution in urban areas.[53]

In addition, people's health will also be affected by malnutrition, forced migration, and conflict—all the result of climate change. According to Jonathan, all the information currently available points to the conclusion that 23% of all deaths—36% among children—are linked to environmental factors influenced by human activity. He cited one striking example: during the Olympic Games in Atlanta in 1996, the organizers restricted the use of cars. One of the consequences of this was that morning rush-hour traffic fell by 23%, and peak ozone levels by 28%. At the same time the number of emergency hospital visits related to asthma in children plummeted by an astonishing 42%.

Conversely, during the warming triggered by the 1997 and 1998 El Niño weather phenomenon, winter temperatures in Lima were 5°C above average, and the number of hospital admissions for acute diarrhea increased by 200% compared with the five previous years.[54]

Malaria kills between 1 and 3 million people worldwide each year, the majority children living in developing countries. As it happens, the transmission of malaria is strongly affected by climate. The time it takes for the parasite to develop inside a mosquito is closely linked to temperature. It can be thirty days if the atmospheric temperature is around 18°C, but just ten days if it is 30°C. What's more, the relationship is not linear: in hot regions, an increase of 0.5°C in temperature can translate into a rise of 30% to 100% in the number of mosquitoes.

Similarly, the incidence rate of malaria is greatly intensified by deforestation. It has been shown that deforestation in the Amazon basin increases the size of the habitat favorable to the reproduction of the *Anopheles darlingi* mosquito, the principal malaria vector in the region. The "bite rate" in deforested areas of the Peruvian Amazon is nearly three hundred times higher than in regions where the forest is intact (taking into account differences in human population density in

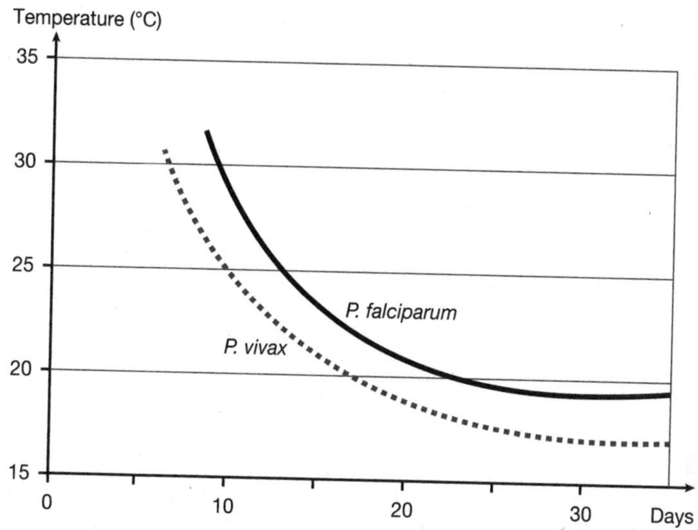

Relationship between temperature and malaria parasite development time inside mosquito ("extrinsic incubation period," or EIP). EIP shortens at higher temps, so mosquitoes infectious sooner.

these differing biotopes).[55] Several studies have also highlighted the correlation between deforestation and increased exposure to malaria in sub-Saharan Africa.[56]

In addition, as the economist Jeffrey Sachs has underlined, there is a clear correlation between the prevalence of malaria and poverty: the poorer a population, the less capable it is of protecting itself against malaria; and the more people are affected by malaria, the less prosperous their economy becomes.[57] The GDP in African countries where malaria is endemic grows by an average of 0.4% per annum, versus 2.3% in countries that are relatively little affected by the disease.

Prompted by the former investor and philanthropist Ray Chambers, now the UN's Special Envoy for Malaria, an ambitious program has been launched in the seven worst affected African countries. Ray and his team have succeeded in raising 6 billion dollars and have distributed 300 million mosquito nets treated with insecticide, bringing protection to 800 million people. This project has already saved the lives of more than 1 million people. The end of 2013 result of approximately 437,000 child deaths from malaria in Africa represents an almost 60% decrease in the mortality rate since this collective fight against malaria began seven years ago. With the expected progress during 2015, a path to reaching the target of fewer than 100,000 child deaths from malaria is now clear.[58] Yet, all these efforts could be compromised in the medium term by global warming if the latter is not contained below 2°C.

A Revealing Example of Interdependence

In conclusion, Jonathan Patz told us this story, which illustrates the extent to which all aspects of the environment are closely interdependent. In the 1950s, the WHO launched a malaria control program in Borneo, using large quantities of dieldrin. The program seemed to be working effectively since the mosquitoes were largely eradicated. But one or two years later, a typhus fever epidemic broke out; and at the same time, all the straw roofs in the villages collapsed. Why?

Dieldrin had indeed killed the mosquitoes, along with all the flies and cockroaches. But that wasn't all. The geckos that feed on the insects in the houses had acquired high levels of dieldrin in their body fat. The cats, who ate the geckos, had all died from that. In the absence of the cats, the rat population had exploded, and with it, the number of typhus-carrying fleas that parasitized the rats. The fleas transmitted the disease to the humans. Already the first catastrophe was under way, but why did the roofs cave in? The dieldrin had not just killed the mosquitos, flies, and cockroaches. It had also virtually wiped out a species of wasp that normally kills a certain type of caterpillar in order to lay its eggs, allowing the incoming larvae to feed off the caterpillar's body. As a result of the decline of the wasp population, the caterpillars had proliferated in the straw roofs, which had disintegrated and then collapsed. This example perfectly illustrates the incredible richness and subtlety of the levels of interdependence that link all Nature's dynamic agents and forces. It also cautions us to take far greater care of the natural equilibrium that has been in place for millennia.

Pessimism Is a Waste of Time: Solutions Exist

As the photographer and environmentalist Yann Arthus-Bertrand rightly said, if we want to preserve the well-being of our biosphere, "it's too late to be a pessimist."[59] Wijkmann and Rockström give two good reasons for optimism: the potential of replacing all fossil fuel energy with renewable energy by 2050; and the dawn of a "triply green" agricultural revolution, which is also quite possible.

The German Advisory Council on Global Change (*Wissenschaftlicher Beirat der Bundesregierung Globale Umweltverväanderungen*, or WGBU) devised a plan to place a limit on the use of fossil fuels—oil, coal, and natural gas—between now and 2050, at the same time as meeting global energy demand. On top of promoting renewable energy, one of the key points in this plan relates to the overall use of vehicles running off hydrogen, methane, gas, electricity, etc.[60]

Implementing such a program of course depends on world leaders rallying to the cause: this plan will require global investment to the tune of 1 billion dollars per year, and will only be profitable in the long term. This massive investment is far from unachievable, since worldwide government subsidies directed at keeping the price of oil at a level below its real cost already represent 400 to 500 billion dollars each year. These subsidies prolong oil and gas consumption, and hinder the technological development of renewable energy sources, which has in the same time period only received subsidies worth 66 billion dollars.[61]

The G20 has now committed to bringing an end to subsidies for fossil fuels, whose usage will decrease as renewable energy sources are made available in poorer countries, so as not to handicap these nations with punitively high rises in energy prices.

We have another reason to be optimistic. In contrast to other irremediable forms of environmental degradation (the loss of animal and plant species in particular), global warming is to an extent reversible: it is possible to cool the atmosphere by capturing enough CO_2. A 2010 report by McKinsey & Company shows that a 40% reduction in greenhouse gas emissions is possible by 2030, thanks to technological advances that would, in addition, lead to savings.[62]

The European Climate Foundation, or ECF, has published a report entitled *Roadmap 2050*, which shows that it is entirely possible to reduce CO_2 by 80% to 95% by 2050, provided that 80% of electricity is generated from renewable sources. What's more, this report convincingly shows that—over time—energy costs would overall become lower than those of energy from fossil fuels.

As far as Rockström and his colleagues are concerned, there is no doubt whatsoever that a tax of 50 to 180 dollars per ton of CO_2 emitted would provide the greatest incentive to speed up the transition to renewable energy. The tax currently applied by the European Union is just 20 dollars per ton, which is inadequate in the eyes of the scientific community. The example of Sweden is revealing. There they have imposed a tax of 100 dollars per ton, which has virtually eliminated the use of hydrocarbons in heating and significantly reduced industrial CO_2 emissions without doing anything to harm national economic growth. In Germany, new feed-in electricity tariffs have brought about a remarkable rise in renewable energy, particularly wind and solar, which now represents 10% of the country's production. In China, the solar energy sector will multiply by a factor of ten by 2015. According to a report by the Climate Commission in Australia, in 2012 China reduced its growth in electricity demand by a half. Considerable progress has also been made in Spain and Scandinavia. Jeremy Rifkin, president of the Foundation on Economic Trends, has stated that in 2009 the European Union installed more wind energy than any other energy source: 38% of all new energy deployment. The sector, which currently employs almost 200,000 people across the EU and produces 4.8% of its electricity, could supply—according to estimates—almost 17% of electricity in the European market in 2020, and 35% in 2030. By then it will employ nearly half a million people.[63] The time has come to roll out this transition across the world.

The cost required to curb greenhouse gas emissions, protect the tropical rainforest, and stabilize the world's climate has been estimated at around 150 to 200 billion dollars per year. This is certainly an enormous sum, but if we consider that each year 400 billion dollars are spent on advertising and that the Iraq war cost the United States 3 trillion dollars,[64] it becomes abundantly clear that businesses and governments are willing to spend colossal sums on things that are either insignificant or destructive.

There are various ways to raise this sum each year—it just requires the necessary political will. A tax of one dollar per barrel of oil, for example, would bring in 30 billion dollars per year, which is not excessive considering that the use of oil is, directly or indirectly, the principal cause of climate change.

Restoring and preserving Earth's ecosystems involves short-term spending, but represents an excellent long-term investment. For example, in the case of the tropical rainforest, the cost of restoration is estimated at 3,450 dollars per hectare, with profits from the restoration reaching 1,620 dollars, i.e. an internal rate of return of 50%. This dividend is 20% for other types of forest, 27% for lakes and rivers, 7% for coral reefs, 12% for marshland, and 79% for grassland.[65]

According to Rockström, companies in the financial, industrial, and banking sectors should produce a balance sheet that includes their environmental impact, and adapt their staff training methods to include education on the environmental effects of their activity.

The Crucial Hydrocarbon Alternative

We have seen that 78% of CO_2 emissions come from the use of fossil fuels. The production of hydrocarbons has multiplied by a factor of ten since 1950. Agriculture too has become increasingly dependent on energy from fossil fuels: calculations carried out in the United States show that 7 to 8 fossil fuel calories are needed for the production of every calorie of food consumed. Today feeding the average American for a year requires 1.6 tons of hydrocarbons.

Until now, economic growth in the richest countries has gone hand in hand with the growth of hydrocarbon consumption.[66] But the age of cheap oil is past. Every year, we consume twice as much oil as we discover, hence the deplorable idea of resorting to the exploitation of shale gas. Different studies by several independent groups have shown that the maximum level of hydrocarbon production will have been reached by 2018, after which we will experience a period of constant price hikes.[67] Most of the focus has been on the exploitation of existing resources and the search for new deposits, an approach which merely pushes back the inevitable deadline. Governments have delayed majorly in terms of creating any alternative solutions.

If we were to succeed in generating almost all of the energy we need from renewable sources, we would have already resolved the best part of the climate challenge. The beauty of energy management, as Rockström remarks, lies in the fact that, once produced, both forms of energy are entirely interchangeable: electricity from coal is exactly the same as electricity produced using wind power.[68]

A Complete Transition Toward Renewable Energy

There is no doubt that renewable energy can comfortably cater to global demand, which currently stands at around 500 exajoules (EJ): the production potential of wind energy is greater than 1000 EJ, and if we factor in the potential of geothermic, solar, and hydroelectric power, the figure is as great as 11,000 EJ.[69]

The DESERTEC project, which saw the light of day in Germany, aims to install a new system for capturing solar energy in the Sahara desert. During the day, the sun's rays can heat oil reservoirs to temperatures of 1,300°C, with the resulting heat producing vapor that in turn drives electricity-generating turbines. The oil cools relatively slowly, and the heat stored during the day is capable of guaranteeing overnight electricity production through the following morning. An area of just 10km² of panels in the Sahara would be enough to supply electricity to North Africa and almost the whole of Europe (via ultra-efficient underwater cables). DESERTEC has already launched pilot projects in Morocco, Tunisia, and Egypt. The technology can be rolled out to any desert in the world, from the center of Spain to Australia via the Gobi Desert. According to another study carried out in Japan, if photovoltaic panels were installed on 4% of the world's total desert area, they would produce energy levels equivalent to global energy consumption.[70]

In 2009, for the first time in Europe, investment in wind and solar energy production overtook investment in conventional electricity production. Overall, renewable energy still only represents a tiny percentage of the energy produced in the world, but even so production is growing by 20% every year. The challenge then is to take renewable energy from where it sits at 2% to 3% and to get it up to 80% or even 100% by 2050.[71]

Residential and commercial buildings currently consume 40% of all energy produced, and they are the main contributors to greenhouse gas emissions. Nowadays it is possible to use "passive energy," and even to fit out buildings in such a way that they produce electricity that can be fed back into the grid.

Supplying Energy to Poor Countries

In the meantime, poorer countries are suffering from chronic energy shortages. In Africa, 85% of the population have no access to electricity. The same goes for 60% of the population of South Asia. Supplying safe, renewable energy to the Third World is essential for alleviating poverty and improving the health of disadvantaged peoples. Better access to renewable energy would also allow schools, medical clinics, and village community buildings to function more efficiently. In Bangladesh, for example, thanks to a program run by Muhammad Yunus's organization Grameen Solar, in 2010 one million people received electricity generated using solar panels. Mass production of solar energy has also led to a considerable fall in electricity prices. Improving people's access to energy sources in poor countries now represents one of the United Nations' main priorities, their objective being to guarantee global energy supply by 2030.[72]

More than a million and a half people die each year from household pollution resulting from the burning of wood, coal, and dried dung inside the home, and from oil or kerosene lighting. The use of electricity and solar cooking equipment, which involves large, cheap, round dishes for boiling water and cooking food, would stamp out these health and accident risks.

Sensible Water Management

It is absolutely essential that we manage our freshwater reserves more rationally. Today, 70% of the freshwater we use comes from dwindling lakes, rivers, and water tables. One-quarter of the world's watercourses no longer reach the ocean, overexploited as they are for agricultural purposes. And the situation is only getting worse.

We have already seen that 70% of world freshwater extraction is dedicated to agriculture. Nothing consumes more water than food production, especially meat (lest we forget, the production of 1kg of meat uses up fifty times more water than for 1kg of cereals). Across the world, the amount of water required each day to produce enough food for one person—*taking every phase into account*—is 3,000–4,000 liters, an astonishingly high figure, while 50 to 150 liters covers our other basic daily needs, such as drinking, washing, and cleaning our houses and clothes.

Two improvements are necessary: collecting more rainwater, and making better use of "green" water. If we refer to water from rivers, lakes, and the water table as "blue" water, "green" water is the invisible water that maintains the dampness of the soil, is found inside plants, evaporates following transpiration, and is released back into the atmosphere. More than 60% of the water that makes up the hydrological cycle is "green" water.[73] It is responsible for making plants grow, and facilitates freshwater-dependent agriculture, which represents 80% of world farming. The best opportunities for improving agricultural practice rest here.

In developing countries, especially South Asia, it is possible to restore water-table levels and resupply exhausted wells in villages by building rainwater dikes, which let the water filter down into the soil rather than evaporate away quickly. What's more, collecting rainwater on the roofs of houses and storing it in large underground cisterns, built using traditional materials, is enough to ensure a plentiful supply in villages that up until now have suffered terrible freshwater shortages. These techniques have been implemented, for instance, in the arid regions of Rajasthan, India, by Bunker Roy's Barefoot College.

Food for All Without Destroying the Biosphere: A Real Green Revolution

Some 40% of Earth's land area is dedicated to agriculture. Agriculture and livestock farming are responsible for 30% of greenhouse gas emissions, and are the principal cause of nitrogen and phosphorous being released into the atmosphere. Several scientific reports present new methods that would lead to *producing enough food at the same time as avoiding the destruction of the environment.*[74]

An executive summary, published by the FAO in 2011, shows that it is possible to produce 70% more food in the world without increasing the area of cultivated land.[75] However, this report emphasizes that growth in production must not come about by resorting to intensive farming methods using chemical fertilizers and pesticides.

According to Wijkmann and Rockström, we require nothing short of a "triply green" revolution. The first green revolution, which occurred in the 1960s, more than doubled our cereal crop production, mainly rice, maize, and wheat. India in particular witnessed a spectacular increase in food resources. But this initial revolution relied heavily on mass use of chemical fertilizers, pesticides, hybrid seeds, and irrigation methods that required diesel pumps to extract water from very deep in the soil.

The long-term consequences of this temporary increase in production were detrimental in several ways: exhausting water tables, soil erosion and impoverishment, chemical pollution, and negative social impacts in rural communities where people's lifestyles were profoundly changed. In her prophetic book *Silent Spring*, Rachel Carson posed the question: "Can anyone believe it is possible to lay down such a barrage of poisons on the surface of the earth without making it unfit for all life?"[76]

We talk about "insecticides," but more apt would be the term "biocides." Agroecologists the world over possess an increasing amount of evidence to show that organic farming can produce roughly the same amount of food as "chemical" farming. This can be achieved by creating a balance between agriculture and livestock farming, which produces natural fertilizer; promoting crop rotation, which allows the soil to regain its levels of organic nitrogen; and avoiding intensive plowing, thus protecting soil quality. Nitrogen loss in the soil is reduced by 30% if farmers grow cover crops in the winter, such as rye or wheat, which also increase carbon capture in the soil.

According to the Stockholm Environment Institute and the Stockholm Resilience Center headed up by Rockström, the next agricultural revolution must add two green revolutions to the first. On the one hand we must gradually move away from the use of chemical fertilizers and pesticides, and on the other, use "green" water from renewable sources so as not to exhaust lakes, rivers, and water tables.

A summary of all these potential outcomes, presented in Jonathan Foley's article "Solutions for a cultivated planet,"[77] which was published in the journal *Nature*, shows that it is possible to feed 9 billion human beings in a way that does not destroy the land still available to us, especially in tropical regions. The authors also stress the importance of reducing wastage at every stage of the food production process: 30% of the food bought in rich countries ends up in the trash (the same applies to medicine). Almost 50% of the food produced in the world never reaches a human stomach for reasons as varied as insufficient infrastructure and storage facilities, overly strict regulations regarding expiry dates, "buy one get one free"–type offers, and the habit among consumers of only selecting food with a perfect appearance.

Revitalizing the Soil

One of the most strongly recommended measures is to stop deep plowing, which exposes the richest elements of the soil to the air: the organic matter heats up in the sun, dries and evaporates, emitting CO_2 and leading to a major depletion of carbon levels. The soil's microfauna—bacteria, acari, earthworms, and other life-giving organisms—is destroyed and erosion becomes more serious. Earth sterilized by plowing also becomes harder and more compact, preventing plants' roots from reaching deeper water. The soil therefore becomes less and less fertile and its yield decreases. Land should therefore only be worked as minimally as possible on the surface, or even not at all: in Uruguay, Paraguay, and Bolivia, in the last ten to fifteen years, 70% of farmers have stopped plowing their fields and in doing so their yields have returned to their highest levels.

These techniques also allow a soft approach to sowing that avoids turning the soil over. They have the advantage of considerably reducing soil erosion and work time (and therefore energy consumption), improving soil structure, bearing capacity, and porosity (making it easier for water to filter through), and enhancing the biological richness of the earth.

In the 1980s in Burkina Faso, the agroecologist Pierre Rabhi showed that it was possible to reverse the desertification process with methods that were easily adoptable for local communities. These techniques involve: revitalizing dry soil with natural compost (humus), which is rich in microorganisms and capable of holding up to five times its weight in water; planting trees; building low stone walls to slow down water run-off; and reintroducing traditional, more durable seeds.[78] These very techniques were implemented by Yacouba Sawadogo, a humble farmer, who has over the course of the last thirty years succeeded in revegetating 6 million hectares in the Sahel region, earning the respect of all the nation's farmers and of big international organizations. Water table levels have risen in these areas, trees are making the landscape greener, and cereal crop harvests have become plentiful.[79]

As we saw in the chapter headed "Individualized Selfishness," the Indian NGO Navdanya operates in sixteen Indian states distributing seeds, including no fewer than 600 varieties of rice and 150 varieties of wheat, to farmers seeking to practice organic farming and reestablish their food self-sufficiency.[80] At present, Navdanya counts half a million farmers among its membership.

Establishing a Circular Economy by Recycling All Rare Metals

Despite various worthy efforts, raw material recycling rates remain extremely poor. According to a 2011 report by the United Nations Environment Programme (UNEP), the transition to a green economy requires a huge step forward from feeble current levels of metal recycling. Just twenty of the sixty metals taken into consideration are recycled at more than a rate of 50%, and for thirty-four of the other forty metals it is lower than 1%, even though many of them play a crucial role in various clean technological devices, such as batteries for hybrid cars or wind turbine magnets.[85] Yet in theory, *metals can be recycled an infinite number of times,* and this process would create new job opportunities.

By recycling aluminum instead of making it from bauxite, CO_2 emissions created in its production could be reduced by 90%. Nowadays, however, just a third of aluminum comes from recycling. In addition, if one were to recycle lead instead of processing it from minerals, the corresponding CO_2 emissions would decrease by 99%. The same applies for iron, copper, nickel, tin, and other metals. Moreover, 50 million tons of electronics are thrown away each year, with only 15% to 20% recycled.[86]

What's more, rare metal deposits are dwindling very quickly. According to one evaluation of the reserves of eighteen rare metals used in key industrial sectors, six will be exhausted in the next fifty years at the current rate of consumption, and thirteen in the same timeframe if the whole world were to use just half the amount consumed by the United States.[87] Ever heard of indium? This element is much in demand for the manufacture of flat-screens used in computers and televisions. It is the most endangered of the eighteen rare metals and, at the current rate of consumption, it will have been exhausted in the next thirteen years. It multiplied in price by a factor of ten between 2006 and 2009. The price of tantalum, used to make mobile telephones, has also increased significantly, and the desire to control its exploitation is one of the main causes of the bloody civil war in Congo.

At this rate—if demand does not increase, which seems unlikely—zinc will be exhausted in the next forty-six years, tin in forty, silver in twenty-nine, and copper in sixty-one. Only aluminum (1,027 years), platinum (360), and chromium (143) are still relatively abundant.

An Intelligent Network for Sharing Renewable Energy

In *The Third Industrial Revolution,*[88] the economist Jeremy Rifkin proposes that all buildings should be transformed into miniature local power plants operating on geothermal, wind, and solar power, and by converting waste. If millions of buildings were to generate renewable energy, store any surplus by turning it into hydrogen (which can then at any moment be reconverted into electricity), or sell it on to millions of other users, the resulting power would far exceed the production capacity of national power plants, whether they are nuclear, coal-fired, or gas. The process would involve producing hydrogen by the simple electrolysis of water using solar electricity, while another system would recombine it with oxygen in a fuel cell to produce electricity on demand. This process has the major advantage of being entirely clean, and, unlike batteries, doesn't use any polluting elements such as cadmium or lithium.

A computerized system would enable the distribution of any excess into areas that do not have electricity at any given moment because of disruptions in production, and supply charging stations for hydrogen-powered cars. Experimental buses and hydrogen-powered vehicles are already in use in Europe. In May 2007, the European Parliament, the legislative body representing the then twenty-seven European Union member states, voted to commit to supporting this third industrial revolution.[89] Several pilot projects have been put in place, notably in Corsica, where a large field of photovoltaic panels have been installed near Ajaccio, along with an almost industrial-scale system for the production and storage of hydrogen, designed to compensate for the inevitable interruptions associated with solar power.

SOME ENCOURAGING SIGNS

Some countries have made laudable efforts in the area of environmental protection. Despite its rapid modernization, Vietnam, for example, has succeeded in increasing its forestry areas from representing 28% of the country's area to 38% between the years 1990 and 2005, thanks to a systematic reforestation program (which is in stark contrast to the savage deforestation carried out in nearby Indonesia). Its rate of reforestation between 1970 and 1980 was twice as fast as the rate of deforestation.[90] In Costa Rica, more than 95% of the country's energy comes from renewable sources. In the Himalayas, Bhutan, a country roughly the size of Switzerland, captures four times more CO_2 than it emits.

The United Nations' biodiversity summit at Nagoya in 2010 resulted in a consensus among world governments to widen the area of biologically protected zones in the world. Some 17% of land area and 10% of the oceans were designated as natural reserves. At a second summit, in Hyderabad, India, in October 2012, signatories of the Convention on Biological Diversity (CBD) elected to double the spending made by developed countries (10 billion dollars) toward developing countries by 2015, so as to implement the plan to save the world's "living systems" and the twenty-point strategy adopted in Nagoya for the period 2010–2020. The plan to protect international waters was quickly approved, and "marine areas of biological or ecological interest" were designated in the southwest Pacific, the Caribbean, the midwest Atlantic, and the Mediterranean.

Another initiative is that of "ethical markets" that use "green transition scorecards" (GTS) and track the private sector's investment development in "green markets." The report published by this organization in 2012 gives the sum of 3.3 trillion dollars of turnover in these markets since 2007.[91]

GREEN CITIES SET THE EXAMPLE

The city of Portland, Oregon, has topped the rankings year after year of America's best cities to live in. In the 1970s, Tom McCall, the state's first eco-minded governor, ripped up the freeway that bisected the city and transformed it into a 4,000-hectare public green space. His successors have continued his initiative. Between 1990 and 2008, the city reduced its CO_2 emissions by 19%. As much as 26% of its total area is planted with trees, and counting (it will be 30% by 2030). This city of 1.4 million inhabitants has built 700 kilometers of cycle lanes, and employees at most companies who walk or cycle to work receive an extra 50 dollars in their monthly salary. A deposit is charged on all glass bottles to encourage recycling, and most fast-food chains (McDonald's, Starbucks, etc.) have shut up shop to give way to restaurants serving local produce. Portland is the only American city where the construction of a Walmart, the world's biggest supermarket, has been blocked by residents.[92]

Stockholm, with a population of 1 million, is another model green city. Some 70% of the city's heating comes from renewable energy sources. It has set itself the target of moving away from all fossil fuels by 2050.[93] Currently 95% of Stockholm's population lives less than three hundred meters from a green space. Many of the city's green zones actively contribute to water purification, noise reduction, biological diversity, and citizen well-being.

Most of the people in Stockholm use non-polluting public transport. The creation of a city toll following a 2007 referendum has considerably reduced traffic and, by consequence, air pollution. As such, since 1990, greenhouse gas emissions have fallen by 25%. The Swedish capital has also implemented an innovative waste management system that has guaranteed better rates of recycling.

An eco-neighborhood in Hamburg is to be heated via a cogeneration system: it will use solar and photovoltaic power as well as collect rainwater.

The Covenant of Mayors is an association bringing together European cities engaged in improving their energy efficiency and increasing the amount of renewable energy they use. The Covenant's signatories aim to achieve, or even overtake, the European Union's target to reduce

CO_2 emissions by 20% before 2020. More than four thousand European cities have agreed to meet these obligations.

Masdar, a city near Abu Dhabi that's been under construction since 2008, will run exclusively on renewable energy, including solar power, a reliable resource given its desert location. It is meant to be completed this year, in 2015, and will have 50,000 inhabitants. The aim is for it to have zero CO_2 emissions and to create no waste, and there will not be any cars. Not bad for the oil capital of the world!

To the north of Shanghai, China, a planned green city called Dongtan will also operate exclusively on renewable energy, and should start off with a population of 50,000 to 80,000, increasing to 500,000 in 2050.

Another example is BedZED (Beddington Zero Emissions Development),[94] a neighborhood of eco-friendly buildings in the Hackbridge area of London, which is a carbon-positive development that produces more energy than it consumes.

Taking Action and Not Looking for Excuses for Doing Nothing

The progress required to relieve these environmental challenges is naturally fraught with obstacles, ranging from inertia to denial via compromise and a "wait-and-see" attitude.

First of all there are the climate-change *deniers,* who refuse to accept either that it is happening or that it is caused by humans. They are becoming more and more unreasonable and absurd even when the scientific data detailing changes to our biosphere mount up in front of us. Indeed, there is easily enough scientific data available to justify determined, sustained action if we are to avoid succumbing to what my father, Jean-François Revel, called "useless knowledge."

After them we have the *skeptical* camp, who declare that decades of warnings about impending disaster have produced nothing of the sort. In 1880, for example, a scientist announced that the streets of Paris would be engulfed in a layer of manure due to the ever increasing number of horses in the capital. But these skeptics who claim to have seen it all will soon realize that these are not merely alarmist proclamations about localized problems, as with industrial pollution in nineteenth-century London, which made the air almost impossible to breathe, and turned the Thames into a putrid cesspit, but rather transformations that are largely irreversible.

It is true that the increase in disquieting news about climate change, the loss of biodiversity, and other serious environmental challenges can create a blasé attitude among some people or, conversely, elicit a feeling of powerlessness about the scale of the transformations and interventions required to overcome the problem. Everyone is sad that the bee population is in full decline, that fish stocks have decreased by 90%, or that only 10% of the forest we had ten thousand years ago remains. "What a shame!" we think, reassuring ourselves by saying, "Oh well, we'll think of something..." Sunita Narain, director of the Centre for Science and Environment in New Delhi, sums up the attitude of our times with the mantra: "Don't worry, just consume!"[95]

In the past, local communities have of course successfully overcome lots of similar difficulties, but the problem we face today is entirely different: it is the first time in human history that our species is associated with such rapid and radical planetary change.

Then there are the *relativists,* such as the Danish statistician Bjorn Lomborg, who think that there are other problems, such as poverty, dwindling food reserves, AIDS, and other contagious diseases, that require greater resources and need fixing more urgently than climate change, which he deems to be unconfirmed anyway.[96] Here we see a twofold error of judgment, since not only is climate change now an undeniable fact, but also, as we have seen time and again, it is precisely the world's poorest people who will suffer the most from diseases whose contagiousness increases the hotter the temperature gets, and that the dwindling of food resources is also made worse by climate change. Human well-being therefore goes hand in hand with the fight against climate change.

To say that the well-being of the current generation of humans is more important than the next is like saying that it is more useful to make your house comfortable instead of extinguishing the approaching fire that is threatening to destroy the entire village.

Next on the list are the *opportunists,* who are disturbed by the idea of prosperity without growth. They would rather maximize growth that benefits the current generation as much as possible. They also see economic opportunities in the melting of the arctic (to exploit oil reserves deep below the North Pole) and eagerly anticipate Siberia becoming the new Riviera for vacationers. In order to do nothing to protect the environment right now, they praise in advance the ingenuity of future generations, who will, they tell us, figure out the solutions. This is not to underestimate the human species' creativity and capacity for innovation, but we must be clear-sighted, and the existence of critical boundaries in a variety of fields will make the task impossible. Today we are, in various places, trying to reintroduce species that have disappeared from them—wolves, Tasmanian devils, and, in parts of Western Europe, bears, lynxes, and vultures—but these frequently unsuccessful cosmetic changes will be eclipsed by the anticipated disappearance of 30% of living species by 2050.

A QUESTION OF COMMON SENSE

The planet is not a fixed entity and never will be. Countless species appeared and became extinct well before *Homo sapiens* arrived on the scene. There is no way, therefore, that we can conceive of an "ideal state" for a planet that is constantly evolving. But a major change has come about—we have entered the period that most scientists have agreed to call the Anthropocene, an epoch in which humans have become a geological force that profoundly alters the natural equilibrium and is significant enough to threaten both the well-being of humankind and the survival of innumerable other species.

In conclusion, it is an urgent imperative that we recognize the links between humans and nature, our economies and the biggest transformations affecting our planet. In other words, we must be more aware than ever of our place in the biosphere. As we approach the boundaries of what Earth can offer us and tolerate, we must realize that our future well-being depends on our capacity to remain within these planetary boundaries. The report entitled "Harmony with Nature," presented in 2010 by the Secretary General of the United Nations, shines a light on this interdependence:

> *Ultimately, environmentally destructive behavior is the result of a failure to recognize that human beings are an inseparable*

> *part of Nature and that we cannot damage it without severely damaging ourselves.*[97]

Implementing the necessary course of action requires the strengthening of governance and international cooperation, but also, and above all, the promotion of the values of altruism and solidarity at community level as well as within ourselves as individuals.

42

Sustainable Harmony

You cannot solve problems with the same thinking used to create the problems.

—Albert Einstein

What good is an extremely rich and all-powerful nation full of unhappy people? An enlightened human society, as we have seen, must provide an appropriate way of life for the present generation by alleviating poverty, and at the same time serve future generations by staving off the planet's destruction. According to this philosophy, growth is secondary to establishing a balance between everyone's aspirations and a "sustainable harmony" that factors in the fortunes of generations to come, and which is only conceivable in a context where altruism and cooperation prevail. Only the realization of these two goals will allow us to overcome the challenge outlined at the beginning of this work and reconcile the demands of prosperity, quality of life, and environmental protection, in the short, medium, and long term. Nowadays, we are better advised to pursue qualitative growth based on better living conditions than a quantitative growth based on ever-increasing consumption.

Neither Growth Nor Decline: A Balanced Prosperity

The majority of contemporary economists define growth in terms of wealth increase—or more specifically wealth increase as an aim in itself—

and exploitation of natural resources. Yet this sort of growth is no longer suited to the realities we face today. Natural resources have satisfied our needs until now, but in the present circumstances they are limited. Even so, the very idea of limiting growth is met with incredulity by most economists and politicians, and, as the English economist Partha Dasgupta highlights, "Nature is treated like any other part of the capital stock whose purpose is to be exploited for humanity's interest."[1] In the eyes of the politician Anders Wijkman and environmentalist Johann Rockström, there can be nothing more perverse than an economy that grows at the expense of the raw materials that allow it to exist: "The world's population is growing. Consumption is growing. The only problem is that the Earth is not growing."[2] He points out that the only truly unlimited natural resources are the wind and the sun—the ones we use least.

In short, as the English-born American economist Kenneth Boulding said: "Those who believe that economic growth can go on forever are either mentally deranged or they are economists."[3] Fortunately this does not apply to all economists. Some have now realized that we need an economy that cares for the poor and cares for future generations.

But that's not all. By choosing to carry on encouraging growth as though it were "business as usual," mainstream economists are loading the odds against future generations. The report published by one of their most eminent members, Sir Nicholas Stern, showed in convincing fashion that the economic cost of inaction toward climate change will essentially be far higher than the investment needed to control or prevent the warming.[4] Stern and others predict that more than 200 million people will be displaced by 2050 because of climate change.

Herman Daly, a professor at the University of Maryland, estimates that the current environmental costs linked to economic growth exceed the profit it generates: beyond a certain threshold, economic growth, which neglects to factor in the harm it causes as an item on its balance sheet, actually makes us poorer instead of richer.[5]

We are facing a serious dilemma. In essence, neither economic growth, which in its current form and at its current rate is unsustainable in terms of the natural resources left to us, nor economic decline, which would harm the poorest, constitute suitable ways of managing the present situation. This is the view expressed by the British economist Tim Jackson, Professor of Sustainable Development at the

University of Surrey, in his book *Prosperity Without Growth: Economics for a Finite Planet.*[6] Jackson identifies three reasons why current growth cannot continue: firstly, the present economic model takes it as given that wealth is an appropriate indicator of prosperity. This is of course a highly narrow and reductive vision of what constitutes quality of life, by virtue of the fact that massive growth often runs contrary to popular well-being, leading to what Jackson calls "social recession."

Secondly, the profit that comes from growth is distributed very unequally, disproportionately benefiting those who are already rich. Let us not forget that 5% of the world's population pocket 75% of global income, while the poorest 5% receive just 2%. In a system that entrenches inequality instead of reducing it, Jackson underlines, "you could grow the world economy for a million years and still not make poverty history."[7]

Thirdly, unlimited economic growth is quite simply impossible because of the planet's ecological boundaries. People living in the second half of the twenty-first century will pay dearly for the selfishness and excess of today's citizens.

Jackson is not an advocate for *decline,* which would bring instability to society by provoking unemployment and, yet again, causing most harm to the poorest people, who as a result would have even less chance of accessing the basic services we have in developed societies. The author does not offer a miracle cure, but demonstrates that the blind pursuit of ever increasing consumption is extremely damaging to the future of humanity.

The middle way between growth and decline can be found in *sustainable harmony,* in other words a situation that guarantees everyone a decent way of life and reduces inequality at the same time as ceasing to exploit the planet at such a drastic speed. To bring about and maintain this harmony, we must on the one hand lift a billion people out of poverty as soon as possible, and on the other, reduce the rampant consumption taking place in rich countries. We must also gain awareness of the fact that unbridled material growth is not remotely necessary for our well-being. We know, for example, that in the coming ten years, economic growth in Europe and many other countries will most likely stagnate. We are therefore better off redirecting our attention to a qualitative conception of growth based on life satisfaction and which prioritizes the protection of the environment.

THE WEAKNESSES OF THE PRESENT ECONOMIC MODEL

According to James Gustave Speth, former dean of the Yale School of Forestry and Environmental Studies and one-time administrator of the United Nations Development Programme (UNDP), Earth's breakneck degradation is not merely the result of deficient policy at the national level or of simple negligence: it is due to the systemic failures of modern capitalism, which, by targeting perpetual economic growth, has led us simultaneously to the verge of plenty and the verge of ruin. In *The Bridge at the Edge of the World,*[8] he identifies as a principal driver of environmental destruction the 60,000 multinational companies that have emerged over the last few decades and who strive for continual growth in size and profitability without any consideration for the fate of future generations. He is of the opinion that the modern capitalist system can only create an increasing environmental threat, and that this will outweigh any efforts made to control it. It is therefore necessary to change tack and commit to building from here on out a "post-growth" society based more on well-being than on economic riches.

The main change in perspective concerns the importance attached to GDP. For Amartya Sen, the economic crisis is an opportunity to think more broadly about our notions of progress and happiness, and to consider other ways of measuring it instead of GDP. For Sen, "GDP is very limited. Used on its own, it's a disaster. Indicators relating to production or goods consumption tell us very little about freedom or well-being, which in turn depend on the organization of a society and on the distribution of wealth."[9] Why? Because, as Robert Costanza and colleagues wrote in *Nature,* "GDP measures mainly market transactions. It ignores social costs, environmental impacts and income inequality."[10] We therefore need several other indicators that reflect, among other things, life expectancy, education, access to care, inequality, subjective well-being, environmental preservation, etc.

The inventor of GDP, the Nobel Prize–winning economist Simon Kuznets, showed sixty years ago that GNP (gross national product) and GDP (gross domestic product), devised to manage the crisis of 1929, only measure some aspects of the economy, and should never be used to assess the well-being, or indeed progress, of a nation: "The welfare of a nation can scarcely be inferred from a measurement of national income," wrote Kuznets in 1934.[11] He emphasized that we could not satisfy ourselves with solely examining what is increasing in quantitative terms, but on the *nature* of what is increasing: "Distinctions must be kept in mind between quantity and quality of growth.... Goals for more growth should specify more growth *of what* and *for what*."[12] GDP quantifies total production value over the course of a year, and the wealth created by economic agents (households, businesses, public spending) resident in a country. Yet true prosperity has a number of parameters that GDP does not take into account. In particular, the way GDP is measured makes no distinction between the increase in volume of goods and services when that increase brings greater well-being and when it works to the detriment of well-being.

In the 1990s, economists started talking more and more about GDP than GNP, which further diminished the correlation between a nation's theoretical wealth and the well-being of its people. GNP corresponds with the annual production of wealth created by a country, whether this took place domestically or abroad. Yet if a country's products are largely exported, which is generally the case with mineral and oil reserves, GDP goes up, while the GNP could decrease if the citizens do not see any of the profit generated by these resources—either because they are exploited by foreign companies, or because an unscrupulous ruling elite keeps hold of them. In other circumstances, GDP might increase greatly while quality of life decreases as a result of environmental damage and conflict linked to seizing control of mineral resources, as has happened in Congo. As the psychologist Martin Seligman points out:

> *At the time of the industrial revolution, economic indicators were a very good approximation of how well a nation was doing. Meeting simple human needs for food, shelter, and clothing was chancy and satisfying these needs moved in lockstep with more wealth. The more prosperous a society becomes, however, the worse an approximation wealth is to how well that society is doing. Basic goods and services, once scarce, became so widely available that in the twenty-first century, many economically developed nations such as the United States, Japan and Sweden experience an abundance, perhaps an overabundance of goods and services. Because simple needs are largely satisfied in modern*

> *societies, factors other than wealth now play an enormous role in how well these societies are doing.... Today the divergence between wealth and quality of life has become glaring.*[13]

We cannot expect quality of life to be a mere by-product of economic growth, since the two things are not based on the same criteria. It would be more appropriate to introduce the concept of "gross national happiness," an idea conceived of by the little Himalayan country Bhutan a few years ago. For three decades they have used a scientific tool to measure various aspects of life satisfaction and its correlation with other extrinsic (financial resources, social standing, education, levels of freedom, violence in society, political situation) and intrinsic factors (subjective well-being, optimism or pessimism, egocentrism or altruism).[14]

Almost forty years ago, when he was running for the US presidency, Senator Robert Kennedy made the following visionary declaration:

> *For too long we seem to have surrendered personal excellence and community value in the mere accumulation of material things. Our gross national product now is over 800 billion dollars a year, but that gross national product, if we judge the United States of America by that, that gross national product counts air pollution, and cigarette advertising, and ambulances to clear our highways of carnage. It counts special locks for our doors and the jails for people who break them. It counts the destruction of the redwoods and the loss of our natural wonder in chaotic squall. It counts Napalm, and it counts nuclear warheads, and armored cars for the police to fight the riots in our city. It counts Whitman's rifles and Speck's knifes and the television programs which glorify violence in order to sell toys to our children.*
>
> *"Yet, the gross national product does not allow for the health of our children, the quality of their education, or the joy of their play; it does not include the beauty of our poetry or the strength of our marriages, the intelligence of our public debate or the integrity of our public officials. It measures neither our wit nor our courage, neither our wisdom nor our learning, neither our compassion nor our devotion to our country; it measures everything in short except that which makes life worthwhile.*[15]

Toward New Criteria of Prosperity

No nation wants to feel that its prosperity is in decline, and any fall in GDP is concerning and leads to a sense of failure. But if a country's prosperity were measured in terms of economic performance, well-being, and environmental integrity, then leaders and citizens could enjoy annual growth in the last two indicators, even if GDP were not going up. Detailed below are several initiatives that, with the support of numerous influential economists[16] and politicians, have attempted to integrate these three elements into a coherent framework.

The *Genuine Progress Indicator (GPI)*, used by the Californian organization Redefining Progress, calculates people's economic input by factoring in domestic and voluntary work, and subtracting pollution and social inequality. In the years 1950 to 2002, the rate of life satisfaction bore no resemblance to that of GDP in the United States, but was much more consistent with that of GPI trends.

The *Human Development Index (IDH)* published by the UNDP covers quality of education, life expectancy, and GDP. It does, however, have the downside of not having an environmental criterion.

Since 1987, two American sociologists from the Fordham Institute, Marc and Marque-Luisa Miringoff, have calculated an *Index of Social Health (ISH)* comprising sixteen criteria, including infant mortality and child poverty, child abuse, teenage suicide and drug abuse as well as high school dropout rates, unemployment, income inequality, access to affordable housing, crime rates, poverty among those aged 65 and over, and life expectancy.[17] It should be noted that these criteria do not include any evaluation of subjective well-being, which is an indicator of life satisfaction levels among citizens.

At the same time, the economists Herman Daly and John Cobb, in their book *For the Common Good*, developed an *Index of Sustainable Economic Welfare (ISEW)* with the aim of addressing the most obvious limitations of GDP.[18] For example, they take GDP and subtract activities that are harmful to sustainable development—first and foremost, pollution and environmental degradation—and add activities that improve the state of the environment. Daly and Cobb observe that, up to a certain point, rising GDP goes hand in hand with increased well-being, especially in poor countries. Yet beyond a certain level, rising

GDP results in decreased well-being and environmental degradation because of the harm caused by excessive consumption.

The Chilean economist Manfred Max-Neef, who took part in the *gross national happiness (GNH)* talks in Bhutan, has for his part proposed a model that incorporates nine fundamental human needs, including not just typical material requirements, but also the need for protection, freedom, participation (in society), and affection. His model is based on six principles:

- The economy is to serve people and people are not to serve the economy;
- Development is about people and not about objects;
- Growth is not the same as development and development does not necessarily require growth;
- No economy is possible without the ecosystem's services;
- The economy is a subsystem of a larger and finite system, the biosphere, hence permanent growth is impossible;
- Under no circumstances whatsoever can an economic process, or interest, take precedence over the reverence of life.

In the United Kingdom, following a 2012 report on the people's well-being, Prime Minister David Cameron was accused of worrying about problems that were of minor importance to the country, to which he issued the following response: "To those who say that all this sounds like a distraction from the serious business of government, I would say, that finding out what will really improve lives and acting on it is actually the serious business of government."

Three Essential Indicators: Balanced Prosperity, Contentment with Life, Quality of the Environment

The most promising aspect of the GNH proposed by Bhutan is that it engenders a long-term vision. As such, it is attracting the attention of a growing number of economists, sociologists, and politicians. In contrast to the indices mentioned above, GNH is closely linked to subjective happiness, and has honed a set of criteria by which to measure and assess it, but it also factors in social wealth indicators (voluntary work, cooperation, etc.) and natural wealth (e.g. valuing unspoiled natural heritage) as a complement to economic prosperity, which ceases to be the sole priority.

The Kingdom of Bhutan, which recently became a constitutional monarchy, is a country in the Himalayas roughly the same size as Switzerland, with a population just over 700,000 people. It entered the age of sustainable development directly from the Middle Ages, skipping the phase of overexploiting natural resources that has so affected most other countries. Their track record is an inspiration: contrary to all other Asian countries (with the exception of Vietnam), where the coverage of natural habitats such as forest, wetlands, prairie, glaciers, etc., has decreased, in Bhutan it has *increased* over the past twenty years, rising from 60% of the country's area to 70%.

The country as a whole absorbs four times more carbon than it emits, and the few chemical fertilizers used in a handful of places are to be banned in the next five years. Nowadays, only 5% of farmers use chemical fertilizers and 2% use pesticides. Recently, Bhutan sent several tons of chemical fertilizers and pesticides to Switzerland to be incinerated.

Hunting and fishing are illegal throughout the country,[19] as is the sale of tobacco. Bhutan is also the only country in the world where advertising is banned. Education and health care are free. What's more, inspired by its Buddhist culture with its emphasis on inner peace, the state has decided to make the pursuit of happiness its absolute priority. The Bhutanese are entirely aware of the fact that they still have a lot of responsibility for improving the quality of life in their country, and that GNH is not some magic formula, but they have the merit of having chosen priorities that are conducive to bringing about a prosperity based on four fundamental pillars: sustainable development, environmental preservation, cultural preservation, and good governance.

The former prime minister of Bhutan, Lyonchen Jigme Thinley, emphasizes the degree to which it is essential to have a long-term future vision. When he asked some of his foreign counterparts what their vision of their country's future was in fifty years' time, he was shocked to notice that they often seemed to be "groping around in the dark."[20]

This adventure began in 1972, when, following his accession to the throne, the country's fourth king, Jigme Singye Wangchuck,[21] declared in a famous speech that "gross national happiness is more important than gross national product." When this concept was first introduced at international conferences, Bhutanese representatives were greeted with wry smiles. Since then, however, this new prosperity paradigm has gained ground and attracted the attention of some of today's biggest economists. As Joseph Stiglitz comments:

> *When Bhutan took up GNH, some people said that it was because they wanted to take attention away from lack of development. I think quite the contrary. The crisis has made us aware of how bad our metrics were even in economics, because US GDP looked good, and then we realized it was all a phantasm.*[22]

In July 2011, a resolution entitled "Happiness: towards a holistic approach to development," tabled by Bhutan and cosponsored by 68 countries, was unanimously adopted by the 193 member-states of the United Nations. In April 2012 at the United Nations headquarters in New York, a full day, which I attended, was set aside to implement this resolution. On this occasion, Secretary-General Ban Ki-moon made the following declaration:

> *While material prosperity is important, it is far from being the only determinant of well-being.... Bhutan has recognized the supremacy of national happiness over national income since the 1970s. It has famously adopted the goal of Gross National Happiness over Gross National Product. Such thinking is now gaining ground in other regions. Costa Rica is well-known for being the "greenest" country in the world—an example of holistic environmentally responsible development. Compared to other countries with similar income levels, it ranks higher in human development, and it is a beacon of peace and democracy.*[23]

That day, at a preparatory meeting organized by The Earth Institute, which is directed by Jeffrey Sachs of Columbia University, three Nobel Prize–winning economists, scientists, philosophers,[24] and representatives from several countries (including the president of Costa Rica and a large Brazilian delegation) implemented an action plan. Since that moment, the movement has not stopped gathering momentum. Besides

Bhutan and Costa Rica, the governments of Brazil and Japan have now taken measures to include gross national happiness in their political agenda. The province of Alberta in Canada has also established a "Canadian well-being index," along with relevant tools for measuring it.

The European Commission has launched its "Beyond GDP" project, while the Organisation for Economic Co-operation and Development (OECD), represented at the United Nations by its chief statistician, Martine Durand, has also drawn up its own guidelines for measuring well-being.

National Accounts That Recognize the Value of Natural and Human Capital

GDP only takes into account the market's monetary transactions. When forests are flattened and the oceans emptied of all life, the results show up as positive growth on the GDP balance sheet. There is a double perversion here, since not only does this system fail to consider the value of natural goods, but also it allows their degradation to represent economic profit.[25] As Lyonchen Jigme Thinley explains:

> *If we were to cut down all our forests in Bhutan, GDP would mushroom, because GDP only counts the timber value of our forests once they are cut and sold at market. GDP takes no account at all of the resources we leave behind, and so it entirely ignores the value of our standing forests.... Because those values are invisible in GDP, it's no wonder the world has accumulated a massive ecological debt that appears in no country's national accounts.*[26]

The sociologist Dominique Méda agrees wholeheartedly: "By driving this logic through to its conclusion, it could be argued that a society that destroys itself completely, that consumes and devastates itself, will get richer and richer, up until the point it has nothing left to sell."[27]

If a country has more crime, pollution, war, and disease, GDP increases as a result of financial transactions relating to expenditure in prisons, policing, weapons, and health care. This increase enters the accounts as a positive indicator of a growing economy, even though it represents a decline in well-being. In addition, Jigme Thinley says that:

> *GDP entirely ignores a whole range of productive economic activity that genuinely does contribute to well-being—ignoring it simply because no money is exchanged. And so, volunteer work, community service, and the vital unpaid work done in households count for nothing in GDP, and the precious free time that we need to meditate, garden, and socialize with family and friends is completely value-less in GDP.*

This point was illustrated by the American psychologist Tim Kasser at a conference on Buddhism and consumer society, which took place in Bangkok in 2008: "Today I spent a wonderful morning in the park with my son. Aside from the pure joy of being together, we discovered all manner of tropical flowers and multicolored birds, and the beauty and calm of the place did us a great deal of good. Imagine if instead I had taken my son to do some shopping at the supermarket, and then afterwards we had taken a *tuk-tuk* that crashed into a car. The driver would have been wounded, nothing serious, but we would have had to take him to hospital, and a fine would have been imposed on the other driver responsible for the crash: all that would have been better in terms of GDP."

One of the first modern economists, Jean-Baptiste Say, stated in 1803 that air, water, and light are not goods that would generally come under the heading of "wealth."[28] Yet it is clear that the quality of both air and water has a marked influence on our quality of life, and that they must, along with the inexhaustible energy source that is sunlight, be considered natural capital. Wijkman and Rockström, the former a politician, the latter an environmental scientist, also direct our attention to the fact that we cannot indefinitely expect artificial goods to take the place of natural goods: a situation where wood is replaced with plastic and human endeavor with machines has its limits.[29] There is no replacement for clean air, intact vegetation, and healthy, fertile land. It is therefore essential to distinguish between and calculate at fair value the different types of capital—industrial, financial, human, and natural—and grant each one the importance it deserves.

Moreover, GDP itself continues to grow for as long as an entire country gets richer, even if that represents the richest 1% that dominates the majority of wealth acquired, while GNH is incompatible with social injustice and rampant inequality between rich and poor.

Recently, some European countries, including Italy, decided to include drug and human trafficking in their GDP, even though these are clearly deeply damaging to the fabric of society. There are plenty of other examples of this absurd way of managing national accounts: according to current economic doctrine, the more fossil fuels we burn and resulting greenhouse gases we produce, the more GDP increases and the "wealthier" we become. The true negative consequences of climate change remain invisible—for the time being, at least. The example of the devastating oil spills in the Gulf of Mexico show that the real cost of petrol is never reflected in the price we see at the pump; the national accounting systems in force take no heed of ecological damage. To top off the irony, even the cost of the cleanup and the repairs to the facilities contribute to an increase in GDP.

The fact that our natural capital has sustained such considerable losses and that certain ecosystems are on the verge of becoming irreversibly degraded does not feature anywhere in the accounts. The only negative figures occasionally taken into consideration are those that pertain to wear and tear to machinery and buildings—but never to the planet.[30]

Economists take particular exception to considering "externalities," a term that refers to the indirect consequences of economic activity. At no point does a forestry company that demolishes 1,000 hectares factor into its accounts the externality represented by the loss of oxygen production and CO_2 absorption, soil erosion, and the loss of biodiversity triggered by the trees' removal.

Even the word "externality" shows the extent to which the nefarious effects of economic activity are considered secondary inconveniences and undesirable irritations in the overall scheme of things. In reality, because of the severity of their impact on living conditions, these externalities have taken on such significance that they are at the point of transcending all the other central concerns of economists. We must therefore discard this notion of externality and factor the variables they represent into our economic evaluations.

In short, natural capital—the value of intact forest, freshwater reserves, wetlands, biodiversity—must be measured at its fair value and included in a nation's balance sheet in the same way as financial returns or gold reserves, for example. It is a priceless treasure, after all, and any economy that does not incorporate this natural capital is fundamentally skewed.

In fact, The Economics of Ecosystems and Biodiversity, or TEEB, a United Nations initiative, engaged in a series of investigations that laid the foundation for a national accounts system that factors in the state of ecosystems.

Back in Bhutan in 2012–2013, under the Gross National Happiness Commission directed by Dasho Karma Ura, many international experts inspired by this unique experiment lent their services to guarantee the success of this new economic data. In particular, Robert Costanza and Ida Kubiszewski carried out the first ever estimation of the value of a country's natural capital—Bhutan, as it happened—settling on the figure of 760 billion ngultrums (the Bhutanese currency), equivalent to 11 billion euros, for the services provided by the ecosystem each year. This is 4.4 times more than Bhutan's GDP. What's more, the services provided by the ecosystem (forestry, first and foremost) extend beyond Bhutan's borders, since their contribution to the regulation of the climate, carbon storage, and river basin protection benefits other countries.

Bhutan's national accounts also incorporate social capital, including the amount of time people spend volunteering to support their fellow citizens by clearing up refuse, repairing important public buildings, fighting fires, or helping the sick, elderly, or handicapped. They also take into account negative health costs linked to alcoholism (instead of regarding alcohol and tobacco sales as positive contributors) and several other harmful consumer goods. If you sell tobacco, the GDP goes up. Then people go to hospital to be treated for lung cancer. The GDP goes up again. Finally those who don't survive die and the funeral director is called in. The GDP goes up yet again. But according to the GNH paradigm, all this would be accounted as a loss of social capital.

This new economic paradigm therefore allows the savings made when crime reduces to be factored into the national accounts, as well as profits arising from the health care system following the ban on selling tobacco (lower mortality rates due to the decrease in lung cancer, heart disease, and respiratory problems).

As for subjective well-being, the Bhutanese, led by Dasho Karma Ura, have developed a set of questionnaires that are much more detailed and sophisticated than most surveys used elsewhere in the world to evaluate happiness. Some of the questions posed to a representative sample of 8,000 inhabitants included: "How many times have you felt jealous in the last two weeks?"; "How well do you sleep?"; "How many people could you count on if you were to fall sick?"; "How many times a day do you drop in and socialize with your neighbors?"; "Do you talk about spirituality often with your children?"; or even, "Do you practice meditation?"

According to the former prime minister: "If we can demonstrate the viability of a national accounts system based on GNH (rather than GDP) to set a course and move forward in a healthy and balanced way, then that will represent one of the greatest contributions our little country has made to the rest of the world."

Contrary to rumors that have gone round, the new Bhutanese prime minister, Lyonchen Tshering Topgay, has not turned his back on the country's implementation of the gross national happiness concept, which is written into the Bhutanese constitution.[31] Following his election in September 2013, at the opening session of the Parliament, he declared: "Some are concerned that I do not believe in GNH. Today, I ask them to put their fears to rest. I am not only a firm believer of GNH, but a practitioner." Likewise, in an interview with *The Guardian* in 2014, he stated that: "What's changed with our government is that we believe our priority must be at home. We must remove the obstacles to GNH and be true to it within the country.... In doing business, companies will need to take GNH very seriously; your business will be respectful and add value to the good of society, respect our values and culture, add to the wealth of our environment, and help us to achieve a green economy, one that is fuelled by sustainable competitiveness.... GNH is a platform to achieve and to excel. It's a platform to dream differently and to articulate a vision that is sustainable for Bhutan and maybe for the world."[32]

An Ecology of Well-Being

We have placed a great deal of emphasis on the environment in terms of natural wealth, and on the essential importance of its preservation for the future prosperity of the biosphere. But we must also highlight the fact that the presence of a healthy natural environment has a remarkable effect on subjective well-being. In his book *An Ecology of Happiness*,

Éric Lambin, professor at the Universities of Louvain and Stanford, presents a summary of several studies showing that despite the contingencies of modern life, we are still intimately linked to Nature.[33]

The Slovenian physicist Aleksander Zidansek has identified a positive correlation between the (subjective) life satisfaction of the inhabitants of a given country and that country's environmental performance indicators.[34] He has also shown that a country's CO_2 emissions are inversely proportional to the well-being of its citizens.

As for the father of sociobiology, E. O. Wilson, he talks of "biophilia" and observes the extent to which mankind has an innate emotional affinity with other living beings, the plant world, and natural landscapes. This timeless, age-old relationship with Nature, a profound part of our own biological make-up, has been the object of a particularly substantial body of scientific research. In addition, when different people are presented with photographs of various landscapes, the ones they appreciate most are those depicting vast, verdant landscapes with a scattering of trees and areas of water.[35]

It is quite astonishing that this preference is observed regardless of the geographical origin of the individual being asked, including among the Inuit, who have never even seen such landscapes. These reactions can undoubtedly be explained by the fact that for our ancestors from sub-Saharan Africa, relatively high open spaces with a few trees for shelter would have offered an ideal opportunity for looking out for both predators, of whom they were fearful, and game, on which they relied for food. The verdant element evokes plenty, and water sources represent vital conditions for survival. Looking at such landscapes instills a sense of peace, safety, and contentment in most of us.

A study published in the journal *Science* by the American geographer Roger Ulrich has also shown that patients convalescing from surgery recover more quickly when their hospital bed looks out on a natural landscape—a park or a lake—than on a brick wall or a building. On average, the former left hospital one day sooner than the latter, had less need for painkillers, and the nurses found that they were more pleasant as patients.[36]

Similarly, in a prison in Michigan, it was observed that prisoners whose cell window looked out on an inner courtyard required medical attention 24% more frequently than those prisoners whose windows gave out onto the countryside.[37]

MUTUALITY: INTEGRATING ECONOMIC, SOCIAL, AND NATURAL CAPITAL WITHIN A COMPANY

Can a capitalist company apply these principles of sustainable harmony and factor the three crucial indicators—namely material prosperity, life satisfaction, and environmental conservation—into its balance sheet? This is, in any event, the plan laid out by the company Mars, best known for its chocolate bars of the same name, even though it sells many other food products, such as Snickers, Bounty, Uncle Ben's rice, Suzi Wan, various tea and coffee brands, and pet food (Pedigree, Petcare, Whiskas), as well as organic seeds (Seeds of Change). Mars directly employs some 80,000 people and owns 160 factories, with 35 billion dollars of capital (twenty times more than Danone, just as a point of reference). A privately held family-owned company, it can be fairly free in deciding how it orients itself.

For about the last ten years, Mars has asked a team headed up by the French economist Bruno Roche to implement a system that lets the company reconcile the three prerequisites for sustainable harmony: economic prosperity; the quality of life of everyone involved in the company's business activities, including small producers; and protecting the environment. In order to do this, Mars had to be open to the idea of limiting its profits in order to accommodate the other two components.

And so Roche came up with the concept of "mutuality," which, according to him, can allow businesses to meet today's challenges relating to dwindling natural resources, environmental degradation, and the pernicious effects of social inequality.

The expression "economics of mutuality" refers to the fact that profit must be *shared mutually* by investors, workers, and the environment. It rests on three pillars that must be constantly respected and upheld: *nature,* which supplies resources and which we must take care of; *work,* which uses and transforms these resources, and which must be fairly rewarded for doing so; and *capital,* which serves to guarantee continuity for several consecutive projects. Nature, work, and capital must be "remunerated," each in its own way, if we are to avoid shaking and destabilizing these pillars of prosperity.

As Roche has explained to me in discussions we've been having over the years, different schools of thought have led to an unbalanced approach to these three pillars: Marxist economics seeks to remunerate work at the expense of capital and nature; free-market economics without any regulation seeks to reward only capital; while purist ecologists focus exclusively on environmental conservation. As far as Roche is concerned, it is essential to integrate these three components constructively, since they are omnipresent in human activity.

The economics of mutuality therefore takes into serious consideration the well-being of those people involved in economic activity; it is also prepared to protect natural resources at the expense of economic gain. Mars has now launched a pilot project in one sector of its activity (coffee), and if all goes according to plan, the idea is to roll the model out across the entire company. Although the company has remained fairly discreet about this initiative, it hopes to inspire others to adopt this alternative model centering on sustainable development.

Somewhere between philanthropy, which requires a donation-based approach, and social enterprise, which takes profit and reinvests it to further a social cause without paying out a dividend to shareholders, the economics of mutuality could allow big businesses to function in a way that is more respectful of gross national happiness and the biosphere.

In his book *The Third Industrial Revolution*, the political commentator Jeremy Rifkin concludes:

> *The critical task at hand is to harness the public capital, market capital, and especially the social capital of the human race to the mission of transitioning the world in a Third Industrial Revolution and a post-carbon era.... Only when we begin to think as an extended global family, that not only includes our own species but all our fellow travelers in this evolutionary sojourn on Earth, will we be able to save our common biosphere community and renew the planet for future generations.*[38]

43

Local Commitment, Global Responsibility

A politician thinks of the next election, a Statesman of the next generation.

—James Freeman Clarke[1]

Nationalism is to nations what individualism is to individuals. In the same way that society's problems can only be resolved when each person takes part in implementing solutions that have been devised on a collective basis, so the world's problems can only be addressed through collaboration between countries and the international institutions whose authority they recognize.

To meet the many challenges that concern us all, particularly those involving the degradation of the environment, heads of state should play a role at the global level that is equivalent to that of provincial authorities within a nation.[2] At the same time as administering their national affairs, they should defer to international authorities the power to make decisions that affect the fate of the planet as a whole.

Global warming, the loss of biodiversity, air and water pollution, the melting of glaciers, and ocean degradation are problems that local bodies acting alone simply do not have the capacity to control. These bodies must, however, be closely involved in the process of implementing global solutions.

All of these phenomena are strongly interconnected, but they are also linked to issues such as health, poverty, social justice, human rights, rampant financial systems, and many other difficulties. It is therefore essential to provide integrated solutions that control the global running of human affairs.

If a World State is, in the opinion of the French philosopher André Comte-Sponville, neither possible nor desirable, we are clearly in need of a world politics that goes "in the direction of a united humanity on a unique planet, which is trying to preserve what is essential.... Global governance will work neither against the State, nor without it."[3]

Pascal Lamy, who was Director-General of the World Trade Organization for eight years, made the following statement: "Global governance describes the system we put in place to help human society achieve its common objective in a sustainable manner, that is to say with fairness and justice."[4] In his view, the best way to install greater fairness and justice is to have more global governance. The management of collective global goods—especially environmental goods—forms the basis of global governance, taking into consideration the fact that purely national responses are no longer sufficient. This opinion is shared by Laurence Tubiana, founder of the Institute for Sustainable Development, and Jean-Michel Severino, former director of the French Development Agency (AFD), for whom "refocusing the doctrine of international cooperation on the concept of public goods offers the possibility... of breaking the deadlock in international negotiations on development, with the perception of shared interests breathing new life into an international solidarity that is running out of steam."[5]

According to an appeal launched by members of Collegium International[6] in March 2012: "A new global order for how the world works has become essential." In order to do this, men and women across the world must recognize that they are interdependent on multiple levels—between continents, nations, and as individuals—and to be aware of our common destiny. The interests of our human community can only be safeguarded by measures that are common to everyone, even if they run contrary to near-sighted national interests, local selfishness, the hegemony of multinationals, and the machinations of lobbyists who meddle with policy, often transforming the international scene into a gathering-place where sordid haggling prevails.

What Government for the World?

The term *governance,* or the "act or manner of governing," was a synonym for *government* in Old French until the fourteenth century. It became obsolete but then reappeared in the 1990s. Although it is a term that irritates certain thinkers, such as the Canadian academic Alain Deneault, who considers it to be a way of justifying private enterprises' stranglehold on the state,[7] the expression "global governance" now describes the set of rules used to organize human society on a planetary scale.[8]

According to Pierre Jacquet, director of the French Institute on International Relations (IFRI), the economist Jean Pisani-Ferry, and Laurence Tubiana: "sustainable economic integration requires that the populations reap the benefits, that the states agree on the objectives, and that the governing institutions are perceived as legitimate."[9] These three conditions are still a long way from being fulfilled.

International authorities with executive power must be able to control everything that is related to global health, human and animal rights, international justice, poverty, arms control measures, and environmental issues.

Building responsible global governance that allows a society's political organization to adapt to globalization involves the formation of legitimate democratic policy at every level: local, state, regional, global. In order to do this, we need a network of international organizations that are fair, transparent, and democratic, and which are bestowed with significant resources and far-reaching capacities for intervention.

We have already mentioned the remarkable advances that have been made in the twentieth century: the adoption of the Universal Declaration of Human Rights, the creation of the United Nations, the WHO, WTO, FAO, the International Labour Organization, the International Court of Justice, the European Community, and many other international organizations. These have already accomplished a great deal, even if they are sometimes hindered by those that promote their own sovereign interests over those of the global community, not to mention other conflicts of interest.

Others are more controversial, such as international financial institutions, especially the World Bank, the IMF, and the Bank for International Settlements (BIS), since they remain for the most part under the control of the United States, which determines their policies. China and India, which now represent almost a quarter of world GDP, only have, on average, 5% of the votes in these institutions.[10] Joseph Stiglitz points out that the need for international institutions like the IMF, the World Bank, and the WTO has never been so great, but people's trust in them has never been so low.[11]

The IMF and the World Bank, for example, help developing countries, but force them in return to open their markets to subsidized Western commodities, such as agricultural products, and to adopt restructuring measures that harm their local economies, particularly with regard to small producers who cannot compete with big multinationals.

Jacquet, Pisani-Ferry, and Tubiana talk of international institutions as being incomplete, which can be attributed to the gap that "has emerged between the nature of the problems to be handled and the international architecture: the latter has not adjusted to the scale of current problems. For example, the environment has become a major area of concern and negotiation, yet it has not been endowed with the adequate institutional structure."[12]

How can we make the step forward from local engagement to global responsibility? It will require three levels of transformation: individual, community, and global.

Transforming Ourselves in Order to Transform the World

This could well be the slogan for an approach that couples personal engagement with global responsibility. My personal experience of being immersed in the world of humanitarian action for the past twelve years has shown me that what throws sand in the gears most often is corruption, battles of egos, and other human imperfections. Setting out with the aim of helping others, people end up completely losing sight of the virtuous goal they hoped to achieve.

To want to rush headlong into working for the good of others, without getting prepared first, is like wanting to carry out a medical operation immediately in the street, without taking the required time to learn medicine and build hospitals. Of course the years of study and the countless tasks required to build a hospital do not heal anyone, but once they are complete, they allow us to care for the sick infinitely more efficiently.

The first thing to do if you want to help others, therefore, is to develop your own compassion, altruistic love, and courage enough to be able to serve these others without betraying your original intention. Remedying our own egocentrism is a powerful way of serving those around us. We must therefore not underestimate the importance of personal transformation.

Community Engagement: The NGO Revolution

After personal transformation comes community engagement. In *Une brève histoire de l'avenir* (A Brief History of the Future), Jacques Attali declares that we are moving toward a formidable increase in the power of altruism thanks to nongovernmental organizations, which, in his opinion, will one day govern the world.[13]

In order to achieve this, NGOs, which have sprung from engagement at the local level and from social movements, must learn to cooperate so as to create a global synergy and build their capacities.

According to the psychologist Paul Ekman, the difference between the highly motivated members of an NGO and those of big international organizations, who are often out of touch, lies in the feeling of an emotional connection with those whose conditions they are trying to improve, as well as with those who share their vision and work alongside them. In *Empathy: A Handbook for Revolution,* philosopher Roman Krznaric gives many inspiring examples of people who have immersed themselves in the lives of the poor, the homeless, and racially discriminated African American or Turkish immigrant workers, in order to gain a truly empathetic insight into their living conditions.

This community engagement is often sparked by the strength of ideas, by imagination and creativity, and the inspirational power of major moral figures such as Nelson Mandela or the Dalai Lama, as well as social entrepreneurs who marry a long-term altruistic vision with astonishingly efficient activity, like Muhammad Yunus, Fazle Abed, Vandana Shiva, Bunker Roy, and many others. It is essential to kindle hope and arouse enthusiasm at the same time as implementing pragmatic solutions capable of being replicated on a broader scale.

Environmental NGOs influenced the decision to adopt the Kyoto Protocol on the reduction of greenhouse gases. The work of Handicap International and the International Campaign to Ban Landmines (ICBL), whose founding coordinator, Jody Williams, won the Nobel Peace Prize, brought about the Ottawa Treaty to ban landmines. Amnesty International and the International Federation for Human Rights (FIDH), for their part, helped found the International Criminal Court. Greenpeace campaigns have led to the adoption of numerous important (though still largely insufficient) measures to protect the environment.

Big international NGOs like Oxfam, Care, Amnesty International, Human Rights Watch, Médecins Sans Frontières, Médecins du Monde, Save the Children, Action Against Hunger, Greenpeace, or Max Havelaar produce public goods all over the world, but still have little influence in countries ruled by dictatorships, for whom the very term "nongovernmental organization" is seen as a threat. In democratic states, however, their independent and objective status allows them to mobilize opinion, offer solutions, and, with more or less success, put pressure on governments.

Smaller NGOs, on the other hand, which have been set up by the million, are often capable of working extremely effectively at the local level by managing to avoid, so far as possible, incurring the wrath of authoritarian regimes, and carrying out work in the realms of health care, education, and social services that would normally be carried out by a functioning state. They embody the spirit of solidarity and determination that can be found among civilian populations in all societies.

Attaching Greater Importance to Civil Society

Henry Mintzberg, a professor at McGill University in Canada with a strong reputation in the field of management, has proposed a radical revitalization of civil society, what he calls the "plural" sector, which comprises charities, foundations, community and nongovernmental organizations, professional associations, cooperatives, mutual funds, health organizations, and nonprofit schools and universities, as well as other organizations for whom it is inherently easier to inspire a group dynamic, create a set of values, and take a more responsible approach with regard to collective goods: natural resources and human communities.[14]

He thinks that we have to transcend the linear politics of left, right, and center, and to understand that a balanced society, like a stool that doesn't wobble, needs to have three solid pillars: a public sector made up of political forces embodied by well-respected governments, a private sector made up of economic forces embodied by responsible businesses, and a plural sector of social forces embodied by robust civilian communities. A harmonious, solidarity-based society is therefore achieved when there is a balance between these three areas. Nowadays, the plural sector is the weakest of the three, and must be strengthened if it is to take its place alongside the other two in order to achieve a balance in society. "Some countries, such as the United States or the United Kingdom, need to develop it in the face of extreme pressure from the private sector; others, like China, must do it under equally extreme pressure from the public sector; Brazil, and maybe India, are in my opinion the closest to achieving a balance between the three sectors, and are in this sense the best examples of the economic model to come."[15]

Mintzberg provocatively defines the capitalist credo as follows: "greed is good, markets are sacrosanct, property is sacred, and governments are suspect." He is no kinder to totalitarian regimes, which are at the opposite extreme, withdrawing power from the hands of the people and placing it entirely in the grip of the state. Both cases lead to imbalance.

For Mintzberg, governance structures are stuck in a form of individualistic democracy that goes back to the eighteenth century, whereas resolving today's problems requires above all else cooperation at the international level. He thinks that community groups in the plural sector are the best suited to creating the social initiatives that we need. A whole host of these are already underway thanks to social media, but many others are needed to dislodge the unhealthy alliance between big business and government.

In *The Third Industrial Revolution,* Jeremy Rifkin describes civil society as the place where humans create social capital. He too deplores the fact that civil society has been relegated to the background and deemed marginal by comparison with the economy or the state, even though it is the principal domain in which civilization develops:

> *There is no example I can think of in history where a people first set up markets and governments, and then later created a culture. Rather, markets and governments are extensions of culture... The civil society is where we generate social capital—which is really accumulated trust—that is invested in markets and governance. If markets and governance destroy the social trust vested in them, people will eventually withdraw their support or force a reorganization of the other two sectors.*[16]

Rifkin reminds us that civil society is also an emerging economic force, and that a 2010 study taking in more than forty countries by the Johns Hopkins Center for Civil Society Studies found that the nonprofit "third" sector represents an average of 5% of GDP in the eight countries investigated most closely,[17] which is more, for example, than that represented by utilities companies (electricity, water, gas), and puts it on par with the building trade (5.1%).[18]

In numerous countries, the "third sector" also represents a large percentage of jobs. Millions of people work in it on a voluntary basis, but millions of others are employed by these organizations on a salaried basis. In the forty-two countries studied, the nonprofit sector employs around 5.6% of the economically active population. At the moment, Europe is experiencing the sharpest growth in the nonprofit sector.[19]

Contrary to what was happening only ten years ago, many young people are spurning traditional careers in the private and public sectors in favor of the nonprofit sector.[20]

Integrating Our Understanding of Interdependence

To make the step from community engagement to global responsibility, it is essential to realize that all things are interdependent, and to assimilate that worldview in such a way that it influences our every action. Altruism and compassion are intimately linked to this understanding of interdependence, since it allows us to bring down the illusory wall that we erect between "myself" and "others," between "I" and "we," making us feel responsible for our world and its inhabitants. As the Dalai Lama explains:

> *To acquire a sense of universal responsibility—to perceive the universal dimension of each of our actions and each person's duty towards happiness and non-suffering—is to acquire a state of mind that, when we see an opportunity to help others, drives us to seize it rather than worrying solely about our own petty self-interest.*[21]

Globalization for Better and for Worse

How can we altruistically link local community action to that which affects the planet as a whole? In *The Path to Hope,* Stéphane Hessel and Edgar Morin examine the frequently incongruous aspects of globalization:

> *We must understand that globalization constitutes both the best and the worst thing that could ever happen to mankind. The best because all the scattered fragments of humanity have become interdependent for the first time, creating a shared fate.... The worst because it has triggered a frantic race toward a succession of catastrophes.*[22]

This view is shared by Joseph Stiglitz, who does not see globalization as an evil in itself, but rather something that becomes perverse when states manage it in such a way that benefits vested interests, especially those of multinationals or dictators. Relying on people, countries, and economies around the world can be just as effective a way of creating prosperity as it can be for spreading greed and exacerbating poverty.[23]

Even though 70% of its population lives below the poverty line, Nigeria has many billionaires who have accrued immense wealth through the worldwide sale of the country's oil reserves. The same is true of many developing countries. In such cases, we see globalization perverted through the alliance between wicked political institutions—which allow oligarchs to accumulate private fortunes—and multinationals whose sole aim is the endless accumulation of profit, even if it means leaving local communities to languish in appalling poverty. As the historian Francis Fukuyama has pointed out, bad institutions exist because it is in the interests of powerful political forces within the poor country itself to maintain the status quo.[24]

For Stiglitz, "globalization as [it is] currently managed promotes neither global efficiency nor equity; even more importantly, it puts our democracy in peril."[25]

Globalization that is unobstructed and does not take into careful consideration the situation of those who are affected by it cannot effectively serve the majority, and benefits only the most powerful.

Harvard professor Dani Rodrik writes in *The Globalization Paradox*[26] that, even though economic globalization has increased the level of prosperity in developed countries and provided employment to hundreds of millions of poor workers in China and elsewhere in Asia—work that often verges on bona fide exploitation—the concept is built on shaky foundations, and its long-term viability is in no way guaranteed. Rodrik's argument centers on a fundamental "trilemma": that we cannot simultaneously pursue democracy, national self-determination, and economic globalization. Give too much power to governments, and you have protectionism. Give markets too much freedom, and you have an unstable world economy with little social and political support for those it is supposed to help. Rodrik argues for smart globalization, not maximum globalization.

What we need is not globalization based on the economic exploitation of Third World countries, but globalization based on access to health care, knowledge (scientific as well as traditional), and bringing about conditions of peace and freedom that let each person realize the fullness of their potential. For Hessel and Morin, it is essential that we work out how to globalize and deglobalize: we must maintain and develop "every aspect of globalization that fosters fellowship and cultural vitality,"[27] but at the same time we must deglobalize in order to restore vital forms of autonomy to local populations and promote cultural diversity, local economies, agroecology, local food supplies, and small-scale artisans and businesses, not to mention safeguarding traditional practices and expertise that have stood the test of centuries.

As Pascal Lamy notes, "That there is a widening gap between global challenges and the ways of working out solutions is no longer in dispute today. One of the most important consequences of this gap is, in my view, the feeling of dispossession which is spreading among the citizens of this planet. Dispossession of their own destiny, dispossession of the means to act on an individual level as well as at a national level—to say nothing of the global one."[28] In his view, it is not globalization that is creating this impression, but the absence of appropriate ways to deal with it—the absence of democratic governance at the required level, that is, the global level.

UNIVERSALITY OF RIGHTS, RESPONSIBILITY OF EACH INDIVIDUAL

Stéphane Hessel, during an interview with the Dalai Lama, made the following remark:

> *The authors of the Universal Declaration were focusing not on the West, but on all humanity. Its authors included people from China, Lebanon, Latin America, and India. It was not for nothing that René Cassin was able to attribute the adjective "universal" to this text, alone among all other international documents. We must not let dictators hide behind accusations of Occidentalism in order to escape the provisions of this text.*[29]

The Dalai Lama unambiguously supported this position:

> *Certain governments in Asia have maintained that the human rights criteria set out in the Universal Declaration were asserted by the West and that they cannot be applied in Asia or other parts of the developing world for reasons of cultural difference and discrepancies in levels of social and economic development. I do not share this perspective... since it is in the nature of all human beings to aspire to liberty, equality, and dignity, and those in the East have the same rights in this respect as anyone else.... Diversity of culture and tradition cannot under any circumstances justify human rights violations. As such, discrimination against women, people from different backgrounds, and people from more vulnerable parts of society, can in some regions stem from tradition, but if they run contrary to*

universally recognized human rights, then these behaviors must change.[30]

AN INFORMED DEMOCRACY AND AN ACCOUNTABLE MERITOCRACY

How do we ensure that people get the best of all possible governments? As the Dalai Lama said after "freely, joyously, and proudly" putting an end to four centuries of collusion between spiritual power and earthly power with the establishment of a fully democratic Tibetan administration in exile: "The time of dictators and religious leaders having a stranglehold on governments is over. The world belongs to 7 billion human beings, and it is them and only them who must decide democratically on the fate of humankind." These words have been uttered many times since 2011, when he handed over the last remnants of political authority that had until then formed part of his station, at the end of a process of democratization of Tibetan institutions that he had undertaken the moment he arrived in exile on Indian soil.

As Winston Churchill quipped, "Democracy is the worst form of Government, except all those other forms that have been tried from time to time."[31] But how do we make sure that the best decisions for an entire population emerge from an immense mass of individuals who do not always have access to the information needed for a complete understanding of a situation? Dictators have answered that question by deciding on everyone's behalf, and religious leaders by deciding according to the dogmas of their respective creeds. With the odd exception, both camps have caused, and continue to cause, immeasurable suffering.

Most primitive tribes, as we have seen, were fundamentally egalitarian in nature. When they settled, the people who became leaders were generally those who were considered the most wise and experienced, and who had proved themselves the most. The choice of leaders therefore involved both consensus and meritocracy. As communities grew, accumulated wealth, and formed hierarchies, other systems emerged, particularly brutal power struggles and the submission of peoples to the authority of potentates. Human history has ultimately shown that democracy is the only form of government capable of respecting the aspirations of a majority of citizens.

But how do we avoid descending into populism and hasty decisions made to satisfy the demands of those who view politics as an instrument of short-term advantages and inconveniences? Politicians guarantee their reelection by acceding to demands and dare not engage in far-reaching reform whose rewards will not be reaped in the immediate future, and which often involve making unpopular decisions.

The threat of demagoguery is today particularly clear in the case of climate change denial, much in vogue in the United States, whose arguments would melt away a hundred times faster than the Arctic ice cap if a majority of people, the media, and politicians took greater heed of scientific evidence, and if those who were correctly informed were in a position to make the decisions needed to bring about long-term human prosperity. It is also essential for the scientific community to be less prone to yielding to the pressures of the financial markets, which draw researchers away from producing meaningful work in favor of seeking economic gain. The commodification of science and medicine often means that greater importance is attached to the interests of pharmaceutical laboratories than to caring for the sick, in the same way that the interests of big food companies are placed before those of farmers and consumers.[32]

The Berggruen Institute on Governance, founded by the German-born philanthropist Nicolas Berggruen, who decided to dedicate his fortune to improving systems of governance across the world, defines "intelligent governance"[33] as finding a balance between a meritocracy built on a series of choices carried out at different levels of society (from local authorities to national positions of responsibility) and a democratic process that allows citizens to prevent potential shifts in power that might lead to corruption, nepotism, abuses of power, and totalitarianism.[34]

According to Berggruen and the political columnist Nathan Gardels, an *informed democracy* involves maximum decentralization of decision-making power, which needs to be entrusted to citizen bodies active in their relevant areas of expertise.[35] In order to manage and integrate these interdependent yet decentralized powers, the authors state that it would be essential to instate a suitably competent and experienced political authority, which would have an overview of the system and take decisions on matters concerning the collective good of its citizens. This authority would constitute an *enlightened meritocracy,* protected from the immediate interests of pressure groups. But in order to retain legitimacy, the authority must be transparent and accountable, and its activity must be monitored by democratically elected civilian representatives.

Berggruen and Gardels conceive of a pyramid structure that would encourage the emergence, at every level of representation, of small-scale elected bodies that know each other and have the relevant skill-sets and experience to assess their peers.[36] Let us imagine this system being applied to a country with 80 million inhabitants. The country is divided into 100 districts of 800,000 people. Each community of 2,000 people, representing a precinct, elects ten deputies. These deputies meet up, deliberate, and elect one of their own to sit on a council made up of twenty members, representing a total of 40,000 inhabitants. They then elect one regional representative, and twenty regional representatives elect one deputy to represent the whole district (800,000 people) and sit at a national parliament of 100 deputies.

Those elected therefore represent groups that, at various levels, reflect the full breadth of the electorate. Good examples of this system can be found in Australia and Ireland. The difference with the direct election of one deputy representing 800,000 people is that at every level the people who elect the individual who will represent them at a higher level know each other and can vouch firsthand for the experience, intelligence, and skills of the people they are electing. At every level, candidates have to prove that they are competent enough (in terms of knowledge and experience) to take on the responsibility required. This solution therefore involves dividing the political system into small manageable units operating on a human scale, with each one electing the next-higher unit.[37]

TOWARD A GLOBAL FEDERATION?

For his part, Jacques Attali, in his book *Demain qui gouvernera le monde?* (Tomorrow, Who Will Govern the World?), states that federalism is the form of administering the world that has the greatest chance of being effective. Global governance must have a supranational dimension without being at all centralized. What is federalism?

"Federalism," Attali explains, "adheres to three principles: separation, which involves dividing up legislative authority between a federal government and several federated governments; autonomy, which allows each level of government to be solely responsible in its field of competence; appropriation, by which federated entities, represented in federal institutions and participating in the adoption of federal laws, feel a sense of belonging within the community and its rules, and have faith in the main body's ability to ensure diversity and compromise."[38] In short, Attali concludes:

> *In order to survive, humanity must go even further than the current, vague realization of an "international community." It must realize the unity of its fate, and primarily of its existence in its present form. It must understand that, together, it can achieve so much more than it can apart.*

Conclusion:

Daring Altruism

It is not because things are difficult that we do not dare; it is because we do not dare that things are difficult.

— Seneca

We have reached the end of this long adventure. For my part, I have passionately devoted myself to it for five fruitful years of research, reading, and encounters.

I had first planned only to deal with two central themes, the existence of real altruism and the way to cultivate it. But was it possible to ignore everything that opposes altruism and threatens it—selfishness, devaluation of the other, violence? Deepening my investigations, little by little I discovered that altruism played a determining role in almost every dimension of our life. It is the essential key to resolving crises we are experiencing now—social, economic, ecological crises. Thus this essay began to fill out. I had to avoid simplifying an infinitely complex reality, in which the various phenomena are massively interdependent.

Over the course of this decade, I have had the good fortune to meet and talk with most of the thinkers, scientists, and economists whose conclusions and studies I have presented here. Nevertheless, I am quite aware that this overview remains imperfect, and that a few additional years of research would have allowed me to offer readers a more complete whole. But as they stand, the ideas and scientific studies I have compiled here do allow us to support the hypothesis that I presented in the beginning of this book, namely, that altruism is the Ariadne's thread allowing us to connect harmoniously the challenges of the economy in the short term, quality of life in the mean term, and our future environment in the long term. I hope from the bottom of my heart that this book can contribute its stone, modest as it may be, to the building of a better world.

For things truly to change, however, we must dare to embrace altruism. Dare to say that real altruism exists, that it can be cultivated by every one of us, and that the evolution of cultures can favor its expansion. Dare, too, to teach it in schools as a precious tool allowing children to realize their natural potential for kindness and cooperation. Dare to assert that the economy cannot content itself with the voice of rationality and strict personal interest, but that it must also listen to the voice of caring and make it heard. Dare to take the fate of future generations seriously, and dare to change the way we are exploiting the planet today that will be their home tomorrow. Dare, finally, to proclaim that altruism is not a luxury, but a necessity.

As we approach a dangerous point of no-return in terms of the environment, we still have the power to overcome these difficulties by fully engaging our extraordinary ability to cooperate with each other: "Cooperation," the evolutionist Martin Nowak reminds us, "was the principal architect of four billion years of evolution. It is the greatest hope for the future of humanity, and it will allow us to meet the serious challenges that lie ahead."[1]

To do this, we must cultivate altruism on an individual level, for that is where everything begins. Altruism shows us what is good to do, but also how one should be, and what qualities and virtues one should cultivate. Starting with a kindly motivation, altruism should be integrated into our everyday lives, and should reflect the unique quality of every being and every situation. We should promote altruism on the level of society through education, through institutions that respect the rights of every individual, and through political and economic systems that allow everyone to flourish without sacrificing the good of future generations. Finally, it is essential to consolidate in a common effort the different movements that try to promote altruism and cooperation: "The only thing that will redeem mankind is cooperation,"[2] said the philosopher and mathematician Bertrand Russell.

Altruism has been the central concept of my research, since it is the most all-encompassing, but we should still not forget that basically it's love that's at stake, love that extends to everyone, including oneself. "The best practical advice I can give to the present generation is to practice the virtue of love," Bertrand Russell also said, joined in this by the Dalai Lama, who so often asserts that love and compassion are the very foundations of society and proclaims, "My religion is kindness." He explains his thinking in his book *Ancient Wisdom, Modern World: Ethics for the New Millennium:*

> *The spiritual revolution I advocate is not a religious revolution. Nor does it have to do with a style of life that, in a way, would be from another world; it has even less to do with anything magical or mysterious. Rather it's a matter of radical re-orientation, far from our usual selfish preoccupations, for the benefit of the community that is ours; it's a kind of conduct that takes into account the interests of others as well as our own.*

This altruistic love is the best guarantee of a life that is full of meaning, a life in which we work for the happiness of others and try to remedy their suffering, a life we can regard with a feeling of serene satisfaction as death approaches. Love and compassion also need to be guided by wisdom. At the heart of the Buddhist teachings one finds the notion that wisdom and compassion have to be intimately united, like the two wings of a bird. A bird cannot fly with just one wing and does not learn how to fly with one wing first and the other next: wisdom has to deepen as compassion becomes vaster.

"I don't know what your destiny will be," said Albert Schweitzer to a group of schoolboys, "but one thing I know: the only ones among you who will be really happy are those who have sought and found how to serve."[3] Real happiness is entwined with altruism, since it is part of an essential kindness that is accompanied by a profound desire that everyone can flourish in life. It is a love that is always available, and that stems from the unchanging simplicity, serenity, and strength of a good heart.

Kathmandu, Nepal,
June 2, 2013

CONCLUSION: DARING ALTRUISM

As long as beings exist,
As long as space lasts,
May I, too, remain
To dissipate the suffering of the world!

— SHANTIDEVA

Acknowledgments

I would like first to express my unending thanks to my spiritual masters, who have given direction, meaning, and joy to every moment of my life: His Holiness the Dalai Lama, Kangyur Rinpoche, Dilgo Khyentse Rinpoche, Dudjom Rinpoche, Trulshik Rinpoche, Pema Wangyal Rinpoche, Jigme Khyentse Rinpoche, and Shechen Rabjam Rinpoche.

Meeting them is by far and wide the best thing that has happened to me in this life, and the fact that I have not progressed further along the spiritual path is due entirely to my own mental confusion and laziness.

An immense debt of gratitude goes also to my dear parents, to whom I owe my life, and to my sister Ève who has taught us a lesson in humanity.

My thanks also to my friends and mentors from the scientific community: Daniel Batson, Richard Davidson, Paul Ekman, Tania and Wolf Singer, Antoine Lutz, Richard Layard, Dennis Snower, as well as François Jacob, who initiated me into the world of scientific thought.

I thank Christian Bruyat, Marie Haeling, Carisse Busquet, and Françoise Delivet with all my heart for their patient and expert editing of the various drafts of this manuscript. By helping me clearly see the weaker points in some of my arguments, and by helping me to order my ideas and considerably improve the style and presentation of the text, they have made a vast contribution to the work as it appears today. Any remaining errors and imperfections are entirely the result of my own limitations.

I wholeheartedly thank the experts who were willing to check so carefully the chapters relevant to their specialism, both in French and English translation: Daniel Batson for the chapters in Part One; Tania Singer, Antoine Lutz, and Olga Klimecki for the chapters on neuroscience; Anaïs Rességuier and Patrick Carré for the chapter on philosophy; Jane Goodall and Frans de Waal for the chapters on evolution and animals; Jacques Van Rillaer for the chapter on psychoanalysis; Gérard Tardy, Tarek Toubale, Cornelius Pietzner, and my cousin David Baverez for the chapters on economics; not to mention those who gave me invaluable suggestions on wider sections of the text: Christophe André, Michael Dambrun, Raphaële Demandre, Jean-François Deschamps, Jacques Lecomte, Caroline Lesire, Ilios Kotsou, Yahne Le Toumelin, Michel Terestchenko, as well as Barbara Maibach, who transcribed the recordings of conversations with my scientist colleagues.

Special thanks to Dennis Snower who took the trouble to read carefully through the whole book and provided very valuable insights.

I am extremely grateful to the Mind & Life Institute, of which I have been a part since 2000, and to its founder, the sorely missed Francisco Varela. It is thanks to this Institute that I have been able to participate in twenty inspiring meetings with scientists, philosophers, economists, and thinkers gathered around His Holiness the Dalai Lama to discuss subjects as varied as destructive emotions, matter and life, quantum physics, neuroplasticity, the nature of consciousness, education, altruism in economic systems, ecology, and ethics. These meetings have led to others, in particular the "Émergences" conferences in Brussels, the "Happiness & Its Causes" forum in Australia, the World Economic Forum (WEF) in Davos, and the Global Economic Symposium (GES), all of which I have attended regularly.

This has enabled me to meet and maintain contact with the many specialists, thinkers, and social entrepreneurs cited in this book: Christophe André, Jacques Attali, Daniel Batson, Aaron Beck, Michel Bitbol, Michael Caldwell, Ray Chambers, Richard Davidson, John Dunne, Nancy Eisenberg, Paul Ekman, Abel Fazle, Ernst Fehr, Barbara Fredrickson, Fred Gage, Paul Gilbert, Daniel Goleman, Jane Goodall, Mark Greenberg, Alexandre Jollien, Jon Kabat-Zinn, Serge-Christophe Kolm, Daniel Kahneman, Stephen Kosslyn, Éric Lambin, Richard Layard, Jacques Lecomte, Diana Liverman, Antoine Lutz,

Michael Meaney, Kristin Neff, Greg Norris, Clare Palmer, Jonathan Patz, Pierre Rabhi, Charles Raison, Jacques Van Rillaer, Bruno Roche, Johan Rockström, Bunker Roy, Cliff Saron, Martin Seligman, Phil Shaver, Tania Singer and her team, Wolf Singer, Dennis Snower, Richard Tremblay, Archbishop Desmond Tutu, Frans de Waal, B. Alan Wallace, Stewart Wallis, Philip Zimbardo, and many more besides.

I am also very grateful to my partners-in-altruism, Christophe and Pauline André, who were kind enough to offer up their home and their table, organizing evenings with thinkers I was keen to meet and hear talk on altruism, as well as to those who attended these dinners for the knowledge and perspectives they were willing to share: André Comte-Sponville, Alexandre Jollien, David Servan-Schreiber, Michel Terestchenko, and Tzvetan Todorov.

My thanks also go to Lyonchen Jigme Thinley, former prime minister of Bhutan, and Dasho Karma Ura, who heads the Gross National Happiness Commission in Bhutan, for including me in their think tank and letting me join in their debates in Bhutan and the United Nations, which also led to me being able to engage in dialogue with other thinkers mentioned in this book, including Jeffrey Sachs and Joseph Stiglitz.

To Jacques Lecomte, thank you for the goodwill of sending me an advance version of the book *La Bonté humaine* (Human Goodness), as I was working to finish the present work that I began over five years ago. I was at once astonished and comforted to discover that our books were inspired by the same reflections and frequently the same sources. We were delighted about this, since there surely cannot be too many voices to project a more positive perspective of human nature.

My thanks also go to the whole team at Karuna-Shechen, the humanitarian organization I founded fifteen years ago, which has successfully completed over a hundred and forty projects in Tibet, Nepal, and India in the fields of education, health care, and social services—friends, collaborators, and benefactors who embody compassion in action. Thanks too to the friends and collaborators who help me greatly in the various activities in which I am involved: Patricia Christin, Raphaële Demandre, and Vivian Kurz.

Finally, words fail me in expressing the gratitude I feel towards my French publisher Nicole Lattès, a friend and an editor who has been a constant source of encouragement over the past four years of work, as well as the entire team at Éditions NiL and Robert Laffont. My profound thanks go to Charlotte Mandell for undertaking the challenging task of translating this large piece of work, and for the wonderful spirit of collaboration that we sustained for more than a year. I am also grateful to Sam Gordon for translating, with equal skill, the final part of the book and to Amanda Brower who insightfully edited the final draft. My heartiest thanks goes to Michael Pietsch, Judy Clain, and the whole team at Little, Brown for bringing about the English-language edition of *Altruism.* And finally, my profound gratitude goes to Vivian Kurz, who has tirelessly assisted our various humanitarian and spiritual projects for nearly two decades, for her dedicated efforts in bringing this book to readers of English around the world.

Karuna-Shechen

Altruism in Action

In 2000, Matthieu Ricard founded Karuna-Shechen, an international non-profit humanitarian organization providing health care, education, sustainable development, and cultural preservation throughout the Himalayan region. These activities help under-served communities in remote areas that have little or no other access to these vital services.

Karuna-Shechen has developed more than 140 humanitarian projects in India, Nepal, and Tibet. These programs are developed in response to the needs and aspirations of these communities, serving them with respect for their unique cultural heritage, and paying special attention to educating and improving the status of girls and women.

Today, Karuna-Shechen treats more than 100,000 patients annually through its clinics and outreach programs, educates over 20,000 children in schools it has helped to build, and benefited thousands through its social programs. In addition it has built homes for the elderly, equipped remote villages with solar power and rainwater collection systems, and built bridges and schools.

Its cultural preservation programs have helped to renew traditional crafts in Tibet through vocational training, rebuilt retreat centers for contemplatives, and reproduced more than 400 volumes of ancient texts.

Karuna-Shechen

All of the author's share of royalties from this, as for all his books and events, are dedicated to furthering the work of Karuna-Shechen.

For further information and to support these activities, please visit www.karuna-shechen.org or write to Karuna-Shechen, 381 Park Avenue South, Suite 820, New York, NY 10016.

Notes

Introduction

1. *The Comedy of Asses*, Plautus, Harvard University Press, 1916.
2. Hobbes, Thomas, *Leviathan*, 1651, Chapter 13.
3. Freud, Sigmund, in a letter to Oskar Pfister, September 10, 1918. http://www3.dbu.edu/mitchell/freud%27sillusion.htm.
4. Lord Tennyson, Alfred, "In Memoriam." In *The Works of Alfred Lord Tennyson*, Wordsworth Editions, 1998.
5. See especially Tremblay, Richard, *Early Learning Prevents Youth Violence*, http://www.excellence-earlychildhood.ca/documents/Tremblay_AggressionReport_ANG.pdf, and the book by Pinker, Steven, *The Better Angels of Our Nature: Why Violence Has Declined*, Penguin, 2012.
6. See especially the writings of the psychologist Batson, C. Daniel, *The Altruism Question* (1991) and *Altruism in Humans* (2011), Oxford University Press, as well as the works by the political commentator and philosopher Monroe, Kristen Renwick, *The Heart of Altruism* (1996), the sociologist Kohn, Alfie, *The Brighter Side of Human Nature, Altruism and Empathy in Everyday Life* (1992), the psychologists Wallach, Michael and Lise, *Psychology's Sanction for Selfishness* (1983), the ethologist Waal de, Frans, *The Age of Empathy: Nature's Lessons for a Kinder Society* (2009), and the psychologist Lecomte, Jacques, *La Bonté humaine: Altruisme, empathie, générosité* (2012), as well as numerous philosophers, including Joseph Butler, David Hume, Charlie D. Broad, & Norman J. Brown.
7. See www.karuna-shechen.org.

8. Kasser, Tim, *The High Price of Materialism*, MIT Press, 2003.
9. Forbes, Stephen, statement during a debate on Fox News, October 18, 2009.
10. These numbers represent the situation in the United States.
11. Notably Dennis Snower, Ernst Fehr, Richard Layard, & Joseph Stiglitz, as well as members of the GNH (Gross National Happiness) movement promulgated by Bhutan and now taken seriously in Brazil, Japan, and other countries.
12. These three pillars correspond to the concept of "mutuality" developed by the economist Bruno Roche.
13. Stemming notably from the studies by David Sloan Wilson, Elliott Sober, E. O. Wilson, & Martin Nowak.
14. On this subject, see the excellent chapters by Lecomte, Jacques, in *La Bonté humaine* (2012), *op. cit.*, on the deformations and exaggerations produced by a number of recent tragedies, as well as Chapter 9 of that book, "La banalité du bien" ["The banality of the good"].
15. Notably the studies by Robert Boyd & Peter J. Richerson. See Richerson & Boyd, *Not By Genes Alone*, 2005.

Chapter 1: The Nature of Altruism

1. *Oeuvres d'Auguste Comte*: *Système de politique positive ou Traité de sociologie* [The Works of Auguste Comte: System of Positive Polity or Treatise on Sociology], Editions Anthropos, 2007, vol. 1, pp. 7–10.
2. Nagel, Thomas, *The Possibility of Altruism*, Princeton University Press, 1978, p. 79.
3. *Ibid.*, p. 80.
4. Post, Stephen G., *Unlimited Love: Altruism, Compassion, and Service*, Templeton Foundation Press, 2003, p. vi.
5. Batson, C. D. (2001), *op. cit.*, p. 20.
6. On this point Batson agrees with Emmanuel Kant, who wrote: "Always act so that you treat humanity... as an end and never simply as a means." *Groundwork of the Metaphysic of Morals* (no page given).
7. Monroe, Kristen Renwick, *The Heart of Altruism: Perceptions of a Common Humanity,* Cambridge University Press, 1996, p. 6.
8. *Ibid.*
9. The complete account of the characteristics of altruistic motivation, of which we have presented a simplified version, can be found in Batson, C. D. (2001), pp. 22–23.
10. In his book devoted to sympathy, the philosopher Max Scheler writes: "Love is a movement, passing from a lower value to a higher one, in which the higher value of the object or person suddenly flashes upon us; whereas

hatred moves in the opposite direction." Later on, Edith Stein would take up Scheler's analyses and envision the question of empathy according to a purely phenomenological approach in the tradition of Husserl, of whom she was a close disciple. See Scheler, Max, *The Nature of Sympathy*, Transaction Publishers, 2008, p. 152, and Stein, Edith, *On the Problem of Empathy: The Collected Works of Edith Stein*, 3d rev. ed., ICS Publications, 1989. I am grateful to Michel Bitbol for drawing my attention to these two books.

11. Hutcheson, Frances, *An Essay on the Nature and Conduct of the Passions and Affections, with Illustrations on the Moral Sense* [1742] http://oll.libertyfund.org/?option=com_staticxt&staticfile=show.php%3Ftitle=885. Quoted by Terestchenko, Michel, *Un si fragile vernis d'humanité: Banalité du mal, banalité du bien*, Editions La Découverte, 2007, p. 60.
12. Hallie, Philip, *Lest Innocent Blood Be Shed: The Story of the Village of Le Chambon and How Goodness Happened There*, Harper Perennial, 1994. Quoted by Terestchenko, M., *op. cit.*, p. 207.
13. Monroe, Kristen, *op. cit.*, p. 3.
14. Deschamps, Jean-François, & Finkelstein, Rémi, Existe-t-il un veritable altruisme basé sur les valeurs personelles? *Les Cahiers internationaux de psychologie sociale* (1), 37–62.
15. Taylor, Charles, *Sources of the Self: The Making of the Modern Identity*, Harvard University Press, 1989, p. 13.

CHAPTER 2: EXTENDING ALTRUISM

1. Alexandre Jollien in conversation with the author, Gstaad, January 29, 2012.
2. The Dalai Lama, *Ancient Wisdom, Modern World: Ethics for a New Millennium*, Little, Brown, 1999.
3. See Ricard, Matthieu, *Happiness: A Guide to Developing Life's Most Important Skill*, Little, Brown, 2007.
4. Aristotle, *Rhetoric*, II, 4, trans. W. Rhys Roberts, online: http://classics.mit.edu/Aristotle/rhetoric.2.ii.html. Quoted by Audi, Paul, in *L'empire de la compassion*, Les Belles Lettres, 2011, p. 37.
5. The Dalai Lama & Vreeland, Nicholas, *An Open Heart: Practicing Compassion in Everyday Life*, Little, Brown, 2001, pp. 96–97.
6. Jean-François Revel, in conversation with the author.
7. Gunaratana, B. H., *Eight Mindful Steps to Happiness: Walking the Path of the Buddha*, Wisdom Publications, p. 74.
8. For Batson, *empathic solicitude* is an emotion directed to the other, engendered by the perception that the other is in need, an emotion in harmony with that perception. See Batson, C. D. (2011), p. 11.

9. Darwin, Charles, *The Descent of Man, and Selection in Relation to Sex*, 1891, Chapter 4.
10. Sober, Elliott, & Wilson, David Sloan, *Unto Others: The Evolution and Psychology of Unselfish Behavior*, Harvard University Press, 1999.
11. I am grateful to Daniel Batson for helping me identify these two points over the course of several conversations.
12. Darwin, *The Descent of Man, and Selection in Relation to Sex*, *op. cit.*, Chapter 5.
13. See Chapter 26, "Having Hatred or Compassion Toward Oneself."
14. Trungpa, Chögyam, *Cutting Through Spiritual Materialism*, Shambhala, 1973.
15. Shantideva, *A Guide to the Bodhisattva Way of Life*, Snow Lion Press, 1997. Online: http://www.fodian.net/world/be_bodsv.html (translation slightly modified).
16. Kohn, Alfie, *The Brighter Side of Human Nature: Altruism and Empathy in Everyday Life*, Basic Books, 1992, p. 156.
17. BBC World Service, Outlook, September 7, 2011.
18. Camus, Albert, *The Plague*, Vintage, 1991, p. 91.
19. Translated from the Tibetan by Matthieu Ricard from the Complete Works: *The Collected Works (gsun 'bum) of the Seventh Dalai Lama blo-bzan-bskal-bzang-rgya-mtsho*, published by Dodrup Sangye, Gangtok, 1975–1983.

CHAPTER 3: WHAT IS EMPATHY?

1. The English word *empathy* was used for the first time in the early twentieth century to translate *Einfühlung*, by the psychologist Edward Titchener.
2. Lipps, Theodor, Einfühlung, innere Nachahmung und Organempfindung. *Archiv für die gesamte Psychologie*, *1*(2), pp. 185–204.
3. Paul Ekman, in conversation, November 2009.
4. Darwin, Charles, *The Expression of Emotion in Man and Animals*, 1872.
5. It is interesting to note that the Greek word *sumpatheia* also means "mutual interdependence."
6. Darwin, Charles, *op. cit.*; Eisenberg, Nancy, & Strayer, Janet, *Empathy and Its Development*, Cambridge University Press, 1990.
7. Waal, Frans de, *The Age of Empathy: Nature's Lessons for a Kinder Society*, Harmony Books, 2009, p. 88.
8. In our day, the abundance and repetition of similar images in the media have ended up eroding empathic reaction and have given rise to

an apathetic resignation in public opinion. See Boltanski, Luc, *La Souffrance à distance*, Gallimard, Folio, 2007.

9. Wilder, D. A., Social Categorization: Implications for Creation and Reduction of Intergroup Bias. *Advances in Experimental Social Psychology, 19*, 1986, pp. 291–355. Quoted in Kohn, Alfie, *op. cit.*, p. 145.
10. Remarque, Erich Maria, *All Quiet on the Western Front*, Ballantine Books, 1987, p. 223.
11. Broad, Charlie Dunbar, Egoism as a theory of human motives. In *Ethics and the History of Philosophy*, Routledge, 1952, pp. 218–31.
12. See especially Kohut, Heinz, *The Restoration of the Self*, University of Chicago Press, 2009.
13. Batson, C. D. "These things called empathy: Eight related but distinct phenomena." In Decety, J., *The Social Neuroscience of Empathy*, MIT Press, 2009.
14. Batson, C. D. (2011), *op. cit.* The many scientific references corresponding to these various definitions of empathy can be found in his book.
15. See Preston, S. D., Waal, F. B. M. de, *et al.* (2002), Empathy: Its ultimate and proximate bases, *Behavioral and Brain Sciences, 25* (1), pp. 1–20. The "Perception-action model" (PAM) was partly inspired by research into mirror neurons, which are present in some sections of the brain and are activated when one sees, for example, someone else making a gesture that interests us (see Chapter 5, sub-heading: "When two brains agree"). Mirror neurons can provide an elementary basis for imitation and intersubjective resonance, but the phenomenon of empathy is much more complex and involves numerous areas of the brain. Rizzolatti, G., & Sinigaglia, C., *Mirrors in the Brain: How Our Minds Share Actions, Emotions, and Experience*, Oxford University Press, 2008.
16. Thompson, R. A. (1987). "Empathy and emotional understanding: The early development of empathy." In *Empathy and Its Development*, 119–145. In Eisenberg, N., & Strayer, J., *Empathy and Its Development*, Cambridge University Press, 1990.
17. Batson, C. D., Early, S., & Salvarani, G. Perspective taking: Imagining how another feels versus imagining how you would feel, *Personality and Social Psychology Bulletin, 23*(7), 1997, pp. 751–758.
18. Mikulincer, M., Gillath, O., Halevy, V., Avihou, N., Avidan, S., & Eshkoli, N. Attachment theory and reactions to others' needs: Evidence that activation of the sense of attachment security promotes empathic responses. *Journal of Personality and Social Psychology, 81*(6), 2001, p. 1205.

19. Coke, J. S., Batson, C. D., & McDavis, K. Empathic mediation of helping: A two-stage model. *Journal of Personality and Social Psychology, 36* (7), 1978, p. 752.
20. According to the various authors, this kind of empathy is called:

    - "Empathic distress," in Hoffman, M. L., "The development of empathy," in J. P. Rushton and R. M. Sorrentino (eds.), *Altruism and Helping Behavior: Social, Personality, and Developmental Perspectives*, Erlbaum, 1981, pp. 41–63.
    - "Distressed sympathy," in McDougall, W., *An Introduction to Social Psychology*, Methuen, 1908.
    - "Personal distress," Batson, C. D., Prosocial motivation: Is it ever truly altruistic? *Advances in Experimental Social Psychology, 20*, 1987, pp. 65–122.
    - "Unpleasant feeling provoked by observation," in Piliavin, J. A., Dovidio, J. F., Gaertner, S. L, & Clark, R. D., III, *Emergency Intervention*, Academic Press, 1981.
    - Empathy, in Krebs, D., Empathy and Altruism. *Journal of Personality and Social Psychology, 32*(6), 1975, p. 1134. Quoted by Batson, C. D. (2011), *op. cit.*

21. Revault d'Allonnes, M., *L'Homme compassionnel*, Seuil, 2008, p. 22. This confusion is understandable if one holds to the Latin etymology of *compassion*, a term derived from the words *compatior*, "to suffer with," and *compassio*, "shared suffering."
22. Batson, C. D., *The Altruism Question: Toward a Social Psychological Answer*, Lawrence Erlbaum, 1991; Batson, C. D. (2011), *op. cit.*
23. Spinoza does not use the terms "pity" and "compassion," but, according to Alexandre Jollien, in the language of the time, he explains that in pity, sadness comes first, and in compassion, love. In his *Ethics*, Book 3, Number 28, he says: "Commiseration is a sadness brought on by the idea of pain experienced by another whom we imagine to be similar to us." And in Number 24, Spinoza writes: "Pity is love as it affects man in such a way that he rejoices at another's happiness and is on the contrary saddened by another's misfortune." Conversation with A. Jollien, January 29, 2012.
24. Zweig, Stefan, epigraph to *Beware of Pity*, trans. Phyllis and Trevor Blewitt, NYRB Classics, 2006, p. xxv.
25. If pain is at stake, the sections of the brain involved will include the anterior insular cortex and the anterior cingulate cortex (ACC). If disgust is at issue, it will also be the anterior insular cortex. If you

experience a neutral tactile sensation, the secondary somatosensory cortex will be activated. If you experience pleasant emotions and agreeable sensations, the insula, the striatum, and the median orbitofrontal cortex can be involved. Cognitive apprehension rests on the medial prefrontal cortex, the temporal parietal junction (TPJ), and the superior temporal sulcus (STS), a network that is activated when one asks people to reflect on their thoughts and beliefs.

26. Which specialists call "theory of mind."
27. See Vignemont, F. de, & Singer, T. The empathic brain: how, when and why? *Trends in Cognitive Sciences, 10*(10), 2006, pp. 435–441. Aside from this article, this chapter is chiefly based on explanations given by Tania Singer, with whom I have collaborated for several years, during the course of conversations in January 2012.
28. Singer, T., Seymore, B., O'Doherty, J. P., Stephan, K. E., Dolan, R. J., & Frith, C. D. Empathic neural responses are modulated by the perceived fairness of others. *Nature, 439*(7075), 2006, pp. 466–469; Hein, G., Silani, G., Preuschoff, K., Batson, C. D., & Singer, T. Neural responses to ingroup and outgroup members' suffering predict individual differences in costly helping. *Neuron, 68*(1), 2010, pp. 149–160; Hein, G., & Singer, T. I feel how you feel but not always: the empathic brain and its modulation. *Current Opinion in Neurobiology, 18*(2), 2008, pp. 153–158.
29. Batson, C. D., Lishner, D. A., Cook, J., & Sawyer, S. Similarity and nurturance: Two possible sources of empathy for strangers. *Basic and Applied Social Psychology, 27*(1), 2005, pp. 15–25.
30. For more details on these different points quoted above, see de Vignemont, F., & Singer, T. (2006), *op. cit.*
31. Singer, T., & Steinbeis, N. Differential roles of fairness and compassion-based motivations for cooperation, defection, and punishment. *Annals of the New York Academy of Sciences, 1167*(1), 2009, pp. 41–50; Singer, T. The past, present and future of social neuroscience: A European perspective. *Neuroimage, 61*(2), 2012, pp. 437–449.
32. Klimecki, O., Ricard, M., & Singer, T. Empathy versus compassion—Lessons from 1st and 3rd person methods. In Singer, T., & Bolz, M. (eds.), *Compassion: Bridging Practice and Science*, a multimedia book [e-book], 2013.
33. Klimecki, O. M., Leiberg, S., Lamm, C., & Singer, T. Functional neural plasticity and associated changes in positive affect after compassion training. *Cerebral Cortex*, 2012.
34. In various pathologies—narcissism, psychopathy, and personality disorders—different components of the chain of affective reactions

involved in social interactions do not function normally, and empathy is inhibited. See Chapter 27, "The Deficiencies of Empathy."

CHAPTER 4: FROM EMPATHY TO COMPASSION IN A NEUROSCIENCE LABORATORY

1. For a summary of the 32 studies on empathy with regard to pain, see Lamm, C., Decety, J., & Singer, T. Meta-analytic evidence for common and distinct neural networks associated with directly experienced pain and empathy for pain. *Neuroimage*, *54*(3), 2011, pp. 2492–2502.
2. The increase of a positive reaction through compassion is associated with an activation of a cerebral network that includes the areas of the median orbitofrontal cortex, the ventral striatum, the ventral tegmental section, the nuclei of the brainstem, the nucleus accumbens, the median insula, the pallidum and putamen, all areas of the brain that were previously associated with love (especially maternal love), feelings of belonging and gratification. In the case of empathy, the areas are the anterior insula and the median cingulate cortex. Klimecki, O. M., *et al.* (2012), *op. cit.*; Klimecki, O., Ricard, M., & Singer, T. (2013), *op. cit.*
3. Felton, J. S. Burnout as a clinical entity—its importance in health care workers. *Occupational Medicine, 48*(4), 1998, pp. 237–250.
4. For a neural distinction between compassion and empathy fatigue, see Klimecki, O., & Singer, T., "Empathic distress fatigue rather than compassion fatigue? Integrating findings from empathy research in psychology and social neuroscience." In Oakley, B., Knafo, A., Madhavan, G., & Wilson, D. S., *Pathological Altruism*, Oxford University Press, 2011, pp. 368–383.
5. Singer, T., & Bolz, M. (eds.) (2013), *op. cit.*; Klimecki, O., Ricard, M., & Singer, T. (2013), *op. cit.* The most recent publication is Klimecki, O., Leiberg, S., Ricard, M., & Singer, T. Differential Pattern of Functional Brain Plasticity after Compassion and Empathy Training. *Social Cognitive and Affective Neuroscience*, 2013.
6. This expression designates a study that observes over a course of months, or even years, the evolution of subjects.
7. Bornemann B., & Singer, T., "The resource study training protocol." In Singer, T., & Bolz, M. (eds.), *Compassion: Bridging Practice and Science*, 2013, a multimedia book [e-book].
8. Klimecki, O. M., *et al.* (2012). *Op. cit.*
9. At the neural level, the researchers observed that training in empathic resonance increased activity in a network that is involved both in empathy for another's pain and in one's own experience of pain. This

network includes the anterior insula and the anterior medial cingulate cortex (MCC). Singer, T., & Bolz, M. (eds.) (2013), *op. cit.*

10. More precisely, these regions include the orbitofrontal cortex, the ventral striatum, and the anterior cingulate cortex. As to the training, our participants received courses on the notion of *metta*, a word that means "altruistic love" in Pali. The instructions the participants received were mostly concentrated on the aspect of kindness and benevolent wishes ("May you be happy, in good health, etc."). The training included one entire day spent with a teacher, followed by daily group practices, one hour every evening. The participants were also encouraged to practice at home.
11. Klimecki, O. M., *et al.* (2012), *op. cit.*
12. Lutz, A., Brefczynski-Lewis, J., Johnstone, T., & Davidson, R. J. Regulation of the neural circuitry of emotion by compassion meditation: Effects of meditative expertise. *PLoS One, 3* (3), 2008, e1897.
13. Christophe André, *Feelings and Moods*, Polity Press, 2012, p. 250.

Chapter 5: Love, Supreme Emotion

1. Fredrickson, B. L. The role of positive emotions in positive psychology: The broaden-and-build theory of positive emotions. *American Psychologist, 56*(3), 2001, p. 218; Fredrickson, B. "Positive emotions." In Snyder C. R., & Lopez, S. J., *Handbook of Positive Psychology*, Oxford University Press, 2002, pp. 122 and 125, for the ensuing quotation.
2. Ekman, Paul, *Emotions Revealed: Recognizing Faces and Feelings to Improve Communication and Emotional Life*, Holt, 2007; Ekman, P., & Davidson, R. J., *The Nature of Emotion: Fundamental Questions*, Oxford University Press, 1994.
3. Atwood, Margaret, *Surfacing*, Anchor, 1998, p. 107.
4. Fredrickson, B. *Love 2.0: How Our Supreme Emotion Affects Everything We Feel, Think, Do, and Become*, Hudson Street Press, 2013, p. 16. I am grateful to Barbara Fredrickson for sending me the proofs of her book before its publication.
5. *Ibid.*, p. 5.
6. *Ibid.*
7. House, J. S., Landis, K. R., & Umberson, D. Social relationships and health. *Science, 241*(4865), 1988, pp. 540–545. See also Diener, E., & Seligman, M. E. P. Very happy people. *Psychological Science, 13*(1), 2002, pp. 81–84.
8. Hegi, K. E., & Bergner, R. M. What is love? An empirically-based essentialist account. *Journal of Social and Personal Relationships, 27(5)*, 2010, pp. 620–636.

9. Fredrickson, B. (2013), *op. cit.*, note 7, p. 186, as well as Fredrickson, B. L., & Roberts, T. A. Objectification theory. *Psychology of Women Quarterly, 21*(2), 1997, pp. 173–206; Fredrickson, B. L., Hendler, L. M., Nilsen, S., O'Barr, J. F., & Roberts, T. A. Bringing back the body: A retrospective on the development of objectification theory. *Psychology of Women Quarterly, 35*(4), 2011, 689–696.
10. At stake here are reactions to the content of the conversation and not simply to the sound of the other's voice, or one's own voice when one is speaking. In fact, the synchronization of cerebral activities stops if the other person is speaking a foreign language, Russian, for instance, which the one listening does not understand.
11. Stephens, G. J., Silbert, L. J., & Hasson, U. Speaker-listener neural coupling underlies successful communication. *Proceedings of the National Academy of Sciences, 107*(32), 2010, 14425–14430; Hasson, U. I can make your brain look like mine. *Harvard Business Review, 88*(12), 2010, 32–33. Quoted and explained by Fredrickson, B. (2013), *op. cit.*, pp. 39–44.
12. See Chapter 4, "From Empathy to Compassion in a Neuroscience Laboratory."
13. Singer, T., & Lamm, C. The social neuroscience of empathy. *Annals of the New York Academy of Sciences, 1156*(1), 2009, pp. 81–96; Craig, A. D. How do you feel—now? The anterior insula and human awareness. *Nature Reviews Neuroscience*, 10, 2009, pp. 59–70.
14. Hasson, U., Nir, Y., Levy, I., Fuhrmann, G., & Malach, R. Intersubject synchronization of cortical activity during natural vision. *Science, 303*(5664), 2004, pp. 1634–1640.
15. Fredrickson B. (2013), *op. cit.*, p. 43.
16. Fredrickson, B., *Positivity: Groundbreaking Research Reveals How to Embrace the Hidden Strength of Positive Emotions, Overcome Negativity, and Thrive*, Crown Archetype, 2001.
17. For a summary of the discovery of these mirror neurons and of the researches into them, see Rizzolatti, G., & Sinigaglia, C., *Mirrors in the Brain: How Our Minds Share Actions, Emotions, and Experience*, Oxford University Press, 2008.
18. Cho, M. M., DeVries, A. C., Williams, J. R., & Carter, C. S. The effects of oxytocin and vasopressin on partner preferences in male and female prairie voles (Microtus ochrogaster). *Behavioral Neuroscience 113* (5), 1999, p. 1071.
19. Champagne, F. A., Weaver, I. C. G., Diorio, J., Dymob, S., Szyf, M., & Meaney, M. J. Maternal care associated with methylation of the estrogen receptor-alpha1b promoter and estrogen receptor-alpha expression in

the medial preoptic area of female offspring. *Endocrinology, 147*(6), 2006, pp. 2909–2915.

20. Francis, D., Diorio, J., Liu, D., & Meaney, M. J. Nongenomic transmission across generations of maternal behavior and stress responses in the rat. *Science, 286*(5442), 1999, pp. 1155–1158.
21. Guastella, A. J., Mitchell, P. B., & Dadds, M. R. Oxytocin increases gaze to the eye region of human faces. *Biological Psychiatry, 63*(1), 2008, p. 3; Marsh, A. A., Yu, H. H., Pine, D. S., & Blaire, R. J. R. Oxytocin improves specific recognition of positive facial expressions. *Psychopharmacology, 209*(3), 2010, pp. 225–232; Domes, G., Heinrichs, M., Michel, A., Berger, C., & Herpertz, S. C. Oxytocin improves "mind-reading" in humans. *Biological Psychiatry, 61*(6), 2007, pp. 731–733.
22. Kosfeld, M., Heinrichs, M., Zak, P. J., Fischbacher, U., & Fehr, E. Oxytocin increases trust in humans. *Nature, 435* (7042), 2005, pp. 673–676.
23. These researchers showed that oxytocin does not increase risk-taking in general (parachute jumping, for instance), but more specifically accepting the fact that one is running a risk when one decides to trust someone else, when our own interests are at stake.
24. Mikolajczak, M., Pinon, N., Lane, A., De Timary, P., & Luminet, O. Oxytocin not only increases trust when money is at stake, but also when confidential information is in the balance. *Biological Psychology, 85*(1), 2010, pp. 182–184.
25. Gamer, M., Zurowski, B., & Büchel, C. Different amygdala subregions mediate valence-related and attentional effects of oxytocin in humans. *Proceedings of the National Academy of Sciences, 107*(20), 2010, pp. 9400–9405. See also: Kirsch, P., Esslinger, C., Chen, Q., Mier, D., Lis, S., Siddhanti, S., & Meyer-Lindenberg, A. Oxytocin modulates neural circuitry for social cognition and fear in humans. *Journal of Neuroscience, 25*(49), 2005, pp. 11489–11493; Petrovic, P., Kalisch, R., Singer, T., & Dolan, R. J. Oxytocin attenuates affective evaluations of conditioned faces and amygdala activity. *Journal of Neuroscience, 28*(26), 2008, pp. 6607–6615.
26. Uvnäs-Moberg, K., Arn, I., & Magnusson, D. The psychobiology of emotion: The role of the oxytocinergic system. *International Journal of Behavioral Medicine, 12*(2), 2005, pp. 281–295.
27. Campbell, A. Oxytocin and human social behavior. *Personality and Social Psychology Review, 14*(3), 2010, pp. 281–295.
28. Lee, H. J., Macbeth, A. H., & Pagani, J. H. Oxytocin: The great facilitator of life. *Progress in Neurobiology, 88*(2), 2009, pp. 127–151.

29. Shamay-Tsoory, S. G., Fischer, M., Dvash, J., Harari, H., Perach-Bloom, N., & Levkovitz, Y. Intranasal administration of oxytocin increases envy and schadenfreude (gloating). *Biological Psychiatry, 66*(9), 2009, pp. 864–870.
30. De Dreu, C. K. W., Greer, L. L., Van Kleef, G. A., Shalvi, S., & Handgraaf, M. J. J. Oxytocin promotes human ethnocentrism. *Proceedings of the National Academy of Sciences, 108*(4), 2011, pp. 1262–1266.
31. Porges, S. W. Social engagement and attachment. *Annals of the New York Academy of Sciences, 1008*(1), 2003, pp. 31–47.
32. Bibevski, S., & Dunlap, M. E. Evidence for impaired vagus nerve activity in heart failure. *Heart Failure Reviews, 16*(2), 2011, pp. 129–135.
33. Kiecolt-Glaser, J. K., McGuire, L., Robles, T. F., & Glaser, R. Emotions, morbidity, and mortality: New perspectives from psychoneuroimmunology. *Annual Review of Psychology, 53*(1), 2002, pp. 83–107; Moskowitz, J. T., Epel, E.S., & Acree, M. Positive affect uniquely predicts lower risk of mortality in people with diabetes. *Health Psychology, 27*(1S), 2008, p. S73.
34. Fredrickson B. (2013), *op. cit.*, p. 10.
35. Fredrickson, B. L., Cohn, M. A., Coffey, K. A., Pek, J., & Finkel, S. M. Open hearts build lives: positive emotions, induced through loving-kindness meditation, build consequential personal resources. *Journal of Personality and Social Psychology, 95*(5), 2008, p. 1045.
36. Kok, B. E., Coffey, K. A., Cohn, M. A., Catalino, L. I., Vacharkulksemsuk, T., Algoe, S. B., Brantley, M., & Fredrickson, B. L. Positive emotions drive an upward spiral that links social connections and health. *Psychological Science, 24*, 2012, p. 1123; Kok, B. E., & Fredrickson, B. L. Upward spirals of the heart: Autonomic flexibility, as indexed by vagal tone, reciprocally and prospectively predicts positive emotions and social connectedness. *Biological Psychology, 85*(3), 2010, pp. 432–436.
37. Fredrickson, B. (2013), *op. cit.*, p. 16.
38. *Ibid.*, p. 23.

CHAPTER 6: THE ACCOMPLISHMENT OF A TWOFOLD BENEFIT, OUR OWN AND OTHERS'

1. Shantideva, *The Way of the Bodhisattva: A Translation of the Bodhicharyavatara*, trans. the Padmakara Translation Group, Shambhala Publications, 1997, p. 129.
2. Butler, Joseph, from "Five Sermons," in *The Whole Works of Joseph Butler*, Ulan Press, 2012, pp. 106–107.

3. See Chapter 25, "The Champions of Selfishness."
4. Khyentse Rinpoche, Dilgo, *The Heart of Compassion: The Thirty-Seven Verses on the Practice of a Bodhisattva*, Shambhala Press, 2007, p. 127.
5. Fromm, Erich, *Man for Himself: An Inquiry into the Psychology of Ethics*, Rinehart and Co., 1947, pp. 134–6.
6. Terestchenko, Michel (2007), *op. cit.*, p. 17.
7. Plato, *Gorgias, Complete Works,* Volume 1, Gallimard, 1940.

CHAPTER 7: SELF-INTERESTED ALTRUISM AND GENERALIZED RECIPROCITY

1. Duc de La Rochefoucauld, François, *Reflections; Or Sentences and Moral Maxims*, trans. Bund and Friswell, Echo Library, 2007, Maxim 85, pp. 34–35.
2. Interviews given to the *Monde des religions*. Statements gathered by Frédéric Lenoir and Karine Papillaud, 2007.
3. Jacques Attali, interview on 20minutes.fr, November 19, 2006.
4. Kolm, S.-C., *La bonne économie*, PUF, 1984 p. 191.
5. André Comte-Sponville, conversations during an evening organized by Christophe and Pauline André.
6. Darwin, Charles, *Descent of Man*, *op. cit.*, online: http://www.infidels.org/library/historical/charles_darwin/descent_of_man/chapter_04.html
7. Wilkinson, G. S. Reciprocal altruism in bats and other mammals. *Ethology and Sociobiology*, 9(2–4), 1988, pp. 85–100.
8. I am grateful to Danielle Follmi for providing me with this information.
9. Ref. http://www.scribd.com/doc/16567239/The-Inca-From-Village-to-Empire
10. Turnbull, Colin M., *The Mountain People*, Simon & Schuster, 1972, p. 146.
11. The various forms of gift exchange ritual in traditional societies have given rise to countless studies. See especially Mauss, M., *Essai sur le don: Forme et raison de l'échange dans les sociétés archaïques*, PUF, 2007, as well as the preface by Florence Weber.
12. Paul Ekman, personal communication, 2009. In 1972, Ekman worked as an anthropologist in a Papuan tribe in New Guinea, where he studied the facial expression of emotions.
13. Kolm, Serge-Christophe (1984), *op. cit.*, p. 11. I am grateful to S.-C. Kolm for having had the kindness to meet me and share his work with me. Serge-Christophe Kolm was Director of the CSERA (Center for

Socio-Economic Research and Analysis), and professor at Harvard and Stanford.

14. Kolm, S.-C. (1984), *op. cit.*, p. 56.

CHAPTER 8: SELFLESS ALTRUISM

1. The Samaritans of New York, *New York Times*, September 5, 1988, p. 26.
2. *Daily Mail,* November 5, 2010, and CBC News, November 4, 2010.
3. Berkowitz, L., & Daniels, L. R. Responsibility and dependency. *Journal of Abnormal and Social Psychology*, *66*(5), 1963, p. 429.
4. Kohn, A. (1992), *op. cit.*, p. 230.
5. Titmuss, R. M. The gift relationship: From human blood to social. *Policy, London*, 1970.
6. Eisenberg, N., & Neal, C. Children's moral reasoning about their own spontaneous prosocial behavior. *Developmental Psychology*, *15*(2), 1979, p. 228.
7. The Carnegie Hero Fund Commission was founded in 1904 by the American philanthropist Andrew Carnegie to reward acts of heroism every year; it has distributed almost 10,000 medals since its foundation.
8. Monroe, K. R. (1996), *op. cit.*, p. 61.
9. Milo, R. D., *Egoism and Altruism*, Wadsworth Publications, 1973 p. 98.
10. France 2, Envoyé special, aired on October 9, 2008.

CHAPTER 9: THE BANALITY OF GOOD

1. It was the philosopher Hannah Arendt who spoke of the "banality of evil" in connection with Adolf Eichmann, the Nazi administrator of the concentration camps who, during his trial, tried to give himself the image of a commonplace functionary, a man like anyone else who was only fulfilling his duties and carrying out orders. Arendt, H., *Eichmann in Jerusalem: A Report on the Banality of Evil*, Penguin, 1963.
2. Marcus Aurelius, *The Meditations.*
3. According to Gaskin, K., Smith, J. D., & Paulwitz, I., *Ein neues Bürgerschaftliches Europa: Eine Untersuchung zur Verbreitung und Rolle von Volunteering in zehn europäischen Ländern,* Lambertus, 1996. In the countries they studied, people who volunteer represent 38% of the population in Holland, 36% in Sweden, 34% in Great Britain, 32% in Belgium, 28% in Denmark, 25% in France and Ireland, and 18% in Germany.
4. Martel, F., *De la culture en Amérique*, Gallimard, 2006, p. 358; Clary, E. G., & Snyder, M. A functional analysis of altruism and prosocial

behavior: The case of volunteerism. In *Prosocial Behavior*, Sage Publications, 1991, pp. 119–148.

5. Laville, J.-L., *Politique de l'association*, Seuil, 2010. They work for 1,100,000 associations, with 21.6 million members.
6. Chatel, Véronique, *Profession: bénévole*, in *L'Express*, special issue, No. 9, May–June 2011, p. 54.
7. The fields of activity are diverse: culture and entertainment (28%), sports (20%), social, sanitary, and humanitarian action (17%), human rights defense (15% in unions, a consumer's defense association, and the like), religion (8%), education (6%), political parties, heritage organizations (3%), environment (2.6%), defense of biodiversity, restoration of natural parks, etc. See Le travail bénévole: un essai de quantification et de valorization, [archive] INSEE. *Economie et statistique*, No. 373, 2004 [pdf].
8. http://www.kiva.org/, http://www.microworld.org/fr/, http://www.globalgiving.org/.
9. Lecomte, J. (2012), *La Bonté humaine. Op. cit.*, Chapter 1.
10. Esterbrook, J. (August 31, 2005), New Orleans fights to stop looting, CBS news. Quoted in Lecomte (2012), *op. cit.*, p. 22.
11. *Arkansas Democrat-Gazette* (September 2, 2005). Quoted in "Governor Kathleen Blanco: Strong leadership in the midst of catastrophe," PDF.
12. Anonymous (September 2, 2005). Troops told "shoot to kill" in New Orleans. ABC News online.
13. Lecomte, *op. cit.*, p. 24.
14. Rosenblatt, S., & Rainey, J. Katrina takes a toll on truth, news accuracy, *Los Angeles Times*, 2005, p. 27.
15. Dwyer, J., & Drew, C. Fear exceeded crime's reality in New Orleans. *New York Times, 25* (2005): A1. See also Rodriguez, H., Trainor, J., & Quarantelli, E. L. Rising to the challenges of a catastrophe: The emergent and prosocial behavior following Hurricane Katrina. *Annals of the American Academy of Political and Social Science, 604*(1), 2006, pp. 82–101, along with Tierney, K., Bevc, C., & Kuligowski, E. Metaphors matter: Disaster myths, media frames, and their consequences in Hurricane Katrina. *Annals of the American Academy of Political and Social Science, 604*(1), 2006, pp. 57–81. Quoted in Lecomte, *op. cit.*, p. 348.
16. Lecomte, *op. cit.*, pp. 25–26.
17. Rodriguez *et al.* (2006), *op. cit.*, p. 84.
18. Barsky, L., Trainor, J., & Torres, M. (2006). Disaster Realities in the Aftermath of Hurricane Katrina: Revisiting the Looting Myth. Retrieved from http://udspace.udel.edu/handle/19716/2367.

19. U.S. House of Representatives (2006), A failure of initiative: Final Report of the Select Bipartisan Committee to Investigate the Preparation for and Response to Hurricane Katrina, Washington, U.S. Government Printing Office, pp. 248–249. Quoted in Lecomte, *op. cit.*, p. 348.
20. Tierney, K., Bevc, C., & Kuligowski, E. (2006). *Op. cit.*, pp. 68, 75.
21. Quarantelli, E. L. The nature and conditions of panic. *American Journal of Sociology*, 1954, pp. 267–275.
22. Der Heide, E. A. Common misconceptions about disasters: Panic, the "disaster syndrome," and looting. *The First*, *72*, 2004, 340–380. Quoted in Lecomte, (2012), *op. cit.*, p. 349.
23. Clarke, L. (2002). Le mythe de la panique. *Sciences humaines*, 16–20. Clarke, L. (2002). Panic: Myth or reality? *Contexts*, *1*(3), 21–26. See also Connell, R. (2001). "Collective behavior in the September 11, 2001 evacuation of the World Trade Center." http://putnam.lib.udel.edu/8080/dspace/handle/19716/683
24. Drury, J., Cocking, C., & Reicher, S. The nature of collective resilience: Survivor reactions to the 2005 London bombings. *International Journal of Mass Emergencies and Disasters*, *27*(1), 2009, pp. 66–95. Summarized in Lecomte, *op. cit.*, pp. 36–37.
25. Quoted by Clarke (2002). *op. cit.*, p. 24.
26. Quarantelli, E. L. Conventional beliefs and counterintuitive realities. *Social Research: An International Quarterly*, *75*(3), 2008, pp. 873–904. Quoted in Lecomte, *op. cit.*, p. 33.

CHAPTER 10: ALTRUISTIC HEROISM

1. According to various articles, mainly one by Buckley, Cara. Man Is Rescued By Stranger on Subway Tracks, *New York Times*, January 3, 2007. In another similar incident, the rescuer did not want to be identified. In March 2009, after a man fell onto the railroad tracks in Pennsylvania Station in New York, a citizen jumped onto the tracks to help him out. As people were crowding around the man to congratulate him, covered in soot and dirt from the tracks, he got into the next train entering the station and refused to speak with a journalist who was there. Wilson, Michael. An Unsung Hero of the Subway, in *New York Times*, March 16, 2009.
2. Oliner, Samuel and Pearl, *Do Unto Others: Extraordinary Acts of Ordinary People*, Basic Books, 2003, p. 21.
3. Monroe, Kristen, *The Heart of Altruism, op. cit.*, pp. 140–1.
4. *Ibid.*

5. Franco, Blau, & Zimbardo, P. Heroism: A conceptual analysis and differentiation between heroic action and altruism. *Review of General Psychology, 15*(2), 2011, pp. 99–113.
6. Hughes-Hallett, L., *Heroes*, London: Harper Collins, 2004; Eagly, A., & Becker, S. Comparing the heroism of women and men. *American Psychologist, 60*, 2005, pp. 343–344.
7. Franco, Z., & Zimbardo, P. The banality of heroism. *Greater Good, 3*, 2006–2007, Fall–Winter, pp. 30–35; Glazer, M. P., & Glazer, P. M. On the trail of courageous behavior. *Sociological Inquiry, 69*, 1999, pp. 276–295; Shepela, S. T., Cook, J., Horlitz, E., Leal, R., Luciano, S., Lutfy, E., . . . Warden, E. Courageous resistance. *Theory and Psychology, 9*, 1999, pp. 787– 805.
8. Robin, M.-M., *The World According to Monsanto: Pollution, Corruption, and the Control of the World's Food Supply*. New Press, 2010. Kindle, pp. 1432–1530.
9. Shepela, S. T., *et al.* (1999), *op. cit.*
10. Monroe, K. R. (1996), *op. cit.*, pp. 66–67.
11. Zimbardo, P., *The Lucifer Effect*, Ebury Digital. Kindle Edition, 2011, p. 1134.

CHAPTER 11: UNCONDITIONAL ALTRUISM

1. Monroe, K. R. (1996), *op. cit.*, pp. ix–xv.
2. Opdyke, I. G., *In My Hands: Memories of a Holocaust Rescuer*, Anchor, 1999.
3. Opdyke, *op. cit.*, p. 111.
4. 90% of the Jewish population of Poland, or 3,000,000 people, were executed during collective massacres or in the concentration camps of Auschwitz, Sobibor, Treblinka, Belzec, and Majdanek, all located in Poland.
5. Oliner, S. P. & P. M., *The Altruistic Personality: Rescuers of Jews in Nazi Europe*, Macmillan, 1988, p. 2.
6. *Ibid.*, p. 166.
7. *Ibid.*, p. 168.
8. *Ibid.*, p. 131.
9. This summary of events is taken from Hallie, P. P., *Lest Innocent Blood Be Shed* (Reprinted edition), Harper Perennial, 1994, p. 12, and Terestchenko, M., *Un si fragile vernis d'humanité*, 2007, *op. cit.*, p. 213.
10. *Ibid.*, p. 173.
11. Hallie, P. P., *op. cit.*, pp. 267–268.
12. Terestchenko, M., *op. cit.*

13. *Ibid.*, p. 140.
14. *Ibid.*, p. 142.
15. *Ibid.*, pp. 206–7.
16. Halter, M., *La Force du bien,* Robert Laffont, 1995, p. 95.
17. Oliner, S. P., & Oliner, P. M. (1988), *op. cit.*, p. 228.
18. *Ibid.*
19. Mordecai Paldiel. Is goodness a mystery? *Jerusalem Post*, October 8, 1989.

CHAPTER 12: BEYOND IMITATIONS, TRUE ALTRUISM: AN EXPERIMENTAL INVESTIGATION

1. Quoted by Harold Schulweis, in the preface to Oliner, S. P., & Oliner, P. M. (1988). *Op. cit,* p. ix–x.
2. Ghiselin, M. T., *The Economy of Nature and the Evolution of Sex*, University of California Press, 1974, p. 247.
3. La Rochefoucauld, F. de (1678/2010), *Reflections; or Sentences and Moral Maxims* (Kindle Locations 483–484). Kindle Edition.
4. Campbell, D. T. On the conflicts between biological and social evolution and between psychology and moral tradition. *American Psychologist*, *30*(12), 1975, 1104. Quoted by Batson, C. D. (1991), *op. cit.*, p. 42.
5. Batson, C. D. (2011), *op. cit.*, p. 4.
6. *Ibid.,* pp. 87–88.
7. Hatfield, E., Walster, G. W., & Piliavin, J. A. Equity theory and helping relationship. In *Altruism, Sympathy and Helping: Psychological and Sociological Principles*, 1978, pp. 115–139. Quoted by Batson, C. D. (1991), p. 39.
8. Batson, C. D. (2011), *op. cit.*, p. 4.
9. *Ibid.,* p. 89.
10. Nagel, T., *Possibility of Altruism*, Princeton University Press, 1979, p. 80.
11. Here, since the subject being observed is a woman, all the observers were women, so as to suppress the effects of politeness or "gallantry." The possibility, for instance, that men might feel "obliged" to help a woman in difficulty would complicate the study by the addition of additional parameters. All these experiments were also undertaken with men and the results are identical in both cases.
12. These two experiments reported in Batson, C. D., *et al.* (1981). *Op. cit.* and two experiments in Batson, C. D., O'Quin, K., Fultz, J., Vanderplas, M., & Isen, A. M. (1983), Influence of self-reported distress and empathy on egoistic versus altruistic motivation to help. *Journal of Personality and Social Psychology*, *45*(3), 706.

13. All sources for the figures found in this book can be found at the end of the book, p. 877.
14. We will return to this point of view at greater length in Chapter 25, "The Champions of Selfishness."
15. Batson, C. D., & Weeks, J. L. (1996), Mood effects of unsuccessful helping: Another test of the empathy-altruism hypothesis. *Personality and Social Psychology Bulletin*, *22*(2), 148–157.
16. Concerning these objections, see Hoffman, M. L. (1991). Is empathy altruistic? *Psychological Inquiry*, *2*(2), 131–133; Sober, E., & Wilson, D. S. (1999), *Unto Others: The Evolution and Psychology of Unselfish Behavior*. Harvard University Press; Wallach, L., & Wallach, M. A. (1991). Why altruism, even though it exists, cannot be demonstrated by social psychological experiments. *Psychological Inquiry*, *2*(2), 153–155.
17. The fact that they can certainly think about Katie's fate *later on*, after the text, does not influence the result of the experiment.
18. For a more detailed description, see Batson, C. D. (2011). *Op. cit.*, pp. 140–145, and Stocks, E. L., Lishner, D. A., & Decker, S. K. (2009), Altruism or psychological escape: Why does empathy promote prosocial behavior? *European Journal of Social Psychology, 39*, 649–665.
19. The subjects with weak empathy, on the other hand, help only when they fear that their inaction will be criticized.
20. Batson, C. D., Dyck, J. L., Brandt, J. R., Batson, J. G., Powell, A. L., McMaster, M. R., & Griffitt, C. (1988), Five studies testing two new egoistic alternatives to the empathy-altruism hypothesis. *Journal of Personality and Social Psychology*, *55*(1), 52. The experiment also shows that altruists do better on the test when Suzann's fate depends on them, and are less attentive when they know that Suzanne isn't risking anything. On the other hand, those who have little empathy have a lower score than the altruists when Suzanne is in danger, but curiously get a higher score when they know she isn't risking anything. The explanation offered is that, in the second case, they are more interested in their own personal score, whereas altruists lost interest in the test since it isn't useful to Suzanne.
21. See especially Cialdini, R. B. Altruism or egoism? That is (still) the question. *Psychological Inquiry*, *2*(2), 1991, 124–126.
22. Interested readers can find these details in C. D. Batson's articles and in the summary he made of them in his recent book, *Altruism in Humans* (2011), *op. cit.*
23. Batson, C. D. Why act for the public good? Four answers. *Personality and Social Psychology Bulletin*, *20*(5), 1994, 603–610. The paper from

which Batson's conclusion is quoted was published in 1994. Between 1978 and 1996, over eighteen years, altogether thirty-one experiments were conducted, all lending support to the empathy-altruism hypothesis.

24. See especially Cialdini, R. B. (1991). *Op. cit.*
25. Batson, Daniel, *Altruism in Humans,* op. cit., p. 161

CHAPTER 13: THE PHILOSOPHICAL ARGUMENTS AGAINST UNIVERSAL SELFISHNESS

1. For a detailed account of the positions of these thinkers, see Batson, C. D., *The Altruism Question: Toward a Social Psychological Answer*, Lawrence Erlbaum, 1991, Chapters 1 and 2.
2. David Hume, *Works of David Hume. A Treatise of Human Nature, An Enquiry Concerning Human Understanding, An Enquiry Concerning the Principles of Morals, The Natural... Dialogues Concerning Natural Religion* (Kindle Locations 3705–3706). MobileReference. Kindle Edition.
3. *Ibid.*
4. Quoted in Kohn, A., *The Brighter Side of Human Nature, op. cit.*, p. 215.
5. Feinberg, J., & Shafer-Landau, R., *Reason and Responsibility: Readings in Some Basic Problems of Philosophy*, Wadsworth, 1971, Chapter 19.
6. Maslow, A. H., *The Psychology of Science, a Reconnaissance*, Henry Regnery, 1966.
7. Kohn, A. (1992). *Op. cit.*, p. 209.
8. Spencer, H. (1892). *The Principles of Ethics*, vol. 1. D. Appleton and Co., pp. 241, 279. Quoted in Kohn, A. (1992). *Op. cit.*, p. 210.
9. As told to Kristen Monroe, Monroe, K. R. (1996). *Op. cit.*, p. 142.
10. For a more detailed exposition, see Broad, C. D., *Ethics and the History of Philosophy* (new edition), 2010, pp. 218–231.
11. Schlick, M., *Problems of Ethics*, Nabu Press, 2011.
12. Feinberg, J. (1971). *Op. cit.*
13. Monroe, K. R. (1996). *Op. cit.*, p. 201.
14. Batson, C. D. (2011). *Op. cit.*, p. 64.
15. Haidt, J., *The Righteous Mind: Why Good People Are Divided by Politics and Religion,* Allen Lane, 2012.
16. Kagan, J., *Unstable Ideas: Temperament, Cognition, and Self*, Harvard University Press, 1989. Quoted by Kohn, A. (1992). *Op. cit.*, p. 41.
17. Mandela, Nelson, *Long Walk to Freedom*, Little, Brown, 1994.

CHAPTER 14: ALTRUISM IN THEORIES OF EVOLUTION

1. Darwin, C., *The Descent of Man, and Selection in Relation to Sex*, Vol. 1, John Murray, 1871, p. 90, http://darwin-online.org.uk/.
2. *Ibid.* p. 100.
3. E. Sober, in Davidson, R. J., & Harrington, A., *Visions of Compassion: Western Scientists and Tibetan Buddhists Examine Human Nature,* Oxford University Press, 2002, p. 50.
4. I am grateful to Frans de Waal for clarifying this point for me.
5. See especially Trivers, R. L., *Social Evolution*, 1985, Benjamin-Cummings.
6. Memoirs of the Society of Naturalists of St. Petersburg. Quoted in Peter Kropotkin, *Mutual Aid: A Factor of Evolution,* London: Freedom Press, 2009.
7. Nowak, M. A., & Highfield, R., *SuperCooperators: Altruism, Evolution, and Why We Need Each Other to Succeed,* Simon & Schuster, 2011, pp. 274–275. Bourke, A. F. G., *Principles of Social Evolution*, Oxford University Press, 2011. See also the excellent article summarizing these arguments by Candau, Joël. Pourquoi coopérer. *Terrain* (1), 2012, pp. 4–25.
8. We know, for instance, that over five hundred species of bacteria colonize the teeth and mucous membranes of humans, offering an obvious potential for cooperation as well as for competition. But it has been demonstrated that it is cooperation between these bacteria that allows them to survive in an environment where a single species is incapable of proliferating. See Kolenbrander, P. E. Mutualism versus independence: Strategies of mixed-species oral biofilms in vitro using saliva as the sole nutrient source. *Infect. Immun.*, *69*, 2001, 5794–5804. Concerning bacteria, see also Koschwanez, J. H., Foster, K. R., & Murray, A. W. Sucrose utilization in budding yeast as a model for the origin of undifferentiated multicellularity. *PLoS Biology*, 2011, *9*(8).
9. See especially Aron, S., Passera, S. & L., *Les Sociétés animales: évolution de la coopération et organisation sociale*, De Boeck University, 2000, as well as Wilson, E. O., *The Social Conquest of Earth* (1st edition), Liveright, 2012.
10. Candau, J. (2012), *op. cit.*, and Henrich, J., & Henrich, N., *Why Humans Cooperate: A Cultural and Evolutionary Explanation*, Oxford University Press, 2007.
11. Darwin, *The Origin of Species*, Chapter 8, http://darwin-online.org.uk/.
12. Ibid., Chapter 6, http://darwin-online.org.uk/.

13. Darwin, C., *The Descent of Man, op.cit.*, p. 82. http://darwin-online.org.uk/.
14. Sober, E., & Wilson, D. S., *Unto Others, op. cit.*, pp. 201–205.
15. Dugatkin, L. A., *Cooperation Among Animals,* Oxford University Press, 1997.
16. Hamilton, W. D. (1963). The evolution of altruistic behavior. *American Naturalist*, *97*(896), 354–356. Hamilton, W. D. (1964). The genetical evolution of social behaviour. *Journal of Theoretical Biology*, *7*(1), 1–16.
17. Wilson, E. O., *The Insect Societies*, Harvard University Press, 1971.
18. Clutton-Brock, T. H., O'Riain, M., Brotherton, P., Gaynor, D., Kansky, R., Griffin, A., & Manser, M. Selfish sentinels in cooperative mammals. *Science*, *284*(5420), 1999, p. 1640.
19. It has also been verified among alpheid shrimp, the naked mole-rat, certain wasps, bees, Coleoptera, and, based on recent discoveries, among certain Trematoda worms. The first of these confirmations came thirteen years after the publication of Hamilton's first article, following research by Robert Trivers and Hope Hare: Trivers, R.L., & Hare, H. Haplodiploidy and the evolution of the social insects. *Science*, *191*(4224), 1976, 249–263.
20. See the biography of George Price: Harman, O. S., *The Price of Altruism,* Norton, 2010.
21. Hamilton, W. D. (1970). Selfish and spiteful behaviour in an evolutionary model. *Nature*, 228, 1218–1219.
22. Price, G. R., & others. (1970). Selection and covariance. *Nature*, *227*(5257), 520.
23. Hill, K. R. (2002). Altruistic cooperation during foraging by the Ache, and the evolved human predisposition to cooperate. *Human Nature*, *13*(1), 105–128; Kelly, R. L., *The Foraging Spectrum: Diversity in Hunter-Gatherer Lifeways,* Smithsonian Institution Press, 1995.
24. Richerson, P. J., & Boyd, R., *Not by Genes Alone: How Culture Transformed Human Evolution,* University of Chicago Press, 2004. Wood, W., & Eagly, A. H. (2002). A cross-cultural analysis of the behavior of women and men: Implications for the origins of sex differences. *Psychological Bulletin*, *128*(5), 699.
25. Trivers, R. L. (1971). The evolution of reciprocal altruism. *Quarterly Review of Biology*, 35–57; Axelrod, R., & Hamilton, W. D. (1981), The evolution of cooperation. *Science*, *211*(4489), 1390; Boyd, R., & Richerson, P. J. (1988). An evolutionary model of social learning: The effects of spatial and temporal variation. *Social Learning: Psychological and Biological Perspectives*, 29–48.

26. Hill, K. R., Walker, R. S., Božičević, M., Eder, J., Headland, T., Hewlett, B., Hurtado, A. M., *et al.* (2011). Co-residence patterns in hunter-gatherer societies show unique human social structure. *Science*, *331*(6022), 1286. The researchers notably studied the Inuit of Labrador, the Ache of Paraguay, the Australian Wanindiljaugwa, and several other communities.
27. Dawkins, R., *The Selfish Gene*, Oxford University Press, (2d ed.), 1990.
28. *Ibid.*, p. ix.
29. *Ibid.*, p. 3.
30. *Ibid.*, p. 139.
31. Warneken, F., & Tomasello, M. (2009). The roots of human altruism. *British Journal of Psychology, 100*, 455–471.
32. Goodall, J., & Berman, P. L. *Reason for Hope: A Spiritual Journey*, Grand Central Publishing, (1999), p. 121.
33. Waal, F. D. de, *The Age of Empathy*, p. 42.
34. McLean, B., & Elkind, P., *The Smartest Guys in the Room: The Amazing Rise and Scandalous Fall of Enron*, Penguin, 2003. Quoted in Waal, F. B. M. de (2009), p. 39. Clarke, T. (2005). Accounting for Enron: shareholder value and stakeholder interests. *Corporate Governance: An International Review*, *13*(5), 598–612.
35. "The Very Human Heroes of Fukushima," *The Guardian*, Thursday, March 24, 2011.
36. Wilson, E. O. (1971). *Op. cit.*
37. Wilson, E. O., *The Social Conquest of Earth*, Liveright, 2012.
38. Cavalli-Sforza, L. L., & Feldman, M. W. (1978). Darwinian selection and "altruism." *Theoretical Population Biology*, *14*(2), 268–280.
39. Nowak, M. A., & Highfield, R. (2011). *Op. cit.*, p. 106.
40. See the detailed "Supplementary Information," doi: 10.1038/nature09205, available at www.nature.com/nature, which accompanies the main article by Nowak, M. A., Tarnita, C. E., & Wilson, E. O. (2010). The evolution of eusociality. *Nature*, *466*(7310), 1057–1062. George Price's covariance equation is also included in this new analysis, which explains it as a mathematical tautology.
41. Hunt, J. H., *The Evolution of Social Wasps*, Oxford University Press, 2007; Gadagkar, R., & Gadagkar, R., *The Social Biology of Ropalidia Marginata: Toward Understanding the Evolution of Eusociality,* Harvard University Press, 2001.
42. Johns, P. M., Howard, K. J., Breisch, N. L., Rivera, A., & Thorne, B. L. (2009). Nonrelatives inherit colony resources in a primitive termite. *Proceedings of the National Academy of Sciences*, *106*(41),

17452–17456. The ethologist Elli Leadbeater has also demonstrated that *Polistes dominulus* wasps built new nests every spring, and often do so in small groups of females that are not all related. She observed that the females who take part in building the nests had more offspring than solitary wasps. Leadbeater, E., Carruthers, J. M., Green, J. P., Rosser, N. S., & Field, J. (2011). Nest inheritance is the missing source of direct fitness in a primitively eusocial insect. *Science*, *333*(6044), 874–876.

43. See the recent books by these two authors, Wilson, E. O., *The Social Conquest of Earth*, Liveright, 2012, and Nowak, M., & Highfield, R., *SuperCooperators*, The Free Press, 2011 which contain all the pertinent scientific references.
44. Nowak, M. A., Tarnita, C. E., & Wilson, E. O. (2010). *Op. cit.* For one of the reactions to this article, see Abbot, P., Abe, J., Alcock, J., Alizon, S., Alpedrinha, J. A. C., Andersson, M.,...Balshine, S. (2011). Inclusive fitness theory and eusociality. *Nature*, *471*(7339), E1–E4. For the authors' reply, see Nowak, M. A., Tarnita, C. E., & Wilson, E. O. (2011). Nowak *et al.* reply, *Nature*, *471*(7339), E9–E10.
45. After the publication of the book by Williams, G. C., *Adaptation and Natural Selection*, Princeton University Press, 1966 which set forth an uncompromising criticism of group selection.
46. These writers offer offer a fascinating general view of the question of altruism in evolution in their book: Sober, E., & Wilson, D. S., *Unto Others*.
47. Hamilton, W. D. (1975), Innate social aptitudes of man: An approach from evolutionary genetics. *Biosocial Anthropology*, *133*, 155.
48. That does not require the group to remain in the same place. If a foreign explorer sits down at their table, he does not form part of their group. On the other hand, a member of the group can decide not to take part in the expedition and can remain at home in order to oversee the logistics of their trip from a distance.
49. Bowles, S., & Gintis, H., *A Cooperative Species: Human Reciprocity and Its Evolution*, Princeton University Press, 2011.
50. We should remember, as we read what follows, that to evolution specialists the word "altruism" designates "behavior that is beneficial to others." It is only when these authors use the expression "psychological altruism" that they refer to the sense of the word "altruism" as Daniel Batson and the present author mean it in these pages.
51. Nowak, M. A., & Highfield, R. (2011). *Op. cit.*, pp. 262–263.

Chapter 15: Maternal Love, Foundation for Extended Altruism?

1. Batson, C. D. (2011). *Altruism in Humans*, *op. cit.*, p. 4.
2. *Ibid.*
3. Darwin, C. (1871). *Op. cit.*, p. 308. In fact, parental care, regarded as one of the main sources of empathy, is itself based on more ancient instincts that preceded the ability to feel empathy, since we also observe it among animal species whose rudimentary nervous system does not allow complex cognitive or emotional faculties. Scorpion mothers, for instance, carry their young on their backs, even though that considerably slows down their movements, thereby exposing them to the danger of being captured by a predator. Shaffer, L. R., & Formanowicz, J. (1996), A cost of viviparity and parental care in scorpions: Reduced sprint speed and behavioural compensation. *Animal Behaviour, 51*(5), 1017–1024.
4. Bell, D. C. (2001). Evolution of parental caregiving. *Personality and Social Psychology Review, 5*(3), 216–229.
5. McDougall, W., *An Introduction to Social Psychology*, Methuen 1908. I owe these various clarifications to Daniel Batson. See also Batson, C. D (1991). *Op. cit.*, Chapters 2 and 3.
6. Sober, E., in Davidson, R. J., & Harrington, A., *Visions of Compassion: Western Scientists and Tibetan Buddhists Examine Human Nature,* Oxford University Press, 2002, p. 99, and Sober, E., & Wilson, D. S. (1998). *Op. cit.*; Waal, F. B. M. de, *Le Bon Singe: Les bases naturelles de la morale*, Bayard, 1997; Churchland, P. S., *Braintrust: What Neuroscience Tells Us about Morality*, Princeton University Press, 2011.
7. Paul Ekman, in conversation with the author.
8. Leopard vs. baboon, http://www.youtube.com/watch?v=Nvp9cELWHhs.
9. Hrdy, S. B., *Mothers and Others: The Evolutionary Origins of Mutual Understanding*, Belknap Press, 2009, pp. 67 and 109.
10. *Ibid.*, p. 66.
11. Marlowe, F., "Who tends Hadza children?" in Hewlett, B., & Lamb, M., *Hunter-Gatherer Childhoods*, 2005, pp. 177–190. Quoted in Hrdy, S. B. (2009). *Op. cit.*, p. 76.
12. Sagi, A., IJzendoorn, M. H., Aviezer, O., Donnell, F., Koren-Karie, N., Joels, T., & Harl, Y. (1995). Attachments in a multiple-caregiver and multiple-infant environment: The case of the Israeli kibbutzim. *Monographs of the Society for Research in Child Development, 60* (2–3), 71–91. Quoted in Hrdy, S. B. (2009). *Op. cit.*, p. 131.

13. Personal communication from Jane Goodall, whom I thank for clarifying this.
14. Sear, R., Mace, R., & McGregor, I. A. (2000). Maternal grandmothers improve nutritional status and survival of children in rural Gambia. *Proceedings of the Royal Society of London. Series B: Biological Sciences, 267*(1453), 1641. Quoted in Hrdy, S. B. (2009). *Op. cit.*, pp. 107–108.
15. Pope, S. K., Whiteside, L., Brooks-Gunn, J., Kelleher, K. J., Rickert, V. I., Bradley, R. H., & Casey, P. H. (1993). Low-birth-weight infants born to adolescent mothers. *JAMA, 269*(11), 1396–1400. Quoted in Hrdy, S. B. (2009). *Op. cit.*, pp. 107–108.
16. Hrdy, S. B. (2009). *Op. cit.*, p. 144.
17. Watson, J., *Psychological Care of Infant and Child*, W. W. Norton, 1928, p. 82. Quoted in Hrdy, S. B. (2009). *Op. cit.*, p. 82.
18. Fernandez-Duque, E. (2007). Cost and benefit of parental care in free ranging owl monkey (*Aotus azarai*). Abstract. Article presented at the 76th annual meeting of the American Association of Physical Anthropologists, March 28–31, Philadelphia; Wolovich, C. K., Perea-Rodriguez, J. P., & Fernandez-Duque, E. (2008). Food transfers to young and mates in wild owl monkeys (*Aotus azarai*). *American Journal of Primatology, 70*(3), 211–221. Quoted in Hrdy, S. B. (2009). *Op. cit.*, pp. 88–89.
19. Boesch, C., Bole, C., Eckhardt, N., & Boesch, H. (2010). Altruism in forest chimpanzees: The case of adoption. *PloS one*, *5*(1), e8901.
20. Busquet, G., *À l'écoute de l'Inde; des mangroves du Bangladesh aux oasis du Karakoram*, Transboréal, 2013, pp. 105ff.
21. Hrdy, S. B. (2009). *Op. cit.*, p. 128.
22. *Ibid.*, pp. 292–293.
23. See especially the exhaustive study on the effect of day care centers, NICHD Early Child Care Research Network, 1997, as well as McCartney, K., "Current research on child care effects," in Tremblay, R. E., *et al.*, *Encyclopedia on Early Childhood Development [online], Centre of Excellence for Early Childhood Development*, 2004, 1–5. This study is ongoing, and one can follow its developments at www.nichd.nih.gov and www.excellence-earlychildhood.ca. Quoted in Hrdy, S. B. (2009). *Op. cit.*, p. 125.
24. The French philosopher and historian Élisabeth Badinter, for example, thinks that the concept of the maternal instinct is "old-fashioned" and that any discourse inspired by naturalism is a step backward. Badinter, É., *Le Conflit: La femme et la mère*, Le Livre de Poche, 2011.

CHAPTER 16: THE EVOLUTION OF CULTURES

1. Some people even go so far as to deny its importance, like the anthropologist Laura Betzig, who states straightforwardly in a scholarly book, "Personally, I find culture useless." Betzig, L. L., *Human Nature: A Critical Reader*, Oxford University Press, 1997, p. 17. Quoted in Richerson, P. J., & Boyd, R. (2004). *Op. cit.*, p. 19.
2. *Ibid.*, p. 5.
3. Tomasello, M., *Why We Cooperate*, MIT Press, 2009, p. xiv.
4. *Ibid.*, p. x.
5. Richerson, P. J., & Boyd, R. (2004). *Op. cit.*, p. 6.
6. Boyd, R., & Richerson, P. J. (1976). A simple dual inheritance model of the conflict between social and biological evolution. *Zygon®*, *11*(3), 254–262, along with their principal book, *Not by Genes Alone* (2004). *Op. cit.*
7. Lydens, L.A. "A Longitudinal Study of Crosscultural Adoption: Identity Development Among Asian Adoptees at Adolescence and Early Adulthood." Northwestern University, 1988. Quoted in Richerson, P. J., & Boyd, R. (2004). *Op. cit.*, p. 39–42.
8. Heard, J. N., & Norman, J., *White into Red: A Study of the Assimilation of White Persons Captured by Indians.* Scarecrow Press, 1973. Quoted in Richerson, P. J., & Boyd, R. (2004). *Op. cit.*, pp. 41–42.
9. According to Richerson, P. J., & Boyd, R. (2004). *Op. cit.*, pp. 139–145, the development of social learning, unique to humans, which is the foundation for the evolution of cultures, could have had as a catalyst unprecedented climatic fluctuations that dominated the second half of the Pleistocene era during the last 500,000 years. There is in fact a correlation between climatic variations and an increase in the volume of the brain in hominids and a number of mammals, which increases their ability to adopt new behavior and, in the case of hominids, to make new tools and acquire transmissible knowledge. Hominids began to make tools about 2.6 million years ago, but these tools changed very little for a long time. Then, 250,000 years ago, the number and especially variety of tools suddenly increased. Finally, 50,000 years ago, the humans of Africa spread throughout the world. See Hofreiter, M., Serre, D., Poinar, H. N., Kuch, M., Pääbo, S., *et al.* (2001), Ancient DNA. *Nature Reviews Genetics*, 2(5), 353–359. Cité in Richerson, P. J., & Boyd, R. (2004). *Op. cit.*, p. 143.

CHAPTER 17: ALTRUISTIC BEHAVIOR AMONG ANIMALS

1. Darwin, C., "On the Origin of Species," in *Works of Charles Darwin* (1st, 2nd, and 6th editions). Kindle Edition locations 53721–53722 and 53732.

2. Darwin, C. (1877). *The Expression of the Emotions in Man and Animals, op. cit.*
3. Darwin, C. (1871) *The Descent of Man, op.cit.* vol. 1, p. 35, http://darwin-online.org.uk/.
4. Jerome Kagan, eminent Harvard professor.
5. Tai National Park, in the Ivory Coast, cited in Waal, F. B. M. de (2010). *Op. cit.*, p. 7.
6. Waal, F. B. M. de (1997). *Le Bon Singe. Op. cit.*
7. Watch on YouTube: www.youtube.com/watch?v=DgjyhKN_35g.
8. Waal, F. B. M. de (2010). *Op. cit.*, p. 56.
9. Savage, E., Temerlin, J., & Lemmon, W. (1975). Contemporary Primatology 5th Int. Congr. Primat., Nagoya, 1974, pp. 287–291. Karger.
10. Waal, F. B. M. de (1997). *Op. cit.*, p. 220.
11. Moss, C., *Elephant Memories: Thirteen Years in the Life of an Elephant Family,* William Morrow & Co., 1988, pp. 124–125.
12. Henderson, J. Y., *Circus Doctor,* P. Davies, 1952, p. 78. Quoted in Masson, J. M., & McCarthy, S., *Quand les éléphants pleurent*, Albin Michel, 1997.
13. See www.animalplace.org/mr-g-and-jellybean-united. Many thanks to Jane Goodall for sending me this information.
14. Waal, F. B. M. de (2010). *Op. cit.*, p. 153.
15. Goodall, J., & Berman, P. L., *Reason for Hope: A Spiritual Journey*, Grand Central Publishing, 1999, p. 139.
16. Jane Goodall, personal communication.
17. Waal, F. B. M. de (2010). *Op. cit.*, pp. 130–131.
18. Köhler, W., & Winter, E., *The Mentality of Apes*, K. Paul, Trench, Trubner, 1925. Quoted in Rollin, B. E., *The Unheeded Cry: Animal Consciousness, Animal Pain and Science,* Oxford University Press, 1989, p. 223.
19. The video can be seen on https://www.youtube.com/watch?v=lf08i5vqIvQ.
20. Lee, P. (1987). Allomothering among African elephants. *Animal Behaviour, 35*(1), 278–291.
21. Bates, L. A., Lee, P. C., Njiraini, N., Poole, J. H., Sayialel, K., Sayialel, S., . . . Byrne, R. W. (2008). Do elephants show empathy? *Journal of Consciousness Studies, 15*(10–11), 204–225.
22. Caldwell, M. C., & Caldwell, D. K., "Epimeletic (Care-Giving) Behavior in Cetacea." In *Whales, Porpoises and Dolphins.* University of California Press, 1966, pp. 755–789.
23. Lilly, J. C. (1963), Distress call of the bottlenose dolphin: Stimuli and evoked behavioral responses. *Science, 139*(3550), 116; Lilly, J. C., *Man and Dolphin*, Gollancz, 1962.

24. Brown, D. H., & Norris, K. S. (1956). Observations of captive and wild cetaceans. *Journal of Mammalogy*, *37*(3), 311–326; Siebenaler, J., & Caldwell, D. K. (1956), Cooperation among adult dolphins. *Journal of Mammalogy*, *37*(1), 126–128.
25. The incident was photographed. See the *Daily Mail*, July 29, 2009. http://www.dailymail.co.uk/news/article-1202941/Pictured-The-moment-Mila-brave-Beluga-whale-saved-stricken-divers-life-pushing-surface.html.
26. According to a report from the New Zealand Press Association, November 22, 2004.
27. Nishiwaki. M. (1962), Aerial photographs show sperm whales' interesting habits. *Nor. Hvalfangstid*. 51:395–398. Davis, W. M., *Nimrod of the Sea; or the American Whaleman*, Harper, 1874.
28. Who Is the Walrus? *New York Times*, May 28, 2008.
29. Mohr, E., *Das Verhalten der Pinnipedier*, W. de Gruyter, 1956.
30. Helfer, R., *The Beauty of the Beasts,* Jeremy P. Tarcher, 1990, pp. 82–83.
31. Romero, T., Castellanos, M. A., & Waal, F. B. M. de (2010). Consolation as possible expression of sympathetic concern among chimpanzees. *Proceedings of the National Academy of Sciences, 107*(27), 12110.
32. See Waal, F. B. M. de, *De la réconciliation chez les primates,* Flammarion, 1992.
33. Moss, C. (1988). *Elephant Memories. Op. cit.*, pp. 272–273.
34. Ryan, M., & Thornycraft, P. Jumbos mourn black rhino killed by poachers, *Sunday Independent*, November 18, 2007, quoted in Bekoff, M., & Pierce, J., *Wild Justice: The Moral Lives of Animals*, University of Chicago Press, 2009, p. 105.
35. Goodall, J., *The Chimpanzees of Gombe: Patterns of Behavior*, Harvard University Press, 1986.
36. Boesch, C., Bole, C., Eckhardt, N., & Boesch, H. (2010). Altruism in forest chimpanzees: The case of adoption. *PloS One*, *5*(1), e8901.
37. McGrew, W. C., *Chimpanzee Material Culture: Implications for Human Evolution*, Cambridge University Press, 1992; McGrew, W. C., *The Cultured Chimpanzee: Reflections on Cultural Primatology*, Cambridge University Press, 2004. See also the article by Dominique Lestel in the journal *Science et Avenir*, special issue, Oct.–Nov. 2005.
38. Menzel, E. W. (1975). Purposive behavior as a basis for objective communication between chimpanzees. *Science*, *189*(4203), 652; Menzel, E. W. (1978). Cognitive mapping in chimpanzees. *Cognitive Processes in Animal Behavior*, 375–422.
39. Premack, D., Woodruff, G., *et al.* (1978). Does the chimpanzee have a theory of mind? *Behavioral and Brain Sciences*, *1*(4), 515–526.

40. Hare, B., Call, J., & Tomasello, M. (2001). Do chimpanzees know what conspecifics know? *Animal Behaviour*, *61*(1), 139–151.
41. Bugnyar, T., & Heinrich, B. (2005). Ravens, *Corvus corax*, differentiate between knowledgeable and ignorant competitors. *Proceedings of the Royal Society B: Biological Sciences*, *272*(1573), 1641.
42. For wolves and dogs, see Virányi, Z., Gácsi, M., Kubinyi, E., Topál, J., Belényi, B., Ujfalussy, D., & Miklósi, Á. (2008). Comprehension of human pointing gestures in young human-reared wolves (*Canis lupus*) and dogs (*Canis familiaris*). *Animal Cognition*, *11*(3), 373–387. For capuchin monkeys, see Kuroshima, H., Fujita, K., Adachi, I., Iwata, K., & Fuyuki, A. (July 3, 2003). A capuchin monkey (*Cebus apella*) recognizes when people do and do not know the location of food. *Animal Cognition*, *6*(4), 283–291.
43. Waal, F. B. M. de (2010). *Op. cit.*, pp. 150–151 and 346–347.
44. Yamamoto, S., Humle, T., & Tanaka, M. (2012). Chimpanzees' flexible targeted helping based on an understanding of conspecifics' goals. *Proceedings of the National Academy of Sciences of the United States of America*.
45. Mischel, W., Ebbesen, E. B., & Raskoff Zeiss, A. (1972). Cognitive and attentional mechanisms in delay of gratification. *Journal of Personality and Social Psychology*, *21*(2), 204.
46. Rohan, A. de (2003). Deep thinkers: The more we study dolphins, the brighter they turn out to be. *The Guardian* (UK). Quoted in Balcombe, J., & Balcombe, J. P., *Second Nature: The Inner Lives of Animals*, Palgrave Macmillan, 2003, p. 33.
47. Described in Waal, F. B. M. de (2010). *Op. cit.*, p. 132.
48. Gallup, G. G. (1970). Chimpanzees: Self-recognition. *Science*, *167*(3914), 86.
49. Nimchinsky, E. A., Gilissen, E., Allman, J. M., Perl, D. P., Erwin, J. M., & Hof, P. R. (1999). A neuronal morphologic type unique to humans and great apes. *Proceedings of the National Academy of Sciences*, *96*(9), 5268.
50. Hakeem, A. Y., Sherwood, C. C., Bonar, C. J., Butti, C., Hof, P. R., & Allman, J. M. (2009), Von Economo neurons in the elephant brain. *The Anatomical Record: Advances in Integrative Anatomy and Evolutionary Biology*, *292*(2), 242–248.
51. Daniel Batson, in conversation.
52. Warneken, F., & Tomasello, M. (2006). Altruistic helping in human infants and young chimpanzees. *Science*, *311*(5765), 1301.
53. Warneken, F., & Tomasello, M. (2007). Helping and cooperation at 14 months of age. *Infancy*, *11*(3), 271–294.

54. Crawford, M. P. (1937). The cooperative solving of problems by young chimpanzees. *Comparative Psychology Monographs*, *14*(2), 1–88. For the video clip, see http://www.emory.edu/LIVING_LINKS/av/nissencrawford_cut.mov.
55. I am grateful to Malini Suchak and Frans de Waal for their clarifications of the interpretations of these experiments.
56. Plotnik, J. M., Lair, R., Suphachoksahakun, W., & Waal, F. B. M. de (2011). Elephants know when they need a helping trunk in a cooperative task. *Proceedings of the National Academy of Sciences*, *108*(12), 5116.
57. Horner, V., Carter, J. D., Suchak, M., & Waal, F. B. M. de (2011). Spontaneous prosocial choice by chimpanzees. *Proceedings of the National Academy of Sciences*, *108*(33), 13847–13851.
58. Rollin, B. E., *The Unheeded Cry: Animal Consciousness, Animal Pain and Science,* Oxford University Press, 1989.
59. Frans de Waal in conversation with Martha Nussbaum: http://www.youtube.com/watch?v=ZL5eONzGIR0.
60. Rollin, B. E. (1989). *Op. cit.*, p. 32.
61. Darwin, C. (1871). *The Descent of Man*, *op.cit.*, p. 35.
62. Frans de Waal coined the English word *anthropodenial* to designate the denial, commonly observed in the scientific community and the public at large, of any similarity between human and animal mental states and emotions.
63. Frans de Waal, *The Age of Empathy*, *op. cit.*, p. 131.
64. Rollin, B. E. (1989). *Op. cit.*, p. 23.
65. Frans de Waal, *The Age of Empathy*, *op. cit.*, p. 90.
66. See his recent book, which retraces the history of his research. Davidson, R. J., & Begley, S., *The Emotional Life of Your Brain,* Hudson Street Press, 2012.

CHAPTER 18: ALTRUISM AMONG CHILDREN

1. Tomasello, M. (2009). *Why We Cooperate. Op. cit.*, p. 3.
2. Tremblay, R. E., *Prévenir la violence dès la petite enfance*, Odile Jacob, 2008. In English: McCord, J., & Tremblay, R. E. (Eds.), *Preventing Antisocial Behavior: Interventions from Birth Through Adolescence*, Guilford Press, 1992.
3. Sagi, A., & Hoffman, M. L. (1976). Empathic distress in the newborn. *Developmental Psychology*, *12*(2), 175.

   For an account of the various phases of development in children, from self-awareness and reaction to others' distress to compassionate behavior, see Hoffman, M. L., *Empathy and Moral Development: Implications for Caring and Justice,* Cambridge University Press, 2000.

4. Martin, G. B., & Clark, R. D. (1982). Distress crying in neonates: Species and peer specificity. *Developmental Psychology, 18*(1), 3.
5. Sagi and Hoffman had deduced the presence of a "rudimentary empathic reaction of distress," which allows the newborn to tune into the emotional state of another infant, without clearly distinguishing its own emotions from those of others. According to the neuroscientist Jean Decety, "these results demonstrate that the newborn possesses the two essential aspects of empathy: 1) the ability to share emotions with people with whom it can identify; and 2) the distinction between self and other." (Decety, J., "L'empathie est-elle une simulation mentale de la subjectivité d'autrui." In Berthoz, A., Jorland, G., *et al. L'Empathie,* Odile Jacob, 2004.) Other researchers, like the neuroscientist Tania Singer, are more cautious in their interpretations, since indubitable signs of distinction between self and other appear only after the age of fourteen months. Questioned about this, Tania Singer thinks the discrimination made between the different cries by the newborn stems simply from the fact that its constitution allows it at birth to distinguish a human voice from an ordinary sound and to grant various degrees of importance to different kinds of voices. The intensity of emotional contagion could be linked to the degree of similarity between the infant and the crying child. According to Singer, the reason newborns do not cry upon hearing a recording of their own cries can be attributed to the fact that our brain anticipates the effects of our own reactions (our tears, for instance) and automatically neutralizes them before these reactions occur. That is why we cannot tickle ourselves. Similarly, placing one of my hands over another as a sign of comfort will have the same calming effect only if someone takes my hand when I am suffering (Tania Singer, in conversation, February 2012).
6. Soltis, J. (2004). The signal functions of early infant crying. *Behavioral and Brain Sciences, 27,* 443–490; Zeifman, D. M. (2001). An ethological analysis of human infant crying: Answering Tinbergen's four questions. *Developmental Psychobiology, 39,* 265–285. Quoted in Batson, R. D. (2011). *Altruism in humans. Op. cit.*
7. Hamlin, J. K., Wynn, K., & Bloom, P. (2007). Social evaluation by preverbal infants. *Nature, 450*(7169), 557–559.

   This experiment had already been successfully carried out in the same laboratory with older children, from twelve to sixteen months. Kuhlmeier, V., Wynn, K., & Bloom, P. (2003). Attribution of dispositional states by 12-month-olds. *Psychological Science*, *14*(5), 402–408. If this experiment is repeated with inanimate objects (instead of figurines presenting a human appearance), none of the objects are preferred over the other.

8. Quoted in Hoffman, M. L. (2000). *Empathy and Moral Development. Op. cit.*, p. 100. The children sometimes call an adult for help, but relationships of alterity remain quite vague, and a fourteen-month-old might take the hand of a crying child to lead it not to the latter's mother, who is present, but to its own mother.
9. Hoffman, M. L. (2000). *Op. cit.*; Lecomte, J. (2012). *La Bonté humaine. Op. cit.*, pp. 232–235.

   Carolyn Zahn-Waxler, who for over thirty years has studied the emergence of empathy among children, observed the way young children react *in daily life* when people close to them find themselves in difficulty. For example, she asked mothers to simulate the pain of bumping into something, or pretend to be sad or exhausted, or to seem to have trouble breathing. Almost always, the children behaved in a consoling way, kissing the mother and giving her other signs of affection, or acting in a considerate way, by bringing, for instance, a bottle to a younger brother or sister, or a blanket to someone shivering with cold. Zahn-Waxler, C., & Radke-Yarrow, M. (1982). The development of altruism: Alternative research strategies. *Development of Prosocial Behavior*, 109–137.
10. The children who pass the mirror test begin to show empathy to someone who is sobbing or seems to be upset (at eighteen months for girls, twenty-one months for boys). Bischof-Köhler, D. (1991), The development of empathy in infants. http://epub.ub.uni-muenchen.de/2915/1/2915.pdf; Bretherton, I., Fritz, J., Zahn-Waxler, C., & Ridgeway, D. (1986). Learning to talk about emotions: A functionalist perspective. *Child Development*, 529–548.
11. Quoted in Kohn, A. (1998). *The Brighter Side of Human Nature. Op. cit.*
12. Voir Barber, N., *Why Parents Matter: Parental Investment and Child Outcomes*, Praeger Pub Text, 2000, p. 124.
13. Rheingold, H. L. (1982). Little children's participation in the work of adults, a nascent prosocial behavior. *Child Development*, 114–125.
14. Report on BBC Radio by Helen Briggs, science correspondent.
15. Aside from the studies by Rheingold, H. L. (1982). *Op. cit.*
16. Piaget, J., *Le Jugement moral chez l'enfant*, F. Alcan, 1932.
17. Eisenberg, N., & Fabes, R. A. (1998). "Prosocial development." In Eisenberg, N., & Damon, W., *Handbook of Child Psychology*, John Wiley & Sons, 3: 701–778, 1998.

18. Svetlova, M., Nichols, S. R., & Brownell, C. A. (2010). Toddlers' prosocial behavior: From instrumental to empathic to altruistic helping. *Child Development*, *81*(6), 1814–1827.
19. Warneken, F., & Tomasello, M. (2006). Altruistic helping in human infants and young chimpanzees. *Science*, *311*(5765), 1301; Warneken, F., & Tomasello, M. (2009). The roots of human altruism. *British Journal of Psychology*, *100*(3), 455–471. Videos of these experiments can also be seen on the site http://email.eva.mpg.de/~warneken/video.
20. Warneken, F., & Tomasello, M. (2009). *Op. cit.* Tomasello, M. (2009). *Op. cit.*
21. *Ibid.*
22. See, for instance, the many studies published by Joan E. Grusec, especially Grusec, J. E., & Redler, E. (1980). Attribution, reinforcement, and altruism: A developmental analysis. *Developmental Psychology*, *16* (5), 525–534.
23. Tomasello, M. (2009). *Op. cit.*
24. Aknin, L. B., Hamlin, J. K., & Dunn, E. W. (2012). Giving leads to happiness in young children. *PLoS One*, *7*(6), e39211.
25. In the first experiment, the experimenter takes a treat out of his pocket, gives it to the child, and asks the child either to keep it for himself, or to give it to someone else: the child shows more happiness in the second case. In the second experiment, the experimenter gives some treats to the child, who puts them in his bowl. A little later, he suggests to the child that he give a treat to someone else: it's in this situation that the child shows the most happiness.
26. Warneken, F., & Tomasello, M. (2009). *Op. cit.*
27. Hay, D. F. (1994). Prosocial development. *Journal of Child Psychology and Psychiatry*, *35*(1), 29–71.
28. Freud, S., *The Interpretation of Dreams*, p. 283. Trans. and ed. by James Strachey, Avon Discus, 1965.
29. Eisenberg, N., Cumberland, A., Guthrie, I. K., Murphy, B. C., & Shepard, S. A. (2005). Age changes in prosocial responding and moral reasoning in adolescence and early adulthood. *Journal of Research on Adolescence*, *15*(3), 235–260.
30. Turiel, E., *The Development of Social Knowledge: Morality and Convention*, Cambridge University Press, 1983; Helwig, C. C., & Turiel, E., *Children's Social and Moral Reasoning. The Wiley-Blackwell Handbook of Childhood Social Development*, 2002, 567–583. Many books and articles have been written about this. For an excellent summary, see Baumard, N., *Comment nous sommes devenus moraux: Une histoire naturelle du bien et du mal*, Odile Jacob, 2010.

31. Greene, J., & Haidt, J. (2002). How (and where) does moral judgment work? *Trends in Cognitive Sciences*, *6*(12), 517–523.
32. Miller, J. G., & Bersoff, D. M. (1994). Cultural influences on the moral status of reciprocity and the discounting of endogenous motivation. *Personality and Social Psychology Bulletin*, *20*(5), 592–602.
33. Kochanska, G. (2002), Mutually responsive orientation between mothers and their young children: A context for the early development of conscience. *Current Directions in Psychological Science*, *11*(6), 191. See also Kochanska, G., & Murray, K. T. (2000). Mother–child mutually responsive orientation and conscience development: From toddler to early school age. *Child Development*, *71*(2), 417–431. Cited by Lecomte, J. (2012). *Op. cit.*, p. 239.
34. Barber, N., *Why Parents Matter: Parental Investment and Child Outcomes*, Praeger Publications, 2000, p. 124.
35. Quoted in Kohn, A. (1998). *Op. cit.*
36. Eisenberg, N., & Fabes, R. A. (1998). Prosocial development. *Op. cit.*
37. Keenan, K., Tremblay, R., Barr, R., & Peters, R. V., "The Development and Socialization of Aggression During the First Five Years of Life." Tremblay, R. E., Barr, R. G., Peters, R. de V. (eds). *Encyclopedia on Early Childhood Development*, 2002, 1–6.
38. Tremblay, R. E., Nagin, D. S., Séguin, J. R., Zoccolillo, M., Zelazo, P. D., Boivin, M., . . . Japel, C. (2004). Physical aggression during early childhood: Trajectories and predictors. *Pediatrics*, *114*(1), e43–e50.
39. Domitrovich, C. E., Greenberg, M. T., Tremblay, R., Barr, R., & Peters, R. V., "Preventive Interventions that Reduce Aggression in Young Children." *Encyclopedia on Early Childhood Development.* Montreal, Quebec: Centre of Excellence for Early Childhood Development, Recuperado El, 2003, p. 25.
40. Tomasello, M. (2009). *Op. cit.*
41. Hoffman, M. L., *Empathy and Moral Development: Implications for Caring and Justice*, Cambridge University Press, 2001.
42. Janssens, J. M., & Gerris, J. R. M., "Child Rearing, Empathy and Prosocial Development." In J. M. Janssens & J. R. M. Gerris (eds.), *Child Rearing: Influence on Prosocial and Moral Development*, Swets & Zeitlinger, 1992, pp. 57–75. Krevans, J., & Gibbs, J. C. (1996). Parents' use of inductive discipline: Relations to children's empathy and prosocial behavior. *Child Development*, *67*(6), 3263–3277.
43. Trickett, P. K., & Kuczynski, L. (1986). Children's misbehaviors and parental discipline strategies in abusive and nonabusive families. *Developmental Psychology*, *22*(1), 115.
44. Ricard, E., *La Dame des mots*, Éditions NiL, 2012.

45. Hoffman M. L. (2008). *Empathy and Moral Development. Op. cit.*; Krevans, J. & Gibbs, J. C. (1996). *Op. cit.*; Stewart, S. M., & McBride-Chang, C. (2000). Influences on children's sharing in a multicultural setting. *Journal of Cross-Cultural Psychology, 31*(3), 333–348.
46. Lecomte, J. (2012). *La Bonté humaine. Op. cit.*, p. 245. See also Crockenberg, S., & Litman, C. (1990). Autonomy as competence in 2-year-olds: Maternal correlates of child defiance, compliance, and self-assertion. *Developmental Psychology, 26*(6), 961.
47. Lecomte, J., *Donner un sens à sa vie*, Odile Jacob, 2007, Chapter 3.
48. Eisenberg-Berg, N., & Geisheker, E. (1979). Content of preachings and power of the model/preacher: The effect on children's generosity. *Developmental Psychology, 15*(2), 168.
49. Lecomte, J. (2012). *La Bonté humaine. Op. cit.*, p. 240.
50. Bekkers, R. (2007). Intergenerational transmission of volunteering. *Acta Sociologica, 50*(2), 99–114; Wilhelm, M. O., Brown, E., Rooney, P. M., & Steinberg, R. (2008). The intergenerational transmission of generosity. *Journal of Public Economics, 92*(10–11), 2146–2156; Rice, M. E., & Grusec, J. E. (1975). Saying and doing: Effects on observer performance. *Journal of Personality and Social Psychology, 32*(4), 584; Rushton, J. P., & Littlefield, C. (1979). The effects of age, amount of modelling, and a success experience on seven-to eleven-year-old children's generosity. *Journal of Moral Education, 9*(1), 55–56; Rushton, J. P., & Teachman, G. (1978). The effects of positive reinforcement, attributions, and punishment on model induced altruism in children. *Personality and Social Psychology Bulletin, 4*(2), 322–325.
51. Bryan, J. H., & Walbek, N. H. (1970). The impact of words and deeds concerning altruism upon children. *Child Development*, 747–757.
52. Howes, C., & Eldredge, R. (1985). Responses of abused, neglected, and nonmaltreated children to the behaviors of their peers. *Journal of Applied Developmental Psychology, 6*(2–3), 261–270; Main, M., & George, C. (1985). Responses of abused and disadvantaged toddlers to distress in agemates: A study in the day care setting. *Developmental Psychology, 21*(3), 407; Miller, P. A., & Eisenberg, N. (1988). The relation of empathy to aggressive and externalizing/antisocial behavior. *Psychological Bulletin, 103*(3), 324.
53. Waal, F. B. M. de, *The Age of Empathy, op. cit.* p. 13.
54. Beckett, C., Maughan, B., Rutter, M., Castle, J., Colvert, E., Groothues, C., . . . Sonuga-Barke, E. J. (2006). Do the effects of early severe deprivation on cognition persist into early adolescence? Findings

from the English and Romanian adoptees study. *Child Development*, *77*(3), 696–711.

55. Nanni, V., Uher, R., & Danese, A. (2012). Childhood maltreatment predicts unfavorable course of illness and treatment outcome in depression: A meta-analysis. *American Journal of Psychiatry*, *169*(2), 141–151.
56. Jacques Lecomte, in conversation. According to him, belief in intergenerational re-occurrence of abuse comes from the statistical angle of inversion of probabilities (most abusive parents were abused, and so it is wrongly deduced that most abused children become abusive). See Lecomte, J., *Guérir de son enfance*, Odile Jacob, 2010.

CHAPTER 19: PROSOCIAL BEHAVIOR

1. Bierhoff, H. W., *Prosocial Behaviour*, Psychology Press, 2002.
2. *Ibid.* Kindle, 216–227.
3. Bierhoff, H. (1983). Wie hilfreich ist der Mensch? [How helpful are humans?]. *Bild der Weissenchaft*, *20*, 118–126.
4. Milgram, S. (1970). The experience of living in cities. *Set*, *167*, 1461–1468. This study is somewhat old, but it was later confirmed; see Amato, P. R. (1983). Helping behavior in urban and rural environments: Field studies based on a taxonomic organization of helping episodes. *Journal of Personality and Social Psychology*, *45*(3), 571; Levine, R. V., Martinez, T. S., Brase, G., & Sorenson, K. (1994). Helping in 36 US cities. *Journal of Personality and Social Psychology*, *67*(1), 69.
5. Piliavin, I. M., Piliavin, J. A., & Rodin, J. (1975). Costs, diffusion, and the stigmatized victim. *Journal of Personality and Social Psychology*, *32*(3), 429–438; Piliavin, J. A., & Piliavin, I. M. (1972). Effect of blood on reactions to a victim. *Journal of Personality and Social Psychology*, *23*(3), 353–361.
6. Latané, B., & Darley, J. M., *The Unresponsive Bystander: Why Doesn't He Help?*, 1970 Appleton-Century Crofts; Latané, B., & Nida, S. (1981). Ten years of research on group size and helping. *Psychological Bulletin*, *89*(2), 308. For a more recent study, see Fischer, P., Krueger, J. I., Greitemeyer, T., Vogrincic, C., Kastenmüller, A., Frey, D., . . . Kainbacher, M. (2011). The bystander-effect: A meta-analytic review on bystander intervention in dangerous and non-dangerous emergencies. *Psychological Bulletin*, *137*(4), 517–537.
7. http://www.dailymotion.com/video/xlq30q_18-enfant-de-2-ans-renverse-et-ignore-par-les-passants_news

8. Quoted in Oliner, S. P., *Do Unto Others: Extraordinary Acts of Ordinary People* (illustrated edition), Basic Books, 2003, p. 93.
9. Schwartz, S. H., & Gottlieb, A. (1976). Bystander reactions to a violent theft: Crime in Jerusalem. *Journal of Personality and Social Psychology, 34*(6), 1188. For a more elaborate model than Latané's, see Schwartz, S. H., & Howard, J. A. (1982). Helping and cooperation: A self-based motivational model. *Cooperation and Helping Behavior: Theories and Research*, 327–353. In an emergency situation, the people who have particular abilities—nurses, team leaders, those who received emergency training, etc.—are much more likely than others to get involved in helping. Cramer, R. E., McMaster, M. R., Bartell, P. A., & Dragna, M. (1988). Subject competence and minimization of the bystander effect. *Journal of Applied Social Psychology, 18*(13), 1133–1148. As for those who think they're too incompetent to intervene directly, they often take the initiative to call for help: Shotland, R. L., & Heinold, W. D. (1985). Bystander response to arterial bleeding: Helping skills, the decision-making process, and differentiating the helping response. *Journal of Personality and Social Psychology, 49*(2), 347.
10. Korte, C., & Kerr, N. (1975). Response to altruistic opportunities in urban and nonurban settings. *Journal of Social Psychology, 95*(2), 183–184.
11. Takooshian, H., Haber, S., & Lucido, D. (1977). Who wouldn't help a lost child? You, maybe. *Psychology Today, 10*, 67.
12. US Census Bureau, *Statistical Abstracts of the United States* (Washington, DC: Author, 2002), quoted in Barber, N. (2004). *Op. cit.*, p. 148.
13. Cameron, C. D., & Payne, B. K. (2012). The cost of callousness regulating compassion influences the moral self-concept. *Psychological Science.*
14. Abbé Pierre famously stormed into a national radio station on a very cold winter in 1954 to give blankets for the homeless, some of whom had died in the street (thousands of blankets were delivered to collecting points within hours).
15. Whiting, B. B., & Whiting, J. W., *Children of Six Cultures: A Psychocultural Analysis*, Harvard University Press, 1975. Moreover, the studies carried out by D. Rosenhan more particularly showed that parental influence played a determining role in readiness to help others. See Rosenhan, D. (1970). The natural socialization of altruistic autonomy. *Altruism and Helping Behavior*, 251–268.

16. Nadler, A., & Jeffrey, D. (1986). The role of threat to self-esteem and perceived control in recipient reaction to help: Theory development and empirical validation. *Advances in Experimental Social Psychology*, *19*, 81–122.
17. Feldman, R. E. (1968). Response to compatriot and foreigner who seek assistance. *Journal of Personality and Social Psychology*, *10*(3), 202.
18. Triandis, H. C., Vassiliou, V., & Nassiakou, M. (1968). Three cross-cultural studies of subjective culture. *Journal of Personality and Social Psychology*, *8*(4p2), 1.
19. Eagly, A. H. (2009). The his and hers of prosocial behavior: An examination of the social psychology of gender. *American Psychologist*, *64*(8), 644. Lecomte, J. (2012). *Op. cit.*, pp. 157–158.
20. Eagly, A. H., & Crowley, M. (1986). Gender and helping behavior: A meta-analytic review of the social psychological literature. *Psychological Bulletin*, *100*(3), 283.
21. Piliavin, I. M., Rodin, J., & Piliavin, J. A. (1969). Good samaritanism: An underground phenomenon? *Journal of Personality and Social Psychology*, *13*(4), 289. A summary based on 99 studies confirms that men help more in emergency situations. See Eagly, A. H., & Crowley, M. (1986). *Op. cit.*, as well as, for situations in daily life, Bierhoff, H. W., Klein, R., & Kramp, P. (1991). Evidence for the altruistic personality from data on accident research. *Journal of Personality*, *59*(2), 263–280.
22. Eagly, A. H. (2009). The his and hers of prosocial behavior: An examination of the social psychology of gender. *American Psychologist*, *64*(8), 644. Lecomte, J. (2012). *Op. cit.*, pp. 157–158.
23. Gaskin, K., Smith, J. D., & Paulwitz, I., *Ein neues bürgerschaftliches Europa: Eine Untersuchung zur Verbreitung und Rolle von Volunteering in zehn europäischen Ländern*, Lambertus, 1996.
24. Rosenhan, D. (1970). The natural socialization of altruistic autonomy. *Altruism and Helping Behavior*, 251–268; Isen, A. M., & Levin, P. F. (1972). Effect of feeling good on helping: Cookies and kindness. *Journal of Personality and Social Psychology*, *21*(3), 384.
25. Watson, D., Clark, L. A., McIntyre, C. W., & Hamaker, S. (1992). Affect, personality, and social activity. *Journal of Personality and Social Psychology*, *63*(6), 1011.
26. Strenta, A., & DeJong, W. (1981). The effect of a prosocial label on helping behavior. *Social Psychology Quarterly*, 142–147.
27. Schwartz, S. H. (1994). Are there universal aspects in the structure and contents of human values? *Journal of Social Issues*, *50*(4), 19–45.

28. Deschamps, J. F., & Finkelstein, R. (2012). Existe-t-il un véritable altruism basé sur les valeurs personnelles? *Les Cahiers internationaux de psychologie sociale* (1), 37–62.
29. Hellhammer, K., Holz, N., & Lessing, J. (2007). Die Determinanten zivilcouragierten Verhaltens. *Zeitschrift Psychologischer Forschung* (Revue de recherche en psychologie), 13.
30. Jeffries, V. (1998). Virtue and the altruistic personality. *Sociological Perspectives*, 151–166.
31. Paluck, E. L. (2009). Reducing intergroup prejudice and conflict using the media: A field experiment in Rwanda. *Journal of Personality and Social Psychology, 96*(3), 574–587. Quoted in Batson, C. D. (2011). *Op. cit.*, p. 179.
32. Galinsky, A. D., Maddux, W. W., Gilin, D., & White, J. B. (2008). Why It Pays to Get Inside the Head of Your Opponent the Differential Effects of Perspective Taking and Empathy in Negotiations. *Psychological Science, 19*(4), 378–384. For more details and all the references, see Batson, C. D. (2011). *Op. cit.*, p. 171–172.
33. Diener, E., & Seligman, M. E. P. (2002). Very happy people. *Psychological Science, 13*(1), 81–84.
34. Luks A., & Payne, P., *The Healing Power of Doing Good: The Health and Spiritual Benefits of Helping Others,* Ballantine, 1991. For a complete overview of the benefits of altruistic and volunteer activities, see Post, S. G., *The Hidden Gifts of Helping: How the Power of Giving, Compassion, and Hope Can Get Us Through Hard Times,* John Wiley & Sons, 2011.
35. Nicholson, H. J., Collins, C., & Holmer, H. (2004). Youth as people: The protective aspects of youth development in after-school settings. *Annals of the American Academy of Political and Social Science, 591*(1), 55–71.
36. Brown, S. L., Brown, R. M., House, J. S., & Smith, D. M. (2008). Coping with spousal loss: Potential buffering effects of self-reported helping behavior. *Personality and Social Psychology Bulletin, 34*(6), 849–861.
37. Batson, C. D. (2011). *Op. cit.*, p. 186, as well as Dovidio, J. F., Piliavin, J. A., Schroeder, D. A., & Penner, L., *The Social Psychology of Prosocial Behavior,* Lawrence Erlbaum Associates Publishers, 2006.
38. Oman, D., "Does Volunteering Foster Physical Health and Longevity?" In S. G. Post (ed.), *Altruism and Health: Perspectives from Empirical Research*, Oxford University Press, 2007, pp. 15–32.
39. Since then, the psychologists Elisabeth Dunn, Lara Aknin, & Michael Norton have amply demonstrated this phenomenon, first in North America, then in many other countries. See Dunn, E. W., Aknin,

L. B., & Norton, M. I. (2008). Spending money on others promotes happiness. *Science, 319*(5870), 1687. Aknin, L. B., Barrington-Leigh, C. P., Dunn, E. W., Helliwell, J. F., Burns, J., Biswas-Diener, R.,… Norton, M. I. (2013). Prosocial spending and well-being: Cross-cultural evidence for a psychological universal. *Journal of Personality and Social Psychology*, *104*(4), 635–652.

40. llen, K. (2003). Are pets a healthy pleasure? The influence of pets on blood pressure. *Current Directions in Psychological Science*, *12*(6), 236–239; Dizon, M., Butler, L. D., & Koopman, C., "Befriending Man's Best Friends: Does Altruism Towards Animals Promote Psychological and Physical Health?" In S. G. Post (ed.), *Altruism and Health: Perspectives from Empirical Research*, Oxford University Press, 2007, p. 277–291. Netting, F. E., Wilson, C. C., & New, J. C. (1987). The human-animal bond: Implications for practice. *Social Work*, *32*(1), 60–64.
41. Halter, M., *La Force du bien*, Robert Laffont, 1995, p. 199.

CHAPTER 20: CAN WE CHANGE?

1. These words of the Dalai Lama's have sometimes been interpreted as an apology for selfishness. He is, of course, not advising people to be actually selfish (he is constantly stressing the danger of cherishing oneself excessively). What he means is that someone who really wants to benefit himself should understand that loving his neighbor and showing altruism is the best way not just to accomplish the benefit of others but also to ensure one's own happiness. Pursuing a basically selfish happiness is, in fact, doomed to failure.
2. André Comte-Sponville, remarks made during a discussion arranged by the kind auspices of Christophe and Pauline André.
3. Begley, S., *Train Your Mind, Change Your Brain: How a New Science Reveals Our Extraordinary Potential to Transform Ourselves*, Ballantine Books, 2007, p. 7.
4. These phenomena were observed among ferrets made deaf at birth, whose auditory cortex dealt with perception of light rays, and among mice blind from birth, whose visual cortex dealt with the perception of sounds. In a way, one could say that the ferrets *heard light* and that the mice *saw sounds.* Begley, S. (2007). *Op. cit.*, pp. 51–53, as well as Sur, M., Leamey, C. A., *et al.* (2001). Development and plasticity of cortical areas and networks. *Nature Reviews Neuroscience*, 2(4), 251–262; Sur, M., & Rubenstein, J. L. R. (2005). Patterning and plasticity of the cerebral cortex. *Science's STKE*, *310*(5749), 805.

5. Altman, J. (1962). Are new neurons formed in the brains of adult mammals? *Science*, *135*(3509), 1127–1128.
6. Nottebohm, F. (1981). A brain for all seasons: Cyclical anatomical changes in song control nuclei of the canary brain. *Science*, *214*(4527), 1368.
7. The hippocampus is an area of the brain that manages knowledge acquired from new experiences, then spreads this knowledge to other areas of the brain where it will be memorized and reused.
8. Kempermann, G., Kuhn, H. G., & Gage, F. H. (1997). More hippocampal neurons in adult mice living in an enriched environment. *Nature*, *386*(6624), 493–495.
9. Eriksson, P. S., Perfilieva, E., Björk-Eriksson, T., Alborn, A. M., Nordborg, C., Peterson, D. A., & Gage, F. H. (1998). Neurogenesis in the adult human hippocampus. *Nature Medicine*, *4*(11), 1313–1317.
10. Fred Gage, during the Mind and Life XII conference in 2004 ("Neuroplasticity: The Neuronal Substrates of Learning and Transformation") in Dharamsala, India, with the Dalai Lama. See Begley, S. (2007), *Train Your Mind, Change Your Brain* (*op. cit.*), p. 65.
11. Elbert, T., Pantev, C., Wienbruch, C., Rockstroh, B., & Taub, E. (1995). Increased cortical representation of the fingers of the left hand in string players. *Science*, *270*(5234), 305–307.
12. Maguire, E. A., Spiers, H. J., Good, C. D., Hartley, T., Frackowiak, R. S. J., & Burgess, N. (2003). Navigation expertise and the human hippocampus: A structural brain imaging analysis. *Hippocampus*, *13*(2), 250–259; Maguire, E. A., Woollett, K., & Spiers, H. J. (2006). London taxi drivers and bus drivers: A structural MRI and neuropsychological analysis. *Hippocampus*, *16*(12), 1091–1101.
13. Carey, N., *The Epigenetics Revolution*, Icon Books, 2011.
14. Epigenetic modifications can occur because of several mechanisms. One of them is the "methylation" of genes. A methyl group fixated on one of the bases that comprise DNA blocks access to the gene in question. This gene can no longer be transcribed into a protein and remains inactive. One could say that the expression of this gene has been "repressed." Researchers think that methylation acts by modifying the tridimensional structure of the DNA, causing a sort of "fold" at gene level, thus preventing access of the RNA that causes transcription of the gene into proteins which will then be active in the cell. I am grateful to Michael Meaney for these explanations.

    Aside from methylation, which is stable, the acetylation of histones, a group of proteins associated with DNA, can cause epigenetic effects lasting a shorter amount of time, while certain types of RNA, which don't encode any protein, can interact with genes and render them silent. See Francis, D., Diorio, J., Liu, D., & Meaney, M. J. (1999). Nongenomic transmission across generations of maternal behavior and stress responses in the rat. *Science, 286*(5442), 1155–1158; Champagne, F. A., Weaver, I. C. G., Diorio, J., Dymov, S., Szyf, M., & Meaney, M. J. (2006). Maternal care associated with methylation of the estrogen receptor-alpha1b promoter and estrogen receptor-alpha expression in the medial preoptic area of female offspring. *Endocrinology, 147*(6), 2909–2915. See also Carey, N. (2011), *The Epigenetics Revolution. Op. cit.*

15. Heim, C., Shugart, M., Craighead, W. E., & Nemeroff, C. B. (2010). Neurobiological and psychiatric consequences of child abuse and neglect. *Developmental Psychobiology, 52*(7), 671–690.
16. In the case of people who committed suicide, postmortem analysis revealed high levels of methylation of genes in the cerebral neurons when the subjects were abused in childhood, but relatively low levels of methylation among those who did not experience such abuse. That means that the fact of having been abused leads to lasting modifications in the expression of genes. McGowan, P. O., Sasaki, A., D'Alessio, A. C., Dymov, S., Labonté, B., Szyf, M., ... Meaney, M. J. (2009). Epigenetic regulation of the glucocorticoid receptor in human brain associates with childhood abuse. *Nature Neuroscience, 12*(3), 342–348. Quoted in Carey, N. (2011). *Op. cit.*
17. Kaliman, P., Álvarez-López, M. J., Cosín-Tomás, M., Rosenkranz, M. A., Lutz, A., & Davidson, R. J. (2013). Rapid changes in histone deacetylases and inflammatory gene expression in expert meditators. *Psychoneuroendocrinology*; doi:10.1016/j.psyneuen.2013.11.004. There was, of course, no question of removing neurons from the meditators, but one can also observe epigenetic changes in blood cells, and it turned out, studying the cells of deceased individuals, that these changes correspond to similar modifications of the neurons in the brain. Studies on the epigenetic effects of meditation on altruistic love are also under way in Barbara Fredrickson's laboratory.
18. Richerson, P. J., & Boyd, R. (2004). *Not by Genes Alone. Op. cit.*, p. 247.

CHAPTER 21: TRAINING THE MIND: WHAT THE COGNITIVE SCIENCES HAVE TO SAY

1. The account of these meetings gave rise to a book: Goleman, D., and the Dalai Lama, *Destructive Emotions: A Scientific Dialogue with the Dalai Lama*, Bantam Books, 2004.

2. Kaufman, M., Meditation gives brain a charge, study finds, *Washington Post*, January 3, 2005, p. A05.
3. See Ricard, M., *Why Meditate?* Hay House, 2010; *The Art of Meditation*, Atlantic, 2011.
4. Davidson, R. J., & Begley, S., *The Emotional Life of Your Brain: How Its Unique Patterns Affect the Way You Think, Feel, and Live—and How You Can Change Them,* Hudson Street Press, 2012, p. xii.
5. Among the many researchers involved in these studies, we'll cite by way of example: Julie Brefczynski-Lewis, Linda Carlson, Richard Davidson, Gaelle Desbordes, Sona Dimidjian, Brooke Dodson-Lavelle, Paul Ekman, Brent Field, Barbara Fredrickson, Brita Hölzel, Amishi Jha, Jon Kabat-Zinn, Olga Klimecki, Bethany Kok, Sara Lazar, Antoine Lutz, Brendan Ozawa-de Silva, David Perlman, Chuck Raison, Cliff Saron, Tania Singer, Heleen Slagter, John Teasdale, Elen Weng, Mark Williams, Fadel Zeidan, to cite only those with whom I have had the opportunity to interact over the past few years.
6. Brefczynski-Lewis, J. A., Lutz, A., Schaefer, H. S., Levinson, D. B., & Davidson, R. J. (2007). Neural correlates of attentional expertise in long-term meditation practitioners. *Proceedings of the National Academy of Sciences, 104*(27), 11483–11488.
7. Lutz, A., Slagter, H. A., Rawlings, N. B., Francis, A. D., Greischar, L. L., & Davidson, R. J. (2009). Mental training enhances attentional stability: Neural and behavioral evidence. *Journal of Neuroscience, 29*(42), 13418–13427.
8. Gyatso, Tenzin (the XIVth Dalai Lama) & Jinpa, G. T., *The World of Tibetan Buddhism: An Overview of Its Philosophy and Practice*, Wisdom Publications, 1995. Wallace, B. A., *The Attention Revolution: Unlocking the Power of the Focused Mind*, Wisdom Publications, 2006; Ricard, M., *The Art of Meditation.*
9. This stems from the fact that the brain is always involved in dealing with consciously perceived stimulus and does not have enough attentive resources to deal with stimuli that follow. The term "attentional blink" is given to the inability to deal with the images that follow. The most surprising discovery was that experienced meditators, even if they were older (attentional blink increases with age because the mechanisms of attention become slower) had remarkably short attentional blinks. One 65-year-old meditator, in particular, didn't have any at all, and perceived all the stimuli, even though they went by very quickly (unpublished results of research carried out at the

laboratories of Anne Treisman and Jonathan Cohen at Princeton University). Heleen Slagter and Antoine Lutz have also shown that after three months of intensive training in meditation on full awareness, attentional blink was considerably reduced. Slagter, H. A., Lutz, A., Greischar, L. L., Francis, A. D., Nieuwenhuis, S., Davis, J. M., & Davidson, R. J. (2007). Mental training affects distribution of limited brain resources. *PLoS Biology*, *5*(6), 138.

10. Gamma waves have rapid oscillation frequencies between 25 and 42 Hz.
11. The first of these articles: Lutz, A., Greischar, L. L., Rawlings, N. B., Ricard, M., & Davidson, R. J. (2004). Long-term meditators self-induce high-amplitude gamma synchrony during mental practice. *Proceedings of the National Academy of Sciences of the United States of America*, *101*(46), 16369.
12. Lutz, A., Greischar, L. L., Perlman, D. M., & Davidson, R. J. (2009). BOLD signal in insula is differentially related to cardiac function during compassion meditation in experts vs. novices. *Neuroimage*, *47*(3), 1038–1046.
13. Other studies suggest that lesions in the amygdala disturb the emotional aspect of empathy, without affecting its cognitive aspect. See Hurlemann, R., Walter, H., Rehme, A. K., *et al.* (2010). Human amygdala reactivity is diminished by the b-noradrenergic antagonist propanolol. *Psychol. Med*, *40*, 1839–1848.
14. Lutz, A., Brefczynski-Lewis, J., Johnstone, T., & Davidson, R. J. (2008). Regulation of the neural circuitry of emotion by compassion meditation: Effects of meditative expertise. *PLoS One*, *3*(3), e1897; Klimecki, O. M., Leiberg, S., Ricard, M., & Singer, T. (2013). Differential pattern of functional brain plasticity after compassion and empathy training. *Social Cognitive and Affective Neuroscience*, doi:10.1093/scan/nst060.
15. Fredrickson, B. L., Cohn, M. A., Coffey, K. A., Pek, J., & Finkel, S. M. (2008). Open hearts build lives: Positive emotions, induced through loving-kindness meditation, build consequential personal resources. *Journal of Personality and Social Psychology*, *95*(5), 1045. The subjects studied have trained according to the Buddhist meditation on *metta*, the Pali word for altruistic love.
16. Pace, T. W. W., Negi, L. T., Adame, D. D., Cole, S. P., Sivilli, T. I., Brown, T. D., Issa, M. J., *et al.* (2009). Effect of compassion meditation on neuroendocrine, innate immune and behavioral responses to psychosocial stress. *Psychoneuroendocrinology*, *34*(1), 87–98.

17. Hofmann, S. G., Grossman, P., & Hinton, D. E. (2011). Loving-kindness and compassion meditation. Potential for psychological interventions. *Clinical Psychology Review*, *31*(7), 1126–1132.
18. Lazar, S. W., Kerr, C. E., Wasserman, R. H., Gray, J. R., Greve, D. N., Treadway, M. T.,... Fischl, B. (2005). Meditation experience is associated with increased cortical thickness. *Neuroreport*, *16*(17), 1893. This growth in volume is caused by an increase of areas of gray matter that contain inter-neural connections and are linked to the process of learning. The number and size of synapses and dendritic ramifications increase phenomena also observed in other forms of training and learning. The term "neuropil" is given to the areas of gray matter situated between neuronal cell bodies, glial cell bodies, and blood vessels. Neuropil is constituted by a complex web of a multiplicity of neuronal cytoplasmic continuations (axons and dendrites) and glials, of varying caliber.
19. Especially in regions associated with sensory perception, emotional and cognitive regulation, and production of neurotransmitters that affect moods, the posterior cingulate cortex, the insula, the temporal parietal junction, the cerebellum, and the brainstem (which produces noradrenaline). See Hölzel, B., *et al.* (2011); Hölzel, B. K., Carmody, J., Evans, K. C., Hoge, E. A., Dusek, J. A., Morgan, L., Pitman, R. K., *et al.* (2010). Stress reduction correlates with structural changes in the amygdala. *Social Cognitive and Affective Neuroscience*, *5*(1), 11–17; Hölzel, B. K., Carmody, J., Vangel, M., Congleton, C., Yerramsetti, S. M., Gard, T., & Lazar, S. W. (2011). Mindfulness practice leads to increases in regional brain gray matter density. *Psychiatry Research: Neuroimaging*, *191*(1), 36–43.
20. Goleman, D., and the Dalai Lama, *Destructive Emotions: A Scientific Dialogue with the Dalai Lama*, pp. 14–15.
21. Weng, H. Y., Fox, A. S., Shackman, A. J., Stodola, D. E., Caldwell, J. Z. K., Olson, M. C., Rogers, G., & Davidson R. J. (in press). Compassion training alters altruism and neural responses to suffering. *Psychological Science*. NIHMSID: 440274. One can predict the degree of prosocial behavior by simply observing differences of brain activity in the amygdala.
22. Leiberg, S., Klimecki, O., & Singer, T. (2011). Short-term compassion training increases prosocial behavior in a newly developed prosocial game. *PloS One*, *6*(3), e17798.
23. Condon, P., Desbordes, G., Miller, W., DeSteno, D., Hospital, M. G., & DeSteno, D. (n.d.). Meditation increases compassionate responses

to suffering. *Psychological Science*. Retrieved from http://daviddesteno.com/page5/files/Condon.etal.2013.pdf.

24. Rudman, L. A., Ashmore, R. D., & Gary, M. L. (2001). "Unlearning" automatic biases: The malleability of implicit prejudice and stereotypes. *Journal of Personality and Social Psychology, 81*(5), 856–868.
25. Dasgupta, N., & Greenwald, A. G. (2001). On the malleability of automatic attitudes: Combating automatic prejudice with images of admired and disliked individuals. *Journal of Personality and Social Psychology, 81*(5), 800–814.
26. Hutcherson, C. A., Seppala, E. M., & Gross, J. J. (2008). Loving-kindness meditation increases social connectedness. *Emotion, 8*(5), 720–724.
27. Kang, Y., Gray, J. R., & Dovidio, J. F. (2013). The nondiscriminating heart: Lovingkindness meditation training decreases implicit bias against stigmatized outgroups. *Journal of Experimental Psychology*; doi:10.1037/a0034150.
28. The activity of the amygdala and the anterior insulate cortex is markedly weaker among meditators than novices.
29. Lutz, A., McFarlin, D. R., Perlman, D. M., Salomons, T. V., & Davidson, R. J. (2012). Altered anterior insula activation during anticipation and experience of painful stimuli in expert meditators. *NeuroImage*; Perlman, D. M., Salomons, T. V., Davidson, R. J., & Lutz, A. (2010). Differential effects on pain intensity and unpleasantness of two meditation practices. *Emotion, 10*(1), 65.
30. Zeidan, F., Martucci, K. T., Kraft, R. A., Gordon, N. S., McHaffie, J. G., & Coghill, R. C. (2011). Brain mechanisms supporting the modulation of pain by mindfulness meditation. *Journal of Neuroscience, 31*(14), 5540–5548. The reduction of subjective intensity of pain was accompanied by increased activity in the areas of the brain associated with cognitive regulation of painful sensations (anterior cingulate cortex and anterior insula), while the reduction of the unpleasant aspect of pain was associated with an activation of the prefrontal orbital cortex that is involved in putting sensations into perspective and reevaluating them. For a recent study, see Zeidan, F., Grant, J. A., Brown, C. A., McHaffie, J. G., & Coghill, R. C. (2012). Mindfulness meditation-related pain relief: Evidence for unique brain mechanisms in the regulation of pain. *Neuroscience Letters*. For an overview of all the studies, see Grant, J. A. (2013). Meditative analgesia: The current state of the field. *Annals of the New York Academy of Sciences*; doi:10.1111/nyas.12282.

31. Fossel, M. (2000). Role of cell senescence in human aging. *Journal of Anti-Aging Medicine*, *3*(1), 91–98; Chan, S. R., & Blackburn, E. H. (2004). Telomeres and telomerase. Philosophical transactions of the Royal Society of London. *Series B: Biological Sciences*, *359*(1441), 109–122.
32. Blackburn, E. H. (1991). Structure and function of telomeres. *Nature*, *350*(6319), 569–573.
33. Cawthon, R. M., Smith, K. R., O'Brien, E., Sivatchenko, A., & Kerber, R. A. (2003). Association between telomere length in blood and mortality in people aged 60 years or older. *Lancet*, *361*(9355), 393–395; Epel, E. S. (2009). Telomeres in a life-span perspective a new "psychobiomarker"? *Current Directions in Psychological Science*, *18*(1), 6–10.
34. Jacobs, T. L., Epel, E. S., Lin, J., Blackburn, E. H., Wolkowitz, O. M., Bridwell, D. A., Zanesco, A. P., *et al.* (2010). Intensive meditation training, immune cell telomerase activity, and psychological mediators. *Psychoneuroendocrinology*. See also Hoge, E. A., Chen, M. M., Metcalf, C. A., Fischer, L. E., Pollack, M. H., & DeVivo, I. (2013). Loving-kindness meditation practice associated with longer telomeres in women. *Brain, Behavior, and Immunity*.
35. Goleman, D., and the Dalai Lama, *Destructive Emotions, op. cit.*, pp. 26–27.

CHAPTER 22: HOW TO CULTIVATE ALTRUISM: MEDITATIONS ON ALTRUISTIC LOVE, COMPASSION, JOY, AND IMPARTIALITY

1. Davidson, R. J., & Lutz, A. (2008). Buddha's brain: Neuroplasticity and meditation [in the spotlight]. *Signal Processing Magazine, IEEE*, *25*(1), 176–174.
2. Etymologically, the Sanskrit and Tibetan words translated as "meditation" are, respectively, *bhavana* ("to cultivate") and *gom pa* ("to become familiar with").
3. Hume, D., *An Enquiry Concerning the Principles of Morals*, in *Works of David Hume*. MobileReference. Kindle Edition. (Kindle Locations 4210–4212).
4. "A Dialogue" in *The Shorter Leibniz Texts*, edited by Lloyd Strickland, Bloomsbury, 2006, p. 170.
5. McCullough, M. E., Emmons, R. A., & Tsang, J.-A. (2002). The grateful disposition: A conceptual and empirical topography. *Journal of Personality and Social Psychology*, *82*(1), 112–127; Mikulincer, M., & Shaver, P. R. (2005). Attachment security, compassion, and altruism. *Current Directions in Psychological Science*, *14*(1), 34–38; Lambert, N. M., & Fincham, F. D. (2011). Expressing gratitude to a partner

leads to more relationship maintenance behavior. *Emotion-APA*, *11*(1), 52; Grant, A. M., & Gino, F. (2010). A little thanks goes a long way: Explaining why gratitude expressions motivate prosocial behavior. *Journal of Personality and Social Psychology*, *98*(6), 946–955.

6. Shantideva (2006), *The Way of the Bodhisattva (Bodhicaryavatara)*, Padmakara Translation Group, Shambhala, stanzas 18–22, pp. 49–50. (Translation slightly modified.)
7. The Dalai Lama, during a lecture given in Porto, Portugal, November 2001.

CHAPTER 23: EGOCENTRISM AND CRYSTALLIZATION OF THE EGO

1. Sociologists speak of *endogroup* and *exogroup.*
2. For more in-depth expositions, see Galin, D., "The Concepts of 'Self', 'Person', and 'I' in Western Psychology and in Buddhism," in Wallace, B. A., *Buddhism and Science: Breaking New Ground*, Columbia University Press, 2003, pp. 107–142; Wallace, B. A., *Science et Bouddhisme: À chacun sa réalité*, 1998, Calmann-Lévy; Damasio, A. R., *Le Sentiment même de soi: Corps, émotions, conscience*, Odile Jacob, 2002.
3. Galin, D. (2003). *Op. cit.*
4. For an expanded explanation of this interaction, see Varela, F. J., *The Embodied Mind: Cognitive Science and Human Experience*, MIT Press, 1991.
5. Descartes, *Meditations on First Philosophy, IV,* trans. Donald A. Cress, Hackett, 1993.
6. We will speak of Freudian theories in the chapter on the "Champions of Selfishness." We have not included them in this chapter because of their lack of validity (that is hard to write without support, so better not speak of it, it seems to me) both from the introspective perspective of Buddhism and from the scientific perspective.
7. The actors used the mouth of the mask like a megaphone, to make their voice carry.
8. Paul Ekman, in conversation. See also Goleman, D., & the Dalai Lama, *Destructive Emotions.*
9. Dambrun, M., & Ricard, M. (2011). Self-centeredness and selflessness: A theory of self based psychological functioning and its consequences for happiness. *Review of General Psychology*, *15*(2), 138.
10. Report heard on "Science in Action," a science broadcast from the BBC World Service, in 2001.

11. LeVine, R. A., & Campbell, D. T., *Ethnocentrism: Theories of Conflict, Ethnic Attitudes, and Group Behavior*, Wiley, 1972.
12. Tajfel, H., *Human Groups and Social Categories: Studies in Social Psychology*, Cambridge University Press, 1981.
13. The experimenters then proposed an evening of reconciliation, the secret aim of which was in fact to accentuate the disagreements. They put fruit and drinks on a table, half of which were intact and nicely presented, the other in poor condition (rotting fruit, etc.). They had one group arrive before the other. The members of that group unhesitatingly chose the good food, leaving the bruised fruit for the second group, which, once they arrived, protested vehemently and insulted the members of the first group. The next day, the wronged group avenged itself by dirtying the cafeteria tables, throwing food at the boys in the other group, and putting up posters with threatening messages.
14. Pettigrew, T. F. (1998). Intergroup contact theory. *Annual Review of Psychology*, *49*(1), 65–85.
15. Sherif, M., Harvey, O. J., White, B. J., Hood, W. E., & Sherif, C. W., *Intergroup Conflict and Cooperation: The Robbers Cave Experiment*, University of Oklahoma Book Exchange, 1961; Sherif, M., Reprinted as *The Robbers Cave Experiment: Intergroup Conflict and Cooperation,* Wesleyan, 1961.

Chapter 24: The Spread of Individualism and Narcissism

1. Hutcherson, C. A., Seppala, E. M., & Gross, J. J. (2008). Loving-kindness meditation increases social connectedness. *Emotion*, *8*(5), 720–724.
2. Cialdini, R. B., Brown, S. L., Lewis, B. P., Luce, C., & Neuberg, S. L. (1997). Reinterpreting the empathy-altruism relationship: When one into one equals oneness. *Journal of Personality and Social Psychology*, *73*, 481–494; Glaeser, E. L., Laibson, D. I., Scheinkman, J. A., & Soutter, C. L. (2000). Measuring trust. *The Quarterly Journal of Economics*, *115*(3), 811–846.
3. Fehr, E., & Rockenbach, B. (2003). Detrimental effects of sanctions on human altruism. *Nature*, *422*(6928), 137–140.
4. Putnam, R. D., *Bowling Alone: The Collapse and Revival of American Community* (1st edition), Touchstone Books / Simon & Schuster; McPherson, M., Smith-Lovin, L., & Brashears, M. E. (2006). Social isolation in America: Changes in core discussion networks over two decades. *American Sociological Review*, *71*(3), 353–375.

5. Rahn, W. M., & Transue, J. E. (1998). Social trust and value change: The decline of social capital in American youth, 1976–1995. *Political Psychology, 19*(3), 545–565.
6. Claeys, Gregory (1986). "Individualism," "Socialism," and "Social Science": Further Notes on a Process of Conceptual Formation, 1800–1850. *Journal of the History of Ideas, 47*(1): 81–93; doi:10.2307/2709596. JSTOR 2709596.
7. Layard, R., & Dunn, J., *A Good Childhood: Searching for Values in a Competitive Age*, Penguin, 2009, p. 6.
8. Twenge, J. M., *Generation Me: Why Today's Young Americans Are More Confident, Assertive, Entitled—and More Miserable Than Ever Before* (1st edition), The Free Press, 2006, p. 20.
9. Bruckner, P., *La Tentation de l'innocence*, Le Livre de Poche, 1996.
10. See the analysis by Lipovetsky, G., *L'Ère du vide: Essais sur l'individualisme contemporain,* Gallimard, 1989.
11. Rousseau didn't claim to describe what actually happened in prehistoric times but offered a theoretical fiction.
12. See Waal, F. B. M. de (2009), *The Age of Empathy. Op. cit.*
13. Barrès, M., *Mes cahiers,* Volume 6, 1907, p. 46.
14. Gasset, J. O., *Man & People,* W. W. Norton, 1963, p. 46.
15. Dumont, L., *Essays on Individualism: Modern Ideology in Anthropological Perspective,* University of Chicago, 1992, p. 263.
16. Alicke, M. D., & Govorun, O., "The Better-Than-Average Effect," in Alicke, M. D., Dunning, D. A., & Krueger, J. I. (eds.), *The Self in Social Judgment*, Psychology Press, 2005, pp. 85–106.
17. Preston, C. E., & Harris, S. (1965). Psychology of drivers in traffic accidents. *Journal of Applied Psychology, 49*(4), 284.
18. Pronin, E., Gilovich, T., & Ross, L. (2004). Objectivity in the eye of the beholder: Divergent perceptions of bias in self versus others. *Psychological Review, 111*(3), 781.
19. According to the *Diagnostic and Statistical Manual of Mental Disorders* (DSM-IV-TR, 2000) of the American Psychiatric Association.
20. Campbell, W. K., Rudich, E. A., & Sedikides, C. (2002). Narcissism, self-esteem, and the positivity of self-views: Two portraits of self-love. *Personality and Social Psychology Bulletin, 28*(3), 358–368; Gabriel, M. T., Critelli, J. W., & Ee, J. S. (1994). Narcissistic illusions in self-evaluations of intelligence and attractiveness. *Journal of Personality, 62*(1), 143–155.
21. Twenge, J. M., & Campbell, W. K., *The Narcissism Epidemic: Living in the Age of Entitlement,* The Free Press, 2010, p. 25; Bosson, J. K.,

Lakey, C. E., Campbell, W. K., Zeigler-Hill, V., Jordan, C. H., & Kernis, M. H. (2008). Untangling the links between narcissism and self-esteem: A theoretical and empirical review. *Social and Personality Psychology Compass*, *2*(3), 1415–1439; Gabriel, M. T., Critelli, J. W., & Ee, J. S. (1994). Narcissistic illusions in self-evaluations of intelligence and attractiveness. *Journal of Personality*, *62*(1), 143–155.

22. Participants were not aware of the different response times or of the significance of these differences: in scientific terms they speak of an *implicit* measure of self-esteem.
23. Campbell, W. K., Bosson, J. K., Goheen, T. W., Lakey, C. E., & Kernis, M. H. (2007). Do narcissists dislike themselves "deep down inside"? *Psychological Science*, *18*(3), 227–229.
24. Jordan, C. H., Spencer, S. J., Zanna, M. P., Hoshino-Browne, E., & Correll, J. (2003). Secure and defensive high self-esteem. *Journal of Personality and Social Psychology*, *85*(5), 969–978.
25. Heatherton, T. F., & Vohs, K. D. (2000). Interpersonal evaluations following threats to self: Role of self-esteem. *Journal of Personality and Social Psychology*, *78*(4), 725.
26. Twenge, J. M., & Campbell, W. K. (2010). *Op. cit.*, p. 199.
27. See http://fr.wikipedia.org/wiki/Kim_Jong-il, which also gives numerous references.
28. Twenge, Jean M., and W. Keith Campbell, *The Narcissism Epidemic: Living in the Age of Entitlement*. According to various studies, the most narcissistic countries are Serbia, Chile, Israel, and the United States, with the least narcissistic countries being South Korea, Switzerland, Japan, Taiwan, and Morocco.
29. Newsom, C. R., Archer, R. P., Trumbetta, S., & Gottesman, I. I. (2003). Changes in adolescent response patterns on the MMPI/MMPI-A across four decades. *Journal of Personality Assessment*, *81*(1), 74–84. Quoted in Twenge, J. M., & Campbell, W. K. (2010). *Op. cit.*, p. 35.
30. Twenge, J. M., & Campbell, W. K. (2001). Age and birth cohort differences in self-esteem: A cross-temporal meta-analysis. *Personality and Social Psychology Review*, *5*, 321, 344; Gentile, B., & Twenge, J. M. "Birth Cohort Changes in Self-Esteem," 1988–2007. Unpublished manuscript. Based on Gentile, B., Master's thesis, San Diego State University, 2008.
31. Grant, B. F., Chou, S. P., Goldstein, R. B., Huang, B., Stinson, F. S., Saha, T. D., ... Pickering, R. P. (2008). Prevalence, correlates, disability, and comorbidity of DSM-IV borderline personality disorder: Results

from the Wave 2 National Epidemiologic Survey on Alcohol and Related Conditions. *Journal of Clinical Psychiatry*, *69*(4), 533.

32. Twenge, J. M., & Campbell, W. K. (2010). *Op. cit.*, p. 34.
33. *Ibid.*, p. 36.
34. *Ibid.*, p. 32.
35. Gentile, B., Twenge, J. M., Freeman, E. C., & Campbell, W. K. (2012). The effect of social networking websites on positive self-views: An experimental investigation. *Computers in Human Behavior, 28*(5), 1929–1933. These results can depend on the style of the various social networks. The same study carried out on Facebook users showed that after thirty-five minutes of use, they showed an increase of self-esteem but not of narcissism.
36. Christophe André, during broadcast of the TV show *Voix bouddhistes* on France 2, February 10, 2013.
37. *Ibid.*, p. 41.
38. Robins, R. W., & Beer, J. S. (2001). Positive illusions about the self: Short-term benefits and long-term costs. *Journal of Personality and Social Psychology*, *80*(2), 340–352.
39. *Ibid.*, p. 14.
40. Mastromarino, D. (ed.)., *The Girl's Guide to Loving Yourself: A Book About Falling in Love with the One Person Who Matters Most… YOU!*, Blue Mountain Arts, 2003.
41. According to the psychologist Bonne Zucker, interviewed in *People*. Field-Meyer, T., Kids out of control, *People*, December 20, 2004. Quoted in Twenge, J. M. (2006). *Op. cit.*, p. 75.
42. According to government statistics of the National Assessment of Eductional Progress, quoted in Twenge, J. M., & Campbell, W. K. (2010). *Op. cit.*, p. 49.
43. Twenge, J. M., & Campbell, W. K. (2010). *Op. cit.*, p. 147.
44. *Ibid.*, p. 81.
45. Nafstad, H. E., Blakar, R. M., Carlquist, E., Phelps, J. M., & Rand-Hendriksen, K. (2007). Ideology and power: The influence of current neo-liberalism in society. *Journal of Community & Applied Social Psychology*, *17*(4), 313–327. Quoted by Twenge, J. M., & Campbell, W. K. (2010). *Op. cit.*, p. 264.
46. Twenge, J. M., & Campbell, W. K. (2010). *Op. cit.*, p. 4.
47. Baumeister, R. (2005), The lowdown on high self-esteem. Thinking you're hot stuff isn't the promised cure-all, *Los Angeles Times*, January 25, 2005. Quoted in Twenge, J. M. (2006). *Op. cit.*, p. 66.
48. Twenge, J. M. (2006). *Op. cit.*, p. 67.

49. James, W., *Précis de psychologie*, Les Empêcheurs de penser en rond, 2003. Quoted in André, C. (2009). *Op. cit.*, p. 88.
50. *Ibid.*, p. 416. Quoting Tangney J. P., "Humility," in Snyder, C. R., & Lopez, S. J., *Handbook of Positive Psychology*, Oxford University Press, 2002, pp. 411–419.
51. Turkle, S., *Alone Together: Why We Expect More from Technology and Less from Each Other*, Basic Books, 2011; Turkle, S., The flight from conversation, *New York Times*, April 24, 2012.
52. *Bhagavad-Gita*, Chapter 13, lines 8–12.
53. According to Nobutaka Inoue, Professor of Shinto Studies at the University of Kokugakuin in Tokyo. See Norrie, J., Explosion of cults in Japan fails to heed deadly past, *The Age*, November 2, 2007.
54. Bellah, R. N., *et al.*, *Habits of the Heart: Individualism and Commitment in American Life* (2nd edition), University of California Press, 1996. Quoted in Twenge, J. M., *et al.* (2010), p. 246.
55. Trungpa, C., *Cutting Through Spiritual Materialism*, Shambhala Publications, 2010.
56. Rand, A., *Atlas Shrugged*, Penguin, 1992, p. 970.
57. La Rochefoucauld, F. de, *Reflections; or Sentences and Moral Maxims* (Kindle Locations 990–991). Maxim 457. Kindle Edition.
58. *Ibid.* (Kindle Locations 578–579). Maxim 147. Kindle Edition.
59. Bushman, B. J., & Baumeister, R. F. (1998). Threatened egotism, narcissism, self-esteem, and direct and displaced aggression: Does self-love or self-hate lead to violence? *Journal of Personality and Social Psychology*, *75*, 219–229.
60. Exline, J. J., & Baumeister, R. F. (2000). Case Western Reserve University. Unpublished data cited by J. P. Tangney, "Humility," in *Handbook of Positive Psychology* (2002). *Op. cit.*, pp. 411–419.

CHAPTER 25: THE CHAMPIONS OF SELFISHNESS

1. Machiavelli, N., "The Morals of the Prince." Online: http://www.umphrey.org/wp-content/uploads/2011/01/Machiavellei-The-Morals-of-the-Prince.pdf
2. Stirner, M., *The Ego and His Own*, trans. by S. T. Byington, A. C. Fifield, 1912, p. 339.
3. Nietzsche, F., *The Gay Science: With a Prelude in Rhymes and an Appendix of Songs*, Random House, 2010, p. 94.
4. Nietzsche, F., *Thus Spoke Zarathustra*, Penguin, 1974 Section XVI.
5. Nietzsche, F. (1888/1927), *Ecce Homo*, p. 862.

6. In the United States, for example, Freud is only discussed when the history of ideas is being studied. According to Steven Kosslyn, former chair of psychology at Harvard, these days, in North America, there is probably not a single doctoral thesis in psychology under way that has the subject of psychoanalysis. (Steven Kosslyn, in conversation.)
7. Ayn Rand (1905–1982) is a pen name. She was born Alissa Zinovievna Rosenbaum; she emigrated from Russia to the United States after the Russian Revolution, and became an American citizen.
8. According to a Gallup poll carried out in 2009, almost 25% of Americans are ultraconservative. This movement is notably supported by the Cato Institute and by the magazine *Reason*, in which some recent headlines are, for example: "She Is Back! Ayn Rand Bigger Than Ever," December 2009, and "How to Slash the Government Before It Slashes You," November 2010.
9. Greenspan, A., *The Age of Turbulence*, Penguin, 2007, p. 51.
10. See the column by Paul Krugman, recipient of the Nobel Prize in Economy: "Galt, Gold and God," editorial in the *New York Times*, August 23, 2012; http://www.nytimes.com/2012/08/24/opinion/krugman-galt-gold-and-god.html.
11. Rand's vision of the ideal hero, the egocentric superman, however, is regarded by philosophers as being closer to Nietzsche than to Aristotle. She scorned all other philosophers, especially Emmanuel Kant, whom she called a "monster," thinking he was "the worst of all," since he advocated an ethics based on duty and responsibility to the collective, the exact opposite of the individualist autonomy she championed.
12. Rand, A., *Anthem*, Public Domain Books, 2009. Kindle Edition, pp. 89–90.
13. Rand, A., *Atlas Shrugged, op. cit.*, p. 1034.
14. Ayn Rand was interviewed by the famous journalist Mike Wallace. See http://youtu.be/1ooKsv_SX4Y.
15. Rand, A., *The Fountainhead*, Plume, 1994, p. 715.
16. Rand, A., *The Virtue of Selfishness*, Signet, 1964, pp. 49–52.
17. Ayn Rand in 1976, quoted by *The Economist*, October 20, 2012, p. 54.
18. See Ayn Rand, *The Nature of Government, in Virtue of Selfishness.* Rand's ideas on "laissez-faire" politics were inspired by the Austrian economist Ludwig von Mises, whom she regarded as the greatest economist of the modern era.

19. Stiglitz, Joseph E., *The Price of Inequality: How Today's Divided Society Endangers Our Future*, Norton, 2012, pp. 93–94. Kindle Edition.
20. *Ibid.*, p. 175.
21. *Ibid.*, as well as Wilkinson, R., & Pickett, K., *The Spirit Level: Why Equality Is Better for Everyone*, Penguin, 2010.
22. Cohen, D., *The Prosperity of Vice: A Worried View of Economics*, trans. Susan Emanuel (translation slightly modified), MIT Press, 2012, p. 169.
23. Rand, A., *The Virtue of Selfishness*, 1964, p. 26.
24. Cavalli-Sforza, F. (1998/2011), *La Science du bonheur*, Odile Jacob.
25. See Chapter 19 of this book, as well as Diener, E., & Seligman, M. E. P. (2002). Very happy people, *Psychological Science*, *13*, 81–84; and Seligman, M. E. P., *Authentic Happiness: Using the New Positive Psychology to Realize Your Potential for Lasting Fulfillment*, The Free Press, 2002. See also Dambrun, M., & Ricard, M. (2011). *Op.cit.*
26. Rachels, J., *The Elements of Moral Philosophy*, McGraw-Hill, 4th edition, 2003, p. 89.
27. Freud, S., *The Interpretation of Dreams,* Trans. and ed. James Strachey, Avon Discus, 1965, p. 283.
28. Freud, S., *Correspondance avec le pasteur Pfister, 1909–1939*, Gallimard, 1991, p. 103. These sources were kindly provided to me by Jacques Van Rillaer.
29. Freud, S., *The Interpretation of Dreams*, Standard Edition, 4, Hogarth, 1978, p. 267. *Gesammelte Werke*, II/III, p. 274.
30. The word "altruism" appears only seven times in the twenty or so volumes of his complete works. Freud, S. *Gesammelte Werke*, Fischer Verlag; *Oeuvres complètes*. PUF.
31. Freud, S., *Civilization and Its Discontents*, trans. J. Riviere, Hogarth Press, 1930, p. 134.
32. Freud, S., *Sur la guerre et la mort*, in *Œuvres complètes,* "Psychanalyse," Vol. 13, PUF, 1915, pp. 1914–1915.
33. Later, the term "altruism" would be used only rarely by psychoanalysts, and does not appear in Haplanche, J., & Pontalis, J.-B., *The Language of Psycho-Analysis*, Norton, 1974.
34. Darwin, C., *The Descent of Man*, CreateSpace Independent Publishing Platform, 1881, p. 72.
35. *Ibid.*, p. 69.
36. Hochmann, J., *Une histoire de l'empathie: Connaissance d'autrui, souci du prochain*, Odile Jacob, 2012, pp. 53–59.

37. Freud, S., *Standard Edition*, Vol. 8, *Jokes and Their Relation to the Unconscious,* Hogarth, 1971. Quoted in Hochmann, J. (2012). *Op. cit.*, p. 54. This laughter is also supposedly set off by the observation that the person has thus managed to conserve the energy we usually use to inhibit our impulses and conform to proper behavior.
38. *Ibid.*, vol. XV, p. 112.
39. See the subchapter "Does an 'Instinct for Violence' Exist?" in Chapter 28, "At the Origin of Violence: Devaluing the Other."
40. Jung, C., *Civilization in Transition*, trans. R. F. C. Hull, Pantheon, 1964.
41. Freud S., *Civilization and Its Discontents,* trans. Joan Riviere, Martino Fine Books, 2011, p. 89.
42. Freud, S., *Gesammelte Werke*, 10,1915, p. 231. In English: Freud, S., *The Unconscious*, trans. Graham Frankland, Penguin Books, 2005, p. 30.
43. Waal, F. B. M. de, *The Bonobo and the Atheist: In Search of Humanism Among the Primates,* W. W. Norton, 2013, p. 39.
44. Haidt, J., *The Righteous Mind: Why Good People Are Divided by Politics and Religion*, Allen Lane, 2012. This does not exclude the fact that social norms later play an important role by shaping the personal morality of individuals in various ways.
45. Turiel, E., Killen, M., & Helwig, C. C., "Morality: Its Structure, Functions, and Vagaries." In *The Emergence of Morality in Young Children*, University of Chicago Press, 1987, pp. 155–243; Hamlin, J. K., Wynn, K., & Bloom, P. (2007). Social evaluation by preverbal infants. *Nature*, *450*(7169), 557–559.
46. Freud, S., " 'Civilized' Sexual Morality and Modern Nervous Illness." In J. Strachey (ed.), *The Complete Psychological Works of Sigmund Freud* (The Standard Edition), Hogarth, 1959, vol. 9, p. 191.
47. Freud, A. (1936). *Das ich und die Abwehrmechanismen.* In English: Freud, A., *The Ego and the Mechanisms of Defense*, International Universities Press, 1946.
48. Golse, Bernard, Altruism article in Mijolla, A. de, Golse, B., Mijolla-Mellor, S. de, & Perron, R., *International Dictionary of Psychoanalysis,* 3 Vols., Macmillan, 2005; Ionescu, S., Jacquet, M.-M., & Lhote, C., *Les Mécanismes de défense: Théorie et clinique*, 2d edition, Armand Colin, 2012.
49. Canceil, O., Cottraux, J., Falissard, B., Flament, M., Miermont, J., Swendsen, J.,...Thurin, J.-M., *Psychothérapie: Trois approches évaluées,* Inserm, 2004.

50. Moscovici, S., *La Psychanalyse, son image et son public.* PUF, 1976, p. 143. Cited by Van Rillaer, J. (1980). *Op. cit.*, p. 374.
51. Baruk, H. (1967). De Freud au néo-paganisme moderne. *La Nef, 3*, p. 143; Baruk, H., in *La Psychiatrie française de Pinel à nos jours*, PUF, 1968, p. 29. During an investigation conducted by the sociologist Dominique Frischer on about thirty Parisian analysands, one of them, "already selfish in the past, acknowledged that analysis developed this tendency, making him a perfect egocentric." Frischer, D., *Les Analysés parlent*, Stock, 1976, p. 312. Quoted in Van Rillaer, J. (1980). *Op. cit.*, p. 373.
52. Lacan, J., *Encore: Le séminaire*, Book 20, Seuil, 1999, p. 64.
53. Quoted in Van Rillaer, J., "Les bénéfices de la psychanalyse," in *Le Livre noir de la psychanalyse*, Les Arènes, 2005, p. 200.
54. Rey, P., *Une saison chez Lacan*, Laffont, 1999, p. 74.
55. *Ibid.*, p. 156.
56. Bettelheim, B., *The Empty Fortress: Infantile Autism and the Birth of the Self*, The Free Press, 1972, p. 66.
57. Autisme: Un scandale français. *Sciences et Avenir*, 782, April 2012.
58. *Ibid.*
59. Franck Ramus, statements gathered by Hervé Ratel, *Sciences et Avenir*, March 29, 2012. Some autistic people have a more voluminous brain, and a recent study, published in the journal *PNAS*, highlighted an overproduction of neurons by 67% in the prefrontal cortex involved in language and thought.
60. Herbert, M. R., & Weintraub, K., *The Autism Revolution: Whole-Body Strategies for Making Life All It Can Be*, Ballantine, 2012.
61. Wallach, M. A., & Wallach, L., *Psychology's Sanction for Selfishness: The Error of Egoism in Theory and Therapy*, W. H. Freeman, 1983.
62. Horney, K., *Neurosis and Human Growth—The Struggle Toward Self-Realization*, Routledge and Kegan Paul, 1951.
63. Wallach, M. A., & Wallach, L. (1983). *Op. cit.*, pp. 116–120.
64. *Ibid.*, p. 162.

CHAPTER 26: HAVING HATRED OR COMPASSION FOR YOURSELF

1. For an excellent overview of all the research, see Gilbert, P., & Irons, C. (2005). Focused therapies and compassionate mind training for shame and self-attacking. *Compassion: Conceptualisations, Research and Use in Psychotherapy*, 263–325.
2. *Ibid.*

3. Gilbert, P., & Irons, C. (2005). *Op. cit.*, p. 271.
4. *Ibid.*
5. Bohus, M., Limberger, M., Ebner, U., Glocker, F. X., Schwarz, B., Wernz, M., & Lieb, K. (2000). Pain perception during self-reported distress and calmness in patients with borderline personality disorder and self-mutilating behavior. *Psychiatry Research*, *95*(3), 251–260.
6. For suicidal tendencies, see Stanley, B., Gameroff, M. J., Michalsen, V., & Mann, J. J. (2001). Are suicide attempters who self-mutilate a unique population? *American Journal of Psychiatry*, *158*(3), 427–432.
7. Gilbert, P., & Irons, C. (2005). *Op. cit.*
8. *Ibid.*, p. 291.
9. Neff, K. D. (2011). *Op. cit.*, p. 41.
10. *Ibid.*, p. 43.
11. Kohut, H., *The Analysis of the Self*, New York University Press, 1971. Neff, K. D. (2011). *Op. cit.*, p. 64. See also Baumeister, R. F., & Leary, M. R. (1995). The need to belong: Desire for Interpersonal Attachments as a fundamental human motivation. *Psychological Bulletin*, *117*(3), 497.
12. Neff, K. D. (2011). *Op. cit.*, p. 69.
13. Gilbert, P., & Irons, C. (2005). *Op. cit.*, p. 312.
14. Kabat-Zinn, J., *Full Catastrophe Living: Using the Wisdom of Your Body and Mind to Face Stress, Pain, and Illness*, Delta, 1990.
15. See Kabat-Zinn, J., Lipworth, L., & Burney, R. (1985). The clinical use of mindfulness meditation for the self-regulation of chronic pain. *Journal of Behavioral Medicine*, *8*(2), 163–190.
16. Davidson, R. J., Kabat-Zinn, J., Schumacher, J., Rosenkranz, M., Muller, D., Santorelli, S. F., . . . Sheridan, J. F. (2003). Alterations in brain and immune function produced by mindfulness meditation. *Psychosomatic Medicine*, *65*(4), 564–570. On the long-term effects of meditation, see Chapter 21, "Training the Mind: What the Cognitive Scientists Have to Say."
17. Shapiro, S. L., Astin, J. A., Bishop, S. R., & Cordova, M. (2005). Mindfulness-based stress reduction for health care professionals: Results from a randomized trial. *International Journal of Stress Management*, *12*(2), 164–176.
18. Gilbert, P., *Mindful Compassion: How the Science of Compassion Can Help You Understand Your Emotions, Live in the Present, and Connect Deeply with Others*, New Harbinger, 2014.
19. Neff, K. D. (2003*a*). Self-compassion: An alternative conceptualization of a healthy attitude toward oneself. *Self and Identity*, *2*(2),

85–101; Neff, K. D. (2003*b*). The development and validation of a scale to measure self-compassion. *Self and Identity*, *2*(3), 223–250.

20. Crocker, J., Moeller, S., & Burson, A. (2010). The costly pursuit of self-esteem. *Handbook of Personality and Self-Regulation*, 403–429.
21. Neff, K. D. (2003*b*). *Op. cit.*
22. Gilbert, P., *Human Nature and Suffering*, Lawrence Erlbaum, 1989; Gilbert, P., & Irons, C. (2005). *Op. cit.*
23. Neff, K. D., Kirkpatrick, K. L., & Rude, S. S. (2007). Self-compassion and adaptive psychological functioning. *Journal of Research in Personality*, *41*(1), 139–154. See also Swann, W. B., *Self-Traps: The Elusive Quest for Higher Self-Esteem*, W. H. Freeman, 1996.
24. Leary, M. R., Tate, E. B., Adams, C. E., Allen, A. B., & Hancock, J. (2007). Self-compassion and reactions to unpleasant self-relevant events: The implications of treating oneself kindly. *Journal of Personality and Social Psychology*, *92*(5), 887.

CHAPTER 27: THE SHORTFALL OF EMPATHY

1. Singer, T., & Lamm, C. (2009). The social neuroscience of empathy. *Annals of the New York Academy of Sciences*, *1156*(1), 81–96.
2. Krasner, M. S., Epstein, R. M., Beckman, H., Suchman, A. L., Chapman, B., Mooney, C. J., & Quill, T. E. (2009). Association of an educational program in mindful communication with burnout, empathy, and attitudes among primary care physicians. *JAMA*, *302*(12), 1284–1293.
3. David Shlim, preface to Rinpoche, C. N., *Medicine and Compassion*, Wisdom Publications, 2006.
4. Harvey Fineberg, Foreword to Rinpoche, C. N., *Medicine and Compassion*, p. ix.
5. *Ibid.*
6. Maslach, C., *Burnout: The Cost of Caring*, Prentice Hall Trade, 1982, p. 3.
7. *Ibid.*, p. 4.
8. Preface by Prof. Patrick Légeron in Maslach, C., & Leiter, M. P., *Burnout: Le syndrome d'épuisement professionnel*, Les Arènes, 2011, p. 16.
9. Maslach, C. (1982). *Op. cit.*, pp. 10 ff.
10. *Ibid.*, p. 58.
11. *Ibid.*, p. 59.
12. *Ibid.*, p. 70.
13. McGrath, M., & Oakley, B., "Codependency and Pathological Altruism," in Oakley, B., Knafo, A., Madhavan, G., & Wilson, D., *Pathological Altruism*, Oxford University Press, Chapter 4, 2011, p. 59.

14. Zanarini, M. C. (2000). Childhood experiences associated with the development of borderline personality disorder. *Psychiatric Clinics of North America*, *23*(1), 89–101.
15. Richard Davidson, in conversation.
16. American Psychiatric Association, *DSM-IV: Diagnostic and Statistical Manual of Mental Disorders*, 4th ed., American Psychiatric Association, 1994.
17. Blair, R. J. R., Jones, L., Clark, F., & Smith, M. (1997). The psychopathic individual: A lack of responsiveness to distress cues? *Psychophysiology*, *34*(2), 192–198.
18. Hare, R. D., McPherson, L. M., & Forth, A. E. (1988). Male psychopaths and their criminal careers. *Journal of Consulting and Clinical Psychology*, *56*(5), 710.
19. Hare, R. D. (1993). *Without Conscience. Op. cit.*
20. Hare's twenty-point list includes: superficial charm, a sense of the grandiose, a need for stimulation and a predisposition to boredom, pathological lying, the art of manipulating others and deceiving them, the absence of remorse and any guilt feeling, interpersonal coldness, lack of empathy, a parasitic lifestyle, weak emotional control, sexual promiscuity, behavioral problems at an early age (lying, theft, deception, vandalism, cruelty to animals), the absence of long-term realistic goals, impulsiveness, irresponsibility, inability to assume responsibility for one's own actions, a large number of short-term romantic relationships, juvenile delinquency, repeat offenses, and multiple, diverse criminal activities. For the most recent version of this list, see Hare, R. D., *Manual for the Revised Psychopathy Checklist*, 2nd ed., Multi-Health Systems, 2003.
21. Hare, R. D. (1993), *Without Conscience. Op. cit.*
22. Raine, A., Lencz, T., Bihrle, S., LaCasse, L., & Colletti, P. (2000). Reduced prefrontal gray matter volume and reduced autonomic activity in antisocial personality disorder. *Archives of General Psychiatry*, *57*(2), 119.
23. Quoted in Pinker, S., *The Better Angels of Our Nature: Why Violence Has Declined,* Viking, 2011, p. 495.
24. Fazle, S., & Danesh, J. (2002). Serious mental disorder in 23,000 prisoners: A systematic review of 62 surveys. *Lancet*, *359*(9306), 545–550. Hart, S. D., & Hare, R. D. (1996). Psychopathy and antisocial personality disorder. *Current Opinion in Psychiatry*, *9*(2), 129–132.
25. Hemphill, J. F., Hare, R. D., & Wong, S. (1998). Psychopathy and recidivism: A review. *Legal and Criminological Psychology*, *3*(1), 139–170.

26. Blair, R. J. R., Peschardt, K. S., Budhani, S., Mitchell, D. G. V., & Pine, D. S. (2006). The development of psychopathy. *Journal of Child Psychology and Psychiatry*, *47*(3–4), 262–276; Blonigen, D. M., Hicks, B. M., Krueger, R. F., Patrick, C. J., & Iacono, W. G. (2005). Psychopathic personality traits: Heritability and genetic overlap with internalizing and externalizing psychopathology. *Psychological Medicine*, *35*(05), 637–648.
27. Muhammad, M, *Scared Silent*, 1st ed., Strebor Books, 2009.
28. Babiak, P., & Hare, R. D., *Snakes in Suits: When Psychopaths Go to Work*, HarperBusiness, 2007.
29. Board, B. J., & Fritzon, K. (2005). Disordered personalities at work. *Psychology, Crime and Law;* and Board, B. "The Tipping Point." *New York Times*, May 11, 2005, Opinion section. http://www.nytimes.com/2005/05/11/opinion/11board.html.
30. Kiehl, K. & Buckholtz, J. Dans la tête d'un psychopathe (November–December 2011). *Cerveau et Psycho*, *48*.
31. Harenski, C. L., Harenski, K. A., Shane, M. S., & Kiehl, K. A. (2010). Aberrant neural processing of moral violations in criminal psychopaths. *Journal of Abnormal Psychology*, *119*(4), 863; and for an overview, see Blair, R. J. R. (2010). Neuroimaging of psychopathy and antisocial behavior: A targeted review. *Current Psychiatry Reports*, *12*(1), 76–82.
32. Ermer, E., Cope, L. M., Nyalakanti, P. K., Calhoun, V. D., & Kiehl, K. A. (2012). Aberrant paralimbic gray matter in criminal psychopathy. *Journal of Abnormal Psychology*, *121*(3), 649.
33. Weng, H. Y., Fox, A. S., Shackman, A. J., Stodola, D. E., Caldwell, J. Z., Olson, M. C., . . . Davidson, R. J. (2013). Compassion training alters altruism and neural responses to suffering. *Psychological Science*. Retrieved from http://pss.sagepub.com/content/early/2013/05/20/0956797612469537.short; Lutz, A., Brefczynski-Lewis, J., Johnstone, T., & Davidson, R. J. (2008). Regulation of the neural circuitry of emotion by compassion meditation: Effects of meditative expertise. *PLoS One*, *3*(3), e1897.
34. Anderson, N. E., & Kiehl, K. A. (2012). The psychopath magnetized: Insights from brain imaging. *Trends in Cognitive Sciences*, *16*(1), 52–60.
35. Aside from the orbitofrontal cortex and the amygdala, the paralimbic system includes the anterior cingulate cortex, which regulates emotional states and helps individuals control their impulses and regulate their behavior, as well as the insula, which plays an essential role in

recognizing a violation of social norms, as well as in feelings of anger, fear, empathy, or disgust. But we know that psychopaths don't care about social norms and have a particularly high threshold of disgust, calmly tolerating repugnant smells and images.

36. Raine, A., Lencz, T., Bihrle, S., LaCasse, L., & Colletti, P. (2000). Reduced prefrontal gray matter volume and reduced autonomic activity in antisocial personality disorder. *Archives of General Psychiatry*, *57*(2), 119.
37. Miller, G. (2008). *Op. cit.*
38. Cleckley, H. (1941). *Op. cit.*; Salekin, R. T. (2002). Psychopathy and therapeutic pessimism: Clinical lore or clinical reality? *Clinical Psychology Review*, *22*(1), 79–112.
39. Caldwell, M., Skeem, J., Salekin, R., & Van Rybroek, G. (2006). Treatment response of adolescent offenders with psychopathy features a 2-year follow-up. *Criminal Justice and Behavior*, *33*(5), 571–596; Caldwell, M. F., McCormick, D. J., Umstead, D., & Van Rybroek, G. J. (2007). Evidence of treatment progress and therapeutic outcomes among adolescents with psychopathic features. *Criminal Justice and Behavior*, *34*(5), 573–587.
40. Michael Caldwell, in conversation with the author, Madison, October 2012.
41. Caldwell, M. F., *et al.* (2006). *Op. cit.*, Kiehl, K., & Buckholtz, J. (2011). *Op. cit.*
42. Testimony taken from the book by Andrew Solomon, *The Noonday Demon: An Atlas of Depression*, Scribner, 2002, p. 346.
43. Milner, J. S., Halsey, L. B., & Fultz, J. (1995). Empathic responsiveness and affective reactivity to infant stimuli in high-and low-risk for physical child abuse mothers. *Child Abuse & Neglect*, *19*(6), 767–780. For comparable results obtained by using physiological methods, see Frodi, A. M., & Lamb, M. E. (1980). Child abusers' responses to infant smiles and cries. *Child Development*, *51*(1), 238. Quoted in Batson, C. D., *Altruism in Humans*, Oxford University Press, 2011.
44. See especially Schewe, P. A., *Preventing Violence in Relationships: Interventions Across the Life Span*, Vol. 8, American Psychological Association, 2002.
45. See especially McCullough, M. E., Worthington Jr., E. L., & Rachal, K. C. (1997). Interpersonal forgiving in close relationships. *Journal of Personality and Social Psychology*, *73*(2), 321; McCullough, M. E., Rachal, K. C., Sandage, S. J., Worthington Jr., E. L., Brown, S. W., &

Hight, T. L. (1998). Interpersonal forgiving in close relationships, II. Theoretical elaboration and measurement. *Journal of Personality and Social Psychology*, *75*(6), 1586; Witvliet, C. V. O., Ludwig, T. E., & Vander Laan, K. L. (2001). Granting forgiveness or harboring grudges: Implications for emotion, physiology, and health. *Psychological Science*, *12*(2), 117–123. Quoted in Batson, C. D. (2011). *Op. cit.*

46. Harmon-Jones and his collaborators evaluated the effect of empathy on anger by measuring by EEG the activity of the left frontal cortex, which we know is related to the intensity of anger. In the initial phase of the experiment, the experimenters influenced the degree of empathy of members of two groups of volunteer students (who took part in the experiment one at a time) by asking some to imagine the feelings of a female student suffering from multiple sclerosis, thus inducing increased empathy for her (she was actually an accomplice of the experimenters), and others to consider the sick person's situation in a detached, objective way, which induced only a weak amount of empathy. Soon after, the volunteer student supposedly suffering from MS gave the volunteers either a rude, insulting report, meant to give rise to an aggressive reaction, of an essay these volunteers had written, or a neutral evaluation. The EEG activity of the volunteers was recorded immediately after they received these evaluations. It turned out that the activity of the frontal cortex that normally increases when one is insulted and that accompanies aggression increased markedly among the subjects of the group who were asked to adopt a detached attitude, but was inhibited in those in whom empathy was induced. This experiment is one of those that show most clearly that empathy can directly inhibit the desire to attack. Harmon-Jones, E., Vaughn-Scott, K., Mohr, S., Sigelman, J., & Harmon-Jones, C. (2004). The effect of manipulated sympathy and anger on left and right frontal cortical activity. *Emotion*, *4*(1), 95. Quoted in Batson, C. D. (2011). *Op. cit.*, p. 167.

Chapter 28: At the Origin of Violence: Devaluing the Other

1. Hare, R. D., *Without Conscience: The Disturbing World of the Psychopaths Among Us*, Pocket Books, 1993, p. 33. Quoted in Baumeister, R. F., *Evil: Inside Human Cruelty and Violence*, Barnes & Noble, 2001, p. 221.
2. Quoted in Pinker, S. (2011). *Op. cit.*, p. 509.

3. Aaron Beck said this during a meeting with the Dalai Lama in Sweden in 2005. This number suggests the importance of the mental superimpositions that affect our perceptions under the influence of anger, but are not a precise, measured evaluation of cognitive distortions.
4. For a detailed explanation of this mechanism, see Beck, A., *Prisoners of Hate: The Cognitive Basis of Anger, Hostility, and Violence*, Harper Perennial, 2000.
5. His Holiness the Dalai Lama, *365 Dalai Lama: Daily Advice from the Heart*, Hampton Roads Publishing, 2012.
6. Pinker, S. (2011). *Op. cit.*, p. 164; Baumeister, R. F. (2001). *Op. cit.*, p. 157.
7. Quoted in Pinker, S. (2011). *Op. cit.*, p. 529.
8. Baumeister, R. F. (2001). *Op. cit.*, p. 167.
9. Brezina, T., Agnew, R., Cullen, F. T., & Wright, J. P. (2004). The code of the street. A quantitative assessment of Elijah Anderson's subculture of violence thesis and its contribution to youth violence research. *Youth Violence and Juvenile Justice*, *2*(4), 303–328.
10. Courtwright, D. T., *Violent Land: Single Men and Social Disorder from the Frontier to the Inner City*, new ed., Harvard University Press, 1998. Quoted in Pinker, S. (2011). *Op. cit.*, p. 103.
11. King James Bible. Deuteronomy, 42–43.
12. The Dalai Lama, in a speech at the Sorbonne, during a meeting of recipients of the Prix de la Mémoire, in 1993.
13. Hillesum, E., *Etty: A Diary 1941–43,* trans. Arnold J. Pomerans, Jonathan Cape, 1983.
14. Dui Hua Foundation (2010). Reducing death penalty crimes in china more symbol than substance. *Dialogue*, 40.
15. Report broadcast on the BBC World Service, October 6, 2006.
16. Vergely, B., *Souffrance*, Flammarion, 1998.
17. Baumeister, R. F. (2001). *Op. cit.*, 1990, pp. 132–134.
18. Scully, D., *Understanding Sexual Violence: A Study of Convicted Rapists*, Routledge, 1990. Quoted in Baumeister, R. F. (2001). *Op. cit.*, p. 138.
19. Baumeister, R. F. (2001). *Op. cit.*, pp. 141, 144.
20. Kernis, M. H., "The Roles of Stability and Level of Self-Esteem in Psychological Functioning," in *Self-Esteem: The Puzzle of Low Self-Regard*, Plenum Press, 1993, pp. 167–182.
21. Baumeister, R. F. (2001). *Op. cit.*, p. 149.
22. Berkowitz, L. (1978). Is criminal violence normative behavior? Hostile and instrumental aggression in violent incidents. *Journal of Research in Crime and Delinquency*, *15*(2), 148–161.

23. Ford, F. L., *Political Murder: From Tyrannicide to Terrorism*, Harvard University Press, 1987, p. 80. Quoted in Baumeister, R. F. (2001). *Op. cit.*, p. 152.
24. Johnson, D. D., McDermott, R., Barrett, E. S., Cowden, J., Wrangham, R., McIntyre, M. H., & Rosen, S. P. (2006). Overconfidence in wargames: Experimental evidence on expectations, aggression, gender and testosterone. *Proceedings of the Royal Society B: Biological Sciences*, *273*(1600), 2513–2520.
25. Beck, A. (2004). *Op. cit.*, p. 34.
26. Baumeister, R. F. (2001). *Op. cit.*, pp. 39–48.
27. Straus, M. (1980). Victims and aggressors in marital violence. *American Behavioral Scientist*, *23*(5), 681. Cited by Baumeister, R. F. (2001). *Op. cit.*, p. 53.
28. Black, D. (1983). Crime as social control. *American Sociological Review*, 34–45. Quoted in Pinker, S. (2011). *Op. cit.*, p. 83.
29. Including Luckenbill, Gottfredson, and Hirschi.
30. Luckenbill, D. F. (1977). Criminal homicide as a situated transaction. *Social Problems*, 176–186; Gottfredson and Hirschi, *A General Theory of Crime,* Stanford University Press, 1990. Quoted in Baumeister, R. F. (2001) *Op. cit.*, p. 53.
31. Baumeister, R. F., (2001), *Op. cit.*, p. 117.
32. *Ibid.*, p. 62.
33. Twitchell, J. B., *Dreadful Pleasures: An Anatomy of Modern Horror*, Oxford University Press, 1985; quoted in Baumeister, R. F. (2001). *Op. cit.*, pp. 64, 66.
34. Baumeister, R. F. (2001). *Op. cit.*, p. 77.
35. Norris, J., *Walking Time Bombs*, Bantam, 1992, p. 53.
36. *Ibid.*, pp. 18–19.
37. Jankowski, M. S., *Islands in the Street: Gangs and American Urban Society*, University of California Press, 1991, p. 177.
38. Finkelhor, D., & Yllö, K., *License to Rape: Sexual Abuse of Wives*, The Free Press, 1987.
39. Toch, H., *Violent Men: An Inquiry into the Psychology of Violence*, 2d rev. ed., American Psychological Association, 1993.
40. Baumeister, R. F. (2001). *Op. cit.*, pp. 232–236.
41. Gottfredson, M., & Hirschi, T., *A General Theory of Crime*, Stanford University Press, 1990, p. 105.
42. Baumeister, R. F. (2001). *Op. cit.*, p. 106.
43. Gelles, R. J., *Intimate Violence*, Simon & Schuster, 1988.
44. Katz, J., *Seductions of Crime: Moral and Sensual Attractions in Doing Evil*, Basic Books, 1990, as well as Baumeister, R. F. (2001). *Op. cit.*, p. 111.

45. Milgram, S. (1963). Behavioral study of obedience. *Journal of Abnormal and Social Psychology*, *67*(4), 371.
46. "Le Jeu de la mort" ["The Game of Death"], broadcast on France 2, March 17, 2010.
47. Zimbardo, P., *The Lucifer Effect: Understanding How Good People Turn Evil*, Random House, 2007.
48. We even thought of repeating the Stanford prison experiment using only longtime Buddhist practitioners, and considered several variants: either all the guards, or all the prisoners, could be Buddhist meditators, or both could. One could also envisage a mixed population of students and meditators. But, according to Phil, it would be almost impossible today to obtain permission from the ethics committees that review research propositions, because of the potentially disturbing effects for the volunteers.
49. Zimbardo, P. (2007). *Op. cit.*
50. Quoted in Pinker, S. (2011). *Op. cit.*, p. 509.
51. See the table in the *New Scientist*, http://www.newscientist.com/embedded/20worst, based on White, M., *The Great Big Book of Horrible Things: The Definitive Chronicle of History's 100 Worst Atrocities*, W. W. Norton, 2012, as well as McEvedy, C., Jones, R., & others, *Atlas of World Population History*, Penguin Books, 1978, for numbers concerning the world population at various times in history.
52. Pinker, S. (2011). *Op. cit.*, p. 196.
53. Fanon, F., *The Wretched of the Earth*, Grove Press, 2007.
54. Baumeister, R. F., *Evil: Inside Human Cruelty and Violence*, Barnes & Noble, 2001, p. 120.
55. Maalouf, A., *The Crusades Through Arab Eyes,* Schocken, 1989.
56. Rummel, R. J., *Death by Government*, Transaction Publishers, 1994.
57. Freud, S., *Reflections on War and Death* (Kindle Locations 341–343), Kindle Edition, 2012.
58. Freud, Sigmund, *Civilization and Its Discontents* (Kindle Locations 825–826), Kindle Edition, 2013.
59. What's more, as Jacques Van Rillaer, a former psychoanalyst who has explored this question in detail in his book *Les Illusions de la psychanalyse*, explains, psychologists today challenge the principle by which living beings basically try to search for a state completely without tension, and to reduce any new tension that arises in them. On the contrary, an animal or a person placed in a comfortable place but completely isolated from any stimulation likely to arouse tension soon experiences this situation as very disagreeable. Van Rillaer, J., *Les Illusions de la psychanalyse*, 1995. *Op. cit.*, p. 289, and note 94.

60. *Ibid.*, p. 296.
61. Lorenz, K., *On Aggression*, Routledge, 2005, p. 5.
62. *Ibid.*, p. 265.
63. *Ibid.*, pp. 232–233.
64. *Ibid.*, p. 48.
65. Waal, F. B. M. de, *Le Bon Singe: Les bases naturelles de la morale*, Bayard, 1997, pp. 205–208.
66. Eibl-Eibesfeldt I., *Contre l'agression*, Stock, 1972. Eibl-Eibesfeldt, I., *Love and Hate: On the Natural History of Basic Behaviour Patterns*, AldineTransaction, 1973, p. 5.
67. Kohn, A., *The Brighter Side of Human Nature*, 1992. *Op. cit.*, p. 51.
68. Davidson, R. J., Putnam, K. M., & Larson, C. L. (2000). Dysfunction in the neural circuitry of emotion regulation—a possible prelude to violence. *Science*, *289*(5479), 591–594; Friedman, H. S., *Hostility, Coping, and Health*, Vol. 16, American Psychological Association, 1992.
69. Williams, R. B., Barefoot, J. C., & Shekelle, R. B. (1985). The health consequences of hostility. In Chesney, M. A., & Rosenman, R. H., *Anger and Hostility in Cardiovascular and Behavioral Disorders*, Hemisphere, 1985.
70. Douglas, J. E., *Mindhunter: Inside the FBI's Elite Serial Crime Unit*, Scribner, 1995. Quoted in Baumeister, R. F. (2001). *Op. cit.*, p. 273.
71. Prunier, G., *Rwanda: Le génocide*, Dagorno, 1998.
72. Adams, D. B. (2006). Brain mechanisms of aggressive behavior: An updated review. *Neuroscience and Biobehavioral Reviews*, *30*(3), 304–318. Cited by Pinker, S. (2011). *Op. cit.*, pp. 495–496.
73. Panksepp, J., *Affective Neuroscience: The Foundations of Human and Animal Emotions*, Vol. 4., Oxford University Press, 2004.
74. Davidson, R. J., Putnam, K. M., & Larson, C. L. (2000). Dysfunction in the neural circuitry of emotion regulation—a possible prelude to violence. *Science*, *289*(5479), 591–594.
75. Strasburger, V. C. (2010). Media education. *Pediatrics*, 126(5), 1012–1017; doi:10.1542/peds.2010-1636. Anderson, C. A., Berkowitz, L., Donnerstein, E., Huesmann, L. R., Johnson, J. D., Linz, D.,… Wartella, E. (2003). The influence of media violence on youth. *Psychological Science in the Public Interest*, 4(3), 81–110. Another study adds: "The changes in aggression are both short term and long term, and these changes may be mediated by neurological changes in the young viewer." Murray, J. P. (2008). Media violence the effects are both real and strong. *American Behavioral Scientist*, 51(8), 1212–1230, doi:10.1177/0002764207312018.

76. Conclusion of a joint report by six of the leading American medical associations, American Academy of Pediatrics, Policy statement. Media violence, in *Pediatrics*, vol. 124, pp. 1495–1503, 2009.
77. In contrast to the thousands of studies that show that violent images and video games increase violent behavior, not a single study has identified any effect of release that would reduce these behaviors (i.e., no cathartic effect). For overviews on the impact of violence in the media, see Christensen, P. N., & Wood, W. (2007). Effects of media violence on viewers' aggression in unconstrained social interaction, in Preiss, R. W., Gayle, B. M., Burrell, N., Allen, M., & Bryant, J., *Mass Media Effects Research: Advances Through Meta-Analysis*, Lawrence Erlbaum, 2007, pp. 145–168. Quoted in Lecomte, J. (2012). *La Bonté humaine. Op. cit.*, p. 316.
78. Desmurget, M. (2012). La télévision creuset de la violence. *Cerveau et Psycho*, *8*, November–January 2012. Desmurget, M., *TV Lobotomie: La vérité scientifique sur les effets de la télévision*, Max Milo Éditions, 2012.
79. Gerbner, G., Gross, L., Morgan, M., & Signorielli, N. (1986). Living with television: The dynamics of the cultivation process. *Perspectives on media effects*, 17–40. Gerbner, G., Gross, L., Morgan, M., Signorielli, N., & Shanahan, J. (2002). Growing up with television: Cultivation processes. *Media effects: Advances in theory and research*, *2*, 43–67.
80. Quoted in Kohn, A. (1992). *Op. cit.*, p. 37.
81. Mares, M. L., & Woodard, E. (2005). Positive effects of television on children's social interactions: A meta-analysis. *Media Psychology*, *7*(3), 301–322.
82. Christakis, D. A., & Zimmerman, F. J. (2007). Violent television viewing during preschool is associated with antisocial behavior during school age. *Pediatrics*, *120*(5), 993–999.
83. Desmurget, M. (2012). La télévision creuset de la violence. These effects are independent of the normal temperament, more or less aggressive, of the individual.
84. Sestir, M. A., & Bartholow, B. D. (2010). Violent and nonviolent video games produce opposing effects on aggressive and prosocial outcomes. *Journal of Experimental Social Psychology*, *46*(6), 934–942; Bartholow, B. D., Bushman, B. J., & Sestir, M. A. (2006). Chronic violent video game exposure and desensitization to violence: Behavioral and event-related brain potential data. *Journal of Experimental Social Psychology*, *42*(4), 532–539; Engelhardt, C. R., Bartholow, B. D., Kerr, G. T., & Bushman, B. J. (2011). This is your brain on violent video

games: Neural desensitization to violence predicts increased aggression following violent video game exposure. *Journal of Experimental Social Psychology*, *47*(5), 1033–1036. Still, when it comes to the authors of serious violent actions, murders especially, the influence of the media affects them especially when they are already predisposed to violence. Compared to the rest of the population, aggressive individuals, in fact, go to see more violent films, and the influence these films exercise on their tendency to become angry and commit violent actions is stronger than among other people. See Bushman, B. J. (1995). Moderating role of trait aggressiveness in the effects of violent media on aggression. *Journal of Personality and Social Psychology*, *69*(5), 950.

85. Desmurget, M. (2012), L'empreinte de la violence, *Cerveau et Psycho*, *8*, November–January 2012.
86. Diener, E., & DeFour, D. (1978). Does television violence enhance program popularity? *Journal of Personality and Social Psychology*, *36*(3), 333. Quoted in Lecomte, J. (2012). *Op. cit.*, p. 314.
87. Lenhart, A., Kahne, J., Middaugh, E., Macgill, A. R., Evans, C., & Vitak, J. (2008). Teens, video games, and civics: Teens. *Pew Internet & American Life Project*, 76; Escobar-Chaves, S. L., & Anderson, C. A. (2008). Media and risky behaviors. *The Future of Children*, *18*(1), 147–180.
88. Anderson, C. A., Shibuya, A., Ihori, N., Swing, E. L., Bushman, B. J., Sakamoto, A.,…Saleem, M. (2010). Violent video game effects on aggression, empathy, and prosocial behavior in eastern and western countries: A meta-analytic review. *Psychological Bulletin*, *136*(2), 151.
89. Gentile, D. A., Lynch, P. J., Linder, J. R., & Walsh, D. A. (2004). The effects of violent video game habits on adolescent hostility, aggressive behaviors, and school performance. *Journal of Adolescence*, *27*(1), 5–22.
90. Anderson, C. A., Sakamoto, A., Gentile, D. A., Ihori, N., Shibuya, A., Yukawa, S.,…Kobayashi, K. (2008). Longitudinal effects of violent video games on aggression in Japan and the United States. *Pediatrics*, *122*(5),1067–1072.
91. Glaubke, C. R., Miller, P., Parker, M. A., & Espejo, E., *Fair Play? Violence, Gender and Race in Video Games*, Children NOW, 2001.
92. Barlett, C. P., Harris, R. J., & Bruey, C. (2008). The effect of the amount of blood in a violent video game on aggression, hostility, and arousal. *Journal of Experimental Social Psychology*, *44*(3), 539–546.
93. Bègue, L. (2012). Jeux video, l'école de la violence, *Cerveau et Psycho*, *8*, November–January 2012.

94. Kutner, L., & Olson, C., *Grand Theft Childhood: The Surprising Truth About Violent Video Games and What Parents Can Do,* Simon & Schuster, 2000.
95. Grossman, D., *On Killing: The Psychological Cost of Learning to Kill in War and Society*, rev. ed., Back Bay Books, 2009, p. 306, 329.
96. *Ibid.*, p. 325.
97. Bègue, L. (2012). Devient-on tueur grâce aux jeux vidéo? *Cerveau et Psycho*, *8*, November–January 2012, 10–11.
98. Anderson, C. A., Gentile, D. A., & Buckley, K. E., *Violent Video Game Effects on Children and Adolescents: Theory, Research, and Public Policy: Theory, Research, and Public Policy*, Oxford University Press, 2007.
99. Green, C. S., & Bavelier, D. (2003). Action video game modifies visual selective attention. *Nature*, *423*(6939), 534–537.
100. Bavelier, D., & Davidson, R. J. (2013). Brain training: Games to do you good. *Nature*, *494*(7438), 425–426.
101. Prosocial games include Chibi Robo, in which the player controls a robot that helps everyone at home and elsewhere. The more the player helps, the more points he earns. In Super Mario Sunshine, the players help clean up a polluted island. The goal of the research teams that are now developing new prosocial games is for the games to be truly attractive and maintain the player's interest.
102. They also verified that violent video games not only increased aggression, but also diminished positive mental states.
103. Saleem, M., Anderson, C. A., & Gentile, D. A. (2012). Effects of prosocial, neutral, and violent video games on college students' affect. *Aggressive Behavior*, *38*(4), 263–271; Greitemeyer, T., Osswald, S., & Brauer, M. (2010). Playing prosocial video games increases empathy and decreases schadenfreude. *Emotion*, *10*(6), 796–802.
104. Bingenheimer, J. B., Brennan, R. T., & Earls, F. J. (2005). Firearm violence exposure and serious violent behavior. *Science*, *308*(5726), 1323–1326.
105. "Broken Bodies, Shattered Minds: Torture and Ill-Treatment of Women." Amnesty International Report ACT 40/001/2001.
106. Amnesty International Report ACT 40/001/2001, based on "Ending Violence Against Women, Based on over 50 Population Surveys," report published by the Johns Hopkins University Population Information Program, 2000.
107. BBC World Service, November 5, 2012. http://www.bbc.com/news/world-asia-20202686.

108. For an exhaustive report on harassment and its causes, see Di Martino, V., Hoel, H., & Cooper, C. L., *Prévention du harcèlement et de la violence sur le lieu de travail*, Office des Publications Officielles des Communautés Européennes, 2003. Victims of harassment generally exhibit some characteristics such as shyness, low self-esteem, a feeling of not being very effective ("I won't be able to do this"), emotional instability, or a sluggish character, marked by passivity. Finally, harassment is facilitated by certain so-called situational characteristics of the victim, such as a vulnerability linked to a precarious economic situation, to social or family difficulties, and to a level of training that is either higher or lower than that of other members of the group. Such characteristics are known to favor being treated as a scapegoat within groups.
109. Keinan, G. (1987). Decision making under stress: Scanning of alternatives under controllable and uncontrollable threats. *Journal of Personality and Social Psychology*, *52*(3), 639.
110. Zillmann, D. "Mental Control of Angry Aggression," in Wegner, D., & Pennebaker, P., *Handbook of Mental Control*, Prentice Hall, 1993.
111. Hokanson, J. E., & Edelman, R. (1966). Effects of three social responses on vascular processes. *Journal of Personality and Social Psychology*, *3*(4), 442.
112. Alain, *Propos sur le bonheur*, Gallimard, 1985, Folio.
113. Baumeister, R. F. (2001). *Op. cit.*, p. 313.
114. *Ibid.*, pp. 304–342.
115. King, M. L., & Jackson, J., *Why We Can't Wait*, Signet Classics, 2000.

Chapter 29: The Natural Repugnance to Kill

1. Marshall, S., *Men Against Fire: The Problem of Battle Command*, University of Oklahoma Press (orig. ed., 1947), 2000, p. 79.
2. See especially the studies by Picq, C. A. du, *Études sur le combat*, Ivrea, 1978, on old wars; Griffith, P., *Battle Tactics of the Civil War*, Yale University Press, 1989, on the Napoleonic wars and the American Civil War; and Holmes, R., *Acts of War: The Behavior of Men in Battle*, The Free Press, 1985, on the behavior of Argentine soldiers during the Falkland war. Quoted in Grossman, D., *On Killing: The Psychological Cost of Learning to Kill in War and Society*, Back Bay Books, 2009.
3. Quoted in Grossman, D. (2009). *Op. cit.*, p. 27.

4. *Ibid.*, p. 28.
5. Keegan, J. (1976). Quoted in Grossman, D. (2009). *Op. cit.*, p. 122.
6. Giraudoux, J., *The Trojan War Will Not Take Place,* trans. Christopher Fry., Methuen, 1983, p. 7.
7. Gray, J. G., *The Warriors: Reflections on Men in Battle,* Bison Books, 1998. Quoted in Grossman, D. (2009). *Op. cit.*, p. 39.
8. Grossman, D. (2009). *Op. cit.*, p. 160.
9. Stouffer, S. A., Suchman, E. A., Devinney, L. C., Star, S. A., & Williams Jr., R. M., *The American Soldier: Adjustment During Army Life*, Princeton University Press, 1999.
10. Grossman, D. (2009). *Op. cit.*, p. 212.
11. Strozzi-Heckler, R., *In Search of the Warrior Spirit*, Blue Snake Books, 2007.
12. Hatzfeld, J., *Machete Season: The Killers in Rwanda Speak*, Macmillan, 2006.
13. Abé, N. (December 14, 2012). Dreams in infrared: The woes of an American drone operator. *Spiegel Online International.* http://www.alipac.us/f19/meet-brandon-bryant-drone-operator-who-quit-after-killing-child-war-crimes-268988/.
14. Marsh, P., & Campbell, A., *Aggression and Violence*, Blackwell, 1982.
15. Gabriel, R. A., *No More Heroes: Madness and Psychiatry in War,* Hill and Wang, 1988.
16. Dyer, G., *War: The Lethal Custom*, Basic Books, 2006. Quoted in Grossman, D. (2009). *Op. cit.*, p. 180.
17. Swank, R. L., & Marchand, W. E. (1946). Combat neuroses: Development of combat exhaustion. *Archives of Neurology & Psychiatry, 55*(3), 236.
18. Quoted in Grossman, D. (2009). *Op. cit.*, pp. 237–238.
19. Dyer, G. (2006). *Op. cit.,* quoting a sergeant in the American Marines, a Vietnam veteran. In Grossman, D. (2009). *Op. cit.*, p. 253.
20. *Ibid.* Quoted in Grossman, D. (2009). *Op. cit.*, p. 19.
21. Grossman, D. (2009). *Op. cit.*, p. 267.
22. Giedd, J. N., Blumenthal, J., Jeffries, N. O., Castellanos, F. X., Liu, H., Zijdenbos, A., . . . Rapoport, J. L. (1999). Brain development during childhood and adolescence: A longitudinal MRI study. *Nature Neuroscience, 2*(10), 861–863.
23. Manchester, W., *Goodbye, Darkness: A Memoir of the Pacific War,* Michael Joseph, 1981. Quoted in Grossman, D. (2009). *Op. cit.*, p. 116.
24. Williams, T. (2012). Suicides outpacing war deaths for troops. *New York Times*, June 8, 2012.

25. Snow, B. R., Stellman, J. M., Stellman, S. D., Sommer, J. F., & others. (1988). Post-traumatic stress disorder among American Legionnaires in relation to combat experience in Vietnam: Associated and contributing factors. *Environmental Research*, *47*(2), 175–192.
26. Interview BBC World Service. 2003.
27. Words uttered by the 14th Dalai Lama during the 25th meeting of the Mind and Life Institute, January 21, 2013, in South India.
28. Swofford, A., *Jarhead: A Soldier's Story of Modern War*, Scribner, 2004.
29. On "just" war, see Bible, Samuel, chapter 23, 8, Exodus, chapter 20, 13; chapter 34, 10–14, Deuteronomy, chapter 7, 7–26.
30. Torah, Book of Numbers, chapter 35, 16–23; Leviticus, chapter 20, 10, Exodus, chapter 22, 20 and 32.
31. Koran, chapter 17, 33 and 186.
32. Boismorand, P. (ed.), *Magda et André Trocmé, Figures de résistance*, selected passages, Éditions du Cerf, 2008, extracts from *Souvenirs*, p. 119.
33. St. Paul, Epistle to the Romans, chapter 13, 8–10.
34. These words were uttered by Desmond Tutu during a meeting with a group of scholars and representatives of various religions at the World Economic Forum in Davos, January 26, 2012.

CHAPTER 30: DEHUMANIZING THE OTHER: MASSACRES AND GENOCIDES

1. Beck, A. T., *Prisoners of Hate: The Cognitive Basis of Anger, Hostility, and Violence*, Perennial, 2000, p. 17.
2. Quoted in Waal, F. B. M. de, *The Bonobo and the Atheist: In Search of Humanism Among the Primates*, W. W. Norton, 2013, p. 212.
3. Miller, S. C., *Benevolent Assimilation: American Conquest of the Philippines, 1899–1903*, Yale University Press, 1982, pp. 188–189, quoted by Charles Patterson. *Eternal Treblinka: Our Treatment of Animals and the Holocaust* (Kindle Locations 493–494). Kindle Edition.
4. Hatzfeld, J., *Machete Season.*
5. Suarez-Orozco, M., & Nordstrom, C. (1992). A Grammar of terror: Psychocultural responses to state terrorism in dirty war and post-dirty war Argentina. *The Paths to Domination, Resistance, and Terror*, 219–259. Quoted in Baumeister, R. F. (2001). *Op. cit.*, p. 226.
6. Binding, K., & Hoche, A., *Die Freigabe der Vernichtung lebensunwerten Lebens*, Bwv Berliner-Wissenschaft (original ed., 1920), 2006; Schank, K., & Schooyans, M., *Euthanasie, le dossier Binding and Hoche*, Le Sarment, 2002.

7. Quoted in Staub, E., *The Roots of Evil: The Origins of Genocide and Other Group Violence*, reprint, Cambridge University Press, 1992, note 21.
8. The Aktion T4 program concerned all patients suffering from schizophrenia, epilepsy, senility, incurable paralysis, weakness of mind, encephalitis, and terminal-phase neurological disorders, as well as patients who had been hospitalized since the age of at least five.
9. Chalk, F., & Jonassohn, K., *The History and Sociology of Genocide: Analyses and Case Studies*, Yale University Press, 1990.
10. Hatzfeld, J. (2005). *Op. cit.*, p. 53.
11. Pinker, S. (2011). *Op. cit.*, p. 326.
12. Chang, I., *The Rape of Nanking: The Forgotten Holocaust of World War II*, Basic Books, 1997, p. 56. Quoted in Charles Patterson, *Eternal Treblinka: Our Treatment of Animals and the Holocaust*, Lantern, 2002, p. 75.
13. Menninger, K. A., "Totemic Aspects of Contemporary Attitudes Toward Animals," *Psychoanalysis and Culture: Essays in Honor of Géza Róheim*, International Universities Press, 1951, pp. 42–74. Quoted in Patterson, C. (2008). *Op. cit.*, p. 70.
14. Sémelin, J., *Purify and Destroy: The Political Uses of Massacre and Genocide*, Columbia University Press, 2007, p. 243.
15. Hodgen, M., *Early Anthropology in the Sixteenth and Seventeenth Centuries*, vol. 1014, University of Pennsylvania Press, 2011, p. 22.
16. Stannard, D. E., *American Holocaust: The Conquest of the New World*, Oxford University Press, 1992, p. 243. Quoted in Patterson, C. (2008). *Op. cit.* (Kindle Locations 448–452). Kindle Edition.
17. From a speech made in January 1886 in South Dakota. Hagedorn, H., *Roosevelt in the Bad Lands*, Houghton Mifflin, 1921, pp. 354–356; 2010 edition, Bilbio Bazar.
18. Patterson, C. (2008). *Op. cit.* (Kindle Locations 375–376). Kindle Edition.
19. Gould, S. J., *La Mal-mesure de l'homme*, Odile Jacob, 1996, p. 135. Quoted in Patterson, C. (2008). Op. cit., p. 58.
20. Levi, P., *If This Is a Man: Remembering Auschwitz*, Little, Brown, 1997.
21. Staub, E. (1992). *Op. cit.*, p. 101.
22. Shirer, William L., *The Rise and Fall of the Third Reich: A History of Nazi Germany*, Simon & Schuster, 2011, p. 236. William Shirer notes: "The great founder of Protestantism was both a passionate anti-Semite and a ferocious believer in absolute obedience to political authority. He wanted Germany rid of the Jews....[Luther's] advice was literally followed four centuries later by Hitler, Goering and

Himmler." The Nazis celebrated their *Luthertag* (Luther Day) and Fahrenhorst, a member of the Organization Committee for Luthertag, dubbed Luther "the first German spiritual Führer."

23. Sémelin, J. (2007). *Purify and Destroy. Op. cit.*
24. Glass, J. M. (1997). Against the indifference hypothesis: The Holocaust and the enthusiasts for murder. *Political Psychology*, *18*(1), 129–145.
25. Sémelin, J., (2007). *Op. cit.*, p. 269.
26. *Ibid.*, p. 41.
27. Jean Hatzfeld, *Machete Season*.
28. Letter from Walter Mattner dated October 5, 1941, in Ingrao, C. (2002). Violence de guerre, violence de génocide. Les pratiques d'agression des *Einsatzgruppen*, pp. 219–241. In Audoin-Rouzeau, S., & Asséo, H. (2002). *La Violence de guerre, 1914–1945: Approches comparées des deux conflits mondiaux*. Complexe. Quoted in Sémelin, J. (2007). *Op. cit.*, p. 250.
29. Hoess, R., *Commandant at Auschwitz: Autobiography*, Weidenfeld & Nicholson, 1959.
30. Browning, C. (2007). *Op. cit.*
31. *Ibid.*, p. 75.
32. Sémelin, J. (2007). *Op. cit.*, p. 246.
33. Bandura, A., Barbaranelli, C., Caprara, G. V., & Pastorelli, C. (1996). Mechanisms of moral disengagement in the exercise of moral agency. *Journal of Personality and Social Psychology*, *71*(2), 364.
34. Todorov, T., *Facing the Extreme: Moral Life in the Concentration Camps*, Holt, 1997.
35. Tillon, G., *Ravensbrück*, Seuil, 2d ed., 1997, p. 109.
36. Langbein, H., *Hommes et femmes à Auschwitz*, Tallandier, 2011, p. 307. Quoted in Todorov, T. (1991). *Op. cit.*, p. 157.
37. Lifton, R. J., *The Nazi Doctors: Medical Killing and the Psychology of Genocide* (new ed.), Basic Books, 1988, pp. 418–422.
38. Arendt, H., *Eichmann in Jerusalem: A Report on the Banality of Evil*, Penguin, 2006, p. 125. Quoted in Todorov, T. (1991). *Op. cit.*, p. 163.
39. Expression suggested by the American psychologist Léon Festinger, Festinger, L., *A Theory of Cognitive Dissonance*, Stanford University Press, 1957. See also Gustave-Nico, F., *La Psychologie sociale*, Seuil, 1997, p. 160. Quoted in Sémelin, J. (2007). *Op. cit.*, p. 301.
40. According to Sémelin, J. (2007). *Op. cit.*, p. 304.
41. Sereny, G., *Into That Darkness: An Examination of Conscience*, Vintage Books, 1983, p. 164.

42. *Ibid.*, p. 200.
43. *Ibid.*, p. 412.
44. Mark F. No hard feelings. Villagers Defend Motives for Massacres, Associated Press, May 13, 1994.
45. Grmek, M. D., Mirko D., Gjidara, M., & Simac, N., *Le Nettoyage ethnique*, Fayard, 1993, p. 320. Quoted in Sémelin, J. (2009). *Op. cit.*, p. 253.
46. Intercepted telephone conversation between Colonel Ljubisa Beara (former head of military security for the *Republika Srpska* from 1992 to 1996) and General Krstic. See Srebrenica: quand les bourreaux parlent, *Le Nouvel Observateur*, March 18–24, 2004. Quoted in Sémelin, J. (2007). *Op. cit.*, p. 254.
47. Sémelin, J. (2007). *Op. cit.*, p. 254.
48. According to Sémelin, J. (2007). *Op. cit.*, p. 312.
49. *Ibid.*, p. 313.
50. Des Forges, ed., *Aucun témoin ne doit survivre: Le génocide au Rwanda*, Karthala, 1999, p. 376. Quoted in Sémelin, J. (2007). *Op. cit.*, p. 313.
51. Tillion, G., *Ravensbruck*, Seuil, 1973, p. 214. Quoted in Todorov, T. (1991). *Op. cit.*, p. 140.
52. Zimbardo, P., *The Lucifer Effect*, Ebury Digital, 2011, pp. 5001–5002.
53. *Ibid.*, pp. 5013–5015.
54. Browning, C. R., *Ordinary Men*, Harper Perennial, 1993, p. 170.
55. Staub, E. (1992). *Op. cit.*
56. Malkki, L. H., *Purity and Exile: Violence, Memory, and National Cosmology Among Hutu Refugees in Tanzania*, University of Chicago Press, 1995.
57. Straus, S. (2004). How many perpetrators were there in the Rwandan genocide? An estimate. *Journal of Genocide Research*, *6*(1), 85–98. Quoted in Sémelin, J. (2005).
58. Mueller, J. (2000). The banality of "ethnic war." *International Security*, *25*(1), 42–70.
59. Langbein, H. (2011). *Op. cit.*, p. 274. Quoted in Todorov, T., *Facing the Extreme*, p. 122.
60. Hatzfeld, J. (2005). *Op. cit.*, p. 13.
61. See Chapter 28, "At the Source of Violence: De-Valuing the Other."
62. Borowski, T., *This Way for the Gas, Ladies and Gentlemen*, Penguin, 1976, p. 168. Quoted in Todorov, T. (1991). *Op. cit.*, p. 38.
63. Levi, P., *Survival in Auschwitz*, CreateSpace Independent Publishing Platform, 2013, p. 101.
64. *Ibid.*, p. 106.

65. Shalamov, V., *Kolyma*, François Maspero, 1980, pp. 11, 31. In Todorov, T. (1991). *Op. cit.*, p. 38.
66. Guinzbourg, E. S., *Le Ciel de la Kolyma*, Seuil, 1980, pp. 21, 179. In Todorov, T. (1991). *Op. cit.*, p. 38–39.
67. Marchenko, A., *Mon témoignage. Les camps en URSS après Staline*, Seuil, 1970, pp. 108–109. In Todorov, T. (1991). *Op. cit.*, p. 45.
68. *Ibid.*, pp. 45–66, 164.
69. Levi, P. *Survival in Auschwitz*, *op. cit.*, p. 128.
70. Laks, S., and Coudy, R., *Musiques d'un autre monde*, Mercure de France, 1948. Republished under the name *Mélodies d'Auschwitz*, Cerf, 2004. Quoted in Todorov, T. (1991). *Op. cit.*, p. 41.
71. Todorov, T. (1991). *Op. cit.*, p. 41.
72. Frankl, V. E., *Viktor Frankl. Un psychiatre déporté témoigne*, Éditions du Chalet, 1967, p. 114. Quoted in Todorov, T. (1996). *Op. cit.*, p. 61.
73. Borowski, T. (1964). *Op. cit.*, p. 135. Quoted in Todorov, T. (1991), *Op. cit.*, p. 40.
74. Baumeister, R. F., *Evil: Inside Human Cruelty and Violence*, Barnes & Noble, 2001, p. 304.
75. Terestchenko, M., *Un si fragile vernis d'humanité: Banalité du mal, banalité du bien*, La Découverte, 2007.
76. Sereny, G., *Into That Darkness: An Examination of Conscience*, Vintage, 2011.
77. *Ibid.*, p. 39.
78. *Ibid.*, p. 37.
79. *Ibid.*, p. 51.
80. *Ibid.*, p. 136.
81. *Ibid.*, p. 157.
82. *Ibid.*, p. 160.
83. Terestchenko, M. (2007). *Op. cit.*, p. 94.
84. *Ibid.*, p. 96.
85. Chalamov, V., & Mandelstam, N., *Correspondance avec Alexandre Soljenitsyne et Nadejda Mandelstam*, Verdier, 1998.
86. See Chapter 11, "Unconditional Altruism."
87. Broz, S., *Good People in an Evil Time: Portraits of Complicity and Resistance in the Bosnian War*, Other Press, 2005.
88. Since he willingly surrendered to the International Criminal Tribunal in The Hague, his case was the first to be tried by that court. See the report of his trial on the Internet: http://www.un.org/icty.
89. The NGO African Rights published, in 2002, a brochure presenting profiles of nineteen Rwandan "Just Ones" who selflessly saved Tutsis

during the genocide: *Tribute to Courage*, African Rights, August 2002. Quoted in Sémelin, J. (2007). *Op. cit.*, p. 266.

90. Alexander, E., *A Crime of Vengeance: An Armenian Struggle for Justice*, The Free Press, 1991.
91. Baumeister, R. F. (2001). *Op. cit.*, p. 292.
92. Sémelin, J. (2007). *Op. cit.*, p. 200. After Kristallnacht "not a single voice from the religious hierarchy was raised in protest against what had happened, either from the Protestant or from the Catholic side" (p. 85). This silence in 1938 "bears witness to a collapsing of religion: religion was no longer capable of calling the population to order by reminding them that murder is prohibited." The same would be true for the Orthodox Church in Serbia and with the Catholic Church in Rwanda.
93. Sémelin, J. (2007). *Op. cit.*, p. 204, translation modified.
94. Sémelin, J. (2007). *Op. cit.*, pp. 149–150.
95. Harff, B., "Assessing Risks of Genocide and Politicide," in Marshall, M. G., & Gurr, T. R., *Peace and Conflict 2005*, Center for International Development and Conflict Management, 2005, 57–61.
96. Harff, B. (2003). No lessons learned from the Holocaust? Assessing risks of genocide and political mass murder since 1955. *American Political Science Review*, *97*(1), 57–73.
97. Levi, P., *The Drowned and the Saved*, Vintage, 1989, p. 44.
98. Mao Zedong Li, Z., *The Private Life of Chairman Mao: The Memoirs of Mao's Personal Physician*, new ed., Arrow Books, 1996, p. 217.
99. A concept initially proposed by my late father, the philosopher and political writer Jean-François Revel.

Chapter 31: Has War Always Existed?

1. Hobbes, T. (1651). *Leviathan*. Online: https://scholarsbank.uoregon.edu/xmlui/bitstream/handle/1794/748/leviathan.pdf P. 218.
2. Churchill, W., "Shall We Commit Suicide?" In *Thoughts and Adventures,* ed. James W. Muller, Intercollegiate Studies, 2009.
3. Buss, D., *Evolutionary Psychology: The New Science of the Mind*, Allyn & Bacon, 1999.
4. Wilson, E. O., "On Human Nature." In D. Barash, ed., *Understanding Violence*, Allyn and Bacon, 2001, pp. 13–20.
5. Fry, D. P., *Beyond War: The Human Potential for Peace*, Oxford University Press, 2007.
6. Wrangham, R., & Peterson, D., *Demonic Males: Apes and the Origins of Human Violence*, Houghton Mifflin, 1996.
7. Ardrey, R., *African Genesis; A Personal Investigation into the Animal Origins and Nature of Man*, Dell, 1967, p. 322.

8. .009 to .016 occurrence per hour, according to the studies. See Goodall, J., *Chimpanzees of Gombe*, Harvard University Press, 1986. In the case of gorillas, this frequency is .20 conflict event per hour. See Schaller, G. B., *The Mountain Gorilla*, University of Chicago Press, 1963.
9. Sussman, R. W., & Garber, P. A., *Cooperation and Competition in Primate Social Interactions*, 2005, p. 640.
10. *Ibid.*, p. 645.
11. Strum, S. C., *Almost Human: A Journey into the World of Baboons*, University of Chicago Press, 2001, p. 158.
12. Waal, F. B. M. de, & Lanting, F., *Bonobo: The Forgotten Ape*, University of California Press, 1998, p. 2.
13. For a detailed summary, see Fry, D. (2007). *Op. cit.*, pp. 34–39.
14. Dart, R. A. (1953). The predatory transition from ape to man. *International Anthropological and Linguistic Review, 1*(4), 201–218; Dart, R. A. (1949). The predatory implemental technique of Australopithecus. *American Journal of Physical Anthropology, 7*(1), 1–38.
15. Studies by Sherry Washburn and Carlton Coon, reviewed in Roper, M. K. (1969). A survey of the evidence for intrahuman killing in the Pleistocene. *Current Anthropology, 10*(4), 427–459.
16. Brain, C. K. (1970). New Finds at the Swartkrans Australopithecine Site. *Nature, 225*(5238), 1112–1119.
17. Fry, D. (2007). *Op. cit.*, p. 38.
18. Berger, L. R., & Clarke, R. J. (1995). Eagle involvement in accumulation of the Taung child fauna. *Journal of Human Evolution, 29*(3), 275–299; Berger, L. R., & McGraw, W. S. (2007). Further evidence for eagle predation of, and feeding damage on, the Taung child. *South African Journal of Science, 103*(11–12), 496–498. See also Stiner, M. C. (1991). The faunal remains from Grotta Guattari: A taphonomic perspective. *Current Anthropology, 32*(2), 103–117; White, T. D., Toth, N., Chase, P. G., Clark, G. A., Conrad, N. J., Cook, J.,...Giacobini, G. (1991). The question of ritual cannibalism at Grotta guattari [commentaries and responses]. *Current Anthropology, 32*(2), 118–138.
19. See, for example, Prosterman, R. L., *Surviving to 3000: An Introduction to the Study of Lethal Conflict*, Duxbury Press, 1972, p. 140.
20. Sponsel, L. E. (1996). The natural history of peace: A positive view of human nature and its potential. *A Natural History of Peace*, 908–12.
21. http://www.census.gov/population/international/data/worldpop/table_history.php.
22. Haas, J., "War." In Levinson, D., & Ember, M., *Encyclopedia of Cultural Anthropology*, vol. 4, Holt, 1996, p. 1360.

23. Waal, F. B. M. de, *The Age of Empathy*, p. 23. Moreover, the human race almost did not survive, since we know, from mitochondrial DNA study, that our species was at one time in its existence reduced to some 2,000 individuals, from whom we are *all* now descendants.
24. See especially Flannery, K. V., & Marcus, J., *The Creation of Inequality: How Our Prehistoric Ancestors Set the Stage for Monarchy, Slavery, and Empire*, Harvard University Press, 2012; Price, T. D., & Brown, J. A. (eds.), *Prehistoric Hunter Gatherers: The Emergence of Cultural Complexity*, Academic Press, 1985; Kelly, R. L., *The Foraging Spectrum: Diversity in Hunter-Gatherer Lifeways*, Smithsonian Institution Press, 1995.
25. Knauft, B. M., Abler, T. S., Betzig, L., Boehm, C., Dentan, R. K., Kiefer, T. M.,...Rodseth, L. (1991). Violence and sociality in human evolution [comments and responses]. *Current Anthropology*, *32*(4), 391–428. Quoted in Fry, D. (2007). *Op. cit.*
26. Boehm, C., Barclay, H. B., Dentan, R. K., Dupre, M.-C., Hill, J. D., Kent, S.,...Rayner, S. (1993). Egalitarian behavior and reverse dominance hierarchy [comments and responses]. *Current Anthropology*, *34*(3), 227–254. Quoted in Sober, E., & Wilson, D. S., *Unto Others: The Evolution and Psychology of Unselfish Behavior*, Harvard University Press, 1999, p. 185.
27. Gardner, P., "The Paliyan." In Lee, R., & Daly, R. (eds.), *The Cambridge Encyclopedia of Hunters and Gatherers*, 1999, 261–264.
28. Flannery, K. V., & Marcus, J., *The Creation of Inequality: How Our Prehistoric Ancestors Set the Stage for Monarchy, Slavery, and Empire*, Harvard University Press, 2012.
29. Boehm, C., *et al.* (1993). *Op. cit.;* Boehm, C., Antweiler, C., Eibl-Eibesfeldt, I., Kent, S., Knauft, B. M., Mithen, S.,...Wilson, D. S. (1996). Emergency decisions, cultural-selection mechanics, and group selection [comments and responses]. *Current Anthropology*, *37*(5), 763–793. Quoted in Sober, E., & Wilson, D. S. (1999). *Op. cit.*, p. 180.
30. Reyna, S. P., & Downs, R. E., *Studying War: Anthropological Perspectives*, vol. 2, Routledge, 1994; Boehm, C., & Boehm, C., *Hierarchy in the Forest: The Evolution of Egalitarian Behavior*, Harvard University Press, 2009.
31. Haas, J., *The Origins of War and Ethnic Violence. Ancient Warfare: Archaeological Perspectives*, Gloucestershire, UK: Sutton Publishing, 1999.
32. Roper, M. (1975). Evidence of warfare in the Near East from 10,000–4,300 B.C. In Nettleship, A., and Nettleship, M. A. (eds.), *War, Its Causes and Correlates*, Mouton, 1975, pp. 299–344.

33. *Ibid.*
34. Bar-Yosef, O. (1986). The walls of Jericho: An alternative interpretation. *Current Anthropology, 27*(2), 157–162.
35. Maschner, H. D., *The Evolution of Northwest Coast Warfare*, vol. 3. In Martin, D., & Frayer, D. (eds.), *Troubled Times: Violence and Warfare in the Past*, 1997, Gordon and Breach, 1997, pp. 267–302.
36. Wrangham, R., & Peterson, D., *Demonic Males.*
37. Fry, D. P., et Söderberg, P. (2013). Lethal aggression in mobile forager bands and implications for the origins of war. *Science*, 341(6143), 270–273.
38. Keeley, L. H., *War Before Civilization*, Oxford University Press, 1997.
39. Fry, D. (2007). *Op. cit.*, p. 16.
40. Ghiglieri, M. P., *The Dark Side of Man: Tracing the Origins of Male Violence*, Da Capo Press, 2000, p. 246.
41. Chagnon, N. A. (1988). Life histories, blood revenge, and warfare in a tribal population. *Science, 239*(4843), 985–992.
42. Chagnon, N. A., *Yanomamo, the Fierce People*, Holt McDougal, 1968.
43. Moore, J. H. (1990). The reproductive success of Cheyenne war chiefs: A contrary case to Chagnon's Yanomamo. *Current Anthropology, 31*(3), 322–330; Beckerman, S., Erickson, P. I., Yost, J., Regalado, J., Jaramillo, L., Sparks, C., Ironmenga, M., & Long, K. (2009). Life histories, blood revenge, and reproductive success among the Waorani of Ecuador. *Proceedings of the National Academy of Sciences, 106*(20), 8134–8139.
44. Lecomte, J. (2012). *La Bonté humaine. Op. cit.*, pp. 199–204.
45. Good, K., & Chanoff, D., *Into the Heart: One Man's Pursuit of Love and Knowledge Among the Yanomama,* Simon & Schuster, 1991. Quoted in Lecomte, J. (2012).
46. *Ibid.*, p. 13.
47. *Ibid.*, pp. 80–83.
48. Four experienced anthropologists made the following declaration in 2001: "In his book *The Fierce People*, Chagnon has fabricated a sensationalist and racist image of the Yanomami, describing them as cunning, aggressive and fearsome, and falsely stating they lived in a state of chronic war.... We have, between all of us, spent over eighty years with the Yanomami. Most of us speak one or more Yanomami dialects. None of us recognizes the society described in Chagnon's books." Albert, B., Ramos, A., Taylor, K. I., & Watson, F., *Yanomami: The Fierce People?*, Survival International, 2001.

49. Lee, R. B., & Daly, R. H., " Introduction." In *The Cambridge Encyclopedia of Hunters and Gatherers*, Cambridge University Press, 1999.
50. Endicott, K., "Property, Power and Conflict Among the Batek of Malaysia." In *Hunters and Gatherers*, vol. 2, 1988, pp. 110–127. Quoted in Fry, D. (2007). *Op. cit.*
51. Quoted in Fry D., *The Human Potential for Peace: An Anthropological Challenge to Assumptions about War and Violence*, Oxford University Press, 2005, p. 73. See also Robarchek, C. A. (1977). Frustration, aggression, and the nonviolent Semai. *American Ethnologist, 4*(4), 762–77; Robarchek, C. A. (1980). The image of nonviolence: World view of the Semai Senoi. *Federated Museums Journal, 25*, 103–117; Robarchek, C. A., & Robarchek, C. J. (1998). Reciprocities and realities: World views. *Aggressive Behavior, 24*, 123–133.
52. Carol Ember, notably, asserts that societies of hunter-gatherers were not at all as peaceful as we are led to believe, and that 90% of them often wage war. But included under the term "war" are any sorts of hostile behavior (just as one could metaphorically describe as "war" a long series of hostilities perpetrated between two families in certain cultures), including revenge murders by a single individual, which scarcely makes sense. What's more, half the societies analyzed by Ember are not in fact itinerant hunter-gatherers, but more sophisticated societies, including hunters on horseback, etc. It is not immaterial to mention this example, since Carol Ember's article has been abundantly quoted. Ember, C. R. (1978). Myths about hunter-gatherers. *Ethnology, 17*(4), 439–448. Quoted in Fry, D. (2007). *Op. cit.*, pp. 195–196.
53. Ember, C. R., & Ember, M. (1992). Warfare, aggression, and resource problems: Cross-cultural codes. *Cross-Cultural Research, 26*(1–4), 169–226. Quoted in Fry, D. (2007). *Op. cit.*, p. 13.
54. Tacon, P., & Chippindale, C. (1994). Australia's ancient warriors: Changing depictions of fighting in the rock art of Arnhem Land, NT. *Cambridge Archaeological Journal, 4*(2), 211–48. Quoted in Fry, D. (2007). *Op. cit.*, p. 133–135.
55. Wheeler, G. C. (1910), *The Tribe, and Intertribal Relations in Australia*, BiblioLife, 2009; Berndt, R. M., & Berndt, C. H., *The World of the First Australians: Aboriginal Traditional Life: Past and Present*, Aboriginal Studies Press, 1988.
56. Warner, W. L., *A Black Civilization: A Social Study of an Australian Tribe*, Gloucester Publications, 1937, 1969.
57. Fry, D. (2007). *Op. cit.*, p. 102.

58. For a series of tables collecting the various data on this subject, see Pinker, S., *The Better Angels of Our Nature: Why Violence Has Declined*, Viking, 2011, pp. 49, 53.
59. *Ibid.*

CHAPTER 32: THE DECLINE OF VIOLENCE

1. Gurr, T. R. (1981). Historical trends in violent crime: A critical review of the evidence. *Crime and Justice*, 295–353. See also Eisner, M. (2003). Long-term historical trends in violent crime. *Crime & Just.*, *30*, 83.
2. Tremblay, R. E., *Prévenir la violence dès la petite enfance*, Odile Jacob, 2008, p. 31. See also Tremblay, R. E., *Developmental Origins of Aggression*, Guilford Press, 2005, as well as Tremblay, R. E., Aken, M. A. G. van, & Koops, W., *Development and Prevention of Behaviour Problems: From Genes to Social Policy*, Psychology Press, 2009.
3. WHO, United Nations Office on Drug and Crime (UNDOC), 2009.
4. Pinker, S. (2011). *Op. cit.*, p. 89.
5. Durant, W. & A., *The Story of Civilization*, vol. 9: *The Age of Voltaire*, Simon & Schuster, 1965. Quoted in Tremblay, R. E. (2008), p. 33.
6. Harris, J. R., *The Nurture Assumption: Why Children Turn Out the Way They Do*, The Free Press, 1998. Quoted in Pinker, S. (2011). *Op. cit.*, p. 437.
7. Finkelhor, D., Jones, L., & Shattuck, A. (2008). Updated trends in child maltreatment, 2010. *Crimes Against Children Research Center* (http://unh.edu/ccrc/Trends/index.html).
8. *Washington Post* on June 19, 2006, referring to Justice Department data, as well as Pinker, S. (2011). *Op. cit.*, p. 408.
9. Numbers at the time of going to press of Matthew White, quoted in Pinker, S. (2011). *Op. cit.*, p. 135. On the site http://necrometrics.com Matthew White presents many statistics on mortality over the course of the centuries.
10. See also the engravings gathered by Norbert Elias, on which we see, beside country life, gibbets, mercenaries burning thatched cottages, and all sorts of tortures and other acts of violence, intermingled with activities of daily life. Elias, N., *The Civilizing Process: Sociogenetic and Psychogenetic Investigations*, Blackwell, 2000.
11. Held, R., *Inquisition*, Qua d'Arno, 1985. Quoted in Pinker, S. (2011). *Op. cit.*, p. 132.
12. Badinter, É., *Les Passions intellectuelles*, vol. 2: *Désirs de gloire (1735–1751)*, Fayard, 1999.
13. *The Diary of Samuel Pepys*, October 13, 1660. http://www.pepysdiary.com/archive/1660/10/13/.

14. Roth, C., *Spanish Inquisition*, reprint, W. W. Norton, 1964.
15. Tuchman, B. W., *A Distant Mirror: The Calamitous 14th Century*, Knopf, 1978.
16. Tuchman, B. W., *A Distant Mirror: The Calamitous 14th Century*, new ed., Ballantine, 1991, p. 135. Quoted in Pinker, S. (2011). *Op. cit.*, p. 67.
17. Beccaria, C., *On Crimes and Punishments*, Hackett, 1986.
18. Rummel, R. J., *Death by Government*, Transaction Publishers, 1994. Added to that are the victims of slavery in the East, which have not been estimated.
19. http://www.un.org/en/documents/udhr/.
20. The United Nations adopted a moratorium on the death penalty in 2007, by a vote of 105 to 54 (including the United States).
21. Payne, J. L., *A History of Force: Exploring the Worldwide Movement Against Habits of Coercion, Bloodshed, and Mayhem*, Lytton, 2003, p. 182.
22. Brecke, P. (2001). "The Long-Term Patterns of Violent Conflict in Different Regions of the World." Prepared for the conference in Uppsala, June 8 and 9, 2005; Uppsala, Sweden; Brecke, P. (1999). Violent conflicts 1400 AD to the present in different regions of the world. "1999, Meeting of the Peace Science Society," unpublished manuscript.
23. Brecke, P. (1999 and 2001). *Op. cit.* See his *Conflict Catalogue*.
24. Pinker, S. (2011). *Op. cit.* See especially Chapters 5 and 6.
25. White, M. (2010). Selected death tolls for wars, massacres, and atrocities before the twentieth century (http://necrometrics.com/pre1700a.htm). Quoted in Pinker. S. (2011). *Op. cit.*, p. 194.
26. See the chart in the journal *New Scientist New Scientist* (http://www.newscientist.com/embedded/20worst) based on White, M. (2012) for the numbers concerning mortality, and on McEvedy, C., Jones, R., *et al.* (1978) for numbers concerning the world population at various times in history. To give an example, the Mongolian invaders massacred the 1.3 million inhabitants of the city of Merv and the 800,000 inhabitants of Baghdad, exploring the ruins to make sure they hadn't left any survivors. See Pinker, S. (2011), p. 196.
27. White, M., *The Great Big Book of Horrible Things: The Definitive Chronicle of History's 100 Worst Atrocities*, W. W. Norton, 2012, as well as the site http://www.atrocitology.com, which contains hundreds of references. According to investigating science journalist Charles Mann, the death toll, 95% of which seems to be due to smallpox and other imported diseases, could have been as high as 100 million, since

he contends that the indigenous population was much greater than generally thought. Mann, C. C., *1491: New Revelations of the Americas Before Columbus*, Vintage, 2006.

28. Gleditsch, N. P. (2008). The liberal moment fifteen years on. *International Studies Quarterly*, *52*(4), 691–712, and diagram in Pinker, S. (2011). *Op. cit.*, p. 366.
29. Human Security Report Project, H. S. R. (2011). See also the Peace Research Institute of Oslo or PRIO, which has also compiled a considerable database on conflicts http://www.prio.no/CSCW/Datasets/Armed-Conflict/Battle-Deaths/. See also Lacina, B., & Gleditsch, N. P. (2005). Monitoring trends in global combat: A new dataset of battle deaths. *European Journal of Population/Revue européenne de démographie*, *21*(2), 145–166; Lacina, B., Gleditsch, N. P., & Russett, B. (2006). The declining risk of death in battle. *International Studies Quarterly*, *50*(3), 673–680.
30. Mueller, J., *The Remnants of War,* Cornell University Press, 2007.
31. Global Terrorism Database at the University of Maryland, see http://www.start.umd.edu/gtd/.
32. http://en.wikipedia.org/wiki/List_of_school_shootings_in_the_United_States#2010s.
33. See http://www.niemanwatchdog.org/index.cfm?fuseaction=ask_this.view&askthisid=00512.
34. Gigerenzer, G. (2006). Out of the frying pan into the fire: Behavioral reactions to terrorist attacks. *Risk Analysis*, *26*(2), 347–351. This evaluation is based on the sudden increase of road traffic and the number of deaths on roads in the months that followed the 9/11 attack.
35. Johnson, E. J., Hershey, J., Meszaros, J., & Kunreuther, H. (1993). Framing, probability distortions, and insurance decisions. *Journal of Risk and Uncertainty*, *7*(1), 35–51.
36. According to the report by the National Counterterrorism Center, available on the site http://www.nctc.gov/.
37. Esposito, J. L., & Mogahed, D., *Who Speaks for Islam? What a Billion Muslims Really Think,* Gallup Press, 2008.
38. Elias, N., *The Civilizing Process: Sociogenetic and Psychogenetic Investigations,* Blackwell, 1993.
39. Pinker, S. (2011). *Op. cit.*, p. 64.
40. Putnam, R. D., Leonardi, R., & Nanetti, R., *Making Democracy Work: Civic Traditions in Modern Italy*, Princeton Universtiy Press, 1994. Quoted in Tremblay, R. E. (2008). *Op. cit.*, p. 27. See also Gatti, U., Tremblay, R. E., & Schadee, H. (2007). Civic community and violent behavior in Italy. *Aggressive Behavior,* *33*(1), 56–62.

41. Pinker, S. (2011). *Op. cit.*, p. 52.
42. Wright, Q. (1942/1983) and the French Wikipedia article "Nombre de pays en Europe depuis 1789."
43. http://en.wikipedia.org/wiki/Number_of_guns_per_capita_by_country.
44. CNN, *Piers Morgan Tonight*, December 18, 2012.
45. Thomas, E. M., *The Harmless People*, 2d rev. ed., Vintage. See also Gat, A., *War in Human Civilization*, annotated ed., Oxford University Press, 2006. Quoted in Pinker, S. (2011). *Op. cit.*, p. 55.
46. See Pinker, S. (2011). *Op. cit.*, pp. 278–87.
47. Pinker, S. (2011). *Op. cit.*, p. 287.
48. Russett, B., Eichengreen, B., Kurlantzick, J., Peterson, E. R., Posner, R. A., Severino, J. M., Ray, O., *et al.* (2010). Peace in the twenty-first century? *Current History.*
49. Pinker, S. (2011). *Op. cit.*, p. 76.
50. Stiglitz, J. E., *The Price of Inequality: How Today's Divided Society Endangers Our Future*, W. W. Norton, 2012, p. 139.
51. Fortna, V. P., *Does Peacekeeping Work? Shaping Belligerents' Choices After Civil War*, Princeton University Press, 2008. Quoted in Pinker, S. (2011). *Op. cit.*, pp. 314–315.
52. Human Security Report Project (2009).
53. Bertens, Jan-Willem. The European movement: Dreams and realities, article presented at the conference "The EC After 1992: The United States of Europe?," Maastricht, January 2, 1994.
54. Mueller, J., *Retreat from Doomsday; The Obsolescence of Major War*, Basic Books, 1989. Quoted in Pinker, S. (2011). *Op. cit.*, p. 242.
55. Memoirs of Ephraïm Grenadou, collected by Alain Prévost, broadcast by France Culture in 1967 and in 2011–2012. See also Grenadou, E., *Vie d'un paysan français*, Seuil, 1966.
56. Mueller, J. (1989). *Retreat from Doomsday. Op. cit.*
57. Analysis of books present on Google Books. See Michel, J. B., Shen, Y. K., Aiden, A. P., Veres, A., Gray, M. K., Pickett, J. P., ... *et al.* (2011). Quantitative analysis of culture using millions of digitized books. *Science*, *331*(6014), 176.
58. Heise, L., & Garcia-Moreno, C. (2002). Violence by intimate partners. *World Report on Violence and Health*, 87–121.
59. Pinker, S. (2011). *Op. cit.*, p. 413.
60. Straus, M. A., & Gelles, R. J. (1986). Societal change and change in family violence from 1975 to 1985 as revealed by two national surveys. *Journal of Marriage and the Family*, 465–479. For the 1999 surveys, PR Newswire, http://:www.nospank.net/n-e62/htm. Quoted in Pinker, S. (2011). *Op. cit.*, p. 439.

61. Singer, P., *Animal Liberation,* Ecco Press, 2001.
62. V-Frog 2.0, made by Tractus Technology. For a scientific report on the introduction of this technique, see Lalley, J. P., Piotrowski, P. S., Battaglia, B., Brophy, K., & Chugh, K. (2008). A comparison of V-Frog and copyright to physical frog dissection. *Honorary Editor, 3*(3), 189. See also Virtual dissection. *Science*, February 22, 2008, 1019.
63. Caplow, T., Hicks, L., & Wattenberg, B. J., *The First Measured Century: An Illustrated Guide to Trends in America, 1900–2000*, American Enterprise Institute Press, 2001. Quoted in Pinker, S. (2011). *Op. cit.*, p. 392.
64. Cooney, M. (1997). The decline of elite homicide. *Criminology, 35*(3), 381–407.
65. Pinker, S. (2011). *Op. cit.*, p. 85.
66. https://commons.wikimedia.org/wiki/File:1477–1799_ESTC_titles_per_decade,_statistics.png.
67. Stowe, H. B., *Uncle Tom's Cabin,* Dover, 2005.
68. Swanee Hunt, in conversation during the meeting for peace organized by the Dalai Lama's Center for Peace and Education in Vancouver in 2009 (Vancouver Peace Summit).
69. Goldstein, J. S., *War and Gender: How Gender Shapes the War System and Vice Versa*, Cambridge University Press, 2003, pp. 329–330 and 396–399. Quoted in Pinker, S. (2011). *Op. cit.*, p. 527.
70. Pinker, S. (2011). *Op. cit.*, p. 528.
71. Dwight Garner, After the bomb's shock, the real horror began unfolding. *New York Times*, January 20, 2010.
72. See Pinker, S. (2011). *Op. cit.*, p. 686.
73. Potts, M., & Hayden, T., *Sex and War: How Biology Explains Warfare and Terrorism and Offers a Path to a Safer World*, BenBella Books, 2010.
74. Hudson, V. M., & Boer, A. D. (2002). A surplus of men, a deficit of peace: Security and sex ratios in Asia's largest states. *International Security, 26*(4), 5–38.
75. See the site http://girlsnotbrides.org/.
76. Only a few high government officials, like the former president Pieter Botha, showed no remorse and provided no explanations. The final report also criticized the behavior of certain leaders of the liberation movement, the ANC (African National Congress).
77. For the Iraq war, see the estimation by Stiglitz, Joseph E., & Bilmes, Linda J., *Washington Post*, March 8, 2008. For the cost of the war in Afghanistan, see www.costofwar.org, as well as the Congressional

Research Service, Brookings Institution, and the Pentagon, according to a file presented by *Newsweek* on October 10, 2011, compiled by Rob Verger and Meredith Bennett-Smith.

78. The Global Peace Index (GPI) attempts to evaluate the relative position of 162 countries' state of peacefulness. It has been elaborated by the Institute for Economics and Peace (IEP), in collaboration with international peace experts, using data collected by the Economist Intelligence Unit. The study is the brainchild of Australian technology entrepreneur Steve Killelea, founder of Integrated Research, and has been endorsed by Kofi Annan, the Dalai Lama, Desmond Tutu, Muhammad Yunus, economist Jeffrey Sachs, former president of Ireland, Mary Robinson, and former US president, Jimmy Carter. The report can be downloaded from www.economicsandpeace.org.
79. What's more, these resources usually fall into the hands of corrupt despots or unscrupulous foreign powers. The fictional movie *Blood Diamond*, based on a real-life situation, shows the tragic complexity of the situation of poor countries rich in precious mineral resources.
80. Human Security Report (2005).
81. Deary, I. J., Batty, G. D., & Gale, C. R. (2008). Bright children become enlightened adults. *Psychological Science*, *19*(1), 1–6.
82. Pinker, S. (2011). *Op. cit.*, p. 668 ff.

Chapter 33: The Instrumentalization of Animals: A Moral Aberration

1. Jussiau, R., Montméas, L., & Parot, J.-C., *L'Élevage en France: 10 000 ans d'histoire*, Educagri Editions, 1993. Quoted in Nicolino, F., Bidoche. *L'industrie de la viande menace le monde*, Les liens qui libèrent, 2009.
2. Television broadcast "Eurêka" on December 2, 1970, titled "Sauver le boeuf..." [Saving steer], with commentaries by Guy Seligman and Paul Ceuzin. See the INA archives, http://www.ina.fr/video/CPF06020231/sauver-le-boeuf.fr.html. Quoted in Nicolino, F. (2009). *Op. cit.*
3. *National Hog Farmer*, March 1978, p. 27. Quoted in Singer, P. (1993). *Op. cit.*, p. 199.
4. *Poultry Tribune*, November 1986, quoted in Singer, P., *Animal Liberation: The Definitive Classic of the Animal Movement*, Harper Perennial, 2009, p. 107.
5. The lifespan for a calf, a cow, and a pig is twenty years. Calves are killed at the age of three, dairy cows are "discharged" (slaughtered)

around the age of six, and pigs at six months of age. The life expectancy for a chicken is seven years in normal conditions, but it is killed at six weeks. This concerns 1 billion animals in France.

6. That is especially the case for animals in the fur trade in Chinese breeding industries, for instance, and it also occurs in slaughterhouses when animals have survived what was supposed to kill them, and are then skinned alive.
7. As defined respectively by the Treaty of Rome (1957) and, until it was changed to "sentient beings" in April 2014, by the French Civil Code.
8. Barrett, J. R., *Work and Community in the Jungle: Chicago's Packing-House Workers, 1894–1922*, University of Illinois Press, 1990, p. 57. Quoted in Patterson, C. (2008). *Eternal Treblinka.*
9. Sinclair, U., *The Jungle*, Signet, 1964, pp. 35–45. Upton Sinclair, a young journalist, was twenty-six when, in 1904, his employer sent him to investigate the work conditions in the slaughterhouses of Chicago. With the complicity of some of the workers, he entered the slaughterhouses and factories secretly, and discovered that as long as he held a bucket, and never stood still, he could walk through the factories without drawing any attention. He went everywhere. He saw everything. *The Jungle* gave its author instantaneous fame, and a committee of eminent intellectuals, led by Albert Einstein, proposed him for the Nobel Prize in Literature. *The Jungle* set off a scandal. Best-seller of the year, the book was translated into seventeen languages. Besieged by journalists, pursued by threats, or promises, of large corporations, carried by the wave of popular unrest, Upton Sinclair was received at the White House by the president of the United States, Theodore Roosevelt. An investigation was ordered, and the exactitude of Sinclair's criticisms recognized. (This information is according to the preface by Jacques Cabau to the French edition of *The Jungle*.)
10. Sinclair, Upton (1994–06–01), *The Jungle,* Public Domain Books, Kindle Edition, pp. 20–21.
11. *Ibid.*, pp. 21–22.
12. David Cantor, Responsible Policies for Animals http://www.rpaforall.org. Quoted in Charles Patterson, *Eternal Treblinka* (Kindle locations 777–778). Kindle Edition.
13. Foer, J. S., *Eating Animals,* Back Bay Books, 2010.
14. *Ibid.*, pp. 50–51.
15. Eisnitz, G. A., *Slaughterhouse: The Shocking Story of Greed. Neglect, and Inhumane Treatment Inside the US Meat Industry*, Prometheus, 1997, p. 82.

16. Quoted in Charles Patterson, *Eternal Treblinka* (Kindle locations 1363–1366). Kindle Edition.
17. According to Singer, P. (1993). *Op. cit.*, p. 163.
18. Foer, J. S. (2012). *Op. cit.*, p. 240.
19. Fontenay, É. de., *Sans offenser le genre humain: Réflexions sur la cause animale*, Albin Michel, 2008, p. 206.
20. Coe, S., *Dead Meat*, Four Walls Eight Windows, 1996, pp. 111–113.
21. Eisnitz, G. A. (1997). *Slaughterhouse. Op. cit.*, p. 182.
22. Coe, S. *Dead Meat, op. cit.*, p. 120.
23. *Ibid.*
24. Carpenter. G., *et al.* (1986). Effect of internal air filtration on the performance of broilers and the aerial concentrations of dust and bacteria. *British Poultry Journal, 27*, 471–480. Quoted in Singer, P. (1993). *Op. cit.*, p. 172.
25. Bedichek, R., *Adventures with a Texas Naturalist*, University of Texas Press, 1961. Quoted in Harrison, R., *Animal Machines: The New Factory Farming Industry*, CABI Publishing, 2013. Original edition (1964), p. 154.
26. Breward, J. & Gentle, M. (1985). Neuroma formation and abnormal afferent nerve discharges after partial beak amputation (beak trimming) in poultry. *Experienta, 41*(9), 1132–1134.
27. *National Geographic Magazine*, February 1970. Quoted in Singer, P. (1993). *Op. cit.*, p. 177.
28. Foer, J. S. (2012). *Op. cit.*, p. 176.
29. *Ibid.*, p. 65.
30. Mississippi State University Extension Services in collaboration with the USDA. Publication No. 384. Dehorming, castrating, branding, vaccinating cattle; see also Beef cattle: dehoming, castrating, branding and marking, USDA, *Farmers' Bulletin, 2141*, September 1972. In Singer, P. (1993). *Op. cit.*, p. 225.
31. Foer, J. S. (2012). *Op. cit.*, p. 187.
32. *Stall Street Journal*, November 1973.
33. *Ibid.*, April 1973.
34. Foer, J. S. (2010). *Op. cit.*, pp. 231–233.
35. *Ibid.*, p. 231.
36. *Ibid.*, p. 233.
37. See *A Shocking Look Inside Chinese Fur Farms*, a documentary filmed by Mark Rissi for Swiss Animals Protection/EAST International, which can be viewed on PETA's website: http://www.peta.org/issues/animals-usedfor-clothing/chinese-fur-industry.aspx.

38. According to the numbers published by *Agreste* (an organization of the French Ministry of Agriculture), we can reasonably estimate that by including fish and marine animals, at least 3 billion animals are killed directly and indirectly every year in France for human consumption. Added to this are about 30 million animals killed for hunting (not counting the wounded ones that die in the woods) and some 3 million used by research (invertebrate animals are not inventoried).
39. Mood, A., & Brooke, P. (July 2010). *Estimating the Number of Fish Caught in Global Fishing Each Year* (amood@fishcount.org.uk). These authors used statistics published by the FAO concerning the tonnage of yearly catches for each species and calculated the number of fish by estimating the average weight of the fish of the species studied.
40. Foer, J. S. (2010). *Op. cit.*, p. 193.
41. Chauvet, D. (2008). La volonté des animaux? *Cahiers antispécistes*, 30–31, December 2008.
42. Vergely, B., *La Souffrance: Recherche du sens perdu*, Gallimard, Folio, 1997, p. 75.
43. *Earthlings*, directed by Shaun Monson, available on the internet: www.earthlings.com.
44. Wells, H. G., *A Modern Utopia*, Penguin, 2008.

Chapter 34: Backfire: Effects of the Meat Industry on Poverty, Environment, and Health

1. I.e., linked to construction (natural resources and energy expenditure used for construction) and to the use (electrical, heating, etc.) of public, industrial, and private buildings.
2. M. E. Ensminger, *Animal Science*, Interstate, 1991.
3. Rifkin, J., *La Troisième Révolution industrielle*, Les liens qui libèrent, 2012.
4. Doyle, J., *Altered Harvest: Agriculture, Genetics and the Fate of the World's Food Supply*, 2d ed., Viking, 1985.
5. The *Worldwatch Institute* is a grass-roots research organization based in the United States. One of their current projects is a comparative analysis of agricultural innovations that are ecologically long-lasting to reduce poverty and hunger.
6. According to Worldwatch.
7. Foer, J. S. (2010). *Op. cit.*, p. 211 and note, p. 322. Calculation by Bruce Friedrich based on US government and academic sources.
8. Moore-Lappé, F., *Diet for a Small Planet*, Ballantine, 1971, pp. 4–11.

9. McMichael, A. J., Powles, J. W., Butler, C. D., & Uauy, R. (2007). Food, livestock production, energy, climate change, and health. *Lancet, 370*(9594), 1253–1263.
10. FAO (2006). *L'Ombre portée de l'élevage. Impacts environnementaux et options pour atténuation*, Rome; FAO (2009). *Comment nourrir le monde en 2050 [Livestock's long shadow: environmental issues and options].*
11. FAO (2006). *Op. cit.*, and (2003), "World Agriculture Towards 2015/2030."
12. Lambin, E., *An Ecology of Happiness*, University of Chicago Press, 2012, p. 70 of the French edition.
13. Moore-Lappé, F. (1976). *Op. cit.*, pp. 11–12 and 21.
14. FAO (2006). *Op. cit.*
15. Boyan, S. (February 7, 2005). How our food choices can help save the environment; www.earthsave.org/environment/foodchoices.htm.
16. Pimentel, D., Williamson, S., Alexander, C. E., Gonzalez-Pagan, O., Kontak, C., & Mulkey, S. E. (2008). Reducing energy inputs in the US food system. *Human Ecology, 36*(4), 459–471.
17. "Compassion in world farming." Quoted by Marjolaine Jolicoeur, AHIMSA, 2004.
18. Kaimowitz, D., *Livestock and Deforestation in Central America in the 1980s and 1990s: A Policy Perspective*, Cifor, 1996; Kaimowitz, D., Mertens, B., Wunder, S., & Pacheco, P. (2004). Hamburger connection fuels Amazon destruction. *Center for International Forest Research*, Bogor, Indonesia.
19. *Amazon Cattle Footprint*, Greenpeace, 2009.
20. Dompka, M. V., Krchnak, K. M., & Thorne, N. (2002). Summary of experts' meeting on human population and freshwater resources. In Karen Krchnak (ed.), *Human Population and Freshwater Resources: U.S. Cases and International Perspective*, Yale University, 2002.
21. According to the World Bank and the McKinsey Global Institute (2011). *Natural Resources.* http://www.mckinsey.com/insights/mgi/research/natural_resources.
22. International Food Policy Research Institute and the United Nations Environment Program.
23. Borgstrom, G., *Harvesting the Earth*, Abelard-Schuman, 1973, pp. 64–65.
24. The browning of America, *Newsweek*, February 22, 1981, p. 26. Quoted in Robbins, J., *Se nourrir sans faire souffrir*, Alain Stanke, 1991, p. 420.

25. Rosegrant, M. W., & Meijer, S. (2002). Appropriate food policies and investments could reduce child malnutrition by 43% in 2020. *Journal of Nutrition*, *132*(11), 3437S–3440S.
26. Jancovici, J.-M., *L'Avenir climatique: Quel temps ferons-nous?* Seuil, 2005.
27. This number is from the most recent evaluation produced by the FAO in *Tackling Climate Change through Livestock*, FAO, October 2013. This report is the most complete produced to date on greenhouse gas emissions linked to the livestock industry. Bovines contribute to two-thirds of these emissions. The number 14.5% is calculated based on an analysis that includes the complete life cycle of the process, that is, it includes the CO_2 emissions associated with deforestation linked to livestock, the production and conditioning of food for livestock, etc. The same method, however, has not been applied to transportation. Another study, which was carried out by researchers at the University of Cambridge, the National University of Australia, and others, asserts that the number would be closer to 17% (McMichael, A.J., *et al.*, 2007. *Op cit.*). Those who refute this number propose the 4% stated by the IPCC; but that concerns direct emissions and not the complete life cycle. It is important to consider the entirety of the life cycle, because indirect emissions coming from livestock constitute a significant proportion of emissions.
28. http://www.conservation-nature.fr/article2.php?id=105.
29. Desjardins, R., Worth, D., Vergé, X., Maxime, D., Dyer, J., & Cerkowniak, D. (2012). Carbon footprint of beef cattle. *Sustainability*, *4*(12), 3279–3301.
30. FAO (2006). *Op. cit.*, p. 125.
31. According to the Worldwatch Institute.
32. US Environmental Protection Agency and General Accounting Office (GAO). Quoted in Foer, J. S. (2010).
33. Steinfeld, H., De Haan, C., & Blackburn, H. (1997). Livestock-environment interactions. *Issues and options. Report of the Commission Directorate General for Development.* Fressingfield, UK, WREN Media.
34. Narrod, C. A., Reynnells, R. D., & Wells, H. (1993). "Potential options for poultry waste utilization: A focus on the Delmarva Peninsula." United States Environmental Protection Agency (EPA).
35. See the data and report provided by the Bloom Association: http://www.bloomassociation.org/en.
36. Pauly, D., Belhabib, D., Blomeyer, R., Cheung, W. W. W. L., Cisneros-Montemayor, A. M., Copeland, D., & Zeller, D. (2013). China's distant-water fisheries in the 21st century. *Fish and Fisheries.*

37. Foer, J. S. (2010). *Op. cit.*, pp. 48–49. Environmental Justice Foundation Charitable Trust, *Squandering the Seas: How Shrimp Trawling Is Threatening Ecological Integrity and Food Security Around the World*, Environmental Justice Foundation, 2003, p. 12.
38. Sinha, R., Cross, A. J., Graubard, B. I., Leitzmann, M. F., & Schatzkin, A. (2009). Meat intake and mortality: A prospective study of over half a million people. *Archives of Internal Medicine, 169*(6), 562. Quoted in Nicolino, F., *Bidoche. L'industrie de la viande menace le monde,* Les liens qui libèrent, 2009, p. 318.
39. Lambin, E. (2009). *Op. cit.*, p. 78.
40. Pan, A., Sun, Q., Bernstein, A. M., Schulze, M. B., Manson, J. E., Stampfer, M. J.,... Hu, F. B. (2012). Red meat consumption and mortality: Results from 2 prospective cohort studies. *Archives of Internal Medicine*, *172*(7), 555. These analyses took into account risk factors for chronic diseases such as age, body mass index, physical activity, family history of heart disease, and major cancers.
41. Haque, R., Kearney, P. C., & Freed, V. H., "Dynamics of Pesticides in Aquatic Environments." In *Pesticides in aquatic environments*, Springer, 1977, pp. 39–52; Ellgehausen, H., Guth, J. A., & Esser, H. O. (1980). Factors determining the bioaccumulation potential of pesticides in the individual compartments of aquatic food chains. *Ecotoxicology and Environmental Safety*, *4*(2), 134–157.
42. Lambin, E. (2009). *Op. cit.*, p. 80.
43. Interview in the *Telegraph*, September 7, 2008.
44. See also Hedenus, F., Wirsenius, S., & Johansson, D. J. A. (forthcoming, 2014). The importance of reduced meat and dairy consumption for meeting stringent climate change targets. *Climatic Change*, 1–13; doi:10.1007/s10584-014-1104-5.

CHAPTER 35: INSTITUTIONALIZED SELFISHNESS

1. Stiglitz, J., *The Price of Inequality,* Kindle location, 205.
2. Oreskes, N., & Conway, E. M. M., *Merchants of Doubt: How a Handful of Scientists Obscured the Truth on Issues from Tobacco Smoke to Global Warming*, Bloomsbury Press, 2011. See also Hoggan, J., *Climate Cover-up: The Crusade to Deny Global Warming*, Greystone Books, 2009. As well as Pooley, E., *The Climate War: True Believers, Power Brokers, and the Fight to Save the Earth*, Hyperion, 2010.
3. Fred Seitz notably directed a program for the R. J. Reynold Tobacco Company that, from 1979 to 1985, distributed 45 million dollars

(equivalent to $98 million today) to compliant researchers to carry out studies that could be used in the courts to defend the harmlessness of tobacco. Oreskes, N., & Conway, E. M. M. (2011). *Op. cit.*, p. 6.

4. Lahsen, M. (2008). Experiences of modernity in the greenhouse: A cultural analysis of a physicist "trio" supporting the backlash against global warming. *Global Environmental Change*, *18*(1), 204–219. Quoted in Oreskes, N., & Conway, E. M. M. (2011). *Op. cit.*, p. 6.
5. Singer, S. F. (1989). My adventures in the ozone layer. *National Review*, *30*. Quoted in Oreskes, N., & Conway, E. M. M. (2011). *Op. cit.*, p. 249.
6. Wynder, E. L., Graham, E. A., & Croninger, A. B. (1953). Experimental production of carcinoma with cigarette tar. *Cancer Research*, *13*(12), 855–864. Quoted in Oreskes, N., & Conway, E. M. M. (2011). *Op. cit.*, p. 15.
7. American Tobacco, Benson and Hedges, Philip Morris, and U.S. Tobacco.
8. United States of America vs. Philips Morris, R. J. Reynolds, *et. al.* (1999), p. 3. Quoted in Oreskes, N., & Conway, E. M. M. (2011). *Op. cit.*, p. 15 and note 24, p. 282.
9. In 1957, for example, one of these pamphlets, entitled "Smoking and Health," was distributed to 350,000 doctors. Tobacco Industry Research Committee: BN2012002363. Legacy Tobacco Document Library. Another pamphlet, published in 1993 for internal circulation in the tobacco industry and entitled *Bad Science: A Resource Book*, contained a mine of information on the most effective ways to fight and discredit scientific researches demonstrating the harmful effects of tobacco, as well as an address book of researchers and journalists sympathetic to the cause and who could be recruited. *Bad Science: A Resource Book*. Quoted in Oreskes, N., & Conway, E. M. M. (2011). *Op. cit.*, pp. 6 and 20.
10. Oreskes, N., & Conway, E. M. M. (2011). *Op. cit.*, p. 34.
11. Michaels, D., *Doubt Is Their Product: How Industry's Assault on Science Threatens Your Health*, Oxford University Press, 2008.
12. Schuman, L. M. (1981). The origins of the Report of the Advisory Committee on Smoking and Health to the Surgeon General. *Journal of Public Health Policy*, 2(1), 19–27. Quoted in Oreskes, N., & Conway, E. M. M. (2011). *Op. cit.*, pp. 21–22.
13. Tobacco smoke contains 4,000 different chemical substances, 60 of which are carcinogenic. The smoke that escapes laterally from the cigarette contains seven times more benzene, seventy times more nitrosamines, and a hundred times more ammonia than smoke inhaled or exhaled by the smoker.

14. According to the data and references gathered by Wikipedia: http://en.wikipedia.org/wiki/Passive_smoking.
15. Hirayama, T. (1981). Passive smoking and lung cancer. *British Medical Journal* (Clinical research ed.), *282*(6273), 1393–1394. Before that, the first major study goes back to 1980. Involving over 2,100 people and published in England, it demonstrated that non-smokers working in offices where their colleagues smoked manifested the same alterations in their lungs as light smokers. This study was abundantly criticized by scientists, all of whom had ties with the tobacco industry. For a recent study, see Öberg, M., Jaakkola, M. S., Woodward, A., Peruga, A., & Prüss-Ustün, A. (2011). Worldwide burden of disease from exposure to second-hand smoke: A retrospective analysis of data from 192 countries. *Lancet*, *377*(9760), 139–146.
16. Glanz, S. A., *The Cigarette Papers Online Wall of History,* UCSF, 2004.
17. Non-Smokers' Rights Association. The Fraser Institute: Economic Thinktank or Front for the Tobacco Industry? April 1999. Quoted in Oreskes, N., & Conway, E. M. M. (2011). *Op. cit.*, p. 140.
18. Quoted in Oreskes, N., & Conway, E. M. M. (2011). *Op. cit.*, p. 242; note 6, p. 335.
19. That is how the journals *Tobacco and Health* and *Science Fortnightly*, to cite only those two, in the case of tobacco, were created. The same methods were used for climate studies. Other articles were formatted exactly like those in the PNAS (Proceedings of the National Academy of Sciences) and distributed to all the media, even though they were neither published nor submitted to a scientific journal. Oreskes, N., & Conway, E. M. M. (2011). *Op. cit.*, p. 244.
20. Associated Press, November 27, 2012.
21. WHO. Fact sheet no. 339, May 2012: http://www.who.int/mediacentre/factsheets/fs339/en/.
22. Not counting the cases of bronchitis and pneumonia among young children, along with an increase of asthma among millions of children. Britton, J., & Godfrey, F. (2006). Lifting the smokescreen. *European Respiratory Journal*, *27*(5), 871–873. The report presented to the European Parliament is available on the site www.ersnet.org.
23. Glantz, S. A., & Parmley, W. W. (2001). Even a little secondhand smoke is dangerous. *JAMA*, *286*(4), 462–463.
24. L'Asie fume à pleins poumouns. *GEO*, October 2011, *292*, p. 102.
25. WHO. Fact sheet No. 339, May 2012.
26. *Ibid.*
27. Oreskes, N., & Conway, E. M. M. (2011). *Op. cit.*, p. 241.

28. West, R. (2006). Tobacco control: Present and future. *British Medical Bulletin*, *77–78*(1), 123–136.
29. Oreskes, N., & Conway, E. M. M. (2011). *Op. cit.*, p. 171 and note 9, p. 320.
30. A group that nicknamed itself the "Jasons" and was mainly composed of physicists, then a commission directed by Jule Charney, an MIT professor.
31. *Ibid.*, p. 174, note 20 and p. 321.
32. The pdf report with numbers and detailed attributions can be downloaded at the Greenpeace site: http://www.greenpeace.org/usa/en/campaigns/global-warming-and-energy/polluterwatch/koch-industries/.
33. Mooney, C., *The Republican War on Science*, Basic Books, 2006. In the investigative journal *Mother Jones*, May–June 2005. http://www.motherjones.com/environment/2005/05/some-it-hot.
34. Wijkman, A., & Rockström, J., *Bankrupting Nature: Denying Our Planetary Boundaries*, Routledge, 2013, p. 96.
35. Santer, B. D., Taylor, K. E., Wigley, T. M. L., Johns, T. C., Jones, P. D., Karoly, D. J., . . . Ramaswamy, V. (1996). A search for human influences on the thermal structure of the atmosphere. *Nature*, *382*(6586), 39–46.
36. Seitz, F. A major deception on global warming. *Wall Street Journal*, June 26, 1996. Quoted in Oreskes, N., & Conway, E. M. M. (2011). *Op. cit.*, p. 3.
37. Statement made on March 14, 2002. http://www.msnbc.msn.com/id/26315908/.
38. Statement made on January 4, 2005. http://inhofe.senate.gov/pressreleases/climateupdate.htm.
39. Statement made on July 28, 2003. http://inhofe.senate.gov/pressreleases/climate.htm.
40. Michele Bachmann assured us that CO_2 emissions are harmless. Herman Cain, one of the last candidates, spoke of the "myth" of global warming, and Rick Perry, governor of Texas, also denounced a "hoax" perpetrated by scientists in need of subventions. Those were the same candidates who also want to ban teaching the theory of evolution in schools and teach "creationism" instead. Mitt Romney finally echoed their voices under the pressure of extreme-right-wing Republicans.
41. Survey carried out by ABC News.
42. Goldacre, B., *Bad Pharma: How Drug Companies Mislead Doctors and Harm Patients*, Fourth Estate, 2012.

43. Gøtzsche, P. C., Hróbjartsson, A., Johansen, H. K., Haahr, M. T., Altman, D. G., & Chan, A. W. (2006). Constraints on publication rights in industry-initiated clinical trials. *JAMA*, *295*(14), 1645–1646. Quoted in Goldacre, B. (2012). *Op. cit.*, p. 38. A survey also shows that 90% of subjects and patients who volunteer for these medical tests think their participation is an important contribution to society, whereas pharmaceutical companies refuse to make their research data public: Wendler, D., Krohmal, B., Emanuel, E. J., & Grady, C. (2008). Why patients continue to participate in clinical research. *Archives of Internal Medicine*, *168*(12), 1294. Quoted in Goldacre, B. (2012). *Op. cit.*, p. 43.
44. Doshi, P. (2009). Neuraminidase inhibitors—the story behind the Cochrane review. *BMJ*, *339*. Quoted in Goldacre, B. (2012). *Op. cit.*, p. 365.
45. Godlee, F. (2012). Open letter to Roche about oseltamivir trial data. *BMJ*, *345*.
46. Medicines and Healthcare Products Regulatory Agency (MHRA). www.mhra.gov.uk. GSK investigation concludes. http://www.mhra.gov.uk/Howweregulate/Medicines/Medicinesregulatorynews/index.htm. Between 1994 and 2002, GSK led nine series of tests on the effects of paroxetine on children that showed that the medication was effective to treat depression among children, but that also revealed harmful side effects. GSK cleverly and knowingly used a legal loophole. The makers are not required to declare undesirable, even serious, effects, of a medication except for specific uses ("usage for adults," for example) for which it received an authorization to market the product. GSK knew the medication was prescribed for children, and it also knew that there were safety problems for these children, but it chose not to reveal this information. Goldacre, B. (2012). *Op. cit.*, p. 58.
47. Juni, P., Nartey, L., Reichenbach, S., Sterchi, R., Dieppe, P., & Egger, M. (2004). Risk of cardiovascular events and rofecoxib: Cumulative meta-analysis. *Lancet*, *364*(9450), 2021–2029. See also *Rédaction* (2005). Comment éviter les prochaines affaires Vioxx. *Prescrire* (2005), *25*(259), 222–225.
48. Psaty, B. M., & Kronmal, R. A. (2008). Reporting mortality findings in trials of rofecoxib for Alzheimer disease or cognitive impairment. *JAMA*, *299*(15), 1813–1817; Le célécoxib encore sur le marché: au profit de qui? *Rescrire* (2005), *25*(263), 512–513.
49. *Prescrire* (2009), *29*(303), 57.
50. In 2004, for example, the International Committee of Medical Journal Editors (ICMJE) announced that starting from 2005, none of them

would publish clinical trials, unless they were correctly registered before their execution (so that one could follow the results of these tests). The problem seemed solved, but everything continued the same as before. The editors didn't put their threats into action, probably due to the financial revenue, amounting to millions of dollars, that these same editors obtain when they publish tens of thousands of offprints from pharmaceutical industry publications. De Angelis, C., Drazen, J. M., Frizelle, P. F. A., Haug, C., Hoey, J., Horton, R.,... Overbeke, A. J. P. M. (2004). Clinical trial registration: A statement from the International Committee of Medical Journal Editors. *New England Journal of Medicine*, *351*(12), 1250–1251. Goldacre, B. (2012). *Op. cit.*, p. 51.

51. Goldacre, B. (2012). *Op. cit.*, p. 71.
52. *Ibid.*, p. 72.
53. *Ibid.*, p. 51–52.
54. Gagnon, M. A., & Lexchin, J. (2008). The cost of pushing pills: a new estimate of pharmaceutical promotion expenditures in the United States. *PLoS Medicine*, *5*(1), e1. For national GDP values, see http://www.indexmundi.com/.
55. Heimans, L., Van Hylckama Vlieg, A., & Dekker, F. W. (2010). Are claims of advertisements in medical journals supported by RCTs? *Neth. J. Med*, *68*, 46–9.
56. Fugh-Berman, A., Alladin, K., & Chow, J. (2006). Advertising in medical journals: Should current practices change? *PLoS Medicine*, *3*(6), e130. Goldacre, B. (2012). *Op. cit.*, p. 305. A recent study in the United States revealed that 60% of hospital department managers received money from the industry to work in its favor as consultants, lecturers, members of advisory councils, etc. Campbell, E. G., Weissman, J. S., Ehringhaus, S., Rao, S. R., Moy, B., Feibelmann, S., & Goold, S. D. (2007). Institutional academic-industry relationships. *JAMA*, *298*(15), 1779–1786. Altogether, 17,700 doctors received money, for a total of 750 million dollars, from AstraZeneca, Pfizer, GSK, Merck, and many others. 384 doctors received over $100,000 each. See Goldacre, B. (2012). *Op. cit.*, p. 331. This information is available on the ProPublica site, http://www.propublica.org/series/dollars-for-docs.
57. Fugh-Berman, A., & Ahari, S. (2007). Following the script: How drug reps make friends and influence doctors. *PLoS Medicine*, *4*(4), e150.
58. Orlowski, J. P., & Wateska, L. (1992). The effects of pharmaceutical firm enticements on physician prescribing patterns. There's no such thing as a free lunch. *Chest*, *102*(1), 270–273.

59. Verispan, Wolters-Kluwer, and IMS Health. The latter company has data on two-thirds of all prescriptions registered in pharmacies
60. Stell, L. K. (2009). Drug reps off campus! Promoting professional purity by suppressing commercial speech. *Journal of Law, Medicine & Ethics*, *37*(3), 431–443. See also Goldacre's interview on the site of the prestigious scientific journal *Nature*, September 28, 2012.
61. Hollis, A. (2004). Me-too drugs: Is there a problem? *WHO report*. In http://cdrwww.who.int/entity/intellectualproperty/topics/ip/Me-tooDrugs_Hollis1.pdf.
62. ALLHAT, Antihypertensive and Lipid-Lowering Treatment to Prevent Heart Attack Trial, which lasted for eight years, was conducted by the US Health Department.
63. Goldacre, B. (2012). *Op. cit.*, p. 149.
64. Helms, R., *Guinea Pig Zero: An Anthology of the Journal for Human Research Subjects*, Garrett County Press, 2006. See also the site http://www.guineapigzero.com/. Quoted in Goldacre, B. (2012). *Op. cit.*, p. 107.
65. PCB, commercialized by Monsanto under the name Aroclor in the United States, is a highly toxic chlorinated oil that was used as insulation in the electric and electronic industries, and that, in the presence of heat, gives off dioxin. Pyralène has been banned in France since 1987.
66. According to a declassified report, written in March 2005 by the Environmental Protection Agency, or EPA, for forty years, 810 tons of PCBs were poured into canals like Snow Creek and 32,000 tons of contaminated waste were dumped out in the open, on the site itself, in the heart of the neighborhood inhabited by the city's African-American community.
67. Robin, M.-M., *The World According to Monsanto*, The New Press, 2012, p. 16.
68. *Ibid.*, p. 18.
69. *Ibid.*
70. *Ibid.*
71. Regular exposure to these products can cause cancer, heart disease, diabetes, a lowering of the immune system, malfunctioning of the thyroid and of sexual hormones, reproductive disorders, and serious neurological disorders. Robin, M.-M. (2010). *Op. cit.*, Kindle location, p. 726 of the French edition.
72. Jensen, S. (1966). Report of a new chemical hazard. *New Scientist*, *32*(612), 247–250.
73. Robin, M.-M. (2012). *Op. cit.*, p. 19.

74. www.chemicalindustryarchives.org/dirtysecrets/annistonindepth/toxicity.asp. Quoted in Robin, M.-M. (2012). *Op. cit.*, p. 19.
75. Robin, M.-M. (2012). *Op. cit.*, p. 22.
76. *Ibid.*, location 685–686 of the French.
77. *Ibid.*, p. 27.
78. *Ibid.*, p. 26.
79. Monsanto's Pledge can be consulted on its website: http://www.monsanto.com/whoweare/pages/monsanto-pledge.aspx.
80. Agent Orange would also be manufactured by other firms like Dow Chemicals, a subsidiary of which, Union Carbide, would, in 1984, be responsible for the Bhopal catastrophe in India that officially killed 3,500 people, but that probably caused 20,000 or 25,000 deaths according to victims' associations. It is estimated that 80 million liters of defoliants were discharged over 3.3 million hectares of forests and land. 90% of the trees and bushes touched were destroyed within two years. Over 3,000 villages were contaminated, and 60% of the defoliants used were Agent Orange, containing the equivalent of 400 kilos of dioxins. According to WHO: "Dioxins are very toxic and can cause problems of reproduction and development, harm the immune system, interfere with the hormonal system, and cause cancer." Stellman, J. M., Stellman, S. D., Christian, R., Weber, T., & Tomasallo, C. (2003). The extent and patterns of usage of agent orange and other herbicides in Vietnam. *Nature*, *422*(6933), 681–687. Quoted in Robin, M.-M. (2010). *Op. cit.*, Kindle location 8038–8040; Stellman, Jane Mager, The extent and patterns of usage of agent orange and other herbicides in Vietnam, *Nature*, April 17, 2003.
81. Monsanto's agent orange: The persistent ghost from the Vietnam war. Organic Consumers Association, 2002. http://www.organicconsumers.org/monsanto/agentorange032102.cfm; Dai, Le Cao, *et al.* A comparison of infant mortality rates between two Vietnamese villages sprayed by defoliants in wartime and one unsprayed village. *Chemosphere*, vol. 20, August 1990, pp. 1005–1012. Robin, M.-M. (2010). *Op. cit.*, Kindle location 8186.
82. Seven companies produced Agent Orange: Dow Chemicals, Monsanto, Diamond Shamrock, Hercules, T-H Agricultural & Nutrition, Thompson Chemicals, and Uniroyal. Robin, M.-M. (2010). *Op. cit.*, pp. 1280–1281.
83. Suskind, R. R. (1983). Long-term health effects of exposure to 2, 4, 5-T and/or its contaminants. *Chemosphere*, *12*(4), 769.
84. Robin, M.-M. (2012). *Op. cit.*, p. 51.

85. Monsanto was warned, no one knows how, and its vice president wrote to the president of the scientific committee of the EPA to protest against the "highly provocative and erroneous information about the epidemiological studies concerning Monsanto's West Virginia plant.... We are very disturbed by the false charges being made against Monsanto and Dr. Suskind." Frustrated, Cate Jenkins sent the report to the press, which was outraged. Monsanto continued to intervene with the EPA to prevent the investigation from concluding and to have Jenkins penalized or even fired. She was finally transferred, and was subjected to harassment for years.
86. This list included various cancers (respiratory, prostate), including some very rare cancers like sarcoma of the soft tissue or non-Hodgkin's lymphoma, but also leukemia, type 2 diabetes, peripheral neuropathy (from which Alan Gibson, the veteran I met, suffers), and chloracne.
87. Robin, M.-M. (2012). *Op. cit.*, Kindle location 1585 of the French.
88. Robin, M.-M. (2012). *Op. cit.*, p. 73.
89. Problems plague the EPA pesticide registration activities, US Congress, House of Representatives, House Report, 98–1147, 1984. Quoted in Robin, M.-M. (2012). *Op. cit.*, p. 337. See also the article in *New York Times*, March 2, 1991.
90. Canada: McDuffie, H. H., Pahwa, P., McLaughlin, J. R., Spinelli, J. J., Fincham, S., Dosman, J. A.,... Choi, N. W. (2001). Non-Hodgkin's lymphoma and specific pesticide exposures in men cross-Canada study of pesticides and health. *Cancer Epiology Biomarkers & Prevention*, *10*(11), 1155–1163. Sweden: Hardell, L., Eriksson, M., & Nordström, M. (2002). Exposure to pesticides as risk factor for non-Hodgkin's lymphoma and hairy cell leukemia: Pooled analysis of two Swedish case-control studies. *Leukemia & Lymphoma*, *43*(5), 1043–1049. United States: De Roos, A. J., Blair, A., Rusiecki, J. A., Hoppin, J. A., Svec, M., Dosemeci, M.,... Alavanja, M. C. (2005). Cancer incidence among glyphosate-exposed pesticide applicators in the Agricultural Health Study. *Environmental Health Perspectives*, *113*(1), 49.
91. When Paul Berg then announced his intention of inserting a carcinogenic virus from a monkey into a cell of *Escherichia coli*, a bacterium that colonizes the human stomach and intestines, the scientific community was alarmed: "What will happen if, by accident, the organism being manipulated escapes from the laboratory?" wondered the geneticist Robert Pollack. A temporary moratorium on genetic manipulations was decreed. But it would not last, and genetic engineering experiments multiplied.

92. Robin, M.-M. (2012). *Op. cit.*, p. 203.
93. Other competitors also entered the fray to file the first patents on most of the main crops in the world: Calgene, a California start-up that had just successfully made tobacco resistant to glyphosate (the component of Roundup), Rhône-Poulenc, Hoechst, Dupont and Ciba-Geigy, and other giants of the chemical industry.
94. *CropChoice News*, November 16, 2003. Robin, M.-M. (2012). *Op. cit.*, p. 140.
95. Food and Drug Administration, "Statement of policy: Foods derived from new plant varieties," *Federal Register*, vol. 57, no. 104, May 29, 1992, p. 22983. Quoted in Robin, M.-M. (2012). *Op. cit.*, p. 145.
96. "The principle of substantial equivalence is an alibi with no scientific basis created out of thin air to prevent GMOs from being considered at least as food additives, and this enabled biotechnology companies to avoid the toxicological tests provided for in the Food, Drug, and Cosmetic Act and to avoid labeling their products." Robin, M.-M. (2012). *Op. cit.*, p. 147.
97. According to the 2007 Center for Food Safety report, Monsanto has a budget of $10 million and a team of 75 people hired full-time to supervise and instigate legal proceedings against the farmers who use its products. As of June 2006, Monsanto had filed between 2,391 and 4,531 suits for "seed piracy" against farmers in 19 countries, obtaining from them between 85 and 160 million dollars.
98. Detoeuf, A., *Propos de O. L. Barenton, confiseur*, Éditions du Tambourinaire, 1962, p. 111.
99. According to www.centerforfoodsafety.org.
100. Robin, M.-M. (2012). *Op. cit.*, p. 259.
101. *Ibid.*, location 6135 of the French.
102. *Ibid.*, p. 291.
103. Shiva, Vendana, From seeds of suicide to seeds of hope, *Huffington Post*, April 28, 2009.
104. Traditional varieties of cotton seeds are ready for harvesting after 150–160 days, unlike Bt varieties, which take 180–200 days. The use of these traditional seeds also reduces the need for fertilizers and pesticides.
105. Shiva, V. J., & Jalees, Kunwar, *Seeds of Suicide: The Ecological and Human Costs of Seed Monopolies and Globalisation of Agriculture*, Navdanya, 2006.
106. Chapelle, Sophie, *Journal des Alternatives*, November 5, 2012.
107. An offshoot of the CIG (Citizen Interest Group), this association includes Greenpeace, ATTAC, and Friends of the Earth.

108. "Agro-ecology and the right to food," report presented by Olivier de Schutter to the UN Human Rights Council on March 8, 2011 in Geneva.

CHAPTER 36: THE VIRTUES OF COOPERATION

1. Extract from a speech made at the General Assembly of the United Nations, September 24, 2001.
2. Candau, J. (2012). Pourquoi coopérer [Why Cooperate?]. *Terrain*, *1*, 4–25.
3. See also Axelrod, R., *The Evolution of Cooperation*, Basic Books, 1984; Kappeler, P. M., & Van Schaik, C., *Cooperation in Primates and Humans: Mechanisms and Evolution*, Springer Verlag, 2006; Henrich, J., & Henrich, N., *Why Humans Cooperate: A Cultural and Evolutionary Explanation*, Oxford University Press, 2007.
4. Candau, J. (2012). *Op. cit.*
5. The contents of this meeting were published in the book Goleman, D. & Dalai Lama, *Destructive Emotions and How We Can Overcome Them: A Dialogue with the Dalai Lama*, Bantam, 2004. See also Ekman, P., Davidson, R. J., Ricard, M., & Wallace, B. A. (2005). Buddhist and psychological perspectives on emotions and well-being. *Current Directions in Psychological Science*, *14*, 59–63.
6. Ekman, D. P., *Moving Toward Global Compassion*, Paul Ekman Group, 2014.
7. Memories of Ephraïm Grenadou, collected by Alain Prévost, broadcast on France Culture in 1967 and in 2011–2012. See also Grenadou, E., *Vie d'un paysan français* [Life of a French Farmer], Seuil, 1966.
8. Paul Ekman, in conversation with the author, 2009.
9. Candau, J. (2012). *Op. cit.*, p. 40.
10. Carpenter, J., Matthews, P., & Schirm, J., *Tournaments and Office Politics: Evidence from a Real Effort Experiment* (SSRN Scholarly Paper No., ID 1011134), Social Science Research Network, 2007.
11. DeMatteo, J. S., Eby, L. T., & Sundstrom, E. (1998). Team-based rwards: current empirical evidence and research in organizational behavior, *20*, 141–183. Tamu.edu.
12. Richard Layard, in a conversation with the author, 2010.
13. Mokyr, J., *The Enlightened Economy: An Economic History of Britain 1700–1850*, Yale University Press, 2009, pp. 384–385.
14. Wilkinson, R., Pickett, K. (2009). *Op. cit.*
15. http://usa2012.coop/about-co-ops/cooperatives-around-world.

16. Hardin, G. (1968). The tragedy of the commons. *Science, 162*(3859), 1243–1248.
17. Cox S. J. (1985). No tragedy on the commons. *Environmental Ethics, 7*, 49–61 (p. 60).
18. Angus, I. (2008). The myth of the tragedy of the commons. *Monthly Review Magazine, 25*(08), 08.
19. Engels, F., *The Mark*, New York Labor News Co., 1902. (Originally published in German in 1892.)
20. Ostrom E., *Governing the Commons: The Evolution of Institutions for Collective Action*, Cambridge University Press, 2010.
21. *Ibid.*, pp. 90–104. Lecomte, J., *La Bonté humaine* [Human Goodness], Odile Jacob, 2012.
22. Elinor Ostrom, cited in Lecomte, J. (2012). *Op. cit.*
23. Rustagi, D., Engel, S., & Kosfeld, M. (2010). Conditional cooperation and costly monitoring explain success in forest commons management. *Science, 330*(6006), 961–965.
24. I am grateful to Dennis Snower for clarifying this point.
25. Hervé Le Crosnier, *Le Monde diplomatique*, July 15, 2012.
26. Tania Singer, Diego Hangartner, and I organized this conference, which included, around the Dalai Lama, among others, the psychologist Daniel Batson, the economist Ernst Fehr, the ethologist Joan Silk, the neuroscientist William Harbaugh, the leadership teacher Bill George, and the social entrepreneur Bunker Roy. The content of this conference has been published in Singer, T., & Ricard, M. (eds.), *Caring Economics: Conversations on Altruism and Compassion, Between Scientists, Economists, and the Dalai Lama*, Picador, 2015.
27. Fehr, E., & Gächter, S. (2000). Cooperation and punishment in public goods experiments. *American Economic Review, 90*(4), 980–994; Fehr, E., Fischbacher, U., & Gächter, S. (2002). Strong reciprocity, human cooperation, and the enforcement of social norms. *Human Nature, 13*(1), 1–25.
28. Fehr, E., & Gächter, S. (2002). Altruistic punishment in humans. *Nature, 415*(6868), 137–140.
29. Boyd, R., Gintis, H., Bowles, S., & Richerson, P. J. (2003). The evolution of altruistic punishment. *Proceedings of the National Academy of Sciences, 100*(6), 3531–3535; Flack, J. C., Girvan, M., Waal, F. B. M. de, & Krakauer, D. C. (2006). Policing stabilizes construction of social niches in primates. *Nature, 439*(7075), 426–429; Mathew, S., & Boyd, R. (2011). Punishment sustains large-scale cooperation in prestate warfare. *Proceedings of the National Academy of Sciences, 108*(28), 11375–11380.

30. Herrmann, B., Thöni, C., & Gächter, S. (2008). Antisocial punishment across societies. *Science, 319*(5868), 1362–1367.
31. Since 1995, the NGO Transparency International has published an annual Corruption Perception Index (or CPI) that classifies countries according to the level of corruption perceived by its citizens. This index is produced with the help of surveys carried out by businesspeople and sociologists.
32. A Danish woman was arrested by New York police for "abandoning her child" after leaving her baby in its stroller outside a restaurant—something she did as a matter of course in her country.
33. Nowak, M. A., Sasaki, A., Taylor, C., & Fudenberg, D. 2004. Emergence of cooperation and evolutionary stability in finite populations. *Nature, 428*, 646–50; Imhof, L. A., Fudenberg, D., & Nowak, M. A. (2005). Evolutionary cycles of cooperation and defection. *Proceedings of the National Academy of Sciences of the United States of America, 102*(31), 10797–10800; Dreber, A., Rand, D. G., Fudenberg, D., & Nowak, M. A. (2008). Winners don't punish. *Nature, 452*(7185), 348–351.
34. Hamlin, J. K., & Wynn, K. (2011). Young infants prefer prosocial to antisocial others. *Cognitive Development, 26*(1), 30–39; Hamlin, J. K., Wynn, K., Bloom, P., & Mahajan, N. (2011). How infants and toddlers react to antisocial others. *Proceedings of the National Academy of Sciences, 108*(50), 19931–19936.
35. Singer, T., Seymour, B., O'Doherty, J. P., Stephan, K. E., Dolan, R. J., & Frith, C. D. (2006). Empathic neural responses are modulated by the perceived fairness of others. *Nature, 439*(7075), 466–469.
36. Rand, D. G., Dreber, A., Ellingsen, T., Fudenberg, D., & Nowak, M. A. (2009). Positive interactions promote public cooperation. *Science, 325*(5945), 1272–1275.
37. Ozouf, M., "Liberté, Égalité, Fraternité, Peuplements de Pays Paix et la Guerre." In *Lieux de mémoire* (dir. Pierre Nora), Quarto Gallimard, book 3, 1997, pp. 4353–4389.
38. Attali, J., *Fraternités*, Fayard, 1999, p. 172.
39. *Ibid.*, p. 173.
40. *Ibid.*, p. 174.
41. *Ibid.*, pp. 170–171.
42. Martin Luther King Jr., speech on March 31, 1968.
43. Tomasello, M., *Why We Cooperate*, MIT Press, 2009.
44. Sober, E., & Wilson, D. S., *Unto Others: The Evolution and Psychology of Unselfish Behavior*, Harvard University Press, p. 166, 1999; Boyd, R., & Richerson, P. J. (1992). Punishment allows the evolution

of cooperation (or anything else) in sizable groups. *Ethology and Sociobiology, 13*(3), 171–195. According to Colin Turnbull, among the Mbuti people in Africa, "even the most insignificant and routine action in the daily life of the family is potentially of major concern to the band as a whole.... It is important that there should be a pattern of behavior that is generally accepted, and which covers every conceivable angle." Turnbull, C. M., *The Mbuti Pygmies: An Ethnographic Survey*, American Museum of Natural History, 1965, vol. 50, p. 118.

45. Nowak, M., & Highfield, R., *SuperCooperators*, The Free Press, 2011, pp. 270–1.

CHAPTER 37: AN ENLIGHTENED EDUCATION

1. Seligman, M. E. P., *Flourish: A Visionary New Understanding of Happiness and Well-Being,* Atria Books, 2012.
2. Dalai Lama, G. T., *Ancient Wisdom, Modern World*, Abacus, 2000.
3. For a critique of "neutralism" in education and the teaching of universally desirable and acceptable values, see also White, J., *Education and the Good Life: Autonomy, Altruism, and the National Curriculum*, Advances in Contemporary Educational Thought, vol. 7, ERIC, 1991.
4. Greenberg, M. T. (2010). School-based prevention: Current status and future challenges. *Effective Education*, 2(1), 27–52.
5. Favre, D., *Transformer la Violence des Élèves: Cerveau, Motivations et Apprentissage* [Tranforming violence in students: The brain, motivations, and learning]. Dunod, 2006; Favre, D., *Cessons de Démotiver les Élèves: 18 Clés pour Favoriser l'Apprentissage* [Let's stop demotivating students: 18 key ways to enhance learning]. Dunod, 2010.
6. Hawkes, N., *From My Heart: Transforming Lives Through Values*, Independent Thinking Press, 2013, p. 66–67. See also Hawkes, N., *Does Teaching Values Improve the Quality of Education in Primary Schools? A Study About the Impact of Values Education in a Primary School,* VDM Verlag, 2010. See also the website www.values-education.com.
7. Farrer, F., *A Quiet Revolution: Encouraging Positive Values in Our Children*, Rider, 2005.
8. Lovat, T., Toomey, R., & Clement, N., *International Research Handbook on Values Education and Student Wellbeing*, Springer, 2010; Lovat, T., & Toomey, R., *Values Education and Quality Teaching: The Double Helix Effect*, Springer-Verlag, 2009.

9. Forms of meditation combining intellectual analysis and attention development, mindfulness, and benevolence are taught in certain educational establishments in North America and various countries in Europe. Greenland, S. K., *The Mindful Child: How to Help Your Kid Manage Stress and Become Happier, Kinder, and More Compassionate,* The Free Press, 2010. Also, regarding the practice of mindfulness in parental education, see Kabat-Zinn, J., *Everyday Blessings: The Inner Work of Mindful Parenting*, Hyperion, 1998.
10. Ozawa-de Silva, B., & Dodson-Lavelle, B. (2011). An education of heart and mind: Practical and theoretical issues in teaching cognitive-based compassion training to children. *Practical Matters*, *1*(4), 1–28.
11. Pléty, R., *L'Apprentissage coopérant* [Cooperative Learning], Presses Universitaires de Lyon (PUL), 1998, p. 7.
12. Johnson, D. W., Johnson, R. T., & Stanne, M. B., *Cooperative Learning Methods: A Meta-Analysis,* Minneapolis, University of Minnesota, 2000. See also this seminal work by two top specialists: Johnson, D. H., & Johnson, R. T., *Learning Together and Alone: Cooperative, Competitive, and Individualistic Learning*, 5th ed., Pearson, 1998.
13. Slavin, R. E., Hurley, E. A., & Chamberlain, A., *Cooperative Learning and Achievement: Theory and Research*, Wiley Online Library, 2003. A more recent study has confirmed that cooperative education improves school results: Tsay, M., & Brady, M. (2010). A case study of cooperative learning and communication pedagogy: Does working in teams make a difference? *Journal of the Scholarship of Teaching and Learning*, *10*(2), 78–89.
14. Johnson, D. W., Johnson, R. T., & Holubec, E. J., *Cooperation in the Classroom*, Interaction Book Company, 1991.
15. Cohen, P. A., Kulik, J. A., & Kulik, C. L. C. (1982). Educational outcomes of tutoring: A meta-analysis of findings. *American Educational Research Journal*, *19*(2), 237–248. See also the section "Enseignment" [Teaching] on the site http://www.psychologie-positive.net, founded by Jacques Lecomte.
16. Barley, Z., Lauer, P. A., Arens, S. A., Apthorp, H. S., Englert, K. S., Snow, D., & Akiba, M., *Helping At-Risk Students Meet Standards,* Mid-Continent Research for Education and Learning, 2002; Finkelsztein, D., *Le Monitorat: S'entraider pour réussir*, Hachette, 1997.
17. Ray Chambers began his career as a successful financier. After tiring of life on Wall Streets he decided to help hundreds of poor, deserving students from New Jersey to further their studies. He is now the

UN's Special Envoy for Malaria. See Perry, A., *Lifeblood: How to Change the World One Dead Mosquito at a Time*, PublicAffairs, 2011.

18. See http://erdcanada.com/.
19. Topping, K. J., & Trickey, S. (2007). Collaborative philosophical enquiry for school children: Cognitive effects at 10–12 years. *British Journal of Educational Psychology*, *77*(2), 271–288; Trickey, S., & Topping, K. J. (2004). Philosophy for children: A systematic review. *Research Papers in Education*, *19*(3), 365–380.
20. Aronson, E., & Patnoe, S., *Cooperation in the Classroom: The Jigsaw Method*, 3d rev. ed., Pinter & Martin, 2011.
21. Lucker, G. W., Rosenfield, D., Sikes, J., & Aronson, E. (1976). Performance in the interdependent classroom: A field study. *American Educational Research Journal*, *13*(2), 115–123; Fini, A. A. S., Zainalipour, H., & Jamri, M. (2011). An investigation into the effect of cooperative learning with focus on jigsaw technique on the academic achievement of second-grade students. *J. Life Sci. Biomed.* 2(2), 21–24.
22. For more on the life of Sanjit "Bunker" Roy, see Chapter 1, "The Nature of Altruism."
23. Jennings, P. A., & Greenberg, M. T. (2009). The prosocial classroom: Teacher social and emotional competence in relation to student and classroom outcomes. *Review of Educational Research*, *79*(1), 491–525; Aspy, D. N., & Roebuck, F. N., *Kids Don't Learn from People They Don't Like*, Human Resource Development Press, 1977.
24. Lecomte, J. (April 2009). Les résultats de l'éducation humaniste [The results of humanist education]. *Sciences humaines*, *203*.
25. Aspy, D. N., & Roebuck, F. N. (1977). *Op. cit.*
26. Gordon, M., *Roots of Empathy: Changing the World Child by Child*, Thomas Allen & Son, 2005.
27. Schonert-Reichl, K. A. (2005). Effectiveness of the roots of empathy program in promoting children's emotional and social competence: A summary of research outcome findings. Appendix B in Gordon, M. (2005). *Op. cit.*
28. Santos, R.G., Chartier M. J., Whalen, J. C., Chateau, D., & Boyd, L. "Effectiveness of the Roots of Empathy (ROE) Program in Preventing Aggression and Promoting Prosocial Behavior: Results from a Cluster Randomized Controlled Trial in Manitoba." Poster presented at the Banff Conference on Behavioral Sciences, Banff, March 2008.
29. *Ibid.*
30. Rivkin, M. S., *The Great Outdoors: Restoring Children's Right to Play Outside*, ERIC, 1995; Karsten, L. (2005). It all used to be better?

Different generations on continuity and change in urban children's daily use of space. *Children's Geographies*, *3*(3), 275–290.

31. George, D. S. Getting lost in the great indoors. *Washington Post*, June 19, 2007. Cited in Rifkin, J. (2012). *The Third Industrial Revolution. Op cit.*, p. 352.
32. Louv, R., *Last Child in the Woods: Saving Our Children from Nature-Deficit Disorder,* Algonquin Books, 2008, p. 10. Cited in Rifkin, J. (2012). *Op. cit.*, p. 353.
33. Kellert S. R., "The Biological Basis for Human Values of Nature." In Kellert, S. R., & Wilson, E. O., *The Biophilia Hypothesis*, Island Press, 1995.
34. Cited in Rifkin, J. (2012). *Op. cit.*, p. 360.
35. Lewinsohn, P. M., Rohde, P., Seeley, J. R., & Fischer, S. A. (1993). Age-cohort changes in the lifetime occurrence of depression and other mental disorders. *Journal of Abnormal Psychology*, *102*(1), 110.
36. For this and the experiment at the Geelong School, see Seligman, M. E. P. (2012). *Flourish, Op.cit.*

CHAPTER 38: FIGHTING INEQUALITY

1. Morin, E., *La Voie: Pour l'avenir de l'humanité*, Fayard, 2011.
2. For details of calculations and sources, see Stiglitz, J. (2011), Stiglitz, J., *The Price of Inequality,* Kindle Edition, Location 103.
3. Occupy Wall Street is a peaceful protest movement condemning the rapacious systems of financial capitalism. It began in September 2011 when one thousand people demonstrated at the New York Stock Exchange on Wall Street. This movement, which resembles that of the *Indignés* in France or the *Indignados* in Spain, taking their name from Stéphane Hessel's essay *Indignez-vous!* [Time for Outrage!], spread rapidly across the whole of the United States, reaching 500 cities in 82 countries.
4. Stiglitz, J. (2012). *Op. cit.*, location 103. See also Stiglitz, J. (2011). Of the 1%, by the 1%, for the 1%. *Vanity Fair,* May 2011.
5. Kuroda, H., & Bank, A. D., *Asian Development Outlook 2012: Confronting Rising Inequality in Asia*, Asian Development Bank, 2012.
6. Cited in Bourguinat, H., & Briys, E., *L'Arrogance de la finance: Comment la théorie financière a produit le krach,* La Découverte, 2009.
7. Piketty, T., & Saez, E., *Income Inequality in the United States, 1913–1998*, National Bureau of Economic Research, 2001.
8. Comment made by Andrew Sheng in Charles Ferguson's documentary *Inside Job*, a startling perspective on the consequences of

deregulation and on the psychology of the individuals at the root of the financial crisis. He won the Oscar for Best Documentary in 2011. Ferguson, C., *Inside Job*, Sony Pictures Entertainment, 2011.

9. Feller, A., Stone, C., & Saez, E. (2009). Top 1 percent of Americans reaped two-thirds of income gains in last economic expansion. Center on Budget and Policy Priorities.
10. http://www.statistiques-mondiales.com/part_du_revenu.htm.
11. Quoted in Special Report, For richer, for poorer, *The Economist*, October 13, 2013, p. 6.
12. Kuroda, H., & Bank, A. D., *Asian Development Outlook 2012: Confronting Rising Inequality in Asia*, Asian Development Bank, 2012.
13. OECD (2014), "Focus on Inequality and Growth—December 2014." The summary of the report as well as figures and underlying data can be downloaded via www.oecd.org/social/inequality-and-poverty.htm
14. Christopher, C., Daly, M., & Hale, G. (2009). Beyond Kutznets: Persistent Regional Inequality in China. FRBSF Working Paper 09–07; Wan, G., Lu, M., & Chen, Z. (2007). Globalization and regional income inequality: Empirical evidence from within China. *Review of Income and Wealth*, *53*(1), 35–59. Recently, a strong anticorruption campaign has been set in motion by the new Chinese president, Xi Jingping, and many high- and low-level officials have been arrested.
15. In the United States, the economists Emmanuel Saez and Thomas Piketty have observed how 94% of the gains made in the post-2009 recovery have gone to the wealthiest 1%. Shaw, H., Stone, C., Piketty, T., & Saez, E. (2010). Tax data show richest 1 percent took a hit in 2008, but income remained highly concentrated at the top. Center on Budget and Policy Priorities.
16. "World of Work Report 2008—Income inequalities in the age of financial globalization." ILO report, October 2008.
17. http://www.weforum.org/issues/global-risks.
18. Lustig, N., Lopez-Calva, L., & Ortiz-Juarez, E. (2012). The decline in inequality in Latin America: How much, since when and why. *Since When and Why* (April 24, 2011).
19. Breceda, K., Rigolini, J., & Saavedra, J. (2009). Latin America and the social contract: Patterns of social spending and taxation. *Population and Development Review*, *35*(4), 721–748.
20. Wilkinson, R., & Pickett, K. (2009). *Op. cit.*
21. National Opinion Research Center. *General Social Survey*. Chicago NORC, pp. 1999–2004.
22. In other words, if the Gini index were to go from 0.36 to 0.29. This index equals 0 if everyone has equal resources, and 1 if a single person owns all

the wealth. See Kondo, N., Sembajwe, G., Kawachi, I., Van Dam, R. M., Subramanian, S. V., & Yamagata, Z. (2009). Income inequality, mortality, and self rated health: Meta-analysis of multilevel studies. *BMJ, 339.*
23. Wilkinson, R. (2009). *Op. cit.*, p. 64.
24. Tocqueville, A. de, *Democracy in America*, trans. Henry Reeve, Part 3, Chapter 1, 1839. Project Gutenberg.
25. Berg, A., Ostry, J. D., & Zettelmeyer, J. (2012). What makes growth sustained? *Journal of Development Economics*, *98*(2), 149–166.
26. Molina, E., Narayan, A., & Saveedra, J. (2013). "Outcomes, Opportunity and Development: Why Unequal Opportunities and Not Outcomes Hinder Economic Development," by Molina, Ezequiel, Narayan, Ambar, & Saveedra, Jaime. World Bank report. Cited by *The Economist*, Special report, October 13, 2012.
27. *Ibid.*
28. Morin, E. (2011). *Op. cit.*, pp. 114–115.
29. Morin, E., & Hessel, S., *Le Chemin de l'espérance,* Fayard, 2011, p. 44.
30. OECD (2014), "Focus on Inequality and Growth—December 2014." The summary of the report as well as figures and underlying data can be downloaded via www.oecd.org/social/inequality-and-poverty.htm.

Chapter 39: Toward a Caring Economy

1. Pennac, D., *La Fée carabine*, Gallimard, 1997.
2. Persky, J. (1995). Retrospectives: The ethology of *Homo economicus*. *Journal of Economic Perspectives*, *9*(2), 221–231.
3. Based on their preferences, they are meant to maximize their satisfaction by using the resources available, calculating both costs and benefits. See Gary Becker's 1976 book *The Economic Approach to Human Behavior*, University of Chicago Press, 2009. This is one of the most representative works of this line of thinking.
4. Samuelson, P. A., & Nordhaus, W. D., *Economics*, 19th ed., edited and revised, McGraw Hill Higher Education, 2009. This quotation is taken from the 12th ed. (1983), p. 903.
5. Kourilsky, P., *Le Temps de l'altruisme*, Odile Jacob, 2009, p. 142.
6. Edgeworth F. Y., *Mathematical Psychics: An Essay on the Application of Mathematics to the Moral Sciences,* A. M. Kelley, 1964, p. 16.
7. Francis Edgeworth (1845–1926) was appointed to a chair in economics at Oxford and is one of the foremost representatives of the so-called neoclassical school of economics.
8. Landes, W. M., & Posner, R., *Altruism in Law and Economics*, National Bureau of Economic Research, 1977.

9. Blau, P., *Exchange and Power in Social Life*, John Wiley and Sons, 1964, p. 17.
10. Walster, E. H., Hatfield, E., Walster, G. W., & Berscheid, E., *Equity: Theory and Research*, Allyn and Bacon, 1978.
11. Sen, A., *Éthique et économie*, PUF, 1993, p. 18. Cited by Lecomte, J. (2012), *La Bonté humaine. Op. cit.*
12. Kourilsky, P. (2009). *Op. cit.*, p. 145.
13. The individual who thinks only of his own gain "is led by an invisible hand to promote an end which was no part of his intention.... By pursuing his own interest, he frequently promotes that of the society more effectually than when he really intends to promote it." Adam Smith, *An Inquiry into the Nature and Causes of the Wealth of Nations*, Book 4, Chapter 2, 1776.
14. Smith, A. *An Inquiry into the Nature and Causes of the Wealth of Nations* (The Project Gutenberg eBook, 2009), p. 12.
15. Friedman, M., *Capitalism and Freedom*, University of Chicago Press, 1962, pp. 133–134.
16. Waal, F. B. M. de (2009). *The Age of Empathy. Op. cit.*, p. 38.
17. Kolm, S.-C. (1984). *Op. cit.*, p. 34.
18. Smith, A. (2011). *The Theory of Moral Sentiments.* Available through Project Gutenberg.
19. Kahneman, D., Slovic, P., & Tversky, A., *Judgment under Uncertainty: Heuristics and Biases*, Cambridge University Press, 1982; Kahneman, D., & Tversky, A. (1979). Prospect theory: An analysis of decision under risk. *Econometrica*, *47*(2), 263–291. Kahneman, D., *Thinking, Fast and Slow*, Farrar, Straus & Giroux, 2011.
20. Kuhnen, C. M., & Knutson, B. (2005). The neural basis of financial risk taking. *Neuron*, *47*(5), 763–770; Knutson, B., & Bossaerts, P. (2007). Neural antecedents of financial decisions. *Journal of Neuroscience*, *27*(31), 8174–8177.
21. Ariely, D., *The Irrational Bundle: Predictably Irrational, the Upside of Irrationality, and the Honest Truth About Dishonesty*, Harper, 2013.
22. Soros, G. (1997). The capitalist threat. *Atlantic Monthly*, *279*(2), 45–58. Cited in Oreskes, N., & Conway, E. M. M. (2011). *Op. cit.*, note 36, p. 338.
23. *Ibid.*
24. Sandel, M., *What Money Can't Buy: The Moral Limits of Markets*, Open Market edition, Allen Lane, 2012.
25. Interview with Michael Sandel by Edward Luce in the *Financial Times*, April 5, 2013.

26. *Le Monde*, June 9, 2009.
27. Stiglitz, Joseph E., *The Price of Inequality*, pp. 178–179.
28. Sen, A., *L'Idée de justice*, Flammarion, 2012; Sen, A., *Repenser l'inégalité*, Seuil, 2012.
29. Stiglitz, Joseph E., *The Price of Inequality.*
30. Piketty, T., *Capital in the Twenty-First Century*, Harvard University Press, 2014.
31. Stiglitz, J. (2012). *Op. cit.*, locations 159–169.
32. In 2000, InfoSpace employed some shady accounting techniques to declare profits of 46 million dollars in spite of the fact that it had lost 46 million dollars.
33. At a Senate hearing, the senator Carl Levin asked the chairman of Goldman Sachs, Lloyd Blankfein: "Is it not a conflict when you sell something to someone, and then are determined to bet against that same security, and you don't disclose that to the person you're selling to?" To which Blankfein responded: "In the context of market making, that is not a conflict." In 2008, Blankfein was earning $825,900 per week. He declared elsewhere that as a banker he was doing "God's work" (*Sunday Times*, November 8, 2010).
34. Including $485 million for their CEO Richard Fuld.
35. Stiglitz, J. (2012). *Op. cit.*, location 209.
36. Ferguson, C. (2011). *Op. cit.*
37. Comment made by N. Roubini in *Inside Job. Op. cit.*
38. Kallas, S. (March 3, 2005). "The Need for an European Transparency." Speech in Nottingham. Cited by Kempf, H. *L'oligarchie ça suffit, vive la démocratie*, Seuil, 2013, p. 78.
39. Galbraith, J. K., *L'État prédateur: Comment la droite a renoncé au marché libre et pourquoi la gauche devrait en faire autant*, Seuil, 2009, p. 185. Cited in Kempf, H. (2013). *Op. cit.*, p. 69.
40. The "City" is located in London and represents one of the world's major financial centers.
41. Cited in Irène Inchauspé, L'État redéfinit son rôle. *Challenges, 179*, September 10, 2009, p. 53.
42. See Chapter 35 on "Institutionalized Selfishness."
43. George Soros, during a presentation at Davos Word Economic Forum, January 2014.
44. Attali, J., *Demain, qui gouvernera le monde?*, Fayard/Pluriel, 2012.
45. Porter, M., & Kramer, M. (January–February 2011). How to fix capitalism. *Harvard Business Review*, p. 74.
46. Filippi, C.-H., *L'Argent sans maître*, Descartes, 2009.

47. Stiglitz, J. (2012). *Op.cit*, p. 154.
48. Frank, R. H., *Passions Within Reason: The Strategic Role of the Emotions*, W. W. Norton, 1988, p. 236.
49. See http://www.global-economic-symposium.org/symposium-2014/download/GES2014OpeningAdressDSnower.pdf.
50. Kolm, S.-C. (1984). *Op. cit.*, p. 109.
51. *Ibid.*
52. *Ibid.*, p. 56.
53. See also Kolm, S.-C., *Reciprocity: An Economics of Social Relations*, Cambridge University Press, 2009; Kolm, S.-C., & Ythier, J. M., *Handbook of the Economics of Giving, Altruism and Reciprocity: Foundations*, North Holland, 2006.
54. Detœuf, A., *Propos de O. L. Barenton, confiseur*, Éditions du Tambourinaire, 1962.
55. Kolm, S.-C. (1984). *Op. cit.*, p. 227.
56. For more information, see "Mondragon" on http://en.wikipedia.org/wiki/Mondragon, as well as the article by Prades, J. (2005). L'énigme de Mondragon. Comprendre le sens de l'expérience. *Revue internationale de l'économie sociale*, *296*, 1–12.
57. Wolff, R. Yes, there is an alternative to capitalism: Mondragon shows the way. *Guardian*, June 24, 2012.
58. Morin, E., *La Voie: Pour l'avenir de l'humanité*, Fayard, 2011.
59. Taken from the author's notes from the event.
60. Personal communication between the author and Muhammad Yunus.
61. Extract from a speech made by Muhammad Yunus at UNESCO's Earth University, Paris, April 27, 2013.
62. Lecomte, T., *Le Commerce equitable*, Éditions d'Organisation, 2004, pp.12, 17.
63. *Ibid.*, p. 20.
64. *Ibid.*, p. 25.
65. *Ibid.*, pp. 48–49.
66. Darnil, S., & Roux, M. L., *80 Hommes pour changer le monde: Entreprendre pour la planète,* Le Livre de Poche, 2006.
67. *Ibid.*
68. According to figures quoted by Eurosif (European Sustainable Investment Forum): European SRI Study, 2012. www.eurosif.org.
69. See http://www.triodos.com/en/about-triodos-bank/ as well as http://www.calvert.com/.
70. "Impact Investments: An Emerging Asset Class," co-authored by Rockefeller Foundation and J. P Morgan Investment Bank, is presented as the first report that rigorously sizes, projects, and defines the current

impact investment opportunity. http://www.rockefellerfoundation.org/blog/impact-investments-emerging-asset.

71. OECD, Development: aid to developing countries falls because of global recession, press statement, April 4, 2012.
72. Despite the undeniably major achievements of the Gates Foundation, several public health experts have highlighted that by investing massively in the fight against certain diseases like malaria and AIDS, other areas have been neglected by the foundation, and, by consequence, also neglected by local health authorities charged with implementing Gates Foundation programs. This is particularly true of the fight against tuberculosis, as well as maternal and child health and other problems affecting the poor. See especially What has the Gates Foundation done for global health? *Lancet*, *373* (9675), 1577.
73. O'Clery, C., *The Billionaire Who Wasn't: How Chuck Feeney Secretly Made and Gave Away a Fortune*, PublicAffairs, 2013.
74. *Forbes*, February 19, 2013.
75. Bertoni, Steven, & Feeney, Chuck. The billionaire who is trying to go broke. *Forbes*, October 8, 2012.
76. *Ibid.*
77. Under the auspices of the Ditchley Foundation; http://www.ditchley.co.uk/page/394/philanthropy.htm. Cited by Vaccaro, A. (2012). Encourager le Renouveau de la Philanthropie, conference held on March 15, 2012 at the École de Paris du Management.
78. Vaccaro, A. (2012). Le renouveau de la philanthropie. *Journal de l'École de Paris du management*, *96*(4), 31–37. See also L'Herminier, Sandrine, *L'Espoir philanthropique*, Lignes de Repères, 2012.
79. According to Broderick, Daniel, Crowdfunding's untapped potential in emerging markets, *Forbes*, August 5, 2014.
80. About us, Kiva.org.
81. Morin, E., & Hessel, S., *Le Chemin de l'espérance*, Fayard, p. 29.
82. Giles, J. (April 13, 2013). Wiki-opoly. *New Scientist*, *2912*, 38–41.
83. Babinet, G. (February 2013), *Pour un new deal numérique*, Institut Montaigne, p. 26.
84. Porter, M., & Kramer, M. (January–February 2011). How to fix capitalism. *Harvard Business Review*, p. 68.
85. *Ibid.*, p. 71.
86. Greenest companies in America. *Newsweek*, October 22, 2012.

Chapter 40: Voluntary, Joyous Simplicity

1. Gandhi, cited by Varinda Tarzie Vittachi, *Newsweek*, January 26, 1976.
2. Stiglitz, J. (2012). *Op. cit.*, p. 318.

3. Elgin, D., *Voluntary Simplicity: Toward a Way of Life That Is Outwardly Simple, Inwardly Rich,* William Morrow, 2010.
4. Elgin, D., & Mitchell, A. (1977). Voluntary simplicity. *The Co-Evolution Quarterly, 3,* 4–19.
5. Rabhi, P., *Vers la sobriété heureuse,* Actes Sud, 2010.
6. Cited by Scott Russell Sanders. To fix the economy, we first have to change our definition of wealth. *Orion,* July/August 2011.
7. Dalai Lama, *Sagesse ancienne, monde moderne,* Fayard, 1999.
8. Sheldon, K. M., & Kasser, T. (1995). Coherence and congruence: Two aspects of personality integration. *Journal of Personality and Social Psychology, 68*(3), 531.
9. Kasser, T., *The High Price of Materialism,* MIT Press, 2003; Kasser, T. (2008). Can buddhism and consumerism harmonize? A review of the psychological evidence. Presented at the International Conference on Buddhism in the Age of Consumerism, Mahidol University, Bangkok, pp. 1–3.
10. Kasser, T. (2003). *Op. cit.*, p. 831.
11. Schwartz, S. H. (1994). Are there universal aspects in the structure and contents of human values? *Journal of Social Issues, 50*(4), 19–45.
12. Schultz, P. W., Gouveia, V. V., Cameron, L. D., Tankha, G., Schmuck, P., & Franvek, M. (2005). Values and their relationship to environmental concern and conservation behavior. *Journal of Cross-Cultural Psychology, 36*(4), 457–475. Transcultural studies reveal that the greater the importance people attach to objectives such as wealth and status, the less likely they are to worry about protecting the environment or of the need for having a "beautiful world." Through their behavior they show less benevolence and sense of connectedness with the rest of humankind. See Schwartz, S. H. (1992). Universals in the content and structure of values: Theoretical advances and empirical tests in 20 countries. *Advances in Experimental Social Psychology, 25*(1), 1–65; Saunders, S., & Munro, D. (2000). The construction and validation of a consumer orientation questionnaire designed to measure Fromms (1955) marketing character in Australia. *Social Behavior and Personality: An International Journal, 28*(3), 219–240.
13. Sheldon, K. M., & Kasser, T. (1998). Pursuing personal goals: Skills enable progress, but not all progress is beneficial. *Personality and Social Psychology Bulletin, 24*(12), 1319–1331.
14. Paul Mazur in a 1927 article in the *Harvard Business Review,* cited by Häring, N., & Douglas, N., *Economists and the Powerful: Convenient Theories, Distorted Facts, Ample Rewards,* Anthem Press, 2012, p. 17.

15. Ruskin, G. (1999). Why they whine: How corporations prey on our children. *Mothering*, November–December 1999. Cited by Kasser, T. (2003). *Op. cit.*, 1127.
16. Reported by Ruskin, G. (1999). *Op. cit.*
17. Rabhi, P. (2010). *Op. cit.*, p. 18.
18. Ellen McArthur Foundation (2012). *Towards the Circular Economy.*
19. Stahel, W. R., *The Performance Economy*, Palgrave Macmillan, 2010.
20. AFP, April 23, 2013.
21. For broader information on relevant books and review articles, see Layard, R., *Happiness: Lessons from a New Science*, Penguin, 2006; Kahneman, D., Diener, E., & Schwarz, N., *Well-being: The Foundations of Hedonic Psychology*, Russell Sage Foundation, 2003.
22. Myers, D. G. (2000). The funds, friends, and faith of happy people. *American Psychologist*, *55*(1), 56.
23. Graham, C., *Happiness Around the World: The Paradox of Happy Peasants and Miserable Millionaires,* Oxford University Press, 2012.
24. Layard, R. (2007). *Op. cit.*
25. Dunn, E. W., Aknin, L. B., & Norton, M. I. (2008). Spending money on others promotes happiness. *Science*, *319*(5870), 1687.
26. Aknin, L. B., Barrington-Leigh, C. P., Dunn, E. W., Helliwell, J. F., Biswas-Diener, R., Kemeza, I., . . . Norton, M. I., *Prosocial Spending and Well-Being: Cross-Cultural Evidence for a Psychological Universal*, National Bureau of Economic Research, 2010.
27. Dunn, E. W., Gilbert, D. T., & Wilson, T. D. (2011). If money doesn't make you happy, then you probably aren't spending it right. *Journal of Consumer Psychology*, *21*(2), 115.
28. Brown, K. W., & Kasser, T. (2005). Are psychological and ecological well-being compatible? The role of values, mindfulness, and lifestyle. *Social Indicators Research*, *74*(2), 349–368.
29. http://www.courrierinternational.com/article/2012/11/28/uruguay-le-vrai-president-normal. Courrier International, "Uruguay, le vrai président normal," No 1152, November 28, 2013.
30. http://www.bbc.com/news/magazine-20243493, 15 November 2012.
31. BBC World Service report, November 15, 2012, Vladimir Hernández, Montevideo.
32. "Human Happiness and the Environment," address by Uruguayan president Jose Mujica at Rio+20 Earth Summit, June 20, 2013. English translation, see http://therightsofnature.org/category/rio20.

CHAPTER 41: ALTRUISM FOR THE SAKE OF FUTURE GENERATIONS

1. Rockström, J., & Klum, M., *The Human Quest: Prospering Within Planetary Boundaries*, Bokförlaget Langenskiöld, 2012, p. 112.
2. Hawks, J., et. al. (1999). Population bottlenecks and Pleistocene human evolution. *Molecular Biology and Evolution, 17*(1). According to another theory, around seventy thousand years ago, the human population may have been reduced to about ten thousand people following a catastrophic volcanic eruption that profoundly altered the world's climate. See Dawkins, Richard, *The Ancestor's Tale: A Pilgrimage to the Dawn of Life*, Houghton Mifflin, 2004, p. 416.
3. McEvedy, C., & Jones, R., *Atlas of World Population History*, Penguin, 1978; Thomlinson, R., *Demographic Problems: Controversy over Population Control*, Dickenson, 1975.
4. Richardson, K., Steffen, W., & Liverman, D., *Climate Change: Global Risks, Challenges and Decisions*, Cambridge University Press, 2011, Chapter 1, p. 4.
5. http://www.ccema-portal.org/article/read/planetary-boundaries-a-safe-operating-space-for-humanity. See also Steffen, W., Persson, Deutsch, L., Zalasiewicz, J., Williams, M., Richardson, K.,...Gordon, L. (2011). The Anthropocene: From global change to planetary stewardship. *Ambio, 40*(7), 739–761.
6. Ellis, E. C., Klein Goldewijk, K., Siebert, S., Lightman, D., & Ramankutty, N. (2010). Anthropogenic transformation of the biomes, 1700 to 2000. *Global Ecology and Biogeography, 19*(5), 589–606; Taylor, L., *The Healing Power of Rainforest Herbs: A Guide to Understanding and Using Herbal Medicinals*, Square One Publishers, 2004. As much as 90% of Western Africa's coastal rainforest has disappeared since 1900. In Southern Asia, around 88% of the tropical rain forest has been lost. A large part of the remainder of the world's tropical rainforest is located in the Amazon basin, covering an area of around 4 million km^5. In Central America, two thirds of the low-altitude tropical rainforest has been transformed into farmland since 1950, and 40% of all forestry has been lost over the course of the last forty years. Madagascar has seen the destruction of 90% of its eastern tropical rainforest. For all scientific references, see the Wikipedia article on "Deforestation."
7. Some scientists place the start of the Anthropocene further back, in the eighteenth century. Most environmentalists, however, consider

the "Great Acceleration" of 1950 as the beginning of this era, by virtue of the wide-ranging ecological shifts that began happening then.

8. Thompson, L. G., Mosley-Thompson, E., & Henderson, K. A. (2000). Ice-core palaeoclimate records in tropical South America since the Last Glacial Maximum. *Journal of Quaternary Science*, *15*(4), 377–394.
9. Deforestation and resulting forest fires represent as much as 20% at least of man-made CO_2 emissions.
10. Wijkman, A., & Rockström, J. (2013). *Op. cit.*; Lenton, T. M., Held, H., Kriegler, E., Hall, J. W., Lucht, W., Rahmstorf, S., & Schellnhuber, H. J. (2008). Tipping elements in the Earth's climate system. *Proceedings of the National Academy of Sciences*, *105*(6), 1786–1793.
11. Wijkman, A., & Rockström, J. (2013). *Op. cit.*, p. 117.
12. Rockström, J., Steffen, W., Noone, K., Persson, Chapin, F. S., Lambin, E. F., . . . Schellnhuber, H. J. (2009). A safe operating space for humanity. *Nature*, *461*(7263), 472–475.
13. *Ibid.*
14. Guinotte, F. (2008), Ocean acidification and its potential effects. *Annals of New York Academy of Sciences*, *1134*, 320–342.
15. Díaz, S., *et al.*, "Biodiversity Regulation of Ecosystem Services" in *Ecosystems and Human Well-being: Current State and Trends* (Hassan, H., Scholes, R. & Ash, N. [eds.]), Island Press, 2005, pp. 297–329.
16. Aerosol particles in the atmosphere are responsible for around 800,000 premature deaths each year worldwide. The quantity of aerosols is significant enough for them to feature among the "planetary boundaries," but the safety threshold has not yet been determined in sufficiently accurate quantitative terms.
17. Mace, G., *et al.*, "Biodiversity" in *Ecosystems and Human Well-being*, pp. 79–115.
18. According to the "2014 Living Planet Report" issued by the WWF.
19. WWF (October 2004). Bad blood? A survey of chemicals in the blood of European ministers. www.worldwildlife.org/toxics/pubs/badblood.pdf. Cited in Rockström, J., & Klum, M. (2012). *Op. cit.*, p. 209.
20. Rockström, J., Steffen, W., Noone, K., Persson, Chapin, F. S., Lambin, E. F., . . . Schellnhuber, H. J. (2009). A safe operating space for humanity. *Nature*, *461*(7263), 472–475.
21. Diana Liverman, personal conversation at the Mind and Life Institute meeting: "Ecology, Ethics, and Interdependence." Dharamsala, October 2011.

22. According to an evaluation by the Millennium Ecosystem Assessment (MEA), a United Nations initiative.
23. Pavan Sukhdev, in the preface of Wijkman, A., & Rockström, J. (2013). *Op. cit.* Sukhdev is also the founder of Corporation 2020, an organization that promotes environmentally friendly business.
24. According to the World Meteorological Organization, press release No. 1002, September 9, 2014.
25. This global warming, which reflects the general changes in climate over the course of the last century, must not be confused with variable meteorological patterns, which—though sometimes extreme—come about whatever the circumstances in some places. The winter of 2010, for example, was particularly cold in Scandinavia, Russia, and the east coast of the United States, but it was hotter than normal in the rest of the world. In the Arctic and in Canada, temperatures were 4°C above average.
26. Battisti, D. S., & Naylor, R. L. (2009). Historical warnings of future food insecurity with unprecedented seasonal heat. *Science*, *323*(5911), 240–244.
27. Shakhova, N., Semiletov, I., Salyuk, A., Yusupov, V., Kosmach, D., & Gustafsson, Ö. (2010). Extensive methane venting to the atmosphere from sediments of the East Siberian Arctic Shelf. *Science*, *327*(5970), 1246–1250.
28. Cazenave, A., & Llovel, W. (2010). Contemporary sea level rise. *Annual Review of Marine Science*, *2*, 145–173; Nicholls, R., and Leatherman, S. (1995), Global sea-level rise. In Strzepek, K., & Smith, J. (eds.), *As Climate Changes: International Impacts and Implications*, Cambridge University Press, 1996, pp. 92–123; Pfeffer, W. T., Harper, J. T., & O'Neel, S. (2008). Kinematic constraints on glacier contributions to 21st-century sea-level rise. *Science*, *321*(5894), 1340–1343.
29. Care, N. S. (2008). Future generations, public policy, and the motivation problem. *Environmental Ethics*, *4*(3), 195–213.
30. Parfit, D., *Reasons and Persons,* Clarendon Press, 1984.
31. I am grateful to Clare Palmer, professor at the University of Texas, for these clarifications and references. She is the author of several books and coeditor of a five-volume collection on environmental philosophy. Palmer, C., & Baird, Callicott J., *Environmental Philosophy*, Routledge, 2005.
32. Degeorge, R. T. (1981). The environment, rights, and future generations. *Responsibilities to Future Generations*, 157–165.
33. Partridge, E. (1990). On the rights of future generations. In Scherer, D., ed., *Issues in Environmental Ethics*, Temple University Press, 1990.

34. Weiss, E., *In Fairness to Future Generations: International Law, Common Patrimony, and Intergenerational Equity*, Transnational Publication and the United Nations University, 1989.
35. Kurzban, R., & Houser, D. (2005). Experiments investigating cooperative types in humans: A complement to evolutionary theory and simulations. *Proceedings of the National Academy of Sciences of the United States of America, 102*(5), 1803–1807.
36. Steven Forbes, statement during a Fox News debate, October 18, 2009.
37. Wijkman, A., & Rockström, J. (2013). *Op. cit.*, p. 145; Wackernagel, M., & Rees, W. E., *Our Ecological Footprint: Reducing Human Impact on Earth*, vol. 9, New Society Publications, 1996.
38. Pacala, S. Cited in Lambin, É., *Une écologie du bonheur*, Le Pommier, 2009, p. 13.
39. Wijkman, A., & Rockström, J. (2013). *Op. cit.* pp.154–155.
40. *Ibid.*, p. 156.
41. *Ibid.*, p. 22.
42. *Ibid.*, p. 19.
43. Diamond, J., *Collapse: How Societies Choose to Fail or Succeed*, Viking, 2005.
44. Wijkman, A., & Rockström, J. (2013). *Op. cit.*, p. 4.
45. Study carried out by the International Assessment of Agricultural Knowledge, Science and Technology for Development (IAASTD), an organization founded by the United Nations and the World Bank.
46. These five boundaries concern: soil usage, levels of nitrogen and phosphorous released into the biosphere, loss of biodiversity, chemical pollution, and climate change.
47. *Ibid.*, p. 54.
48. Robin, M.-M., *Les Moissons du Futur: Comment l'Agroécologie Peut Nourrir le Monde*, La Découverte, 2012.
49. Caillat, Sophie, "Le grand entretien," Rue 89, *Le Nouvel Observateur*, October 15, 2012.
50. Schneider, S. H., & Lane, J. (2006). Dangers and thresholds in climate change and the implications for justice. *Fairness in adaptation to climate change*, 23–51. In Adger, W. N., Paavola, J., Hug, S., & Mace, M. J., eds., *Fairness in Adaptation to Climate Change*, MIT Press, 2006; Thomas, D. S., & Twyman, C. (2005). Equity and justice in climate change adaptation amongst natural-resource-dependent societies. *Global Environmental Change, 15*(2), 115–124.
51. Patz, J. A., Gibbs, H. K., Foley, J. A., Rogers, J. V., & Smith, K. R. (2007). Climate change and global health: Quantifying a growing ethical crisis. *EcoHealth, 4*(4), 397–405; Myers, S. S., & Patz, J. A. (2009).

Emerging threats to human health from global environmental change. *Annual Review of Environment and Resources*, *34*, 223–252; as well as the IPCC report, 2009, and *Climate Change*, Oxford University Press, 2015, Chapter 10.

52. McMichael, A. J., Levy, B., & Patz, J., *Climate Change and Human Health: Risks and Responses*, WHO, 2003.
53. Patz, J. A., Olson, S. H., Uejio, C. K., & Gibbs, H. K. (2008). Disease emergence from global climate and land use change. *Medical Clinics of North America*, *92*(6), 1473–1491.
54. Checkley, W., Epstein, L. D., Gilman, R. H., Figueroa, D., Cama, R. I., Patz, J. A., & Black, R. E. (2000). Effects of EI Niño and ambient temperature on hospital admissions for diarrhoeal diseases in Peruvian children. *Lancet*, *355*(9202), 442–450.
55. Vittor, A. Y., Gilman, R. H., Tielsch, J., Glass, G., Shields, T. I. M., Lozano, W. S., . . . Patz, J. A. (2006). The effect of deforestation on the human-biting rate of Anopheles darlingi, the primary vector of falciparum malaria in the Peruvian Amazon. *American Journal of Tropical Medicine and Hygiene*, *74*(1), 3–1.
56. Guerra, C. A., Snow, R. W., & Hay, S. I. (2006). A global assessment of closed forests, deforestation and malaria risk. *Annals of Tropical Medicine and Parasitology*, *100*(3), 189; Cohuet, A., Simard, F., Wondji, C. S., Antonio-Nkondjio, C., Awono-Ambene, P., & Fontenille, D. (2004). High malaria transmission intensity due to *Anopheles funestus* (Diptera: Culicidae) in a village of savannah-forest transition area in Cameroon. *Journal of Medical Entomology*, *41*(5), 901–905; Coluzzi, M. (1994). Malaria and the Afrotropical ecosystems: Impact of man-made environmental changes. *Parassitologia*, *36*(1–2), 223.
57. Sachs, J., & Malaney, P. (2002). The economic and social burden of malaria. *Nature*, *415*(6872), 680–685.
58. Ray Chambers, via personal communication.
59. Statement by Yann Arthus Bertrand in his movie *Home*. http://www.homethemovie.org/
60. WBGU (2011), A vision for a renewable energy future by 2050.
61. According to a report by the International Energy Agency, in 2010, 37 governments spent $409 billion in subsidies to keep fossil fuel energy prices below the cost price. IEA (International Energy Agency), *Energy Technology Perspectives*, annual report. Cited in Wijkman, A., & Rockström, J. (2013). *Op. cit.*, p. 78.
62. See in particular the following reports McKinsey CO_2 Abatement: Exploring Options for Oil and Natural Gas Companies; Carbon &

Energy Economics; Roads Toward a Low-Carbon Future; www.mckinsey.com.

63. European Wind Energy Association, or EWEA: Factsheets, 2010. Cited in Rifkin, J. (2012), *Op. cit.*, p. 63.
64. According to estimates by Joseph Stiglitz and Linda Bilmes. The true cost of the Iraq war. *Washington Post*, September 5, 2010.
65. TEEB, Sukhdev, 2008. Cited by Wijkman, A., & Rockström, J. (2013). *Op. cit.*, p. 290.
66. Wijkman, A., & Rockström, J. (2013). *Op. cit.*, p. 60.
67. Including Fredrick Robelius, a member of the Swedish team headed up by Kjell Aleklett (Global Energy System in Uppsala), who looked into the world's entire oil reserves; the APSO (Association for the Study of Peak Oil and Gas), also presided over by Professor Aleklett; the German Central Bank and Merrill Lynch & Co.; the "Sustainable Energy and Security" report published by the insurance market Lloyd's; "The Oil Crunch," a report written by several business heads assembled by Richard Branson; and the UK Industry Task Force on Peak Oil and Energy Security. All cited in Wigkman, A., & Rockström, J., *Bankrupting Nature: Denying Our Planetary Boundaries*, Routledge, 2013, p. 69.
68. Rockström, J., & Klum, M. (2012). *The Human Quest. Op. cit.*, p. 281.
69. WBGU (2012), "World in Transition—A Social Contract for Sustainability, Flagship Report 2011. German Advisory Council on Climate Change.
70. Kurokawa, K., Komoto, K., Van Der Vleuten, P., & Faiman, D., *Energy from the Desert: Practical Proposals for Very Large Scale Photovoltaic Systems*, Earthscan London.
71. Wijkman, A., & Rockström, J. (2013). *Op. cit.*, p. 74.
72. *Ibid.*, p. 65.
73. Rockström, J., & Klum, M. (2012). *Op. cit.*, pp. 286–287.
74. Including reports from the IAASD, the UN Water Development Report, "Water in a Changing World" (2010); the GGIAR Comprehensive Assessment (CA 2007), cited by Wijkman, A., & Rockström, J. (2013). *Op. cit.*, p. 55; WWAP, United Nations (2009). "Water in a Changing World" (vol. 3). United Nations Educational; Jackson, R. B., Carpenter, S. R., Dahm, C. N., McKnight, D. M., Naiman, R. J., Postel, S. L., & Running, S. W. (2001). Water in a changing world. *Ecological applications*, *11*(4), 1027–1045.
75. Rockström, J., & Falkenmark, M. (2000). "Semiarid Crop Production from a Hydrological Perspective" (FAO) 2011. *Save and Grow: A Policymaker's Guide to the Sustainable Intensification of Smallholder Crop Production*, FAO (Rome), 2011, 7369, 337–342.

76. Carson, R., *Silent Spring*, Houghton Mifflin, 1962.
77. Foley, J. A., Ramankutty, N., Brauman, K. A., Cassidy, E. S., Gerber, J. S., Johnston, M.,... West, P. C. (2011). Solutions for a cultivated planet. *Nature, 478*(7369), 337–342.
78. Rabhi, P., *Du Sahara aux Cévennes: Itinéraire d'un homme au service de la Terre-Mère,* Albin Michel, 2002.
79. See Dubesset-Chatelain, L. (February 2003). L'homme qui a réussi à faire reculer le desert. *GEO, 408*, p. 20.
80. There are about twenty species of rice numbering thousands of varieties often classified according to the speed with which they ripen (precocity) and the length of their vegetative cycle (which ranges from ninety to over two hundred and ten days).
81. Carson, R. (1963). *Op. cit.*
82. Darnil, S., & Le Roux, M., *80 Hommes pour changer le monde. Op. cit.*
83. Boys, A. (2000). "Food and Energy in Japan." Interview with Takao Furuno.
84. Furuno, T., *The Power of Duck: Integrated Rice and Duck Farming*, Tagari Publications, 2001. Cited in Darnil, S., & Le Roux, M. (2006). *Op. cit.*
85. UNEP (2011). Report on "Recycling Rates of Metals."
86. Evaluation report by the US Environmental Protection Agency (EPA). Cited in Wijkman, A., & Rockström, J. (2013). *Op. cit.*, p. 164.
87. How long will it last? (2007). *New Scientist*. Cited in Rockström, J., & Klum, M. (2012). *The Human Quest. Op. cit.*, p. 221.
88. Rifkin, J. (2012). *The Third Industrial Revolution. Op. cit.*
89. *Ibid.*, p. 79, 105.
90. Meyfroidt, P., & Lambin, É. (2008). The causes of the reforestation in Vietnam. *Land Use Policy*, *25*(2), 182–197.
91. Ethical Markets 2012. *The Green Transition Scorecard.* Ethical Markets Media.
92. Portland, America's eco-capital. *GEO, 392*, October 2011.
93. Morin, E. (2011). *Op. cit.*, p. 256.
94. See http://www.bbc.co.uk/learningzone/clips/the-beddington-zero-energy-development-a-sustainable-design-solution/6338.html.
95. Sunita Narain. Cited in Wijkman, A., & Rockström, J. (2013). *Op. cit.*
96. Lomborg, B., *The Skeptical Environmentalist: Measuring the Real State of the World*, Cambridge University Press, 2001, pp. 165–172.
97. "Harmony with Nature" report, presented by the Secretary General of the United Nations on August 19, 2010. This aspect of the report is

based on a study contributed by Chivian, Éric (dir.), *Biodiversity: Its Importance to Human Health—Interim Executive Summary*, Center for Health and the Global Environment, Harvard Medical School, 2002.

CHAPTER 42: SUSTAINABLE HARMONY

1. Partha Dasgupta, cited in Wijkman, A., & Rockström, J. (2013), *Op. cit.*, p. 125.
2. Wijkman, A., & Rockström, J. (2013), *Op. cit.*, p. 37.
3. *Ibid.*
4. Stern, N., *The Economics of Climate Change: The Stern Review*, Cambridge University Press, 2007.
5. Daly, H. E., *Beyond Growth: The Economics of Sustainable Development*, Beacon Press, 1997.
6. Jackson, T., *Prosperity Without Growth: Economics for a Finite Planet*, Routledge, 2010.
7. *Ibid.*
8. Speth, J. G., *The Bridge at the Edge of the World: Capitalism, the Environment, and Crossing from Crisis to Sustainability*, Yale University Press, 2009.
9. *Le Monde*, June 9, 2009.
10. Costanza, R., Kubiszewski, I., Giovannini, E., Lovins, H., McGlade, J., Pickett, K. E.,... Wilkinson, R. (2014). Time to leave GDP behind. *Nature*, (505), 283–285.
11. Kuznets, S., "National Income, 1929–1932," 73rd Congress, 2nd session, Senate document no. 124, 1934, p. 7.
12. Kuznets, S. How to judge quality. *New Republic*, October 20, 1962, pp. 29–32.
13. Seligman, M., *Flourish*, Belfond, 2013. Kindle locations 4829–4854; Diener, E., & Seligman, M. E. (2004). Beyond money toward an economy of well-being. *Psychological Science in the Public Interest*, *5*(1), 1–31.
14. Personal communication, Dasho Karma Ura of the Centre for Bhutan Studies & GNH Research, http://www.bhutanstudies.org.bt/. See also the GNH Centre, http://www.gnhbhutan.org/.
15. Kennedy, R. Speech on March 18, 1968, at the University of Kansas. In *The Gospel According to RFK*, Westview Press, p. 41.
16. Including Herman Daly, Robert Costanza, Manfred Max-Neef, and Charles Hall, as well as progressive economists like Joseph Stiglitz, Nicholas Stern, Dennis Snower, Partha Dasgupta, and Amartya Sen.

17. Their studies are summarized in Miringoff, M. L., & Miringoff, M.-L., *The Social Health of the Nation: How America is Really Doing*, Oxford University Press, 1999.
18. Daly, H. E., Cobb, Jr., J. B., & Cobb, C. W., *For the Common Good: Redirecting the Economy toward Community, the Environment, and a Sustainable Future*, Beacon Press, 1994.
19. The Bhutanese do, however, slaughter animals for meat, and only a small number of them are vegetarian. Former kings used to engage in hunting as a form of special privilege, but that practice has now been abandoned.
20. H. E. Lyonchen Jigme Thinley, personal communication.
21. Up to the end of the nineteenth century, Bhutan was a federation of small provinces overseen by a central government. The first king, Ugyen Wangchuck, reigned from 1907 to 1952. Bhutan joined the United Nations in 1971. In 2006, the fourth king, Jigme Sengye Wangchuck, announced his intention to introduce democracy, abdicating in favor of his son, Jigme Khesar Namgyel Wangchuck, who in 2010 became the fifth king at the head of a constitutional monarchy similar to the British monarchy.
22. Cited in Jyoti Thottam. The pursuit of happiness. *Time*, October 22, 2012, p. 49.
23. The discussions can be viewed on the site http://www.gnhc.gov.bt/2012/04/un-webcast-on-happiness-and-wellbeing-high-level-panel-discussion/. My modest contribution occurs at 1:58:30 of Part 1.
24. Among them the Nobel Prize winner Daniel Kahneman, Joseph Stiglitz, and George Akerlof, the economists Jeffrey Sachs and Richard Layard, along with eminent scientists including Richard Davidson, Daniel Gilbert, Martin Seligman, Robert Putnam, John Helliwell, and many others.
25. Wijkman, A., & Rockström, J. (2013). *Op. cit.*, p. 3.
26. H. E. Lyonchen Jigme Thinley, "Bhutan will be the first country with expanded capital accounts." Press conference at the occasion of the release of the first national accounts factoring in natural, social, and human capital, February 10, 2012.
27. Meda, D., *Au-delà du PIB: Pour une autre mesure de la richesse*, Flammarion, 2008, p. 98.
28. Say, J. B., *Traité d'économie politique, ou simple exposition de la manière dont se forment, se distribuent, et se consomment les richesses*, Adamant Media, 2001 (original edition, 1803).
29. Wijkman, A., & Rockström, J. (2013). *Op. cit.*, pp. 132–133.
30. *Ibid.*, p. 3.

31. Article 9, section 2, of the Constitution of the Kingdom of Bhutan reads, "The State shall strive to promote those conditions that will enable the pursuit of Gross National Happiness."
32. Interview with Lyonchen Tshering Topgay by Jo Cofino for the *Guardian*, April 2014.
33. Lambin, É., *Une écologie du bonheur,* Le Pommier, 2009. Éric Lambin shares his time between the Georges-Lemaître Centre for Earth and Climate Research, the Université catholique de Louvain, and the School of Earth Sciences at Stanford University, California.
34. Zidansek, A. (2007). Sustainable development and happiness in nations. *Energy, 32*(6), 891–897. Cited in Lambin, É. (2009). *Op. cit.*, p. 38.
35. Kellert, S. R., & Wilson, E. O., *The Biophilia Hypothesis*, Island Press, 1995.
36. Lambin, É. (2009). *Op. cit.*, p. 51.
37. Ulrich, R. (1984). View through a window may influence recovery. *Science*, *224*, 224–225. Cited in Lambin, É. (2009). *Op. cit.*, p. 52.
38. Rifkin, J. (2012). *The Third Industrial Revolution. Op. cit.*, p. 380.

CHAPTER 43: LOCAL COMMITMENT, GLOBAL RESPONSIBILITY

1. James Freeman Clarke (1810–1888) was an American theologian, a human rights defender, and a social activist.
2. My thanks go to my friend Thierry Lombard, philanthropist and partner of Lombard Odier & Co, for the discussions we have had on this subject.
3. Comte-Sponville, A. (September 10, 2009). *Challenges*, 179, p. 51.
4. Lamy, P. (2005). "Global Governance: Lessons from Europe." Gunnar Myrdal lecture, UN, Geneva.
5. Tubiana, L., Severino, J.-M. (2002). "Biens publics globaux, gouvernance mondiale et aide publique au développement," CAE (Conseil d'Analyse Économique) report on global governance.
6. Collegium International counts, or counted, among its principal members Edgar Morin, Michel Rocard, Mireille Delmas-Marty, Richard von Weizsäcker, Stéphane Hessel, Fernando Henrique Cardoso, Peter Sloterdijk, Patrick Viveret, Ruth Dreifuss, and many others.
7. Deneault, A., *Gouvernance: Le Management totalitaire,* Lux, 2013.
8. Forum on New World Governance; http://www.world-governance.org/spip.php?article144.
9. Jacquet, P., Pisani-Ferry, J., & Tubiana, L. (2003). À la recheche de la gouvernance mondiale. *Revue d'économie financière*, 70, January 2003.

10. Attali, J., *Demain, qui gouvernera le monde?*, Fayard/Pluriel, 2012.
11. Stiglitz, J. E. (2006). "Global public goods and global finance: does global governance ensure that the global public interest is served?" In Touffut, J.-P., *Advancing Public Goods*, Edward Elgar, 2006.
12. *Ibid.*
13. Jacques Attali, interview on 20minutes.fr, November 19, 2006, following the release of *Brève histoire de l'avenir*, Fayard, 2009.
14. See his manifesto *Rebalancing Society* on the site http://www.mintzberg.org.
15. Reverchon, A. Henry Mintzberg contre l'entreprise arrogante, *Le Monde/économie. LeMonde.fr.*, May 21, 2012.
16. Rifkin, J. (2012). *The Third Industrial Revolution. Op cit.*, p. 374.
17. Salamon, L. M. (2010). Putting the civil society sector on the economic map of the world. *Annals of Public and Cooperative Economics, 81*(2), 167–210. Cited in Rifkin, J. (2012). *Op. cit.*, p. 374. The eight countries that were studied most fully were the United States, Canada, France, Japan, Australia, the Czech Republic, Belgium, and New Zealand.
18. Kurzweil, R., *The Singularity Is Near,* M21 éditions, 2005, p. 30.
19. *Ibid.*
20. Rifkin, J. (2012). *Op. cit.*, p. 377.
21. Dalai Lama, *Sagesse ancienne, monde moderne,* Fayard, 1999.
22. Morin, E., & Hessel, S., *Le Chemin de l'espérance*, Fayard, 2011, p. 11.
23. Stiglitz, J. E., *The Price of Inequality*, Norton, 2012.
24. Francis Fukuyama, Acemoglu and Robinson on Why Nations Fail, *The American Interest,* March 26, 2012.
25. Stiglitz, J. (2012). *Op. cit.*, p. 145.
26. Rodrik, D., *The Globalization Paradox: Democracy and the Future of the World Economy,* W. W. Norton, 2011.
27. Morin, E., & Hessel, S. (2011). *Op. cit.*, p. 12.
28. Pascal Lamy, "Towards Global Goverance?" Conference at the Institut d'Études Politiques de Paris, October 21, 2005. Lamy, P., *La Démocratie-monde: Pour une autre gouvernance globale*, Seuil, 2004.
29. Dalai Lama, & Hessel, S., *Déclarons la paix! Pour un progrès de l'esprit*, Indigène Éditions, 2012.
30. *Ibid.*
31. Winston Churchill, in a speech on November 11, 1947 in the House of Commons, London. *The Official Report, House of Commons* (5th series), November 11, 1947, vol. 444, pp. 206–207.
32. Presentation at a workshop by the French NGO Fondation Sciences Citoyennes at the World Social Forum; http://sciencescitoyennes.org/.

33. Berggruen, N., & Gardels, N., *Intelligent Governance for the 21st Century: A Middle Way Between West and East*, Polity, 2012.
34. 21st Century Council, a Berggruen Institute initiative, has a number of distinguished members, including Gordon Brown, Gerhard Schröder, Amartya Sen, Joseph Stiglitz, Francis Fukuyama, and Pascal Lamy.
35. Berggruen, N., & Gardels, N. (2012). *Op. cit.*, pp. 172–3.
36. *Ibid.*, p. 181.
37. *Ibid.*, p. 183.
38. Attali, J., *Demain, qui gouvernera le monde?* Fayard/Pluriel, 2012, pp. 305–6.

Conclusion: Daring Altruism

1. Nowak, M., & Highfield, R. (2011), *SuperCooperators. Op. cit.*, pp. 271–2 and 280.
2. The origin of this famous quote, attributed to Bertrand Russell, has not been traced.
3. Albert Schweitzer, from a speech given at Silcoates School in Great Britain, December 1935.

Sources for Figures

Chapter 12, p. 128.

From the presentation by Daniel Batson at the conference entitled "Altruism and Compassion in Economic Systems: A Dialogue at the Interface of Economics, Neuroscience and Contemplative Sciences," organized in Zurich by Mind & Life Institute in April 2009. Based on Batson, C. D., Duncan, B. D., Ackerman, P., Buckley, T., & Birch, K. (1981). Is empathic emotion a source of altruistic motivation? *Journal of Personality and Social Psychology, 40* (2), 290–302, and Batson, C. D., O'Quint, K., Fultz, J., Vanderplas, M., & Isen, A. M. (1983). Influence of self-reported distress and empathy on egoistic versus altruistic motivation to help. *Journal of Personality and Social Psychology, 45* (3), 706. This graph corresponds to a compilation of data from four experiments.

Chapter 24, p. 427.

From Pinker, S., *The Better Angels of Our Nature: Why Violence Has Declined*, Viking, 2011, p. 63. From data in Eisner, M. (2003). Long-term historical trends in violent crime. *Crime & Just., 30*, 83. Table 1, p. 99.

Chapter 24, p. 428.

From Finkelhor, D., Jones, L., & Shattuck, A. (2008). Updated trends in child maltreatment, 2006. *Crimes Against Children Research Center.*

Chapter 32, p. 433.

From Pinker, S. (2011). *Op. cit.*, p. 149. Based on Hunt, L., *Inventing Human Rights: A History*, W. W. Norton, 2008, pp. 76, 179, and Mannix, D. P., *The History of Torture*, Dell paperback, 1964, pp. 137–38.

Chapter 32, p. 434.

From Brecke, P. (1999). Violent conflicts 1400 AD to the present in different regions of the world. In "1999 Meeting of the Peace Science Society" (unpublished manuscript).

Chapter 32, p. 436.

From Lacina, B., & Gleditsch, N. P. (2005). Monitoring trends in global combat: A new dataset of battle deaths. *European Journal of Population, 21*(2), 145–166.

Chapter 32, p. 436.

From UCDP/PRIO Armed Conflict Dataset, Lacina, B., & Gleditsch, N. P. (2005). Monitoring trends in global combat: A new dataset of battle deaths. *European Journal of Population, 21*(2), 145–166. Adapted from the *Human Security Report Project*; Human Security Centre, 2006. Cited in Pinker, S. (2011). *Op. cit.*, p. 304.

Chapter 32, p. 437.

From Pinker, S. (2011). *Op. cit.*, p. 338 (adapted). Data up to 1987 comes from Rummel (1997), data after 1987 from various sources. Data for the gray line, 1900–1987, from Rummel, 1997. Data for the black line, 1955–2008, from the Political Instability Task Force (PITF) State Failure Problem Set, 1955–2008, Marshall, Gurr, & Harff, 2009; Center for Systemic Peace, 2010. The death tolls for the latter were geometric means of the ranges in table 8.1 in Harff, 2005, distributed across years according to the proportions in the Excel database. World population figures from U.S. Census Bureau, 2010c. Population figures for the years 1900–1949 were taken from McEvedy & Jones, 1978, and multiplied by 1.01 to make them commensurable with the rest.

Chapter 32, p. 442.

From Pinker, S. (2011). *Op. cit.*, p. 294, based on data from Cederman, L.-E., & Rao, M. P. (2001). Exploring the dynamics of the democratic peace. *Journal of Conflict Resolution,* 45(6), 818–833.

Chapter 32, p. 444.

From Gleditsch, N. P. (2008). The liberal moment fifteen years on. *International Studies Quarterly, 52*(4), 691–712. Based on research from Siri Rustad. Cited in Pinker, S. (2011). *Op. cit.*, p. 314.

Chapter 36, p. 525.

From Fehr, Gächter, S. (2000). Cooperation and punishment in public good experiments, *American Economic Review*, *90*(4), p. 989.

Chapter 38, p. 557.

From Gasparini, L. & Lustig, N. (2011). "The Rise and Fall of Income Inequality in Latin America." CEDLAS, Working Paper 0118, Universidad Nacional de La Plata.

Chapter 40, p. 611.

From Myers, D. G. (2000). The funds, friends, and faith of happy people. *American Psychologist*, *55*(1), 56.

Chapter 41, p. 617.

Stockholm Resilience Center, based on data from the GRIP (European Greenland Ice Core Project), and on Oppenheimer, S., *Out of Eden: The Peopling of the World*, Constable & Robinson, 2004.

Chapter 41, pp. 619–622.

Same source applies to all 9 graphs
From Steffen, W., Sanderson, A., Tyson, P. D., Jäger, J., Matson, P. A., Moore III, B., Oldfield, F., Richardson, K., Schellnhuber, H.-J., Turner, II, BL, & Wasson, R. J. (2004) *Global Change and the Earth System: A Planet Under Pressure.* The IGBP Book Series, Springer-Verlag, Berlin, Heidelberg, New York. This article also contains the scientific references on which each of these diagrams is founded. Adapted and kindly supplied by Diana Liverman.

Chapter 41, pp. 625–626.

Same source applies to all 3 graphs
Stockholm Resilience Center, from Rockström, J., Steffen, W., Noone, K., Persson, ÄAA, Chapin, F. S., Lambin, E. F., Schellnhuber, H. J. (2009). A safe operating space for humanity. *Nature*, 461 (7263), 472–475.

Chapter 41, p. 628.

From NASA Goddard Institute for Space Studies. NASA Earth Observatory / Robert Simmon.

Chapter 41, p. 629.

From Guinehut, S., and G. Larnicol (2008); CLS/Cnes/Legos. NASA Global Change Master Directory http://gcmd.nasa.gov/records/GCMD_CLS-LEGOS-CNES_MeanSeaLevel1992-2008.html.

Chapter 41, pp. 637 and 639.

Diagrams kindly supplied by Jonathan Patz.

Select Bibliography

André, C. (2012). *Feelings and Moods*. Polity.

Arendt, H. (2006). *Eichmann in Jerusalem: A Report on the Banality of Evil*. Penguin.

Aronson, E., & Patnoe, S. (2011). *Cooperation in the Classroom: The Jigsaw Method*. Pinter & Martin.

Axelrod, R., & Dawkins, R. (2006). *The Evolution of Cooperation* (rev. ed.). Basic Books.

Babiak, P., & Hare, R. D. (2007). *Snakes in Suits: When Psychopaths Go to Work*. HarperBusiness.

Barber, N. (2000). *Why Parents Matter: Parental Investment and Child Outcomes*. Praeger.

Batson, C. D. (1991). *The Altruism Question: Toward a Social Psychological Answer*. Lawrence Erlbaum.

Batson, C. D. (2011). *Altruism in Humans*. Oxford University Press.

Baumeister, R. F. (2001). *Evil: Inside Human Cruelty and Violence*. Barnes & Noble.

Baumeister, R. F. (2005). *The Cultural Animal: Human Nature, Meaning, and Social Life*. Oxford University Press.

Beck, A. T. (1979). *Cognitive Therapy and the Emotional Disorders*. Plume.

Beck, A. T. (2000). *Prisoners of Hate: The Cognitive Basis of Anger, Hostility, and Violence*. Perennial.

Beck, J. S., & Beck, A. T. (2011). *Cognitive Behavior Therapy: Basics and Beyond* (2d ed.). Guilford Press.

Begley, S. (2007). *Train Your Mind, Change Your Brain: How a New Science Reveals Our Extraordinary Potential to Transform Ourselves*. Ballantine Books.

Bekoff, M., & Goodall, J. (2008). *The Emotional Lives of Animals: A Leading Scientist Explores Animal Joy, Sorrow, and Empathy—and Why They Matter.* New World Library.

Berggruen, N., & Gardels, N. (2012). *Intelligent Governance for the 21st Century: A Middle Way Between West and East*. Polity Press.

Bierhoff, H. W. (2002). *Prosocial Behaviour.* Psychology Press.

Borch-Jacobsen, M., & Shamdasani, S. (2012). *The Freud Files: An Inquiry into the History of Psychoanalysis.* Cambridge University Press.

Borgstrom, G. (1973). *Harvesting the Earth.* Abelard-Schuman.

Bourke, A. F. G. (2011). *Principles of Social Evolution*. Oxford University Press.

Bowles, S., & Gintis, H. (2011). *A Cooperative Species: Human Reciprocity and Its Evolution*. Princeton University Press.

Carey, N. (2011). *The Epigenetics Revolution*. Icon Books.

Carson, R. (1963). *Printemps silencieux*. Plon.

Chang, J., & Halliday, J. (2007). *Mao: The Unknown Story.* Vintage.

Coe, S. (1996). *Dead Meat.* Four Walls Eight Windows.

Comte, A. (1988). *Introduction to Positive Philosophy.* (F. Ferré, trans.). Hackett.

Comte-Spoonville, A. (2002). *A Small Treatise on the Great Virtues: The Uses of Philosophy in Everyday Life* (reprint ed.). Picador.

Costanza, R., Cumberland, J. H., Daly, H., Goodland, R., Norgaard, R. B., Kubiszewski, I., & Franco, C. (2014). *An Introduction to Ecological Economics* (2d ed.). CRC Press.

Crocker, J., Moeller, S., & Burson, A. (2013). "The Costly Pursuit of Self-Esteem." In *Handbook of Personality and Self-Regulation*, Wiley-Blackwell, pp. 403–429.

Cyrulnik, B. (2011). *Resilience: How Your Inner Strength Can Set You Free from the Past* (orig. ed.). Tarcher.

Dalai Lama, (2000). *Ancient Wisdom: Ethics for the New Millennium*. Abacus.

Dalai Lama (2012). *365 Daily Advice from the Heart*. Hampton Roads.

Dalai Lama & Vreeland, N. (2002). *An Open Heart: Practicing Compassion in Everyday Life* (reprint ed.). Back Bay Books.

Dalai Lama, & Cutler, H. C. (1999). *The Art of Happiness: A Handbook for Living*. Hodder.

Daly, H. E. (1997). *Beyond Growth: The Economics of Sustainable Development*. Beacon Press.

Daly, H. E., Cobb, Jr., J. B., & Cobb, C. W. (1994). *For the Common Good: Redirecting the Economy toward Community, the Environment, and a Sustainable Future*. Beacon Press.

Darwin, C. (2013). *The Descent of Man and Selection in Relation to Sex—Primary Source Edition*. Nabu Press.

Darwin, C., Ekman, P., & Prodger, P. (2002). *The Expression of the Emotions in Man and Animals*. Oxford University Press.

Davidson, R. J., & Begley, S. (2012). *The Emotional Life of Your Brain: How Its Unique Patterns Affect the Way You Think, Feel, and Live and How You Can Change Them*. Hudson Street Press.

Davidson, R. J., & Harrington, A. (2002). *Visions of Compassion: Western Scientists and Tibetan Buddhists Examine Human Nature*. Oxford University Press.

Dawkins, R. (1989). *The Selfish Gene*. Oxford Universtiy Press.

Decety, J. (2009). *The Social Neuroscience of Empathy*. MIT Press.

Desmurget, M. (2012). *TV Lobotomie: La vérité scientifique sur les effets de la télévision*. Max Milo Éditions.

Diamond, J. (2011). *Collapse: How Societies Choose to Fail or Succeed* (rev. ed.). Penguin Books.

Dovidio, J. F., Piliavin, J. A., Schroeder, D. A., & Penner, L. A. (2006). *The Social Psychology of Prosocial Behavior*. Psychology Press.

Doyle, J. (1985). *Altered Harvest: Agriculture, Genetics and the Fate of the World's Food Supply*. Viking.

Dugatkin, L.A. (1997). *Cooperation Among Animals*. Oxford University Press.

Eibl-Eibesfeldt, I. (1973). *Love and Hate: On the Natural History of Basic Behaviour Patterns*. AldineTransaction.

Eibl-Eibesfeldt, I. (1979). *The Biology of Peace and War: Men, Animals and Aggression*. Viking.

Eisenberg, N. (1992). *The Caring Child*. Harvard University Press.

Eisenberg, N., & Damon, W. (1998). *Handbook of Child Psychology*. John Wiley & Sons.

Eisnitz, G. A. (1997). *Slaughterhouse: The Shocking Story of Greed, Neglect, and Inhumane Treatment Inside the U.S. Meat Industry*. Prometheus.

Ekman, P. (2007). *Emotions Revealed: Recognizing Faces and Feelings to Improve Communication and Emotional Life*. Holt.

Ekman, P. (2014). *Moving Toward Global Compassion*. Paul Ekman Group.

Ekman, P. E., & Davidson, R. J. (1994). *The Nature of Emotion: Fundamental Questions*. Oxford University Press.

Elgin, D. (2010). *Voluntary Simplicity: Toward a Way of Life That Is Outwardly Simple, Inwardly Rich*. William Morrow.

Farrer, F. (2005). *A Quiet Revolution: Encouraging Positive Values in Our Children*. Rider.

Fehr, B. A., Sprecher, S., Underwood, L. G., & Gordon, L. U. (2008). *The Science of Compassionate Love: Theory, Research, and Applications.* Blackwell.

Festinger, L. (1957). *A Theory of Cognitive Dissonance.* Stanford University Press.

Filippi, C.-H. (2009). *L'Argent sans maître.* Descartes.

Foer, J. S. (2010). *Eating Animals.* Back Bay Books.

Fontenay, E. de. (2012). *Without Offending Humans: A Critique of Animal Rights.* (W. Bishop, trans.) University of Minnesota Press.

Fredrickson, B. (2001). *Positivity: Groundbreaking Research Reveals How to Embrace the Hidden Strength of Positive Emotions, Overcome Negativity, and Thrive.* Crown Archetype.

Fredrickson, B. (2013). *Love 2.0: How Our Supreme Emotion Affects Everything We Feel, Think, Do, and Become.* Hudson Street Press.

Fromm, E. (1947). *Man for Himself: An Inquiry into the Psychology of Ethics.*

Fry, D. P. (2007). *Beyond War: The Human Potential for Peace.* Oxford University Press.

Galbraith, J. K. (2008). *The Predator State: How Conservatives Abandoned the Free Market and Why Liberals Should Too.* The Free Press.

Gandhi, M. K. (1980). *All Men Are Brothers.* Continuum.

Gerhardt, S. (2004). *Why Love Matters: How Affection Shapes a Baby's Brain.* Brunner-Routledge.

Germer, C. K. (2009). *The Mindful Path to Self-Compassion: Freeing Yourself from Destructive Thoughts and Emotions.* Guilford Press.

Gilbert, P. (1989). *Human Nature and Suffering.* Lawrence Erlbaum.

Gilbert, P. (2005). *Compassion: Conceptualisations, Research and Use in Psychotherapy.* Psychology Press.

Gilbert, P. (2009). *Violence et compassion: Essai sur l'authenticité d'être.* Cerf.

Gilbert, P. (2010). *The Compassionate Mind: A New Approach to Life's Challenges.* New Harbinger.

Gilbert, P. (2014). *Mindful Compassion: How the Science of Compassion Can Help You Understand Your Emotions, Live in the Present, and Connect Deeply with Others.* New Harbinger.

Goldacre, B. (2012). *Bad Pharma: How Drug Companies Mislead Doctors and Harm Patients.* Fourth Estate.

Goleman, D. (2000). *Working with Emotional Intelligence.* Bantam.

Goleman, D. (2005). *Emotional Intelligence: Why It Can Matter More Than IQ* (10th anniversary ed.). Bantam Books.

Goleman, D. (2007). *Social Intelligence: The New Science of Human Relationships.* Bantam.

Goleman, D. (2009). *Ecological Intelligence: How Knowing the Hidden Impacts of What We Buy Can Change Everything.* Crown Business.

Goodall, J. (1986). *The Chimpanzees of Gombe: Patterns of Behavior.* Harvard University Press.

Goodall, J. (2011). *Through a Window: Thirty Years with the Chimpanzees of Gombe.* Phoenix.

Goodall, J., & Bekoff, M. (2013). *The Ten Trusts: What We Must Do to Care for the Animals We Love.* HarperOne.

Goodall, J., & Berman, P. L. (1999). *Reason for Hope: A Spiritual Journey.* Grand Central.

Gordon, M. (2005). *Roots of Empathy: Changing the World Child by Child.* Thomas Allen.

Graham, C. (2012). *Happiness Around the World: The Paradox of Happy Peasants and Miserable Millionaires.* Oxford University Press.

Greenland, S. K. (2010). *The Mindful Child: How to Help Your Kid Manage Stress and Become Happier, Kinder, and More Compassionate.* The Free Press.

Grossman, D. (2009). *On Killing: The Psychological Cost of Learning to Kill in War and Society.* Back Bay Books.

Gunaratana, B. H. (2001). *Eight Mindful Steps to Happiness: Walking the Path of the Buddha.* Wisdom Publications.

Gunaratana, B. H. (2011). *Mindfulness in Plain English* (20th anniversary ed.). Wisdom Publications.

Haidt, J. (2012). *The Righteous Mind: Why Good People Are Divided by Politics and Religion.* Allen Lane.

Hallie, P. P. (1994). *Lest Innocent Blood Be Shed* (reprint ed.). Harper Perennial.

Hare, R. D. (1999). *Without Conscience: The Disturbing World of the Psychopaths Among Us.* Guilford Press.

Harman, O. S. (2010). *The Price of Altruism.* Norton.

Hatzfeld, J. (2006). *Machete Season: The Killers in Rwanda Speak.* Macmillan.

Hatzfeld, J. (2007). *Life Laid Bare: The Survivors in Rwanda Speak.* Other Press.

Hawkes, N. (2013). *From My Heart: Transforming lives Through values.* Independent Thinking Press.

Hawkes, N., Redsell, C., & Barnes, R. (2003). *How to Inspire and Develop Positive Values in Your Classroom.* Wisbech: LDA.

Henrich, J., & Henrich, N. (2007). *Why Humans Cooperate: A Cultural and Evolutionary Explanation*. Oxford University Press.

Herbert, M., & Weintraub, K. (2013). *The Autism Revolution: Whole-Body Strategies for Making Life All It Can Be*. Ballantine Books.

Hessel, S., & Morin, E. (2012). *The Path to Hope*. Other Press.

Hillesum, E., & Hoffman, E. (1996). *Etty Hillesum: An Interrupted Life: The Diaries, 1941–1943,* and *Letters from Westerbork*. Picador.

Hobbes, T. (2002). *Leviathan*. Public Domain Books.

Hoffman, M. L. (2001). *Empathy and Moral Development: Implications for Caring and Justice*. Cambridge University Press.

Hoggan, J. (2009). *Climate Cover-Up: The Crusade to Deny Global Warming*. Greystone.

Hrdy, S. B. (2009). *Mothers and Others: The Evolutionary Origins of Mutual Understanding*. Belknap Press.

Hume, D., & Beauchamp, T. L. (1998). *An Enquiry Concerning the Principles of Morals: A Critical Edition* (vol. 4). Oxford University Press.

Hutcheson, F., & Garrett, A. (2003). *An Essay on the Nature and Conduct of the Passions and Affections, with Illustrations on the Moral Sense.* (K. Haakonssen, ed.). Liberty Fund.

Jablonka, E., & Lamb, M. J. (2005). *Evolution in Four Dimensions: Genetic, Epigenetic, Behavioral, and Symbolic Variation in the History of Life*. MIT Press.

Jackson, T. (2012). *Prosperity Without Growth: Economics for a Finite Planet*. Routledge.

James, W. (1981). *The Principles of Psychology, vols. 1–2* (annotated ed.). Harvard University Press.

Johnson, D. H., & Johnson, R. T. (1998). *Learning Together and Alone: Cooperative, Competitive, and Individualistic Learning*. Pearson.

Johnson, D. W., Johnson, R. T., & Holubec, E. J. (1991). *Cooperation in the Classroom*. Interaction Book Company.

Kabat-Zinn, J. (1998). *Everyday Blessings: The Inner Work of Mindful Parenting* (reprint ed.). Hyperion.

Kabat-Zinn, J. (2013). *Full Catastrophe Living: Using the Wisdom of Your Body and Mind to Face Stress, Pain, and Illness*. Bantan.

Kahneman, D. (2013). *Thinking, Fast and Slow* (reprint ed.). Farrar, Straus & Giroux.

Kahneman, D., Slovic, P., & Tversky, A. (1982). *Judgment Under Uncertainty: Heuristics and Biases*. Cambridge University Press.

Kappeler, P. M., & Van Schaik, C. (2006). *Cooperation in Primates and Humans: Mechanisms and Evolution*. Springer Verlag.

Kasser, T. (2003). *The High Price of Materialism*. MIT Press.

Kasser, T. (2008). "Can Buddhism and Consumerism Harmonize? A Review of the Psychological Evidence." In International Conference on Buddhism in the Age of Consumerism, Mahidol University, Bangkok (pp. 1–3).

Kellert, S. R., & Wilson, E. O. (1995). *The Biophilia Hypothesis*. Island Press.

Keltner, D. (2009). *Born to Be Good: The Science of a Meaningful Life*. W. W. Norton.

Kempf, H. (2013). *L'oligarchie ça suffit, vive la démocratie*. Seuil.

Khyentse, D. (2006). *Enlightened Courage: An Explanation of the Seven-Point Mind Training*. (P. T. Group, trans.). Snow Lion.

Khyentse, D. (2013). *The Heart of Compassion: The Thirty-Seven Verses on the Practice of a Bodhisattva*.

Kohn, A. (1992). *The Brighter Side of Human Nature: Altruism and Empathy in Everyday Life*. Basic Books.

Kolm, S.-C. (2009). *Reciprocity: An Economics of Social Relations*. Cambridge University Press.

Kolm, S.-C., & Ythier, J. M. (2006). *Handbook of the Economics of Giving, Altruism and Reciprocity: Foundations*. North Holland.

Kropotkin, P., & Kropotkin, P. A. (1989). *Mutual Aid: A Factor of Evolution*. Black Rose Books.

Krznaric, R. (2014). *Empathy, A Handbook for Revolution*. Riders Books.

Lambin, E. (2012). *An Ecology of Happiness*. University of Chicago Press.

Lappe, F. M. (1985). *Diet for a Small Planet* (20th Anniversary ed.). Ballantine Books.

Layard, R. (2011). *Happiness: Lessons from a New Science* (2d rev. ed.). Penguin.

Layard, R., & Dunn, J. (2009). *A Good Childhood: Searching for Values in a Competitive Age*. Penguin.

Leary, M. R. (2007). *The Curse of the Self: Self-Awareness, Egotism, and the Quality of Human Life*. Oxford University Press.

Levi, P. (1995). *Survival in Auschwitz* (reprint ed.). Touchstone.

Levi, P., & Bailey, P. (1991). *If This Is a Man* and *The Truce*. (S. Woolf, trans.). Little, Brown.

Lilly, J. C. (1962). *Man and Dolphin*. Gollancz.

Lorenz, K. (2005). *On Aggression*. Routledge.

Louv, R. (2008). *Last Child in the Woods: Saving Our Children from Nature-Deficit Disorder*. Algonquin Books.

Mandela, N. (1995). *Long Walk to Freedom: The Autobiography of Nelson Mandela*. Back Bay Books.

Margulies, A. (1989). *The Empathic Imagination*. W. W. Norton.

Maslach, C. (1982). *Burnout: The Cost of Caring*. Prentice Hall.

Masson, J. M., & McCarthy, S. (1996). *When Elephants Weep: The Emotional Lives of Animals*. Random House Digital.

Mauss, M. (2000). *The Gift: The Form and Reason for Exchange in Archaic Societies*. (W. D. Halls, trans.). W. W. Norton.

McCord, J., & Tremblay, R. E. (eds.). (1992). *Preventing Antisocial Behavior: Interventions from Birth Through Adolescence*. Guilford Press.

McDougall, W. (1908). *An Introduction to Social Psychology*. Methuen.

Miller, A. G. (2005). *The Social Psychology of Good and Evil*. Guilford Press.

Milo, R. D. (1973). *Egoism and Altruism*. Wadsworth.

Monroe, K. R. (1996). *The Heart of Altruism: Perceptions of a Common Humanity*. Princeton University Press.

Monroe, K. R. (2006). *The Hand of Compassion: Portraits of Moral Choice During the Holocaust*. Princeton University Press.

Mooney, C. (2006). *The Republican War on Science*. Basic Books.

Moore-Lappé, F. (1971). *Diet for a Small Planet*. Ballantine.

Morin, E., & Hessel, S. (2011). *The Path to Hope*. Other Press (A. Shugaar, trans.).

Moss, C. (1988). *Elephant Memories: Thirteen Years in the Life of an Elephant Family*. William Morrow.

Nagel, T. (1970/1979). *Possibility of Altruism*. Princeton University Press.

Neff, K. (2011). *Self-Compassion: Stop Beating Yourself Up and Leave Insecurity Behind*. William Morrow.

Nowak, M. A., & Highfield, R. (2011). *SuperCooperators: Altruism, Evolution, and Why We Need Each Other to Succeed*. Simon & Schuster.

O'Clery, C. (2013). *The Billionaire Who Wasn't: How Chuck Feeney Secretly Made and Gave Away a Fortune*. PublicAffairs.

Oliner, S. P. (2003). *Do unto Others: Extraordinary Acts of Ordinary People*. Basic Books.

Oliner, S. P., & Oliner, P. M. (1988). *The Altruistic Personality: Rescuers of Jews in Nazi Europe*. Macmillan.

Opdyke, I. G. (1999). *In My Hands: Memories of a Holocaust Rescuer*. Anchor.

Oreskes, N., & Conway, E. M. M. (2011). *Merchants of Doubt: How a Handful of Scientists Obscured the Truth on Issues from Tobacco Smoke to Global Warming*. Bloomsbury.

Ostrom E. (2010). *Gouvernance des biens communs: Pour une nouvelle approche des ressources naturelles*. De Boeck.

Patterson, C. (2002). *Eternal Treblinka: Our Treatment of Animals and the Holocaust*. Lantern Books.

Perry, A. (2011). *Lifeblood: How to Change the World One Dead Mosquito at a Time*. PublicAffairs.

Piliavin, J. A., Dovidio, J. F., Gaertner, S. L., & Clark III, R. D. (1981). *Emergency Intervention*. Academic Press.

Pinker, S. (2011). *The Better Angels of Our Nature: Why Violence Has Declined*. Viking.

Pooley, E. (2010). *The Climate War: True Believers, Power Brokers, and the Fight to Save the Earth*. Hyperion.

Post, S. G. (2003). *Unlimited Love: Altruism, Compassion, and Service*. Templeton Foundation Press.

Post, S. G. (2011). *The Hidden Gifts of Helping: How the Power of Giving, Compassion, and Hope Can Get Us Through Hard Times*. John Wiley.

Post, S., & Neimark, J. (2007). *Why Good Things Happen to Good People: The Exciting New Research That Proves the Link Between Doing Good and Living a Longer, Healthier, Happier Life*. Broadway Books.

Rabhi, P., & Menuhin, Y. (2006). *As in the Heart, So in the Earth: Reversing the Desertification of the Soul and the Soil*. Park Street Press.

Rand, A. (1964). *The Virtue of Selfishness*. Signet.

Rand, A. (1997). *Atlas Shrugged*. Signet.

Remarque, E. M. (1982). *All Quiet on the Western Front*. Ballantine.

Ricard, M. (2007). *Happiness: A Guide to Developing Life's Most Important Skill* (reprint). Little, Brown.

Ricard, M. (2010). *Why Meditate?* Hay House.

Richardson, K., Steffen, W., & Liverman, D. (2011). *Climate Change: Global Risks, Challenges and Decisions*. Cambridge University Press.

Richerson, P. J., & Boyd, R. (2004). *Not by Genes Alone: How Culture Transformed Human Evolution*. University of Chicago Press.

Rifkin, J. (1992). *Beyond Beef: The Rise and Fall of the Cattle Culture*. Penguin.

Rifkin, J. (2009). *The Empathic Civilization: The Race to Global Consciousness in a World in Crisis*. Tarcher.

Rifkin, J. (2009). *The Empathic Civilization: The Race to Global Consciousness in a World in Crisis*. Tarcher.

Rifkin, J. (2013). *The Third Industrial Revolution: How Lateral Power Is Transforming Energy, the Economy, and the World*. Palgrave Macmillan.

Rifkin, J. (2014). *The Zero Marginal Cost Society: The Internet of Things, the Collaborative Commons, and the Eclipse of Capitalism*. Palgrave Macmillan.

Robin, M.-M. (2010). *The World According to Monsanto: Pollution, Corruption, and the Control of the World's Food Supply*. New Press.

Rochefoucauld, F. de L., & Brotier, A. C. (2012). *Reflexions ou sentences et maximes morales...* Nabu Press.

Rockström, J., & Klum, M. (2012). *The Human Quest: Prospering Within Planetary Boundaries.* Bokförlaget Langenskiöld.

Rodrik, D. (2011). *The Globalization Paradox: Democracy and the Future of the World Economy.* W. W. Norton.

Rollin, B. E. (1989). *The Unheeded Cry: Animal Consciousness, Animal Pain and Science.* Oxford University Press.

Russett, B. M., & Oneal, J. R. (2001). *Triangulating Peace: Democracy, Interdependence, and International Organizations* (vol. 9). Norton.

Salzberg, S. (2002). *Lovingkindness: The Revolutionary Art of Happiness* (revised ed.). Shambhala.

Sandel, M. (2012). *What Money Can't Buy: The Moral Limits of Markets.* Allen Lane.

Scheler, M. (1954/2008). *The Nature of Sympathy.* Transaction.

Schumacher, E. F. (1979). *Small Is Beautiful.* Seuil.

Seligman, M. E. P. (2002). *Authentic Happiness: Using the New Positive Psychology to Realize Your Potential for Lasting Fulfillment.* The Free Press.

Seligman, M. E. P. (2012). *Flourish: A Visionary New Understanding of Happiness and Well-Being* (reprint ed.). Atria Books.

Sémelin, J. (2007). *Purify and Destroy: The Political Uses of Massacre and Genocide.* Columbia University Press.

Sen, A. (1991). *On Ethics and Economics* (reprint ed.). Wiley-Blackwell.

Sen, A. (1995). *Inequality Reexamined* (reprint ed.). Harvard University Press.

Sen, A. (2010). *The Idea of Justice.* Penguin.

Sereny, G. (1983). *Into That Darkness: An Examination of Conscience.* Vintage Books.

Shantideva. (2006). *The Way of the Bodhisattva* (P. T. Group, trans.) (rev. ed.). Shambhala.

Sherif, M. (1961). *The Robbers Cave Experiment: Intergroup Conflict and Cooperation.* Wesleyan.

Shirer, W. L. (1990). *Le III[e] Reich.* Stock.

Shiva, V., Kunwar, J., Navdanya (2006). *Seeds of Suicide: The Ecological and Human Costs of Seed Monopolies and Globalisation of Agriculture.* Navdanya.

Sinclair, U. (1964). *The Jungle.* Signet.

Singer, P. (2009). *Animal Liberation: The Definitive Classic of the Animal Movement.* Harper Perennial.

Singer, T., & Bolz, M. (eds.) (2013). *Compassion: Bridging Practice and Science.* A multimedia book [e-book].

Singer, T., Ricard, M., (eds.) (2015). *Caring Economics: Conversations on Altruism and Compassion, Between Scientists, Economists, and the Dalai Lama.* Picador.

Slavin, R. E., Hurley, E. A., & Chamberlain, A. (2003). *Cooperative Learning and Achievement: Theory and Research.* Wiley Online Library.

Smith, A. (2002). *Adam Smith: The Theory of Moral Sentiments.* Cambridge University Press.

Smith, A., & Krueger, A. B. (2003). *The Wealth of Nations.* Bantam.

Snel, E., Kabat-Zinn, M., & Kabat-Zinn, J. (2013). *Sitting Still Like a Frog: Mindfulness Exercises for Kids.* Shambhala.

Snyder, C. R., & Lopez, S. J. (2002). *Handbook of Positive Psychology.* Oxford University Press.

Sober, E., & Wilson, D. S. (1999). *Unto Others: The Evolution and Psychology of Unselfish Behavior.* Harvard University Press.

Speth, J. G. (2009). *The Bridge at the Edge of the World: Capitalism, the Environment, and Crossing from Crisis to Sustainability.* Yale University Press.

Staub, E. (1992). *The Roots of Evil: The Origins of Genocide and Other Group Violence.* Cambridge University Press.

Stein, E. (1917/1989). *On the Problem of Empathy.* ICS Publications.

Stern, N. (2007). *The Economics of Climate Change: The Stern Review.* Cambridge University Press.

Stiglitz, J. E. (2003). *Globalization and Its Discontents.* W. W. Norton.

Stiglitz, J. E. (2012). *The Price of Inequality: How Today's Divided Society Endangers Our Future.* W. W. Norton.

Strum, S. C. (2001). *Almost Human: A Journey into the World of Baboons.* University of Chicago Press.

Swofford, A. (2004). *Jarhead: A Soldier's Story of Modern War.* Scribner.

Tajfel, H. (1981). *Human Groups and Social Categories: Studies in Social Psychology.* Cambridge University Press.

Taylor, C. (1989). *Sources of the Self: The Making of the Modern Identity.* Harvard University Press.

Terestchenko, M. (2007). *Un si fragile vernis d'humanité: Banalité du mal, banalité du bien.* Découverte.

Thomas, E. M. (1990). *The Harmless People.* Vintage.

Tillion, G. (1997). *Ravensbrück.* Seuil.

Todorov, T. (1996). *Facing the Extreme: Moral Life in the Concentration camps.* Metropolitan Books.

Tomasello, M. (2009). *Why We Cooperate*. MIT Press.

Tremblay, R. E., Aken, M. A. G. van, & Koops, W. (2009). *Development and Prevention of Behaviour Problems: From Genes to Social Policy*. Psychology Press.

Trivers, R. L. (1985). *Social Evolution*. Benjamin-Cummings.

Turkle, S. (2011). *Alone Together: Why We Expect More from Technology and Less from Each Other*. Basic Books.

Turnbull, C. M. (1972). *The Mountain People*. Simon & Schuster.

Twenge, J. M. (2006). *Generation Me: Why Today's Young Americans Are more Confident, Assertive, Entitled—and More Miserable than Ever Before*. The Free Press.

Twenge, J. M., & Campbell, W. K. (2010). *The Narcissism Epidemic: Living in the Age of Entitlement*. The Free Press.

Varela, F. J. (1991). *The Embodied Mind: Cognitive Science and Human Experience*. MIT Press.

Varela, F. J. (1999). *Ethical Know-How: Action, Wisdom, and Cognition*. Stanford University Press.

Waal, Frans B. M. de (1997). *Good Natured: The Origins of Right and Wrong in Humans and Other Animals*. Harvard University Press.

Waal, F. B. M. de (1997). *Le Bon Singe: Les bases naturelles de la morale*. Bayard.

Waal, F. B. M. de (2009). *The Age of Empathy: Nature's Lessons for a Kinder Society*. Harmony Books.

Waal, F. B. M. de (2013). *The Bonobo and the Atheist: In Search of Humanism Among the Primates*. W. W. Norton.

Waal, F. B. M., & Lanting, F. (1997). *Bonobo: The Forgotten Ape*. University of California Press.

Wallach, M. A., & Wallach, L. (1983). *Psychology's Sanction for Selfishness: The Error of Egoism in Theory and Therapy*. W. H. Freeman.

White, J. (1991). *Education and the Good Life: Autonomy, Altruism, and the National Curriculum. Advances in Contemporary Educational Thought* (vol. 7). ERIC.

White, M. (2010). Selected death tolls for wars, massacres and atrocities before the 20th century. http://necrometrics.com/pre1700a.htm.

White, M. (2012). *The Great Big Book of Horrible Things: The Definitive Chronicle of History's 100 Worst Atrocities*. W. W. Norton.

Wijkman, A., & Rockström, J. (2013). *Bankrupting Nature: Denying Our Planetary Boundaries*. Routledge.

Wilkinson, R., & Pickett, K. (2009). *The Spirit Level: Why Equality Is Better for Everyone*. Bloomsbury.

Wilson, E. O. (2012). *The Social Conquest of Earth*. Liveright.

Zhi-Sui, L., & Zhisui, L. (1996). *The Private Life of Chairman Mao*. Random House.

Zimbardo, P. (2011). *The Lucifer Effect*. Ebury Digital.

Zolli, A., & Healy, A. M. (2013). *Resilience: Why Things Bounce Back*. Simon & Schuster.

About the Author

Born in France in 1946, Matthieu Ricard is a Buddhist monk who left a career in cellular genetics to study Buddhism in the Himalayas over forty-five years ago. He is an internationally bestselling author and a prominent speaker on the world stage, celebrated at the World Economic Forum at Davos, the NGH forums at the United Nations, and at TED, where his talk on happiness has been viewed by more than seven million people.

His previous books have been translated into more than twenty languages and include *The Monk and the Philosopher, The Quantum and the Lotus, Happiness: A Guide to Developing Life's Most Important Skill,* and *Why Meditate?,* as well as seven photography books.

Ricard is an active participant in the current scientific research on the effects of meditation on the brain. He lives in Nepal and devotes much of his time to 140 humanitarian projects in Tibet, India, and Nepal.

altruismbook.com

www.matthieuricard.com

www.karuna-shechen.org